# Differentiating Normal and Abnormal Personality

**Stephen Strack, PhD,** is Assistant Director of Training at the VA Ambulatory Care Center in Los Angeles, and holds faculty appointments at Alliant International University, Los Angeles, and Fuller Graduate School of Psychology in Pasadena, CA. As a graduate student at the University of Miami he worked with Theodore Millon, the late Robert B. Meagher Jr., and Catherine Greene. After receiving his doctorate in 1983, Dr. Strack has continued to work in the area of personality theory and assessment. He has published five edited books and over 50 articles and chapters, including *Pioneers of Personality Science: Autobiographical Perspectives,* Strack and Kinder, Eds. (Springer Publishing Company, 2005). He is a Fellow of the American Psychological Association and Society for Personality Assessment and a Board member of the Millon Institute for Advanced Studies in Personology and Psychopathology.

# Differentiating Normal and Abnormal Personality

**Edition 2**

## Editor
## Stephen Strack, PhD

SPRINGER PUBLISHING COMPANY

New York

Springer Publishing Company, Inc.
11 West 42nd Street
New York, NY 10036

*Acquisitions Editor: Sheri W. Sussman*
*Production Editor: Print Matters, Inc.*
*Cover design by Joanne Honigman*
*Typeset by Compset*

06 07 08 09 10 / 5 4 3 2 1

Library of Congress Cataloging-in-Publication Data

Differentiating normal and abnormal personality / Stephen Strack, editor.—2nd ed.
    p. cm.
    Includes bibliographical references and indexes.
    ISBN 0-8261-3206-5
    1. Personality tests. 2. Personality disorders—Diagnosis. 3. Personality assessment. I. Strack, Stephen.

  BF698.5.D54 2006
  155.2'8—dc22
    2005057903

Printed in the United States of America by Bang Printing.

*This book is dedicated
to the memory of Maurice Lorr (1910–1998),
gentle giant in the field of personality psychology.*

# Contents

Contributors  xiii

Foreword by Auke Tellegen  xv

Introduction by Stephen Strack  xvii

Acknowledgments  xxviii

# Part 1: Theoretical Perspectives

1    Millon's Evolutionary Model for Unifying the Study of Normal and
     Abnormal Personality  3
     *Theodore Millon and Seth D. Grossman*
     Differentiating Normal and Abnormal Personality  8
     Conceptualizing Personality  11
     Manifest and Latent Taxa  16
     An Evolutionary Scaffold for Personality Theory  23
     Personological Assessment  38
     Concluding Comment  46

2    Psychopathology from the Perspective of the Five-Factor Model  51
     *Robert R. McCrae*
     The Definition of Personality  53
     AXIS I Psychopathology and the FFM  54
     AXIS II Psychopathology and the FFM  54
     A Proposed Definition of Personality-Related Disorders  56
     An Example: The Obsessive-Compulsive Style  59
     Personality-Related Problems and the *DSM*  60
     Acknowledgments  61

3    Differentiating Personality Deviance, Normality, and Well-Being by the
     Seven-Factor Psychobiological Model  65
     *C. Robert Cloninger*
     Definition and Range of Personality  69
     Content and Movement of Thought  71
     Differentiating Levels of Maturity and Well-Being  73

Practical Issues and Supports for Professional TCI Use   77
Summary and Conclusions   78
Acknowledgments   79

4   Interpersonal Theory and the Interpersonal Circumplex: Evolving Perspectives
    on Normal and Abnormal Personality   83
    *Aaron L. Pincus and Michael B. Gurtman*
    The Interpersonal Tradition in Personality   84
    Differentiating Normal and Abnormal Personality: Individual Differences in Traits   92
    Differentiating Normal and Abnormal Personality: Interpersonal Transaction and
    Reciprocity   100
    Differentiating Normal and Abnormal Personality: Covert Internal Processes   104
    Concluding Remarks   106

5   Cognitive Theory of Personality and Personality Disorders   113
    *Marjorie E. Weishaar and Aaron T. Beck*
    Theory of Personality   113
    Personality and Psychopathology   119
    Assessment Instruments for Personality Disorders   125
    Tests of the Cognitive Theory of Personality Disorders   127
    Tests of Cognitive Behavior Therapy   128
    Principles of Cognitive Therapy with Personality Disorders   130
    Acknowledgments   132

6   Psychobiological Models and Issues   137
    *Gordon Claridge*
    Reductionism, Asymmetry, and Continuity   141
    Temperament, Personality, and Deviance   145
    Dimensionality of Psychosis   151
    Final Remarks   157

7   Differentiating Normal and Abnormal Personality from the Perspective of
    the *DSM*   165
    *Douglas B. Samuel and Thomas A. Widiger*
    Personality Disorder Diagnoses via *DSM-IV*   165
    Personality Disorder Diagnostic Thresholds   168
    Conceptual Distinction Between Normal and Abnormal Personality   169
    Deviation from Cultural Expectations   170
    Behavioral, Psychological, or Biological Dysfunction   171
    Inflexibility and Dyscontrol   174
    Clinically Significant Impairment   176
    Conclusions   180

# Part 2: Methodology

8   Problems and Pitfalls in Designing Research on Normal–Abnormal
    Personality   187
    *Stephen Strack*
    General Design Issues   188

Specific Design Issues   194
Conclusions   205
Acknowledgments   206

9    Principles of Exploratory Factor Analysis   209
     *Lewis R. Goldberg and Wayne F. Velicer*
     Decisions to Be Made Prior to Collecting the Data   212
     Decisions to Be Made After the Data Have Been Obtained   215
     Decisions Directly Related to Factor Analysis   217
     Vertical and Horizontal Aspects of Factor Structures in Personality   230
     Summary and Conclusions   232
     Acknowledgments   234

10   Latent Variable Modeling: Representing the Structural Continuity and
     Discontinuity of Normal and Abnormal Personality   239
     *Kristian E. Markon and Robert F. Krueger*
     Generalized Linear Latent Variable Models   239
     Estimating Latent Variable Models   243
     Modeling Latent Distributions   245
     Comparing Models   247
     Summary   254

11   Methods for Understanding Genetic and Environmental Influences in
     Normal and Abnormal Personality   257
     *Laura A. Baker*
     Quantitative Genetic Methods   258
     Molecular Genetic Methods   273
     Future Directions   278

12   Taxometrics   283
     *Nick Haslam and Ben Williams*
     Overview of Taxometric Methods   286
     Taxometric Studies of Personality   288
     How to Do It   297
     The Future of Taxometrics   304
     Conclusions   305

# Part 3: Measurement and Assessment

13   Assessment of Maladaptive Personality Traits   311
     *Thomas A. Widiger, Paul T. Costa Jr., and Douglas B. Samuel*
     Assessment Strategy   312
     Which Instruments to Use?   315
     Convergent and Discriminant Validity   327

14   Differentiating Normal from Abnormal Personality with the MMPI-2   337
     *Yossef S. Ben-Porath*
     Theoretical Underpinnings and Construction of the MMPI   337
     Evolution of the Original MMPI   341

The MMPI-2: 2001 Update   357
The MMPI-2: Post-2001 Developments   362
Future Directions for the MMPI-2   373
Conclusions   374
Acknowledgment   375

**15   Interpersonal Circumplex Measures   383**
*Kenneth D. Locke*
Measures   385
Scoring and Interpreting IPC Inventories   391
Using IPC Measures to Assess Abnormality   392
Caveats and Conclusions   397

**16   The Dimensional Assessment of Personality Pathology (DAPP)
Approach to Personality Disorder   401**
*W. John Livesley*
Overview of the DAPP Constructs and Measures   402
Conceptual Foundations   402
Constructing a Theoretical Taxonomy: A Lexical Approach   403
Scale Construction   405
Preliminary Psychometric Analyses   405
Structure of Personality Disorder   406
Primary Structure   407
Primary Traits   408
Secondary Structure   410
Genetic Architecture of the DAPP   412
Genetic Influences on Basic Traits   413
Relationship with Other Models of Normal and Disordered Personality   414
Personality Disorder   414
Normal Personality   415
The Distinction Between Normal and Disordered Personality   419
Extreme Variation   419
Maladaptive Trait Expression   420
Specific Trait Constellations   421
Personality Failure   422
Classification and Diagnosis   424
Concluding Comments   425

**17   The Schedule for Nonadaptive and Adaptive Personality (SNAP):
A Dimensional Measure of Traits Relevant to Personality and
Personality Pathology   431**
*Leonard J. Simms and Lee Anna Clark*
Dimensional Assessment   433
The SNAP   434
Other SNAP Scales   441
Potential Research Applications   442
Clinical Case Example   444
Summary and Conclusions   447
Acknowledgments   448

18    The Personality Assessment Inventory and the Measurement of Normal and Abnormal Personality Constructs   451
*Leslie C. Morey and Christopher J. Hopwood*
An Overview of the PAI   451
Theoretical Basis and Test Development   452
Normative Data   454
Reliability   455
Validity   456
Summary   467

19    Rorschach Assessment of Normal and Abnormal Personality   473
*Ronald J. Ganellen*
Symptoms, Diagnoses, and the Rorschach   475
Implicit and Explicit Measures of Personality   476
Dimensions of Personality Functioning Assessed by the Rorschach   480
Reliability   485
Validity   487
Racial and Ethnic Differences   492
Directions for Future Research   495

Name Index   501
Subject Index   517

# Contributors

Laura A. Baker, PhD
Department of Psychology
University of Southern California
Los Angeles, CA

Aaron T. Beck, MD
Department of Psychiatry
University of Pennsylvania
Philadelphia, PA

Yossef S. Ben-Porath, PhD
Department of Psychology
Kent State University
Kent, OH

Gordon Claridge, PhD
Department of Experimental Psychology
University of Oxford
Oxford, UK

Lee Anna Clark, PhD
Department of Psychology
University of Iowa
Iowa City, IA

C. Robert Cloninger, MD
Department of Psychiatry
Washington University School of Medicine
St. Louis, MO

Paul T. Costa Jr., PhD
Gerontology Research Center
National Institute on Aging
Baltimore, MD

Ronald J. Ganellen, PhD
Department of Psychiatry and Behavioral
  Sciences
Northwestern University
Chicago, IL

Lewis R. Goldberg, PhD
Senior Scientist
Oregon Research Institute
Eugene, OR

Seth D. Grossman, PsyD
Assistant Dean
Institute for Advanced Studies in Personology
  and Psychopathology
Coral Gables, FL

Michael B. Gurtman, PhD
Department of Psychology
University of Wisconsin–Parkside
Kenosha, WI

Nick Haslam, PhD
Department of Psychology
University of Melbourne
Parkville, VIC, Australia

Christopher J. Hopwood, MS
Department of Psychology
Texas A&M University
College Station, TX

Robert F. Krueger, PhD
Department of Psychology
University of Minnesota
Minneapolis, MN

W. John Livesley, MD, PhD
Department of Psychiatry
University of British Columbia
Vancouver, BC, Canada

Kenneth D. Locke, PhD
Department of Psychology
University of Idaho
Moscow, ID

Kristian E. Markon, BA
Department of Psychology
University of Minnesota
Minneapolis, MN

Robert R. McCrae, PhD
Gerontology Research Center
National Institute on Aging
Baltimore, MD

Theodore Millon, PhD, DSc
Dean and Scientific Director
Institute for Advanced Studies in
Personology and Psychopathology
Coral Gables, FL

Leslie C. Morey, PhD
Department of Psychology
Texas A&M University
College Station, TX

Aaron L. Pincus, PhD
Department of Psychology
Pennsylvania State University
University Park, PA

Douglas B. Samuel, MA
Department of Psychology
University of Kentucky
Lexington, KY

Leonard J. Simms, PhD
Department of Psychology
State University of New York
Buffalo, NY

Auke Tellegen, PhD
Department of Psychology
University of Minnesota
Minneapolis, MN

Wayne F. Velicer, PhD
Professor and Co-director
Cancer Prevention Research Center
University of Rhode Island
Kingston, RI

Marjorie E. Weishaar, PhD
Clinical Professor, Psychiatry and
    Human Behavior
Brown BioMed Division of
Biology and Medicine
Brown University
Providence, RI

Thomas A. Widiger, PhD
Department of Psychology
University of Kentucky
Lexington, KY

Ben Williams, MA
Department of Psychology
University of Melbourne
Parkville, VIC, Australia

**T**his second edition of *Differentiating Normal and Abnormal Personality* is a timely sequel to its distinguished predecessor published a dozen years ago. Based on my own reading, I can say that Dr. Strack and his co-authors have given us a thoroughly and thoughtfully updated revision. It surveys, as intended, three connected subjects: (a) major current theories about the contrasts, continuities, and commonalities between normal and abnormal personality; (b) potentially powerful analytic methods for future explorations and developments; and (c) available assessment instruments intended to map the basic individual differences defining this vast domain.

I expect the information-rich, yet concisely written, chapters of this book will motivate professionals, as they did in my case, to reflect on recent developments and ponder future trends and changes. However, as Dr. Strack stresses in his Introduction, this volume is definitely also written to be "accessible to neophytes." Those who are ready to explore and appraise diverse perspectives and approaches with open minds and energy will find this to be true.

In my Foreword to the first edition of this book, I took note of the variety of viewpoints found in it. The same holds for this second edition. Striking pluralism continues to characterize the field of normal–abnormal personality. Given its basic subject matter, namely, human nature viewed from the perspective of its marked adaptive and maladaptive range, and given the many different ways an inventive thinker can make sense of her observations by initially focusing on different salient aspects, the existing diversity of viewpoints and methods cannot be surprising. I also noted that a personality psychology harboring a wide variety of perspectives might worry psychologists who wish it to be a cumulatively progressive discipline but fear that divisions will compromise its credibility.

But diverse models provide opportunities for empirical comparisons allowing informed choices, which can be especially consequential if the subject matter itself is important. In fact, had there been no alternative models we would have had to invent them. Vigorous and repeated advocacy of a single favorite model, while admissible if it is reasonably plausible, is not enough (Paul Meehl once told me that the great philosopher of science Paul Feyerabend called it the Big Mouth strategy). And certainly, advancing one's model as if there were no serious alternatives would bring back the cultism of earlier days.

Furthermore, the increasing emphasis on "evidence-based practice," including evidence-based assessment, reminds us that comparative evaluations of alternative approaches are critical not only to the continued health and growth of personality psychology as a scientific discipline but also to its acceptance as a societally useful enterprise. The two concerns are related. Demonstrated comparative usefulness in diverse real-world settings confers greater credibility on the underlying constructs.

As Dr. Strack points out, very few rigorous and potentially decisive "head-to-head" comparisons have so far appeared in the literature. Such studies are much needed. The tripartite organization of this book (and of its predecessor) underscores the value of combining conceptual creativity, the use of strong methods for modeling and testing one's conceptions, and the development of measures that implement these constructs in real-world settings. It instructs the reader that all three are essential to maximally informative and decisive comparisons. The built-in endorsement of this integrative three-pronged approach is one of its important contributions.

Auke Tellegen, PhD
*Department of Psychology*
*University of Minnesota*
*Minneapolis, Minnesota*

**S**tudy of the interface between normal and abnormal personality was brought center stage following publication in 1980 of the third edition of the *Diagnostic and Statistical Manual of Mental Disorders* (*DSM-III*; American Psychiatric Association, 1980). There, for the first time, personality was separated from other mental disorders, and clinicians were asked to consider additional forms of psychiatric pathology (e.g., depression) in the context of their patients' enduring patterns of experience and behavior. *DSM-III* and subsequent editions (now *DSM-IV-TR*; American Psychiatric Association, 2000) authorized clinicians to diagnose personality disorders (PDs), not normal personality styles, but definitional criteria for PDs assumed knowledge of healthy functioning:

> Personality traits are enduring patterns of perceiving, relating to, and thinking about the environment and oneself that are exhibited in a wide range of social and personal contexts. Only when personality traits are inflexible and maladaptive and cause significant functional impairment or subjective distress, do they constitute Personality Disorders. (American Psychiatric Association, 2000, p. 686)

The personality types diagnosed as disorders in the current manual (*DSM-IV-TR*; American Psychiatric Association, 2000) were not derived from an empirically based taxonomy or comprehensive theory. Rather, they are the product of a consensus of opinion among the scientists and practitioners who made up the PDs work group authorized by the American Psychiatric Association to develop Axis II. Reports from those who participated in the work groups for *DSM-III* (Millon, 1981) and *DSM-IV* (Livesley, 1995) indicated that their decisions about which PDs to include were informed by then current summaries of personality theory and empirical research. For example, the *DSM-IV* PD work group used empirically based reports to become informed about such issues as definitional clarity of the PDs, overlap and relationship with each other, and the appropriateness of categorical versus dimensional classification. Extensive literature searches were conducted, and both published and unpublished data were scrutinized (in some cases they were reanalyzed). Although field trials were advocated, only one was actually carried out (for the antisocial disorder), and it proved to be controversial. The reports that were issued skillfully documented existing problems, but minimal changes were actually made because the task force was asked to be conservative and to make changes only when clear empirical support was available. Because most of the research directly relevant to the *DSM* was begun after 1980, there were few opportunities to make research-based calls for change (Livesley, 1995).

By the standards of most scientists, Axis II of the *DSM* remains a failure in many respects. It is not a taxonomy because it lacks a coherent structure and a sound empirical base. There are still many problems with definition, overlap of diagnostic criteria, and differentiation of PDs from normal personality. There is amazing agreement about these problems (see Kupfer, First, & Regier, 2002; Widiger & Simonsen, 2005). Essentially all believe that, in general, personality style is more a matter of degree than kind, meaning that dimensionalized traits are more useful for understanding personality than categorical distinctions. They argue that a sound foundation is needed to conceptualize the nature and range of PDs, and that diagnostic criteria must be linked more closely than they are now to their definitional base as pervasive, inflexible, and maladaptive patterns of feelings, thoughts, and behaviors.

The path to DSM-V is clear. We are searching for an empirically validated taxonomy that will encompass the range of personalities seen in the clinic, an articulate set of diagnostic criteria that includes a rationale for fuzzy boundaries and inevitable overlap, and a clear understanding of the relationship between normal and abnormal personality functioning (Livesley, 2001a; Kupfer, First, & Regier, 2002; Widiger & Simonsen, 2005).

The purpose of this book is to inform readers about the central issues that are now being addressed by researchers and clinicians in the realm of normal–abnormal personality, with the aim of providing individuals new to this area some of the basic tools they need to become participants in this important area of scientific inquiry. Written with graduate students and novice professionals in mind, contributors were asked to provide state-of-the-art summaries of their topic areas. They were instructed not to simply report on their subject matter, but to *teach* what is essential and important so that readers can become comfortable with terminology, ideas, and methods that are unique to this scientific arena.

Divided into three parts, the volume offers an overview of major theories, statistical methods, and measurement instruments being used by today's researchers in their quest to understand and differentiate normal and abnormal personality. Part I, Theoretical Perspectives, covers seven influential models of personality and psychopathology that take a variety of perspectives in addressing their common subject matter; that is, dimensional, categorical, interpersonal, cognitive, biological, and evolutionary. Part II, Methodology, offers accessible introductions to four statistical methods that have proved useful in answering many questions about taxonomy, diagnosis, similarities and differences between normal and abnormal personality, and the genetic and environmental influences that cause some people to develop PDs when others do not. To assist beginning researchers, the first chapter of Part II identifies problems and pitfalls that commonly face those who design empirical studies in the realm of normal–abnormal personality. Part III, Measurement and Assessment, includes empirically based introductions to five widely used instruments for assessing normal–abnormal personality, and a review of measures used to study the interpersonal circumplex. Although self-report questionnaires are clearly the most popular type of instrument employed by today's researchers, interviews and performance-based assessments are also important because of the unique behavioral samples they yield. These methods are highlighted in a chapter on the Rorschach, and the first chapter of Part III that discusses a variety of structured and semi-structured interviews as well as some important issues to consider when selecting instruments to measure various personality traits, types, and styles.

# Normal and Abnormal Personality in Historical Context

Anthropologists and sociologists speculate that the behavioral consistencies we refer to as *personality* were recognized by the prehistoric peoples who formed the first stable groups and societies. Philosophical accounts of individual differences in human character appeared over 2500 years ago (e.g., Thales, Empedocles, Plato), and by the time of Christ several writers from Greece (e.g., Heraclitus, Socrates, Hippocrates, Aristotle, Galen) had created sophisticated theories that explained normal and abnormal behaviors as a function of ethereal manipulation, social pressures, personal choices, and physical characteristics such as the quantity of fluids or "humors" in the body. Although many of the observations made by these pioneers were eclipsed long ago, several important ideas remain current in the twenty-first century; for example, the concepts of temperament, type, taxonomy, and continuity between normal and abnormal behaviors (Durant, 1939; Hergenhahn, 1992; Millon, 2004; Russell, 1945).

Progress in understanding personality from a scientific perspective took a giant leap forward following Darwin's (1859) discovery of the evolution of species. The process of natural selection provided an intriguing explanation for the development of complex behavior patterns as means for survival, adaptation, and procreation. Although Darwin did not elaborate on the origin of group and individual differences at the phenotypic (observed) level, his contemporaries and followers (e.g., Galton, Helmholtz, Wundt, James) helped create the fledgling science of psychology from philosophy as the study of human behavior. In the late nineteenth and early twentieth centuries, scientific and technological advances helped psychologists develop complex explanations for behavioral consistencies as stemming from a mixture of evolutionary, biological, social, and personal variables (Goodwin, 1998; Koch & Leary, 1992).

Based on his training in neurology, clinical observations of neurotic patients, and appreciation of Darwinian theory, Sigmund Freud (1895/1966; 1915/1957) sought to develop a comprehensive model of normal and abnormal human behaviors based on neurological evolution. Although many aspects of Freud's neurobiological model did not take hold among his contemporaries, his method of understanding behavior from a psychodynamic perspective did, and later spawned rival paradigms that viewed behavior as stemming from social, familial, interpersonal, cognitive, and learning factors (e.g., Freud, 1923/1961; Goodwin, 1998; Hergenhahn, 1992).

Like Darwin, Freud gave us ideas that allowed people from many disciplines to discuss human behavior from a completely new viewpoint. Freud could explain normal as well as abnormal behavior, and he could treat people with a variety of ailments using his psychoanalytic methods. However, his ideas seemed to explain some behaviors better than others; he lacked a comprehensive taxonomy, and he discouraged experimental validation.

The study of personality went in many directions after Freud. In America, the psychologists Gordon Allport (1937) and Henry Murray (1938) developed a science of personology that was independent of abnormal behavior. European psychologists continued to be influenced by psychodynamic thinkers like Fenichel (1945) and Reich (1949), but some rejected Freud and his followers in favor of the taxonomic, biological observations of those such as Kraepelin (1904), Bleuler (1924), Kretschmer (1925), and Jaspers (1948). The comprehensive models of normal and abnormal personality begun in the 1930s and 1940s by Cattell (1946) and Eysenck (1947) exemplify this latter group.

The Second World War (WWII) shifted the heart of science to America as well as to theories that could explain behavior from sociocultural and interpersonal perspectives (e.g., Fromm, Horney, Sullivan). Another consequence of WWII was the proliferation of nonmedically trained mental health practitioners, particularly clinical psychologists, who helped shape the future of mental health theory and treatment.

By the last quarter of the twentieth century, students of human behavior could pick from dozens of theories that explained various forms of normal and abnormal functioning from intrapsychic, biological, behavioral, interpersonal, phenomenological, and sociocultural perspectives (Hall & Lindzey, 1979; Lanyon & Goodstein, 1997). Too often these theories focused on specific phenomena or global aspects of functioning, normal or abnormal behavior, and either etiology or treatment of dysfunction. In many ways, the person got lost in an effort to explain behavioral details or outside shaping forces.

The atheoretical, multiaxial *DSM-III* (American Psychiatric Association, 1980) separated personality from other mental disorders and asked practitioners to consider the pathology they were treating from whatever vantage point they felt was appropriate, in the context of the whole person. Just as Darwin and Freud had galvanized the attention of scientists from many walks of life, and created a flurry of new ideas and research, *DSM-III* radically changed the way behavioral scientists conducted themselves in the clinic and laboratory. Like deregulation in the modern economic marketplace, by cutting itself loose from the past *DSM-III* gave free reign to the scientific community to step in and fill the knowledge gaps created by the new system. This alone brought a stampede of new theorists and researchers into the area. But just as central is that by giving PDs their own axis, and asking clinicians to consider the stable trait characteristics of all their patients, personality was elevated to a level of importance it had never had before. A consequence of this is that many more patients were diagnosed with PDs (e.g., Loranger, 1990). With more PD patients to treat, better treatments were needed. More money poured into PD research, and of course, this attracted more people into the area.

After *DSM-III* researchers began focusing on the interface between normal and abnormal behaviors. They started questioning the need for separate theories that addressed symptoms outside the scope of personality, or health beyond the scope of pathology, and helped people begin to see the similarities in theories that previously seemed different. The hope of integrating ideas about the nature of human development, personality functioning, psychopathology, and treatment is again pushing through. People from different disciplines and schools of thought are now working toward a comprehensive, biopsychosocial understanding of normal and abnormal behaviors that can encompass, or be compatible with, the many perspectives that have shown promise in the past, including biological, psychodynamic, sociocultural, and interpersonal (Strack & Lorr, 1994a).

In the first decade of the twenty-first century the study of personality has moved beyond the confines of the *DSM* (Livesley, 2001a; Widiger & Simonsen, 2005). As noted previously, the *DSM* model does not offer an empirically based taxonomy, and it has kept its categorical distinction between normality and pathology in the face of scientific evidence that argues against this. But just as contemporary personologists have moved away from atheoretical, dualistic conceptions of human behavior, they no longer expect a single model of behavior to encompass the vast array of human features, both normal and abnormal. There is greater tolerance for, and interest in, dimensional conceptualizations of personality and psychopathology that have empirical backing, as well as models that predict and demonstrate discontinuity in some behaviors and disorders (e.g., schizotypy; Lenzenweger & Korfine, 1992).

## Developments in Normal–Abnormal Personality Science Since 1994

In our survey of the field in 1994 (Strack & Lorr, 1994a), Maurice Lorr and I marveled at the integrative process spawned by *DSM-III* (American Psychiatric Association, 1980). Previously segregated groups of theorists and researchers, academics and clinicians, psychologists and psychiatrists, were brought together on the new playing field of normal–abnormal personality. We envisioned a bright future where the entire spectrum of personality might eventually be understood, but we also recognized that the complex problems and issues facing researchers might take generations to resolve. We called for tolerance of diverse theories, methods, and measures, and greater clarity in how researchers specified their assumptions and goals.

At that time we made a number of specific suggestions for improving the field (Strack & Lorr, 1994b):

- Although a variety of personality theories and personality assessment measures were available to researchers, many showed lopsided treatment of either normal or abnormal functioning (i.e., focused on one side or the other but not both). We believed that these theories and measures should be expanded to encompass a full range of normal and abnormal personality features.
- Although considerable progress had been made in identifying a taxonomy of normal personality traits (e.g., Five-Factor Model [FFM]), there was no counterpart in the realm of PDs. We argued that researchers should focus their attention on mapping the domain of traits in clinical samples to see if a taxonomy could be developed that would encompass normal *and* abnormal personality.
- Although the stability of normal personality had been well documented by the 1990s, we did not know how PDs faired over time. We encouraged the start of longitudinal studies to map the course of PDs over the life span.
- Given the variety of competing personality theories, measures, and statistical techniques, studies should be launched to compare and contrast some of these in well-matched groups of normals and patients, to help determine which are best for addressing particular questions and issues.
- Because most people in the field agree on the problems in the *DSM* model of personality, *DSM-V* should be updated to reflect dimensional traits (not just personality categories) as well as the importance of normal personality in understanding psychiatric pathology.

In the past dozen years significant progress has been made in each of these areas. In fact, there have been enough new developments in theory and research to spawn several recent books and journal issues to review the progress (see, for example, Cloninger, 1999; Livesley, 2001; Strack, 2005; Widiger & Simonsen, 2005). Focusing on the improvement areas just presented, let me summarize the major changes.

Today's theories, models, and measures of normal–abnormal personality are improved over what they were a dozen years ago because many now focus more evenly on normal and abnormal behaviors. For example, Millon (1996, this volume, chapter 1) and Cloninger (2004, this volume, chapter 3) have expanded their views to include more sophisticated, detailed descriptions of the domain of normal behavior and how personality pathology is differentiated from it.[1] Interpersonal theory has also expanded (Pincus & Gurtman, this volume, chapter 4), and dimensional approaches like the Five-Factor Model (FFM) are now more thoroughly linked to traits in the clinical range (McCrae, this volume, chapter 2). We now have more, and better, measures of normal–abnormal personality, including interviews and self-report forms addressing whole theories and models, as well as specific personalities, traits, and subtraits. For reports on changes to major instruments, see the chapters in Part III as well as Clark and Harrison (2001), Widiger and Coker (2002), and Morey (2003).

In the previous edition of this book, Harkness and McNulty (1994) introduced their counterpart to the FFM, called the PSY-5 (Psychopathology-5), a set of five dimensions encompassing abnormal personality. Since then the PSY-5 have been incorporated as standard measures in the Minnesota Multiphasic Personality Inventory-2 (MMPI-2; Ben-Porath, this volume, chapter 14; Butcher et al., 2001), making them accessible to a wide audience of clinicians and researchers. As well, a number of studies have examined the dimensional trait structure of personality in both normal and abnormal populations. Findings indicate that there are at least four dimensions relevant across the board, namely neuroticism/emotional stability, agreeableness/disagreeableness, introversion/extraversion, and conscientiousness (Livesley, 2005; Mulder & Joyce, 1997; O'Connor & Dyce, 1998). Because major factor-based models of personality encompass these dimensions in one form or another, none have become obsolete as a consequence of the new findings. Much of the work now focuses on the hierarchy of traits needed to encompass normal-abnormal personality, that is, the combination of higher order and lower order traits and facets needed to address individual differences in behavior, cognition, and experience (Markon, Krueger, & Watson, 2005; Paunonen, 1998).

It is remarkable that in just 12 years a handful of longitudinal studies have been launched to examine the course of PDs over time (e.g., Gunderson, et al., 2000). Results of a 2-year study of avoidant, obsessive-compulsive, borderline, and schizotypal PDs gave us evidence for strong trait stability during this time interval "even though noteworthy changes in the categorical diagnosis . . . were observed in these patients." (Warner et al., 2004; p. 224). Other studies covering a 2- to 6-year time frame hint that at

---

[1]The personality theories of Cattell (e.g., 1946; Cattell & Bolton, 1969) and Eysenck (e.g., 1947, 1994) continue to be important in research on normal–abnormal personality, but the deaths of these pioneers in 1998 and 1997, respectively, put an end to additional theorizing, and thus possible changes since the last edition of this book. Readers can refer to chapters by Krug (1994, on Cattell) and Eysenck (1994) for a summary of their work as it applies to differentiating normal and abnormal personality.

least some PD traits, and psychosocial functioning in persons with borderline PD, are not as stable as previously thought (Shea & Yen, 2003; Zanarini, Frankenburg, Hennen, Reich, & Silk, 2005). We will have to wait another 5–10 years before data from longer periods of time can be analyzed and described.

Numerous comparative studies have been published since 1994 but very few of them provided head-to-head comparisons of theories, models, measures, and statistical techniques with normal and abnormal subjects, to predict specific outcomes. The most common among these were those assessing factor structure of traits in various samples (see above; Livesley, 2005; O'Connor & Dyce, 1998). Tests of specific hypotheses concerning genetic, biological, and molecular connections to personality traits and styles have also been relatively common (Kluger, Siegfried, & Ebstein, 2002; Livesley, 2005; Plomin & Caspi, 1999), but these have yielded conflicting, rather than clarifying, results. Except for the stable finding that broad personality traits have a genetic (heritable) basis, hypothesized connections between traits and molecular and biological variables have not been unequivocally borne out (Loehlin, 1992; Livesley, 2005). For example, a hypothesized link between novelty seeking and dopamine was tested in over 20 studies but no clear relationship has thus far emerged (Kluger, Siegfried, & Ebstein, 2002).

Axis II of the current diagnostic manual (*DSM-IV-TR*; American Psychiatric Association, 2000) was informed by research findings that accumulated after 1980, but a dimensional model was not adopted because there were many unanswered questions about such fundamental issues as how many traits should be included (Livesley, 1995, 2001). A concerted effort is now underway to see if a validated dimensional model of PDs can be used in place of the categorical model for *DSM-V* (Livesley, 2005; Widiger & Simonsen, 2005). Unfortunately, it appears that much less progress has been made in convincing clinical scientists of the importance of normal functioning for understanding PDs (Sabshin, 2005), so it seems unlikely at the moment that *DSM-V* will concern itself with nondisordered personalities, or criteria for what is normal and healthy.

This latter conclusion is bothersome because it is obvious to many that a definition of abnormality is incomplete without reference to what is normal. Perhaps because of its medical heritage psychiatry has avoided focusing on the domain of healthy functioning: "In psychiatry...the concepts of normality have been distinctly secondary to concepts of pathology" (Sabshin, 2005, p. 233). PDs are diagnosed when trait-related behaviors and experiences are viewed as *problematic* by the individual or *deviate markedly* from what is expected by those who make up his or her social milieu. This skirts the issue of what is normal, yet as Sabshin (2005), former Executive Director of the American Psychiatric Association, recognizes, "as psychiatry develops toward a more objectifiable etiological system in the twenty-first century, it must begin to find a more rational conceptual basis for normality" (p. 233). From early history personality models have addressed both normal and abnormal behaviors. The two realms of functioning seem to be inherently intertwined, so it seems highly unlikely that abnormal personality can ever be fully explained without reference to what is normal and healthy. As Widiger and Simonsen (2005) recently observed,

> The inclusion of normative, adaptive traits [in *DSM-V*] will facilitate the provision of a more comprehensive (and accurate) description of each patient's general personality structure; it will facilitate an integration of the diagnostic manual with basic science research on general

personality structure; and it will facilitate treatment decisions through the recognition of traits that contribute to an understanding of treatment responsivity. (p. 126)

# Concepts of Normality and Pathology

In the first edition of this book Maurice Lorr and I cited five models of normality–abnormality described by Offer and Sabshin (1991b) that encompass the viewpoints of practically all people in the field. The first of these conceptualizes *normality as health and pathology as illness.* Consistent with the traditional medical model, this perspective defines disorder by symptoms, syndromes, and physical and/or laboratory abnormalities. To be healthy is to be reasonably free of bothersome symptoms or disease—and this includes most people. Optimal or ideal functioning is not considered.

*Normality as pathology, health as utopia* is a viewpoint that conceptualizes the large majority of persons as being to some extent unhealthy. Health is defined as a perfect condition that few ever attain. According to this perspective, the average person falls considerably short of the ideal and is therefore viewed as suffering at least some pathology (e.g., possessing neurotic traits; Freud, 1937/1959).

Defining *normality as average and pathology as deviant* takes into account cultural definitions of what is normal and healthy and what is not. In this perspective, behavior is defined according to what is acceptable and unacceptable within a given culture. The term "normal" is applied to typical or average behavior, whereas the term "abnormal" is applied to behavior outside this range.

The fourth model, *normality and pathology as transactional systems,* defines health and disorder according to an individual's ability to change and adapt within a social system that also changes. Patterns of adjustment are observed over long periods of time. Normal, healthy behavior is ascribed to those who adapt and respond effectively to ongoing internal (biological, psychological) and external (social) demands. Abnormal, unhealthy behavior occurs in persons who fail to adapt or respond adequately.

*Normality and pathology as pragmatism* asserts that consensual definition determines what is normal and what is abnormal. Relativistic in nature, this model suggests that any condition we recognize and treat as unhealthy or maladaptive is abnormal, whereas conditions that rarely, if ever, bring people in for help are normal. According to this perspective, normality and pathology are in the eye of the beholder and a given culture may have several definitions of what is healthy and unhealthy.

In addition to these broad, philosophical perspectives, most clinicians and researchers hold one of four views concerning the interface between normal and abnormal personality. The first asserts that *normal and disordered personalities are categorically distinct.* Holders of this viewpoint assert that normal and abnormal personalities can be readily distinguished based on objective (ultimately biological or genetic) criteria. This perspective underlies the current system of *DSM* (American Psychiatric Association, 2000) PD diagnosis. A second point of view holds that *normal and abnormal personalities are dimensionally linked*; that is, they exist on the same plane and merge at some point on one or more sets of trait dimensions. Proponents of this viewpoint would agree that healthy and disordered personalities can sometimes be distinguished according to consensual definitions, but that these definitions are inherently arbitrary because no sharp line of demarcation separates normal from abnormal.

Two additional perspectives combine elements of the categorical and dimensional approaches. The third viewpoint asserts that *quantitative differences in dimensional traits can produce qualitatively different normal and abnormal personality types*. For example, certain combinations of extraversion, introversion, and emotional stability can lead to habitual patterns of behavior that are so pervasive and distinct that they can be defined as particular normal and abnormal personality styles (e.g., compulsive, histrionic). A fourth view holds that *normal personality is based on dimensional traits, but abnormal personality results from biological processes and/or genetic elements that interact with these traits to produce categorically distinct disorders*. For example, the presence of a genetic marker for schizophrenia in an otherwise normal introvert might result in disturbed thinking, a predisposition to psychotic breakdowns, and a schizotypal PD.

The conceptual systems just described are not always mutually exclusive, and some researchers may espouse beliefs that are a hybrid mixture of different perspectives. As normal–abnormal personality research becomes more advanced and sophisticated, the empirical reality that emerges is likely to encompass multiple points of view. For example, current evidence suggests that most PDs can be accounted for by a set of dimensional traits, yet the field is also becoming convinced that schizotypal PDs develop only in persons who have a particular genetic makeup. Not all persons with this genetic makeup actually develop problems. Other factors, including dimensional traits and psychosocial stressors, are likely to be important in determining who becomes abnormal and who does not (Lenzenweger & Korfine, 1992; Livesley, 2001b, 2005; Millon, 1996).

# Toward the Future

Readers of this book have an opportunity to make meaningful contributions to the rapidly evolving field of normal–abnormal personality. Although answers to some of our questions may take generations to obtain, studies conducted in this area over the next several years will significantly impact what is contained in the next diagnostic manual (*DSM-V*). Unlike many "closed" areas of science that require contributors to have highly specialized knowledge and experience, normal–abnormal personality is wide open to creative contributions by students and novice professionals. Many of the testable hypotheses, statistical methods, and measures are accessible to neophytes, and I particularly believe that open mindedness, which is a characteristic of people new to the field, is a good fit to the mélange of ideas and methods found here.

In this regard, I do not agree with a few observers who see a mounting crisis in the gap between our empirical knowledge base and the awesome requirements of a valid diagnostic manual. The extraordinary progress in the field since 1980, and especially during the past 10–12 years is, I believe, akin to what Kuhn (1996) called a *scientific revolution*. The old paradigms in this area do not fit with the data, and new ones are emerging to take their place. Shifts in science like this take time to evolve, and it is often impossible to see the process clearly until after the dust has settled. I trust that in another 10–15 years significant progress will be made in establishing the empirical foundation needed to have a valid taxonomy of normal and abnormal personality traits, styles, types, and disorders, as well as knowledge of how people develop personality problems and how individuals with PDs can be restored to healthy functioning. Readers of this book will help pave the way.

Stephen Strack, PhD
*Los Angeles, CA*

## REFERENCES

Allport, G. (1937). *Personality: A psychological interpretation*. New York: Henry Holt.

American Psychiatric Association. (1980). *Diagnostic and statistical manual of mental disorders* (3rd ed.). Washington, DC:Author.

American Psychiatric Association. (2000). *Diagnostic and statistical manual of mental disorders* (4th ed., text revision). Washington, DC: Author.

Bleuler, E. (1924). *Textbook of psychiatry*. New York: Macmillan.

Butcher, J. N., Graham, J. R., Ben-Porath, Y. S., Tellegen, A., Dahlstrom, W. G., & Kaemmer, B. (2001). *The Minnesota Multiphasic Personality Inventory-2 (MMPI-2): Manual for administration and scoring* (rev. ed.). Minneapolis, MN: University of Minnesota Press.

Cattell, R. B. (1946). *Description and measurement of personality*. Yonkers, NY: World Book.

Cattell, R. B., & Bolton, L. S. (1969). What pathological dimensions lie beyond the normal dimensions of the 16PF? A comparison of MMPI and 16PF factor domains. *Journal of Consulting and Clinical Psychology, 33*, 18–29.

Clark, L. A., & Harrison, J. A. (2001). Assessment instruments. In W. J. Livesley (Ed.), *Handbook of personality disorders* (pp. 277–306). New York: Guilford Press.

Cloninger, C. R. (Ed.). (1999). *Personality and psychopathology*. Washington, DC: American Psychiatric Press.

Cloninger, C. R. (2004). *Feeling good: The science of well-being*. New York: Oxford.

Darwin, C. R. (1859). *On the origin of species by means of natural selection*. London: Murray.

Durant, W. (1939). *The story of civilization, Part II: The life of Greece*. New York: Simon & Schuster.

Eysenck, H. J. (1947). *Dimensions of personality*. London: Routledge & Kegan Paul.

Eysenck, H. J. (1994). Normality-abnormality and the three-factor model of personality. In S. Strack, & M. Lorr (Eds.), *Differentiating normal and abnormal personality* (pp. 3–25). New York: Springer.

Fenichel, O. (1945). *The psychoanalytic theory of neurosis*. New York: Norton.

Freud, S. (1957). Instincts and their vicissitudes. In *The standard edition* (Vol. XIV). London: Hogarth. (Original work published 1915)

Freud, S. (1959). Analysis terminable and interminable. In J. Strachey (Ed.), *Collected papers of S. Freud* (Vol. 5, pp. 316–358). New York: Basic Books. (Original work published 1937)

Freud, S. (1961). The ego and the id. In *The standard edition* (Vol. XIX). London: Hogarth. (Original work published 1923)

Freud, S. (1966). Project for a scientific psychology. In *The standard edition* (Vol. I). London: Hogarth. (Original work published 1895)

Goodwin, C. J. (1998). *A history of modern psychology*. New York: Wiley.

Gunderson, J. G., Shea, M. T., Skodol, A. E., McGlashan, T. H., Morey, L. C., Stout, R. L., et al. (2000). The Collaborative Longitudinal Personality Disorders Study. I: Development, aims, design, and sample characteristics. *Journal of Personality Disorders, 14*, 300–315.

Hall, C. S., & Lindzey, G. (1979). *Theories of personality* (3rd ed.). New York: Wiley.

Harkness, A. R., & McNulty, J. L. (1994). The personality psychopathology five (PSY-5): Issue from the pages of a diagnostic manual instead of a dictionary. In S. Strack, & M. Lorr (Eds.), *Differentiating normal and abnormal personality* (pp. 291–315). New York: Springer.

Hergenhahn, B. R. (1992). *An introduction to the history of psychology* (2nd ed.). Belmont, CA: Wadsworth.

Jaspers, K. (1948). *General psychopathology*. London: Oxford.

Kluger, A. N., Siegfried, Z., & Ebstein, R. P. (2002). A meta-analysis of the association between DRD4 polymorphism and novelty seeking. *Molecular Psychiatry, 7*, 712–717.

Koch, S., & Leary, D. E. (Eds.). (1992). *A century of psychology as science*. Washington, DC: American Psychological Association.

Kraepelin, E. (1904). *Lectures on clinical psychiatry*. New York: Wood.

Kretchmer, E. (1925). *Physique and character*. New York: Harcourt Brace.

Krug, S. E. (1994). Personality: A Cattellian perspective. In S. Strack, & M. Lorr (Eds.), *Differentiating normal and abnormal personality* (pp. 65–78). New York: Springer.

Kuhn, T. S. (1996). *The structure of scientific revolutions* (3rd ed.). Chicago: University of Chicago Press.

Kupfer, D. J., First, M. B., & Regier, D. A. (Eds.). (2002). *A research agenda for DSM-V.* Washington, DC: American Psychiatric Press.

Lanyon, R. I., & Goodstein, L. D. (1997). *Personality assessment* (3rd ed.). New York: Wiley.

Leary, T. (1957). *Interpersonal diagnosis of personality.* New York: Ronald Press.

Lenzenweger, M. F., & Korfine, L. (1992). Confirming the latent structure and base rate of schizotypy: A taxometric analysis. *Journal of Abnormal Psychology, 101,* 567–571.

Livesley, W. J. (Ed.). (1995). *The DSM-IV personality disorders.* New York: Guilford Press.

Livesley, W. J. (2001a). Conceptual and taxonomic issues. In W. J. Livesley (Ed.), *Handbook of personality disorders* (pp. 3–38). New York: Guilford Press.

Livesley, W. J. (Ed.). (2001b). *Handbook of personality disorders.* New York: Guilford Press.

Livesley, W. J. (2005). Behavioral and molecular genetic contributions to a dimensional classification of personality disorders. *Journal of Personality Disorders, 19,* 131–155.

Loehlin, J. C. (1992). *Genes and environment in personality development.* Newbury Park, CA: Sage.

Loranger, A. W. (1990). The impact of DSM-III on diagnostic practice in a university hospital: A comparison of DSM-II and DSM-III in 10,914 patients. *Archives of General Psychiatry, 47,* 672–675.

Markon, K. E., Krueger, R. F., & Watson, D. (2005). Delineating the structure of normal and abnormal personality: An integrative hierarchical appraisal. *Journal of Personality and Social Psychology, 88,* 139–157.

Millon, T. (1981). *Disorders of personality.* New York: Wiley.

Millon, T. (1994). *Masters of the mind.* Hoboken, NJ: Wiley.

Millon, T. (1996). *Disorders of personality* (2nd ed.). New York: Wiley.

Morey, L. C. (2003). Measuring personality and psychopathology. In J. Schinka, & W. Velicer (Eds.), *Handbook of psychology: Research methods in psychology* (Vol. 2, pp. 377–406). New York: Wiley.

Mulder, R. T., & Joyce, P. R. (1997). Temperament and the structure of personality disorder symptoms. *Psychological Medicine, 27,* 1315–1325.

Murray, H. A. (1938). *Explorations in personality.* New York: Oxford.

O'Connor, B. P., & Dyce, J. A. (1998). A test of models of personality disorder configuration. *Journal of Abnormal Psychology, 107,* 3–16.

Offer, D., & Sabshin, M. (1991). Introduction. In D. Offer, & M. Sabshin (Eds.), *The diversity of normal behavior* (pp. xi–xxi). New York: Basic Books.

Panounen, S. V. (1998). Hierarchical organization of personality and prediction of behavior. *Journal of Personality and Social Psychology, 74,* 538–556.

Plomin, R., & Caspi, A. (1999). Behavioral genetics and personality. In L. A. Pervin, & O. P. John (Eds.), *Handbook of personality* (2nd ed., pp. 251–276). New York: Guilford Press.

Reich, W. (1949). *Character analysis* (3rd ed.). New York: Farrar, Straus, & Giroux.

Russell, B. (1945). *A history of Western philosophy.* New York: Simon & Schuster.

Sabshin, M. (2005). Concepts of normality and the classification of psychopathology. In S. Strack (Ed.), *Handbook of personology and psychopathology* (pp. 229–237). Hoboken, NJ: Wiley.

Shea, M. T., & Yen, S. (2003). Stability as a distinction between Axis I and Axis II disorders. *Journal of Personality Disorders, 17,* 373–386.

Strack, S. (Ed.). (2005a). *Handbook of personology and psychopathology.* Hoboken, NJ: Wiley.

Strack, S. (Ed.). (2005b). *Pioneers of personality science: Autobiographical perspectives.* New York: Springer.

Strack, S., & Lorr, M. (Eds.). (1994a). *Differentiating normal and abnormal personality.* New York: Springer.

Strack, S., & Lorr, M. (1994b). Summary and perspective. In S. Strack, & M. Lorr (Eds.), *Differentiating normal and abnormal personality* (pp. 421–414). New York: Springer.

Warner, M. B., Morey, L. C., Finch, J. F., Gunderson, J. G., Skodol, A. E., Sanislow, C. A., et al. (2004). The longitudinal relationship of personality traits and disorders. *Journal of Abnormal Psychology, 113,* 217–227.

Widiger, T. A., & Coker, L. A. (2002). Assessing personality disorders. In J. N. Butcher (Ed.), *Clinical personality assessment: Practical approaches* (2nd ed., pp. 407–434). New York: Oxford University Press.

Widiger, T. A., & Simonsen, E. (2005). Alternative dimensional models of personality disorder: Finding a common ground. *Journal of Personality Disorders, 19,* 110–130.

Zanarini, M. C., Frankenburg, F. R., Hennen, J., Reich, B., & Silk, K. R. (2005). Psychosocial functioning of borderline patients and Axis II comparison subjects followed prospectively for six years. *Journal of Personality Disorders, 19,* 19–29.

# Acknowledgments

The death of Maurice Lorr, co-editor of the first edition of this book, in 1998, was a tremendous loss to the field of personality psychology and to me as an individual. Maury was a pioneer in developing psychometrically sound measures of psychopathology, interpersonal behavior, and mood, and for creating empirical models of psychotic syndromes and personality. Like many gifted persons, Maury had abundant talents. He was a sculptor who created a number of bronze busts of prominent people in psychology and psychiatry, as well as family members and friends. He was a wonderful teacher who inspired two generations of budding psychologists. He was a warm, gentle man who made people feel welcome and comfortable in his presence, and he had a great sense of humor.

With Maury gone a follow-up volume seemed to be out of the question. It was only through the encouragement and inspiration of colleagues and friends that this edition was made possible. First among these supporters was Dr. Joan Lorr, Maury's widow and a talented psychologist in her own right. Maury's spirit lives on in the pages of this book, and I thank Joan for her giving me thumbs-up. Dr. James Hennessy of Fordham University was a fan of the first edition. His steadfast interest in a second edition and help in formulating the content of, and target audience for, this volume, were important contributions. Thank you, Jim. Readers who are familiar with the first edition will note that many of the contributors returned to write follow-up pieces. This vote of confidence was very important to me during the early phases of the project, and I thank each of them for their support and advice: Y. S. Ben-Porath, G. Claridge, C. R. Cloninger, L. R. Goldberg, M. B. Gurtman, T. Millon, R. R. McCrae, L. C. Morey, A. L. Pincus, and T. A. Widiger. Finally, my chief at the VA Outpatient Clinic in Los Angeles since 1993, Dr. Gary Wolfe, helped in providing necessary resources for my work on both editions—including the most precious, time. Thank you, Gary.

# 1

# Theoretical Perspectives

# Millon's Evolutionary Model for Unifying the Study of Normal and Abnormal Personality

Theodore Millon
Seth D. Grossman

This is a time of rapid scientific and clinical advancement, a time that seems propitious for ventures designed to bridge new ideas and syntheses. The intersection between the study of "psychopathology" and the study of "personality" is one of these spheres of significant intellectual activity and clinical responsibility. Theoretical formulations that bridge this intersection would represent a major and valued conceptual step, but to limit efforts to this junction alone will lead to overlooking the solid footings necessary for fundamental progress, and which are provided increasingly by more mature sciences (e.g., physics and evolutionary biology). By failing to coordinate propositions and constructs to principles and laws established in these advanced disciplines, psychological science will continue to float, so to speak, at its current level, an act that will ensure the need to return to this task another day.

The goal of this chapter is to connect the conceptual structure of personology to its foundations in the natural sciences. What is proposed herein is akin to Freud's (1895) abandoned *Project for a Scientific Psychology* and Wilson's (1975) highly controversial *Sociobiology*. Both were worthy endeavors to advance our understanding of human nature; this was to be done by exploring interconnections among disciplines that evolved ostensibly unrelated bodies of research and manifestly dissimilar languages.

It is necessary, we believe, to go beyond current conceptual boundaries in psychology, more specifically to explore carefully reasoned, as well as "intuitive" hypotheses that draw their principles, if not their substance, from more established, "adjacent" sciences. Not only may such steps bear new conceptual fruits, but also they may provide a foundation that can undergird and guide our own discipline's explorations. Much of personology, no less psychology as a whole, remains adrift, divorced from broader spheres of scientific knowledge, isolated from firmly grounded, if not universal principles, leading one to continue building the patchwork quilt of concepts and data domains that characterize the field. Preoccupied with but a small part of the larger puzzle, or fearing accusations of reductionism, many fail thereby to draw on the rich possibilities to be found in other realms of scholarly pursuit. With few exceptions, cohering concepts that would connect this subject to those of its sister sciences have not been developed.

Despite the shortcomings of historic and contemporary theoretical schemas of most sciences, systematizing principles and abstract concepts can "facilitate a deeper seeing, a more penetrating vision that goes beyond superficial appearances to the order underlying them" (Bowers, 1977). For example, pre-Darwinian taxonomists such as Linnaeus limited themselves to "apparent" similarities and differences among animals as a means of constructing their categories. Darwin was not "seduced" by appearances. Rather, he sought to understand the principles by which overt features came about. His classifications were based not only on descriptive qualities but also on explanatory ones.

We see our task in the evolutionary model to be that of peeling back the manifest character of the observable personological and clinical world of overt behaviors, thoughts, and emotions, to jettison its veneer, and to expose its latent or underlying functions. In so doing we hope to discover and articulate a set of coherent principles and procedures that may advance and facilitate our understanding and assessment of both normal and abnormal subject domains. Some have said that our evolutionary model seeks "to read the mind of God"; we would rather acquire a somewhat less presumptuous characterization, that of seeking "to read the mind of human nature."

A unifying model for personology and psychopathology must coalesce the field's disparate schools of thought, not, however, in a haphazard way that simply identifies the alternatives or records their separate contributions, but in a manner that truly integrates each of these seemingly contradictory perspectives at a "deeper level," that is, one that synthesizes the alternative components intrinsically. Although, random, eclectic, or broad-based theories have, as their benefit, the advantages of open-mindedness and comprehensiveness, they are likely to be generative of little more than providing a measure of illusory psychic comfort. A substantively unifying paradigm will interweave fundamental relationships that exist among the cognitive, biological, intrapsychic, and behavioral components that are inherent in the person. This will, in effect, generate integrative theoretical and assessment strategies. This desirable advantage has been achieved partially in psychotherapy by efforts to employ combinatorial treatment approaches (e.g., CBT, pharmacological/family interventions). However, even more synergy is possible and desirable. A unified paradigm for the science of normal and abnormal personology must be based conceptually and pragmatically on interweaving the "whole person."

It may be a useful digression to refer to scientific developments of this character in other person- and treatment-oriented fields. Medicine, for example, has recently begun to focus on matters beyond surface symptomatology. Diseases in the past were "understood" and named only in accord with their overtly observable qualities (e.g., smallpox), in much the same way as we now refer to psychiatric entities such as "dysthymia" or "anxiety." Late in the 19th century, a paradigm shift occurred when biologists and physicians recognized that unseen "infectious agents" were central to the etiology and understanding of disease manifestation. Symptom-labeled entities such as "smallpox" were no longer to be approached with superficial palliatives (e.g., bloodletting), but as infiltrating microbial agents in otherwise healthy individuals and, as further technical knowledge advanced, to be treated at their roots with appropriately targeted antibiotics.

An additional conceptual development in medical science occurred this past quarter of a century in response to the HIV/AIDS epidemic. Never before had the immune system been known to play so vital a role in differentiating normal versus abnormal functioning. It has been illustrated recently, for example, that constitutional differences exist among individuals in their susceptibility to the immunodeficiency virus; some are resistant to its effects whereas others will succumb to full-blown AIDS. Here again we may draw a parallel to our personological model from our sister science of medicine. Personality disorders may be seen as representing different vulnerabilities in people's "psychic immune system," that is, defects or deficiencies in a person's longstanding pattern of perceiving and coping with the psychic stressors in his or her mental life. The different personality disorders are signs of different psychic vulnerabilities. The task of personologists is to decode (diagnose) these vulnerabilities on the basis of a patient's symptoms, and then engage in therapy that not only removes the symptoms but also works through the individual's underlying vulnerabilities. Assessing and understanding the vulnerabilities—the patient's weakened intrapsychic defenses, neurochemical imbalances, cognitive misinterpretations, and interpersonal difficulties—will enable us to take steps to effect, with all these domains of vulnerability in focus, a synergisitic and "personalized therapy."

The desire for and potential in personological unification calls for at least one additional consideration. Again, the parallel between medicine and personology points to an issue often alluded to, but rarely addressed directly: On what basis should a unifying paradigm of a "personality" science be grounded?

In our view, all basic or applied sciences (physics, engineering, personology) are expressions of common functions grounded and understood from the conceptual principles of evolution theory. All disciplines of science, once achieving sufficient maturity, are natural outgrowths of, as well as demonstrations of, the operation of evolutionary processes. Formally structured, each of these sciences is composed of *subject-relevant theories* (e.g., particle physics, personology), *component classified taxonomies* (e.g., synaptic neurochemicals, International Classification of Diseases), *operational measuring tools* (e.g., cyclotrons, Minnesota Multiphasic Personality Inventory [MMPI]), and, when required, *efficacious instruments* of effecting change (e.g., locomotives, cognitive therapy). As we see it, only when all four of the preceding elements that provide a structure to a science are articulated and coordinated can our assessment tools and our therapeutic techniques demonstrate or achieve full empirical validity and instrumental efficacy.

Unfortunately, most of our theories and studies have existed largely as independent and often contradictory approaches to a modestly formed science; that is, they have little to no relationship to the assessment measures we employ to identify interventional targets, nor do they stem from explanatory principles of theories employed to understand the individuals who seek our clinical efforts. We lack the means found in subjects such as physics where physicists possess the ability to apply the equations of theory to their taxonomy of elementary particles and possess measurement instruments that can test whether theoretically generated properties exist in fact.

It is our belief that we are reaching a time when we can begin to systematize our knowledge of personology in a manner akin to more advanced sciences. Specifically, it is our judgment that we would do well to employ the universal principles of evolutionary theory to guide our understanding of the properties of human functioning, that is, to enable us to formulate theoretical propositions that "explain" our subject domain. These principles should also enable us to construct a taxonomic system that is derived from such a theory, which, in turn, will facilitate the development of assessment tools that identify properties composing the taxonomy, and then point to those clinical characteristics that should serve as therapeutic targets. In effect, a unified personological paradigm such as this will serve as an ever-present guide as to where, how, and which assessment tools and interventions are best employed.

A few words should be said at the outset outlining the logic and steps we will follow as we proceed in this chapter. First, let us note that the ontological position of the personality *prototypes* is unchanging and invariant. They are derived by a series of direct and simple deductions from the evolutionary model, resting on what we believe to be the three fundamental and indispensable essentials of life: "existential *survival*" (pleasure/pain), ecological *adaptation* (active/passive), and species *replication* (propagation/nurturance). As an inevitable deduction, the several derived personality prototypes are the final word, real and definitive, given that they neither change nor can be altered by the impact of such extrascientific conditions as social or political considerations. That the *prevalence* of prototypal personalities can and will vary as a function of cultural influences is both possible and expected, but their enduring and inextinguishable character, as derived from the essentials of evolution, is immutable.

Second, what *is* variable are what we refer to as personality *subtypes*. Personality subtypes are essentially combinations of the several immutable prototypes. The subtypes are not derived directly from the imperatives of evolution's processes. They take shape as the adventitious impact of life's experiences generate admixtures of composites of the prototypes, compounds, and blendings that result from the influence of familial and cultural forces. Also among these mosaic amalgamations are subtype variants that differ in their degree of "normality or abnormality." Thus, the exigencies of evolution can sequentially and ultimately generate, in interaction with sociocultural experiences, several pure prototypes, numerous subtypes, and well as any number of levels of healthy and unhealthy multiforms.

Third, there is a need to develop a schema of trait characteristics and associated quantitative tools by which we can differentiate and assess the personality types and subtypes. Numerous theories have been advanced from which selective trait features are highlighted; for example, those that give primacy to interpersonal relations, or cognitive beliefs, or intrapsychic processes, or neurologically based dispositions. Each of these is productive as a source of personological or clinical study. But, the singularity of their focus is severely limiting. We believe a trait format should incorporate and subsume all of these part function characteristics in an overarching schema of *trait domains*, e.g., interpersonal conduct, cognitive style, mood temperament. Similarly, mathematical efforts have been employed to deduce traits from covariant data sources, the most popular of these being several factorial procedures. As will be noted later, numerical procedures, in our judgment, of either a simple arithmetic character or a more complex algebraic formula, are likely to be a more productive methodological resource than factor analysis for assessing quantitative gauges of the several trait domains. These will be touched upon in later paragraphs as well.

To restate our essential thesis, and sound somewhat Mosaic about the matter, let us be reminded that "Nature is One." We humans, understandingly, have subdivided nature's intrinsic oneness into spheres of attention and focus in order to simplify our task of understanding it; hence, we have physics, chemistry, geology, and the like. In doing so, however, *we have overlooked or bypassed those deeper and essential commonalities they share.* As addressed in earlier books and articles of ours, we judge that principles of an evolutionary character underlie all of them, that is, laws and processes that all our man-made distinct sciences share in common. Though "discovered" initially in the biological sciences, evolution reflects a set of natural laws applicable to both the physical and the psychological sciences. To us, these common rudiments and universal operations of nature also undergird our science's study of the problems of persons, as well as the logic we should follow, when needed, to select the focus and modes for their treatment. It is our view that much of psychological science remains adrift, obsessed with horizontal refinements and passing fads, a patchwork quilt of dissonant concepts and methods, rather than a unified tapestry that interweaves (unifies) its components to these deeper fundamental and common principles of nature. Table 1.1 provides an outline of the five components the senior author has articulated as a unifying paradigm for the

 **Table 1.1**

## Personology and Psychopathology Cohering the Science of Clinical Psychology

     I. *Universal scientific principles* (evolution)

       Grounded in ubiquitous laws of nature

       A guiding framework for diverse subject realms

    II. *Subject-oriented theories* (personology/psychopathology)

       Heuristic structure of explanatory propositions

       Deduction and understanding of clinical conditions

   III. *Classification of styles and syndromes* (nosology/taxonomy)

       Theory-derived traits, typologies and pathologies

       Prototypes differentiated, grouped, and interrelated

   IV. *Clinical instruments* (assessment/diagnosis)

       Empirically-grounded and quantitatively sensitive tools

       Identify/measure prototypes/syndromes/domain attributes

       Investigate theory validity and utility

    V. *Personalized interventions* (treatment/therapy)

       Plan goals and strategies

       Balance polarities/counter perpetuations

       Select domain modalities (neurochemical/cognitive, etc.)

       Synergize therapeutic integrations

subject domains of personology and psychopathology. It recommends that these fields be grounded in evolutionary principles and be designed thereby to cohere the elements and functions that comprise a science of clinical psychology.

To fail to build such a unifying paradigm of personology and psychopathology will keep us on the same unprogressive course that has plagued the field since time immemorial. Brilliant theoretical ideas have been proposed in the past, articulate classification systems and quantitatively sensitive assessment instruments have been generated, as well as imaginative therapies developed, but we remain stuck in a babble of conflict and confusion in which little is synthesized or structured logically. Integrating the several prime components comprising a clinically oriented personological science, grounded in the generative paradigm provided by evolutionary principles, will provide an undergirding framework for integrative assessment and treatment interventions. It is a task worthy of collaborative efforts on our part.

# Differentiating Normal and Abnormal Personality

Numerous attempts have been made to develop definitive criteria for distinguishing personological normality from abnormality. Some of these criteria focus on features that characterize the so-called normal, or ideal, state of mental health, as illustrated in the writings of Offer and Sabshin (1974, 1991); others have sought to specify criteria for concepts such as abnormality or psychopathology. The most common criterion employed is a statistical one in which normality is determined by those behaviors that are found most frequently in a social group, and pathology or abnormality by features that are uncommon in that population. Accordingly, normality and pathology may be seen as relative concepts; they represent arbitrary points on a continuum or gradient. No sharp line divides normal from pathological behavior. Moreover, personality is so complex that certain areas of personological functioning operate normally, although others do not. In addition, behaviors that prove adaptive at one time fail to do so at another. As the focus of this chapter is on personality, both normal and abnormal, we should ask at the outset, how do we conceive the subject of personality?

The word *personality* derives from the Greek term *persona* and was chosen to represent the theatrical mask used by dramatic players. This meaning has changed. As a mask assumed by an actor it suggested a pretense of appearance, that is, the possession of traits other than those which actually characterized the individual behind the mask. In time, the term persona lost its connotation of pretense and illusion, and began to represent, not the mask, but the real person, his/her apparent, explicit, and manifest features. A third meaning that the term personality acquired delves "beneath" the surface impression of the person and turns the spotlight on the inner, less revealed, and hidden psychological qualities of the individual. Thus, the term shifted from meaning external illusion to surface reality, to opaque or veiled inner traits. This third meaning comes closest to contemporary psychoanalytic use. *Personology*, a term coined by Murray (1938), was selected to represent a field of study, one that sees the subject as a complex pattern of deeply embedded psychological characteristics that cannot be eradicated easily and express themselves automatically in most facets of functioning. Intrinsic and pervasive, they are composed of traits that emerge from a complicated matrix of biological dispositions and experiential learnings and now comprise the individual's distinctive pattern of perceiving, feeling, thinking, and coping.

Murray also stressed the developmental perspective of personology. As he and his followers saw it, each child displays a wide variety of behaviors in the first years of life. Although exhibiting a measure of consistency consonant with his or her constitutional disposition, the way in which the child responds to and copes with the environment tends to be largely spontaneous, changeable, and unpredictable. These seemingly random and capricious behaviors serve an important exploratory function. The child is "trying out" a variety of behavioral alternatives for dealing with his/her environment. Over time the child begins to discern which of these actions enable him to achieve his or her desires and avoid discomforts. Endowed with certain capacities, energies, and temperaments, and through experience with parents, sibs, and peers, the child learns to discriminate which activities are both permissible and rewarding, and which are not.

Tracing this personological sequence of development over time, be it normal or abnormal, shows that a shaping process has taken place in which the child's initial range of diverse behaviors gradually becomes narrowed, selective, and finally crystallized into preferred ways of relating to others and coping with this world. These learned behaviors not only persist but also are accentuated as a result of being repetitively reinforced by a limited social environment. Given continuity in constitutional equipment and a narrow band of experiences for learning behavioral alternatives, the child acquires a pattern of traits that are deeply etched and difficult to modify. These characteristics comprise his/her personality—that is, ingrained and habitual ways of psychological functioning that emerge from the individual's entire developmental history, and which over time come to characterize the child's "style."

It is important to note that the traits of which both normal and abnormal personalities are composed are not a potpourri of unrelated perceptions, thoughts, and behaviors but a tightly knit organization of attitudes, habits, and emotions. Although all of us may start in life with more or less random and diverse feelings and reactions, the repetitive sequences of reinforcing experiences to which we are exposed narrow our repertoire to particular behavioral strategies that become prepotent and characterize our personally distinctive way of coping with others and relating to ourselves.

This conception of personality breaks the long-entrenched habit of conceiving syndromes of abnormal personality, or what are called "disorders" in the *Diagnostic and Statistical Manual of Mental Disorders (DSM)*, to be one or another variant of a disease as if some "foreign" entity or lesion intruded insidiously within the person to undermine his or her so-called normal functions. The archaic notion that mental disorders represent external intrusions or internal disease processes is an offshoot of prescientific ideas such as demons or spirits that ostensibly "possess" or cast spells on the person. The role of infectious agents and anatomical lesions in physical medicine has reawakened this archaic view. Of course we no longer see demons, but many still see some alien or malevolent force as invading or unsettling the patient's otherwise healthy status. This view is an appealing simplification to the layman, who can attribute his/her irrationalities to some intrusive or upsetting agent. It also has its appeal to the less sophisticated clinician, for it enables him or her to believe that the insidious intruder can be identified, hunted down, and destroyed.

Such naive notions should carry little weight among modern-day medical and behavioral scientists. Given our increasing awareness of the complex nature of both normality and abnormality, we now recognize, for example, that most abnormalities, physical and psychological, result from a dynamic and changing interplay between individuals' capacities to cope and the environment within which they live. It is the patients' overall constitutional makeup that serves as a substrate that inclines them to resist or to succumb to potentially troublesome environmental forces. To illustrate: Infectious viruses and bacteria proliferate within the environment; it is the person's immunological defenses that determine whether or not these microbes will take hold, spread, and, ultimately, be experienced as illness. Individuals with robust immune activity will counteract the usual range of infectious microbes with ease, whereas those with weakened immune capacities will be vulnerable, fail to handle these "intrusions," and quickly succumb. Psychic pathology should be conceived as reflecting the same interactive pattern. Here, however, it is not the immunological defenses but the patient's personality pattern—that is, coping skills and adaptive flexibilities—that will determine whether or not the person will master or succumb to his/her psychosocial environment. Just as physical ill health is likely to be less a matter of some alien virus than it is a dysfunction in the body's capacity to deal with infectious agents, so too is psychological ill health likely to be less a product of some intrusive psychic strain than it is a dysfunction in the personality's capacity to cope with life's difficulties. Viewed this way, the structure and characteristics of personality, normal or abnormal, become the foundation for the individual's capacity to function in a mentally healthy or ill way.

Abnormal personality results from the same forces as involved in the development of normal personality. Important differences in the character, timing, and intensity of these influences will lead some individuals to acquire pathological traits and others to develop adaptive traits. When an individual displays an ability to cope with the environment in a flexible manner, and when his or her typical perceptions and behaviors foster increments in personal satisfaction, then the person may be said to possess a normal or healthy personality. Conversely, when average or everyday responsibilities are responded to inflexibly or defectively, or when the individual's perceptions and behaviors result in increments in personal discomfort or curtail opportunities to learn and to grow, then we may speak of a pathological or maladaptive pattern. Despite the tenuous and fluctuating nature of the normality–pathology distinction, certain features may be abstracted from the flow of personality characteristics to serve as differentiating criteria; notable among them are an adaptive inflexibility, a tendency to foster vicious or self-defeating circles, and a tenuous emotional stability under conditions of stress (Millon, 1969, 1981, 1991).

No less significant for a science of personology and psychopathology is the specification of useful personological and clinical realms in which the characteristics of persons can be systematically differentiated and compared. We have termed these as functional and structural trait domains, for example, interpersonal conduct, cognitive style, and self-image (Millon & Davis, 1996).

Similarly, we have recently articulated 15 different personality *spectra*, each based on evolutionary deductions (e.g., passive-self). Each of the 15 spectra comprises a distinctive continuum of personality variants or subtypes that range from normal/healthy styles to those who are conceived as abnormal/disordered. For example, one spectrum reflects the evolutionary active-detached pattern. Among those at the normal end of the spectrum continuum are those referred to as "shy" personalities, whereas at the abnormal extreme we find those termed as "avoidant" personalities.

As noted previously, we will attempt to present several key topics comprising our approach in sequence. First, we intend to outline the orientation we have taken to conceptualize personality, an orientation that argues in favor of grounding a prototypal concept in a firm theoretical foundation. We contend that the most sturdy scaffolding for understanding personality, normal or abnormal, will be best constructed with reference to the principles of evolutionary theory. We will record the 15 personological/clinical spectra with reference to a *circulargram* figure, and then record their functional and structural domains on two additional figures. Finally, we will describe, albeit briefly, a number of "operational" instruments to gauge these constructs, that is, assessment tools that take the form of specific instruments and quantitative measures.

## Conceptualizing Personality

How can we best conceptualize and organize the data that comprise normal and abnormal personality?

Clearly, personality characteristics express themselves in a variety of ways. Not only are they complex, but also they can be approached at different levels and can be viewed from many frames of reference. For example, behaviorally, personality can be conceived as complicated response patterns to environmental stimuli. At phenomenological or emotional levels, they can be understood as experiences of joy or anguish. Approached physiologically, they can be analyzed as sequences of complex neural and chemical activity. And intrapsychically, they can be inferred as unconscious processes that enable the person to enhance life or to defend against anxiety and conflict.

Given these diverse possibilities, we can readily understand why both normal and pathological states or processes may be classified in terms of any of several data levels we may wish to focus on, and any of a variety of attributes we may wish to identify and explain. Beyond this, each data level lends itself to a number of specific concepts and categories, the usefulness of which must be gauged by their ability to help solve the particular problems and purposes for which they were created. That the subject matter of personality is inherently diverse and complex is precisely the reason why we must not narrow the data comprising a conceptual scheme to one level or one approach. Each source and each orientation has a legitimate and potentially fruitful contribution to make. It should be clear from these considerations that no single classification of personality traits or disorders will "carve nature at its joints," that is, an inevitable representation of the "real world." Rather, our classifications are, at best, interim tools for advancing knowledge and facilitating scientific or clinical goals. They serve to organize our scientific work in a logical manner, and function as explanatory propositions to give meaning to our clinical experiences.

The subject areas that subdivide the natural world differ in the degree to which their phenomena are inherently differentiated and organized. Some areas are "naturally" more articulated and quantifiable than others. To illustrate: The laws of physics relate to highly probabilistic processes in many of its most recondite spheres, but the features of our everyday physical world are highly ordered and predictable. Theories in this latter realm of physics (e.g., mechanics, electricity) serve largely to *uncover* the lawful relationships that do, in fact, exist in nature; it was the task of turn-of-the-century physicists to fashion a network of constructs that faithfully mirrored the universal nature of the phenomena they studied. By contrast, probabilistic realms of physical analysis (e.g., short-lived elementary particles) or systems of recent evolutionary development (e.g., human interactions) are inherently weakly organized, lacking either articulated or invariant connections among their constituent elements. In knowledge domains that relate to these less ordered spheres of nature (the softer sciences), classifiers and theorists find it necessary to *impose* a somewhat arbitrary measure of systematization; in doing so, they construct a degree of clarity and coherence that is not fully consonant with the naturally unsettled and indeterminate character of their subject. Rather than equivocate strategically, or succumb to the "futility of it all," noble or pretentious statistical or theoretical efforts are made to arrange and categorize these inexact and probabilistic elements so that they simulate a degree of precision and order transcending that which they intrinsically possess. To illustrate: In fields such as economics and personology, categories and classifications are, in considerable measure, splendid fictions, compelling notions, or austere formulas devised to give coherence to their *inherently imprecise* subjects.

Is conceptual definition and classification possible in organizing the data of normality and abnormality? Can these most fundamental scientific activities be achieved in subjects that are inherently inexact, of only modest levels of intrinsic order, ones in which even the very slightest variations in context or antecedent conditions—often of a minor or random character—produce highly divergent outcomes (Bandura, 1982)? Because this "looseness" within the network of variables in normality and psychopathology is unavoidable, are there any grounds for believing that such endeavors could prove more than illusory? Persuasive answers to this question of a more philosophical nature must be bypassed in this all-too-concise chapter; those who wish to pursue this line of analysis would gain much by reading, among others, Hempel (1965), Meehl (1978), and Pap (1953). Let us touch, albeit briefly, on a more tangible and psychologically based rationale for believing that formal classification in normal and abnormal personality may prove to be at least a moderately fruitful venture.

There is a clear logic to classifying "syndromes" in medical disorders. Bodily changes wrought by infectious diseases and structural deteriorations repeatedly display themselves in a reasonably uniform pattern of signs and symptoms that "make sense" in terms of how anatomic structures and physiological processes are altered and dysfunction. Moreover, these biological changes provide a foundation not only for identifying the etiology and pathogenesis of these disorders but also for anticipating their course and prognosis. Logic and fact together enable us to construct a rationale to explain why most medical syndromes express themselves in the signs and symptoms they do, as well as the sequences through which they unfold.

Can the same be said for personality classifications? Is there a logic, perhaps evidence, for believing that certain traits (e.g., behaviors, cognitions, affects, mechanisms) cluster together as do medical syndromes, that is, not only covary frequently, but also make sense as a coherently organized and reasonably distinctive group of characteristics? Are there theoretical and empirical justifications for believing that the varied features of personality display a configurational unity and expressive consistency over time? Will the careful study of individuals reveal congruency among attributes such as overt behavior, intrapsychic functioning, and biophysical disposition? Is this coherence and stability of psychological functioning a valid phenomenon, that is, not merely imposed upon observed data by virtue of clinical expectation or theoretical bias?

There are reasons to believe that the answer to each of the preceding questions is yes. Stated briefly and simply, the observations of covariant patterns of signs, symptoms, and traits may be traced to the fact that people possess relatively enduring biophysical dispositions which give a consistent coloration to their experience, and that the range of experiences to which people are exposed throughout their lives is both limited and re-petitive (Millon, 1969, 1981). Given the limiting and shaping character of these biogenic and psychogenic factors, it should not be surprising that individuals develop clusters of prepotent and deeply ingrained behaviors, cognitions, and affects that clearly dis-tinguish them from others of dissimilar backgrounds. Moreover, once a number of the components of a particular clinical pattern are identified, knowledgeable observers are able to trace the presence of other, unobserved but frequently correlated features com-prising that pattern.

A related question that must be addressed may be phrased best as follows: Why does the possession of characteristic A increase the probability, appreciably beyond chance, of also possessing characteristics B, C, and so on? Less abstractly, why do particular behav-iors, attitudes, mechanisms, and so on, covary in repetitive and recognizable ways rather than exhibit themselves in a more or less haphazard fashion? And, even more concretely, why do each of the following: behavioral defensiveness, interpersonal provocativeness, cognitive suspicion, affective irascibility, and excessive use of the projection mechanism, co-occur in the same individual, rather than be uncorrelated and randomly distributed among different individuals?

The "answers" are, first, that temperament and early experience simultaneously affect the development and nature of several emerging psychological structures and functions; that is, a wide range of behaviors, attitudes, affects, and mechanisms can be traced to the *same origins*, leading thereby to their frequently observed covariance. Second, once an individual possesses these initial characteristics, they set in motion a series of derivative life experiences that shape the acquisition of new psychological attributes causally related to the characteristics that preceded them in the sequential chain. Common origins and successive linkages increase the probability that certain psychological characteristics will frequently be found to pair with specific others, re-sulting thereby in repetitively observed trait clusters, or what we term "personality styles" or "clinical syndromes."

The following paragraphs will provide a reasonably balanced overview of the alter-nate and rival methods of personality conceptualization, but it is our bias that "natural" and scientific classifications are best derived from the systematic principles of a theo-retical schema (Hempel, 1965). As is well known, classifications have been proposed in personality since time immemorial. Why is it that only a small number of schemas in most fields of science endure and prove informative, whereas others are patently useless or fail to withstand the test of time?

In the early stages of knowledge, conceptual categories rely invariably on observed similarities among phenomena (Tversky, 1977). As knowledge advances, overt similari-ties are discovered to be an insufficient, if not false basis for cohering categories and imbuing them with scientific meaning (Smith & Medin, 1981). As Hempel (1965) and Quine (1977) have pointed out, it is theory that provides the glue that holds concepts together and gives them both their scientific and clinical relevance. In his discussion of classificatory concepts, Hempel (1965) wrote that

> The development of a scientific discipline may often be said to proceed from an initial "natural history" stage . . . to subsequent more and more "theoretical stages. . . . The vocabulary required in the early stages of this development will be largely observational. . . . The shift toward theoretical systematization is marked by the introduction of new, "theoretical" terms . . . more or less removed from the level of directly observable things and events. . . .
>   These terms have a distinct meaning and function only in the context of a corresponding theory. (pp. 139–140)

More will be said in later paragraphs concerning our view that scientific concepts and classifications must *ultimately* be based on theoretically anchored constructs (Wright & Murphy, 1984).

No issue in personality, be it normal or abnormal, has raised deeper or more persistent epistemological questions than those related to classification. The present chapter touches on a few of these questions, but it cannot undertake a thorough examination of the deeper and more problematic philosophical issues involved in the elements of the subject. No matter how noble and compelling the goal it may be, there is no hope that a universal conceptual system can be achieved; different purposes (e.g., diagnostic, administrative, statistical) call for different solutions. There is a complex network of purposes and a correspondingly varied set of contexts and methods, both pragmatic and theoretical, which will bear on the efficacy and utility of a categorical, dimensional, or prototypal schema. It is hoped that the remainder of this chapter will guide the reader to recognize more clearly the delicate balance required among these complexities and alternatives.

Important differences separate medical from psychological traditions in their approach to classifying their primary subject domains. Psychology's substantive realms have been approached with considerable success by employing methods of dimensional analysis and quantitative differentiation (e.g., intelligence measures, aptitude levels, trait magnitudes, etc.). By contrast, medicine has made its greatest progress by increasing its accuracy in identifying and categorizing discrete "disease" entities. The issue separating these two historic approaches as it relates to the subject domain of normal and abnormal personality may best be stated in the form of a question: Should personality be conceived and organized as a series of *dimensional* traits that combine to form a unique profile for each individual, or should certain central characteristics be selected to exemplify and *categorize* personality types found commonly in clinical populations?

The view that personality might best be conceived in the form of dimensional traits has only recently begun to be taken as a serious alternative to the more classic categorical approach. Certain trait dimensions have been proposed in the past as relevant to these disorders (e.g., dominance–submission, extraversion–introversion, and rigidity–flexibility), but these have not been translated into the full range of personality syndromes. Some traits have been formulated so that one extreme of a dimension differs significantly from the other in terms of their clinical implications; an example here would be emotional stability versus emotional vulnerability. Other traits are psychologically curvilinear such that both extremes have negative implications; an example of this would be found in an activity dimension such as listlessness versus restlessness.

Despite their seeming advantages, dimensional systems have not taken strong root in the formal diagnosis of abnormal personality. Numerous complications and limitations have been noted in the literature.

First is the fact that there is little agreement among dimensional theorists concerning the number of traits necessary to represent personality. Historically, for example, Menninger (1963) contended that a single dimension would suffice; Eysenck (1960) asserted that three are needed, whereas Cattell (1965) claimed to have identified as many as 33 and believes there are many more. However, recent models, most notably the Five-Factor Model (FFM) (Costa & McCrae, 1990; Goldberg, 1990; Goldberg & Velicer, this volume; McCrae, this volume; Norman, 1963) have begun to achieve a modest level of consensus. The problem here is that theorists may "invent" dimensions in accord with their expectations rather than "discovering" them as if they were intrinsic to nature, merely awaiting scientific detection. The number of traits or factors required to assess personality may not be determined by the ability of our research to disclose some inherent truth but rather by predilections for conceiving the studies we undertake and organizing the data they generate (Kline & Barrett, 1983; Millon, 1990).

Categorical models appear to have been the preferred schema for representing both clinical syndromes and personality disorders. It should be noted, however, that most contemporary categories neither imply nor are constructed to be all-or-none typologies. Although singling out and giving prominence to certain features of behavior, they do not overlook the others but merely assign them lesser significance. It is the process of assigning centrality or relative dominance to particular characteristics that distinguishes a schema of categories from one composed of trait dimensions. Conceived in this manner, *a type simply becomes a superordinate category that subsumes and integrates psychologically covariant traits that, in turn, represent a set of correlated habits that, in their turn, stand for a response displayed in a variety of situations.*

There are of course objections to the use of categorical typologies in personality. They contribute to the fallacious belief that syndromes of abnormality are discrete entities, even medical "diseases," when, in fact, they are merely concepts that help focus and coordinate observations. Numerous classifications have been formulated in the past century and one may question whether any system is worth utilizing if there is so little consensus among categorists themselves. Is it possible to conclude from this review that categorical or dimensional schemas are potentially more useful for personality classifications? An illuminating answer may have been provided by Cattell (1970), who wrote:

> The description by attributes [traits] and the description by types must be considered face and obverse of the same descriptive system. Any object whatever can be defined either by listing measurements for it on a set of [trait] attributes or by sequestering it to a particular named [type] category. (p. 40)

In effect, Cattell has concluded that the issue of choosing between dimensional traits and categorical types is both naive and specious because they are two sides of the same coin. The essential distinction to be made between these models is that of comprehensiveness. Types are higher order syntheses of lower order dimensional traits; they encompass a wider scope of generality. For certain purposes it may be useful to narrow attention to specific traits; in other circumstances a more inclusive level of integration may be appropriate (Grove & Tellegen, 1991).

An endeavor to resolve some of these issues has been described in earlier reports (Millon, 1984, 1986, 1990). Termed *prototypal trait domains*, it mixes categorical and dimensional elements in a personological classification. As in the official schema, several criteria are specified for each disorder, but these criteria encompass a large set of clinical domains, e.g., mood/temperament, cognitive style. The diagnostic criterion is conceived to be prototypal, as is the personality-as-a-whole. Each specific domain is given a prototypal standard for each personality. To illustrate: If the clinical attribute "interpersonal conduct" was deemed of value in assessing personality, then a specific prototypal criterion would be identified to represent the characteristic or distinctive manner in which each personality ostensibly conducts its interpersonal life.

By composing a classification schema that includes all relevant personality trait domains that are *well-known and commonly used by clinicians* (e.g., self-image, interpersonal conduct, cognitive style), and specifies a prototypal feature for every domain for each personality prototype or subtype, the proposed format would then be fully comprehensive in its scope, *useful to experienced and sophisticated clinical assessors*, as well as possess directly comparable prototypal features for its parallel categories. *A schema of this nature would not only be accepted by practitioners, but would also furnish both detailed substance and symmetry to its assessment taxonomy.* The 15 spectra of the model and its associated functional and structural domains are noted in Figures 1.2 and 1.3, portrayed later in the chapter.

To enrich its qualitative categories (the several prototypal features comprising the trait range seen in each domain) with *quantitative discriminations* (numerical intensity ratings), personologists would not only identify which prototypal features (e.g., woeful, hostile, labile) in a personological trait domain (e.g., mood/temperament) best characterizes a person, but also record a rating or number (e.g., from 1 to 10) to represent the degree of prominence or pervasiveness of the chosen feature(s). Personologists would be encouraged in such a prototypal schema to record and quantify more than one feature per psychological domain (e.g., if suitable, to note both "woeful" and "labile" moods, should their observations lead them to infer the presence of these two prototypal characteristics in that domain). Reference to the descriptive trait domains of all but one personality may be found in Millon and Davis (1996).

The prototypal domain model illustrates that *categorical* (qualitative distinction) and *dimensional* (quantitative distinction) approaches need not be framed in opposition, no less be considered mutually exclusive. Assessments can be formulated, first, to recognize qualitative (categorical) distinctions in what prototypal features best characterize a person, permitting the multiple listing of several such features, and second, to differentiate these features quantitatively (dimensionally) so as to represent their relative degrees of clinical prominence or pervasiveness. The prototypal domain approach includes the specification and use of categorical attributes in the form of distinct prototypal characteristics, yet allows for a result that permits the diversity and heterogeneity of a dimensional schema.

# Manifest and Latent Taxa

The elements that comprise a classification system are called taxa (singular: taxon); they may be differentiated in a number of different ways. What may be labeled as *manifest* taxa involve classes that are based on observable or phenotypic commonalities (e.g., overt behaviors). *Latent* taxa pertain to groupings formed on the basis of abstract mathematical derivations (factor or cluster analysis) or the propositional deductions of a theory, each of which ostensibly represents the presence of genotypic commonalities (e.g., etiological origins or constitutional dispositions).

The polar distinction between manifest taxa, at the one end, and latent taxa, at the other, represents in part a broader epistemological dichotomy that exists between those who prefer to employ data derived from observational contexts versus those who prefer to draw their ideas from more theoretical or mathematically deduced sources. A parallel distinction was first drawn by Aristotle when he sought to contrast the understanding of disease with reference to knowledge of latent principles—which ostensibly deals with all instances of a disease, however diverse—versus direct observational knowledge—which deals presumably only with specific and individual instances. To Aristotle, knowledge based on direct experience alone represented a more primitive type of knowledge than that informed by mathematics or conceptual theory which could, through the application of principles, not only explain why a particular disease occurs but also illuminate commonalities among seemingly diverse ailments.

For the greater part of history, taxonomies of both normal and abnormal persons were formed on the basis of systematic observation—the witnessing of repetitive patterns of behavior and emotion among a small number of carefully studied persons or patients. Etiological hypotheses were generated to give meaning to these patterns of covariance (e.g., Hippocrates anchored differences in observed temperament to his humoral theory and Kraepelin distinguished two major categories of severe pathology, dementia praecox and manic-depressive disease, in terms of their ostensive divergent prognostic course). The elements comprising these theoretic notions were *post hoc*, however, imposed after the fact on prior observational data, rather than serving as a generative source for taxonomic categories. The most recent example of a clinical taxonomy, one tied explicitly to phenomenal observation and constructed by intention to both atheoretical and nonquantitative, is of course the *DSM*. Spitzer, chairperson of the Task Force, stated in the *DSM-III* manual (American Psychiatric Association, 1980) that "clinicians can agree on the identification of mental disorders on the basis of their clinical manifestations without agreeing on how the disturbances came about" (p. 7). Albeit implicitly, the *DSM* is a product of speculation regarding latent causes or structures. Nevertheless, a major goal of its Task Force committee was to eschew theoretic notions, adhering to as strict an observational philosophy as possible. In doing so, only those attributes that could be readily seen or consensually validated were to be permitted as diagnostic criteria. Numerous derelictions from this epistemology are notable, nevertheless, especially among the personality disorders, where trait ascriptions call for inferences beyond direct sensory inspection.

Not all who seek to render taxa on the basis of observational clinical data insist on keeping latent inferences to a minimum (Tversky, 1977). And by no means do those who draw their philosophical inspiration from a manifest mindset restrict themselves to the mere specification of surface similarities (Medin, Altom, Edelson, & Freko, 1982). It is not only those who employ mathematical procedures and who formulate theoretically generated nosologies who "succumb" to the explanatory power and heuristic value of pathogenic or statistical inferences. Feinstein (1977) a distinguished internist, provides an apt illustration of how one man's "factual" observations may be another's latent inference. As Feinstein put it:

> In choosing an anchor or focus for taxonomy, we can engage in two distinctly different types of nosological reasoning. The first is to form names, designations or denominations for the observed evidence, and to confine ourselves exclusively to what has actually been observed. The second is to draw inferences from the observed evidence, arriving at inferential titles representing entities that have not actually been observed. For example, if a patient says "I have substantial chest pain, provoked by exertion, and relieved by rest," I, as an internist, perform a denomination if I designate this observed entity as angina pectoris. If I call it coronary artery disease, however, I perform an inference, because I have not actually observed coronary artery disease. If a radiologist looking at a coronary arteriogram or a pathologist cutting open the coronary vasculature uses the diagnosis coronary artery disease, the decision is a denomination. If the radiologist or pathologist decides that the coronary disease was caused by cigarette smoking or by a high fat diet, the etiological diagnosis is an inference unless simultaneous evidence exists that the patient did indeed smoke or use a high fat diet. (p. 192)

In large measure, observationally based taxa gain their import and prominence by virtue of consensus and authority. Cumulative experience and habit are crystallized and subsequently confirmed by official bodies such as the various *DSM* committees (Millon, 1986). Specified criteria are denoted and articulated, acquiring definitional, if not stipulative powers, at least in the eyes of those who come to accept the manifest attributes selected as infallible taxonomic indicators.

Inasmuch as manifest taxa stem from the observations and inferences of, for example, clinical diagnosticians, they comprise, in circular fashion, the very qualities that clinicians are likely to see and deduce. Classes so constructed not only will direct future observers to focus on and to mirror these same taxa in their patients but also may lead future nosologists away from potentially more useful constructs with which to fathom less obvious patterns of attribute covariation. It is toward the end of penetrating beneath the sensory domain to more latent commonalities that taxonomists have turned either to numerical methods or to theoretical principles.

There has been a rapid proliferation of new and powerful mathematical techniques for both analyzing and synthesizing vast bodies of clinical data. This expansion has been accelerated by the ready availability of inexpensive computer hardware and software programs. Unfortunately, such mushrooming has progressed more rapidly than its fruits can be digested.

There are numerous purposes to which this growing and diverse body of quantitative methods can be put, of which only a small number are relevant to the goal of aiding in taxonomic construction. The designation "factor analysis" is a generic term encompassing a variety of numerical procedures which serve to achieve different goals, the details of which are not relevant to this chapter. In essence, it seeks to reveal the underlying structure of its attributes by identifying factors which account for their covariation. Toward this end, linear combinations of the attributes are sequentially chosen to cumulate as much variance as possible. Factors derived in this manner are often "rotated" after their initial mathematical solution in order to increase their psychological meaning.

Despite the ostensively productive lines of investigation that factorial techniques have demonstrated (a book such as this is clear evidence for its popularity, if not clinical utility), several problems continue to be raised concerning its applicability as an instrument of conceptualization. Thus, early in its application, Kendall (1975) reported that skepticism in the field remains high,

> . . . largely because of the variety of different factor solutions that can be obtained from a single set of data and the lack of any satisfactory objective criterion for preferring one of these to the others. The number of factors obtained and their loadings are often affected considerably by relatively small changes in the size or composition of the subject sample, or in the range of test employed. (p. 108)

And Sprock and Blashfield (1984) concluded that

> . . . deciding when to stop the process of selecting the number of factors, rotating the solutions, and interpreting the factors are all highly subjective and at the discretion of the user. Therefore, many distrust the results (p. 108).

In addition to these methodological caveats, a number of conceptual forewarnings must be kept in mind regarding the structural implications of these mathematical approaches. As is known among those involved in the development of psychometric instruments (Loevinger, 1957; Millon, 1977, 1986), a reasonable degree of "fidelity" should exist between the pattern of relationships among the scales of a test and its structural model of normality or pathology.

Hence, despite its popularity with many a distinguished current psychometrician, the psychological composition of factorial structures is far from universally accepted. Not only do few personological or psychopathological entities give evidence of factorial "purity" or attribute independence, but factorial solutions tend to be antithetical to the predominant polythetic structure and overlapping relationships that exist among normal personalities and clinical conditions. Neither personological nor syndromic taxa consist of entirely homogeneous and discrete attributes. Rather, taxa comprised diffuse and complex characteristics that share many attributes in common, factorially derived or otherwise.

Nevertheless, there is a growing literature supportive of one such model, the FFM (Costa & McCrae, 1990; Digman, 1990; Goldberg, 1990; McCrae & Costa, 1985; Norman, 1963). Costa and McCrae have provided strong evidence for the power of the "Big Five" as a latent mathematical framework for unraveling diverse and more complex structures of numerous, other personality instruments. In their recent writings they have extended the applicability of these five factors as descriptive underpinnings for the *DSM* personality disorders. This is not the chapter or setting for such purposes, but it should be noted in passing that other equally astute and productive investigators have registered a measure of dissent from both the sufficiency of scope of the Big Five, and its adequacy as a latent explicator of normal or abnormal personality (Benjamin, 1993; Block, 1995; Carson, 1993; Davis & Millon, 1993; Grove & Tellegen, 1991; Hough, 1992; Livesley, 1991; Paunonen & Jackson, 2000; Saucier & Goldberg, 1998; Tellegen, 1993; Waller & Ben-Porath, 1987).

According to the FFM proponents, their favorite instrument, the NEO–PI, has been replicated across multiple data sources, in children and adults, and in several different languages. Indeed, the FFM is usually put forward on the strength of its considerable convergence. But convergence does not signify clinical utility, nor is convergence either construct or theoretical validity. In the same way that judgments can be consistent and wrong, judgments can converge without yielding anything beyond the reliability of surface impressions. Perhaps an example from another descriptive domain would illustrate for the reader the potentially trivial nature of the FFM for both science and clinical work. Let us gather the responses of a wide range of subjects from every culture and language to a comprehensive set of descriptive terms of human physical (not psychological) characteristics. How many and what factors would be likely to emerge? Our guess is that five or six highly loaded dimensions (traits) would be identified and converge, that is, be replicated in all of these diverse settings. To specify: (a) gender; male to female, (b) race; black to white, (c) age; young to old, (d) height; short to tall, (e) physique; thin to heavy, (f) appearance; beautiful to ugly. Despite its convergence across cultures and languages, would this finding be of value in anything but the most superficial characterizations?

And for purposes of clinical science would such characterizations prove useful in the science of anatomy or physiology? Would such a lexicon of naive surface impressions reflect internal morphology or biochemistry such that surgeons could orient themselves to achieve their purposes in clinical diagnosis and treatment? We think not.

The conclusion to be drawn is that the instruments and concepts undergirding the FFM *contain no personality-relevant information beyond the judgments of normal persons, as encoded in our ordinary everyday lexicon.* The FFM should be compared to the judgments of mental health professionals about patients. Encoded in the evolving professional language of the last hundred years or so, we must ask whether our professional language, concepts, and assessment instruments contain information incremental to the superficialities of our everyday lexicon.

Clinical languages differ from everyday language because they serve different and more sophisticated purposes. Indeed, clinical languages reflect the contributions of numerous historical schools of thought (Millon, Tringone, Millon, & Grossman, 2005) that have identified numerous latent structures, as well as diverse and complex psychic processes that operate in our mental life. Surely these clinical lexicons are not reducible to the five superficial dimensions drawn from the vocabulary of nonscientists analyzed by a simplistic statistical methodology.

In fact, using such a factorial methodology, Livesley, Jackson, and Schoeder (1989) set out to identify personality dimensions based on the language of clinical thinkers. A content analysis of their research revealed that 79 dimensions were required to represent personality features. An oblique factorial rotation of these dimensions yielded no less than 15 interpretable factors, not 5. The point of this critical excursion is to point out that clinicians have access to a much more sophisticated lexicon than that employed in the FFM.

Beyond skeptics of the fruitfulness of the FFM are those who question the wisdom of employing latent mathematical methods at all or, at the very least, argue that we should employ methods more suitable to the complexities and interactions of the subject domain, such as taxometrics or structural equation models. Thus, in his usual perspicacious manner, Kendall's (1975) comment of three decades ago, upon reviewing the preceding 20 year period of statistical methods to decode personality dimensions or typologies, is no less apt today as it was then:

> Looking back on the various studies published in the last twenty years it is clear that many investigators, clinicians and statisticians, have had a naive, almost Baconian, attitude to the statistical techniques they were employing, putting in all data at their disposal on the assumption that the computer would sort out the relevant from the irrelevant and expose the underlying principles and regularities, and assuming all that was required of them was to collect the data assiduously beforehand....
>
> Moreover, any statistician worth his salt is likely to be able, by judicious choice of patients and items, and of factoring or clustering procedures, to produce more or less what he wants to. (p. 118)

The task of combining factor attributes into patterns and configurations that correspond to the personality, normal and abnormal, is one, we contend, that transcends the powers of any mathematical technique. Today, we must face the task of counteracting the tyranny of scientifically disingenuous mathematics that falsely misleads naive psychologists into thinking that the addition of pretentious or specious statistics provides them with a meaningful base for useful clinical or personological work. To achieve this task we must still depend on either a measure of logic and clinical "artistry," or the deductive powers of a theory-based model, the other potentially useful approach to uncovering latent principles for constructing and classifying the elements of our subject, and one to which we turn next.

Whereas the biases of statisticians in shaping data are likely to be implicit or arcane, those of theorists are explicit and straightforward. For the most part, the concepts and orientations of theorists are stated as plainly as their subject permits, although the propositions and deductions they derive therefrom rarely are as empirically clear as one might wish.

Nevertheless, as discussed in prior pages, distinguished philosophers such as Hempel (1965) and Quine (1977) consider that mature sciences must progress from an observationally based stage to one that is characterized by abstract concepts or theoretical systemizations. It is their judgment that classification alone does not make a true scientific taxonomy, and that overt similarity among attributes does not necessarily comprise a scientific category (Smith & Medin, 1981). The card catalog of the library or an accountant's ledger sheet, for example, is a well-organized classification, but hardly to be viewed as a taxonomy or a science.

The first purpose of a theoretical model is to cull the relevant from the irrelevant, to separate what predicts from what merely describes, and to discard the latter. What remains are constructs that form a parsimonious model of comparatively great explanatory power. Models derived through factor-analytic means, however, achieve simplicity mechanically, essentially by projecting data into some geometric space. If one is willing to go to the next step, to assume that the axes of this geometric space drive behavior, then one has only to name the axes to feel that something of fundamental importance has been discovered.

The characteristic that distinguishes what we term a latent theoretical as contrasted to a latent mathematical taxonomy is its success in grouping its elements according to logically consonant *explanatory* propositions. These propositions are formed when certain attributes, which have been isolated or categorized, have been shown or have been hypothesized to be dynamically or causally related to other attributes or categories. *The latent taxa comprising a theoretical nosology are not, therefore, mere collections of overtly similar factors or categories, but are linked or unified into a pattern of known or presumed relationships among them.* This theoretically grounded configuration of relationships would be the foundation and essence of a heuristic taxonomy.

Before proceeding with our own substantive model, we should ask what it is that distinguishes a theoretically grounded personality system from one that provides a mere explanatory summary of known observations and inferences.

Simply stated, the answer lies in its power to *generate* observations and relationships other than those used to construct it. This generative power is what Hempel (1965) terms the "systematic import" of a scientific classification. In contrasting what are familiarly known as natural (theoretically guided, deductively based) and "artificial" (conceptually barren, similarity-based) classifications, Hempel (1965) wrote:

> Distinctions between natural and artificial classifications may well be explicated as referring to the difference between classifications that are scientifically fruitful and those that are not; in a classification of the former kind, those characteristics of the elements which serve as criteria of membership in a given class are associated, universally or with high probability, with more or less extensive clusters of other characteristics.
>
> Classification of this sort should be viewed as somehow having objective existence in nature, as "carving nature at the joints" in contradistinction of artificial classifications, in which the defining characteristics have few explanatory or predictive connections with other traits.
>
> In the course of scientific development, classifications defined by reference to manifest, observable characteristics will tend to give way to systems based on theoretical concepts. (pp. 116–148)

Ostensibly toward the end of pragmatic sobriety, those of an antitheory bias have sought to persuade the profession of the failings of premature formalization, warning us that we cannot arrive at the future we yearn for by lifting our science by its own bootstraps. To them, there is no way to traverse the road other sciences have traveled without paying the dues of an arduous program of empirical research. Formalized axiomatics, they say, must await the accumulation of "hard" evidence that is simply not yet in. Shortcutting the route with ill-timed theoretical systematics, such as a latent taxonomy, will lead us down primrose paths, preoccupying our attentions as we wind fruitlessly through endless detours, each of which could be averted by holding fast to an empirical philosophy or a clinical methodology.

No one argues against the view that theories that float, so to speak, on their own, unconcerned with the empirical domain or clinical knowledge, should be seen as the fatuous achievements they are and the travesty they may make of the virtues of a truly coherent nosological system. Formal theory should not be "pushed" far beyond the data, and its derivations should be linked at all points to established clinical observations. Given the vast scope of personalities as well as the extent of knowledge still to be gathered, nosological theories are best kept limited today both in their focus and in specificity. As the senior author has written elsewhere (Millon, 1987), structurally weak theories make it impossible to derive systematic and logical nosologies; this results in conflicting derivations and circular reasoning. Most nosological theories of psychopathology have generated brilliant deductions and insights, but few of these ideas can be attributed to their structure, the precision of their concepts, or their formal procedures for hypothesis derivation.

Despite the shortcomings of historic concepts of personality pathology, it is latent mathematical models and latent theories that may "facilitate a deeper seeing, a more penetrating vision that goes beyond superficial appearances to the order underlying them" (Bowers, 1977). We will turn next to a model that may provide us with this "deeper and more penetrating vision."

# An Evolutionary Scaffold for Personality Theory

As noted at the beginning of this chapter, one of its major goals is to connect the conceptual structure of personology to its foundations in the natural sciences. As said previously, what is proposed herein is akin to Freud's (1895) abandoned *Project for a Scientific Psychology* and Wilson's (1975) highly controversial *Sociobiology*. Both were worthy endeavors to advance our understanding of human nature; this was to be done by exploring interconnections among disciplines that evolved ostensibly unrelated bodies of research and manifestly dissimilar languages.

We seem trapped in (obsessed with?) horizontal refinements. A search for integrative schemas and cohesive constructs that link its seekers closely to relevant observations and laws developed in more advanced fields is needed. The goal—albeit a rather "grandiose" one—is to refashion the patchwork quilt into a well-tailored and aesthetic tapestry that interweaves the diverse forms in which nature expresses itself.

And what better sphere is there within the psychological sciences to undertake such syntheses than with the subject matter of personology? Persons are the only organically integrated system in the psychological domain, evolved through the millennia and inherently created from birth as natural entities, rather than culture-bound and experience-derived gestalts. The intrinsic cohesion of persons is not merely a rhetorical construction, but an authentic substantive unity. Personological features may often be dissonant, and may be partitioned conceptually for pragmatic or scientific purposes, but they are segments of an inseparable biopsychosocial entity, as well as a natural outgrowth of evolution's progression.

What makes evolutionary principles as relevant as we propose? Owing to the mathematical and deductive insights of our colleagues in physics, we have a deeper and clearer sense of the early evolution and structural relations among matter and energy. So too has knowledge progressed in our studies of physical chemistry, microbiology, evolutionary theory, population biology, ecology, and ethology. How odd it is (is it not?) that we have only now again begun to investigate—as we did at the turn of the last century—the interface between the basic building blocks of physical nature and the nature of life as we experience and live it personally? How much more is known today, yet how hesitant are people to undertake a serious rapprochement? As Barash (1982) has commented:

> Like ships passing in the night, evolutionary biology and the social sciences have rarely even taken serious notice of each other. Although admittedly, many introductory psychology texts give an obligatory toot of the Darwinian horn somewhere in the first chapter . . . before passing on to discuss human behavior as though it were determined only by environmental factors. (p. 7)

It is clear that each evolved species displays commonalities in its adaptive or survival style. Within each species, however, there are differences in style and differences in the success with which its various members adapt to the diverse and changing environments they face. In these simplest of terms, personality would be conceived as representing the more-or-less distinctive style of adaptive functioning that an organism of a particular species exhibits as it relates to its typical range of environments. "Disorders" of personality, so formulated, would represent particular styles of maladaptive functioning that can be traced to deficiencies, imbalances, or conflicts in a species' capacity to relate to the environments it faces.

Before elaborating where these disorders arise within the human species, a few more words must be said concerning analogies between evolution and ecology, on the one hand, and personality, on the other.

During its life history an organism develops an assemblage of traits that contribute to its individual survival and reproductive success, the two essential components of "fitness" formulated by Darwin. Such assemblages, termed "complex adaptations" and "strategies" in the literature of evolutionary ecology, are close biological equivalents to what psychologists have conceptualized as personality styles and structures. In biology, explanations of a life history strategy of adaptations refer primarily to biogenic variations among constituent traits, their overall covariance structure, and the nature and ratio of favorable to unfavorable ecological resources that have been available for purposes of extending longevity and optimizing reproduction. Such explanations are not appreciably different from those used to account for the development of personality styles or functions.

Bypassing the usual complications of analogies, a relevant and intriguing parallel may be drawn between the phylogenic evolution of a species' genetic composition and the ontogenic development of an individual organism's adaptive strategies (i.e., its personality style). At any point in time, a species will possess a limited set of genes that serve as trait potentials. Over succeeding generations the frequency distribution of these genes will likely change in their relative proportions depending on how well the traits they undergird contribute to the species' "fittedness" within its varying ecological habitats. In a similar fashion, individual organisms begin life with a limited subset of their species' genes and the trait potentials they subserve. Over time the *salience* of these trait potentials—not the proportion of the genes themselves—will become differentially prominent as the organism interacts with its environments. It "learns" from these experiences which of its traits "fit" best, that is, most optimally suited to its ecosystem. In phylogenesis, then, actual gene *frequencies* change during the generation-to-generation adaptive progress, whereas in ontogenesis it is the *salience* or prominence of gene-based traits that changes as adaptive learning takes place. Parallel evolutionary processes occur, one within the life of a species, the other within the life of an organism. What is seen in the individual organism is a shaping of latent potentials into adaptive and manifest styles of perceiving, feeling, thinking, and acting; these distinctive ways of adaptation, engendered by the interaction of biological endowment and social experience, comprise the elements of what is termed as personality styles. It is a formative process in a single lifetime that parallels gene redistributions among species during their evolutionary history.

Humans are notable for unusual adaptive pliancy, acquiring a wide repertoire of "styles" or alternate modes of functioning for dealing with both predictable and novel environmental circumstances. Unfortunately, the malleability of early potentials for diverse learnings diminishes as maturation progresses. As a consequence, adaptive styles acquired in childhood, and usually suitable for comparable later environments, become increasingly immutable, resisting modification and relearning. Problems arise in new ecological settings when these deeply ingrained behavior patterns persist, despite their lessened appropriateness; simply stated, what was learned and was once adaptive, may no longer fit. Perhaps more important than environmental diversity, then, is the divergence between the circumstances of original learning and those of later life, a schism that has become more problematic as humans have progressed from stable and traditional to fluid and inconstant modern societies.

Lest the reader assume that those seeking to wed the sciences of evolution and ecology find themselves fully on solid ground, there are numerous conceptual and methodological impediments that face those who wish to bring these fields of biological inquiry into fruitful synthesis—no less employing them to construe the styles and disorders of personality. Despite such concerns, recent developments bridging ecological and evolutionary theory are well underway, and hence do offer some justification for extending their principles to human styles of adaptation. To provide a conceptual background from these sciences, and to furnish a rough model concerning the styles of personality, normal and abnormal, four spheres in which evolutionary and ecological principles can be applied are labeled as *Existence, Adaptation, Replication*, and *Abstraction*. The first relates to the serendipitous transformation of random or less organized states into those possessing distinct structures of greater organization; the second refers to homeostatic processes employed to sustain survival in open ecosystems; the third pertains to reproductive styles that maximize the diversification and selection of ecologically effective attributes; and the fourth concerns the emergence of competencies that foster anticipatory planning and reasoned decision making. We will restrict this brief discussion to the first three principles to illustrate normal and abnormal processes. The various components of the fourth will be noted in our description of the theory's coordinated assessment instruments. A more detailed explication of "abstraction" and its related cognitive attributes may be found in the senior author's chapter of the Wiley *Handbook of Personality* (Millon & Lerner, 2002).

## Aims of Existence

The following pages summarize the rationale and characteristics of the first of the three segments of the polarity model to be described. In each section we will draw on the model as a basis for establishing criteria for "normality" grounded in modern evolutionary and ecological theory.

### Life Enhancement and Life Preservation: Pleasure–Pain Polarity

Two intertwined strategies are required: one to achieve existence, the other to preserve it. The aim of the first is the enhancement of life, that is, creating or strengthening ecologically survivable organisms; the aim of the second is the preservation of life, that is, avoiding events that might terminate it. Although we disagree with Freud's concept of a death instinct (Thanatos), we believe he was essentially correct in recognizing that a balanced yet fundamental biological bipolarity exists in nature, a bipolarity that has its parallel in the physical world. As he wrote in one of his last works, "The analogy of our two basic instincts extends from the sphere of living things to the pair of opposing forces—attraction and repulsion—which rule the inorganic world" (Freud 1940, p. 72).

Among humans, the former may be seen in life-enhancing acts that are "attracted" to what we experientially record as "pleasurable" events (positive reinforcers), the latter in life-preserving behaviors oriented to repel events experientially characterized as "painful" (negative reinforcers).

Existence reflects a to-be or not-to-be issue. In the inorganic world, "to be" is essentially a matter of possessing qualities that distinguish a phenomenon from its surrounding field, that is, not being in a state of entropy. Among organic beings, to be is a matter of possessing the properties of life as well as being located in ecosystems that facilitate the enhancement and preservation of that life. In the phenomenological or experiential world of sentient organisms, events that extend life and preserve it correspond largely to metaphorical terms such as pleasure and pain, that is, recognizing and pursuing positive sensations and emotions on the one hand, and recognizing and eschewing negative sensations and emotions on the other.

The pleasure–pain bipolarity not only places sensations, motivations, feelings, emotions, moods, and affects on two contrasting dimensions but also recognizes that each possesses separate and independent quantitative extremes. That is, events such as attractive, gratifying, rewarding, or positively reinforcing may be experienced as weak or strong, as those that are aversive, distressful, sad, or negatively reinforcing can also be experienced as weak or strong.

Efforts to identify specific events or experiences that fit each pole of the pleasure–pain bipolarity are likely to distract from the essential distinction. Thus, the particular actions or objects that people find pleasurable (for example, sex, sports, art, or money) are legion, and for every patient who experiences a certain event as rewarding, one can find another who experiences that same event as distasteful or painful; for example, some patients who are driven to seek attention are sexually promiscuous, whereas others are repelled by sexuality in any form. In short, categorizations based on the specific properties of what may be subsumed under the broad constructs of pain or pleasure will prove not only futile and cumbersome but misguiding as well.

Although there are many philosophical and metapsychological issues associated with the nature of pain and pleasure as constructs, it is neither our intent nor our task to inquire into them here. That they recur as a polar dimension time and again in diverse psychological domains (for example, learned behaviors, unconscious processes, emotion and motivation as well as their biological substrates) has been elaborated in another publication (Millon, 1990). Let us examine their role as constructs for articulating criteria that may usefully define normality.

An interweaving and shifting balance between the two extremes that comprise the pain–pleasure bipolarity typifies normality. Both of the following criteria should be met in varying degrees as life circumstances require. In essence, a synchronous and coordinated personal style would have developed to answer the question of whether the person should focus on experiencing only the pleasures of life versus concentrating his or her efforts on avoiding its pains.

**Life Preservation: Avoiding Danger and Threat.** One might assume that a criterion based on the avoidance of psychic or physical pain would be sufficiently self-evident not to require specification. As is well known, debates have arisen in the literature as to whether mental health/normality reflects the absence of mental disorder, being merely the reverse side of the mental illness or abnormality coin. That there is a relationship between health and disease cannot be questioned; the two are intimately connected, conceptually and physically. On the other hand, to define health solely as the absence of disorder will not suffice. As a single criterion among several, however, features of behavior and experience that signify both the lack of (for example, anxiety, depression) and an aversion to (for example, threats to safety and security) pain in its many and diverse forms provide a necessary foundation upon which other, more positively constructed criteria may rest. Substantively, positive normality must comprise elements beyond mere non-normality or abnormality. And despite the complexities and inconsistencies of personality, from a definitional point of view normality does preclude non-normality.

Notable here are the contributions of Maslow (1968, 1970), particularly his hierarchic listing of "needs." Best known are the five fundamental needs that lead to self-actualization, the first two of which relate to our evolutionary criterion of life preservation. Included in the first group are the "physiological" needs such as air, water, food, and sleep, qualities of the ecosystem essential for survival. Next, and equally necessary to avoid danger and threat, are what Maslow terms the *safety needs*, including the freedom from jeopardy, the security of physical protection and psychic stability, as well as the presence of social order and interpersonal predictability.

That pathological consequences can ensue from the failure to attend to the realities that portend danger is obvious; the lack of air, water, and food are not issues of great concern in civilized societies today, although these are matters of considerable import to environmentalists of the future and to contemporary poverty-stricken nations.

It may be of interest next to record some of the normal and abnormal personalities that reflect aberrations in meeting this first criterion. For example, among those characterized in the *shy-avoidant* (SA) spectrum, the pie shape at two o'clock in Figure 1.1 (Millon 1969, 1981), we see an excessive preoccupation with threats to one's psychic security, an expectation of and hyperalertness to the signs of potential rejection that leads these persons to disengage from everyday relationships and pleasures; here we see the fundamental basis of what FFM proponents use the archaic term (neurosis) to represent. At the other extreme of this criterion we see a risk-taking attitude, a proclivity to chance hazards and to endanger one's life and liberty, a behavioral pattern characteristic of those we find in the *nonconforming-antisocial* (NA) personality spectrum (at about seven o'clock in Figure 1.1). Here there is little of the caution and prudence expected in the criterion of avoiding danger and threat; rather, we observe its opposite, a willingness to put one's safety in jeopardy, to play with fire and throw caution to the wind.

**Life Enhancement: Seeking Rewarding Experiences.** At the other end of the "existence polarity" are attitudes and behaviors designed to foster and enrich life, to generate joy, pleasure, contentment, fulfillment, and thereby strengthen the capacity of the individual to remain vital and competent physically and psychically. This criterion asserts that existence/survival calls for more than life preservation alone; beyond pain avoidance is pleasure enhancement.

This criterion asks us to go at least one step further than Freud's parallel notion that life's motivation is chiefly that of "reducing tensions" (that is, avoiding/minimizing pain), maintaining thereby a steady state, if you will, a homeostatic balance and inner stability. In accord with our view of evolution's polarities, we would assert that normal humans are driven also by the desire to enrich their lives, to seek invigorating sensations and challenges, to venture and explore, all to the end of magnifying if not escalating the probabilities of both individual viability and species replicability.

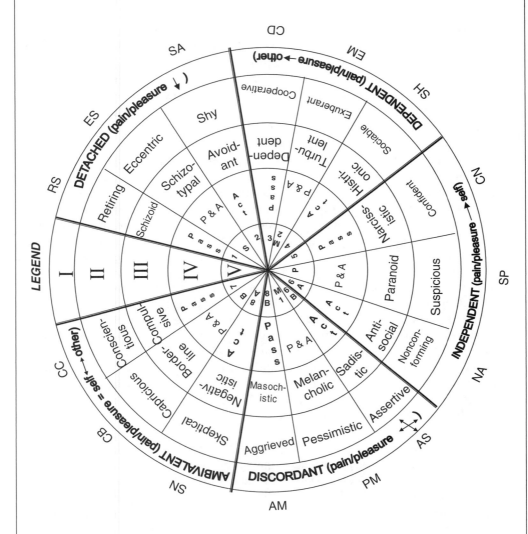

Personality Circulargram I: Normal and abnormal personality patterns. Evolutionary foundations of the normal and abnormal extremes of each personality prototype of the 15 spectra. I: Existential orientation; II: normal prototype; III: abnormal prototype; IV: adaptation style; V: MCMI-III-E Scale number/letter.

Regarding the key instrumental role of "the pleasures," Spencer (1870) put it well more than a century ago: "pleasures are the correlatives of actions conducive to [organismic] welfare . . . the incentives to life supporting acts" (pp. 279, 284). The view that there exists an organismic striving to expand one's inherent potentialities (as well as those of one's kin and species) has been implicit in the literature for ages. That the pleasures may be both sign and vehicle for this realization was recorded even in the ancient writings of the Talmud, where it states: "everyone will have to justify himself in the life hereafter for every failure to enjoy a legitimately offered pleasure in this world" (Jahoda, 1958, p. 45).

Turning to more recent psychological formulations, both Rogers (1963) and Maslow (1968) have proposed concepts akin to the criterion of enhancing pleasure. In his notion of "openness to experience," Rogers asserts that the fully functioning person has no aspect of his or her nature closed off. Such individuals are not only receptive to the experiences that life offers but are also able to use them in expanding all of life's emotions, as well as being open to all forms of personal expression. Along a similar vein, Maslow speaks of the ability to maintain a freshness to experience, to keep up one's capacity to appreciate relationships and events. No matter how often events or persons are encountered, one is neither sated nor bored but is disposed to view them with an ongoing sense of "awe and wonder."

As before, a note or two should be recorded on the personality attributes associated with a failure to meet a criterion. These are seen most clearly in the two personality spectra we have labeled *retiring–schizoid* (RS) and SA. In the former there is an hedonic deficiency, stemming either from an inherent deficit in affective substrates or the failure of stimulative experience to develop either or both attachment behaviors or affective capacity (Millon, 1981). Among those located in the SA spectrum, constitutional sensitivities or abusive life experiences have led to an intense attentional sensitivity to psychic pain and a consequent distrust in either the genuineness or durability of the pleasures, such that these individuals can no longer permit themselves to experience them. Both of these personality spectra tend to be withdrawn and isolated, joyless and grim, neither seeking nor sharing in the rewards of life. By contrast, the *exuberant–manic* (EM) spectrum is characterized by a goodly measure of joyful and enthusiastic moods and behaviors; here we see the old Jungian term adopted by FFM proponents, "extroversion."

## Modes of Adaptation

To maintain their unique structure, differentiated from the larger ecosystem of which they are a part, to be sustained as a discrete entity among other phenomena that comprise their environmental field, requires good fortune and the presence of effective modes of functioning.

### Ecological Accommodation and Ecological Modification: The Passive–Active Polarity

This evolutionary stage relates to what we have termed the modes of adaptation; it is also framed as a two-part polarity. The first may best be characterized as the mode of ecological accommodation, signifying inclinations to passively "fit in," to locate and remain securely anchored in a niche, subject to the vagaries and unpredictabilities of the environment, all acceded to with one crucial proviso: that the elements comprising the surroundings will furnish both the nourishment and the protection needed to sustain existence. Though based on a somewhat simplistic bifurcation among adaptive strategies, this passive and accommodating mode is one of the two fundamental methods that living organisms have evolved as a means of survival. It represents the core process employed in the evolution of what has come to be designated as the plant kingdom, a stationary, rooted, yet essentially pliant and dependent survival mode. By contrast, the second of the two major modes of adaptation is seen in the lifestyle of the animal kingdom. Here we observe a primary inclination toward ecological modification, a tendency to change or rearrange the elements comprising the larger milieu, to intrude upon otherwise quiescent settings, a versatility in shifting from one niche to another as unpredictability arises, a mobile and interventional mode that actively stirs, maneuvers, yields, and, at the human level, substantially transforms the environment to meet its own survival aims.

Both modes—passive and active—have proven impressively capable to both nourishing and preserving life. Whether the polarity sketched is phrased in terms of accommodating versus modifying, passive versus active, or plant versus animal, it represents, at the most basic level, the two fundamental modes that organisms have evolved to sustain their existence. This second aspect of evolution differs from the first stage, which is concerned with what may be called existential "becoming," in that it characterizes modes of "being," that is, how what has become endures.

Broadening the model to encompass human experience, the active–passive polarity means that the vast range of behaviors engaged in by humans may fundamentally be grouped in terms of whether initiative is taken in altering and shaping life's events or whether behaviors are reactive to and accommodate those events.

Normal or optimal functioning, at least among humans, appears to call for a flexible balance that interweaves both polar extremes. In the first evolutionary stage, that relating to existence, behaviors encouraging both life enhancement (pleasure) and life preservation (pain avoidance) are likely to be more successful in achieving survival than actions limited to one or the other alone. Similarly, regarding adaptation, modes of functioning that exhibit both ecological accommodation and ecological modification are likely to be more successful than either by itself.

As with the pair of criteria representing the aims of existence, a balance should be achieved between the two criteria comprising modes of adaptation, those related to ecological accommodation and ecological modification, or what we have termed the passive–active polarity. Normality calls for a synchronous and coordinated personal style that weaves a balanced answer to the question of whether one should accept what the fates have brought forth or take the initiative in altering the circumstances of one's life.

**Ecological Accommodation: Abiding Hospitable Realities.** On first reflection, it would seem to be less than optimal to submit meekly to what life presents, to "adjust" obligingly to one's destiny. As described earlier, however, the evolution of plants is essentially grounded (no pun intended) in environmental accommodation, in an adaptive acquiescence to the ecosystem. Crucial to this adaptive course, however, is the capacity of these surroundings to provide the nourishment and protection requisite to the thriving of a species.

To the extent that the events of life have been and continue to be caring and giving, is it not perhaps wisest, from an evolutionary perspective, to accept this good fortune and "let matters be"? This accommodating or passive life philosophy has worked extremely well in sustaining and fostering those complex organisms that comprise the plant kingdom. Hence passivity, the yielding to environmental forces, may be in itself not only unproblematic but also where events and circumstances provide the "pleasures" of life and protect against their "pains," positively adaptive and constructive.

The humanistic psychologist Maslow (1970) states that "self-actualized" individuals accept their nature as it is, despite personal weaknesses and imperfections. Comfortable with themselves and the world around them, they do not seek to change "the water because it is wet, or the rocks because they are hard . . ." (p. 153). They have learned to accept the natural order of things. Passively accepting nature, they need not hide behind false masks or transform others to fit "distorted needs." Accepting themselves without shame or apology, they are equally at peace with the shortcomings of those with whom they live and relate.

Where do we find personological variants that reflect problematic characteristics associated with the accommodating/abiding criterion?

One example of an inability to leave things as they are is seen in what we describe as the *sociable–histrionic* (SH) spectrum. These individuals demonstrate a persistent manipulation of events designed to maximize the receipt of attention and favors as well as to avoid social disinterest and disapproval. They show an indiscriminate search for stimulation and approval. Their clever and often artful social behaviors may give the appearance of an inner confidence and self-assurance; but beneath this guise lies a fear that a failure on their part to ensure the receipt of attention will, in short order, result in indifference or rejection, and hence their need for reassurance and repeated signs of approval. Tribute and affection must be replenished and may be sought from every interpersonal source. Extreme variants of this disposition are found in the EM spectrum. These personalities are quickly bored and sated; they keep stirring up things, becoming enthusiastic about one activity and then another. There is a restless stimulus-seeking quality in which they cannot leave well enough alone.

At the other end of the polarity are abnormal personalities that exhibit an excess of passivity, failing thereby to give direction to their own lives. Several Axis II disorders demonstrate this passive style, although their passivity derives from and is expressed in appreciably different ways. Those in the *cooperative–dependent* (CD) spectrum typically are average on the pleasure/pain polarity. Passivity for them stems from a lack of self-confidence and competence, leading to deficits in initiative and autonomous skills as well as a tendency to wait passively while others assume leadership and guide them. Passivity among those in the *conscientious–compulsive* (CC) personality spectrum stems from their fear of acting independently, owing to intrapsychic resolutions they have made to quell hidden oppositional thoughts and emotions generated by their intense self–other ambivalence. Dreading the possibility of making mistakes or engaging in disapproved behaviors, they became indecisive, immobilized, restrained, and passive. High on pain and low on both pleasure and self, those in the *aggrieved–masochistic* (AM) spectrum operate on the assumption that they dare not expect or deserve to have life go their way; giving up any efforts to achieve a life that accords with their "true" desires, they passively submit to others' wishes, acquiescently accepting their fate. Finally, those in the *confident–narcissistic* (CN) spectrum, especially high on self and low on others, benignly assume that "good things" will come their way with little or no effort on their part; this passive exploitation of others is a consequence of the unexplored confidence that underlies their self-centered presumptions.

**Ecological Modification: Mastering One's Environment.** The active end of the bipolarity signifies the taking of initiative in altering and shaping life's events. As stated previously, such persons are best characterized by their alertness, vigilance, liveliness, vigor, and forcefulness, their stimulus-seeking energy and drive.

White (1959), in his concept of effectance, sees it as an intrinsic motive that activates persons to impose their desires upon environments. de Charms (1968) elaborates his theme with reference to man as "Origin" and as "Pawn," constructs akin to the active polarity on the one hand and to the passive polarity on the other. He states this distinction as follows:

> That man is the origin of his behavior means that he is constantly struggling against being confined and constrained by external forces, against being moved like a pawn into situations not of his own choosing. . . . An Origin is a person who perceives his behavior as determined by his own choosing; a Pawn is a person who perceives his behavior as determined by external forces beyond his control. . . . An Origin has strong feelings of personal causation, a feeling that the locus for causation of effects in his environment lies within himself. The feedback that reinforces this feeling comes from changes in his environment that are attributable to personal behavior. This is the crux of personal causation, and it is a powerful motivational force directing future behavior. (pp. 273, 274)

In a similar vein, Fromm (1955) proposed a need on the part of man to rise above the roles of passive creatures in an accidental if not random world. To him, humans are driven to transcend the state of merely having been created; instead, humans seek to become the creators, the active shapers of their own destiny. Rising above the passive and accidental nature of existence, humans generate their own purposes and thereby provide themselves with a true basis of freedom.

## Strategies of Replication

If an organism merely duplicates itself prior to death, then its replica is "doomed" to repeat the same fate it suffered. However, if new potentials for extending existence can be fashioned by chance or routine events, then the possibility of achieving a different and conceivably superior outcome may be increased. And it is this co-occurrence of random and recombinant processes that does lead to the prolongation of a species' existence. This third hallmark of evolution's procession also undergirds another of nature's fundamental polarities, that between self and other.

### Reproductive Propagation and Reproductive Nurturance: The Self–Other Polarity

Recombinant replication, with its consequential benefits of selective diversification, requires the partnership of two "parents," each contributing its genetic resources in a distinctive and species-characteristic manner. Similarly, the attention and care given to the offspring of a species' matings is also distinctive. Worthy of note is the difference between the mating parents in the degree to which they protect and nourish their joint offspring. Although the investment of energy devoted to upbringing is balanced and complementary, rarely is it identical or even comparable in either devotion or determination. This disparity in reproductive "investment" strategies, especially evident among animal species (insects, reptiles, birds, mammals), underlies the evolution of the male and female genders, the foundation for the third cardinal polarity we propose to account for evolution's procession.

Somewhat less profound than that of the first polarity, which represents the line separating the enhancement of order (existence–life) from the prevention of disorder (nonexistence–death), or that of the second polarity, differentiating the adaptive modes of accommodation (passive–plant) from those of modification (active–animal), the third polarity, based on distinctions in replication strategies, is no less fundamental in that it contrasts the maximization of reproductive propagation (self–male) from that of the maximization of reproductive nurturance (other–female).

Evolutionary biologists (Cole, 1954; Trivers, 1974; Wilson, 1975) have recorded marked differences among species in both the cycle and pattern of their reproductive behaviors. Of special interest is the extreme diversity among *and* within species in the number of offspring spawned and the consequent nurturing and protective investment the parents make in the survival of their progeny. Designated the *r*-strategy and *K*-strategy in population biology, the former represents a pattern of propagating a vast number of offspring but exhibiting minimal attention to their survival; the latter is typified by the production of few progeny followed by considerable effort to assure their survival.

Not only do species differ in where they fall on the *r*- to *K*-strategy continuum, but *within* most animal species an important distinction may be drawn between male and female genders. It is this latter differentiation that undergirds what has been termed the self-versus other-oriented polarity.

In effect, males tend to be self-oriented owing to the fact that competitive advantages that inhere within themselves maximize the replication of their genes. Conversely, females tend to be other-oriented owing to the fact that their competence in nurturing and protecting their limited progeny maximizes the replication of their genes. The consequences of the male's *r*-strategy are a broad range of what may be seen as self-as opposed to other-oriented behaviors, such as acting in an egotistic, insensitive, inconsiderate, uncaring, and noncommunicative manner. In contrast, females are more disposed to be other-oriented, affiliative, intimate, empathic, protective, and solicitous (Gilligan, 1982; Rushton, 1985; Wilson, 1978).

As before, we consider both of the following criteria necessary to the definition and determination of normality. We see no necessary antithesis between the two. Humans can be both self-actualizing and other-encouraging, although most persons are likely to lean toward one or the other side. A balance that coordinates the two provides a satisfactory answer to the question of whether one should be devoted to the support and welfare of others or fashion one's life in accord with one's own needs and desires.

**Reproductive Nurturance: Constructively Loving Others.** As described earlier, recombinant replication achieved by sexual mating entails a balanced though asymmetric parental investment in both the genesis and nurturance of offspring.

Before we turn to some of the indices and views of the self–other polarity, let us be mindful that these conceptually derived extremes do not evince themselves in sharp and distinct gender differences. Such proclivities are matters of degree, not absolutes, owing not only to the consequences of recombinant "shuffling" and gene "crossing over" but also to the influential effects of cultural values and social learning. Consequently, most "normal" individuals exhibit intermediate characteristics on this as well as on the other two polarity sets.

More eloquent proposals related to this criterion have been formulated by the noted psychologists Maslow, Allport, and Fromm.

According to Maslow (1970), once humans' basic safety and security needs are met, they next turn to satisfy the belonging and love needs. Here we establish intimate and caring relationships with significant others in which it is just as important to give love as it is to receive it. Noting the difficulty in satisfying these needs in our unstable and changing modern world, Maslow sees the basis here for the immense popularity of communes and family therapy. These settings are ways to escape the isolation and loneliness that result from our failures to achieve love and belonging.

One of Allport's (1937, 1961) criteria of the "mature" personality, which he terms a warm relating of self to others, refers to the capability of displaying intimacy and love for a parent, child, spouse, or close friend. Here the person manifests an authentic oneness with the other and a deep concern for his or her welfare. Beyond one's intimate family and friends, there is an extension of warmth in the mature person to humankind at large—an understanding of the human condition and a kinship with all peoples.

To Fromm (1968), humans are aware of the growing loss of their ties with nature as well as with each other, feeling increasingly separate and alone. Fromm believes humans must pursue new ties with others to replace those that have been lost or can no longer be depended on. To counter the loss of communion with nature, he feels that health requires that we fulfill our need by brotherliness with mankind, a sense of involvement, concern, and relatedness with the world. And with those with whom ties have been maintained or re-established, humans must fulfill their other-oriented needs by being vitally concerned with their well-being as well as fostering their growth and productivity.

The consequences of a failure to embrace the polarity criterion of "others" are seen most clearly in two personality spectra, the NA and the CN. Both personality spectra exhibit an imbalance in their replication strategy; in this case, however, there is a primary reliance on self rather than others. They have learned that reproductive success as well as maximum pleasure and minimum pain is achieved by turning primarily to themselves. The tendency to focus on self follows two major lines of development.

In the CN group of personalities, development reflects the acquisition of a self-image of superior worth, learned largely in response to an admiring and doting parent. Providing self-rewards is highly gratifying if one values oneself or possesses either a "real" or inflated sense of self-worth. Displaying manifest confidence, arrogance, and an egocentricity in social contexts, this self-orientation has been termed the passive-independent style in the evolutionary theory, as the individual "already" has all that is important—him- or herself. They blithely assume that others will recognize their specialness. Hence, they maintain an air of self-assurance and, without much thought or even conscious intent, benignly exploit others to their own advantage. Although the tributes of others are both welcome and encouraged, their air of pretentious superiority requires little confirmation through either genuine accomplishment or social approval. Their sublime confidence that things will work out well provides them with little incentive to engage in the reciprocal give-and-take of social life.

Those whom the evolutionary theory characterizes as exhibiting the active-independent orientation resemble the outlook, temperament, and socially questionable behaviors of the NA personality. They act to counter the expectation of pain at the hand of others; this is done by actively engaging in duplicitous, even illegal behaviors in which they seek to exploit others for self-gain. Doubtful regarding the motives of others, they desire autonomy and wish revenge for what are felt as past injustices. Many are irresponsible and impulsive, actions they see as justified because they judge others to be unreliable and disloyal. Insensitivity and ruthlessness with others are the primary means they have learned to head off abuse and victimization.

**Reproductive Propagation: Individuating and Actualizing Self.** The converse of reproductive nurturance is not reproductive propagation but rather the lack of reproductive nurturance. Thus, to fail to love others constructively does not assure the actualization of one's potentials. Both may and should exist in normal/healthy individuals.

Carl Jung's (1961) concept of individuation shares important features with that of actualization in that any deterrent to becoming the individual one may have become would be detrimental to life. Any imposed "collective standard is a serious check to individuality," injurious to the vitality of the person, a form of "artificial stunting."

Perhaps it was the senior author's own early mentor, Goldstein (1939, 1940), who first coined the concept under review with the self-actualization designation. As he phrased it, "There is only one motive by which human activity is set going: the tendency to actualize oneself" (1939, p. 196).

The early views of Jung and Goldstein have been enriched by later theorists, notably Fromm, Rogers, and Maslow.

Following the views of his forerunners, Maslow (1970) stated that self-actualization is the "supreme development" and use of all our abilities, ultimately becoming what we have the potential to become. Noting that self-actualists often require detachment and solitude, Maslow asserted that such persons are strongly self-centered and self-directed, make up their own mind and reach their own decisions, without the need to gain social approval.

In like manner, Rogers (1963) posited a single, overreaching motive for the normal/healthy person—maintaining, actualizing, and enhancing one's potential. The goal is not that of maintaining a homeostatic balance or a high degree of ease and comfort, but rather to move forward in becoming what is intrinsic to self and to enhance further that which one has already become. Believing that humans have an innate urge to create, Rogers stated that the most creative product of all is one's own self.

Where do we see problems in the achievement of self-actualization, a giving up of self to gain the approbation of others? One personality spectrum may be drawn upon to illustrate forms of self-denial.

Those falling in the CD personalities spectrum have learned that feeling good, secure, confident, and so on—that is, those feelings associated with pleasure or the avoidance of pain—is provided almost exclusively in their relationship with others. Behaviorally, these persons learn early that they themselves do not readily achieve rewarding experiences; the experiences are secured better by leaning on others. They learn not only to turn to others as their source of nurturance and security but also to wait passively for others to take the initiative in providing safety and sustenance. Clinically, most are characterized as searching for relationships in which others will reliably furnish affection, protection, and leadership. Lacking both initiative and autonomy, they assume a dependent role in interpersonal relations, accepting what kindness and support they may find and willingly submitting to the wishes of others in order to maintain nurturance and security.

The reader may wish to review Figures 1.2 and 1.3 to examine the eight *functional* and *structural* clinical domains that characterize each of the 15 personality spectra.

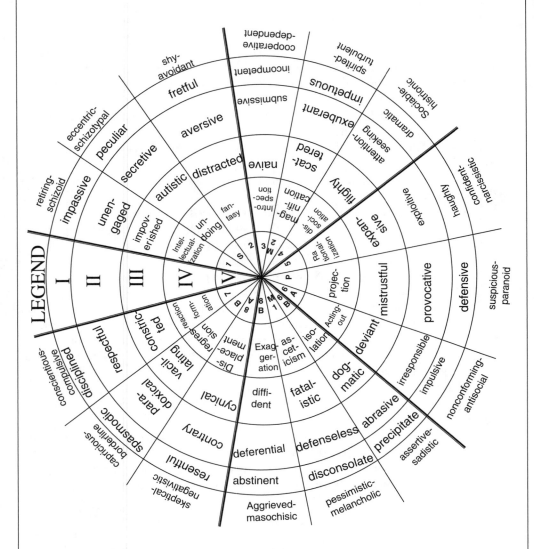

Personality Circulargram IIA: Functional personological domains I: expressive behavior; II: interpersonal conduct; III: cognitive style; IV: regulatory mechanisms; V: MCMI-III Scale.

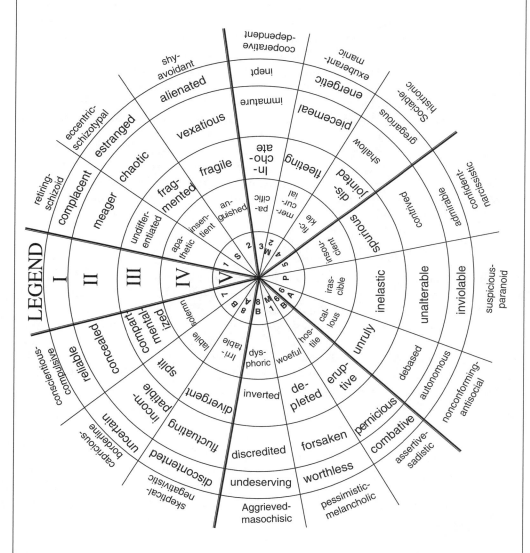

Personality Circulargram IIB: Structural personological domains. I: self-image; II: object representations; III: morphological organization; IV: mood–temperament; V: MCMI–III Scale.

# Personological Assessment

How do we measure the constructs we have proposed in prior pages? Are there "operational" gauges available that can appraise whether persons are suitably self-oriented, active in organizing their lives, over-reactive to the possibility of psychic pain, and so on?

The answer to these questions is yes! Instruments exist to assess whether persons are clinically problematic in one or another combination of polarity extremes. Best known among these is the MCMI (Millon Clinical Multiaxial Inventory, either versions I, II, or III) or the forthcoming MCMI-III; 2nd edition, 2006 (see Grossman & del Rio, 2005). Recent instruments geared to the theoretical model, but focused essentially on nonclinical or normal populations, have also been published. The Personality Adjective Check List (PACL) (Strack, 1987) was the first and most direct form of these tools. More recent is the Millon Index of Personality Styles (MIPS-R), developed by the authors and their associates (Millon, Davis, & Weiss, 1993; Millon, Millon, & Weiss, 2003). Both clinical and normal personality gauges will be briefly described in the following paragraphs. Note should be made to a section earlier in this chapter where we discussed the use of a quantitative measure (1–10) for each distinctive feature (e.g., hostile, labile) for every functional and structural trait domain that characterizes the 15 personality spectra (see Figures 1.2 and 1.3).

## Abnormally Oriented Clinical Instruments

The initial tools developed on the basis of the evolutionary model were oriented primarily to assess abnormal personality, termed disorders in the DSM, although other clinical syndromes were appraised by these instruments as well. Three initial diagnostic inventories instruments were constructed and published, the MCMI (Millon Clinical Multiaxial Inventory), the MBHI (Millon Behavioral Health Inventory), updated a short time ago as the MBMD (Millon Behavioral Medicine Diagnositc) and the MAPI (Millon Adolescent Personality Inventory), replaced in recent years with the MACI (Millon Adolescent Clinical Inventory).

### MCMI

A 175-item true–false self-report inventory, the MCMI and its subsequent revisions, MCMI-II (Millon, 1987), MCMI-III (Millon, 1994), and MCMI-III, 2nd edition, 2006, (Millon, in press) include 14 abnormal personality scales [all of the personality disorders included in the main texts and appendices of the *DSM-III, III-R*, and *IV*; American Psychiatric Association (APA), 1980, 1987, 1994)], nine clinical syndrome scales, as well as three "modifying indices" to appraise problematic response tendencies.

Within the restrictions on validity set by the limits of the self-report mode, the narrow frontiers of psychometric technology, as well as the slender range of consensually shared diagnostic knowledge, all steps were taken to maximize the MCMIs concordance with its generative theory and the official classification system. Pragmatic and philosophical compromises were made where valued objectives could not be simultaneously achieved (e.g., instrument brevity versus item independence; representative national patient norms versus local base rate specificity; theoretical criterion considerations versus empirical data).

A major goal in constructing the MCMI was to keep the total number of items comprising the inventory small enough to encourage use in all types of diagnostic and treatment settings, yet large enough to permit the assessment of a wide range of clinically relevant behaviors. At 175 items, the final form is much shorter than comparable instruments. Potentially objectionable statements were screened out, and terminology was geared to an eighth-grade reading level. As a result, the great majority of patients can complete the MCMI in 20–30 minutes.

Unfortunately, as many have noted (Butcher, 1972), assessment techniques and personality theorizing have developed almost independently. As a result, few diagnostic measures either have been based on or have evolved from clinical theory. The MCMI is different. Each of its personality disorder and clinical syndrome scales was constructed as an operational measure of a syndrome derived from a theory of personality and psychopathology (Millon, 1969, 1981, 1990).

No less important than its link to theory is an instrument's coordination with the official diagnostic system and its syndromal categories. With the advent of the various recent *DSM*s (APA, 1980, 1987, 1994), diagnostic categories and labels have been precisely specified and defined operationally. Few diagnostic instruments currently available are as consonant with the nosological format and conceptual terminology of this official system as the MCMI.

Separate scales of the MCMI have been constructed in line with the DSM to distinguish the more enduring personality characteristics of patients (Axis II) from the acute clinical disorders they display (Axis I), a distinction judged to be of considerable use by both test developers and clinicians (Dahlstrom, 1972). This distinction should enable the clinician to separate those syndrome features of psychopathological functioning that are persistent and pervasive from those that are transient or circumscribed. Moreover, profiles based on all 23 clinical scales illuminate the interplay between long-standing characterological patterns and the distinctive clinical symptomatology a patient manifests under psychic stress.

Similarly, it seemed useful to construct scales that distinguish syndromes in terms of their levels of psychopathological severity. For example, the premorbid personality pattern of a patient is assessed independently of its degree of pathology. To achieve this in the recently published MCMI-III (see Figures 1.1–1.3), separate scales are used to determine the style of traits comprising the basic personality structure (Scales 1–8B) and the greater level of pathology of that structure (Scales S, B $M_1$, $M_2$ and P). In like manner, moderately severe clinical syndromes (Scales A, H, D, B, and T), notably those referred to traditionally as "neurotic," are separated and independently assessed from those with parallel features but more of a so-called "psychotic" nature (Scales SS, CC, and PP).

Worthy of note in the just published MCMI-III, 2nd edtition, is the inclusion of *facet scales* designed to identify and measure several of the functional and structural personological domains shown in Figures 1.2 and 1.3.

Cross-validation data gathered with nondevelopment samples supported the measure's generalizability, dependability, and accuracy of diagnostic scale cutting lines and profile interpretations. Large and diverse samples have been studied with the MCMI, but it is still necessary to achieve full domain coverage in ongoing cross-validation studies. Local base rates and cutting lines may continue to be developed for special settings. Nevertheless, validation data with a variety of populations (e.g., outpatients and inpatients; alcohol and drug centers) suggest that the various forms of the MCMI can be used with a reasonable level of confidence in most clinical settings.

The MCMI is not a general personality instrument to be used for normal populations or for purposes other than diagnostic screening or clinical assessment. Hence, it contrasts with other, more broadly applied, inventories whose presumed utility for diverse populations is often highly questionable. Normative data and transformation scores for the MCMI are based on presumed clinical samples and are applicable therefore only to persons who evince psychological symptoms or are engaged in a program of professional psychotherapy or psychodiagnostic evaluation.

As should be noted, there are distinct boundaries to the accuracy of the self-report method of clinical data collection; by no means is it a perfect data source. The inherent psychometric limits of the tools, the tendency of similar patients to interpret questions differently, the effect of current affective states on trait measures, the effort of patients to effect certain false appearances and impression, all narrow the upper boundaries of this method's potential accuracy. However, by constructing a self-report instrument in line with accepted techniques of validation (Loevinger, 1957), an inventory should begin to approach these upper boundaries.

## MBMD

In a manner similar to the various MCMI forms, these instruments are best employed with persons also being seen in a clinical or medical setting. In this regard, they differ from the PACL and the MIPS-R, to be discussed shortly. Let us briefly describe the Millon Behavioral Medicine Diagnostic (MBMD:Millon, Antoni, Millon, Meagher, & Grossman, 2001) first.

**MBMD.** Using psychiatrically oriented psychological tests in settings primarily of a medical nature requires that their concepts and indices be translated to fit new populations and purposes. Medical populations are not psychiatric populations, and viewing patients within traditional mental health constructs may prove neither valid nor useful. Of course, standard techniques can provide general information, such as levels of emotional health, or the presence of distinctive symptoms, such as depression or anxiety. Problems arise, however, because of the unsuitability of norms, the questionable relevance of clinical signs, and the consequent inapplicability of interpretations. In brief, a "standard" interpretation of results obtained with a medical sample on a diagnostic test developed on and designed to assess a psychiatric population may not characterize sound test use.

**MBHI.** Developed in 1979, the MBHI was replaced by the Millon Behavior Medicine Diagnostic (MBMD) in 2001. Both were developed specifically with physically ill patients and medical–behavioral decision-making issues in mind. Brevity, clarity, and ease of administration were added to the goal of elucidating salient and relevant dimensions of functioning.

The MBMD includes a series of *negative health habit indicators* (e.g., smoking) and several *psychiatric indicators* (e.g., depression). Also, 11 basic coping styles scales are included, each derived from the evolutionary theory of personality (1969, 1974, 1981, 1990, 1996). Other scales were developed additionally to reflect *stress moderators* found in the research literature to be significant precipitators or exacerbators of physical illness. A final group of *treatment prognostic* scales were derived either to appraise the extent to which emotional factors are likely to complicate therapeutic efforts and to predict psychological complications associated with such efforts. All items were selected with data comparing groups of general medical populations or differentiating among subgroups of patients. This shift to a general medical reference population, rather than the usual psychiatric comparison groups, was expected to optimize the discrimination efficiency of the scales; the assumption that these steps should heighten diagnostic accuracy was supported by cross-validation evidence.

**MAPI, MACI, and M-PACI.** A variety of psychological tests have been developed through the years for use with adolescents and preadolescents. Often constructed in accord with the sophistication then available, their shortcomings are now evident as psychometric advances have taken place. Although these older instruments provide useful information, they tend not to be tuned to current issues and behaviors, and lack a theoretically grounded system of personality traits that can integrate the diverse features salient to the teen years. The Millon Adolescent Personality Inventory (Millon, Green, & Meagher, 1982), also known as the MAPI, was normed on both abnormal (seen in clinical settings) and normal (seen in school and church settings) teenagers. The Millon Adolescent Clinical Inventory (Millon, Millon, & Davis, 1993) was based on 13–19-year old abnormal adolescents only, and developed to quantify relationships between traits and clinical states. The M-PACI or Millon PreAdolescent Clinical Inventory was designed as a self-report tool for youngsters between 9 and 12 years of age (Millon, Tringone, Millon & Grossman, 2005).

The items that comprise these inventories were drafted in a language that teenagers and preteenagers use; they deal with matters teens can understand and find relevant to their concerns and experiences. The most elegantly constructed psychometric tool is not likely to be widely accepted if its content, length, and linguistic style make it unwieldy. A major goal for the MAPI, MACI, and M-PACI was to construct inventories with enough items to assess and illuminate accurately a variety of personality traits, psychological concerns, and clinically relevant behaviors, yet be of sufficient brevity to encourage its use in a variety of outpatient and residential settings. Both reading level and vocabulary were set to allow for ready comprehension by the vast majority of youngsters. The final 160-item MACI inventory, geared to the sixth-grade reading level and the 97-item M-PACI test, geared to the third-grade level, can be completed by most youngsters in less than 20 minutes. The brevity and clarity of the instrument facilitates rapid administration with a minimum of client resistance.

Counselors, clinical psychologists, and psychiatrists were involved with the M-PACI and MACI throughout all phases of their development. At an early stage, clinicians were interviewed to ascertain issues relevant to both typical and troubled adolescents. The M-PACI has seven "emerging personality" scales and seven "clinical syndrome" scales. The MACI includes 12 personality scales that seek to parallel the *DSM-IV* disorders. It also possesses eight "expressed concern" scales that address the attitudes teenagers have regarding significant developmental problems. In addition, there are seven clinical syndrome scales that reflect major diagnostic categories associated with behaviors and thoughts that may pose serious difficulties for the adolescent (e.g., suicide ideation, substance abuse).

The capacity to differentiate each of the various clinical problem areas is a key to the effectiveness of the inventory. Hence, MACI item selections were made by comparing the targeted criterion group with a general, but troubled adolescent population. The use of reference groups such as these should substantially increase diagnostic discrimination efficiency. The M-PACI items were selected following substantial evidence of their correlation with clinician judgments of psychologists well-acquainted with their psychological problems.

## Normality-Oriented Personality Instruments

As noted, the first group of instruments generated by the theoretical model focused on abnormality and clinical diagnosis. As the theory was broadened to encompass personality traits and characteristics that fell within the so-called normal range (Millon, 1991), attention was directed to the development of suitability coordinated nonclinical assessment tools. Two such instruments have been constructed in line with this goal— the PACL (Strack, 1987), and the Millon Index of Personality Styles and its revision (Millon, 2004; Millon, Millon, & Davis, 1993).

**PACL.** The first instrument specifically designed to assess the theoretically derived personality types in a normal population was developed by a graduate research group led by the senior author in the early 1980s. As the project progressed through its early revisions, the major responsibility for its further development was undertaken by one of its members, Stephen Strack. Using the adjective checklist format, the initial forms (both clinician-rated and self-reported) were composed of 405 items that were intended to reflect the theory's original basic personality types and its three more severe personality variants.

Item refinements and initial validation studies were based on data from over 2000 normal adults from a variety of diverse national settings. A wide range of validity data have been gathered and reported (Strack, 1987, 1991), including correlations with various other gauges of personality and biographic data on current and past behavior. Each scale of the PACL appears consonant with theoretical expectations and their expected personality characterizations. Thus, the PACL Inhibited scale (which reflects a milder variant of the theory's active-detached pattern and the *DSM*'s avoidant personality disorder) is positively correlated with measures of shyness, submissiveness, and social anxiety, although being negatively correlated with measure of sociability, dominance, and emotional well-being. Similarly, the PACL Forceful scale (a milder version of the theory's and *DSM*'s antisocial and sadistic disorders) is positively related to gauges of aggressiveness, arrogance, dominance, and negatively related to gauges of deference, submissiveness, and conscientiousness.

Owing to the common linkage in theory there is a possibility that the results of the PACL might be erroneously confused with parallel revisions of the MCMI. High scores on the PACL scales do not signify the presence of personality *disorders*, as they do on the MCMI; rather, they suggest the presence of distinctive personality traits. As Strack (1991) notes, all persons in the PACL development group were presumed to have normal personalities, hence the special utility of the instrument as a measure of normality rather than abnormality.

**MIPS-R.** This is a self-report inventory composed of sentence-length items rather than an adjective checklist, as is the PACL. Both are anchored to the theoretical model formulated by Millon from the mid-1960s to the early 2000s. However, the PACL, as with the MCMI, focused its scales on personality *types* as a composite or whole, be they normal (PACL) or abnormal (MCMI). In contrast, the MIPS-R focuses on the constructs that *underlie* these personality types, the latent components that combine to give rise to them. To illustrate: The histrionic personality disorder (MCMI), termed "sociable" personality style (PACL), are the manifest abnormal and normal personality forms that take shape among those who are latently "active" on the active–passive polarity, and oriented to other on the self–other polarity. Focusing on these latent components, the first set of scales of the MIPS measure the three polarity pairs of the theory directly (e.g. pleasure–pain, active–passive, and self–other), rather than the manifest forms into which various combinations of these are exhibited.

Beyond breaking down the theory's manifest personality types into their constituent latent constructs, the theory, as described in previous pages, has been expanded substantially. Whereas the three polarities of the theory are still considered crucial elements of the model and serve as a particularly important gauge of personality *abnormality*, they are now judged to be insufficient as a comprehensive scaffold for encompassing the highly diverse styles of *normal* personality.

This is not the chapter to elaborate both the full rationale and specifics of the expanded model; recent essays on this theme may be found in the MIPS or MIPS-R manuals (Millon, Millon, Davis, & Weiss, 1993; Millon, Millon, & Weiss, 2003).

Briefly, we should note that cognitive differences among individuals and the manner in which they are expressed have not been a sufficiently appreciated domain for generating personality traits. We have added a set of four polarities that reflect different "thinking styles" to the MIPS and MIPS-R. These follow the initial three polarities (e.g., self-other), which have been termed as "motivating styles." Similarly, we have added a third domain of polarities to those of "motivation" and "cognition," that are termed as "behaving styles." We share the view of many who give the manifest forms of the interpersonal dimension a degree of centrality in their personality gauges; in fact, we do judge them no less significant than either motivation or thinking styles, especially if they are organized in terms of the latent polarities they express. Thus, a third domain, comprising five interpersonal behavior polarities, concludes the MIPS-R test form, although work has begun on the inclusion of "character styles" to further advance the utility of the instrument in identifying positive and healthy orientations.

The following précis of the tripartite structure of the MIPS scales divides the test in the manner in which organisms function in their environment, one which we believe may be a useful theory-based schema for purposes of normal personological analysis.

As noted previously, we have termed the first segment in this tripartite sequence as *motivating styles*, to signify that the behaviors of organisms are prompted, energized, and directed by particular purposes and goals they wish to achieve. The second component of the sequence is labeled *thinking styles* to indicate the manner in which human organisms seek out, regulate, internalize, and transform information about their environment and themselves, a step necessary if organisms are to achieve their aims effectively. The third segment in the sequence is referred to as *behaving styles* to represent the different ways in which human organisms relate to and negotiate with other humans in their social environment in light of the aims that motivate them and the cognitions they have formed. To capture personality more-or-less fully we must find ways to characterize all three components of the sequence: the deeper motives which orient individuals, the characteristic sources they utilize to construct and to transform their cognitions, and the particular behaviors they have learned to relate to others interpersonally. By dimensionalizing and quantifying these three elements, we should be able to represent individual differences in accord with the major features that characterize normal personality styles.

1  Motivating styles are most closely akin to concepts such as need, drive, affect, and emotion in that they pertain to the strivings and goals that spur and guide the organism; that is, the purposes and ends that stir them into one or another course of behavior. The aims of motivation reflect strivings for survival, which I see as composed of three elements, those I have referred to previously as "existence," "adaptation," and "replication" (Millon, 1990). In a manner akin to Freud (1915), these three elements are organized as bipolarities, each of which comprise two contrasting scales. At one extreme of the first bipolarity is a motivation-based scale pertaining to the existential aim of strengthening one's life or reinforcing one's capacity to survive (phrased as *pleasure-enhancing*); at the other extreme is an emotion-based scale that reflects the need to protect one's survival against life-threatening events (referred to as *pain-avoiding*). The second of the motivating aim bipolarities relates to adaptation, that is, methods by which one operates in one's environment to enhance and preserve life. One end of this bipolarity represents tendencies to actively and energetically alter the conditions of one's life, (termed *actively modifying*); the other end represents the inclination to passively accept in a neutral and nonresponsive manner ones' life circumstances as they are given (referred to as *passively accommodating*). The third bipolarity comprising the motivating domain also differentiates two scales; one scale represents those who seek to realize and fulfill their own potentials before those of others (spoken of as *self-indulging*), as contrasted to those who are disposed to value the fortunes and potentials of relatives and companions to a greater degree than their own (called *other-nurturing*).

2  The second group of bipolarity scales relates to *thinking styles*, incorporating both the sources employed to gather knowledge about life, and the manner in which this information is transformed. In a manner akin to Jung (1923), four bipolarities, the constructs they reflect, and the eight scales developed to represent them comprise this section of the MIPS. Here we are looking at contrasting "modes of cognizing", differences among people, first, in what they attend to in order to experience and learn about life and, second, what they habitually do to make this knowledge meaningful and useful to themselves. The first two of these bipolarities refer to the *information sources* to which attention and perception are drawn to provide cognitions. One pair of scales contrasts individuals who are disposed to look outward or external-to-self for information, inspiration, and guidance (termed *externally focused*), versus those inclined to turn inward or internal-to-self (referred to as *internally focused*). The second pair of scales contrasts predilections for direct observational experiences of a tangible, material, and concrete nature (labeled *realistic-sensing*) with those geared more toward inferences regarding phenomena of an intangible, ambiguous, symbolic, and abstract character (named *imaginative-intuiting*). The second set of thinking style bipolarities relate to *processes of transformation*; that is, ways in

which information and experiences, once apprehended and incorporated, are subsequently evaluated and reconstructed mentally. The first pair of the transformation scales differentiates processes based essentially on intellect, logic, reason, and objectivity (entitled *thought-guided*) from those which depend on affective empathy, personal values, sentiment, and subjectivity (designated *feeling-guided*). The second of the transformational scales are likewise divided into a bipolar pairing. At one end are reconstruction modes that transform new information so as to make it assimilate to preconceived formal, tradition-bound, well-standardized, and conventionally structured schemas (called *conservation-seeking*); at the other bipolar scale are represented inclinations to avoid cognitive preconceptions, to distance from what is already known and to originate new ideas in an informal, open-minded, spontaneous, individualistic, and often imaginative manner (termed *innovation-seeking*).

3 The third group of bipolar scales represents *behaving styles*, reflecting how individuals prefer to relate to and conduct their transactions with others. These styles of social behavior derive in part from the interplay of the person's distinctive pattern of motivating styles and thinking styles. Five bipolarities have been constructed to represent contrasting styles of interpersonal behaviors; in a broader context these styles of behavior may be considered to be located at the normal end of a spectrum continuum that shades progressively into the more problematic or abnormal personality disorders recorded in the *DSM*, Axis II. The *first* pair of scales in this, the third section of MIPS-R, pertains to a bipolar dimension characterized by contrasting degrees of sociability. At one bipolar end are those persons whose high scale scores suggest that they relate to others in a socially distant, disengaged, affectless, and coolly indifferent manner (termed *asocial-withdrawing*); on the other high scale end are those who seek to be engaged, are lively, talkative, and actively engaged interpersonally (called *gregarious-outgoing*). The *second* polarity pair relates to ones' comfort and poise in social settings; it contrasts those who tend to be uncertain and fearful, are unsure of their personal worth, and are inclined to feel insecure and to withdraw socially (named *anxious–hesitating*), with those who are socially comfortable and self-possessed, as well as bold and decisive in their relationships (entitled *confident-asserting*). The *third* pairing relates to contrasting degrees of conventionality and social deference; it differentiates those who are disinclined more than most to adhere to public standards, cultural mores, and organizational regulations, act autonomously and insist on functioning socially on their own terms (labeled *unconventional-dissenting*), as compared to those who are notably tradition-bound, socially compliant and responsible, respectful of authority, as well as appropriately diligent and reliable (termed *dutiful-conforming*). Facets of the interpersonal dimension of dominance–submission are tapped in the *fourth* polarity. High on one polar scale are those who are not only docile but also self-demeaning, diffident, overly modest, and self-depriving (designated *submissive-yielding*), as compared to those who, beyond being overbearing and arrogant, are also willful, ambitious, forceful, and power-seeking (termed *dominant-controlling*). The *fifth* and final set of polarities pertains to features of a dimension of social negativism versus social congeniality. The former is seen among those who are dissatisfied with both themselves and others, who are generally displeased with the status quo, and tend to be resentful

and oppositional (designated *dissatisfied-complaining*); they contrast with those who are helpful and compromising, not only considerate of others, but also highly obliging, and willingly adapting their behaviors to accord with the wishes of others (named *cooperative-agreeing*). As noted, scales reflecting several "character styles" associated with constructive and positive orientations will be added to the forthcoming revision of the MIPS.

## Concluding Comment

Our goal in this chapter was to connect the conceptual structure of both normal and abnormal personalities to their latent and common foundations in the natural world. What was proposed is akin to Freud's (1895) unfulfilled *Project for a Scientific Psychology*, an endeavor to advance our understanding of human behavior by exploring interconnections among diverse disciplines. It is also akin to Jung's effort to explicate the foundations of personality with reference to deeply rooted or latent polarities. In recent times, we have seen the emergence of sociobiology, a new "science" that explores the interface between human social functioning and evolutionary biology (Wilson, 1975, 1978). Our formulations, as briefly summarized here, have likewise proposed that substantial progress may be achieved by applying evolutionary notions to the study of both normal and abnormal personality traits.

## REFERENCES

Allport, G. (1937). *Personality: A psychological interpretation*. New York: Holt.

Allport, G. (1961). *Pattern and growth in personality*. New York: Holt, Rinehart, and Winston.

American Psychiatric Association. (1980). *Diagnostic and statistical manual of mental disorders* (3rd ed.). Washington, DC: Author.

American Psychiatric Association. (1987). *Diagnostic and statistical manual of mental disorders* (3rd ed., *rev.*) Washington, DC: Author.

American Psychiatric Association. (1994). *Diagnostic and statistical manual of mental disorders* (4th ed.). Washington, DC: Author.

Bandura, A. (1982). The psychology of change encounters and life paths. *American Psychologist, 37*, 747–755.

Barash, D. P. (1982). *Sociobiology and behavior* (2nd ed.). New York: Elsevier.

Benjamin, L. S. (1993). *Interpersonal diagnosis and treatment of personality disorders*. New York: Guilford Press.

Block, J. (1995). A contrarian view of the five-factor approach to personality description. *Psychological Bulletin, 117*, 187–215.

Bowers, K. S. (1977). There's more to Iago than meets the eye: A clinical account of personality consistency. In D. Magnusson, & N. S. Ender (Eds.), *Personality at the crossroads*. Hillsdale, NJ: Erlbaum.

Butcher, J. N. (Ed.). (1972). *Objective personality assessment*. New York: Academic Press.

Carson, R. (1993). Can the big-five help salvage the DSM? *Psychological Inquiry, 4*, 98–100.

Cattell, R. B. (1965). *The scientific analysis of personality*. Chicago: Aldine.

Cattell, R. B. (1970). The integration of function and psychometric requirements in a quantitative and computerized diagnostic system. In A. R. Mahrer (Ed.), *New approaches to personality classification* (pp. 9–52). New York: Columbia University Press.

Cole, L. C. (1954). The population consequences of life history phenomena. *Quarterly Review of Biology, 29*, 103–137.

Costa, P. T., & McCrae, R. R. (1990). Personality disorders and the five-factor model of personality. *Journal of Personality Disorders, 4*, 362–371.

Dahlstrom, W. G. (1972). Whither the MMPI? In J. N. Butcher (Ed.), *Objective personality assessment* (pp. 85–116). New York: Academic Press.

Davis, R. D., & Millon, T. (1993). The five-factor model for personality disorders: Apt or misguided? *Psychological Inquiry, 4*, 104–109.

de Charms, R. (1968). *Personal causation: The internal affective determinants of behavior.* New York: Academic Press.

Digman, J. M. (1990). Personality structure: Emergence of the five-factor model. *Annual Review of Psychology, 41*, 417–440.

Eysenck, H. (1960). *The structure of human personality.* London: Routledge and Kegan Paul.

Feinstein, A. R. (1977). A critical overview of diagnosis in psychiatry. In V. M. Rakoff, H. C. Stancer, & H. B. Kedward (Eds.), *Psychiatric diagnosis* (pp. 189–206). New York: Bruner/Mazel.

Freud, S. (1895). *Project for a scientific psychology* (Standard Edition, English translation, Vol. 1). London: Hogarth.

Freud, S. (1915). *The instincts and their vicissitudes* (Collected Papers, English translation, Vol. 4, 1925). London: Hogarth.

Freud, S. (1940). *An outline of psychoanalysis.* New York: Liveright.

Fromm, E. (1955). *The sane society.* New York: Holt, Rinehart, & Winston.

Fromm, E. (1968). *The revolution of hope: Toward a humanized technology.* New York: Harper & Row.

Gilligan, C. (1982). *In a different voice.* Cambridge, MA: Harvard University Press.

Goldberg, L. R. (1990). An alternative "Description of personality": The Big-Five factor structure. *Journal of Personality and Social Psychology, 59*, 1216–1229.

Goldberg, L. R., & Velicer, W. F. (chapter 9, this volume). Principles of exploratory factor analysis. In S. Strack (Ed.), *Differentiating normal and abnormal personality* (2nd ed.). New York: Springer.

Goldstein, K. (1939). *The organism.* New York: American Book.

Goldstein, K. (1940). *Human nature in the light of psychopathology.* Cambridge, MA: Harvard University Press.

Grossman, S. D., & del Rio, C. (2005). The MCMI-III facet subscales. In R. Craig (Ed.), *New directions in interpreting the Millon Clinical Multiaxial Inventory-III (MCMI-III)* (pp. 3–31). New York: Wiley.

Grove, W. M., & Tellegen, A. (1991). Problems with classification of personality disorders. *Journal of Personality Disorders, 5*, 31–41.

Hempel, C. G. (1965). *Aspects of scientific explanation.* New York: Free Press.

Hough, L. M. (1992). The "Big Five" personality variables—construct confusion: Description versus prediction. *Human Performance, 5*, 139–155.

Jahoda, M. (1958). *Current concepts of positive mental health.* New York: Basic Books.

Jung, C. G. (1923). *Psychological types.* Zurich: Rasher.

Jung, C. G. (1961). *Memories, dreams, reflections.* New York: Vintage Books.

Kendall, R. E. (1975). *The role of diagnosis in psychiatry.* Oxford: Blackwell.

Kline, P., & Barrett, P. (1983). The factors in personality disorders: Ideal types, prototypes, or dimensions? *Journal of Personality Disorders, 5*, 52–59.

Livesley, W. J. (1991). Classifying personality disorders: Ideal types, prototypes, or dimensions? *Journal of Personality Disorders, 5*, 52–59.

Livesley, W. J., Jackson, D. N., & Schroeder, M. L. (1989). A study of the factorial structure of personality pathology. *Journal of Personality Disorders, 3*, 292–306.

Loevinger, J. (1957). Objective tests as instruments of psychological theory. *Psychological Reports, 3*, 635–694.

Maslow, A. H. (1968). *Toward a psychology of being* (2nd ed.). New York: Van Nostrand.

Maslow, A. H. (1970). *Motivation and personality* (2nd ed.). New York: Harper & Row.

McCrae, R. R. (chapter 2, this volume). Psychopathology from the perspective of the five-factor model. In S. Strack (Ed.), *Differentiating normal and abnormal personality* (2nd ed.). New York: Springer.

McCrae, R. R., & Costa, P. T. (1985). Updating Norman's "adequate taxonomy": Intelligence and personality dimensions in natural language and in questionnaires. *Journal of Personality and Social Psychology, 49*, 710–721.

Medin, D. L., Altom, M. W., Edelson, S. M., & Freko, D. (1982). Correlated symptoms and simulated medical classification. *Journal of Experimental Psychology: Learning, Motivation, and Cognition, 8*, 37–50.

Meehl, P. E. (1978). Theoretical risks and tabular asterisks: Sir Karl, Sir Ronald, and the slow progress of soft psychology. *Journal of Consulting and Clinical Psychology, 46*, 806–834.

Menninger, K. (1963). *The vital balance.* New York: Viking.

Millon, T. (1969). *Modern psychopathology: A biosocial approach to maladaptive learning and functioning.* Philadelphia: W.B. Saunders.

Millon, T. (1977). *Millon clinical multiaxial inventory (MCMI) manual.* Minneapolis, MN: National Computer Systems.

Millon, T. (1981). *Disorders of personality: DSM-III, Axis II.* New York: Wiley.

Millon, T. (1984). On the renaissance of personality assessment and personality theory. *Journal of Personality Assessment, 48*, 450–466.

Millon, T. (1986). Personality prototypes and their diagnostic criteria. In T. Millon, & G. L. Klerman (Eds.), *Contemporary directions in psychopathology: Toward the DSM-IV.* New York: Guilford Press.

Millon, T. (1987). On the nature of taxonomy in psychopathology. In C. Last, & M. Hersen (Eds.), *Issues in diagnostic research.* New York: Plenum.

Millon, T. (1990). *Toward a new personology: An evolutionary model.* New York: Wiley-Interscience.

Millon, T. (1991). Classification in psychopathology: Rationale, alternatives, and standards. *Journal of Abnormal Psychology, 100*, 245–261.

Millon, T. (1994) *Millon Clinical Multiaxial Inventory-III (MCMI-III) manual.* Minneapolis, MN: National Computer Systems.

Millon, T. (2006). *Millon clinical multiaxial inventory III (MCMI-III) manual* (2nd ed.). Minneapolis, MN: Pearson Assessments.

Millon, T., Antoni, M., Millon, C., Meagher, S., & Grossman, S. (2001). *Millon behavioral medicine, diagnostic (MBMD) manual.* Minneapolis, MN: Pearson Assessments.

Millon, T., & Davis, R. D. (1996). *Disorders of personality: DSM-IV and beyond.* New York: Wiley.

Millon, T., Green, C. J., & Meagher, R. B., Jr. (1982). *Millon Adolescent Personality Inventory manual.* Minneapolis: National Computer Systems.

Millon, T., & Lerner, M. (2002). Evolution: A generative source for conceptualizing the attributes of personality. In T. Millon, & M. Lerner (Eds.), *Handbook of psychology: Personality and social psychology* (Vol. 5, pp. 3–30). New York: Wiley.

Millon, T., Millon, C., & Davis, R. (1993). *Millon Adolescent Clinical Inventory manual.* Minneapolis: National Computer Systems.

Millon, T., Millon, C., Davis, R. D., & Weiss, L. (1993). *Millon index of personality styles (MIPS) manual.* San Antonio: The Psychological Corporation.

Millon, T., Millon, C., & Weiss, L. (2003). *Millon index of personality styles-revised (MIPS-R) manual.* Minneapolis, MN: Pearson Assessments.

Millon, T., Tringone, R., Millon, C., & Grossman, S. (2005). *Millon pre-adolescent clinical inventory (M-PACI) manual.* Minneapolis, MN: Pearson Assessments.

Murray, H. A. (1938). *Explorations in personality.* New York: Oxford.

Norman, W. (1963). Toward an adequate taxonomy of personality attributes: Replicated factor structure in peer nomination personality ratings. *Journal of Abnormal and Social Psychology, 66*, 574–583.

Offer, D., & Sabshin, M. (Eds.). (1974). *Normality.* New York: Basic Books.

Offer, D., & Sabshin, M. (Eds.). (1991). *The diversity of normal behavior.* New York: Basic Books.

Pap, A. (1953). Reduction sentences and open concepts. *Methods, 5*, 3–30.

Paunonen, S. V., & Jackson, D. N. (2000). What is beyond the Big Five? Plenty! *Journal of Personality, 68*, 821–835.

Quine, W. V. O. (1977). Natural kinds. In S. P. Schwartz (Ed.), *Naming, necessity, and natural groups.* Ithaca: Cornell University Press.

Rogers, C. R. (1963). Toward a science of the person. *Journal of Humanistic Psychology, 3*, 79–92.

Rushton, J. P. ( 1985). Differential K theory: The sociobiology of individual and group differences. *Personality and Individual Differences, 6*, 441–452.

Saucier, G., & Goldberg, L. (1998). What is beyond the Big Five? *Journal of Personality, 66*, 495–524.

Smith, E. E., & Medin, D. L. (1981). *Categories and concepts.* Cambridge, MA: Harvard University Press.

Spencer, H. (1870). *The principles of psychology.* London: Williams and Norgate.

Sprock, J., & Blashfield, R. K. (1984). Classification and nosology. In M. Hersen, A. Kazdin, & A. Bellack (Eds.), *The clinical psychology handbook.* New York: Pergamon Press.

Strack, S. (1987). Development and validation of an adjective check list to assess the Millon personality types in a normal population. *Journal of Personality Assessment, 51*, 572–587.

Strack, S. (1991). *Manual for the Personality Adjective Check List (PACL)* (Rev.). South Pasadena, CA: 21st Century Assessment.

Tellegen, A. (1993). Folk concepts and psychological concepts of personality and personality disorder. *Psychological Inquiry, 4*, 122–130.

Trivers, R. L. (1974). Parental investment and sexual selection. In B. Campbell (Ed.). *Sexual selection and the descent of man 1871–1971*. Chicago: Aldine.

Tversky, A. (1977). Features of similarity. *Psychological Review, 84*, 327–352.

Waller, N. G., & Ben-Porath, Y. S. (1987). Is it time for clinical psychology to embrace the Five-Factor Model of personality? *American Psychologist, 42*, 887–889.

White. R. W. (1959). Motivation reconsidered: The concept of competence. *Psychological Review, 66*, 297–323.

Wilson, E. O. (1975). *Sociobiology: The new synthesis*. Cambridge: Harvard University Press.

Wilson, E. O. (1978). *On human nature*. Cambridge: Harvard University Press.

Wright, J. C., & Murphy, G. L. (1984). The utility of theories in intuitive statistics: The robustness of theory-based judgments. *Journal of Experimental Psychology: General, 113*, 301–322.

# Psychopathology from the Perspective of the Five-Factor Model

## Robert R. McCrae

The Five-Factor Model (FFM; Digman, 1990; McCrae, 1992) is a comprehensive classification of personality traits in terms of five broad dimensions: neuroticism (N), extraversion (E), openness to experience (O), agreeableness (A), and conscientiousness (C). It was first discovered in analyses of scales based on natural language trait terms (Tupes & Christal, 1961/1992), but it has been shown to account as well for the major dimensions underlying inventories based on a variety of formal personality theories. Jung's functions, Murray's needs, Guilford's temperaments, and Gough's folk concepts can all be understood in terms of these five factors (McCrae, 1989; McCrae, Costa, & Piedmont, 1993).

Strong links have also been shown between the FFM and measures of psychopathology (Costa & Widiger, 2002). In a series of studies in community samples (Costa & McCrae, 1990, 1992a; McCrae, 1991) using the NEO Personality Inventory (NEO-PI; Costa & McCrae, 1985) to operationalize the FFM, meaningful correlations were shown with the scales of the Minnesota Multiphasic Personality Inventory (MMPI; Hathaway & McKinley, 1983), the Millon Clinical Multiaxial Inventory (MCMI; Millon, 1983), the Basic Personality Inventory (BPI; Jackson, 1989), and the Personality Assessment Inventory (PAI; Morey, 1991). Across all these instruments, only two scales—BPI Thinking Disorder and PAI Drug Problems—were unrelated to any of the five factors, and all five factors were related to at least one scale in each inventory of psychopathology.

In the past decade, research on psychopathology and the FFM has been extended in two ways. First, there has been considerable research relating FFM measures to psychopathology in clinical populations (Bagby et al., 1999), including patients diagnosed with psychoses (Bagby et al., 1997), anxiety disorders (Hyer et al., 2003), and substance abuse disorders (Ball, 2002). Second, many of the associations reported in American samples have now been replicated in patient groups from around the world (Egger, De Mey, Kerksen, & van der Staak, 2002; Yang et al., 1999, 2002).

Were it not for the fact that there is a long tradition of segregating "normal" personality from "abnormal" personality, most of these associations would be considered unremarkable. In the NEO-PI, N is assessed by summing scales for anxiety, angry hostility, depression, self-consciousness, impulsiveness, and vulnerability. Small wonder that it is related to measures of borderline personality disorder (Trull, 1992)! Individuals low in A are described as being suspicious, aggressive, and arrogant; the negative correlations of A with scales measuring paranoid, antisocial, and narcissistic personality disorders (Costa & McCrae, 1990) are confirmations of the continuity of normal and abnormal characteristics.

Further, personality traits are not mere correlates of personality disorder scales; they share with them the same five-factor structure. In 1989, Wiggins and Pincus showed that five and only five factors were needed to account for the communalities among personality disorder scales, and these five corresponded to the factors of the FFM. Clark (1990) and Livesley, Jackson, and Schroeder (1989) began at the level of individual personality disorder symptoms and found symptom dimensions that are readily interpretable in terms of the FFM (Clark & Livesley, 2002).

Many researchers have concluded from these data that the FFM can be a uniquely valuable tool for understanding the *Diagnostic and Statistical Manual of Mental Disorders* (*DSM-IV*; American Psychiatric Association, 1994) personality disorders in psychiatric patients. On a theoretical level, analyses of the personality disorders in terms of the FFM can help to explain patterns of prevalence and comorbidity (Widiger & Trull, 1992), and to clarify divergences between alternate measures of the personality disorders (Costa & McCrae, 1990). On a practical level, assessment of individuals on measures of the FFM can facilitate personality disorder diagnoses (Costa & McCrae, 2005; McCrae et al., 2001; Widiger, Trull, Clarkin, Sanderson, & Costa, 2002). These possibilities have generated enormous interest in both researchers and clinicians (Costa & Widiger, 2002).

But there is also a more radical way to interpret the same data. We might conclude that normal and abnormal personality are not merely related phenomena, but in fact equivalent; and that the personality disorders of the *DSM-IV* are not qualitatively new forms of personality but merely descriptions of individual differences in personality as they are seen in psychiatric patients.

Adopting this position does not require that we abandon the concept of psychopathology or deny that there are some kinds of psychopathology specifically related to personality. It does, however, change the nature of the problem posed by this book. Instead of differentiating normal from abnormal personality, it presumes that all individuals have personalities that can be adequately described in terms of standing on the five basic factors (and the more specific traits that define them), and then ask how, if at all, these general personality traits are related to the various forms of psychopathology that some individuals manifest.

Thus, the FFM can be seen either as a way of understanding the *DSM-IV* personality disorder categories or as the basis for an entirely different approach to personality and psychopathology (McCrae, 1994). The more radical approach is justified by serious problems with the *DSM-IV* system, which has been criticized as being arbitrary, overlapping, and without a clear empirical basis (e.g., Livesley, 1991; Widiger, 1993). In this chapter I will note some of the problems of the *DSM* personality disorders and address ways of understanding personality-related psychopathology.

I was asked to approach the topic of abnormal personality from the theoretical perspective of the FFM. Insofar as the FFM is intended to be a comprehensive taxonomy of personality traits, collapsing normal and abnormal traits into a unified field of personality described by these five factors seems to be consistent with this request. But the FFM is not itself a theory of psychopathology, and many different theories of psychopathology would be compatible with it. I will discuss some of my own ideas on the nature of psychopathology and its relation to personality, but other advocates of the FFM might have different and equally valid approaches to the topic.

# The Definition of Personality

Some readers may be puzzled by the assertion that there are no qualitative differences between normal and abnormal personality. Surely a hebephrenic schizophrenic or a severely demented individual has a psychological organization qualitatively different from the average person's. If personality is defined broadly as, for example, "the entire mental organization of a human being at any stage of his development" (Warren & Carmichael, 1930, p. 333, cited in Allport, 1961) this objection is entirely appropriate. However, in the psychometric tradition of the FFM and of such measures of psychopathology as the MCMI, personality is more narrowly defined in terms of traits, that is, relatively enduring and pervasive dispositions to act, think, and feel in consistent and characteristic ways.

The scope of personality traits, however, can also be broadly or narrowly construed. Traditionally, cognitive abilities (which clearly fit the above definition of traits) are excluded, and in joint analyses, general intelligence forms a sixth factor alongside the five personality factors (McCrae & Costa, 1985). A more difficult discrimination concerns specific psychiatric symptoms, which may also have traitlike qualities. Some individuals experience chronic hallucinations, which dramatically affect their thoughts, feelings, and behaviors; other people have long-standing paraphilias that are consistent and characteristic. Yet, most trait psychologists would probably not consider hallucination-proneness or transvestic fetishism to be personality traits.

One distinctive feature of personality traits seems to be that they are quasinormally distributed. We can rate all people meaningfully on a scale of 1–10 on traits, such as nervousness and orderliness, but hallucination-proneness and transvestic fetishism appear to be relevant constructs only for a small minority of individuals. In the language of Baumeister and Tice (1988), most people are untraited with respect to these characteristics. By contrast, everyone seems to be traited with respect to the dimensions of the FFM (McCrae, 1993).

McCrae and Costa (1999) have proposed a theory of personality—Five-Factor Theory—that locates traits within the "entire mental organization" of the person. Traits are conceived as biologically based basic tendencies that interact with external influences over time to create characteristic adaptations, which include skills, interests, roles, habits, and attitudes. For example, an individual high on the trait of Openness to Aesthetics may learn to play a musical instrument, form a string quartet, and rehearse every

Saturday afternoon. Such acquired skills, roles, and habits reflect both the dispositions of the individual and the opportunities presented by the environment.

However, individuals may also develop irrational beliefs, dysfunctional roles, and bad habits—characteristic maladaptations. Much of what we consider personality-related psychopathology can be interpreted as characteristic maladaptations, and it is useful to distinguish these acquired problems from the biologically based dispositions that contribute to them. As Harkness and McNulty (2002) have argued, that distinction leads clinicians to realistic expectations for therapeutic change and a focus on relatively tractable problems in living.

# AXIS I Psychopathology and the FFM

In the *DSM-IV*, mental disorders are divided into clinical syndromes (Axis I) and maladaptive and inflexible traits that constitute personality disorders (Axis II). At least superficially, this appears to be a useful distinction. Clinical syndromes are distinguishable from personality traits because they are acute rather than chronic (such as major depressive episode), focalized rather than pervasive (such as nicotine dependence), or categorically distinct from normal behavior (such as Tourette's disorder). A few of the disorders currently classified on Axis I do not fit these criteria—notably dysthymia and social phobia—and some writers have suggested that they might better be classified on Axis II (e.g., Widiger, 1992).

The fact that clinical syndromes are distinguishable from personality traits does not mean that they are unrelated. Widiger and Trull (1992) suggest four ways in which traits may be related to Axis I disorders: They may predispose individuals to a disorder, they may be consequences of the disorder, they may share a common etiology with the disorder, or they may affect the manifestation and course of the disorder. Empirical examples of all these have been offered. Prospective studies have shown that high N predisposes individuals to experience depressive episodes as well as other psychiatric disorders (Hirschfeld et al., 1989; Zonderman, Herbst, Schmidt, Costa, & McCrae, 1993). Personality traits, notably C, are themselves altered in the course of dementing disorders (Siegler et. al., 1991). Jang and Livesley (1999) have shown a common genetic basis for traits and psychopathology.

Perhaps of most clinical importance, personality traits affect response to therapy. T. Miller (1991) showed that high C scores predict better therapy outcomes, perhaps because conscientious patients work harder to solve their problems. In a randomized study of treatments for clinical depression, Shea (1988) found that drug treatment was more effective for introverts, whereas interpersonal therapies were more effective for extraverts. The comprehensive taxonomy offered by the FFM provides a framework for systematic exploration of such trait-by-treatment interactions.

# AXIS II Psychopathology and the FFM

Although personality traits may be associated with Axis I disorders, they are, by definition, central features of Axis II personality disorders. *DSM-IV* provides both a definition and a taxonomy of personality disorders that form the starting point of the remainder of this discussion. Personality disorders are defined as "inflexible and maladaptive" traits that "cause significant functional impairment or subjective distress" (p. 630). The *DSM-IV* taxonomy is a set of 10 disorders thought to meet this definition, together with "not otherwise specified" personality disorders.

The specified personality disorders are a nonsystematic collection of syndromes derived from clinical lore and literature. On the one hand, the *DSM-IV* is officially neutral on issues of etiology, so the diagnostic criteria tend to be simple descriptions of behaviors and reactions. On the other hand, it is an open secret that many of the personality disorders had their theoretical origins in psychoanalysis, where clinical formulations are often highly inferential. This discrepancy means that the *DSM-IV* descriptions sometimes fail to capture the psychopathological essence of a disorder (cf. Kernberg, 1984).

For example, many clinicians have treated patients with severe psychological and interpersonal problems that might be attributed to a histrionic style. But the *DSM-IV* histrionic personality disorder merely describes individuals who are excessively emotional and attention seeking. They are self-centered, vain, and dramatic, and their speech is impressionistic. Some of us would find the company of such individuals annoying, but it is by no means clear why these features themselves constitute a mental disorder. There is no clear implication of subjective distress, and although individuals meeting the *DSM-IV* criteria for histrionic personality disorder might not be ideal candidates for occupations like forest ranger or accountant, it can hardly be considered a significant functional impairment. Of all the ways in which individuals can be distressed or impaired, why single out this one? The answer, of course, is that histrionic personality disorder is also called hysterical personality and evokes psychoanalytic associations stretching back to Breuer and Freud (1895).

Psychoanalysts often have brilliant clinical insights—as I will illustrate with Shapiro's (1965) treatment of the obsessive–compulsive style—but psychoanalytic theory often lacks empirical support, and the characteristics that define the histrionic personality disorder do not in fact covary as one would expect if they identified a naturally occurring category (Clark, 1990; Livesley, Jackson, & Schroeder, 1989). This creates problems for researchers who wish to develop internally consistent scales to measure the disorder, and item selection procedures typically result in scales that measure a narrower construct dominated by attention seeking (i.e., preference for social interaction) and emotionality (i.e., enthusiasm and excitement seeking). Thus, Millon's (1983) Histrionic scale includes items like "I think I am a very sociable and outgoing person" and is so strongly correlated with measures of E (Costa & McCrae, 1990) that its discriminant validity is questionable. These versions of the Histrionic personality disorder seem even further from psychopathology than the *DSM-IV* description.[1]

Given their many conceptual and empirical problems, it would probably be a mistake to attempt to understand personality pathology by analyzing *DSM-IV* syndromes. The DSM definition of personality disorders—inflexible and maladaptive traits causing

---

[1]Millon avoids this problem in part by restricting the recommended use of the MCMI to clinical populations, in which psychopathology can be assumed; the MCMI then need only identify the form of the pathology.

distress or impairment—is less controversial, but it begs the question of what makes a trait maladaptive. I will consider three possibilities, two of which seem viable. To distinguish the conditions I will describe from the categorical personality disorders, I will use the term personality-related disorders. My basic premise is that when patients are characterized as having a personality disorder, they in fact do not have a pathologic personality, but a personality-related pathology.

# A Proposed Definition of Personality-Related Disorders

All individuals have personalities that can be characterized in terms of the five basic factors, and they are likely to encounter characteristic kinds of life problems, especially when there are conflicts between their dispositions and their life circumstances. To take a relatively benign example, individuals high in O (who value variety) may be frustrated by the monotony of their jobs; those who are low in O (and cherish tradition) may be upset by technological innovation. Impaired occupational performance might result in either case. It is these problems, rather than the underlying traits, that bring people to psychotherapy. To define personality-related disorders, we need to understand the nature of these problems and their relation to personality traits. First, however, we must consider whether extremeness or inflexibility is a necessary criterion, and examine the roles of neuroticism and cognitive distortion.

## Extremeness and Inflexibility

The tradition of research associated with the interpersonal circumplex (Kiesler, 1983; Wiggins, 1979) has usually assumed that pathological interpersonal behavior is the result of extreme standing on interpersonal traits. Although Kiesler (1983) described normal and abnormal interpersonal behaviors as being qualitatively different, he appears to have regarded the abnormal versions as being merely exaggerations of the normal. Moderate levels of dominance are normal, but extremely high levels take on a pathological quality, much as extreme levels of body weight become clinically significant obesity.

One basis of this argument is the presumed association of extremeness with inflexibility. If one exhibited dominant behavior in every social situation whether appropriate or not, one would score very high on measures of dominance and one would also be judged inflexible. Short of this absolute extreme, however, extremeness and inflexibility are essentially independent. A very dominant individual may be assertive in almost all aspects of life, but submissive in the few situations that realistically require it. Conversely, an individual could be average on the warm–cold dimension of the interpersonal circumplex, but show inflexibility by being equally lukewarm to close friends and bitter foes.

Wakefield (1992) has discussed limitations of the statistical deviance view of mental disorders, arguing that it is neither a necessary nor a sufficient criterion. Extremeness is not, however, irrelevant. To the extent that problems are associated with a personality trait, those who rank higher on the trait will have a greater risk of encountering those problems. If open individuals require an occasional break from the monotony of routine at work, extremely open individuals may be unable to tolerate any routine.

## The Contribution of Neuroticism

Subjective distress is one of the hallmarks of a personality disorder, and the tendency to experience distress is central to the definition of neuroticism (Watson & Clark, 1984). We might therefore argue that high standing on this dimension is prima facie evidence of a personality-related disorder. Trull (1992) noted that the borderline personality disorder in particular, with its symptoms of depression, hostility, and impulsiveness, is virtually isomorphic with N as measured by facets of the NEO-PI. Individuals with extremely high scores on scales measuring chronic anxiety, angry hostility, depression, self-consciousness, impulsiveness, and vulnerability would surely be at high risk for receiving a diagnosis of borderline personality disorder.

The combination of N with other personality factors could give rise to other kinds of disorder. Individuals with a diagnosis of Histrionic personality disorder may in fact be extraverts who are also high in N. If so, we would expect that their distinctive features would have distressing implications not explicitly noted in *DSM-IV*. They might be vain, but secretly terrified that they are losing their looks. They might seek out social contacts, but be painfully self-conscious when they receive the attention they seek.[2]

Distress is by far the most common reason individuals have for seeking psychotherapy, and patients with many different disorders share high levels of N (e.g., Fagan et al., 1991; Mutén, 1991). It is hard to understand why else an individual with Schizoid characteristics—solitary, indifferent to social opinion, constricted in affect—would ever be found in treatment. Although antisocial patients are often thought to be callous and indifferent to psychological pain, those in voluntary treatment are in fact exceptionally high in N (as well as being low in A and C; Brooner et al., 1991). Trull (1992) found that 9 of the 11 personality disorders as assessed by the Personality Disorder Questionnaire, Revised (Hyler & Rieder, 1987) were significantly associated with N in a clinical sample.

The idea that personality disorders are merely the expression of different levels of E, O, A, and C in combination with high levels of N has considerable appeal; certainly most individuals diagnosed as having personality disorders could be described by that formula. The problem is that it is too broad. There are many individuals who have high N scores, yet do not seek and probably do not need psychotherapy. Jung (1933) noted this fact long ago:

> People whose own temperaments offer problems are often neurotic, but it would be a serious misunderstanding to confuse the existence of problems with neurosis. There is a marked distinction between the two in that the neurotic is ill because he is unconscious of his problems; while the man with a difficult temperament suffers from his conscious problems without being ill. (p. 101)

We may not wish to adopt Jung's view that psychopathology can be equated with unconscious problems, but there is a useful insight here: All people have problems—high N people more than most—but problems become disorders only when they exceed

---

[2]This apparently incongruous combination of gregariousness and self-consciousness is not really implausible: Revised NEO-PI scales measuring these traits are only modestly negatively correlated, $r = -.23$ (Costa & McCrae, 1992b).

the individual's ability to deal with them. The borderline who is simply overwhelmed by affect, the abusive husband who cannot control his temper despite the likelihood of legal consequences, the narcissist who cannot understand why she has alienated all her friends, the passive–aggressive individual whose career never advances all have problems that require professional assistance. These people can be regarded as having personality-related disorders.

## The Contribution of Disordered Cognition

Most people solve their own problems, or require only temporary assistance in adjusting to new circumstances. People with personality-related disorders have chronic problems that they are unable to deal with effectively. The difference might be attributed to disturbances in thinking.

This is perhaps clearest from a consideration of the *DSM-IV* schizotypal personality disorder. Although some aspects of this disorder (e.g., extreme social anxiety) can be described in terms of the FFM, the most characteristic features are aberrant cognition: odd beliefs, unusual perceptions, ideas of reference. Very open individuals often entertain unconventional ideas of the sort measured by Epstein and Meier's (1989) Esoteric Thinking scale (McCrae & Costa, 1997), but the resemblance of these ideas to schizotypal thinking is merely superficial. Schizotypal individuals are not open-minded, they are out of touch with conventional reality. This is not a feature captured by the FFM, and it is not surprising that there is no correlation between any of the five factors and Jackson's (1989) Thinking Disorder scale.

Cognitive distortions of one kind or another are also features of many of the other *DSM-IV* disorders. Borderlines have identity disturbances, Histrionics have impressionistic thinking, Narcissists have an inflated sense of self-importance, Paranoids have groundless suspicions, Schizoids are vague and absent-minded. There is a sense in which all these disorders reflect misperceptions of reality, whether this is due to some defect in cognitive apparatus (as is perhaps the case with schizotypals), to the motivated repression hypothesized by psychoanalysts, or to a simple lack of insight into one's own personality traits and their interaction with the world.

Such cognitive distortions would help explain the persistence of maladaptive behaviors. Normal behavior is characterized by flexible adaptation. When we discover that our high opinions of ourselves are not shared by those around us, we may change our evaluations of ourselves or of them, but we will not continue to be unpleasantly surprised by their lack of esteem for us. When our outbursts of temper fail to win others' submission, we learn to control our temper. But when we cannot understand the reasons for our problems we are likely to remain unable to resolve or accept them.

The presence of some form of cognitive distortion makes it readily understandable why personality-related disorders should be regarded as mental disorders: Those who suffer from them are, in greater or lesser degree, out of touch with reality—they are irrational. This requirement is also consistent with (though broader than) cognitive–behavioral views, which identify dysfunctional cognitive schema as the source of personality disorders (Beck & Freeman, 1990).

In practice, deciding when a view of reality is a misperception can be difficult, although this difficulty is unavoidable in many psychiatric diagnoses. In practice, also, psychological distress is probably sufficient to warrant treatment, whether or not there is cognitive distortion. But a more theoretically satisfying (if tentative) definition of a personality-related disorder is *a set of life problems that (a) are characteristically related to the individual's personality traits; (b) cause the individual significant distress; and (c) are maintained by misperceptions of reality.* Extreme standing on a trait makes it more likely that one will encounter the specific kinds of problems that are associated with the trait, and extreme standing on N makes it more likely that one will be significantly distressed by them, but neither of these is required by the proposed definition.

This definition might be elaborated by allowing *functional impairment* as an alternative to *distress* in (b), or by adopting some criterion of social harm as an alternative to personal impairment (to accommodate such conditions as Antisocial personality disorder). But it seems likely that the basic definition would be suitable for the majority of individuals who appear for psychotherapy.

One notable feature of this definition is that it makes personality-related disorders in principle curable. *DSM-IV* personality disorders by definition are "stable over time" (p. 629), but that is not implied in the definition offered here. Although the underlying personality traits are very stable in adulthood (McCrae & Costa, 2003), the particular problems they give rise to may be acute. Psychotherapeutic interventions (e.g., Beck & Freeman, 1990) that give people insight into their problems or teach them methods of dealing with distress may justify discontinuation of the diagnosis.

## An Example: The Obsessive-Compulsive Style

Many of these ideas were anticipated by Shapiro in his 1965 classic, *Neurotic Styles*. His description of styles as "forms of functioning—ways of thinking, experiencing, and behaving" is consistent with modern definitions of traits, and the neurotic styles he so vividly described would probably be generally accepted today as instances of personality disorders.

Consider the obsessive–compulsive style. Among the hallmarks of this style are attention to detail; a strong sense of obligation, making "I should . . ." a preoccupying thought; intense and continuous work; ceaseless efforts at self-regulation; and a lack of spontaneity. These characteristics clearly call to mind Conscientiousness, a factor defined by traits such as order, dutifulness, achievement striving, self-discipline, and deliberation. It is thus not surprising that the Compulsive scale of the MCMI is strongly related to C (Costa & McCrae, 1990). But traits related to C are normally considered desirable characteristics, contributing to a productive and fulfilling life (McCrae & Costa, 1991). If these are the same traits, why are they pathological in the obsessive–compulsive's case?

Shapiro makes it clear that one difference is in the associated distress-proneness. Although they work ceaselessly, such people take little pleasure in their work. Instead, they do it because they feel that they must, and they suffer from an overwhelming sense of pressure, living a life "characterized by a more or less continuous experience of tense deliberateness, a sense of effort, of trying" (p. 31). At the same time, on vacations or weekends, "those occasions when the regular duties, responsibilities, and burdens of work, about which they have complained, are lifted, they show unmistakable signs of discomfort until they have located some new pressure or compelling duty" (p. 40). This damned-if-you-do, damned-if-you-don't phenomenon is characteristic of individuals high in N, who misattribute their intrinsic distress-proneness to some feature of their environment. High N is also seen in the obsessive's worry about making the "right" decision, and in the common fear of losing control.

Shapiro also noted a loss of contact with reality in such individuals. They are preoccupied with detail to such an extent that they lose all perspective on their actions, devoting as much time and effort to trivial tasks as to major life concerns. Their thinking is dominated by "technical signs and indicators" (p. 52) rather than by a direct perception of their social reality, and this indirect view of the world can lead to either dogmatism or doubt when the signs and indicators misrepresent the reality of the situation. Technical, rule-guided thinking is consistent with the orderliness of high C individuals and contributes to disciplined thinking, notably in the sciences. Unless it is grounded in reality, however, it leads instead to maladaptive absurdities. For example, an obsessive–compulsive may believe that he "should" be more spontaneous, and set about deliberately trying to act spontaneously, oblivious to the inherent contradiction in the attempt.

These elements of high C, high N, and cognitive distortion do not covary to form a discrete category. Livesley, Jackson, and Schroeder (1989), for example, found a "Compulsive Behaviors" factor defined by orderliness, precision, and organization, but they noted that "some dimensions usually associated with obsessive–compulsive personality disorder, namely, Perfectionism, Compulsive Activity, Frugality, Rigid Cognitive Style, and Restricted Expression of Affect, were not salient on this component" (p. 299). But high C, high N, and cognitive distortion are also not mutually exclusive, and when they happen to coincide in the same individual, the obsessive–compulsive style may emerge.

# Personality-Related Problems and the *DSM*

The definition of personality-related disorders described and illustrated in the two preceding sections was initially proposed in the first edition of this book, but it appears to have had very little impact on the field. In particular, there has been scant attention to the issue of cognitive distortions as defining characteristics of personality-related disorders, perhaps because the assessment of cognitive distortions is difficult (but see Barriga & Gibbs, 1996).

Instead, what has evolved is a broader perspective. Instead of tightly defining personality-related disorders by a set of necessary and sufficient criteria, current thinking points out that there is a continuum of problems-in-living associated with personality traits, and that researchers and practitioners need a flexible system that can be applied anywhere along the continuum.

Widiger, Costa, and McCrae (2002) have proposed a four-step process to meet this need. Diagnosis of individual patients begins with an assessment of standing on each of the five factors and their associated facets, either by clinical judgment (M. J. Miller, 1990) or by self-reports or observer ratings on standardized measures of the FFM. Such an assessment would be clinically useful in understanding the strengths and weaknesses of the individual and in developing rapport in almost any therapeutic setting (T. Miller, 1991).

The second step is to identify personality-related problems. This might include the presenting problems, but it would also be possible to use a systematic screening. Widiger, Costa, et al. (2002) provided a list of problems that are likely to be associated with the low and high poles of each of the factors and facets. That list could guide a diagnostic interview. For example, a client who scored low on Trust might be asked if he had a sense of being exploited or victimized; one who was high on assertiveness might be asked if she was perceived as being domineering and bossy. Ultimately, this process should yield a list of issues that could become the focus of counseling or therapy.

Counselors might find no need to proceed beyond Step 2. Clinical psychologists or psychiatrists, who may be required to give a formal, *DSM* diagnosis, would need to ascertain if the problems identified were serious enough to warrant classification as a personality disorder. Step 3 requires a judgment of whether the personality-related problems cause clinically significant personal distress or social or occupational impairment. The Global Assessment of Functioning (*DSM-IV* Axis V; American Psychiatric Association, 1994) scale might be used to make this judgment. If impairment is judged significant—and until the *DSM* offers a new system more in line with the four-step process—the condition can be diagnosed as a Personality Disorder Not Otherwise Specified.

Finally, clinicians or researchers who are interested in more detailed syndromes can use personality profiles (McCrae et al., 2001) or prototypes (J. D. Miller, Pilkonis, & Morse, 2004) to help make categorical judgments. Under the *DSM-IV*, these profiles or prototypes would need to be considered hypotheses that specify the particular disorders that the individual might have; a detailed interview would probably be needed to confirm that *DSM* criteria for a diagnosis are met. If a future *DSM* adopted this four-step procedure, the fourth step would be an optional description of a personality pattern, and would be defined by scores on a personality inventory (Costa & McCrae, 2005). For example, Widiger, Trull, et al. (2002) asserted that the obsessive–compulsive personality disorder is characterized by high levels of assertiveness, competence, order, dutifulness, and achievement striving, and by low levels of openness to values and compliance. An individual showing that pattern of personality traits in Step 1 and diagnosed as having a personality disorder in Step 3 would be classified as having an obsessive–compulsive personality pattern in Step 4.

At this point in scientific history, we know much more about the FFM—its heritability, development, longitudinal stability, universality, and consensual validity (Costa & McCrae, in press)—than we do about the shifting categories of personality disorders that have been offered in a series of *DSM*s. Future *DSM*s should base their description of personality pathology on the solid foundation the FFM supplies. The four-step process is one way to do that.

# Acknowledgments

This chapter benefited from the comments of Paul T. Costa, Jr., and Thomas A. Widiger. Official contribution of the National Institutes of Health; not subject to copyright in the United States.

## REFERENCES

Allport, G. W. (1961). *Pattern and growth in personality*. New York: Holt, Rinehart and Winston.
American Psychiatric Association. (1994). *Diagnostic and statistical manual of mental disorders* (4th ed.). Washington, DC: Author.

Bagby, R. M., Bindseil, K., Schuller, D. R., Rector, N. A., Young, L. T., Cooke, R. G., et al. (1997). Relationship between the Five-Factor Model of personality and unipolar, bipolar and schizophrenic patients. *Psychiatry Research, 70*, 83–94.

Bagby, R. M., Costa, P. T., Jr., McCrae, R. R., Livesley, W. J., Kennedy, S. H., Levitan, R. D., et al. (1999). Replicating the Five-Factor Model of personality in a psychiatric sample. *Personality and Individual Differences, 27*, 1135–1139.

Ball, S. A. (2002). Big Five, Alternative Five, and Seven personality dimensions: Validity in substance-dependent patients. In P. T. Costa, Jr., & T. A. Widiger (Eds.), *Personality disorders and the Five-Factor Model of personality* (2nd ed., pp. 177–201). Washington, DC: American Psychological Association.

Barriga, A. Q., & Gibbs, J. C. (1996). Measuring cognitive distortion in antisocial youth: Development and preliminary validation of the "How I Think" Questionnaire. *Aggressive Behavior, 22*, 333–343.

Baumeister, R. F., & Tice, D. M. (1988). Metatraits. *Journal of Personality, 56*, 571–598.

Beck, A. T., & Freeman, A. (1990). Cognitive therapy of personality disorders. New York: Guilford Press.

Breuer, J., & Freud, S. (1895). *Studies on hysteria* (Collected works, Vol. II). London: Hogarth.

Brooner, R. K., Costa, P. T., Jr., Fetch, L. J., Rousar, E. E., Bigelow, G. E., & Schmidt, C. W. (1991). The personality dimensions of male and female drug abusers with and without antisocial personality disorder. In L. S. Harris (Ed.), *Problems of drug dependence*. Proceedings of the 53rd Annual Scientific Meeting, Committee on Problems of Drug Dependence. Rockville, MD: National Institute on Drug Abuse.

Clark, L. A. (1990). Toward a consensual set of symptom clusters for assessment of personality disorder. In J. N. Butcher, & C. D. Spielberger (Eds.), *Advances in personality assessment* (Vol. 8, pp. 243–266). Hillsdale, NJ: Erlbaum.

Clark, L. A., & Livesley, W. J. (2002). Two approaches to identifying dimensions of personality disorder: Convergence on the Five-Factor Model. In P. T. Costa, Jr. & T. A. Widiger (Eds.), *Personality disorders and the Five-Factor Model of personality* (2nd ed., pp. 161–176). Washington, DC: American Psychological Association.

Costa, P. T., Jr., & McCrae, R. R. (1985). *The NEO Personality Inventory manual.* Odessa, FL: Psychological Assessment Resources.

Costa, P. T., Jr., & McCrae, R. R. (1990). Personality disorders and the Five-Factor Model of personality. *Journal of Personality Disorders, 4*, 362–371.

Costa, P. T., Jr., & McCrae, R. R. (1992a). Normal personality assessment in clinical practice: The NEO Personality Inventory. *Psychological Assessment, 4*, 5–13, 20–22.

Costa, P. T., Jr., & McCrae, R. R. (1992b). *Revised NEO Personality Inventory (NEO-PI-R) and NEO Five-Factor Inventory (NEO-FFI) professional manual.* Odessa, FL: Psychological Assessment Resources.

Costa, P. T., Jr., & McCrae, R. R. (2005). A Five-Factor Model perspective on personality disorders. In S. Strack (Ed.), *Handbook of personology and psychopathology* (pp. 257–270). Hoboken, NJ: JWiley.

Costa P. T., Jr., & McCrae, R. R. (in press). Trait and factor theories. In J. C. Thomas, & D. L. Segal (Eds.), *Comprehensive handbook of personality and psychopathology* (Vol. I). New York: Wiley.

Costa, P. T., Jr., & Widiger, T. A. (Eds.). (2002). *Personality disorders and the Five-Factor Model of personality* (2nd. ed.). Washington, DC: American Psychological Association.

Digman, J. M. (1990). Personality structure: Emergence of the Five-Factor Model. *Annual Review of Psychology, 41*, 417–440.

Egger, J. I. M., De Mey, H. R. A., Kerksen, J. J. L., & van der Staak, C. P. F. (2002). Cross-cultural replication of the Five-Factor Model and comparison of the NEO-PI-R and MMPI-2 PSY-5 scales in a Dutch psychiatric sample. *Psychological Assessment, 15*, 81–88.

Epstein, S., & Meier, P. (1989). Constructive thinking: A broad coping variable with specific components. *Journal of Personality and Social Psychology, 57*, 332–350.

Fagan, P. J., Wise, T. N., Schmidt, C. W., Ponticas, Y., Marshall, R. D., & Costa, P. T., Jr. (1991). A comparison of five-factor personality dimensions in males with sexual dysfunction and males with paraphilia. *Journal of Personality Assessment, 57*, 434–448.

Harkness, A. R., & McNulty, J. L. (2002). Implications of personality individual differences science for clinical work on personality disorders. In P. T. Costa, Jr. & T. A. Widiger (Eds.), *Personality disorders and the Five-Factor Model of personality* (2nd ed., pp. 391–403). Washington, DC: American Psychological Association.

Hathaway, S. R., & McKinley, J. C. (1983). *The Minnesota Multiphasic Personality Inventory manual*. New York: Psychological Corporation.

Hirschfeld, R. M. A., Klerman, G. L., Lavori, P., Keller, M. B., Griffith, P., & Coryell, W. (1989). Premorbid personality assessments of first onset of major depression. *Archives of General Psychiatry, 46*, 345–350.

Hyer, L., Braswell, L., Albrecht, B., Boyd, S., Boudewyns, P., & Talbert, S. (2003). Relationship of NEO-PI to personality styles and severity of trauma in chronic PTSD victims. *Journal of Clinical Psychology, 59*, 1295–1304.

Hyler, S. E., & Rieder, R. O. (1987). *Personality Diagnostic Questionnaire-Revised (PDQ-R)*. New York: Author.

Jackson, D. N. (1989). *Basic Personality Inventory manual*. Port Huron, MI: Sigma Assessment Systems.

Jang, K. L., & Livesley, W. J. (1999). Why do measures of normal and disordered personality correlate? A study of genetic comorbidity. *Journal of Personality Disorders, 13*, 10–17.

Jung, C. G. (1933). *Modern man in search of a soul* (W. S. Dell, & C. F. Baynes, Trans.). New York: Harcourt Brace Jovanovich.

Kernberg, O. F. (1984). *Severe personality disorders*. New Haven, CT: Yale University Press.

Kiesler, D. J. (1983). The 1982 interpersonal circle: A taxonomy for complementarity in human transactions. *Psychological Review, 90*, 185–214.

Livesley, W. J. (1991). Classifying personality disorders: Ideal types, prototypes, or dimensions? *Journal of Personality Disorders, 5*, 52–59.

Livesley, W. J., Jackson, D. N., & Schroeder, M. L. (1989). A study of the factorial structure of personality pathology. *Journal of Personality Disorders, 3*, 292–306.

McCrae, R. R. (1989). Why I advocate the Five-Factor Model: Joint analyses of the NEO-PI and other instruments. In D. M. Buss, & N. Cantor (Eds.), *Personality psychology: Recent trends and emerging directions* (pp. 237–245). New York: Springer-Verlag.

McCrae, R. R. (1991). The Five-Factor Model and its assessment in clinical settings. *Journal of Personality Assessment, 57*, 399–414.

McCrae, R. R. (Ed.). (1992). The Five-Factor Model: Issues and applications [Special issue]. *Journal of Personality, 60*(2).

McCrae, R. R. (1993). Moderated analyses of longitudinal personality stability. *Journal of Personality and Social Psychology, 65*, 577–585.

McCrae, R. R. (1994). A reformulation of Axis II: Personality and personality-related problems. In P. T. Costa, Jr., & T. A. Widiger (Eds.), *Personality disorders and the Five-Factor Model of personality* (pp. 303–310). Washington, DC: American Psychological Association.

McCrae, R. R., & Costa, P. T., Jr. (1985). Updating Norman's "adequate taxonomy": Intelligence and personality dimensions in natural language and in questionnaires. *Journal of Personality and Social Psychology, 49*, 710–721.

McCrae, R. R., & Costa, P. T., Jr. (1991). Adding *Liebe und Arbeit*: The full Five-Factor Model and well-being. *Personality and Social Psychology Bulletin, 17*, 227–232.

McCrae, R. R., & Costa, P. T., Jr. (1997). Conceptions and correlates of openness to experience. In R. Hogan, J. A. Johnson, & S. R. Briggs (Eds.), *Handbook of personality psychology* (pp. 269–290). Orlando, FL: Academic Press.

McCrae, R. R., & Costa, P. T., Jr. (1999). A Five-Factor Theory of personality. In L. A. Pervin, & O. P. John (Eds.), *Handbook of personality: Theory and research* (2nd ed., pp. 139–153). New York: Guilford.

McCrae, R. R., & Costa, P. T., Jr. (2003). *Personality in adulthood: A Five-Factor Theory perspective* (2nd. ed.). New York: Guilford Press.

McCrae, R. R., Costa, P. T., Jr., & Piedmont, R. L. (1993). Folk concepts, natural language, and psychological constructs: The California Psychological Inventory and the Five-Factor Model. *Journal of Personality, 61*, 1–26.

McCrae, R. R., Yang, J., Costa, P. T., Jr., Dai, X., Yao, S., Cai, T., & Gao, B. (2001). Personality profiles and the prediction of categorical personality disorders. *Journal of Personality, 69*, 121–145.

Miller, J. D., Pilkonis, P. A., & Morse, J. Q. (2004). Five-Factor Model prototypes for personality disorders: The utility of self-reports and observer ratings. *Assessment, 11*, 127–138.

Miller, M. J. (1990). The power of the "OCEAN": Another way to diagnose clients. *Counselor Education and Supervision, 29*, 283–290.

Miller, T. (1991). The psychotherapeutic utility of the Five-Factor Model of personality: A clinician's experience. *Journal of Personality Assessment, 57*, 415–433.

Millon, T. (1983). *Millon Clinical Multiaxial Inventory manual* (3rd ed.). Minneapolis: Interpretive Scoring Systems.

Morey, L. (1991). *Personality Assessment Inventory: Professional manual.* Odessa, FL: Psychological Assessment Resources.

Mutén, E. (1991). Self-reports, spouse ratings, and psychophysiological assessment in a behavioral medicine program: An application of the Five-Factor Model. *Journal of Personality Assessment, 57,* 449–464.

Shapiro, D. (1965). *Neurotic styles.* New York: Basic Books.

Shea, M. T. (1988, August). *Interpersonal styles and short-term psychotherapy for depression.* Paper presented at the American Psychological Association Annual Convention, Atlanta, GA.

Siegler, I. C., Welsh, K. A., Dawson, D. V., Fillenbaum, G. G., Earl, N. L., Kaplan, E. B., & Clark, C. M. (1991). Ratings of personality change in patients being evaluated for memory disorders. *Alzheimer Disease and Associated Disorders, 5,* 240–250.

Trull, T. J. (1992). DSM-III-R personality disorders and the Five-Factor Model of personality: An empirical comparison. *Journal of Abnormal Psychology, 101,* 553–560.

Tupes, E. C., & Christal, R. E. (1992). Recurrent personality factors based on trait ratings. *Journal of Personality, 60,* 225–251. (Original work published 1961)

Wakefield, J. C. (1992). The concept of mental disorder: On the boundary between biological facts and social values. *American Psychologist, 47,* 373–388.

Warren, H. D., & Carmichael, L. (1930). *Elements of human psychology* (rev. ed.). Boston: Houghton Mifflin.

Watson, D., & Clark, L. A. (1984). Negative affectivity: The disposition to experience aversive emotional states. *Psychological Bulletin, 96,* 465–490.

Widiger, T. A. (1992). Generalized social phobia versus avoidant personality disorder: A commentary on three studies. *Journal of Abnormal Psychology, 101,* 340–343.

Widiger, T. A. (1993). The DSM-III-R categorical personality disorder diagnoses: A critique and an alternative. *Psychological Inquiry, 4,* 75–90.

Widiger, T. A., Costa, P. T., Jr., & McCrae, R. R. (2002). A proposal for Axis II: Diagnosing personality disorders using the Five-Factor Model. In P. T. Costa, Jr. & T. A. Widiger (Eds.), *Personality disorders and the Five-Factor Model of personality* (2nd ed., pp. 431–456). Washington, DC: American Psychological Association.

Widiger, T. A., & Trull, T. J. (1992). Personality and psychopathology: An application of the Five-Factor Model. *Journal of Personality, 60,* 363–393.

Widiger, T. A., Trull, T. J., Clarkin, J. F., Sanderson, C., & Costa, P. T., Jr. (2002). A description of the DSM-III-R and DSM-IV personality disorders with the Five-Factor Model of personality. In P. T. Costa, Jr., & T. A. Widiger (Eds.), *Personality disorders and the Five-Factor Model of personality* (pp. 89–99). Washington, DC: American Psychological Association.

Wiggins, J. S. (1979). A psychological taxonomy of trait-descriptive terms: The interpersonal domain. *Journal of Personality and Social Psychology, 37,* 395–412.

Wiggins, J. S., & Pincus, A. L. (1989). Conceptions of personality disorders and dimensions of personality. *Psychological Assessment: A Journal of Consulting and Clinical Psychology, 1,* 305–316.

Yang, J., Dai, X., Yao, S., Cai, T., Gao, B., McCrae, R. R., & Costa, P. T., Jr. (2002). Personality disorders and the Five-Factor Model of personality in Chinese psychiatric patients. In P. T. Costa, Jr., & T. A. Widiger (Eds.), *Personality disorders and the Five-Factor Model of personality* (2nd ed., pp. 215–221). Washington, DC: American Psychological Association.

Yang, J., McCrae, R. R., Costa, P. T., Jr., Dai, X., Yao, S., Cai, T., & Gao, B. (1999). Cross-cultural personality assessment in psychiatric populations: The NEO-PI-R in the People's Republic of China. *Psychological Assessment, 11,* 359–368.

Zonderman, A. B., Herbst, J. H., Schmidt, C., Jr., Costa, P. T., Jr., & McCrae, R. R. (1993). Depressive symptoms as a non-specific, graded risk for psychiatric diagnoses. *Journal of Abnormal Psychology, 102,* 544–552.

# Differentiating Personality Deviance, Normality, and Well-Being by the Seven-Factor Psychobiological Model

## C. Robert Cloninger

In this chapter, I will describe my psychobiological model of personality development, which can be assessed using the *Temperament and Character Inventory* (TCI; Cloninger & Przybeck, 1994) as a means of differentiating personality deviance from the personalities of people who are flourishing or who are merely average. It is only possible, in my opinion, to understand the nature of abnormal personality or personality disorder fully by reference to the state of human well-being, not what is average in a contemporary society in which most people are confused about what gives their life satisfaction and meaning (Cloninger, 2004; Huppert & Baylis, 2004).

The central hypotheses in my approach are that (a) human thoughts, feelings, and actions are influenced about equally by the soma and the psyche of a person; (b) personality refers to average patterns of thinking over the range of situations in which a person lives; (c) it is possible to quantify both the processes within individuals and the processes external of them that influence their way of adapting to life experiences; (d) changes in human thoughts, feelings, and actions are dynamic expressions of complex adaptive systems that change discretely from moment to moment, and can be characterized by not only their averages but also their range; and (e) it is possible to identify specific genes and brain networks that are activated by the psychobiological processes underlying the interactions between person and situation, and to show that these nonlinear dynamic interactions are strongly correlated with individual differences in TCI dimensions of personality. The influence of the soma (i.e., the body of a person) is shown by the importance of genetic influences on human personality (Gillespie & Cloninger, 2003; Heath &

Cloninger, 1994). The influence of the psyche (i.e., the spirit or immaterial intelligent aspect of a person as a spontaneous self-aware agent) is shown by the importance of the rich innate endowment of human beings, which is characterized by individual differences that are unique to each person, including freedom of will, varying levels of self-aware consciousness, intuitive insight that is neither acquired by experience nor algorithmically deduced, and spontaneous creative gifts, such as Mozart's musical capacity and Gandhi's spiritual insight, which are innate but not inherited (Cloninger, 2004).

The psyche is sometimes called the soul or spirit (i.e., mind-2) to distinguish it from analytical reasoning (i.e., mind-1"), but the term "psyche" is preferred in psychology and psychiatry. Hence, psychologists and psychiatrists are literally students and healers of the spirit, but both fields have usually neglected their spiritual role. Pioneers in psychology like Allport (1937) were not afraid to use the term "spirituality," but recent generations of mainstream psychologists have been trained professionally with little or no reference to faith and spirituality. Even now that positive psychology is addressing character and virtue as valid psychometric features, faith is often relegated to an alternative path to well-being (Cloninger, 2005a, 2005b). In fact, the theological virtues of hope, love, and faith correspond to the three TCI character dimensions of Self-Directedness (i.e., purposeful, resourceful, and hopeful), Cooperativeness (i.e., helpful, forgiving, and loving), and Self-Transcendence (i.e., insightful, intuitive, and faithful). Each of these character traits interacts synergistically with the others to produce well-being: Only individuals who are high on *all three* traits have frequent positive emotions and infrequent negative emotions (Cloninger, 2004). In other words, underdevelopment of any one aspect of character leaves an individual vulnerable to negative emotions like anxiety, depression, and anger, and leaves him or her unfulfilled and dissatisfied with life.

Behavioral, cognitive, and social approaches to well-being are inadequate without addressing the deeper questions of spirituality that allow us to confront the ultimate questions about suffering and death that we must eventually face. The failure to integrate biological, cognitive, and spiritual approaches in mental health is unfortunate because genetic factors and psychic variables unique to each individual are approximately equally important in their influence on human personality, with environmental factors shared by siblings accounting for less than 10% of variance in personality (Gillespie & Cloninger, 2003). Variables unique to each individual cannot be reduced to cognitive and behavioral factors. The rich innate endowment of human beings includes spiritual variables that are neither inherited nor acquired. Individual differences in spirituality are indicated by freedom of will, nonalgorithmic intuitive processes that lead to creative invention, and spontaneous creative gifts (Cloninger, 2004).

In other words, the TCI (Cloninger & Przybeck, 1994) provides a quantitative model of the psychobiological processes *within a person* that regulate adaptation to changes in his or her internal and external environments. Each human being has unique personality characteristics, but all people share a common structure and path to personality development. The path of human personality development is a spiral of increasing self-awareness and coherence (see Figure 1.1) that is measurable in terms of both changes in thought from moment to moment and in terms of longitudinal studies across the life span (Cloninger, 2003, 2004; Vaillant & Milofsky, 1980). The same path to well-being is evident regardless of the time scale of observation. The patterns of personality change and development are described by the dynamics of nonlinear adaptive

The spiral path of consciousness. Adapted from *Feeling Good: The Science of Well-Being* (Cloninger, 2004).

systems of latent psychobiological processes, not by the linear relationships assumed in factor analysis. Consequently, trait models determined by factor analysis confound the effects of multiple psychobiological processes, which should be distinguished for a true understanding and treatment of personality development. Nonlinear dynamic systems often generate strong correlations among distinct processes, so correlation is not a valid sign of identity or causation. For example, neuroticism is a heterogeneous trait that confounds anxiety and personality disorders; that is, it is a composite of high TCI Harm Avoidance (i.e., anxiety proneness) and low TCI Self-Directedness (i.e., purposefulness). Nevertheless, within-person models of personality can be used to measure the between-person perspective of factor analytically derived traits, so information content of multidimensional personality inventories, like the NEO and the TCI, is largely overlapping, as I will show later.

The TCI is intended to provide measures of the components of a comprehensive model of human personality. It measures temperament, which is defined as the emotional core of personality. The TCI also measures character, which is defined as the attitudes and higher cognitive processes that regulate conflicts among the temperament dimensions so that a person can achieve meaningful goals and maintain human relationships in accordance with his or her values and needs. Hence, the harmonious integration of personality depends on the coherence of character, not on the temperament configuration.

The four temperament dimensions measure individual differences in basic emotions and drives that are independently inherited and moderately stable throughout life: Harm Avoidance (anxious and pessimistic versus careless and risk-taking), Novelty Seeking (anger-prone and impulsive versus stoical and rigid), Reward Dependence (warm and sociable versus cold and aloof), and Persistence (ambitious and perfectionistic versus easily discouraged and spoiled). These temperaments correspond to the ancient humors described by Pythagoras and Hippocrates except they are quantitative variables that are approximately normally distributed, not mutually exclusive qualitative categories.

The TCI also measures three dimensions of character, which can be understood as the three branches of a person's mental self-government: Self-Directedness (executive functions, such as being purposeful, resourceful, and hopeful), Cooperativeness (legislative functions, such as being helpful, agreeable, and loving), and Self-Transcendence (judicial functions, such as being intuitive, insightful, and faithful). Each of the seven dimensions is composed of four or five subscales in its most recent form, as described in the TCI Web site (www.tci.wustl.edu) and elsewhere (Cloninger, 2004).

Measures of general personality traits like the TCI can be used effectively to measure personality disorders (Svrakic & Whitehead, 1993). By "general" I refer to traits that span the range from personality disorder to well-being. However, it is questionable whether quantitative measures of abnormal traits (i.e., those restricted to range from deviant to merely average) can be used to quantify human well-being. Well-being is more than the absence of deviant traits: It involves the expression of human virtues and positive emotions that go beyond what is average in contemporary society (Fredrickson, 2004; Peterson & Seligman, 2004; Seligman & Parks, 2004).

The inclusiveness of TCI content allows consideration of the body, mind, and spirit of a person, so that the integration of all these aspects can be facilitated. Other contemporary personality models tend to reduce humanity to cognitive and behavioral processes, neglecting spirituality as measured by TCI Self-Transcendence or trying to explain it as an emergent property of algorithmic brain functions. Empirically, the three TCI character dimensions (i.e., Self-Directedness, Cooperativeness, and Self-Transcendence) interact synergistically to produce human well-being, whether measured in terms of life satisfaction, virtue, or positive emotions (Cloninger, 2004). As a result, neglect of spirituality presents an obstacle to the understanding and development of well-being and hence of personality in general. Absorption in Tellegen's Multidimensional Personality Questionnaire (Tellegen & Waller, in press) is moderately related to the flow-like self-forgetfulness subscale of Self-Transcendence, but does not measure the transpersonal or spiritual aspects of the scale (Tellegen & Lykken, 1988). Openness, as measured by the NEO Personality Inventory (NEO-PI; Costa & McCrae, 1985) and the updated NEO-PI-R (Costa & McCrae, 1992), is weakly correlated with TCI Self-Transcendence, TCI Novelty Seeking, and TCI Reward Dependence. In other words, NEO Openness corresponds to a materialistic concept of aesthetic and hedonistic interests, rather than a measure of flow, transpersonal awareness, or spirituality. It is fortunate that more work is now being done in positive psychology to measure and study virtues and positive emotions, but up to now even that work has failed to face the crucial role of spiritual faith in the development of well-being (Cloninger, 2005a,b). When faith is neglected, well-being is reduced to reports of hedonistic pleasure, openness of interests, and generativity (Fredrickson, 2004; Seligman & Parks, 2004). These reduced concepts of well-being fail to include transcendence of the fear of death and suffering, which are markers of integrity, enlightenment, and unitive consciousness (Cloninger, 2004; Vaillant, 1993; Vaillant & Milofsky, 1980).

# Definition and Range of Personality

Because different approaches to personality vary in their scope, it is essential to consider just what is the proper scope of personality. Personality can be defined as the dynamic organization within the individual of those psychobiological processes by which an individual uniquely adapts to changing internal and external environments (Cloninger & Svrakic, 1993). This definition corresponds closely to that chosen by Gordon Allport after a thorough study of many alternative definitions (Allport, 1937), so it is a reasonable definition for psychology. Each aspect of the definition is significant: (a) personality refers to *psychobiological* processes within the person, which are not directly observed or based merely on overt behavioral differences between people; (b) personality is *dynamic*, not fixed or necessarily stable across time; (c) personality is unique to each individual, so its optimal description is *idiographic*; and (d) personality is *adaptive* to changes in internal and external environments. Thus personality includes the full range of human adaptation in which a person interacts with his or her changing internal milieu and changing external environment. The internal and external environments vary as a result of changes in biopsychosocial context, such as age, illness, and various opportunities and challenges, which operate at the time scale varying from milliseconds, circadian cycles, monthly cycles, on up through the whole life span.

A general personality model must attend to the full range from abnormal traits seen in personality disorders to the well-being observed when human beings are flourishing. Some may consider deviation from the average as deviant in a statistical sense, so that both personality disorders and well-being would be statistically deviant. On the other hand, if well-being is what is naturally adaptive, then the contemporary average may be considered abnormal in terms of functional fitness. In any case, focus on either abnormal or average characteristics is inadequate for a general understanding of personality.

The TCI is intended to measure the components of a comprehensive model of personality. Does the TCI really cover the full range of human personality, or will there be other traits to add, subtract, or modify with further study? Work carried out since the TCI manual was first published (Cloninger & Przybeck, 1994) suggests that the TCI is quite close to comprehensive as a measure of traditional personality, which excludes intelligence and some aspects of mood that will be mentioned later. This strong claim about the inclusiveness of the TCI is based on a thorough study of the evolution and scope of human thought and related feelings and actions (Cloninger, 1994, 2004). The full scope of human thoughts spans five planes of content: the sexual, material, emotional, intellectual, and spiritual, as I have described in detail elsewhere (Cloninger, 2004). I use the term "planes" here because each corresponds to a level in the spiral of personality development: There are five planes or levels as thought increases in coherence, as illustrated in Table 3.1.

Each of these planes has aspects related to the others, so that the content of thought can be approximately described in terms of a 5 × 5 matrix with 25 compartments, a number close to the number of subscales in broad inventories like the TCI and NEO. It is

**Table 3.1** 5 × 5 Matrix of Elevation of Conflicts in Human Thought (Dualistic Consciousness)[a]

| Subplane of Thought | Plane of Sexuality | Plane of Materiality | Plane of Emotionality | Plane of Intellect | Plane of Spirituality |
|---|---|---|---|---|---|
| Spiritual aspects | Scorn or exhibition (shy) | Power or sarcasm (exploratory) | Contentment or relief of grief (attached) | [Self-actualization + oceanic feelings] (perfectionistic) | [Coherence-seeking] |
| Intellectual aspects | Devaluation or idealization (pessimistic) | Pride or inferiority (impulsive) | Tender-minded or tough-minded (sentimental) | Self-Transcendence & patience (achieving) | [Truth-seeking] |
| Emotional aspects | Harm avoidance—worry or denial | Novelty Seeking—anger/ envy or stoicism | Reward Dependence, warmth or coldness | Persistence—calmness & conscience | [Peace-seeking] |
| Material aspects | Vulnerability or eroticism (fearful) | Greed/competition or submission (extravagant) | Sociability or aloofness (aloof) | Cooperativeness or nonprejudice (eager effort) | [Merit-seeking] |
| Sexual aspects (2) | Emptiness or lust (fatigable) | Desire/fight or aversion/flight (disorderly) | Succorance or rejection (dependent) | Self-Directedness or irresponsibility (spoiled) | [Mastery-seeking] |

[a]Experiences that are unlikely to be explicitly clear in the consciousness of most people are labeled in brackets. Adjectives in parenthesis indicate the TCI temperament subscales that provide quantitative measures of the emotional aspects of the conflict within each subplane of thought observed in dualistic consciousness.

Adapted from Cloninger (2004).

presumably not accidental that these five domains of thought also correspond to the five senses, which provide the sensory information for perceptual processing: There is direct correspondence between touch and sexuality, taste and materiality, smell and emotionality, hearing and intellectuality, and seeing and spirituality. Vision is the only sense that provides a contemplative detachment for viewing of wholes and their components at a distance, which leads to insight as well as sight. Most of the human brain is devoted to processing of visual information, so it is not surprising that most human beings spend more time in prayer or meditation than having sex or eating (Cloninger & Svrakic, 1993).

## Content and Movement of Thought

The content of the first four planes is well measured by the subscales of the four TCI temperament dimensions, whereas the spiritual plane is determined entirely by character. The relation of the TCI temperament scales and subscales to the emotional conflicts in human thought is summarized in Table 3.1. The emotional aspects of the first four planes are specified by Harm Avoidance for sexuality, Novelty Seeking for materiality, Reward Dependence for emotionality, and Persistence for intellectuality. In other words, Harm Avoidance moderates the sexual drive, Novelty Seeking moderates the drive for power and possessions, Reward Dependence moderates the drive for social security, and Persistence moderates the drive for intellectual control. Furthermore, a specific TCI temperament subscale regulates other aspects of each of these drives, as shown in Table 3.1. For example, in the material plane, there is a progressive elevation of the drive for power and possessions from its sexual aspects at the bottom of the column (i.e., fight or flight, as measured by the disorderliness subscale of TCI Novelty Seeking) to its purely material aspects (i.e., greed or submission, as measured by the extravagance subscale of TCI Novelty Seeking), to its intellectual aspects (i.e., superiority or inferiority, as measured by the impulsiveness subscale of TCI Novelty Seeking), to its spiritual aspects (i.e., power or sarcasm, as measured by the exploratory excitability subscale of TCI Novelty Seeking). The description of the content of the subplanes of thought was derived by work on the thoughts associated with hierarchical ranking of fears and on the elevation of thought through relaxation and meditation, as described elsewhere (Cloninger, 2004). Consequently, the correspondence of the subscales of the TCI to the content modules of thought provides systematic support for the structure of the TCI (Cloninger & Svrakic, 1993), which was developed a decade before the matrix structure of human thought was recognized (Cloninger, 2004).

The three TCI character dimensions regulate the movement of thought through the planes of thought content. Each of the three TCI character dimensions has five subscales, one for its regulatory role in each plane, as shown in Table 3.2. For example, the modulation of sexual urges involves the elevation of thought from the basic conflict of emptiness versus lust (shown at the bottom of column one in Table 3.1) up to basic confidence (shown at the top of column one in Table 3.1). The Self-Directedness subscale for responsibility lifts thought from blaming one's problems on external circumstances (characteristic of the bottom of the sexual plane) to acceptance of responsibility for one's actions (which is characteristic of the top of the sexual plane and higher). Likewise, the Cooperativeness subscale for tolerance measures the degree to which a person is able

**Table 3.2** Five Stages of Human Thought and Underlying Dynamic Processes Measured by TCI Character Subscales of Self-Directedness (SD), Cooperativeness (CO), and Self-Transcendence (ST)

| Plane of Self-aware Consciousness | TCI Measures of Functional Processes | | |
|---|---|---|---|
| | Agency (SD) | Flexibility (CO) | Understanding (ST) |
| Sexuality | Responsible vs. controlled | Tolerant vs. prejudiced | Sensible vs. repressive |
| Materiality | Purposeful vs. aimless | Forgiving vs. revengeful | Idealistic vs. practical |
| Emotionality | Accepting vs. approval-seeking | Empathic vs. inconsiderate | Transpersonal vs. individual |
| Intellectual | Resourceful vs. inept | Helpful vs. unhelpful | Faithful vs. skeptical |
| Spiritual | Hopeful sublimation vs. compromising deliberation | Charitable principles vs. self-serving opportunism | Spiritual awareness local realism |

to broaden his or her social tolerance (characteristic of the top of the sexual plane and higher), rather than be prejudiced in intolerance (characteristic of giving in to one's sexual urges and resenting those who frustrate or threaten them). Finally, the Self-Transcendence subscale for self-forgetfulness measures the degree to which a person is able to deepen his or her awareness and understanding sensibly (characteristic of thought elevated to the top of the sexual plane or higher), rather than repressing whatever is unacceptable from consciousness (characteristic of thought at the bottom of the sexual plane). After the subscales were developed intuitively, this structure was inferred empirically in a longitudinal study of the development of character (Cloninger & Svrakic, 1997a, b, c). Still later the 5 × 5 matrix of thought was recognized as an ontogenetic recapitulation of the phylogeny of human cognitive processes (Cloninger, 2003, 2004).

To better understand the regulatory effects of character on temperament configurations, the character scales can be visualized as defining the three dimensions of a spiral with five planes of increasing height, width, and depth, which correspond to increasing levels of well-being and coherence of personality. The planes correspond to the hierarchical progression from sexually motivated thought to spiritually motivated thoughts, as shown in Table 3.2. The degree of a person's Self-Directedness specifies her or his height in the spiral (that is, his or her level of hopefulness in regulating conflicts about what is pleasant or unpleasant). The degree of a person's Cooperativeness specifies the broadening or width of the spiral (that is, her or his capacity for love, which is the acceptance of self-sacrifice in regulating conflicts about what is overarousing or underarousing). Finally, the degree of a person's Self-Transcendence specifies the depth of the spiral (that is, the depth of insightful awareness of what is adaptive). Theoretically, the interactions among the component processes of all three character dimensions is nonlinear and dynamic, so that a stress or problem (i.e., anything you do not understand and regulate, such as habits, memories, fears) can pull a person's thoughts down to a lower level, whereas protective environments or special psychosocial supports may allow their his or her thoughts to rise despite latent vulnerabilities. Empirically, analysis of the longitudinal development of character showed that maturity of character is a spiral in which people can move up as they increase in the height, width, and depth of their awareness (Cloninger & Svrakic, 1997a, b, c). The spiral path to wisdom and well-being is empirically supported by much independent observational and experimental work (Cloninger, 2004; Fredrickson, 2004; Vaillant & Milofsky, 1980). In addition, character and momentary thoughts can spiral down in reaction to violence, addiction, or other stressors as described in detail elsewhere (Cloninger, 2004; Gandhi, 1957; Koob & LeMoal, 2001).

Individual differences in each of the temperament and character dimensions are strongly correlated ($r > 0.7$) with individual differences in specific brain receptor densities measured by positron emission tomography or differences in specific brain networks according to functional brain imaging using magnetic resonance imaging (fMRI) (Cloninger, 2004). The temperament dimensions are correlated with differences in limbic and cortico-striatal regions primarily, as expected because these instantiate brain systems for procedural learning and associative conditioning of habits predicted to be the neurobiological basis for individual differences in temperament (Cloninger, 1987, 2002). For example, Persistence is strongly correlated ($r = 0.8$) with a circuit regulating the expectation of intermittent reward involving the ventral striatum, orbitofrontal cortex, and anterior cingulate cortex (Gusnard & Ollinger, 2003). Harm Avoidance is strongly correlated with individual differences in serotonin receptors 5-HT1A and 5-HT2A in the subgenual prefrontal cortex (Bailer, 2004; Bailer & Frank, 2005). Novelty Seeking is strongly correlated ($r = 0.8$) with individual differences in D2 receptor binding in the insula, amygdala, and dorsal caudate nucleus (Kaasinen & Aalto, 2004; Ursula Bailer & Walter Kaye, personal communication, June 30, 2005). The TCI character scales are strongly correlated primarily with individual differences in specific regions of the neocortex involved in higher cognitive processing, particularly the prefrontal cortex, as described elsewhere (Cloninger, 2004). For example, TCI Self-Directedness is correlated ($r = 0.75$) with individual differences in activation of medial prefrontal cortex (Brodmann areas 9/10) during an executive function task requiring evaluation of internal cues (Cloninger, 2004; Gusnard & Akbudak, 2001; Gusnard & Ollinger, 2001). TCI Self-Transcendence is strongly negatively correlated with density of 5-HT1A receptors in frontal cortex, cerebellum, and the brainstem raphe nuclei (Borg & Andree, 2003). These functional brain findings are also supported by findings about related genetic polymorphisms and individual differences in the TCI dimensions (Cloninger, 2004). Cognitive and behavioral neurogenetic studies show that multiple genetic and environmental factors interact in nonlinear adaptive responses to experience so as to buffer and maintain behaviors characteristic of well-being, but these buffering systems may fail in the psychobiological extremes of person–situation interactions (Cloninger, 2004; Keltikangas-Jaervinen & Raeikkoenen, 2004). Our current cultural and world situation does not provide an optimal situation for well-being, so the contemporary average is unhealthy.

# Differentiating Levels of Maturity and Well-Being

Given that TCI character dimensions provide measures of the higher cognitive processes of mental self-government, what are the best practical ways to measure individual differences in levels of maturity and well-being with the TCI? The answer depends on the complexity of the behavior to be measured.

At the low end of maturity, the simplest distinction is between individuals with a personality disorder and others. The temperament dimensions specify subtypes of personality disorders: high Harm Avoidance is characteristic of people in the C cluster of disorders, who are anxious; high Novelty Seeking is characteristic of people with cluster B disorders, who are impulsive and erratic; low Reward Dependence is characteristic of the C cluster of disorders, which are aloof; and high Persistence is characteristic of compulsive disorders, who are perseverative. Different configurations of these disorders differ in their probability of personality disorder, but any configuration of temperament can occur in a person who is not mature. Only the character dimensions distinguish those with and without personality disorders consistently (Cloninger, 2000), as is expected from their role in insight learning of goals and values (Cloninger & Svrakic, 1993).

The TCI Self-Directedness character scale is the most powerful predictor of the presence or absence of personality disorders. For example, in a study of 136 psychiatric inpatients assessed independently with the TCI and a structured interview for *DSM-III-R* (*Diagnostic and Statistical Manual of Mental Disorders*, 3rd ed., rev.; American Psychiatric Association, 1987) personality disorders, the percentage of observed patients with personality disorder increases from 22% in those with Self-Directedness scores above 39 up to 94% in those with Self-Directedness scores below 16 (Svrakic & Whitehead, 1993). In the 34 patients with Self-Directedness scores below 20 there was a high risk of personality disorder regardless of their Cooperativeness score: Personality disorder was observed in 16 of the 17 patients with Cooperativeness scores higher than 30 and in 15 of the 17 patients with lower Cooperativeness. The crucial role of Self-Directedness suggests that it measures the first task of early adulthood, that is, acceptance of responsibility to support oneself by work. Becoming self-directed also corresponds to the first stage of self-awareness, which may still be highly egocentric (Cloninger, 2004).

When the Self-Directedness score was higher than 30, personality disorder was diagnosed in only 13% of the 16 with Cooperativeness scores higher than 37, compared to 31% or the 16 with next higher cooperativeness scores. In other words, high Cooperativeness reduces the risk of personality disorder in those with moderate to high Self-Directedness. Thus, Cooperativeness measures the second set of tasks of adult maturation, which is to love and care for family and friends. Cooperativeness is crucial for allocentric thinking or mindfulness, which is characteristic of the second stage of self-awareness (Cloninger, 2004).

Self-Directedness scores also predicted the number and certainty of personality disorder diagnoses (Table 3.3), suggesting that current *DSM-III-R* criteria are arbitrary cut-offs. Sixty-six patients with definite PDs were divided into 34 with only one PD and 32 with two or more definite diagnoses. Seventy patients with no definite PD were divided into 17 with "mixed" PD (i.e., too few criterion symptoms for each of two diagnoses) and those with no definite or mixed PD. Patients with high scores had an average of 0.6 diagnoses, those with medium scores had 0.9 diagnoses, and those with low scores had 2.3 diagnoses on average. Personality disorder, as defined in the *DSMIV* (American Psychiatric Association, 1994), corresponds to approximately the lowest 10% of the general population in TCI Self-Directedness, but people who are in the lowest third of Self-Directedness are noticeably immature and have an increased likelihood

| Table 3.3 | Relationship of Self-Directedness Scores to the Number of Personality Disorder Diagnoses |
|---|---|

|  |  | Number of Personality Disorder Diagnoses | | | |
|---|---|---|---|---|---|
| Self-directed Scores | # Pts | None Row % | Mixed Row % | One Only Row % | Two+Row % |
| High (44−30) | 51 | 61 | 14 | 15 | 10 |
| Medium (29−20) | 51 | 39 | 18 | 16 | 16 |
| Low (<20) | 34 | 6 | 3 | 35 | 56 |

Adapted from Svrakic and Whitehead (1993).

of psychiatric treatment and suicide attempts (Cloninger & Bayon, 1997; Cloninger & Svrakic, 1997a, b, c, 2000).

Using both Self-Directedness and Cooperativeness traits, the risk of personality disorder in a clinical sample varies from 11 to 94%, so the relationship to diagnosis is strong. The best measure is the simple sum of TCI Self-Directedness and Cooperativeness scores: The lowest 10% in the general population can be used to define personality disorder and the lowest third are noticeably immature and vulnerable to psychopathology. In addition, character can be used to quantify the number, certainty, and severity or personality disorder diagnoses, thereby avoiding arbitrary cut-off points, multiple diagnoses, and overlap of categorical criteria.

The Self-Transcendence character trait is predictive of the total number of personality disorder symptoms, but is less relevant to the distinction between the presence and absence of any personality disorder than are Self-Directedness and Cooperativeness. This probably reflects the fact that Self-Transcendence and personality deviance follow different, age-specific developmental lines. Personality disorders usually develop in adolescence or early adulthood and the most severe symptoms tend to diminish after 35–40 years of age. In contrast, Self-Transcendence has little impact on the major tasks of early adulthood (e.g., to work and to love), but it becomes a major concern as we face death and misfortune (Cloninger & Svrakic, 1993). For example, people over 35 years of age tend to increase their private religious and spiritual activity (Hamer, 2004; Koenig & Kvale, 1988; Woodward & Springen, 1992).

In other words, high Self-Transcendence is essential for distinguishing integrity and well-being from average adjustment, rather than distinguishing individuals with personality disorders from those who are average. In a sample of 804 individuals representative of the general population of the St. Louis area (Cloninger & Bayon, 1998), we related quantitative measures of positive emotionality and negative emotionality to individual differences in personality. Well-being, as measured by the presence of positive emotions (e.g., cheerful, happy, contented) and the absence of negative emotions (sad, distressed, dissatisfied), occurred only if people had coherence of character. Coherence of character was measured by the presence of high scores on all three of the TCI character traits of Self-Directedness, Cooperativeness, and Self-Transcendence. Our findings are illustrated in Figure 3.2.

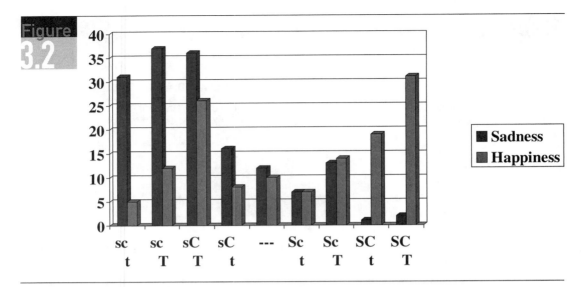

Positive and negative emotions depend on three aspects of character: the percentages of people with prominent sadness or prominent happiness, according to their character profile. Adapted from *Feeling Good: The Science of Well-Being* (Cloninger, 2004).

One of six people was classified as "sad" based on high scores on the depression scale of the Center for Epidemiological Studies (Radloff, 1977). One of six people was classified as "happy" based on high scores on the positive emotionality scale of the Inventory of Personal Characteristics (Tellegen & Grove, 1990). Character was rated using the TCI, distinguishing those who were in the top third of Self-Directedness (S), Cooperativeness (C), and Self-Transcendence (T), from those in the lowest third of Self-Directedness (s), Cooperativeness (c), and Self-Transcendence (t), or in the middle third on each test (—). As can be seen in Figure 3.2, 12% of people who are near average on all three traits of character report being depressed and 10% report being happy. In contrast, about a third (31–37%) of people who are low in Self-Directedness are depressed (see first three sets of bars on the left in Figure 3.2). The percentage of those low in Self-Directedness who are happy is 5% if people are also neither cooperative nor transcendent, and increases to 26% if they are both cooperative and transcendent. Furthermore, if Self-Directedness or Cooperativeness is high, but not both, then people do not differ much in mood from those with average character profiles (see middle three bars in Figure 3.2). If both Self-Directedness and Cooperativeness are elevated, then happiness is much more frequent than sadness (19 versus 1%). Finally, people who are elevated on all three aspects of character have the highest percentage of happiness (26%). In other words, the development of well-being (i.e., presence of positive emotions and absence of negative emotions) depends on the combination of all three TCI character dimensions, which measure the three aspects of mental self-government that regulate self-aware consciousness (Cloninger, 2004). Lack of development of any one of the three factors leaves a person vulnerable to the emergence of conflicts that can lead to a downward spiral of thought into a state of misery, such as depression, substance dependence, eating disorder, or personality disorder.

# Practical Issues and Supports for Professional TCI Use

Several different forms of the TCI are available, varying in length, response set (true/false or 5-point Likert), and age-appropriateness (preschool, juniors 10–14, and adult). These will be briefly described with answers to the most frequently asked questions, but more information is available at the TCI Web site (tci.wustl.edu) and in the TCI manual (Cloninger & Przybeck, 1994), which can be ordered along with forms from the TCI Web site. I will first describe information about the tests for adults.

The first test in this series to be developed was called the Tridimensional Personality Questionnaire (TPQ), which measures only the temperament dimensions. It is a 100-item true/false self-report inventory with well-established psychometric properties and norms from a national area probability sample in the United States (Cloninger & Przybeck, 1991). It measures Harm Avoidance, Novelty Seeking, Reward Dependence, plus a short scale for Persistence. I usually recommend it only for research on temperament because without the character scales of the TCI there is no adequate information for clinical assessments distinguishing people with personality disorder from others. Translations of the TPQ are available in most languages.

The original TCI is a 240-item true/false inventory that retains the TPQ temperament dimensions and adds the three character dimensions. This includes 12 subscales for temperament (HA 4, NS 4, RD 3, PS 1). There are 13 subscales for character (SD 5, CO 5, ST 3). The American language version of the test has been normed in three large samples representative of St. Louis with a 1-year follow-up in one of these samples. Internal consistency and test–retest reliabilities are strong for the total scales, but only moderate for the subscales. Automated scoring and interpretation are available, suitable for both clinicians and clients, accompanied by a detailed validity analysis based on subtle performance-based scales (Cloninger & Svrakic, 1997a, b, c). Scoring and interpretation are available through the TCI Web site or through a personal computer program that is available through the Web site. Factor-analytic studies show strong congruence of the predicted factor structure in different cultures. Causal analyses of the factor structure in twins have shown that there is a common environmental factor for temperament, which distinguishes the temperament and character domains. A short form of 125 items is also available, as are translations of the TCI in most languages.

The TCI-revised (TCI-R) is a 240-item self-report inventory using a 5-point Likert response set (definitely true, probably true, neither true nor false/cannot say, probably false, definitely false). Additional scales were developed so that there are four subscales for all four temperament dimensions, and five for each of the character dimensions. The additional subscales for Persistence improve its reliability substantially. The American test was normed in a large sample representative of the St. Louis metropolitan area. Translations in several languages have also been normed, including Spanish, French, German, and Finnish. Automated scoring and interpretation are available through the TCI Web site.

A junior version of the TCI (JTCI) was developed for children 10–14 years of age. Three versions are available: parent-report, self-report, and rater (teacher)-report. The test measures only the seven higher-order dimensions, not subscales, in order to keep the length near 100 true/false items. Age-appropriate questions were developed in consultation with child psychiatrists. Validity studies and norms are available for the USA,

Germany, and Japan. A preschool version for parent-report is also available for children 3 years of age and older.

At the present time, the Center for Well-being is developing a series of CDs and DVDs that present treatment modules describing mental exercises designed to elevate thought and self-aware consciousness, as described in part elsewhere (Cloninger, 2004). These are intended as enjoyable adjuncts to regular psychotherapy for character development and facilitation of well-being. Information about the availability of these materials will be regularly updated on the TCI Web site.

# Summary and Conclusions

The general population can be approximately divided into thirds in terms of their level of well-being: one third are immature and at least moderately vulnerable to psychopathology; one third are average and getting by without much disability or happiness; and one third are flourishing with high frequency of positive emotions, low frequency of negative emotions, and satisfaction with their life. These three groups can be distinguished on the basis of their three TCI character scores. The combination of high Self-Directedness, high Cooperativeness, and high Self-Transcendence is what characterizes these happy individuals. The extreme deciles (upper and lower 10%s) of personality disorder and of well-being represent the extremes of the human capacity to spiral down into misery or to spiral up into happiness, wisdom, and virtue. The path to well-being involves increasing each of the three components of mental self-government measured by the TCI. Neglect of any of these three aspects of healthy character development leaves a person vulnerable to a wide variety of deficits in well-being.

The TCI allows differentiation of individuals with personality disorder from those who are average or higher in maturity, as well as between individuals who are happy and satisfied with their life from those who are average or lower. Self-Directedness alone can distinguish individuals with severe personality disorders from others, particularly distinguishing those who are irresponsible in work and other aspects of life, resulting in frequent psychiatric treatment and psychosocial disability. Self-Directedness and Cooperativeness together distinguish individuals who are merely average from those who are moderately impaired in the two major tasks of early adulthood, work, and love. Self-Transcendence must be combined with the other two character dimensions to distinguish human beings who are flourishing, happy, and satisfied with their lives, from those who are merely getting by in an average way.

The validity of the TCI measures of maturity and well-being is supported by their success in predicting response to both antidepressants and psychotherapy (Cloninger, 2000, 2004, 2005a, b), their improvement with effective treatment (Cloninger, 2005a, b), and their associations with well-being and absence of psychopathology in the general population (Cloninger & Bayon, 1997). Therefore, the TCI can be used as a screening test, a predictor of response to treatment, and a change measure for monitoring progress. This combination of uses suggests that the TCI is directly measuring what is essential in the process of development of well-being and coherence of personality, providing a reliable and practical instrument for applying my psychobiological approach (Cloninger, 2004).

The opportunity to measure the psychological core of spiritual processes reliably using the TCI means that psychiatry and psychology no longer need neglect spirituality. Spirituality is an important part of human life: People spend more time in prayer or meditation than they do having sex (Cloninger & Svrakic, 1993). The development of an enlarged worldview is not easy but it is essential for a radical transformation of personality with reduced vulnerability to negative emotion. High self-esteem and good social relationships are important foci for psychosocial development, but alone they can never provide access to a transcendental level of serenity that is unconditional. Limiting the scope of the mind to cognitive–behavioral variables trivializes human beings. Yet we all suffer and die, so we all eventually face the spiritual questions that psychiatry and psychology have neglected for too long. If we are willing to face the full scope of human existence in our personal lives, we need not be afraid to face it in our professional lives (Cloninger, 2004).

# Acknowledgments

Supported in part by grants from the US Public Health Service AA-08403, MH-71616, and MH-60879, and the Sansone Family Center for Well-Being.

## REFERENCES

Allport, G. W. (1937). *Personality: A psychological interpretation*. New York: Holt Rinehart & Winston.

American Psychiatric Association. (1987). *Diagnostic and statistical manual of mental disorders* ( 3rd ed., rev.). Washington, DC: American Psychiatric Press.

American Psychiatric Association. (1994). *Diagnostic and statistical manual of mental disorders* (4th ed.). Washington, DC: American Psychiatric Press.

Bailer, U. F. (2004). Altered 5-HT2A receptor binding after recovery from bulimia-type anorexia nervosa: relationships to harm avoidance and drive for thinness. *Neuropsychopharmacology, 29*, 1143–1155.

Bailer, U. F., & Frank, G. K. (2005). Persistent alterations of 5-HT1A receptor binding after recovery from Anorexia Nervosa. *World Journal of Biological Psychiatry, 6*(Suppl. 1), 89.

Borg, J., & Andree, B. (2003). The serotonin system and spiritual experiences. *American Journal of Psychiatry, 160*, 1965–1969.

Cloninger, C. R. (1987). A systematic method for clinical description and classification of personality variants: a proposal. *Archives of General Psychiatry, 44*, 573–587.

Cloninger, C. R. (1994). The genetic structure of personality and learning: aphylogenetic perspective. *Clinical Genetics, 46*, 124–137.

Cloninger, C. R. (2000). A practical way to diagnose personality disorder: A proposal. *Journal of Personality Disorders, 14*(2), 99–108.

Cloninger, C. R. (2002). Functional neuroanatomy and brain imaging of personality and its disorders. In H. D'haenen, J. A. den Boer, & P. Willner (Eds.), *Biological psychiatry* (Vol. 2, pp. 1377–1385). Chichester, UK: Wiley.

Cloninger, C. R. (2003). Completing the psychobiological architecture of human personality development: Temperament, Character, & Coherence. In U. M. Staudinger, & U. E. R. Lindenberger (Eds.), *Understanding human development: Dialogues with lifespan psychology* (pp. 159–182). Boston: Kluwer .

Cloninger, C. R. (2004). *Feeling good: The science of well being*. New York: Oxford University Press.

Cloninger, C. R. (2005a). Antisocial personality disorder: A review. In M. Maj, H. S. Akiskal, J. E. Mezzich, & A. Okasha (Eds.), *Personality disorders: Evidence and experience in psychiatry* (Vol. 8, pp. 125–129). London: Wiley.

Cloninger, C. R. (2005b). Book review of Peterson and Seligman's character and human virtues. *American Journal of Psychiatry, 162*, 820–821.

Cloninger, C. R., & Bayon, C. (1997). Epidemiology and Axis 1 comorbidity of antisocial personality disorder. In D. M. Stoff, J. Breiling, & J. D. Maser (Eds.), *Handbook of antisocial behavior* (pp. 12–21). New York: John Wiley. Cloninger, C. R., & Bayon, C. (1998). Measurement of temperament and character in mood disorders: A model of fundamental states as personality types. *Journal of Affective Disorders, 51,* 21–32.

Cloninger, C. R., & Przybeck, T. R. (1991). The tridimensional personality questionnaire: U.S. normative data. *Psychological Reports, 69,* 1047–1057.

Cloninger, C. R., & Przybeck, T. R. (1994). *The temperament and character inventory: A guide to its development and use.* St. Louis, MO: Washington University Center for Psychobiology of Personality.

Cloninger, C. R., & Svrakic, D. M. (1993). A psychobiological model of temperament and character. *Archives of General Psychiatry, 50,* 975–990.

Cloninger, C. R., & Svrakic, D. M. (1997a). Integrative psychobiological approach to psychiatric assessment and treatment. *Psychiatry, 60,* 120–141.

Cloninger, C. R., & Svrakic, D. M. (1997b). Personality disorders. In S. B. Guze (Ed.), *Washington University adult psychiatry* (pp. 301–318). St. Louis: Mosby.

Cloninger, C. R., & Svrakic N. M. (1997c). Role of personality self-organization in development of mental order and disorder. *Development and Psychopathology, 9,* 881–906.

Cloninger, C. R., & Svrakic, D. M. (2000). Personality disorders. In B. J. Sadock, & V. A. Sadock (Eds.), *Comprehensive textbook of psychiatry* (pp. 1723–1764). New York: Lippincott Williams & Wilkins.

Costa, P. T., Jr., & McCrae, R. R. (1985). *The NEO Personality Inventory manual.* Odessa, FL: Psychological Assessment Resources.

Costa, P. T., Jr., & McCrae, R. R. (1992). *Revised NEO Personality Inventory (NEO-PI-R) and NEO Five-Factor Inventory (NEO-FFI) professional manual.* Odessa, FL: Psychological Assessment Resources.

Fredrickson, B. L. (2004). The broaden-and-build theory of positive emotions. *Philosophical Transactions of the Royal Society of London–Series B: Biological Sciences, 359,* 1367–1377.

Gandhi, M. K. (1957). *An autobiography: The story of my experiments with truth.* Boston: Beacon Press.

Gillespie, N. A., & Cloninger, C. R. (2003). The genetic and environmental relationship between Cloninger's dimensions of temperament and character. *Personality & Individual Differences, 35,* 1931–1946.

Gusnard, D. A., & Akbudak, E. (2001). Medial prefrontal cortex and self-referential mental activity: relation to a default mode of brain function. *Proceedings of the National Academy of Sciences USA, 98,* 4259–4265.

Gusnard, D. A., & Ollinger, J. M. (2001). Personality differences in functional brain imaging. *Society of Neuroscience Abstracts, 27*(80), 11.

Gusnard, D. A., & Ollinger, J. M. (2003). Persistence and brain circuitry. *Proceedings of the National Academy of Sciences USA, 100,* 3479–3484.

Hamer, D. H. (2004). *The God gene: How faith is hardwired into our genes.* New York: Doubleday.

Heath, A. C., & Cloninger, C. R. (1994). Testing a model for the genetic structure of personality: A comparison of the personality systems of Cloninger and Eysenck. *Journal of Personal and Social Psychology, 66,* 762–775.

Huppert, F. A., & Baylis, N. (2004). Why do we need a science of well-being. *Philosophical Transactions of the Royal Society of London–Series B: Biological Sciences, 359,* 1331–1332.

Kaasinen, V., & Aalto, S. (2004). Insular dopamine D2 receptors and novelty seeking personality in Parkinson's disease. *Movement Disorders, 19,* 1348–1351.

Keltikangas-Jaervinen, L., & Raeikkoenen, K. (2004). Nature and nurture in novelty seeking. *Molecular Psychiatry, 9,* 308–311.

Koenig, H. G., & Kvale, J. N. (1988). Religion and well-being in later life. *Gerontologist, 28,* 18–28.

Koob, G. F., & LeMoal, M. (2001). Drug addiction, dysregulation of reward, and allostasis. *Neuropsychopharmacology, 24,* 97–129.

Peterson, C., & Seligman, M. E. P. (2004). *Character strengths and virtues: Handbook and classification.* New York: American Psychological Association and Oxford University Press.

Radloff, L. S. (1977). The CES-D scale: a self-report depression scale for research in the general population. *Applied Psychological Measurement, 36,* 749–760.

Seligman, M. E. P., & Parks, A. C. (2004). A balanced psychology and a full life. *Philosophical Transactions of the Royal Society of London–Series B: Biological Sciences, 359,* 1379–1381.

Svrakic, D. M., & Whitehead, C. (1993). Differential diagnosis of personality disorders by the seven factor model of temperament and character. *Archives of General Psychiatry, 50*, 991–999.

Tellegen, A., & Grove, W. (1990). *Inventory of personal characteristics No. 7*. Minneapolis, MN: Department of Psychology, University of Minnesota.

Tellegen, A., & Lykken, T. D. (1988). Personality similarity in twins reared apart and together. *Journal of Personal and Social Psychology, 54*, 1031–1039.

Tellegen, A., & Waller, N. G. (in press). Exploring personality through test construction: Development of the Multidimensional Personality Questionnaire. In S. R. Briggs & J. M. Cheek (Eds.), *Personality measures: Development and evaluation*. Greenwich, CT: JAI Press.

Vaillant, G. E. (1993). *The wisdom of the ego*. Cambridge, Massachusetts: Harvard University Press.

Vaillant, G. E., & Milofsky, E. (1980). Natural history of male psychological health: IX. Empirical evidence for Erikson's model of the life cycle. *American Journal of Psychiatry, 137*, 1348–1359.

Woodward, K. L., & Springen, K. (1992, January). Talking to God. *Newsweek, 6*, 39–44.

# Interpersonal Theory and the Interpersonal Circumplex

## Evolving Perspectives on Normal and Abnormal Personality

4

Aaron L. Pincus

Michael B. Gurtman

**T**he title of this chapter may appear to include a redundancy that we would like to immediately address. There is a common misconception that the structural model of interpersonal behavior known as the circumplex and the interpersonal theory of personality are one and the same. They are in fact distinct entities.[1] As such, the historical development of each can be traced separately; but if this is done, a complication emerges. Although the psychologists developing the structural model were clearly guided *by interpersonal theory*, the model is not exactly an operationalization *of interpersonal theory*. However, since the articulation of the interpersonal circumplex, this structural model has had a significant impact on the evolution of its progenitor—interpersonal theory itself. This is particularly clear when issues of normality and abnormality are discussed. It is fitting that this state of affairs exists, as interpersonalists have consistently asserted that human behavior is best understood within the context of transactional causality and reciprocal influence (Brokaw & McLemore, 1991; Kiesler, 1996; Pincus & Ansell, 2003). Persons A and B mutually and reciprocally influence each other, in that the behavior of each is both a response to and a stimulus for the other's behavior. It seems the same state of affairs applies to the ongoing evolution of both interpersonal theory and the interpersonal circumplex. In combination, we refer to this nomological net as the *interpersonal tradition* in personality.

---

[1]The present discussion is limited to the *interpersonal circumplex*. Other circumplex models have been articulated in diverse areas such as mood (Russell, 1980), vocational interests (Tracey & Rounds, 1995), and personality disorders (Millon, 1987).

The present chapter reviews a variety of interpersonal approaches to defining, describing, and assessing normal and abnormal personality that have arisen throughout the 50-year history of the interpersonal tradition. These approaches can be usefully categorized in terms of (a) individual differences; (b) interpersonal transaction and reciprocity; and (c) internal psychological processes. We begin with a review of the salient theoretical and empirical history of the interpersonal tradition to introduce its fundamental assumptions, basic structural model, and potential conceptual scope.

# The Interpersonal Tradition in Personality

The origins of the interpersonal tradition in personality are found in Sullivan's (1953a, b, 1954, 1956, 1962, 1964) highly generative interpersonal theory of psychiatry, which considered interpersonal relations and the self-concept to be core emphases in understanding normal and abnormal personality. The interpersonal tradition that emerged from Sullivan's work (e.g., Anchin & Kiesler, 1982; Benjamin, 1974; Carson, 1969; Leary, 1957; Lorr & McNair, 1963, 1965; McLemore & Benjamin, 1979; Schaefer, 1959, 1961; Wiggins, 1979, 1980, 1982) has dramatically evolved in the last 20 years, increasing in scope (e.g., Locke, 2000; Moskowitz, Pinard, Zuroff, Annable, & Young, 2001; Trobst, 2000), level of theoretical integration (e.g., Benjamin, 2003; Horowitz, 2004; Pincus, 2005a, b; Pincus & Ansell, 2003; Wiggins, 1991, 1997; Wiggins & Trapnell, 1996), and methodological sophistication (e.g., Ansell & Pincus, 2004; Gurtman, 1994, 2001; Gurtman & Balakrishnan, 1998; Gurtman & Pincus, 2003; Moskowitz & Zuroff, 2004; Sadler & Woody, 2003). While this evolution is vital and ongoing, Sullivan's commitment to the study of interpersonal phenomena remains at the forefront of these developments. This allows the diverse efforts in the interpersonal tradition to be interconnected and reciprocally influential. Thus, we begin with a clear articulation of Sullivan's views on interpersonal phenomena.

## Sullivan and the Interpersonal Situation

> I had come to feel over the years that there was an acute need for a discipline that was determined to study not the individual organism or the social heritage, but the interpersonal situations through which persons manifest mental health or mental disorder. (Sullivan, 1953b, p. 18)
>
> Personality is the relatively enduring pattern of recurrent interpersonal situations which characterize a human life. (Sullivan, 1953b, pp. 110–111)

Sullivan's emphasis on the interpersonal situation as the focus for understanding both normal and abnormal personality set an elemental course for psychology and psychiatry. Interpersonal theory thus begins with the assumption that the most important expressions of personality occur in phenomena involving more than one person. Sullivan (1953a, b) suggested that individuals express "integrating tendencies" which bring them together in the mutual pursuit of satisfactions (generally a large class of biologically grounded needs), security (i.e., anxiety-free functioning), and self-esteem. These integrating tendencies develop into increasingly complex patterns or "dynamisms" of interpersonal experience. From infancy throughout the life span, these dynamisms are encoded in memory via age-appropriate learning. According to Sullivan, interpersonal learning of self-concept and social behavior is based on an "anxiety gradient" associated with interpersonal situations. All interpersonal situations range from rewarding (highly secure) through various degrees of anxiety and ending in a class of situations associated with such severe anxiety that they are dissociated from experience. The interpersonal situation underlies genesis, development, maintenance, and mutability of personality through the continuous patterning and repatterning of interpersonal experience in relation to the vicissitudes of satisfactions, security, and esteem. Over time, this gives rise to lasting conceptions of self and other (Sullivan's "personifications"), as well as to enduring patterns of interpersonal relating.

Individual variation in learning occurs due to the interaction between the developing person's level of cognitive maturation (i.e., Sullivan's prototaxic, parataxic, and syntaxic modes of experience) and the characteristics of the interpersonal situations encountered. Interpersonal experience is understood differently depending on the developing person's grasp of cause and effect logic and the use of consensual symbols such as language. This affects how one makes sense of the qualities of significant others (including their "reflected appraisals" of the developing person), as well as the ultimate outcomes of interpersonal situations characterizing a human life. Pincus and Ansell (2003) summarized Sullivan's concept of the interpersonal situation as "the experience of a pattern of relating self with other associated with varying levels of anxiety (or security) in which learning takes place that influences the development of self-concept and social behavior" (p. 210). In one way or another, all perspectives on normal and abnormal personality within the interpersonal tradition address elements of the interpersonal situation. These include the individual differences, reciprocal interpersonal patterns of behavior, and internal psychological processes that we review in this chapter.

A second major assumption of interpersonal theory is that the term *interpersonal* is meant to convey a sense of primacy, directing theory to a set of fundamental phenomena important for personality development, structuralization, function, and pathology. The term is not meant as a geographical indicator of locale; it does not imply a dichotomy between what is inside the person and what is outside the person, nor does it limit the scope of interpersonal theory to observable interactions between two proximal people (Pincus, 2005a, b; Pincus & Ansell, 2003).

Mitchell (1988) pointed out that Sullivan was quite amenable to incorporating internal psychological structures and processes into interpersonal theory as he viewed the most important contents of the mind to be the consequence of lived interpersonal experience. For example, Sullivan (1964) asserted that "everything that can be found in the human mind has been put there by interpersonal relations, excepting only the capabilities to receive *and elaborate* the relevant experiences" (p. 302; see also Stern, 1985, 1988). Sullivan clearly viewed the interpersonal situation as equally likely to be found within the mind of the person as it is to be found in the observable interactions between two people. For example, Sullivan (1964) defined psychiatry as "the study of phenomena that occur in configurations of two or more people, all but one of whom may be more or less completely illusory" (p. 33). These illusory aspects of the interpersonal situation involve mental structures, i.e., personifications of self and others. Sullivan (1953b) was forceful in asserting that personifications are elaborated organizations of past interpersonal experience, stating "I would like to make it forever clear that the relation of the personifications to that which is personified is always complex and sometimes multiple; and that personifications are not adequate descriptions of that which is personified" (p. 167).

Thus, interpersonal theory asserts that interpersonal situations occur between proximal interactants and within the minds of those interactants via the capacity for mental representation of self and others (e.g., Benjamin, 1993; Blatt, Auerbach, & Levy, 1997; Heck & Pincus, 2001; Pincus, 2005a). Interpersonal theory does suggest that the most important personality phenomena are relational in nature, but it does not suggest that such phenomena are limited to contemporaneous, observable behavior. They also occur in perceptions of contemporaneous interpersonal experiences, memories of past interpersonal experiences, and fantasies of future interpersonal experiences. Regardless of the level of accuracy or distortion in these perceptions, memories, and fantasies, both internal and proximal interpersonal situations continuously influence an individual's learned relational strategies and self-concept. Abnormal personality is therefore inherently expressed via disturbed interpersonal relations (Sullivan, 1953b).

## Leary and Beyond: The Origins and Evolution of the Interpersonal Circumplex

The first articulation of the interpersonal circumplex was developed from an extensive investigation of group psychotherapy conducted by graduate students, clinicians, and faculty associated with the University of California and the Kaiser Foundation Health Plan in Oakland, California. Guided by the theoretical influences of Sullivan and Kurt Lewin, the clinical goal was to understand the relations between group interaction and personality structure and the research approach was an attempt to systematize and operationally define many of Sullivan's terms and concepts (LaForge, 2004; LaForge, Freedman, & Wiggins, 1985; Wiggins, 1996). The results of this work is documented in a series of articles which appeared in the early 1950s (Coffey, Freedman, Leary, & Ossorio, 1950; Freedman, Leary, Ossorio, & Coffey, 1951; LaForge, Leary, Naboisek, Coffey, & Freedman, 1954; Laforge & Suczek, 1955; Leary & Coffey, 1955) and comprehensively summarized and expanded by Leary (1957). It is of significance that from the beginning, the structural model emerged from what Lewin (1931) referred to as a "Galileian mode of thought" (see also, Wicklund & Gollwitzer, 1987). As noted by LaForge, "We recognized the value of focusing on gross molar beginning-and-end situations mediating hypothetical inner forces. We understood that typological classification was of little utility, that psychological processes had to be related in terms of molar, integrated, goal-directed, dynamic laws" (LaForge et al., 1985, p. 618). The goal was not simply a classification system, but a system of personality (LaForge, 2004); and thus, the reciprocal influence between interpersonal theory and the interpersonal circumplex had begun.

The initial set of interpersonal variables was derived from behavioral observations of patients engaged in group psychotherapy, whereby the investigators attempted to define "interpersonal mechanisms" of overt behavior. The definitions were developed to answer the question, "What is the subject of the activity, e.g., the individual whose behavior is being rated, doing to the object or objects of the activity?" (Freedman et al., 1951, p. 149). In this regard, topical content was not of specific interest. Instead,

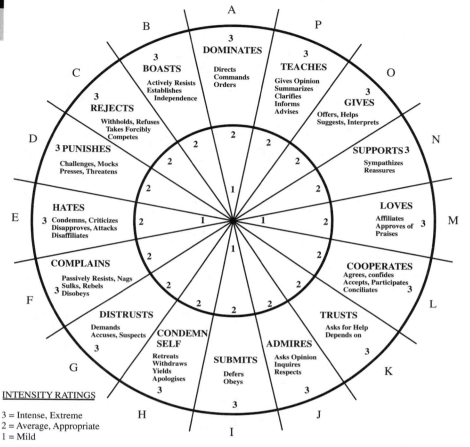

An adaptation of the original circumplex of interpersonal mechanisms (Freedman et al., 1951). Reprinted from Pincus (1994).

interpersonal mechanisms reflected the interaction process between group members. The assumption was that behavior could be functionally understood when related to a dynamic theory of personality.

The comprehensive list of interpersonal mechanisms observed in patients was first presented on a circular continuum by Freedman et al. (1951). The most basic aspects of this circular structure representing interpersonal behavior have remained the same (see Figures 4.1 and 4.2), although a variety of interpersonal circumplex models have been elaborated over the years. However, the circumplex was not a direct operationalization of theory:

> The circular continuum utilized to organize or systematize the interpersonal mechanisms did not emerge out of a priori or deductive reasoning. The first step after evolution of the concept of interpersonal mechanism was to list all the mechanisms that my colleagues and I could discern or distinguish at the beginning. The mechanisms

Figure
4.2

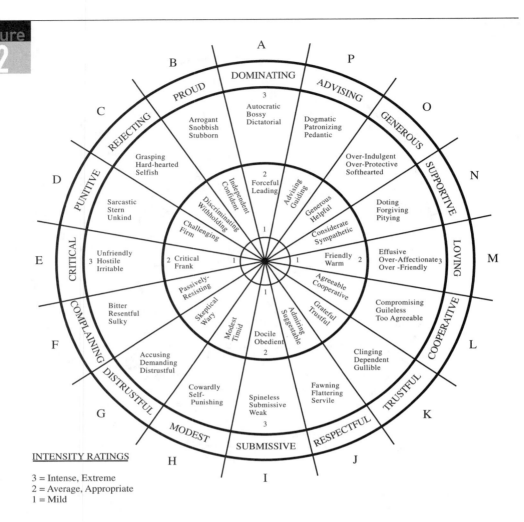

INTENSITY RATINGS

3 = Intense, Extreme
2 = Average, Appropriate
1 = Mild

An adaptation of the original circumplex of interpersonal traits (Freedman et al., 1951). Reprinted from Pincus (1994).

were simply a list of verbs. Thousands of manipulations yielded a system and an orderly arrangement. Slowly the nodal points or axes of affiliation vs. aggression and dominance vs. submission emerged. (LaForge et al., 1985, p. 624)

Figure 4.1 presents an adaptation of the original circumplex of interpersonal mechanisms. Sixteen interpersonal variables are arranged in a circular continuum around the orthogonal dimensions of dominance—submission and hostility—affiliation. The circular arrangement of variables is meant to imply that, in some sense, variables close to each other are more "similar" than are variables further away from each other. As can be noted in Figures 4.1 and 4.2, the original circumplexes were marked by "intensity" values increasing from the center of the circle. Wiggins (1982) pointed out that this feature implies a formal geometric model of two-dimensional Euclidean space where variables located opposite to each other are considered bipolar contrasts (e.g., to dominate is the opposite of to submit). The basic dimensions making up the axes can be considered latent variables, which give rise to the circular continuum (Carson, 1996; Gurtman & Pincus, 2003). From this perspective, each of the interpersonal mechanisms (Figure 4.1) and interpersonal traits (Figure 4.2) may be thought of as representing a particular blend of dominance and affiliation. The implications of this formal geometric model provide psychometric foundations for a variety of interpersonal assessment methods (e.g., Gurtman, 1994; Gurtman & Balakrishnan, 1998; Pincus & Gurtman, 2000; 2003; Tracey, 2000; Wiggins, Phillips, & Trapnell, 1989).

The first interpersonal circumplex was thus developed out of observations of specific behavior in group psychotherapy settings and "the interpersonal mechanisms are regarded as process variables of personality as distinguished from structural variables of personality. They are regarded as descriptive of immediate interpersonal processes, the 'personality in action,' so to speak" (Freedman et al., 1951, p. 156; see also Leary, 1957). This focus on behavior remains a significant emphasis for many contemporary interpersonalists (e.g., Moskowitz, 1994, 2005; Fournier, Moskowitz, & Zuroff, 2002; Tracey, 1994; Tracey & Schneider, 1995). When the circumplex of interpersonal mechanisms is viewed as a formal geometric model, it gives rise to one of the first interpersonal perspectives on abnormal personality. The metric increasing from the center of the circle represents *behavioral intensity*.

The original circular ordering of interpersonal mechanisms was evaluated and translated with reference to adjectival trait descriptors (see Figure 4.2). The concept of *interpersonal trait* has been developed to systematize the structural variables or enduring tendencies of personality. The interpersonal mechanisms displayed by an individual in a social situation may be considered the outcome of an interplay between environmental forces impinging upon him and those enduring tendencies to action which he brings to the situation" (Freedman et al., 1951; see also Leary, 1957). The circumplex of interpersonal traits allows the model to describe enduring patterns of interpersonal behavior and the metric increasing from this level of analysis represents a second perspective on abnormal personality—*behavioral rigidity*.

Of note, while the original concept of an interpersonal trait was conceived of in relation to the consistency of an individual's observable behavior, advances in both trait theory and interpersonal theory have expanded this perspective (Pincus, 1994). Modern trait theory conceives of traits as descriptions of how a person behaves in certain situations, and of equal importance, traits describe something about the intrapsychic functioning of the individual's mind (Funder, 1991; Tellegen, 1991). Within the interpersonal tradition in personality, the trait concept has similarly expanded such that a variety of enduring individual differences are now represented or implied by the interpersonal circumplex structure, including interpersonal problems (Alden, Wiggins, & Pincus, 1990; Horowitz, 1996), interpersonal motives, values, and goals (Horowitz, 2004; Locke, 2000), social support behaviors (Trobst, 2000), and an individual's enduring tendencies to organize perceptions of new interpersonal experience in particular ways (Benjamin, 1995; Kiesler, Schmidt, & Wagner, 1997; Pincus, 1994).

The circumplex structures representing specific interpersonal behaviors and enduring patterns of interpersonal behavior (i.e., traitlike individual differences) share the perspective that normal and abnormal personality lie on a continuum. Thus, adaptive and maladaptive behaviors and behavior patterns can be described and measured along common dimensions. Carson (1991) summarized the interpersonal perspective at the time, stating,

> Abnormality consists of the rigid reliance on a limited class of interpersonal behaviors regardless of situational influences or norms, that often are enacted at an inappropriate level of intensity. Normality, then, is simply the flexible and adaptive deployment, within moderate ranges of intensity, of behaviors encompassing the entire circle, as varied interpersonal situations dictate. (p. 190)

This remains a fundamental interpersonal perspective on normal and abnormal personality. In addition, recent advances in the interpersonal tradition have generated several new and evolving perspectives on normal and abnormal personality.

## Agency and Communion: Integrative Metaconcepts

A major influence on the expansion and evolution of interpersonal perspectives on normal and abnormal personality is Wiggins' (1991, 1997, 2003) seminal review and integration of the nature and broad application of Bakan's (1966) metaconcepts of "agency" and "communion." Wiggins argued that these two superordinate dimensions have propaeduetic explanatory power across fields as diverse as philosophy, linguistics, anthropology, sociology, psychiatry, gender studies, and the subdisciplines of personality psychology, evolutionary psychology, cross-cultural psychology, social psychology, and clinical psychology. Agency refers to the condition of being a differentiated individual, and it is manifested in strivings for power and mastery which can enhance and protect ones' differentiation. Communion refers to the condition of being part of a larger social or spiritual entity, and is manifested in strivings for intimacy, union, and solidarity with the larger entity. Bakan (1966) noted that a key issue for understanding human existence is to comprehend how the tensions of this duality in the human condition are managed.

Wiggins (2003) proposed that agency and communion are most directly related to Sullivan's theory in terms of the goals of human relationship: security (communion) and self-esteem (agency). As can be seen in Figure 4.3, these metaconcepts (concepts about concepts) form a superordinate structure which can be used to derive explanatory and descriptive concepts at different levels of specificity. At the broadest and most interdisciplinary level, metaconcepts serve to classify the motives, strivings, conflicts, and goals of human existence. When the structure is applied to the interpersonal situation, we may consider what agentic or communal motives or goals drive human relationship. At this level, they address the nature of relations between self and other (and self and society), i.e., what states of being and fundamental goals are important to the person?

At more specific levels, the structure provides conceptual coordinates for describing and measuring interpersonal traits and behaviors (Wiggins, 1991). The intermediate level includes the evolving set of interpersonal taxonomies of individual differences noted previously. Agentic and communal traits and problems imply enduring patterns of perceiving, thinking, feeling, and behaving that are probabilistic in nature, and describe an individual's interpersonal tendencies aggregated across time, place, and relationships. At the most specific level, the structure can be used to classify the

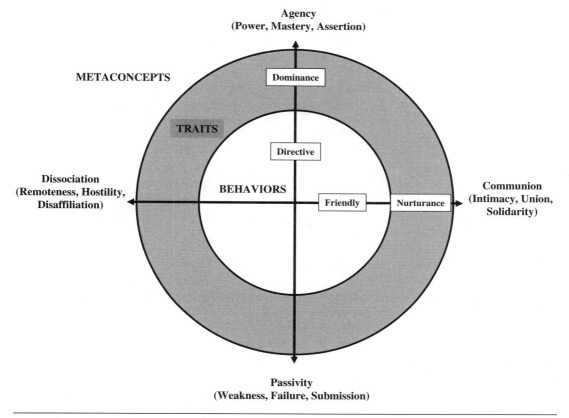

Agency and communion. From Pincus (2005a), reprinted with permission.

nature and intensity of specific interpersonal behaviors or acts. Wiggins' theoretical analysis simultaneously allows for the integration of descriptive levels within the interpersonal tradition as well as expansion of the conceptual scope and meaning of interpersonal functioning. The interpersonal tradition in personality proposes that (a) agency and communion are the fundamental metaconcepts of personality, providing a superordinate structure for conceptualizing interpersonal situations, (b) explicatory systems derived from agency and communion can be used to understand, describe, and measure interpersonal traits and behaviors, and (c) such systems can be applied equally well to the objective description of contemporaneous interactions between two or more proximal individuals (e.g., Markey, Funder, & Ozer, 2003) and to interpersonal situations within the mind evoked via perception, memory, fantasy, and mental representation (e.g., Heck & Pincus, 2001). Figure 4.4 presents a contemporary version of a trait-level interpersonal circumplex that may serve as a prototype for discussions in the following sections.

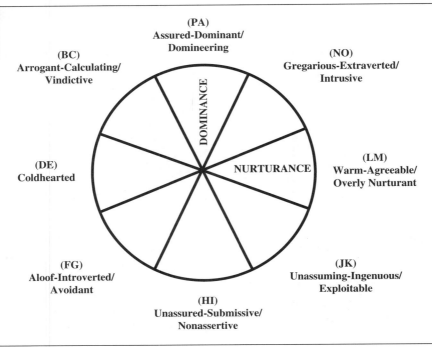

An interpersonal circumplex. From Pincus & Ansell (2003), reprinted with permission.

# Differentiating Normal and Abnormal Personality: Individual Differences in Traits

In this section, we review various approaches for differentiating normal and abnormal personality using personality trait constructs and their derivatives. These include both traditional viewpoints, for example, as reflected in the previous summary offered by Carson (1991) and focusing on personality rigidity and extremity as critical variables (e.g., Kiesler, 1983; Wiggins et al., 1989), and in newer conceptions organized around the metaconcepts of Agency and Communion (e.g., Helgeson, 1994; Horowitz, 2004; Wiggins, 1991).

Regardless of approach, the central individual difference variable here is the personality trait, as typically defined, an enduring, dispositional attribute of the individual expressed in distinctive patterns of thought, behavior, and feeling. As McAdams (1995) points out, traits typically describe individual differences at a fairly broad or general level; they are inherently "decontextualized" and relatively "nonconditional" (p. 365). Hence, the variables of interest here are assumed to reflect a general feature of the person's tendencies (e.g., "I am aggressive"), which would presumably be relatively stable in time and found in an aggregate of interpersonal situations. Importantly, however, a certain trait (whether adaptive or maladaptive) may not necessarily be expressed in a particular interpersonal situation, relationship, or episode; or dictate a particular emergent process. For this level of specificity, interpersonalists have generally relied on other constructs; these will be covered later in this chapter.

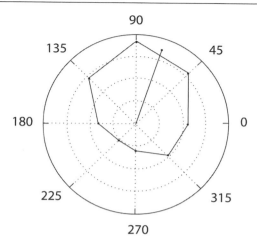

A circular profile, including resultant vector. Reprinted from Gurtman (1994).

## Summarizing Interpersonal Tendencies in the Circumplex Space

The basic methods for depicting individual differences within a circular space have now been described and articulated in many places (see, e.g., Gurtman, 1994; Gurtman & Balakrishnan, 1998; Horowitz, 2004; Kiesler, 1996; Leary, 1957; Wiggins et al., 1989). Here we will cover only the necessary essentials.

The circular profile (Figure 4.5) is the starting point. It represents the individual's pattern of scores as vectors in a circular space; the length of each vector corresponds to the person's score on that trait dimension, and the vector's orientation, or angle, indicates the corresponding scale's angular position on the circumplex, usually theoretically determined.

Using vector addition, it is possible to create a resultant vector that, in effect, summarizes the profile pattern, reducing it to two descriptive statistics: (a) the resultant vector's *angle* (theta) suggests the predominant interpersonal theme or typology (Gurtman, 1994) of the profile, its circular mean (Mardia, 1972), and (b) the vector's magnitude, or *vector length* (*VL*), is essentially an indication of the distinctiveness or extremity of the profile, which relates to the circular standard deviation (e.g., Gurtman, 1994; Mardia, 1972). The profile's elevation (or linear mean value) can also be calculated, and may have interpretive significance for some circumplex measures (as will be discussed later, with reference to interpersonal problems).

## Normal Personality, Extremity, and Rigidity

Leary (1957) was among the first interpersonalists to articulate the view that normal and abnormal interpersonal behaviors lie on the same continuum, and that differences between (what he termed) "adjustive" and "maladjustive" personality are quantitative rather than qualitative in nature (p. 59). This leads to the assumption that normal personality traits—those common dimensions of individual difference descriptive of the average or typical person, and on which people can vary from high to low—provide the basic currency for differentiating normal from abnormal. Today, the same perspective is held by many personality disorder (PD) researchers, who argue that PDs represent maladaptive variations of normal personality traits, such as those comprising the Five-Factor Model of personality (e.g., Costa & Widiger, 1994; Widiger & Costa, 1994).

In the interpersonal realm, an important tool for this kind of analysis and approach are circumplex-based measures of normal interpersonal traits. Optimally, such measures offer a taxonomy of interpersonal variables and give coherence to their assumed structural (circular) relations (Wiggins, 1979). The Interpersonal Adjective Scales, or IAS (Wiggins, 1979, 1995), is notable in this respect. Developed, in part, on the basis of the circumplex model and a conceptual analysis of the interpersonal domain, the IAS has been the de facto standard for assessing normal personality traits within the circumplex tradition (Adams & Tracey, 2004; Gurtman & Pincus, 2000). Figure 4.4 includes the variables of the IAS.

When referenced to the circumplex model, extremity and rigidity are critical variables for conceptualizing abnormal personality within the interpersonal tradition. Although the two are assumed to co-occur, they are conceptually distinct (O'Connor & Dyce, 2001). In the context of the circumplex, extremity reflects a person's deviance from a normative position on a particular dimension, and is represented, geometrically, by a person's (or, literally, the behavior's) distance from the origin of the circle. Behaviors can vary from relatively mild expressions of a trait dimension (close to the origin) to extreme or intense versions at the periphery of the circle. This intensity dimension is an inherent feature of the circle originally conceived by the Kaiser group (Figure 4.1) and, more recently, by Kiesler's (1983, 1996) refined articulation of that model. As a quick glance at the earlier Figure 4.1 would suggest, the extreme behaviors that populate the circle's periphery are likely to be undesirable for both self and others. Their lack of moderation would rarely make them situationally appropriate or successful. (For theoretical elaborations, consult Carson, 1969; Horowitz, 2004; or Kiesler, 1996.)

As Pincus (1994) points out, whereas extremity (or intensity) is a property of an individual's *behavior*, rigidity is a characteristic of a *person*, or more specifically, a summary of his or her limited repertoires across various interpersonal situations. From Leary (1957) on, interpersonalists have argued that disordered individuals tend to enact or rely on a limited or restricted range of behaviors, failing to adapt or conform their behaviors to the particular demands of a given situation. From a circumplex perspective, they tend to draw from a small segment of the interpersonal circle, rather than draw broadly as the situation requires. In contrast, interpersonally flexible individuals are capable of adjusting their behaviors appropriately to the cues of others in order to act effectively (see, e.g., Paulhus & Martin, 1987, 1988). Hence, they are more likely to engage in and sustain complementary behavior patterns that are mutually satisfying to their relational partners (e.g., Kiesler, 1996). In a sense, then, rigidity can be construed as a kind of global interpersonal skill deficit.

Traditionally, rigidity has been assessed using methods of scoring a person's circular profile that derive originally from LaForge et al. (1954). Specifically, the profile's vector length, or VL, has been used as an index of rigidity (e.g., Leary, 1957; O'Connor & Dyce, 1997, 2001; Wiggins et al., 1989). Figure 4.5 illustrates how VL essentially reflects the "peakedness" of a person's profile in the circumplex space, and, as indicated earlier, is obtained through simple vector arithmetic (although, as Gurtman, 1994 has shown, curve fitting can also be used). High VL profiles tend to have greater variance across scales, which is caused by a pronounced elevation in a single region of the circumplex.

Gurtman and Balakrishnan (1998) have extensively discussed and critiqued the presumed link between VL and rigidity, drawing the distinction between VL as statistical index (known properties) and as potential clinical indicator (hypothesis). As a statistic, VL is technically a measure of a profile's variability moderated by the profile's "fit" to a circular model (cosine curve).[2] Whether VL is a valid indicator of rigidity, however, is an ongoing empirical matter, although evidence to date suggests that it is not highly correlated with general maladjustment (e.g., Paulhus & Martin, 1988; Gurtman, 1996; Gurtman & Balakrishnan, 1998; cf. O'Connor & Dyce, 2001; Ruiz et al., 2004; Wiggins et al., 1989). Strangely, we know of no evidence to date that directly addresses whether VL is indeed related to rigid (limited, inflexible) interpersonal repertoires. However, because VL does not, in its calculation, include interpersonal behaviors sampled across time or situations (seemingly central to the meaning of rigidity; see next subsection), we think that its connection to rigidity is inferential and indirect at best.

## New Developments: Flux, Spin, and Pulse

A limitation of traditional measures of interpersonal functioning (specifically, those based on the circumplex) is that they involve assessments at a single point in time. Recently, however, Moskowitz and Zuroff (2004) suggested that intraindividual variability (or fluctuations) in interpersonal behavior may be an important and stable individual difference variable, and offered three new "dynamic additions" to "the lexicon" of interpersonal assessment, which they referred to as flux, spin, and pulse. They defined flux as the variability (standard deviation) of the individual's mean score on a particular interpersonal dimension. Spin indicates the variability of the person's angular position across time, and pulse refers to the variability in vector length. Figure 4.6, reproduced from Moskowitz and Zuroff (2004), provides a visual representation of several possible combinations of spin and pulse.

To explore the properties of these constructs, Moskowitz and Zuroff (2004) conducted a study in which they used an event-contingent recording method to have individuals assess their own interpersonal behaviors over a 20-day period. Personality traits were also assessed initially through a measure of the Five-Factor Model. Two sets of findings were especially noteworthy. First, the results showed that intraindividual variability in interpersonal behavior could serve as a reliable individual difference variable. Second, the results revealed interesting correlations of flux, spin, and pulse with basic personality traits. For example, trait extraversion predicted flux in agreeableness, which, to the authors, suggested that extraverts are relatively flexible in their agreeable behaviors, hence responsive to aspects of social situations that promote positive interactions and well-being. Trait agreeableness, in turn, predicted flux in quarrelsome behaviors, suggesting the possibility of negative reciprocation patterns with others among

---

[2] Consistent with Gurtman (1994), it can be shown that: $VL^2 = k \times R^2 SS_{total}$, where $k$ is a constant, $SS_{total}$ is the total variability of the profile scores as the sum-of-squares, and $R^2$ is goodness-of-fit to a cosine curve.

Figure
4.6

Interpersonal flux, pulse, and spin. From Moskowitz and Zuroff (2004), reprinted with permission.

disagreeable individuals. Neuroticism seemed to serve as a predictor of behavioral lability, especially in submissive behavior.

Flux, spin, and pulse have obvious connections to interpersonal flexibility and rigidity. For example, the rigid individual should be characterized by less spin in interpersonal space (and perhaps less flux and pulse). Arguably, however, the assessment of rigidity should go beyond behavioral variability and include consideration of the specific requirements of the interpersonal situations in which those behaviors occur. Thus, it should also be informed by an understanding of interpersonal situations (Kelley et al., 2003; Rusbult & Van Lange, 2003). As Paulhus & Martin (1988) have noted, the flexible individual not only varies behavior, but tailors the behavior to suit the situation. Comprehensive sampling of situations, along with the knowledge of their evocative properties, would therefore seem to be prerequisites for proper assessment.

## Interpersonal Problems

Measures of normal interpersonal traits are generally not designed to differentiate normal and abnormal personality, except perhaps through the theoretical extensions of extremity and rigidity. Measures that involve the assessment of abnormal personality traits and processes provide a more direct path. In this respect, the development of the Inventory of Interpersonal Problems, or IIP (Horowitz, Rosenberg, Baer, Ureño, & Villaseñor, 1988), along with explication of the interpersonal problems construct, have been critical events in the recent history of interpersonal assessment (Gurtman, 1996; Gurtman & Balakrishnan, 1998).

The evolution of the IIP has been described in detail by Horowitz and his colleagues in a number of articles and chapters (e.g., Horowitz, 1979, 1996; Horowitz & Vitkus, 1986; Horowitz, Rosenberg, & Kalehzan, 1992; Horowitz et al., 1988; Horowitz, Weckler, & Doren, 1983). It was conceived with the assumption that interpersonal problems or difficulties often form the underlying basis of psychiatric complaints and symptoms (Horowitz, 1979; Horowitz et al., 1983). The IIP's item set was originally developed by transcribing and then cataloging the complaints voiced by prospective psychotherapy patients during intake interviews. Complaints judged by a panel of experts as interpersonal were compiled, then reduced, and rewritten to have a common, standardized format. On this basis, Horowitz et al. (1988) published a 127-item version of the IIP (a superset of the current 64-item version; Horowitz, Alden, Wiggins, & Pincus, 2000). Each item on the test was in the form of a self-statement; the first section included statements concerning interpersonal deficits, or "things you find hard to do" (e.g., "It is hard for me to join in on groups"), and the second half concerned problems in interpersonal excess, or "things you do too much" (e.g., "I argue with people too much"). Respondents indicate the degree of "distress" associated with each statement. Thus, interpersonal problems were implicitly conceived as a kind of interpersonal deficit or excess (a behavior, feeling, or attitude) associated with personal distress. The statements are deliberately general, rather than phrased in relation to specific others in the person's life.

The test construction method yielded a test with two particularly appealing features: (a) because the items are based on actual patient complaints, the test possesses a measure of "ecological validity" (Gurtman, 1996) that may be lacking in other instruments; and (b) perhaps on the same basis, the test offers a fairly broad and comprehensive "universe of content" for delineating an individual's specific interpersonal difficulties.

Although the development of the IIP was not guided or informed by a prescriptive theoretical model (e.g., the interpersonal circumplex), subsequent structural analyses of the item content suggested that both agentic and communal contents were important thematic dimensions in the problem set (e.g., Gurtman, 1995; Horowitz, 1996, 2004). Capitalizing on that, Alden et al. (1990) proposed a 64-item subset of the IIP (the IIP-C) designed explicitly to have strong circumplex properties. The test, also illustrated in Figure 4.4, consists of eight scales (or "octants") each consisting of eight items, and thus the test has parallel structure to the IAS. Alden et al.'s (1990) analyses indicated a close empirical fit to the circumplex model, a finding that has been replicated in other studies (e.g., Gurtman, 1994; Gurtman & Balakrishnan, 1998; Horowitz et al., 2000; Pincus, Gurtman, & Ruiz, 1998; Tracey, Rounds, & Gurtman, 1996; Vittengl, Clark, & Jarrett, 2003). In 2000, the IIP-C was repackaged and reintroduced as the IIP, with slight modifications to the scale labels and with new normative data (Horowitz et al., 2000).

Given the circumplex structure of the IIP, the basic methods of circular profile analyses described earlier can be meaningfully applied to elucidate an individual's interpersonal features. Again, this essentially involves calculating a resultant vector from the circular distribution of (IIP scale) scores. Relevant issues have been extensively discussed in Gurtman and Balakrishnan (1998). Specifically, for IIP data, three variables are of potential clinical interest: (a) the resultant vector's angle, or orientation, in the circular space, which, in the case of interpersonal problems, signifies the predominant theme of the individual's interpersonal distress. For example, an angle of 225° would suggest problems in hostile-submissiveness, such as social avoidance; (b) the vector's length, which is a measure of the distinctiveness of the distress. High VL profiles are well-defined or delineated, with a clear peak and trough, and thus suggest a particular interpersonal problem "typology" for the individual; and (c) mean level, or elevation (Gurtman, 1994), which relates to the total amount of reported interpersonal distress (averaged across all regions of the circumplex). Because the IIP, unlike the IAS, includes a large "general factor" in its factor structure, elevation is a potentially important source of individual differences on the IIP. Indeed, Gurtman (1996) and Gurtman and Balakrishnan (1998) have shown that, among the three indices, elevation seems most strongly related to general maladjustment, for example, as reflected in psychiatric ratings of global functioning and in self-reported neuroticism. (See also Vittengl et al., 2003.) However, IIP distress does not appear to be simply a measure of general symptomatology, but retains an interpersonal quality. Horowitz et al. (1992), for example, have shown that individuals high in IIP distress (vs. more nonspecific distress) have a greater capacity to describe others clearly, which may, in turn, make them more likely to profit from interpersonally focused therapies, such as psychodynamic treatment.

### New Developments: Unmitigated Agency and Unmitigated Communion

At a broad level of analysis, interpersonal problems contain thematic elements of agency and communion. Helgeson and her colleagues's work on unmitigated agency (UA) and unmitigated communion (UC) (e.g., Helgeson, 1994; Helgeson & Fritz, 1998) offers a new way of conceptualizing interpersonal maladjustment, and linking maladjustment to both psychological and physical health outcomes.

As noted earlier, Bakan (1966) described agency and communion as the "fundamental modalities" in human existence, and argued that a balance between the two (one "mitigating" the other) was optimal for psychological well-being. Agency, in this sense, involves a focus on self and separation, and communion, a focus on others and connection. These can function as personality traits defining individual differences (e.g., Helgeson & Fritz, 2000); as such, they are also closely tied to traditional conceptions of psychological masculinity and femininity (e.g., Helgeson, 1994; Spence, 1984).

In a series of both theoretical and research papers, Helgeson and others have argued that, whereas agency and communion are generally positive and desirable, extreme manifestations of traits can lead to psychological distress and health problems (e.g., Fritz & Helgeson, 1998; Helgeson, 1994; Helgeson & Fritz, 1998, 2000). Agency, in particular, is theoretically related to psychological well-being, and communion, to positive relationship outcomes. However, high levels of each are maladaptive, in part, because they preclude the expression of the other. Thus, Helgeson (1994) defines UA as agency, or focus on self, to the exclusion of others; and UC as communion, or focus on others, to the exclusion of self. Although normal and extreme versions of each lie on the same continuum (e.g., agency and UA are related, conceptually and empirically), there are also qualitative differences that may account for their differential impacts on health outcomes.

A significant number of studies have now been conducted on the correlates of UA and UC, with perhaps slightly greater attention to UC (for summaries see Helgeson & Fritz, 1998, 2000; for a more general test of the model see Saragovi, Koestner, Di Dio, & Aubé, 1997). Research on UC has been aided by the development of a 9-item self-report measure, the Revised UC Scale (e.g., "I always place the needs of others above my own," and "For me to be happy, I need others to be happy"). Fritz and Helgeson (1998), for example, have shown that UC, unlike (normal) communion, is associated with negative views of self, interpersonal difficulties, and psychological distress. They identify two core dimensions that seem to underlie the UC construct—self-neglect and over-involvement with others. The over-involvement dimension, in particular, seems to provide an important link between UC (as measured by their scale) and the communion (love) axis of the interpersonal problem circumplex (as measured, in part, by the IIP). In this regard, Fritz and Helgeson (1998) obtained a correlation of 0.74 between the UC and a composite scale constructed largely from IIP items from the intrusiveness (NO) and overly nurturant (LM) octants. Similar findings were later reported by Helgeson and Fritz (1999).

Research on UA has been complicated by the lack of a parallel measure of this construct. Typically, UA is assessed using the Extended Version of the Personal Attributes Questionnaire (EPAQ; Spence, Helmreich, & Holahan, 1979), which consists of personality trait adjectives (e.g., "arrogant," "boastful," "cynical") representing negative, stereotypically masculine characteristics. Helgeson and Fritz (1998) found (perhaps not surprisingly) that this measure related most strongly to the domineering (PA) and vindictive (BC) octants of the IIP. (This suggests the possibility that a nonadjectival measure of UA could conceivably be constructed from the IIP item pool.) Other research using this measure has linked UA to poor health behaviors and outcomes, and to interpersonal difficulties such as lack of social support (see Helgeson & Fritz, 2000).

Although not based on either of the traditional UA or UC measures, a recent study by Fournier and Moskowitz (2000) tested an important assumption of the "mitigation" hypothesis. They found that what they referred to as "intradimensional mitigation," or moderation in levels of either agency or communion, was a predictor of positive affect experiences over time. Interdimensional mitigation (e.g., agency mitigating communion, or vice versa) did not predict affect levels, contrary to Helgeson's model. This alternative model of mitigation may therefore prove worthy of further exploration.

Are UA and UC simply subsets of the interpersonal problem circumplex, or do they have surplus meaning beyond the defining dimensions of the traditional interpersonal space? This issue was discussed by Helgeson and Fritz (1999), who related UA and UC specifically to the Wiggins IAS circumplex. They noted that UA appears to be most closely related to the IAS's arrogant-calculating dimension (BC), but they were less clear about the possible location of UC, which, in their view, theoretically has elements of being unassuming (FG) and submissive (HI). More significantly, however, they raise the interesting point that UC, in particular, may be associated with a lack of personal, rather than interpersonal agency (p. 155). Personal agency, with its focus on self, involves separation from others and achieving independence or autonomy. As Hmel and Pincus (2002) have demonstrated, this aspect of autonomy is not captured by the traditional interpersonal circumplex model, although it is a defining feature of some alternative models, such as the SASB system (Benjamin, 1996). In contrast, interpersonal agency involves dominance or control over others, which may or may not be part of the UC constellation for a given individual.

# Differentiating Normal and Abnormal Personality: Interpersonal Transaction and Reciprocity

Individual differences in interpersonal personality traits that give rise to normal and abnormal behaviors must be contextualized to fully inform psychological theory. We must go beyond identifying the constructs and our ability to describe and measure them with reference to the circumplex. Sullivan (1948) provided an early vision of such a context by suggesting that two personalities interacting with each other generate conjunctive and disjunctive forces that lead to integration or disintegration of the interpersonal situation. This view has continued to evolve and we now refer to this context as an "interpersonal field" (Wiggins & Trobst, 1999). Within the interpersonal field, a variety of transactional influences and reciprocal interpersonal patterns have been posited to influence the interactants as they resolve, negotiate, or disintegrate the interpersonal situation.[3] Interpersonal behaviors tend to pull, elicit, evoke, or invite restricted classes of responses from the other, and this is a continual, dynamic transactional process. Thus, interpersonal theory uniquely emphasizes field–regulatory processes in addition to self-regulatory and affect-regulatory processes (Mitchell, 1988; Pincus, 2005a).

Sullivan further developed the field concept in the "theorem of reciprocal emotions," which stated that

> . . . integration in an interpersonal situation is a process in which (1) complementary needs are resolved (or aggravated); (2) reciprocal patterns of activity are developed (or disintegrated); and (3) foresight of satisfaction (or rebuff) of similar needs is facilitated. (Sullivan, 1953b, p. 129)

---

[3]It is useful to remember that an interpersonal situation, and thus the field concept, apply equally well to proximal interactions and mental representations of self and other.

Kiesler (1983) pointed out that although this theorem was a powerful interpersonal assertion, it lacked specificity, and "the surviving general notion of complementarity was that actions of human participants are redundantly interrelated (i.e., have patterned regularity) in some manner over the sequence of transactions" (p. 198).

Leary's (1957) "principle of reciprocal interpersonal relations" provided a more systematic declaration of the patterned regularity of interpersonal behavior, stating,

> . . . interpersonal reflexes tend (with a probability greater than chance) to initiate or invite reciprocal interpersonal responses from the "other" person in the interaction that lead to a repetition of the original reflex. (p. 123)

Learning in interpersonal situations takes place, in part, because social interaction is reinforcing (Leary, 1957). Carson (1991) referred to this as an interbehavioral contingency process where, "there is a tendency for a given individual's interpersonal behavior to be constrained or controlled in more or less predictable ways by the behavior received from an interaction partner" (p. 191).

## Reciprocal Interpersonal Patterns

The interpersonal circumplex provides conceptual anchors and a lexicon to systematically describe the patterned regularity of reciprocal interpersonal processes in relation to individuals' expressions of agentic and communal tendencies. The most basic of these processes is referred to as interpersonal complementarity (Carson, 1969; Kiesler, 1983). Interpersonal complementarity occurs when there is a match between the field-regulatory goals of each person. That is, reciprocal patterns of activity evolve where the agentic and communal needs of both persons are met in the interpersonal situation, leading to stability and likely recurrence of the pattern. Carson (1969) first proposed that complementarity could be defined via the interpersonal circumplex. He proposed that complementarity was based on the social exchange of status (agency) and love (communion) as reflected in reciprocity for the vertical dimension (i.e., dominance pulls for submission; submission pulls for dominance) and correspondence for the horizontal dimension (friendliness pulls for friendliness; hostility pulls for hostility). Kiesler (1983) extended this by adapting complementarity to the geometry of the circumplex model. Given the continuous nature of the circular model's descriptions of behavior (i.e., all interpersonal behaviors are blends of dominance and nurturance), the principles of reciprocity and correspondence could be employed to specify complementary points along the entire perimeter of the circumplex. Thus, beyond the cardinal points, hostile dominance pulls for hostile submission, friendly dominance pulls for friendly submission, etc., which can be further described by the lower-level traits in these segments of the model. Kiesler also proposed that complementarity involves behavioral intensity. Reciprocity on dominance, correspondence on nurturance, and equivalent intensity thus define complementary behaviors.

Although early investigations of interpersonal complementarity generated equivocal results (Orford, 1986), empirical studies employing recent methodological developments, such as bootstrapping techniques, the randomization test of hypothesized order relations, and structural equation modeling consistently find support for its probabilistic predictions (e.g., Gurtman, 2001; Markey et al., 2003; Sadler & Woody, 2003; Tracey, 1994, 2004; Tracey, Ryan, & Jaschik-Herman, 2001; Woody & Sadler, 2005).

The two other broad classes of reciprocal interpersonal patterns anchored by the interpersonal circumplex are referred to as *acomplementary* and *anticomplementary* patterns (Kiesler, 1983, 1996). When reciprocal interpersonal patterns meet one of the two rules of complementarity, this is referred to as an acomplementary pattern. In such a case, interactants may exhibit correspondence with regard to nurturance or reciprocity with regard to dominance, but not both. When interactants exhibit neither reciprocity on dominance nor correspondence on nurturance, this is referred to as an anticomplementary pattern. The patterned regularity in human transaction directly affects the outcomes of interpersonal situations. Complementary reciprocal patterns are considered to promote relational stability; that is, such interpersonal situations are resolved, mutually reinforcing, and recurring. Acomplementary patterns are less stable and instigate negotiation toward or away from greater complementarity. Finally, anticomplementary patterns are the most unstable and lead to avoidance, escape, and disintegration of the interpersonal situation (i.e., disrupted interpersonal relations).

## Adaptive and Maladaptive Transaction Cycles

Complementarity is the reciprocal interpersonal pattern that anchors most theoretical discussions of interpersonal interaction. If we are to regard interpersonal behavior as influential or "field regulatory," there must be some basic goals toward which our behaviors are directed. Sullivan (1953b) viewed the personification of the self to be a dynamism that is built up from the positive reflected appraisals of significant others allowing for relatively anxiety-free functioning and high levels of felt security and self-esteem. The self-dynamism becomes relatively stable over time due to the self-perpetuating influence it has on awareness and organization of interpersonal experience (input), and the field-regulatory influences of interpersonal behavior (output). Sullivan proposed that both our perceptions of others' behaviors toward us and our enacted behaviors are strongly affected by our self-concept. When we interact with others, a proximal interpersonal field is created where behavior serves to present and define our self-concept and negotiate the kinds of interactions and relationships we seek from others. Sullivan's (1953b) theorem of reciprocal emotion and Leary's (1957) principle of reciprocal interpersonal relations have led to the formal view that what we attempt to regulate in the interpersonal field are the responses of the other.

> Interpersonal behaviors, in a relatively unaware, automatic, and unintended fashion, tend to invite, elicit, pull, draw, or entice from interactants restricted classes of reactions that are reinforcing of, and consistent with, a person's proffered self-definition. (Kiesler, 1983, p. 201; see also Kiesler, 1996)

To the extent that individuals can mutually satisfy their agentic and communal needs via interaction that is congruent with their self-definitions (i.e., complementarity), the interpersonal situation remains integrated. To the extent this fails, negotiation or disintegration of the interpersonal situation is more probable. Complementarity is most helpful if considered a common baseline for the field-regulatory pulls and invitations of interpersonal behavior rather than a universal law. Used this way, chronic deviations from complementary reciprocal patterns may be indicative of abnormal functioning.

Interpersonal complementarity (or any other reciprocal pattern) should not be conceived of as some sort of stimulus-response process based solely on overt behavioral actions and reactions (Pincus, 1994). Interpersonal theorists have proposed a variety of intrapsychic processes that mediate individuals' perceptions of the interpersonal situation (input) and their overt reactions to others (output). A comprehensive account of the contemporaneous interpersonal situation must somehow bridge the gap between the proximal interpersonal situation and the internal interpersonal situation of mental representation (e.g., Pincus, 2005a, b; Pincus & Ansell, 2003; Safran, 1992). Kiesler's (1986, 1988, 1991, 1996) "Interpersonal Transaction Cycle" is the most widely applied framework to describe the relations among proximal and internal interpersonal situations within the interpersonal tradition. He proposed that the basic components of an interpersonal transaction are (a) person A's covert experience of person B, (b) person A's overt behavior toward person B, (c) person B's covert experience in response to person A's action, and (d) person B's overt behavioral response to person A. These four components are part of an ongoing transactional chain of events cycling toward resolution, further negotiation, or disintegration. Within this process, overt behavioral output serves the purpose of regulating the proximal interpersonal field via elicitation of complementarity overt responses in the other. An interpersonal transaction is adaptive when the interbehavioral contingencies mutually satisfy the agentic and communal needs of both interactants. That is, interpersonal input and output are relatively contingent upon each other.

An interpersonal transaction becomes maladaptive when one interactant (person A) relies on a limited class of interpersonal behaviors, reducing the potential for mutual complementary interbehavioral contingency and thus limiting the other interactant (person B) to a restricted class of responses complementary to person A's narrow repertoire. The impact of person B's complementary responses is to confirm or validate person A's covert experiences of self, other, and relationship, and thus escalate A's repetition of the rigid, and often extreme interpersonal behaviors that began the cycle. Kiesler points out that the initial complementary responses feel mutually satisfying and the interpersonal situation remains integrated. However, as the transaction recycles, the rigidity and extreme behaviors of person A will have an aversive impact on person B. If interaction cannot satisfy the agentic and communal needs of both people, either disintegration or negative affect or both are likely (Kiesler et al., 1997). If person B cannot disintegrate the situation, the transaction cycles to "impasse—locked into a recurrent enactment of the cycle of maladaptive self-fulfilling prophecy and behavior" (Kiesler, 1986, p. 59).

Psychotherapy with personality-disordered patients provides a clear example (Pincus, 2005a). Therapists generally attempt to work in the patient's best interest and promote a positive therapeutic alliance. Patients who are generally free of personality pathology typically enter therapy hoping for relief of their symptoms and are capable of experiencing the therapist as a potentially helpful and benign expert. Thus, the overt (proximal) and covert (internal) interpersonal situations are consistent with each other and the behavior of therapist and patient is likely to develop into a complementary reciprocal pattern (i.e., a therapeutic alliance in which the therapist exhibits helpful friendly dominance and the patient exhibits receptive friendly submissiveness). Despite psychotherapists taking a similar stance with PD patients, the beginning of therapy is often quite rocky as the patients tend to view the therapists with suspicion, fear, contempt, etc. The covert (internal) interpersonal situation is not consistent with the overt (proximal) interpersonal situation and the patient and therapist likely begin treatment by experiencing noncomplementary reciprocal patterns requiring further negotiation of the therapeutic relationship.

To understand abnormal personality, we must combine concepts anchored to the interpersonal circumplex with a theory of interpersonal functioning. Kiesler (1991) described the nature of this interface. The circumplex specifies the range of individual differences in normal and abnormal interpersonal personality traits and behaviors, and the model can be used to assess and describe the specific nature of an individual's agentic and communal tendencies. The transaction cycle provides a framework to capture the full range of overt and covert human experience of interpersonal situations.

# Differentiating Normal and Abnormal Personality: Covert Internal Processes

In addition to new individual difference constructs (e.g., flux, pulse, spin, interpersonal problems, UA, and UC), the most important theoretical developments for differentiating normal and abnormal personality from the interpersonal tradition focus on the internal processes which mediate overt behaviors in human transaction (i.e., the covert components of the interpersonal transaction cycle). We complete this review by highlighting relevant concepts and several recent advances.

## Parataxic Distortions, Interbehavioral Contingency, and Disturbed Interpersonal Relations

It is perhaps no surprise that we again find Sullivan's work prescient with regard to the evolving perspectives on covert internal processes within the interpersonal tradition. Specifically, Sullivan's (1953a) concept of "parataxic distortion" describes the mediation of proximal relational behavior by internal interpersonal situations, and he suggested that this occurs

> . . . when, beside the interpersonal situation as defined within the awareness of the speaker, there is a concomitant interpersonal situation quite different as to its principal integrating tendencies, of which the speaker is more or less completely unaware. (p. 92).

The effects of parataxic distortions on interpersonal relations are chronic distortions of new interpersonal experiences in the covert phase of an ongoing transaction cycle (input) and the consequent generation of rigid, extreme, and/or chronically non-normative interpersonal behavior in the overt phase of an ongoing transaction cycle (output).

Normal and abnormal personalities may be differentiated by their enduring tendencies to organize interpersonal experience in particular ways, leading to integrated or disturbed interpersonal relations. Pincus (2005a, b) proposed that healthy interpersonal relations are promoted by the capacity to organize and elaborate incoming interpersonal input in generally undistorted ways, allowing for the mutual agentic and communal needs of self and other to be met. That is, the proximal interpersonal field and the internal interpersonal field are relatively consistent (i.e., free of parataxic distortion). Abnormal interpersonal functioning is promoted when the proximal interpersonal field is chronically encoded in distorted or biased ways, leading to behavior that disrupts interpersonal relations due to conflicting or disconnected field-regulatory influences.

We propose that the key aptitude distinguishing normal and abnormal personality is the capacity to enter into new proximal interpersonal situations without parataxic distortion. In other words, normal personalities can flexibly enter a broad range of proximal interpersonal situations in which they exhibit anxiety-free functioning (security) and maintain self-esteem. When this is the case, mediating internal interpersonal situations are not activated and the person can focus on the proximal situation, encode incoming interpersonal input without distortion, respond in adaptive ways that integrate interpersonal relations (i.e., meet the agentic and communal needs of self and other), and establish complementary patterns of reciprocal behavior by fully participating in the proximal interpersonal field. The individual's current behavior will exhibit relatively strong contingency with the proximal behavior of the other and the normative contextual press of the situation. Normal interpersonal functioning is promoted by relatively trauma-free development in a culturally normative facilitating environment that has allowed the person to achieve most developmental milestones in normative ways, leading to full capacity to encode and elaborate incoming interpersonal input without bias from competing psychological needs (Benjamin, 2003; Pincus, 2005a).

In contrast, when the individual develops in a non–normative or traumatic environment, significant non-normative interpersonal learning around basic agentic and communal motives (Benjamin, 2003; Horowitz, 2004), as well as a variety of developmental milestones (Pincus & Ansell, 2003), may lead to difficulties maintaining integrated interpersonal relations. In contrast to the normal personality, personality abnormality is reflected in a broad range of proximal interpersonal situations that elicit anxiety, threaten self-esteem, and disrupt interpersonal relations. When this is the case, internal interpersonal situations are activated and the individual is prone to exhibit various forms of parataxic distortion as his or her interpersonal learning history dictates. Thus, the perception of the proximal interpersonal situation is mediated by internal experience, incoming interpersonal input is distorted, behavioral responses (output) disrupt interpersonal relations (i.e., fail to meet the agentic and communal needs of self and other), and relationships tend toward noncomplementary patterns of reciprocal behavior. The individual's current behavior will exhibit relatively weak contingency with the proximal behavior of the other.

## Impact Messages

In our opinion, conceptions of the covert processes mediating overt relational behavior have mainly been theoretical propositions, reflecting much less consensus among interpersonal theorists than the fundamental organizing metaconcepts of agency and communion, and the circular nature of structural models. The processes proposed have not been comprehensively subjected to empirical evaluation, nor have their influences on the proximal interpersonal field been fully developed. In a significant step forward, Kiesler (1996) has synthesized many concepts (i.e., emotion, behavior, cognition, and fantasy) in his evolving perspective on the construct referred to as the "impact message" (see also Kiesler, 1979; Kiesler et al., 1997). Impact messages are fundamental covert aspects of the interpersonal situation, encompassing feelings (e.g., elicited emotions), action tendencies (pulls to do something, i.e., "I should calm him down" or "I should get away"), perceived evoking messages (i.e., subjective interpretations of the other's intentions, desires, affect states, or perceptions of interpersonal situation), and fantasies (i.e., elaborations of the interaction beyond the current situation). Kiesler and his colleagues view the link between the covert and overt aspects of the interpersonal situation to be emotional experience. Impact messages are part of a "transactional emotion process that is peculiarly essential to interpersonal behavior itself" (Kiesler, 1996, p. 71). Impact messages are registered covertly by person A in response to person B's interpersonal behavior, imposing complementary demands on the behavior of person A through elicited cognition, emotion, and fantasy. Notably, the underlying structure of impact messages parallels that of the interpersonal circumplex (Kiesler et al., 1997; Wagner, Kiesler, & Schmidt, 1995), allowing for description of covert processes that are on a common metric with the description of overt interpersonal behavior.

The covert impact messages evoked within a contemporaneous interpersonal transaction cycle are primarily associated with the encoding of overt behaviors of the other. It is assumed that interactants are generally aware of such covert experience, as the development of the self-report Impact Message Inventory (IMI; Kiesler & Schmidt, 1993) suggests. However, Sullivan's concept of parataxic distortion suggested that individuals may be more or less aware of the mediating influence of internal interpersonal situations. It is clear that the nature of such covert responses, i.e., feelings, action tendencies, interpretations, and fantasies, are not evoked completely in the moment due solely to the interpersonal behavior of the other, but arise in part from enduring organizational tendencies of the individual (Benjamin, 1993; 1995; Pincus & Ansell, 2003). In our view the IMI and the impact message construct may be just as useful to empirically assess person A's enduring ways of organizing new interpersonal experience (input) as it is to assess complementary demands communicated by person B's behavior (see e.g., Mallinckrodt & Chen, 2004). Issues from the person perception literature, partitioning perceiver and target sources of variance may also be of relevance (e.g., Kenny, Mohr, & Levesque, 2001).

## Concluding Remarks

In our view, the evolving perspectives on normal and abnormal personality have clearly matured over the 50-year history of the interpersonal tradition, due in large part to the remarkable catalysis between interpersonal theory and the interpersonal circumplex. There is now a clearly articulated nomological net integrating (a) the interpersonal situation, (b) the interpersonal circumplex structure, (c) explicatory systems based on the metaconcepts of agency and communion, (d) individual differences in traits, (e) reciprocal interpersonal patterns, and (f) covert internal processes. These diverse elements provide a theoretically cohesive approach to differentiating normal and abnormal personality, extend the insights of Sullivan and Leary, and continue to widely inform psychology and psychiatry (Wiggins, 2003).

In many ways, behavioral intensity, behavioral rigidity, flux, pulse, spin, interpersonal problems, unmitigated agency, and unmitigated communion are all possible indicators, or perhaps consequences, of abnormal personality. All of these constructs have been related to various forms of maladjustment, including psychiatric symptomology and diagnoses, psychotherapeutic alliance and outcome, marital and social functioning, and physical health status. They are solid anchors for the continuing evolution of the interpersonal tradition. Future directions for the field include further interconnection between the structural elements of interpersonal functioning (traits) and the dynamic aspects of interpersonal functioning (overt and covert processes) (e.g., Gurtman, 1996, 2001; Moskowitz & Zuroff, 2004), as well as increased articulation and incorporation of uniquely interpersonal perspectives on personality development (e.g., Benjamin, 2003; Pincus, 2005a; Pincus & Ansell, 2003). We have no doubt that such efforts will be facilitated by the continuing reciprocity between interpersonal theory and the interpersonal circumplex.

## REFERENCES

Adams, R. S., & Tracey, T. J. G. (2004). Three versions of the Interpersonal Adjective Scales and their fit to the circumplex model. *Assessment, 11*, 263–270.

Alden, L. E., Wiggins, J. S., & Pincus, A. L. (1990). Construction of circumplex scales for the Inventory of Interpersonal Problems. *Journal of Personality Assessment, 55*, 521–536.

Anchin, J. C., & Kiesler, D. J. (1982). *Handbook of interpersonal psychotherapy*. New York: Pergamon.

Ansell, E. B., & Pincus, A. L. (2004). Interpersonal perceptions of the five-factor model of personality: An examination using the structural summary method for circumplex data. *Multivariate Behavioral Research, 39*, 167–201.

Bakan, D. (1966). *The duality of human existence: An essay on psychology and religion*. Chicago: Rand McNally.

Benjamin, L. S. (1974). Structural analysis of social behavior. *Psychological Review, 81*, 392–425.

Benjamin, L. S. (1993). Every psychopathology is a gift of love. *Psychotherapy Research, 3*, 1–24.

Benjamin, L. S. (1995). Good defenses make good neighbors. In H. Conte & R. Plutchik (Eds.), *Ego defenses: Theory and measurement* (pp. 38–78). New York: Wiley.

Benjamin, L. S. (1996). *Interpersonal diagnosis and treatment of personality disorders* (2nd ed.). New York: Guilford Press.

Benjamin, L. S. (2003). *Interpersonal reconstructive therapy*. New York: Guilford Press.

Blatt, S. J., Auerbach, J. S., & Levy, K. N. (1997). Mental representations in personality development, psychopathology, and the therapeutic process. *Review of General Psychology, 1*, 351–374.

Brokaw, D. W., & McLemore, C. W. (1991). Interpersonal models of personality and psychopathology. In D. G. Gilbert, & J. J. Connolly (Eds.), *Personality, social skills, and psychopathology: An individual differences approach.* (pp. 49–83). New York: Plenum Press.

Carson, R. C. (1969). *Interaction concepts of personality*. Chicago: Aldine.

Carson, R. C. (1991). The social–interactional viewpoint. In M. Hersen, A. Kazdin, & A. Bellack (Eds.), *The clinical psychology handbook* (pp. 185–199). New York: Pergamon.

Carson, R. C. (1996). Seamlessness in personality and its derangements. *Journal of Personality Assessment, 66*, 240–247.

Coffey, H. S., Freedman, M. B., Leary, T. F., & Ossorio, A. G. (1950). Community service and social research—group psychotherapy in a church setting. *Journal of Social Issues, 6*, 1–65.

Costa, P. T., & Widiger, T. A. (1994). *Personality disorders and the five-factor model of personality*. Washington, DC: American Psychological Association.

Fournier, M. A., & Moskowitz, D. S. (2000). The mitigation of interpersonal behavior. *Journal of Personality and Social Psychology, 79*, 827–836.

Fournier, M. A., Moskowitz, D. S., & Zuroff, D. C. (2002). Social rank strategies in hierarchical relationships. *Journal of Personality and Social Psychology, 83*, 425–433.

Freedman, M. B., Leary, T., Ossorio, A. G., & Coffey, H. S. (1951). The interpersonal dimension of personality. *Journal of Personality, 20*, 143–161.

Fritz, H. L., & Helgeson, V. S. (1998). Distinctions of unmitigated communion from communion: Self-neglect and overinvolvement with others. *Journal of Personality and Social Psychology, 75*, 121–140.

Funder, D. C. (1991). Global traits: A neo–Allportian approach to personality. *Psychological Science, 2*, 31–39.

Gurtman, M. B. (1994). The circumplex as a tool for studying normal and abnormal personality: A methodological primer. In S. Strack, & M. Lorr (Eds.), *Differentiating normal and abnormal personality* (pp. 243–263). New York: Springer.

Gurtman, M. B. (1995). Personality structure and interpersonal problems: A theoretically-guided item analysis of the Inventory of Interpersonal Problems. *Assessment, 2*, 343–361.

Gurtman, M. B. (1996). Interpersonal problems and the psychotherapy context: The construct validity of the Inventory of Interpersonal Problems. *Psychological Assessment, 8*, 241–255.

Gurtman, M. B. (2001). Interpersonal complementarity: Integrating interpersonal measurement with interpersonal models. *Journal of Counseling Psychology, 48*, 97–110.

Gurtman, M. B., & Balakrishnan, J. D. (1998). Circular measurement redux: The analysis and interpretation of interpersonal circle profiles. *Clinical Psychology: Science and Practice, 5*, 344–360.

Gurtman, M. B., & Pincus, A. L. (2000). Interpersonal Adjective Scales: Confirmation of circumplex structure from multiple perspectives. *Personality and Social Psychology Bulletin, 26*, 374–384.

Gurtman, M. B., & Pincus, A. L. (2003). The circumplex model: Methods and research applications. In J. A. Schinka, & W. F. Velicer (Eds.), *Handbook of psychology: Research methods in psychology* (Vol. 2, pp. 407–428). New York: Wiley.

Heck, S. A., & Pincus, A. L. (2001). Agency and communion in the structure of parental representations. *Journal of Personality Assessment, 76*, 180–184.

Helgeson, V. S. (1994). Relation of agency and communion to well-being: Evidence and potential explanations. *Psychological Bulletin, 116*, 412–428.

Helgeson, V. S., & Fritz, H. L. (1998). A theory of unmitigated communion. *Personality and Social Psychology Review, 2*, 173–183.

Helgeson, V. S., & Fritz, H. L. (1999). Unmitigated agency and unmitigated communion: Distinctions from agency and communion. *Journal of Research in Personality, 33*, 131–158.

Helgeson, V. S., & Fritz, H. L. (2000). The implications of unmitigated agency and unmitigated communion for domains of problem behavior. *Journal of Personality, 68*, 1031–1057.

Hmel, B. A., & Pincus, A. L. (2002). The meaning of autonomy: On and beyond the interpersonal circumplex. *Journal of Personality, 70*, 277–310.

Horowitz, L. M. (1979). On the cognitive structure of interpersonal problems treated in psychotherapy. *Journal of Consulting and Clinical Psychology, 47*, 5–15.

Horowitz, L. M. (1996). The study of interpersonal problems: A Leary legacy. *Journal of Personality Assessment, 66*, 283–300.

Horowitz, L. M. (2004). *Interpersonal foundations of psychopathology*. Washington, D.C.: American Psychological Association.

Horowitz, L. M., Alden, L. E., Wiggins, J. S., & Pincus, A. L. (2000). *IIP-64/IIP-32 professional manual*. San Antonio, TX: The Psychological Corporation.

Horowitz, L. M., Rosenberg, S. E., Baer, B. A., Ureño, G., & Villaseñor, V. S. (1988). Inventory of Interpersonal Problems: Psychometric properties and clinical applications. *Journal of Consulting and Clinical Psychology, 56*, 885–892.

Horowitz, L. M., Rosenberg, S. E., & Kalehzan, B. M. (1992). The capacity to describe other people clearly: a predictor of interpersonal problems in brief dynamic psychotherapy. *Psychotherapy Research, 2*, 37–51.

Horowitz, L. M., & Vitkus, J. (1986). The interpersonal basis of psychiatric symptoms. *Clinical Psychology Review, 6*, 443–469.

Horowitz, L. M., Weckler, D. A., & Doren, R. (1983). Interpersonal problems and symptoms: A cognitive approach. In P. Kendall (Ed.), *Advances in cognitive-behavioral research and therapy* (pp. 81–125). London: Academic Press.

Kelley, H. H., Holmes, J. G., Kerr, N. L., Reis, H. T., Rusbult, C. E., & Van Lange, P. A. M. (2003). *An atlas of interpersonal situations*. New York: Cambridge University Press.

Kenny, D. A., Mohr, C. D., & Levesque, M. J. (2001). A social relations variance partitioning of dyadic behavior. *Psychological Bulletin, 127*, 128–141.

Kiesler, D. J. (1979). An interpersonal communication analysis of relationship in psychotherapy. *Psychiatry, 42*, 299–311.

Kiesler, D. J. (1983). The 1982 Interpersonal Circle: A taxonomy for complementarity in human transactions. *Psychological Review, 90*, 185–214.

Kiesler, D. J. (1986). Interpersonal methods of diagnosis and treatment. In R. Michels, & J. O. Cavenar (Eds.), *Psychiatry* (pp. 53–75). Philadelphia: Lippincott.

Kiesler, D. J. (1988). *Therapeutic metacommunication: Therapist impact disclosure as feedback in psychotherapy.* Palo Alto, CA: Consulting Psychological Press.

Kiesler, D. J. (1991). Interpersonal methods of assessment and diagnosis. In C. R. Snyder, & D. R. Forsyth (Eds.), *Handbook of social and clinical psychology* (pp. 438–468). New York: Guilford Press.

Kiesler, D. J. (1996). *Contemporary interpersonal theory and research: Personality, psychopathology, and psychotherapy.* New York: Wiley.

Kiesler, D. J., & Schmidt, J. A. (1993). *The Impact Message Inventory: Form IIA octant scale version.* Palo Alto, CA: Mind Garden.

Kiesler, D. J., Schmidt J. A., & Wagner C. C. (1997). A circumplex inventory of impact messages: An operational bridge between emotion and interpersonal behavior. In R. Plutchik & H. Contes (Eds.), *Circumplex models of personality and emotions* (pp. 221–244). Washington, DC: American Psychological Association.

LaForge, R. (2004). The early development of the interpersonal system of personality (ISP). *Multivariate Behavioral Research, 39*, 359–378.

LaForge, R., Freedman, M. B., & Wiggins, J. S. (1985). Interpersonal circumplex models: 1948–1983. *Journal of Personality Assessment, 49*, 613–631.

LaForge, R., Leary, T. F., Naboisek, H., Coffey, H. S., & Freedman, M. B. (1954). The interpersonal dimension of personality: II. An objective study of repression. *Journal of Personality, 23*, 129–153.

LaForge, R., & Suczek, R. F. (1955). The interpersonal dimension of personality: III. An interpersonal check list. *Journal of Personality, 24*, 94–112.

Leary, T. (1957). *Interpersonal diagnosis of personality.* New York: Ronald Press.

Leary, T., & Coffey, H. S. (1955). Interpersonal diagnosis: Some problems of methodology and validation. *Journal of Abnormal and Social Psychology, 50*, 110–124.

Lewin, K. (1931). The conflict between Aristotlian and Galileian modes of thought in contemporary psychology. *Journal of General Psychology, 5*, 141–177.

Locke, K. D. (2000). Circumplex scales of interpersonal values: Reliability, validity, and applicability to interpersonal problems and personality disorders. *Journal of Personality Assessment, 75*, 249–267.

Lorr, M., & McNair, D. M. (1963). An interpersonal behavior circle. *Journal of Abnormal and Social Psychology, 67*, 68–75.

Lorr, M., & McNair, D. M. (1965). Expansion of the interpersonal behavior circle. *Journal of Personality and Social Psychology, 2*, 68–75.

Mallinckrodt, B., & Chen, E. C. (2004). Attachment and interpersonal impact perceptions of group members: A social relations model analysis of transference. *Psychotherapy Research, 14*, 210–230.

Mardia, K. V. (1972). *Statistics of directional data.* New York: Academic Press.

Markey, P. M., Funder, D. C., & Ozer, D. J. (2003). Complementarity of interpersonal behaviors in dyadic interactions. *Personality and Social Psychology Bulletin, 29*, 1082–1090.

McAdams, D. P. (1995). What do we know when we know a person? *Journal of Personality, 63*, 365–396.

McLemore, C. W., & Benjamin, L. S. (1979). Whatever happened to interpersonal diagnosis? *American Psychologist, 34*, 17–34.

Millon, T. (1987). *Manual for the MCMI-II* (2nd ed.). Minneapolis, MN: National Computer Systems.

Mitchell, S. A. (1988). The intrapsychic and the interpersonal: Different theories, different domains, or historical artifacts? *Psychoanalytic Inquiry, 8*, 472–496.

Moskowitz, D. S. (1994). Cross-situational generality and the interpersonal circumplex. *Journal of Personality and Social Psychology, 66*, 921–933.

Moskowitz, D. S. (2005). Unfolding interpersonal behavior. *Journal of Personality, 73*, 1607–1632.

Moskowitz, D. S., Pinard, G., Zuroff, D. C., Annable, L., & Young, S. N. (2001). The effect of trytophan on social interaction in everyday life: A placebo-controlled study. *Neuropsychopharmacology, 25*, 277–289.

Moskowitz, D. S., & Zuroff, D. C. (2004). Flux, pulse, and Spin: Dynamic additions to the personality lexicon. *Journal of Personality and Social Psychology, 86*, 880–893.

O'Connor, B. P., & Dyce, J. A. (1997). Interpersonal rigidity, hostility, and complementarity in musical bands. *Journal of Personality and Social Psychology, 72*, 362–372.

O'Connor, B. P., & Dyce, J. A. (2001). Rigid and extreme: A geometric representation of personality disorders in five-factor model space. *Journal of Personality and Social Psychology, 81,* 1119–1130.

Orford, J. (1986). The rules of interpersonal complementarity: Does hostility beget hostility and dominance, submission? *Psychological Review, 93,* 365–377.

Paulhus, D. L., & Martin, C. L. (1987). The structure of personality capabilities. *Journal of Personality and Social Psychology, 52,* 354–365.

Paulhus, D. L., & Martin, C. L. (1988). Functional flexibility: A new conception of interpersonal flexibility. *Journal of Personality and Social Psychology, 55,* 88–101.

Pincus, A. L. (1994). The interpersonal circumplex and the interpersonal theory: Perspectives on personality and its pathology. In S. Strack & M. Lorr (Eds.), *Differentiating normal and abnormal personality* (pp. 114–136). New York: Springer.

Pincus, A. L. (2005a). A contemporary integrative interpersonal theory of personality disorders. In J. Clarkin & M. Lenzenweger (Eds.), *Major theories of personality disorder* (2nd ed., pp. 282–331). New York: Guilford Press.

Pincus, A. L. (2005b) The interpersonal nexus of personality disorders. In S. Strack (Ed.), *Handbook of personology and psychopathology* (pp. 120–139). New York: Wiley.

Pincus, A. L., & Ansell, E. B. (2003). Interpersonal theory of personality. In T. Millon, & M. Lerner (Eds.), *Handbook of psychology: Personality and social psychology* (Vol. 5, pp. 209–229). New York: Wiley.

Pincus, A. L., & Gurtman, M. B. (2003). Interpersonal assessment. In J. S. Wiggins (Ed.), *Paradigms of personality assessment* (pp. 246–261). New York: Guilford Press.

Pincus, A. L., Gurtman, M. B., & Ruiz, M. A. (1998). Structural analysis of social behavior (SASB): circumplex analyses and structural relations with the interpersonal circle and the Five-Factor Model of personality. *Journal of Personality and Social Psychology, 74,* 1629–1645.

Ruiz, M. A., Pincus, A. L., Borkovec, T. D., Echemendia, R. J., Castonguay, L. G., & Ragusea, S. A. (2004). Validity of the inventory of interpersonal problems (IIP-C) for predicting treatment outcome: An investigation with the Pennsylvania Practice Research Network. *Journal of Personality Assessment, 83,* 213–222.

Rusbult, C. E., & Van Lange, P. A. M. (2003). Interdependence, interaction, and relationships. *Annual Review of Psychology, 54,* 351–375.

Russell, J. A. (1980). A circumplex model of affect. *Journal of Personality and Social Psychology, 39,* 1161–1178.

Sadler, P., & Woody, E. (2003). Is who you are who you're talking to? Interpersonal style and complementarity in mixed-sex interactions. *Journal of Personality and Social Psychology, 84,* 80–96.

Safran, J. D. (1992). Extending the pantheoretical applications of interpersonal inventories. *Journal of Psychotherapy Integration, 2,* 101–105.

Saragovi, C., Koestner, R., Di Dio, L., & Aubé, J. (1997). Agency, communion, and well-being: Extending Helgeson's (1994) model. *Journal of Personality and Social Psychology, 73,* 593–609.

Schaefer, E. S. (1959). A circumplex model for maternal behaviors. *Journal of Abnormal and Social Psychology, 59,* 226–235.

Schaefer, E. S. (1961). Converging conceptual models for maternal behavior and child behavior. In J. C. Glidwell (Ed.), *Parental attitudes and child behavior* (pp. 124–146). Springfield, IL: Charles C Thomas.

Spence, J. T. (1984). Masculinity, femininity, and gender-related traits: A conceptual analysis and critique of current research. In B. A. Maher, & W. Maher (Eds.), *Progress in experimental research* (Vol. 13, pp. 2–97). San Diego, CA: Academic Press.

Spence, J. T., Helmreich, R. L., & Holahan, C. K. (1979). Negative and positive components of psychological masculinity and femininity and their relationships to self-reports of neurotic and acting out behaviors. *Journal of Personality and Social Psychology, 37,* 1673–1682.

Stern, D. N. (1985). *The interpersonal world of the infant.* New York: Basic Books.

Stern, D. N. (1988). The dialectic between the "interpersonal" and the "intrapsychic": With particular emphasis on the role of memory and representation. *Psychoanalytic Inquiry, 8,* 505–512.

Sullivan, H. S. (1948). The meaning of anxiety in psychiatry and life. *Psychiatry, 11,* 1–13.

Sullivan, H. S. (1953a). *Conceptions of modern psychiatry.* New York: Norton.

Sullivan, H. S. (1953b). *The interpersonal theory of psychiatry.* New York: Norton.

Sullivan, H. S. (1954). *The psychiatric interview.* New York: Norton.

Sullivan, H. S. (1956). *Clinical studies in psychiatry.* New York: Norton.

Sullivan, H. S. (1962). *Schizophrenia as a human process.* New York: Norton.

Sullivan, H. S. (1964). *The fusion of psychiatry and social science.* New York: Norton.

Tellegen, A. (1991). Personality traits: Issues of definition, evidence, and assessment. In W. M. Grove & D. Cicchetti (Eds.), *Thinking clearly about psychology: Personality and psychopathology* (Vol. 2, pp. 10–35). Minneapolis: University of Minnesota Press.

Tracey, T. J. G. (1994). An examination of complementarity of interpersonal behavior. *Journal of Personality and Social Psychology, 67,* 864–878.

Tracey, T. J. G. (2000). Analysis of circumplex models. In H. E. A. Tinsley & S. Brown (Eds.), *Handbook of applied multivariate statistics and mathematical modeling* (pp. 641–664). San Diego: Academic Press.

Tracey, T. J. G. (2004). Levels of interpersonal complementarity: A simplex representation. *Personality and Social Psychology Bulletin, 30,* 1211–1225.

Tracey, T. J. G., & Rounds, J. (1995). The arbitrary nature of Holland's RIASEC types: Concentric circles as a structure. *Journal of Counseling Psychology, 42,* 431–439.

Tracey, T. J. G., Rounds, J., & Gurtman, M. (1996). Examination of the general factor with the interpersonal circumplex structure: Application to the inventory of interpersonal problems. *Multivariate Behavioral Research, 31,* 441–466.

Tracey, T. J. G., Ryan, J. M., & Jaschik-Herman, B. (2001). Complementarity of interpersonal circumplex traits. *Personality and Social Psychology Bulletin, 27,* 786–797.

Tracey, T. J. G., & Schneider, P. L. (1995). An evaluation of the circular structure of the checklist of interpersonal transactions and the checklist of psychotherapy transactions. *Journal of Counseling Psychology, 42,* 496–507.

Trobst, K. K. (2000). An interpersonal conceptualization and quantification of social support transactions. *Personality and Social Psychology Bulletin, 26,* 971–986.

Vittengl, J. R., Clark, L. A., & Jarrett, R. B. (2003). Interpersonal problems, personality pathology, and social adjustment after cognitive therapy for depression. *Psychological Assessment, 15,* 29–40.

Wagner, C. C., Kiesler, D. J., & Schmidt, J. A. (1995). Assessing the interpersonal transaction cycle: Convergence of action and reaction interpersonal circumplex measures. *Journal of Personality and Social Psychology, 69,* 938–949.

Wicklund, R. A., & Gollwitzer, P. M. (1987). The fallacy of the private—public self-focus distinction. *Journal of Personality, 55,* 491–523.

Widiger, T. A., & Costa, P. T. (1994). Personality and personality disorders. *Journal of Abnormal Psychology, 103,* 78–91.

Wiggins, J. S. (1979). A psychological taxonomy of trait descriptive terms: he interpersonal domain. *Journal of Personality and Social Psychology, 37,* 395–412.

Wiggins, J. S. (1980). Circumplex models of interpersonal behavior. In L. Wheeler (Ed.), *Review of personality and social psychology* (Vol. 1, pp. 265–293). Beverly Hills, CA: Sage.

Wiggins, J. S. (1982). Circumplex models of interpersonal behavior in clinical psychology. In P. C. Kendall, & J. N. Butcher (Eds.), *Handbook of research methods in clinical psychology* (pp. 183–221). New York: Wiley.

Wiggins, J. S. (1991). Agency and communion as conceptual coordinates for the understanding and measurement of interpersonal behavior. In W. M. Grove, & D. Cicchetti (Eds.), *Thinking clearly about psychology: Personality and psychopathology* (Vol. 2, pp. 89–113). Minneapolis: University of Minnesota Press.

Wiggins, J. S. (1995). *Interpersonal Adjective Scales: Professional manual.* Odessa, FL: Psychological Assessment Resources, Inc.

Wiggins, J. S. (1996). An informal history of the interpersonal circumplex tradition. *Journal of Personality Assessment, 66,* 217–233.

Wiggins, J. S. (1997). Circumnavigating Dodge Morgan's interpersonal style. *Journal of Personality, 65,* 1069–1086.

Wiggins, J. S. (2003). *Paradigms of personality assessment.* New York: Guilford.

Wiggins, J. S., Phillips, N., & Trapnell, P. (1989). Circular reasoning about interpersonal behavior: Evidence concerning some untested assumptions underlying diagnostic classifications. *Journal of Personality and Social Psychology, 56,* 296–305.

Wiggins, J. S., & Trapnell, P. D. (1996). A dyadic interactional perspective on the five-factor model. In J. S. Wiggins (Ed.), *The five-factor model of personality: Theoretical perspectives* (pp. 88–162). New York: Guilford Press.

Wiggins, J. S. & Trobst, K. K. (1999). The fields of interpersonal behavior. In L. Pervin and O.P. John (eds.). *Handbook of Personality: Theroy and Research* (2nd ed.) pp. 653–670. New York: Guilford Press.

Woody, E., & Sadler, P. (2005). Structural equation models for interchangeable dyads: Being the same makes a difference. *Psychological Methods, 10,* 139–158.

# Cognitive Theory of Personality and Personality Disorders

## Marjorie E. Weishaar
## Aaron T. Beck

Cognitive therapy is based on a theory of personality that emphasizes the role of information processing in activating a person's cognitive, affective, motivational, and behavioral responses to the physical and social environments. These responses are based in genetic evolution and shaped by one's biological temperament, developmental experiences, and learning history.

These cognitive, affective, motivational, and physiological/behavioral components are conceptualized as response systems, each comprising parts and roles, that act adaptively and in synchrony to meet environmental demands. The cognitive system involves perception, appraisal, abstraction, recall, memory, self-evaluation, prediction, expectancies, interpretation, and attribution of events. It interacts with the other systems to process information from the environment and mobilize a response. Responses may be maladaptive when misconceptions, misinterpretations, faulty appraisals, or dysfunctional and highly idiosyncratic interpretations occur on a consistent basis.

This chapter presents the cognitive theory of personality and personality disorders; assessment tools for measuring personality constructs such as sociotropy, autonomy, and schemas; clinical research findings in cognitive therapy for personality disorders; and an integrative treatment approach to treating personality disorders.

## Theory of Personality

The cognitive theory of personality is anchored in human evolution and emphasizes the adaptive function of genetically determined "strategies" that facilitate survival and reproduction. Generally speaking, humans take in information from the environment, synthesize it, and develop a plan of action in order to survive in the physical and social environments. Escape, self-defense, conservation of resources, display behavior, attraction, and bonding are all genetically predetermined strategies necessary for survival and finding a mate. These strategies, however primitive, require the integrated contributions of the cognitive, behavioral, affective, and motivational systems. Each system is composed of relatively stable structures called *schemas*. Cognitive schemas (Beck, 1967) select and synthesize incoming data and hold core beliefs derived from past experience. They contain people's perceptions of themselves and others, goals and expectations, memories, and previous learning (Beck, 1967; Beck, Freeman, & Associates, 1990; Beck, Freeman, Davis, & Associates, 2004). Schemas are not conscious, but their content and products can be identified with introspection.

As the *cognitive system* assigns meaning and causal attribution to events, the motivational and behavioral systems mobilize or inhibit action. In cognitive therapy, "motivation" refers to automatic impulses and inhibitions that are tied to primal strategies (Beck, 1996). These include appetite, sexuality, and urges to flee, attack, avoid, or inhibit risk taking.

The *affective system* is the source of emotions, and shapes behavior by reinforcing adaptive behavior. Positive emotions or pleasure reward goal attainment, and negative emotions cause people to pay attention to the circumstances that are diminishing or threatening to their well-being.

The *physiological system* refers to the autonomic nervous system, the motor system, and the sensory system. Physiological symptoms prepare for action and provide feedback on one's internal state. In all these systems, schemas are triggered automatically.

Beck identifies two additional "control" systems: the conscious control system (Beck, 1996) and the internal control system (Beck et al., 1990, 2004). The conscious control system, unlike those mentioned above, is not automatic or out of awareness. It applies logic to problems, and is reflective, deliberate, and capable of making plans. It can gain perspective over automatic cognitive reactions and, thus, is the primary system engaged in cognitive therapy.

The internal control system modifies and inhibits impulsive reactions through the implementation of rules that guide behavior. Such rules might include prohibitions like, "Do not trust strangers" or "Do not take risks." Many of these beliefs are adaptive, but some are dysfunctional, especially when applied in a rigid or generalized manner. The internal control system is important in personality and personality disorders, for it contains cognitive schemas relating to both self-concept and interpersonal relatedness.

Cognitive therapy once posited a linear relationship between the activation of cognitive schemas and changes in the other systems. In other words, cognitive schemas were conceptualized as triggering affect, motivation, and behavior (Beck et al., 1990). A more recent formulation, however, (Beck, 1996), drawing from advancements in evolutionary and cognitive psychology, views all systems acting simultaneously in a *mode*. Modes are networks of cognitive, affective, motivational, and behavioral schemas that compose personality and interpret ongoing situations (Beck, 1996). In the anxiety mode, for example, *orienting schema* acts as a signal that identifies a situation as dangerous. It activates all the systems in the mode to form an integrated response to the demands of the situation. The affective response of fear works in conjunction with the motivation to flee, fight or freeze, and the behavioral/physiological system prepares the body to act through activation of the nervous and the motor systems. The cognitive system assesses the risks involved and the resources available to cope (Beck, Emery, & Greenberg, 1985).

The anxiety mode is considered primal because it is tied to survival. Other modes, like working, studying, or conversing, are minor modes and more amenable to conscious control. The anxiety mode provides a good example of how a primal mode is no longer as adaptive in modern situations as it was in the past. The flight–fight–freeze response was more efficient when environmental threats were largely physical in nature and required a physical response. In the current environment, most threats are psychosocial, so physiological mobilization is an unnecessary, exaggerated response (Beck et al., 1985). Personality disorders also may be viewed as stereotyped responses or exaggerated versions of formerly adaptive strategies in which primal modes are operating almost continuously (Beck, 1996). For example, a dependent personality is constantly seeking help; a histrionic personality goes to extremes for attention and attraction.

Thus, personality is viewed as an organization of integrated systems–cognitive, affective, motivational, and behavioral–each comprising stable structures called schemas and programs called modes, which work together to maintain homeostasis and promote adaptation to the environment. Personality traits, like autonomy or dependency, are the overt expression of schemas. The stability of schemas in a person is reflected in the consistency of systemic responses across a range of situations. In personality disorders, the schemas, and thus the responses, are dysfunctional and operate almost continuously, yielding chronic, self-defeating patterns (Beck et al., 1990, 2004).

## Schemas

The schema concept has been used by previous theorists, such as Bartlett (1932, 1958) and Piaget (1926, 1936/1952), to describe cognitive structures that integrate and assign meanings to events. In cognitive therapy, the concept of schemas is most similar to Kelly's (1955) notion of "personal constructs." Schemas may be adaptive or dysfunctional. They are generally latent, but become active when stimulated by specific, relevant circumstances or stressors.

Cognitive therapy, in theory and in clinical practice, focuses on the role of cognitive schemas in normal and abnormal functioning. Particular attention is paid to the content of schemas and the bias in information processing that occurs in psychological disorders.

Core beliefs about the self, other people, and one's personal world are held in cognitive schemas. In this chapter, "core beliefs" and "schemas" will be used interchangeably. These beliefs sensitize a person to particular stimuli and direct their responses. Our ability to self-correct perceptions and adjust our responses requires cognitive flexibility. During psychological distress, however, cognitive flexibility is lost and judgments become more absolute and rigid. Errors in cognitive processing, termed *cognitive distortions*, proliferate. This is especially the case in situations that are personally meaningful, yet ambiguous. For example, in depression, a negative bias in thinking is most likely to occur when data are not immediately present, are not concrete, are ambiguous, and are relevant to self-evaluation (Riskind, 1983). In paranoid personality, for example, mistrust is easily triggered in vague or ambiguous situations that seem threatening. Cognitive distortions include dichotomous thinking, overgeneralization, minimization and maximization, personalization, selective abstraction, and arbitrary inference (Beck, 1967).

Dysfunctional core beliefs are seen as cognitive vulnerabilities to psychopathology. Beliefs such as, "I am unlovable" or "I am helpless" contribute to the stereotyped responses evident in the syndrome disorders (e.g., the social withdrawal in depression) and in the interpersonal strategies seen in personality disorders (e.g., clinging in dependent personality disorder). While the contents of schemas are typically out of a person's awareness, cognitions such as attitudes, values, and conditional beliefs derived from schemas are more easily identified and changed. Conditional beliefs can be positive or negative (Beck, 1995). They are "if-then" statements that help a person cope with a core belief. If a woman has a schema, "I am unlovable", for example, a positive conditional belief or assumption that would help her cope with that negative core belief might be, "If I do all that my partner wishes, I will be lovable." A corresponding negative conditional belief might be, "If my partner rejects me, then I am unlovable." Negative conditional beliefs may be viewed as ancillary to core beliefs; they are the manifestation of the core belief, the test that proves the rule. Schemas are more rigid, less accessible, and more tied to affect than are conditional beliefs.

Each person has a unique personality profile based on one's innate disposition or temperament and environmental influences. One's temperament, types of which are relatively stable at birth, such as shyness (Kagan, 1989), is accentuated or diminished by experiences with others. Widiger (2003) defines temperament as a person's characteristic manner of affective regulation. One can imagine how negative interactions with caregivers and other negative life experiences might be mediated differently by a highly reactive person and by a placid person. Cognitive theory holds that both identification with significant others and repeated negative life experiences interacting temperament can yield dysfunctional beliefs (Beck et al., 1990, 2004). Repeated exposures to negative experiences (both impersonal and interpersonal) solidify these dysfunctional beliefs in schemas. Maladaptive behavior driven by these schemas leads to mutually reinforcing patterns between the person and others. Over time, the behaviors become compulsive yet self-defeating, dysfunctional yet imperative, overgeneralized, and resistant to change, as are the beliefs underlying them. Schemas holding these beliefs become hypervalent, override more adaptive beliefs and flexible thinking, and operate across most, if not all, situations (Beck et al., 1990).

In addition to *valence* (from latent to hypervalent), which reflects the degree to which a particular schema is engaged at a given point in time, schemas have other characteristics. They have *breadth*, referring to how discrete or broad they are, *flexibility* or rigidity in terms of their capacity for modification, and *density* or relative prominence in the cognitive system (Beck, 1967; Beck et al., 1990, 2004). Cognitive therapy works to identify the content of hypervalent, dysfunctional schemas and to teach people to modify the activity of those schemas and the beliefs contained in them.

Cognitive schemas can be thought of as constructed of subsystems (Beck et al, 1990, 2004). Some are centered on self-evaluation, others on the evaluation of other people. Some schemas prepare for situations through expectancies, predictions, and long-range forecasts. Two sets of schemas that are particularly related to personality and personality disorders are self-schemas (Beck, 1967) and interpersonal schemas (Safran, 1984, 1990; Safran & McMain, 1992; Safran & Segal, 1990).

## Self-Schemas and Interpersonal Schemas

The diagnosis of personality disorder is warranted when an individual's interactions with others create (a) suffering to himself or herself (e.g., avoidant personality disorder) or (b) difficulties for other people or with society (e.g., antisocial personality) (Beck et al., 1990, 2004). Individuals who have personality disorders usually only regard them as problematic when they lead to symptom disorders or when they interfere with the attainment of social or occupational goals. Two types of cognitive schemas—self-schemas or self-concept and interpersonal schemas—play a major role in personality and personality disorders.

The internal control system relates to self-schemas or one's view of self, for it directs self-monitoring, self-appraisal, self-evaluation, self-warnings, and self-instructions (Beck, 1976). These processes relate to personality disorders in general and specific ways. Generally speaking, people who excessively self-monitor tend to be inhibited and those who self-monitor loosely or infrequently tend to behave impulsively or with few constraints. In addition, negative self-evaluations, common in depression, are often found in personality disorders.

Self-evaluations and self-instructions are based in self-schemas or self-concepts. "An exaggerated negative (or positive) self-concept may be the factor that moves a person from being a 'personality type' into having a 'personality disorder'" (Beck et al., 2004, p. 31). Liotti (1992) takes a developmental perspective and emphasizes the central role of egocentrism in personality disorders, defined as "the inability to deal with multiple perspectives simultaneously, and therefore the lack of capacity to differentiate one's point of view from the point of view of others" ( p. 43). Egocentrism, normal in young children, declines over one's lifetime commensurate with cognitive growth. Egocentrism may increase during times of interpersonal crisis and is maintained when accompanied by dysfunctional attitudes.

The rules one develops to get through life, based in part on how one sees oneself (e.g., incompetent, helpless, superior), form the basis for expectations, standards and plans of action, including ways of relating to others. A rigid view of self often results in similarly rigid rules of behavior toward others. This lack of flexibility can result in psychological distress and interpersonal problems.

Cognitive therapy follows Horney's (1950) formulation that one can view personality disorders in terms of how personality types relate to and act toward other people. Safran and his colleagues (Safran, 1984, 1990; Safran & McMain, 1992; Safran & Segal, 1990) theorize that individuals develop internal models of self–other interactions based on early interactions with significant others. These become the person's interpersonal schemas. They hypothesize that maladaptive developmental experiences can lead to the formation of interpersonal schemas that are dysfunctional in later contexts. The more rigid a person's expectations about others and the more constricted his or her sense of how to behave in order to maintain an interpersonal connection or relatedness, the more redundant the person's patterns of interaction are likely to be (Safran & McMain, 1992). Thus, in personality disorders both the self-schemas and the interpersonal schemas are rigid and constricted, resulting in stereotyped responses to others. Cognitive therapy would concur with Blatt and Zuroff's (1992) definition of normal personality as an integration of the capacity to develop meaningful and satisfying interpersonal relations and a consolidated, realistic, essentially positive self-concept.

### Young's Schema Therapy

In Beck's cognitive therapy, the content of schemas is particular to each individual. An alternative model, schema therapy (Young, 1990, 1999), focuses on Early Maladaptive Schemas (EMS), defined as broad, pervasive themes about the self and relationships that comprised memories, emotions, cognitions, and bodily sensations, developed during childhood and adolescence, elaborated through one's lifetime, and dysfunctional to a significant degree (Young, Klosko, & Weishaar, 2003). The content of EMS is seen as common to all who suffer from chronic Axis I symptoms and personality disorders. Young's 18 EMS are grouped according to categories of unmet emotional needs, called *schema domains*. The domains and their corresponding schemas are as follows (Young et al., 2003):

1 *Disconnection and Rejection*: Abandonment/Instability, Mistrust/Abuse, Emotional Deprivation, Defectiveness/Shame, Social Isolation/Alienation
2 *Impaired Autonomy and Performance*: Dependence/Incompetence, Vulnerability to Harm or Illness, Enmeshment/Undeveloped Self, Failure
3 *Impaired Limits*: Entitlement/Grandiosity, Insufficient Self-Control/Self-Discipline
4 *Other-Directedness*: Subjugation, Self-Sacrifice, Approval Seeking/Recognition Seeking
5 *Overvigilance and Inhibition*: Negativity/Pessimism, Emotional Inhibition, Unrelenting Standards/Hypercriticalness, Punitiveness

EMS develop from the frustration of universal emotional needs resulting from the interplay of the child's temperament and any of the following: toxic frustration of needs, trauma or victimization, too much of a good thing or overindulgence, and identification with significant others. EMS crosscut *Diagnostic and Statistical Manual of Mental Disorders (DSM-IV*; American Psychiatric Association, 1994) diagnostic categories of personality disorder. Although some EMS are hallmarks of certain personality disorders (e.g., Abandonment/Instabiltiy and Mistrust/Abuse are often found in borderline personality disorder), any person might have several EMS of varying degrees of activation or primacy.

In response to schema activation, a person responds in one of three coping styles: *schema surrender* or thinking, feeling, and acting as if the schema is true; *schema avoidance* or trying not to think about, feel, or be in situations that trigger the EMS; and *schema overcompensation* or trying to fight back or counterattack the schema.

Mode has a different definition in schema therapy. In cognitive therapy modes are structural and operational units, suborganizations of personality. Beck describes examples such as the anxiety mode and the autonomous mode as programs of coordinated systems that contribute to a syndrome disorder or personality disorder (Beck, 1983, 1996). In schema therapy, a schema mode is a moment-to-moment emotional state and coping response that all people experience. A particular schema mode is determined by the schemas and schema operations active at that time (Young et al., 2003). As a person shifts from one mode to another, different schemas or coping responses become activated. As with EMS, Young has identified 10 schema modes grouped into four broad categories: child modes, dysfunctional coping modes, dysfunctional parent modes, and healthy adult modes.

## Personality and Psychopathology

According to cognitive therapy, the onset of symptom disorders (Axis I) is accompanied by a "cognitive shift" away from normal cognitive processing and to processing controlled by an energized mode. In the depressive mode, the cognitive shift is dominated by negative schemas (Beck, 1967); in generalized anxiety disorder, the danger mode is energized along with schemas focused on threat (Beck et al., 1985). When particular schemas are hypervalent, they are easily triggered by personally relevant life events. They readily take over more adaptive schemas (Beck, 1967). Thus, in depression, the person interprets events negatively, ignores or minimizes positive information, is more likely to recall negative events than positive ones, and predicts failure or loss more frequently than positive outcomes. Normal personality modes appear to play a role in the development of clinical syndromes. Specifically, the personality dimensions of sociotropy and autonomy may be sensitive to particular types of life events in the onset of depression and anxiety. These personality dimensions will be discussed in the text that follows.

We agree with Widiger's (2003) statement that personality disorders increase the likelihood of the development of particular Axis I disorders and often affect their course and treatment. In abnormal personality modes, dysfunctional schemas are more easily triggered than in normal personality and lead to Axis I disorders; they predispose the person to clinical symptoms. In both normal and abnormal personalities, people have access to positive information about themselves when not depressed or anxious, and with both normal and abnormal personalities there is a gradual impairment of reality testing with the onset of an Axis I disorder. The difference between those with normal personalities and those with abnormal personalities is that those with abnormal personalities have long-standing, dysfunctional core beliefs or schemas that are more easily triggered by a range of events, more generalized, more stable, and more resistant to change than those with normal personalities (Beck et al., 1990, 2004). As dysfunctional beliefs are reinforced over time by negative interactions with others, they play a larger role in cognitive processing. Positive or adaptive schemas become less accessible.

With the remission of an Axis I disorder, individuals return to their premorbid cognitive mode (Beck et al., 2004). For individuals with personality disorders, dysfunctional thoughts are less intense and frequent, but are likely to continue in specific situations because these beliefs form the substrate for their orientation to reality.

> The most plausible explanation for the difference between Axis I and the personality disorders is that the extreme faulty beliefs and interpretations characteristic of the symptomatic disorders are relatively plastic—and indeed, become more moderate as

the depression subsides even without therapeutic intervention. However, the more persistent dysfunctional beliefs of the personality disorder are "structuralized"; that is, they are built into the "normal" cognitive organization. (Beck et al., 2004, pp. 69–70)

## Cognitive Profiles of Personality Disorders

Each personality disorder has a distinctive set of cognitive, affective, and behavioral schemas. These include the view of self, the view of others, main beliefs, and main strategies. Some have characteristic thinking styles as well, such as the global, impressionistic thinking of histrionic personality disorder or the "cannot see the forest for the trees" style of obsessive–compulsive personality disorder. These features form a *cognitive profile* for each personality disorder (Beck et al., 1990, 2004). They are most apparent when a situation prevents the person from using his or her idiosyncratic strategy; for example, when an avoidant college student must give a class presentation or when a dependent person is separated from a significant other.

Cognitive profiles for each personality disorder are presented according to *DSM-IV* diagnoses for purely practical reasons; thus, a prototype view of personality is implicit in cognitive therapy's description of personality disorders (Pretzer & Beck, 1996). Cognitive profiles appear in Table 5.1).

Following is an example of a cognitive profile for passive–aggressive personality disorder (Beck et al., 2004, p. 48): The view of self is self-sufficient, yet vulnerable to control or interference. The view of others is intrusive, demanding, interfering, controlling, and dominating. The main belief is, "Others interfere with my freedom of action," "Control by others is intolerable," or "I have to do things my own way." The main strategy is passive resistance, surface submissiveness, and evasiveness or circumvention of the rules. The person's beliefs about self and others contribute to basic strategies for getting through life. Some of these strategies are manifest as overt behaviors; others may be less obvious such as the cognitive or emotional avoidance of disturbing thoughts, memories, or affect.

Because most individuals with a specific personality disorder have attitudes and behaviors that overlap other disorders (Beck et al., 2004), a *cognitive conceptualization* based on a complete evaluation can guide therapists in addressing things such as basic beliefs, conditional beliefs, and compensatory strategies.

## The Personality Dimensions of Sociotropy and Autonomy

In response to Bowlby's (1977) theory of attachment and loss in relation to depression, Beck conducted research on personality as vulnerability to certain types of depression. Beck theorized that two personality features or dimensions, sociotropy and autonomy, were vulnerabilities for reactive depressions when life events congruent with the relevant personality characteristics occurred. This is the basis for his stressor-vulnerability or diathesis-stress model of depression (Beck, 1987). Sociotropy or social dependency involves intense social needs and feelings of helplessness. Autonomy refers to the person's investment in preserving and increasing his or her independence, mobility, and personal rights (Beck, 1983). Although the person high in sociotropy derives gratification from social interactions, the highly autonomous person is gratified by self-direction and goal achievement. A sociotropic person would react negatively to situations involving social

## Cognitive Profiles of Personality Disorders

| Personality Disorder | View of Self | View of Others | Main Beliefs | Main Strategy |
|---|---|---|---|---|
| Avoidant | Vulnerable to depreciation, rejection<br>Socially inept<br>Incompetent | Critical<br>Demeaning<br>Superior | It's terrible to be rejected, put down<br>If people know the "real" me, they will reject me<br>I can't tolerate unpleasant feelings | Avoid evaluative situations<br>Avoid unpleasant feelings or thoughts |
| Dependent | Needy<br>Weak<br>Helpless<br>Incompetent | (Idealized)<br>Nurturant<br>Supportive<br>Competent | I need people to survive, be happy<br>I need to have a steady flow of support, encouragement | Cultivate dependent relationships |
| Passive-aggressive | Self-sufficient<br>Vulnerable to control, interference | Intrusive<br>Demanding<br>Interfering<br>Controlling<br>Dominating | Others interfere with my freedom of action<br>Control by others is intolerable<br>I have to do things my own way | Passive resistance<br>Surface submissiveness<br>Evade, circumvent rules |
| Obsessive-compulsive | Responsible<br>Accountable<br>Fastidious<br>Competent | Irresponsible<br>Casual<br>Incompetent<br>Self-indulgent | I know what's best<br>Details are crucial<br>People *should* do better, try harder | Apply rules<br>Perfectionism<br>Evaluate, control<br>"Shoulds," criticize, punish |
| Paranoid | Righteous<br>Innocent, noble<br>Vulnerable | Interfering<br>Malicious<br>Discriminatory<br>Abusive motives | Others' motives are suspect<br>I must always be on guard<br>I cannot trust people | Be wary<br>Look for hidden motives<br>Accuse<br>Counterattack |
| Antisocial | A loner<br>Autonomous<br>Strong | Vulnerable<br>Exploitative | I'm entitled to *break* rules<br>Others are patsies, wimps<br>I'm better than others | Attack, rob<br>Deceive, manipulate |
| Borderline | Vulnerable (to rejection, betrayal, domination)<br>Deprived (of needed emotional support)<br>Powerless<br>Out of control<br>Defective | (Idealized) Powerful, loving, perfect<br>(Devalued) Rejecting, controlling, betraying, abandoning | I can't cope on my own<br>I need someone to rely on.<br>I cannot bear unpleasant feelings<br>If I rely on someone I'll be mistreated, found wanting, and abandoned | Subjugate own needs to maintain connection<br>Protest dramatically, threaten, and/or become punitive toward those that signal possible rejection |

*(Continued)*

**Table 5.1**  **(Continued)**

| Personality Disorder | View of Self | View of Others | Main Beliefs | Main Strategy |
|---|---|---|---|---|
| Borderline (*Cont.*) | Unlovable Bad | | The worst possible thing would be to be abandoned It's impossible for me to control myself I deserve to be punished | Relieve tension through self-mutilation and self-destructive behavior Attempt suicide as an escape |
| Narcissistic | Special, unique Deserve special rules; superior Above the rules | Inferior Admirers | Since I'm special, I *deserve* special rules I'm above the rules I'm better than others | Use others Transcend rules Manipulate Compete |
| Histrionic | Glamorous Impressive | Seducible Receptive Admirers | People are there to serve or admire me People have no right to deny me my just deserts I can go by my feeling | Use dramatics, charm; temper tantrums, crying; suicide gestures |
| Schizoid | Self-sufficient Loner | Intrusive | Others are unrewarding Relationships are messy, undesirable | Stay away |
| Schizotypal | Unreal, detached, loner Vulnerable, socially conspicuous Supernaturally sensitive and gifted | Untrustworthy Malevolent | (Idiographic, odd, superstitious, magical thinking; for instance, beliefs in clairvoyance, telepathy, or "sixth sense" are central in the belief structure) It's better to be isolated from others. | Watch for and neutralize malevolent attention from others Stay to self Be vigilant for supernatural forces or events. |

From Beck et al. (2004). Reprinted with permission of The Guilford Press.

acceptance and attractiveness. Typical negative thoughts would be, "Nobody cares about me," "I am ugly," or "I made a fool of myself" (Beck, 1987). Depression would likely follow the loss of a relationship, a rejection, or an experience of social deprivation (Beck, 1983). An autonomous personality would be sensitive to situations that appear to limit independent action, mobility, or physical or mental functioning. Typical thoughts would be "I am incompetent," "I am defeated," and "I will never be able to do what I need to do." Thus, the autonomous personality type is likely to become depressed when he or she has been thwarted in achievement, has failed to reach a goal, or is forced to conform (Beck, 1983, 1991).

Sociotropy and autonomy are pure types, with most people having characteristics of both. They are viewed as vulnerabilities that get activated by personally relevant life events and contribute to the development of depression. These personality dimensions illustrate the vulnerability hypothesis—that the sets of circumstances that precipitate depression vary from person to person depending on his or her specific personality organization based in schemas.

The vulnerability hypothesis and the role of schemas in the onset of depression relate to two models of depression: the structural model and the stressor-vulnerability or diathesis-stress model. These are two of the six separable, but overlapping models in the cognitive theory of depression (Beck, 1987). The structural model posits that certain negatively biased schemas become hypervalent in depression and shift the cognitive processes to create a systematic bias in abstraction, interpretation, and memory. The stressor-vulnerability model maintains that specific patterns of schemas make a person sensitive to certain stressors.

A number of theorists from other modalities have developed constructs similar to Beck's sociotropy and autonomy. All of them distinguish a depression initiated by disturbed interpersonal relationships and focused on interpersonal issues (e.g., dependency, helplessness, feelings of loss and abandonment) from a depression initiated by some disruption of self-concept or identity and focused on issues of self-definition (e.g., autonomy, self-criticism, feelings of failure and guilt) (Blatt & Zuroff, 1992). The various theories include the aforementioned ethological and object relations perspective of Bowlby (1977, 1980, 1988), who described anxiously attached and compulsively self-reliant individuals and their predispositions to depression. Blatt's (Blatt, 1974; Blatt & Zuroff, 1992) psychoanalytic and cognitive developmental theory describes anaclitic (dependent) and introjective (self-critical) types, and Arieti and Bemporad's (1978, 1980) interpersonal theory refers to "dominant-other" and "dominant-goal" types of individuals in relation to depression. In all these theories, an excessive preoccupation with either dimension can create a selective vulnerability to a particular series of life events that can lead to depression (Blatt & Zuroff, 1992).

## The Sociotropy–Autonomy Scale

The Sociotropy–Autonomy Scale (SAS; Beck, Epstein, Harrison, & Emery, 1983) is a 60-item, self-report questionnaire that was constructed to assess the personality dimensions of sociotropy and autonomy, specifically to study their relationships to life stress events in the development of symptomotology. Other measures of these constructs are the Depressive Experiences Questionnaire (DEQ; Blatt, D'Afflitti, & Quinlan, 1978) and the Personal Styles Inventory (PSI; Robins, Ladd, Welkowitz, & Blaney, 1994). The most recent factor analysis of the SAS yielded two subfactors of sociotropy, Preference for Affiliation and Fear of Criticism, and two subfactors for autonomy, Independent Goal Attainment and Sensitivity to Others' Control (Bieling, Beck, & Brown, 2004). Beck et al. (1983) report the psychometric properties of the SAS. An expanded and revised SAS was constructed by Clark and Beck (1991) to increase its convergent validity, especially for the autonomy scale. However, most research has relied on the original SAS (Bieling, Olshan, Beck, & Brown, 1998).

The SAS has been used in a number of studies to examine the relationship between life events and depression. Support for the "congruency hypothesis" (Sociotropic individuals would respond to interpersonal disruption and autonomous individuals would respond to negative achievement events) has found support in clinical (Hammen, Ellicott, & Gitlin, 1992; Robins, 1990) and college student samples (Robins, 1990) for sociotropy. Robins and Block (1988) found that autonomous individuals experienced more negative achievement events than non-autonomous subjects, but only Robins and associates (Robins, Hayes, Block, & Kramer, 1995) found that autonomy moderated the relationship of depression and life events for both achievement and interpersonal events. Bieling et al. (1998) provide a summary of this research. Generally speaking, the interaction between sociotropy and negative interpersonal events has been found to be significant in the prediction of depression more frequently than has the interaction between autonomy and negative achievement events.

Recent research by Bieling et al. (2004) followed depressed patients through 12 sessions of cognitive therapy and found that both subscales of sociotropy were positively associated with depression at intake and decreased significantly over time in those who responded to treatment. One subscale of autonomy, independent goal attainment, actually increased significantly with treatment response. The other autonomy subscale, sensitivity to others' control, showed no change. These results indicate that the use of the SAS subscales is informative, for an increase in one suggests improvement and a decrease in the other may be a sign of improvement. This difference would be lost in a total score. The authors conclude that Independent Goal Attainment is a sign of psychological health. Moreover, there was stability in these personality variables as well as clinically meaningful change with cognitive therapy.

Research has demonstrated that sociotropy is related to anxiety as well as depression. Clark and Beck (1991), using a college sample, found that sociotropy predicted both current dysphoria and current anxiety, but autonomy predicted only depression symptoms. Persons and her colleagues (Persons, Burns, Perloff, & Miranda, 1993) found a relationship between dependency beliefs and anxiety symptoms in a clinical sample. Alford and Gerrity (1995) also found sociotropy to be predictive of anxiety in college students. Haaga, Fine, Terril, Stewart, and Beck (1995) found an association between sociotropy and levels of both anxiety and depression in a college student sample. Fresco and colleagues (Fresco, Sampson, Craighead, & Koons, 2001) looked at life stress, depression, anxiety, and personality dimensions over 8 weeks among college students. Sociotropy correlated positively with anxiety symptoms while autonomy correlated positively with depression symptoms. Sociotropy moderated the relationship between life events and depression for both negative interpersonal stress and achievement stress, which suggests that sociotropy may be a general (non-specific) vulnerability factor to depression.

## Sociotropy—Autonomy and Other Personality Measures

Sociotropy and autonomy have been examined in relation to measures in personality psychology, such as the NEO Personality Inventory (NEO-PI; Costa & McCrae, 1985) and the Eysenck Personality Questionnaire (EPQ; Eysenck & Eysenck, 1975). Sociotropy appears related to other measures of theoretically congruent constructs like dependency, lack of assertion, and introversion (Cappeliez, 1993; Gilbert & Reynolds, 1990; Haaga, Fine, Terril, Stewart, & Beck 1995; Moore & Blackburn, 1994; Robins, Block, & Peselow, 1989; Robins et al., 1995). Autonomy appears less strongly related to other measures of pathology, although it is correlated with the theoretically consistent constructs of conscientiousness and extraversion (Cappeliez, 1993; Gilbert & Reynolds, 1990). Gilbert and Reynolds (1990) hypothesized that sociotropy, with its links to depression and neuroticism, may be a more sensitive measure of psychopathology than is autonomy.

Sociotropy and autonomy are complex constructs, each with adaptive and maladaptive aspects. It has been argued that sociotropy may tap into pathological aspects of dependency, but also into a general interpersonal orientation (Rude & Burnham, 1995). Pincus and Gurtman (1995) found that each subscale of sociotropy represents a distinct combination of warmth and dominance, reflecting a range of aspects of dependency. The authors point out that certain types of interpersonal loss would be associated with one aspect of sociotropy, but not another. Although autonomy has positively correlated with conscientiousness, some hypothesize that it may be conceptually related to impulsivity (Gilbert & Reynolds, 1990) and perfectionism (Fresco , Sampson, Craighead, & Koons, 2001). Thus, the complexity of these constructs points to their dimensional nature and to the difficulties inherent in predictive and criterion studies (Bieling et al., 1998).

# Assessment Instruments for Personality Disorders

Cognitive therapy uses both categorical and dimensional measures for the assessment of normal and abnormal personalities. Categorical measures, such as structured clinical interviews to determine and document the presence or absence of an Axis II disorder (e.g., SCID-II; First, Spitzer, Gibbon, Williams, & Benjamin, 1994), are often required in clinical and research settings (Beck et al., 2004). Dimensional approaches, such as the SAS discussed above, the Personality Belief Questionnaire (PBQ; Beck & Beck, 1995), and the Young Schema Questionnaire (YSQ; Young & Brown, 1990) involve the assessment of personality traits or trait-like constructs. The advantage of these self-report questionnaires is that they can provide idiographic data to improve the cognitive conceptualization. Axis II categories and even cognitive profiles are prototypes and, since many patients with personality pathology vary from the prototypical pattern, detailed information about an individual's core beliefs, thinking style, and problematic behaviors are necessary for a compete assessment.

## Personality Belief Questionnaire

The Personality Belief Questionnaire (PBQ; Beck & Beck, 1995) is a 126-item, self-report measure that contains the prototypical schema content of the Axis II disorders. Respondents are asked to rate how much they believe each statement (from 0 "I do not believe it at all" to 4 "I believe it totally"). A belief ascribed to avoidant personality disorder, for example, is "I am socially inept and socially undesirable in work and social activities."

Beck et al. (2004) report that the psychometrics for the PBQ show good internal consistency for the various subscales among college students and psychiatric patients, and a modest correlation between the PBQ and both the Personality Disorder Questionnaire–Revised (PDQ-R; Hyler & Rieder, 1987) and the Minnesota Multiphasic Personality Inventory-Personality Disorder (MMPI-Personality Disorder; Morey, Waugh,

& Blashfield, 1985). Somewhat high intercorrelations were found among many of the PBQ scales. It may be that some sets of beliefs overlap and are not as conceptually distinct as conceived by cognitive theory, or perhaps the shared variance between belief sets is due to a general distress factor (Beck et al., 2004).

The PBQ is used clinically to identify dysfunctional beliefs, construct a cognitive profile, and target those beliefs in treatment.

## Young Schema Questionnaire

Unlike the PBQ, which is designed to correlate with Axis II disorders, the Young Schema Questionnaire YSQ (Young & Brown, 1990) assesses EMS, which cross-cut *DSM–IV* categories and appear in normal personalities as well. EMS are trait-like constructs that are theorized to underlie personality disorders and chronic depressions and anxiety. They are present in normal personalities and contribute to psychopathology depending on their pervasiveness, persistence, and degree of impairment caused by their activity.

The YSQ is a 205-item, self-report questionnaire that asks respondents to rate, on a 6-point Likert scale, the degree to which each item describes them (from 1 "Completely untrue of me" to 6 "Describes me perfectly"). YSQ items are grouped by each of the 16 original schemas identified by Young (1990), and it is not necessary for respondents to be "blind" to the EMS they are endorsing. The YSQ is used primarily for clinical purposes. Total scores are not calculated; rather, clinicians look for high-scoring items and patterns. Scores of 5's and 6's alert the clinician to the likelihood of and EMS. If a patient has three or more high scores for a particular schema, the schema is usually relevant and worthy of exploration (Young et al., 2003). The clinician then uses the high-scoring items to direct a clinical interview for relevant history in order to build a case conceptualization.

A short form of the YSQ (YSQ–S1; Young, 1998) contains 75 items, the five highest loading items found in factor analysis for each schema on the original form (Schmidt, Joiner, Young, & Telch, 1995). The short form has levels similar to those of the long form of internal consistency, parallel forms reliability, and concurrent validity (Stopa, Thorne, Waters, & Preston, 2001), and is used in research studies.

The psychometric properties of the YSQ have been investigated by Schmidt et al. (1995) who found support, in factor analysis, for 12 of Young's 16 original schemas. Another factor, Fear of Losing Control, not hypothesized by Young, was found in a student sample, but not in a patient sample. Social Undesirability did not emerge as a factor in either sample. In the student sample, three higher order factors were identified: Disconnection, Overconnection, and Exaggerated Standards.

A large-scale Australian study of a clinical sample found Social Undesirability to be the only factor hypothesized by Young that failed to emerge (Lee, Taylor, & Dunn, 1999). An additional factor, containing items from Emotional Inhibition, reflected inhibition of emotional expression and thus related to Fear of Loss of Control rather than Emotional Inhibition.

In this sample, a higher order factor analysis yielded factors labeled Impaired Autonomy, Disconnection, Impaired Limits, and Overcontrol. Comparisons were made between patients with Axis I and Axis II disorders. Those with Axis II diagnoses had significantly higher scores on all of the derived scales except Subjugation and Vulnerability. The scales with the largest mean differences loaded on two of the higher order factors, Disconnection and Impaired Limits. "This is consistent with the view that people with a personality disorder are much more likely to have a disturbance in their primary attachment and problems in limit setting than people with only an Axis I diagnosis "(Lee et al., 1999, p. 450).

In addition, the higher order factors of Disconnection and Impaired Autonomy are very similar to sociotropy and autonomy, respectively. Thus, the study by Lee et al. (1999) demonstrates that the YSQ has good internal consistency and that its primary factor structure is stable across clinical samples from different countries and for varying degrees of psychopathology (Axis I and Axis II). The higher order factor structure is consistent with the theoretical distinction between interpersonal relatedness and autonomous achievement, as is Beck's sociotropy and autonomy.

# Tests of the Cognitive Theory of Personality Disorders

According to cognitive theory, the essence of a personality disorder is revealed in the dysfunctional beliefs that characterize and perpetuate it (Beck et al., 1990; Pretzer & Beck, 1996). Early investigations of the association between dysfunctional cognitions and personality disorders provide general support for the cognitive model. O'Leary et al. (1991) found that scores on the Dysfunctional Attitude Scale (DAS; Weissman, 1979) of patients with borderline personality disorder were significantly higher than those of normal controls. The scores of the borderline patients were not related to current major depression, a history of prior major depression, or to clinical status (outpatients and inpatients admitted for research studies vs. inpatients admitted because of clinical necessity). The authors conclude that dysfunctional attitudes may be trait phenomena in personality disorders, related to depressive symptoms rather than major depression. Later work by Arntz, Dietzel, and Dreessen (1999) found that assumptions characteristic of borderline personality disorder appeared stable even with mood induction.

Gasperini et al. (1989) used factor analysis of the Automatic Thoughts Questionnaire (ATQ; Hollon & Kendall, 1980) and the Self-Control Schedule (SCS; Rosenbaum, 1980) to identify the relationships among mood disorders, cognitive patterns, and personality disorders. They found that the first factor that emerged from the factor analysis of the ATQ and the SCS items reflected Cluster B (narcissistic, histrionic, borderline, and antisocial) personalities. The second factor that emerged reflected Cluster C (obsessive–compulsive, dependent, avoidant, and passive–aggressive) personalities. The authors speculate that studying personality traits, rather than clusters, might be more useful in understanding the relationship between personality and cognitive characteristics.

More recently, studies have examined the relationships between maladaptive beliefs and personality disorders. Arntz et al. (1999) found that a subscale of the Personality Disorder Beliefs Questionnaire (PDBQ; Dreessen & Arntz, 1995), hypothesized to contain beliefs characteristic of borderline personality disorder, did indeed differentiate those with borderline personality disorder from subjects with Cluster C personality disorders.

Beck and associates (Beck et al., 2001) used the PBQ (Beck & Beck, 1995) in a study of 756 outpatients who were assessed for personality disorders using standardized clinical interviews. The results showed that avoidant, dependent, obsessive–compulsive, narcissistic, and paranoid personality-disordered subjects preferentially endorsed sets of beliefs theoretically linked to their specific disorders and scored significantly higher on the relevant subscale than did patients without a personality disorder. The other personality disorders were not examined in this study due to a lack of subjects. Nevertheless, these findings support the hypothesis that dysfunctional beliefs are related to at least some personality disorders.

Two studies support the relationship between EMS and personality disorders. A study of 41 methadone-maintained outpatients who met criteria for either antisocial, borderline, avoidant, or depressive personality disorder found that each personality disorder was associated with a unique profile of presenting problems, underlying traits, and schemas (Ball & Cecero, 2001). The YSQ (Young & Brown, 1990), the NEO-Five Factor Inventory (NEO-FFI; Costa & McCrae, 1992), and the Multiple Affect Adjective Checklist-Revised, Trait Version (MAACL-R; Zuckerman & Lubin, 1985) were administered along with a measure of presenting problems to subjects who received personality diagnoses based on the Structural Clinical Interview for *DSM-IV* Axis II (SCID-II; First et al., 1994). The five personality traits assessed on the NEO-FFI are neuroticism, extraversion, openness to experience, agreeableness, and conscientiousness. The MAACL-R was analyzed for Positive Affect and Sensation-Seeking.

Antisocial personality disorder severity was found associated with very low Agreeableness and high Sensation-Seeking. Borderline personality disorder severity was not associated with the NEO-FFI or MAACL-R traits. Avoidant severity was associated with higher Neuroticism and lower Extraversion, Openness to Experience, Sensation-Seeking, and Positive Affect. Depressive severity was associated with lower Extraversion.

In terms of EMS, antisocial personality was linked to Mistrust/Abuse, Vulnerability to Harm, and Emotional Inhibition. Borderline severity was linked with Abandonment/Instability and Mistrust/Abuse schemas. Avoidant severity was associated with Subjugation, and depressive severity was associated with Mistrust/Abuse, Social Isolation, Defectiveness/Shame, Failure to Achieve, and Subjugation schemas.

Loper (2003) examined the relationship among the schema domains of the YSQ-S1 (Young, 1998), behavioral adjustment, and personality disorders among female prison inmates. The Impaired Limits domain score, representing Entitlement and Poor Self-Control, was associated with paranoid, antisocial, borderline, histrionic, and narcissistic personality disorders. The Disconnection/Rejection domain score was associated with a wide array of symptoms. A significant relationship was found between the Impaired Autonomy domain score and dependent personality disorder. This study suggests that specific belief systems are associated with specific personality (and behavior) patterns.

# Tests of Cognitive Behavior Therapy

## Outcome Studies of Cognitive Behavior Therapy for Axis II

A number of studies have looked at the influence of subjects' personality disorders on the outcome of therapy for Axis I disorders (see Dreessen & Arntz, 1998 and Reich, 2003 for reviews). For cognitive therapy, treatment for an Axis I disorder when an Axis II disorder is also present is sometimes effective, sometimes ineffective, and sometimes results in improvement in the Axis II disorder as well (Beck et al., 2004).

The efficacy of cognitive behavioral treatments for personality disorders has been investigated for three personality disorders: antisocial, avoidant, and borderline. Woody, McLellan, Luborsky, and O'Brien (1985), in a study of opiate addicts, found that those diagnosed with major depression and antisocial personality disorder responded well to cognitive therapy and to supportive expressive therapy and showed improvement across a number of psychiatric and behavioral markers.

Stravyski and colleagues (Greenberg & Stravynski, 1985; Stravynsk, Marks & Yule, 1982) used short-term social skills training and social skills training plus a single cognitive intervention (i.e., disputation of irrational beliefs) to treat avoidant personality disorder. The treatments were found to be equivalent in terms of increasing frequency of social interaction and decreasing social anxiety. Another study (Felske, Perry, Chambless, Renneberg, & Goldstein, 1996) found that patients with avoidant personality disorder improved significantly with an exposure-based cognitive behavioral treatment.

A well-researched cognitive behavioral treatment for personality disorders is Linehan's Dialectical Behavior Therapy (DBT; Linehan, 1993). Developed for the treatment of borderline personality disorder, and especially to reduce parasuicidal behavior, DBT combines cognitive behavioral interventions with dialectical materialism and Buddhism. The cognitive and behavioral strategies include collaboration, skills training, problem solving, contingency clarification, and the cognitive restructuring that is part of the dialectical strategies (Linehan, 1987). DBT has been found to be effective in reducing the parasuicidal behavior of patients with borderline personality disorder. Compared to a group of borderline patients who received "treatment as usual" in the community mental health system, those receiving DBT for 1 year had a significantly lower dropout rate, were less self-injurious, and had fewer hospitalizations than the comparison group (Linehan, Armstrong, Suarez, Allmon, & Heard, 1991). Those receiving DBT also had significantly better scores on measures of interpersonal and social adjustment, anger, work performance, and anxious rumination (Linehan, Tutek, & Heard, 1992). The superiority of DBT over treatment as usual in terms of parasuicidal behavior, number of inpatient hospital days, and interviewer rated social adjustment persisted during a 1-year follow-up (Linehan, Heard, & Armstrong. 1993). For a current review of the theory and research findings on DBT, the reader is referred to Robins and Chapman (2004). The efficacy of DBT may be relevant to the role of temperament in abnormal personality, for DBT conceptualizes parasuicidal behaviors as maladaptive attempts at problem solving, the primary problem being unbearable emotional distress (Linehan, 1993). Two of the foci for treatment are emotion regulation and distress tolerance. In contrast with the DBT emphasis on affect regulation, cognitive therapy emphasizes modifying dysfunctional core beliefs in the treatment of personality disorders. A preliminary trial of cognitive therapy for borderline personality disorder (Brown et al., 2004) found that after a year of treatment, subjects had a significant reduction in their symptoms. Moreover, at follow-up, 55% of the participants no longer met diagnostic criteria for borderline personality disorder.

## Comparison with Other Therapies

Comparisons of the efficacy of cognitive therapy and other approaches are few and inconclusive. As mentioned previously, Woody et al. (1985) found that cognitive therapy and supportive expressive therapy were both effective in the treatment of depressed, antisocial subjects. Hardy and colleagues (Hardy et al., 1995) found that subjects with Cluster B personality disorder had significantly poorer outcomes in interpersonal therapy than in cognitive therapy. Black and associates (Black, Monahan, Wesner, Gabel, & Bowers, 1996) found that cognitive therapy resulted in a greater decrease in scores on a self-report measure of personality disorder characteristics than fluvoxamine or pill placebo. Recently, a meta-analysis by Leichsenring and Leibling (2003) examined 11 cognitive behavioral studies and 14 studies of psychodynamic therapy. The authors conclude that psychodynamic psychotherapy and cognitive behavior therapy are both effective treatments for personality disorders.

# Principles of Cognitive Therapy with Personality Disorders

Because of the rigidity and primacy of dysfunctional schemas in individuals with personality disorders, cognitive therapy goes beyond the cognitive and behavioral interventions used in the treatment of Axis I disorders and includes strategies to increase collaboration and confront schemas. Specifically, cognitive therapy for personality disorders integrates cognitive, behavioral, interpersonal, and experiential techniques. Compared to the treatment of uncomplicated Axis I disorders, cognitive therapy for personality disorders places a greater emphasis on the therapy relationship, pays greater attention to childhood experiences and memories, and uses experiential techniques to gain access to painful emotions linked to schemas.

Cognitive therapy for personality disorders begins with a cognitive conceptualization that outlines the patient's core beliefs and relevant life history from which they are derived, conditional beliefs, compensatory strategies and current situations in which they are triggered, and the thoughts, feelings, and behaviors that accompany the activation of core beliefs ( Beck, 1995). By identifying core beliefs and relating them to current distress, a patient's reactions to stressful life events are more understandable and predictable. The cognitive conceptualization is developed collaboratively with the patient and is elaborated over the course of therapy as new information is learned. Similarly, treatment goals are determined collaboratively.

Collaboration is often difficult with patients who have personality disorders, for their same sensitivities and vulnerabilities in other relationships impinge on the therapy relationship. The therapist must consider to the patient's interpersonal schemas, adjust to them, and introduce them to therapy as appropriate.

A number of strategies are used to unravel the meaning of experiences for the patient. Because cognitive and emotional avoidance are common in personality disorders, imagery of past events and present states can reduce avoidance and gain access to core beliefs.

Specific treatment strategies for working with various personality disorders (Beck et al., 1990, 2004) and EMS (Young et al., 2003) are explained at length elsewhere. The following discussion offers a very brief description of techniques to confront schemas.

Confronting schemas is the keystone of cognitive therapy for personality disorders. This is done in several steps. First of all, labeling a schema or core belief as such is less stigmatizing than a diagnostic label. It allows the patient to gain some distance from the distress that feels so much a part of his or her identity and conceptualizes it as something that is learned. Education about how schemas operate and working together on a cognitive conceptualization further build an alliance between therapist and patient and against the schemas.

Experiential techniques of reliving painful childhood experiences through imagery or roleplay can motivate schema change and are often necessary before cognitive and behavioral techniques can be implemented.

Beck et al. (2004) identify three approaches to challenging dysfunctional schemas: schematic restructuring, schematic modification, and schematic reinterpretation.

*Schematic restructuring* entails decreasing the power of dysfunctional schemas and developing more adaptive ones. To decrease the authority of a negative schema, a historical test or review of how the schema has directed a person's life is conducted (Padesky, 1994; Young, 1990). Evidence supporting the schema and evidence contradicting the schema is listed for each age period of the patient's life. Evidence that supports the schema can be challenged by looking for biases in interpretations or alternative explanations of events. For example, a woman who believed, "I am unlovable" used her mother's lack of attention during childhood as evidence. In reviewing the patient's history, it was clear that the mother had been very young, uninterested in parenting, and out of the house frequently. In addition, the patient was able to identify other family members and caregivers who had been very attentive. This examination of evidence helped to decrease the intensity of her belief.

Unlike people with normal personalities, many people with personality disorders have never formed adequate schemas to incorporate positive beliefs, so they are typically unable to recognize and remember positive information that would contradict their negative beliefs. To build new schemas, an alternative, positive belief is first identified. The patient then keeps a diary or "positive data log" of any evidence, however small, that supports the new belief. Sometimes skills training can increase the power of the new belief by improving the behavior congruent with it. For patients who have begun to change, keeping a diary of events along with their old and new perspectives is helpful. For example, a patient might write about a performance, "In the past I would have seen this as a failure, but my new view is that I tried something difficult and achieved a partial success." The Schema Diary (Young, 1993) and Schema Flashcard (Young, Wattenmaker, & Wattenmaker, 1996) are forms used to identify old beliefs and new ways of responding.

*Schematic modification* has the patient gradually test small increments of change. Padesky (1994) describes a number of ways to develop continua for breaking rigid thinking and for making gradual behavioral changes, such as taking small steps to increase trust.

*Schematic reinterpretation* helps the patient to use their schemas in more functional ways; for example, someone who wants admiration might contribute to the community rather than striving for status.

These are just a few specific cognitive interventions. A complete course of cognitive therapy requires the integration of behavioral, interpersonal and experiential techniques as well. As mentioned, there are protocols based on a cognitive conceptualization for each of the personality disorders and EMS. Despite the unique features of the various personality disorders, however, the general principles of schema identification and change prevail.

# Acknowledgments

The authors thank Peter Bieling for sharing his unpublished manuscript on sociotropy and autonomy and Amy Wenzel for her comments on a draft of this chapter.

## REFERENCES

Alford, B. A., & Gerrity, D. M. (1995). The specificity of scoiotropy-autonomy personality dimensions to depression vs. anxiety. *Journal of Clinical Psychology, 51*(2), 190–195.

American Psychiatric Association. (1994). *Diagnostic and statistical manual of mental disorders* ( 4th ed.). Washington, DC: American Psychiatric Press.

Arieti, S., & Bemporad, J. (1978). Severe and mild depression: The psychotherapeutic approach. New York: Basic Books.

Arieti, S., & Bemproad, J. (1980). The psychological organization of depression. *American Journal of Psychiatry, 136,* 1365–1369.

Arntz, A., Dietzel, R., & Dreessen, L. (1999). Assumptions in borderline personality disorder: Specificity, stability and relationship with etiological factors. *Behaviour Research and Therapy, 37,* 545–557.

Ball, S. A., & Cecero, J. J. (2001). Addicted patients with personality disorders: Traits, schemas, and presenting problems. *Journal of Personality Disorders, 15*(1), 72–83.

Bartlett, F. C. (1932). *Remembering.* New York: Columbia University Press.

Bartlett, F. C. (1958). *Thinking: An experimental and social study.* New York: Basic Books.

Beck, A. T. (1967). *Depression: Causes and treatment.* Philadelphia: University of Pennsylvania Press.

Beck, A. T. (1976). *Cognitive therapy and the emotional disorders.* New York: International Universities Press.

Beck, A. T. (1983). Cognitive therapy of depression: New perspectives. In P. Clayton, & J. E. Barnett (Eds.), *Treatment of depression: Old controversies and new approaches* (pp. 265–290). New York: Raven Press.

Beck, A. T. (1987). Cognitive models of depression. *Journal of Cognitive Psychotherapy: An International Quarterly, 1*(1), 5–37.

Beck, A. T. (1991). Cognitive therapy: A 30-year retrospective. *American Psychologist, 46,* 368–375.

Beck, J. S. (1995). *Cognitive therapy: Basics and beyond.* New York: Guilford Press.

Beck, A. T. (1996). Beyond belief: A theory of modes, personality, and psychopathology. In P. M. Salkovskis (Ed.), *Frontiers of cognitive therapy* (pp. 1–25). New York: Guilford Press.

Beck, A. T., & Beck, J. S. (1995). *The Personality Belief Questionnaire.* Bala Cynwyd, PA: Beck Institute for Cognitive Therapy and Research.

Beck, A. T., Butler, A. C., Brown, G. K., Dahlsgaard, K. K., Newman, C. F., & Beck, J. S. (2001). Dysfunctional beliefs discriminate personality disorders. *Behaviour Research and Therapy, 39,* 1213–1225.

Beck, A. T., Emery, G., & Greenberg, R. L. (1985). *Anxiety disorders and phobias: A cognitive perspective.* New York: Basic Books.

Beck, A. T., Epstein, N., Harrison, R. P., & Emery, G. (1983). Development of the sociotropy-autonomy scale: A measure of personality factors in psychopathology. Unpublishedmanuscript. University of Pennsylvania, Philadelphia.

Beck, A. T., Freeman, A., & Associates. (1990). *Cognitive therapy of personality disorders.* New York: Guilford Press.

Beck, A. T., Freeman, A., Davis, D. D., & Associates. (2004). *Cognitive therapy of personality disorders* (2nd ed.). New York: Guilford Press.

Bieling, P. J., Beck, A. T., & Brown, G. K. (2004). Stability and change of sociotropy and autonomy subscales in cognitive therapy of depression. *Journal of Cognitive Psychotherapy: An International Quarterly, 18,* 135–148.

Bieling, P. J., Olshan, S., Beck, A. T., & Brown, G. K. (1998). *The sociotropy-autonomy scale: A review of the extant literature.* Unpublished manuscript, University of Pennsylvania, Philadelphia.

Black, D. W., Monahan, P., Wesner, R., Gabel, J., & Bowers, W. (1996). The effect of fluvoxamine, cognitive therapy, and placebo on abnormal personality traits in 44 patients with panic disorder. *Journal of Personality Disorders, 10*(2), 185–194.

Blatt, S. J. (1974). Levels of object representation in anaclitic and introjective depression. *The Psychoanalytic Study of the Child, 24*, 107–157.

Blatt, S. J., D'Afflitti, J. P., & Quinlan, D. M. (1978). *Depressive Experiences Questionnaire*. Unpublished manuscript, Yale University, New Haven, CT.

Blatt, S. J., & Zuroff, D. C. (1992). Interpersonal relatedness and self-definition: Two prototypes for depression. *Clinical Psychology Review, 12*, 527–562.

Bowlby, J. (1977). The making and breaking of affectional bonds:1. Etiology and psychopathology in light of attachment theory. *British Journal of Psychiatry, 130*, 201–210.

Bowlby, J. (1980). Attachment and loss: Loss, separation, and depression (Vol. 3). New York: Basic Books.

Bowlby, J. (1988). Developmental psychiatry comes of age. *American Journal of Psychiatry, 145*, 1–10.

Brown, G. K., Newman, C. F., Charlesworth, S. E., Crits-Christoph, P., & Beck, A. T. (2004). A preliminary clinical trial of cognitive therapy for borderline personality disorder. *Journal of Personality Disorders, 18*, 257–271.

Cappeliez, P. (1993). The relationship between Beck's concepts of sociotropy and autonomy and the NEO–Personality Inventory. *British Journal of Clinical Psychology, 32*, 78–80.

Clark, D. A., & Beck, A. T. (1991). Personality factors in dysphoria: A psychometric refinement of Beck's sociotropy-autonomy scale. *Journal of Psychopathology and behavioral assessment, 13*, 369–388.

Costa, P. T., & McCrae, R. R. (1985). *The NEO–Personality Inventory manual*. Odessa, FL: Psychological Assessment Resources.

Costa, P. T., & McCrae, R. R. (1992). *Revised NEO Personality Inventory and NEO Five Factor Inventory*. Odessa, FL: Psychological Assessment Resources.

Dreessen, L., & Arntz, A. (1995). *The Personality Disorder Beliefs Questionnaire* (short version). Maastricht, The Netherlands: Author.

Dreessen, L., & Arntz, A. (1998). The impact of personality disorders on treatment outcome of anxiety disorders: Best evidence synthesis. *Behaviour Research and Therapy, 36*, 483–504.

Eysenck, H. J., & Eysenck, S. B. G. (1975). *Manual of the Eysenck Personality Questionnaire*. London: Hodder & Stoughton.

Felske, U., Perry, K. J., Chambless, D. L., Renneberg, B., & Goldstein, A. J. (1996). Avoidant personality disorder as a predictor for treatment outcome among generalized social phobics. *Journal of Personality Disorders, 10*, 174–184.

First, M. B., Spitzer, R. L., Gibbon, M., Williams, J. B. W., & Benjamin, L. (1994). *Structured Clinical Interview for DSM-IV Axis II* (v. 4). New York: Biometrics Research Department.

Fresco, D. M., Sampson, W. S., Craighead, L. W., & Koons, A. N. (2001). The relationship of sociotropy and autonomy to symptoms of depression and anxiety. *Journal of Cognitive Psychotherapy: An International Quarterly, 15*(1), 17–31.

Gasperini, M., Provenza, M., Ronchi, P., Scherillo, P., Bellodi, L., & Smeraldi, E. (1989). Cognitive processes in personality disorders in affective patients. *Journal of Personality Disorders, 3*(1), 63–71.

Gilbert, P., & Reynolds, S. (1990). The relationship between the Eysenck Personality Questionnaire and Beck's concepts of sociotropy and autonomy. *British Journal of Clinical Psychology, 29*, 319–325.

Greenberg, D., & Stravynski, A. (1985). Patients who complain of social dysfunction: I. Clinical and demographic features. *Canadian Journal of Psychiatry, 30*, 206–211.

Haaga, D. F., Fine, J. A., Terril, D. R., Stewart, B. L., & Beck, A. T. (1995). Social problem-solving deficits, dependency, and depressive symptoms. *Cognitive Therapy and Research, 19*, 147–158.

Hammen, C., Ellicott, A., & Gitlin, M. (1992). Stressors and sociotropy/autonomy: A longitudinal study of their relationship to the course of bipolar disorder. *Cognitive Therapy and Research, 16*, 409–418.

Hardy, G., Barkham, M., Shapiro, D. A., Stiles, W. B., Rees, A., & Reynolds, S. (1995). Impact of Cluster C personality disorders on outcomes of contrasting brief psychotherapies for depression. *Journal of Consulting and Clinical Psychology, 63*, 997–1004.

Hollon, S., & Kendall, P. (1980). Cognitive self-statements in depression: Development of an automatic thoughts questionnaire. *Cognitive Therapy and Research, 4*, 383–395.

Horney, K. (1950). *Neurosis and human growth*. New York: Norton.

Hyler, S. E., & Rieder, R. O. (1987). *PDQ-R: Personality Diagnostic Questionnaire-Revised*. New York: New York State Psychiatric Institute.

Kagan, J. (1989). Temperamental contributions to social behavior. *American Psychologist, 44*(4), 668–674.

Kelly, G. (1955). *The psychology of personal constructs*. New York: Norton.

Lee, C. W., Taylor, G., & Dunn, J. (1999). Factor structure of the Schema Questionnaire in a large clinical sample. *Cognitive Therapy and Research, 23*, 441–451.

Leichsenring, F., & Liebing, E. (2003). The effectiveness of psychodynamic therapy and cognitive behavior therapy in the treatment of personality disorders: A meta-analysis. *American Journal of Psychiatry, 160*, 1223–1232.

Linehan, M. M. (1987). Dialectical behavior therapy: A cognitive behavioral approach to parasuicide. *Journal of Personality Disorders, 1*, 328–333.

Linehan, M. M. (1993). *Cognitive-behavioral treatment of borderline personality disorder*. New York: Guilford Press.

Linehan, M. M., Armstrong, H. E., Suarez, A., Allmon, D., & Heard, H. L. (1991). Cognitive-behavioral treatment of chronically parasuicidal borderline patients. *Archives of General Psychiatry, 48*, 1060–1064.

Linehan, M. M., Heard, H. L., & Armstrong, H. E. (1993). Naturalistic follow-up of a behavioral treatment for chronically parasuicidal borderline patients. *Archives of General Psychiatry, 50*, 971–974.

Linehan, M. M., Tutek, D. A., & Heard, H. L. (1992, November). Interpersonal and social treatment outcomes in borderline personality disorder. Paper presented at the annual conference of the Association for Advancement of Behavior Therapy, Boston.

Liotti, G. (1992). Egocentrism and the cognitive psychotherapy of personality disorders. *Journal of Cognitive Psychotherapy: An International Quarterly, 6*(1), 43–58.

Loper, A. B. (2003). The relationship of maladaptive beliefs to personality and behavioral adjustment among incarcerated women. *Journal of Cognitive Psychotherapy: An International Quarterly, 17*, 253–266.

Moore, R. G., & Blackburn, I.- M. (1994). The relationship of sociotropy and autonomy to symptoms, cognition and personality in depressed patients. *Journal of Affective Disorders, 32*, 239–245.

Morey, L. C., Waugh, M. H., & Blashfield, R. K. (1985). MMPI scores for the DSM-III personality disorders: Their derivation and correlates. *Journal of Personality Assessment, 49*, 245–251.

O'Leary, K. M., Cowdry, R. W., Gardner, D. L., Leibenluft, E., Lucas, P. B., & deJong-Meyer, R. (1991). Dysfunctional attitudes in borderline personality disorder. *Journal of Personality Disorders, 5*, 233–242.

Padesky, C. A. (1994). Schema change processes in cognitive therapy. *Clinical Psychology and Psychotherapy, 1*, 267–278.

Persons, J. B., Burns, D. D., Perloff, J. M., & Miranda, J. (1993). Relationships between symptoms of depression and anxiety and dysfunctional beliefs about achievement and attachment. *Journal of Abnormal Psychology, 102*, 518–524.

Piaget, J. (1926). *The language and thought of the child*. New York: Harcourt, Brace.

Piaget, J. (1952). *The origin of intelligence in children*. New York: International Universities Press. (Original work published 1936)

Pincus, A. L., & Gurtman, M. B. (1995). The three faces of interpersonal dependency: Structural analysis of the self-report dependency measures. *Journal of Personality and Social Psychology, 4*, 744–758.

Pretzer, J. L., & Beck, A. T. (1996). A cognitive theory of personality disorders. In J. E. Clarkin, & M. F. Lenzenwegner (Eds.), *Major theories of personality disorder* (pp. 36–105). New York: Guilford Press.

Reich, J. (2003). The effect of Axis II disorders on the outcome of treatment of anxiety and unipolar depressive disorder: A review. *Journal of Personality Disorders, 17*, 387–405.

Riskind, J. H. (1983, August). Misconceptions of the cognitive model of depression. Paper presented at annual convention of the American Psychological Association, Anaheim, CA.

Robins, C. J. (1990). Congruence of personality and life events in depression. *Journal of Abnormal Psychology, 99*, 393–397.

Robins, C. J., & Block, P. (1988). Personal vulnerability, life events, and depressive symptoms: A test of a specific interactional model. *Journal of Personality and Social Psychology, 54*, 847–852.

Robins, C. J., Block, P., & Peselow, E. D. (1989). Relations of sociotropic and autonomous personality characteristics to specific symptoms in depressed patients. *Journal of Abnormal Psychology, 98*, 86–88.

Robins, C. J., & Chapman, A. L. (2004). Dialectical behavior therapy: Current status, recent developments, and future directions. *Journal of Personality Disorders, 18*(1), 73–89.

Robins, C. J., Hayes, A. M., Block, P., & Kramer, R. J. (1995). Interpersonal and achievement concerns and the depressive vulnerability and symptom specificity hypotheses: A prospective study. *Cognitive Therapy and Research, 19,* 1–20.

Robins, C. J., Ladd, J., Welkowitz, J., & Blaney, P. H. (1994). The Personal Style Inventory: Preliminary validation studies of new measures of sociotropy and autonomy. *Journal of Psychopathology and Behavioral Assessment, 16,* 277–300.

Rosenbaum, M. (1980). A schedule for assessing self-control behaviors: Preliminary findings. *Behavior Therapy, 11,* 109–121.

Rude, S. S., & Burnham, B. L. (1995). Connectedness and neediness: Factors of the DEQ and SAS dependency scales. *Cognitive Therapy and Research, 19,* 323–340.

Safran, J. D. (1984). Assessing the cognitive-interpersonal cycle. *Cognitive Therapy and Research, 87,* 333–348.

Safran, J. D. (1990). Towards a refinement of cognitive theory in light of interpersonal theory: I. Theory. *Clinical Psychology Review, 10,* 87–105.

Safran, J. D., & McMain, S. (1992). A cognitive–interpersonal approach to the treatment of personality disorders. *Journal of Cognitive Psychotherapy: An International Quarterly, 6*(1), 59–68.

Safran, J. D., & Segal, Z. V. (1990). *Interpersonal processes in cognitive therapy.* New York: Basic Books.

Schmidt, N. B., Joiner, T. E., Young, J. E., & Telch, M. J. (1995). The Schema Questionnaire: Investigation of psychometric properties and the hierarchical structure of a measure of maladaptive schemas. *Cognitive Therapy and Research, 19,* 295–321.

Stopa, L., Thorne, P., Waters, A., & Preston, J. (2001). Are the short and long forms of the Young Schema Questionnaire comparable and how well does each version predict psychopathology scores? *Journal of Cognitive Therapy: An International Quarterly, 15,* 253–272.

Stravynski, A., Marks, I., & Yule, W. (1982). Social skills problems in neurotic outpatients: Social skills training with and without cognitive modification. *Archives of General Psychiatry, 39,* 1378–1385.

Weissman, A. N. (1979). The Dysfunctional Attitude Scale: A validation study, PhD dissertation, University of Pennsylvania.

Widiger, T. A. (2003). Personality disorder and Axis I psychopathology: The problematic boundary of Axis I and Axis II. *Journal of Personality Disorders, 17*(2), 90–108.

Woody, G. E., McLellan, T., Luborsky, L., & O'Brien, C. P. (1985). Sociopathy and psychotherapy outcome. *Archives of General Psychiatry, 42,* 1081–1086.

Young, J. E. (1990). Cognitive therapy for personality disorders. Sarasota, FL: Professional Resources Press.

Young, J. E. (1993). *The schema diary.* New York: Cognitive Therapy center of New York.

Young, J. E. (1998). The Young Schema Questionnaire-short form [on-line]. Available at: www.homesprynet.com/sprynet/schema/ysqs1.htm

Young, J. E. (1999). *Cognitive therapy for personality disorders: A schema-focused approach* (rev. ed.). Sarasota, FL: Professional Resources Press.

Young, J. E., & Brown, G. (1990). *Young Schema Questionnaire.* New York: Cognitive Therapy Center of New York.

Young, J. E., Klosko, J. S., & Weishaar, M. E. (2003). *Schema therapy: A practitioner's guide.* New York: Guilford Press.

Young, J. E., Wattenmaker, D., & Wattenmaker, R. (1996). *Schema therapy flashcard.* New York: Cognitive Therapy Center of New York.

Zuckerman, M., & Lubin, B. (1985). *Manual for the Multiple Affect Adjective Checklist*—Revised. San Diego, CA: Educational and Industrial Testing Service.

# Psychobiological Models and Issues

## 6

### Gordon Claridge

**M**ost observers would surely agree that human personality variations, normal as well as abnormal, are "psychobiological," in the broad sense that for a complete understanding of an individual's uniqueness we require information about both psychological and biological functioning. It would be even more accurate to say that the span of necessary knowledge is "biosocial," and therefore still wider in scope. In practice, accounts of personality are not as integrative as this and, although theorists sometimes pay lip-service to the psychobiological (or biosocial) ideal, their actual formulations are more focused and self-contained within an experiential, cognitive, physiological, psychometric, or other model. The result is a patchwork of differing perspectives that have so far failed to piece together entirely to form a recognizable whole. Among the more obvious reasons for this one is the sheer complexity of the subject matter. In such circumstances, researchers are often understandably tempted, in the interests of coherence, to concentrate on some limited aspect of the phenomena to be explained; personality psychology, clinical psychology, and psychiatry are no exceptions in this regard; another reason is that various viewpoints genuinely are difficult to assimilate to one another; research inevitably generates its own concepts, methods, and terminology and translating between theories, even from reasonably adjacent domains (e.g., cognitive and behavioral) can be tricky. Finally, it also has to be said that there is sometimes a reluctance to attempt such assimilation anyway: theory builders have a habit of believing in the all-inclusive explanatory power of their own models!

Another reason why the field under review has a rather untidy appearance is that, as in all scientific endeavor (but probably more so here), research on personality and psychological deviance is open to the influence of sociocultural factors, which may shape, even distort, the interpretation of apparently "objective" data. Construction of the person and of personhood vary over time as well as geographically; and scientific ideas that chime with expectations and attitudes—or serve professional or other needs—in one social climate might not do so in another. Consequently, quite different interpretations can be arrived at even among theoreticians starting from the same factual origin. Illustrating the point is a historical example I once quoted (Claridge, 1995), concerning the contrasting messages that European and North American psychologists drew from Pavlovian theory at the birth of and during the heyday of behaviorism. For J. B. Watson, Pavlov's account of the conditioned reflex offered a formula for elaborating a heavily environmentalist view of individual differences consonant with the North American philosophy of personal equality and social opportunity. In contrast, it was left to writers in Europe—and in Western Europe especially, Eysenck—to exploit on behalf of a more stratified social order Pavlov's concept of "nervous types" as a biological and, by inference, more genetically preprogrammed explanation of human personality.[1]

Of course, the particular point at issue in the above example is now out-of-date: extreme behaviorism is dead and so, hopefully, is crude hereditarianism. Yet, over time several *general* themes in the psychobiological debate have scarcely changed; indeed, as we shall see, differences of opinion on some of them have actually sharpened, ever since the first edition of this chapter was written a decade ago. Appropriately spanning the divide, a source of tension continues to be between those who seek descriptions in the nervous system and those who prefer more macroscopic, whole person accounts, whether the latter are formulated in behavioral or, as is now more often the case, in cognitive terms. Furthermore, although not a necessary conjunction, these two positions have also been aligned with differing emphases on the relative influences of nature and nurture in human variation. Biological theorists are predictably drawn to the notion of genetic underpinning of the individual differences they study; for the more psychologically minded, whose primary explanatory constructs lie further from the nervous system, the extrapolation has less appeal.

An increasingly important element in this dialogue is the rapid advance in the methodologies of neuroscience and genetics: if they have not already done so, both of these disciplines promise to resolve questions that have hitherto necessarily remained the subject of speculation and fuzzy thinking. Questions like: "Is there a gene for impulsivity?" Stated like that the answer is almost certainly "No"—and in any case it is inaccessible to the methodology of biometrical behavioral genetic analysis on which researchers in the area previously relied. But applying molecular genetics and posing the question in another way—for example, "How do genes contribute to the novelty-seeking traits that can result in impulsive behavior?"—some sense is beginning to emerge; as witnessed in a recent study by Berman and his colleagues (Berman, Ozkaragoz, Young, & Noble, 2002). These investigators examined D2 dopamine receptor gene polymorphisms in relation to Cloninger's temperament dimensions of novelty seeking and harm avoidance (Cloninger, Svrakic, & Przybeck, 1993). They found that the gene

---

[1]It is instructive to note that, although it has taken a long time, there are now signs of a healthy rapprochement of the two traditions, at least in the domain of therapy. I am referring here to recent attempts to introduce personality as a guiding treatment principle into behavior therapy (Farmer & Nelson-Gray, 2005) and cognitive-behavior therapy (Rasmussen, 2005).

was coded not for either trait taken in isolation, but rather for their profile.Crucially, it was shown that one of the DRD2 alleles was more common in individuals scoring high in *both* novelty seeking *and* harm avoidance, an intuitively dysfunctional combination that could account for, and indeed is found, in personality disorders associated with unhealthy impulsivity. A feature of the authors' analysis was their readiness to see the distinction between adaptive and maladaptive forms of novelty seeking, both occurring in nonclinical subjects, but having different consequences in the event of disorder and possibly having different genetic bases.

The greater precision of molecular (as compared to behavioral) genetics is also making it possible to address with more confidence the diathesis–stress issue and nature–nurture questions about the risk for disorder. A good example, with regard to depression, is to be found in the work of Caspi and his collaborators (Caspi et al., 2003). They showed how a functional polymorphism of the serotonin transporter (5-HTT) gene could modify the impact of stressful life events in the latters' effect on the emergence of clinical depression and suicidality. The source of subjects for this research was the famous "Dunedin study," forming a cohort of individuals who had first been assessed at the age of three and followed-up at intervals into adulthood.

By virtue of its longitudinal design, the second of the two studies, just described neatly, illustrates how the psychobiology debate is now taking on a new slant, as events on the biological side of the equation assume an even greater objective reality than when I last visited this topic in 1994. Anticipating this scientific shift in psychobiology, I suggested then that there could be one of two quite opposite consequences. One might be to promote a more sophisticated, empirically based, and integrated psychobiology.The other might be to reinforce the expectation that most features of individual variation, especially in their pathological form, will soon yield entirely to a biological probe of one kind or another, making discussion of their psychology redundant.How would things look some eleven years later? The impression is that, in some quarters at least, the second of these two reactions is now very firmly in place.

That is definitely true on the psychiatric side of the equation, particularly with respect to the psychotic states; these are now quite routinely spoken of as diseases whose organic etiology is, if not known, certain. Thus, it took very little searching of recent issues of *Schizophrenia Bulletin* to discover the following:

> Because most researchers agree that schizophrenia is a brain disorder that may be developmental in origin, it makes sense to take cues from neurology in designing an assessment plan.

The authors, Conklin and Iacono (2003) were writing in the journal's "At Issue" section under the heading *Assessment of Schizophrenia: Getting Closer to the Cause*. The "cue from neurology" they chose to quote as a paradigm for understanding schizophrenia was Parkinson's disease. In doing so they articulated the most commonly held view of the functional psychoses to be found currently in psychiatry and certain parts of abnormal psychology. Yet, as discussed later, it is a view of psychosis that is seriously open to challenge.

In clinical psychology the picture has quite the opposite appearance. There the increasing (and increasingly successful) use of cognitive behavioral treatments, even in psychosis, has led to a new confidence that *explanations* of disorder can also get by without considering biology. This is certainly the impression given by some of the major players in the field of cognitive clinical psychology. For example, Salkovskis (1999), writing about his own area of expertise—obsessive-compulsive disorder—makes no reference whatsoever to its biology, despite quite convincing neuroimaging evidence for some form of deviant brain circuitry in OCD (Saxena, Brody, Schwartz, & Baxter, 1998). As for psychosis, biological explanations fare little better. Typical are the writings of Bentall, a prominent exponent of the cognitive approach to schizophrenia. In his recent book, *Madness Explained*, Bentall (2003) certainly pays lip-service to biology, but it gets short shrift in his overall construction of psychotic behavior; indeed, as mentioned later, at one point he even misunderstands it.

As implied earlier, it is understandable that for one motive or another people trying to peddle their own wares usually neglect to mention or play down alternatives: Eclecticism does not shift stock! Opinions across the psychobiological divide are no exception. This does not mean, however, that no discussion exists. On the contrary, among thoughtful commentators there is a clear awareness of the issues put forth by the psychobiological perspective on personality and psychopathology. Admittedly here the debate often seems to be one-sided, taking the form of challenges to hard core biological explanations of behavior, rather than vice versa. There is an obvious reason for this: an apparent objectivity and precision of measurement gives the less thoughtful of those who make biological pronouncements a confident (almost smug) air, as if to imply that more reflective discussion is redundant. That that is not actually the case, however, is evidenced by the fact that the past decade has seen a renewed interest in questions that go beyond purely physicalistic interpretations of human nature, including its deviations. In relation to psychiatry, personality, and abnormal psychology there are several signs of this. Representative is the founding, in 1994, of the journal *Philosophy, Psychiatry, & Psychology*, a publication designed to address issues that sit at the cusps between these three disciplines. Among such issues are the value-laden nature of psychiatric diagnosis and the notion that psychological disorders differ from physical (e.g., neurological) diseases in needing to be judged as healthy or unhealthy according to the context in which they occur (Fulford, Broome, Stanghellini, & Thornton, 2005; Jackson & Fulford, 2003). Convergent on that topic are even more fundamental questions about the phenomenology of psychiatric illness and the validity of construing disorders like schizophrenia separately from their biology, as disturbances of consciousness and the subjective experience. In 1989, *Schizophrenia Bulletin* devoted a whole issue to that subject which, in a more sophisticated form, continues to be debated (e.g., Sass & Parnas, 2003).

At the end of the introduction to the 1994 version of this chapter, I expressed a concern that science might even then have already gone too far in dehumanizing the person. In the interim—and making the question even more urgent—the "revolution" in the biological sciences has proceeded at an accelerating pace. This inevitably alters the shape of the debate so that although some issues remain much as before, others allow a different interpretation in the light of new facts or new conceptual insights.

Those who read the earlier version of the chapter will realize that it was illustrative, rather than comprehensive, focusing on a particular set of concerns and following certain themes to do with the dimensionality of personality, the disease concept, the psychosis spectrum, the personality disorders, and the biological underpinnings of these individual differences. The rest of the chapter follows a similar structure and tries to provide an update on these issues and to seek a reconciliation of some continuing points of disagreement.

# Reductionism, Asymmetry, and Continuity

For reasons referred to above, a properly rounded psychobiology of personality is, ironically, in some ways becoming less easy to establish as more and more psychological events prove to have a distinctive biological correlate. Often such phenomena appear to be potentially reducible entirely to physiological, biochemical, and genetic descriptors, giving satisfaction to those experimental psychologists who look forward to the day when their discipline is redefined as a branch of neuroscience. In psychiatry, including its clinical practice, that progression seems already almost to have been achieved. As witness the heavy medicalization of everyday behaviors evident in the *Diagnostic and Statistical Manual of Mental Disorders* (*DSM-IV, DSM-IV-TR*) (American Psychiatric Association, 1994, 2000) and the consequences this has had for the management of deviant moods and habits; for example, the widespread abuse of SSRIs, like Prozac, as so-called "happiness pills," and the massive prescription of stimulant drugs for overactive children loosely diagnosed with ADHD. There is surely something to worry about here. It is what Willner (1985), in a still topical analysis of the problem in relation to psychobiological explanations of depression, discussed under the heading, the "reductionist fallacy."

Willner criticized reductionism on several grounds. He pointed out, for example, that where there is a hierarchical organization of function, such as we have in psychology and most psychological disorders, substituting a lower level of explanation of a phenomenon for an explanation at a higher level is generally not feasible, if only because the account gets too detailed and complex the further one moves down the hierarchy. For example, to describe even a simple perceptual experience would involve specifying an impossibly large number of neuronal connections: The opportunity and availability of data to describe it at a higher—in this case psychological—level is indispensable, and in any case more meaningful. Willner's most telling criticism, however, made use of the well-known phenomenon of emergent properties, whereby new qualities, not evident in simpler systems and not predictable from the latters' own features, become apparent as the level of organization increases in complexity. Here, the psychological data not only have *validity* in their own right but also their own *uniqueness*, simply by virtue of being psychological. Furthermore, as Willner stressed, they also have a certain precedence in psychobiological investigation; unless and until the variables at the psychological level are successfully specified they cannot sensibly be examined at a biological level. To use an example from a different field from the one in which Willner was writing, no amount of search for genes or neural circuitry supposedly "responsible" for schizophrenia will pay dividends until agreed upon answers are found to such elementary questions as the core clinical features of the disorder, or its boundaries *vis-à-vis* normality or other psychoses.

Then there is another important issue within the reductionist debate about human variation. This concerns an apparent difference in the readiness with which biological reductionism is resorted to, and considered acceptable, according to whether the psychological phenomena to be explained fall within the domain of normal or abnormal experience. Sass (1992), in his far-reaching exposition on madness, refers to this as an "asymmetry" of explanation. He elaborates the idea as follows:

> Normal (or healthy) forms of consciousness are assumed to be, to a great extent, under one's intentional control and, in addition, to operate according to rational principles and

> to be oriented toward the objective world. While these normal mental processes are certainly assumed to be *correlated* with physical events occurring in the brain, seldom are they viewed as being *mere* causal by-products of such events. . . . But *abnormal* modes of consciousness . . . have often been seen very differently: as involving a "fall into determinism," a lapse from dualism whereby the malfunctioning physical processes (in brain and nervous system) disrupt the mental or psychic stream, depriving it of its intrinsic rationality and meaningfulness. (p. 375)

Sass' reference at the end here is to the so-called "broken brain" theory of mental illness (Andreasen, 1984) and echoes our earlier observation on how manifest neurological diseases are taking increasing hold as the preferred research model in psychiatry. Of course, it could be argued that it has never been otherwise: As Berrios and Marková (2002b) point out, the idea that "mental disorders are disorders of the brain" can be traced at least to the 17th century medical literature and, although taking different forms in different social and historical contexts, has generally prevailed. So, apart from brief periods of aberration,—such as the radical movements in the middle of the last century (e.g., Laing, 1960)—psychiatry has almost always been predominantly *neuro*psychiatry, seeking to establish "causes" in the nervous system. This is not surprising, given the marked discontinuities in behavior and psychological experience evident in most mental illness, especially serious mental illness. Faced with such breaks in function, investigators will naturally be tempted to look outside the domain of what is presumed to define health, for explanations beyond those that account for normal activity; searching instead for what might cause really big changes in the person. Here the medical analogy has usually seemed the most apt and neurology, the nearest clinical neighbor to psychiatry, the most likely to provide the answer. This is particularly so when, as is sometimes the case, it is possible to point to clearly demonstrable forms of brain pathology that have associated with them psychological symptoms similar to those found in disorders otherwise primarily diagnosed as psychiatric. An example is damage to the temporal lobe producing symptoms not easily distinguishable from those found in schizophrenia. Such "behavioral phenocopies," as Berrios & Markova (2002a) call them, can cause conceptual confusion when trying to distinguish fact from fallacy in biological data about psychological disorder. Thus, while tempting to make the leap, it does not follow, because impulsivity is extremely high in both frontal lesion patients and in those with borderline personality disorder, that the latter therefore must have damaged frontal lobes. In the absence of direct evidence (in this case not forthcoming), all that we can actually conclude is that some dysfunctional, probably frontolimbic, circuitry is implicated in borderline personality—a useful, but much more limited, generalization from the brain injury data. Such examples of reasoning by analogy can be replicated many times over in neuropsychiatry and biological abnormal psychology.

Biological reductionism in normal personality theory has a different, somewhat less brash, feel about it. This is partly because, paraphrasing Sass, the healthy individual—unlike the psychiatric patient—cannot so easily be seen as the victim of some neurological process. He and she are more in control of their behavior and their felt experience, leaving room for a more dualistic perspective on brain/mind relationships. In psychology a greater range of explanatory models—social, humanist, cognitive, existentialist—have continued to flourish, having little or no need to call upon physiological data. Biological models can therefore claim no particular priority in general psychology, though they are highly relevant here because of the real part they have played in trying to explain the connection between personality and psychological disorders (Claridge & Davis, 2003).

A central issue is that of continuity, of which there are several facets. One raises the question of whether psychological disorders are simple extensions of normal personality. That is to say, whether, contradicting Sass' attempt to separate the two domains, abnormal functioning is merely *normal* functioning writ large—or, put slightly the other way around, whether the evident brain disturbance in psychological disorder is represented to lesser degree in normal personality, making the latter's biological underpinnings of special importance to study. Or, if there is not complete quantitative continuity between normal and abnormal, how much is there, what is the relationship between the two, and how do we visualize the transition from one to the other? And we also need to ask whether the answers to such questions apply equally to all forms of abnormality; what, if any, is the connection between different disorders; and how relevant to each case are theories and evidences drawn from normal personality psychology.

An important starting point for trying to answer the above questions is to consider what issues surround the way in which, from a purely descriptive point of view, we construe psychological disorders, and personality, and the intersection between them. The perspective from the abnormal side is formally represented in the diagnostic manuals—the *International Classification of Diseases* (*ICD*; WHO, 1992) and the *DSM-IV-TR* (2000)—and the nosological systems they represent. One relevant point is that both make the distinction between the mental illnesses *per se* and disorders of the personality. This separation is more explicit in the *DSM* with its division into Axis I and Axis II conditions, a distinction that should help in reminding us that a potentially different model might be required to deal with continuity as it relates to the personality disorders (Axis II) as compared with the more convincingly categorical illnesses subsumed under Axis I.

For most people prepared to think outside the medical box personality disorders will no doubt look like extreme variations in normal personality, opening them up to a range of methods of enquiry drawn from individual differences research. Widiger, one of the most prominent writers on this topic, has repeatedly taken this position (Widiger & Costa, 1994; Widiger & Simonsen, 2005a). But the authors of the *DSM* toy, only tentatively, with the idea. In a very short single paragraph in the *DSM-IV* they discuss the possibility of viewing Axis II dimensionally but then reject it. They even start by curtly saying:

> The diagnostic approach used in this manual represents the categorical perspective that Personality Disorders represent qualitatively distinct clinical syndromes. (p. 633)

Compounding its nervousness on the dimensionality issue the *DSM* makes matters worse by a lack of clarity about the relationship between Axis I and Axis II disorders, failing to offer us a really consistent model for studying it. Diagnostically the two axes are intended in principle to be unconnected, in that high ratings on one can exist without high ratings on the other. For some disorders in Axis II this is manifestly unlikely. Schizotypal Personality Disorder (SPD), for example, has a well-established place along the schizophrenia spectrum, with strong clinical and etiological connections to schizophrenia (Maier, Falkei, & Wagner, 1999). Compare that with, say, Narcissistic Personality

Disorder, although having roots in personality psychology, has no obvious Axis I counterpart; indeed its very presence in Axis II seems almost serendipitous, underlining the haphazard way in which the list appears to have been drawn up. Then take Antisocial Personality Disorder. That seems to have no reliable anchor in either normal individual differences or major mental illness and is a rather shapeless, poorly conceived descriptor, comparing badly with attempts elsewhere in the literature to define precise personality characteristics associated with antisocial behavior; for example, primary psychopathy (Hare et al, 1990).

Equally unsatisfactory are some aspects of the grouping of the Axis II disorders into their three Clusters of A (odd/eccentric), B (dramatic/emotional), and C (anxious/fearful). The presence of Borderline Personality Disorder (BPD) in Cluster B, rather than Cluster A, looks strange given that part of the history of the borderline concept lies firmly in the psychosis literature, for example, as "borderline schizophrenia." It also goes against the results of the original APA task force exercise that led to two forms of borderline being recognized (Spitzer, Endicott, & Gibbon, 1979). Although statistically separable it was nevertheless observed in that study that the two forms showed considerable overlap, a finding supported by other evidence at the time that BPD and SPD are closely linked (George & Soloff, 1986). The validity of the borderline concept has continued to be called into question (Parnas, 1994), suggesting that it might be premature to insist on the degree of definitiveness and separateness of BPD and SPD as that imposed by Axis II. The BPD/SPD connection is just one instance of a general problem with Axis II, *viz.* a strong comorbidity both within and across the Axis II clusters (Marinangeli et al, 2000). This does little to inspire confidence in the clinical and theoretical sharpness of the *DSM* system for classifying the personality disorders.

It should be mentioned that many of the concerns about the *DSM*, particularly the dimensional versus categorical approach to Axis II disorders, are the subject of ongoing debate in the context of preparations for the eventual publication of the DSM-*V.* This has occupied a recent whole special issue of the *Journal of Personality Disorders* and brings together contributions from a conference in which several research strategies for investigating the dimensional model were discussed. In introducing the collection of papers Widiger and Simonsen (2005b) draw attention to the very long history of criticism of the categorical model and freely cite sources arguing for the alternative, dimensional classification. Yet their final remarks remain rather cautious:

> One should not infer [from this debate] that the existing categories of personality disorder would be replaced in the next edition of the diagnostic manual by a dimensional classification. (p.106)

A long-standing, vociferous critic of psychiatry's reluctance to embrace dimensionality was the late Hans Eysenck, who argued its case not just for the personality disorders (Eysenck, 1987) but, from the very beginning, in relation to all forms of psychological abnormality (Eysenck, 1960; see also his contribution to the first edition of this book). As one of his former disciples, it is therefore appropriate at this point to introduce a perspective on the issue that will unashamedly help to shape the rest of this chapter. The ideas in question have been developed in several previous publications (Claridge, 1995, 1997a; Claridge & Davis, 2003) and have their origins in—but represent a radical remodeling and reinterpretation of—Eysenck's theory of personality. They contain three main assumptions crucial to the debate about continuity. First, that the personality dimensions can be construed in two ways: as parameters of healthy personality and as risk indicators for psychological disorders. Secondly, that these dimensions have a substantial, though not exclusive, biological underpinning. And, thirdly, that despite the envisaged continuity between normal and abnormal, there is a (varying) degree of discontinuity between healthy personality and psychological disorder, requiring ways of conceptualizing this.

With regard to the third point a significant feature is the distinction that needs to be made between traits and symptoms. This owes much to the early writings of the British psychologist, Foulds (1965, 1971), who was also very concerned with the relationship between personality and mental illness. As Foulds noted, traits are universal, normally distributed in the population, and ego-syntonic, *viz.* adapted to the healthy needs of the person; in contrast, symptoms are relatively rare, mostly temporary in nature, statistically skewed, and ego-dystonic. However, Foulds also recognized the existence of *deviant* traits, characteristics that seem to fall midway between traits and symptoms, describing behaviors that look mildly discontinuous, as though on a continuum with normal, but too extreme for us to be comfortable with them as entirely healthy. The intermediate nature of this descriptor will be familiar to anyone who has tried to find a suitable form of wording for items in rating scales or questionnaires—for example, of anxiety—intended to measure characteristics that lie in the borderland between normal and abnormal behavior. The concept of deviant traits makes the symptom/trait distinction rather messy. But it represents the reality that discontinuity can proceed in imperceptibly small steps which become bigger and bigger until a truly observable break in functioning occurs.

It is clear from the above that there are several subtexts in the ideas described. One is about the apparent paradox of normal personality dimensions acting simultaneously as predispositions to mental illnesses. Another asks whether there might be any difference in that regard for mild as against severe forms of disorders; for example, can the same dimensional model apply equally to anxiety reactions as to illnesses like schizophrenia? Third, how does one reconcile the continuity of personality dimensions with the evident discontinuity inherent in mental illness? And where do the personality disorders fit in, given that, compared with the Axis I conditions, they are more obviously continuous with normal individual variation? Finally, as a corollary to that, we can ask about the connection between the personality disorders and the mental illnesses and whether *DSM*'s present commitment to a categorical model for Axis II, as well as Axis I, helps or hinders the debate.

These themes will be touched upon at various points in the following two sections, which are arranged under two broad headings. One examines the contribution of biological personality theory to our understanding of personality disorder and mild mental illness. The other considers how far it is possible to extrapolate those ideas to serious mental illness and what implications that might have for models of psychological disorder.

# Temperament, Personality, and Deviance

The notion that a substantial part of human individuality is rooted in biology has a long heritage, found in the prescientific era as the humoral theory of temperaments and, in more modern times, as Pavlov's "theory of nervous types," according to which differences in the behavior of his laboratory dogs could be explained (Pavlov claimed) as due to natural variations in certain hypothetical properties of the nervous system. This basic idea has since become the guiding principle for an identifiable school of biological personality theorists, who share a common interest in chasing personality to the nervous system. The father of this movement was undoubtedly Hans Eysenck whose theorizing and empirical work was unique in its time for logically combining three essential elements. The first was his early use of factor analysis to identify the main dimensions of personality (Eysenck, 1947). The second was, once having established what he believed these to be, postulating a biological basis for them—originally derived loosely from Pavlovian nervous typological theory (Eysenck, 1957) and then revised to be more in line with Western notions of the "conceptual nervous system" (Eysenck, 1967). Third, was Eysenck's proposal that the extreme points of his personality dimensions were defined by—or, put in another way, anchored in—major forms of psychological abnormality (Eysenck, 1947).[2] This combination of features provided Eysenck with a strategy for validating his dimensions at a descriptive trait level, as well as offering a potential biological model for simultaneously explaining normal personality differences and the etiology of their associated abnormal variants.

Eysenck's pioneering efforts have in one way or another influenced almost everyone else who has come to think about normal and abnormal personality broadly in the way that he did. The inspiration was sometimes very immediate, as for those of us who modified some parts of Eysenck's own theory (Claridge, 1967; Gray, 1981). In other cases it was simply combatative, as in the challenges to Eysenck's descriptive three-factor solution to personality structure—most notably from Five-Factor theory proponents (Costa & McCrae, 1992). Or it was implicit and occurred in parallel with developments in the Eysenckian "school" proper—in the construction of alternative or complementary biological theories (Depue & Collins, 1999; Depue & Lezenweger, 2001; Zuckerman, 1994).

The exact details of these various theories do not concern us here. Suffice it to comment briefly on their main features. The first point to note is their apparent agreement on a small number of quite similar explanatory constructs, or dimensions. Two clusters in particular stand out. One, having something to do with negative affect, appears in all of them as anxiety (Gray), N-anxiety (Zuckerman), harm avoidance (Cloninger, Depue & Lezenweger), neuroticism (Costa & McCrae). Another cluster represents impulsivity (Gray), sensation seeking (Zuckerman), novelty seeking (Cloninger), nonaffective constraint (Depue & Lezenweger). It would naturally be unwise to conclude from these similarities that there is complete isomorphism among the theories: for example, the term "harm avoidance" is used slightly differently by Cloninger and by Depue; and impulsivity is a heterogeneous concept that is notoriously difficult to define (Revelle, 1997). Nevertheless there is a satisfying degree of convergence between the theories, suggesting that their originators are all looking in roughly the same direction. The greater problem sometimes lies in the "competitiveness" among

---

[2]It is worth noting that in making this connection Eysenck did not distinguish between what in *DSM* eventually came to be labeled Axis I and Axis II conditions. Thus, introversion and neuroticism were associated with anxiety based *neuroses* whereas extraversion and neuroticism were associated with hysterical and psychopathic *personality disorders*.

theorists, which can make it difficult to compare across models, especially when compounded by the use of a different label for the same idea or, as in the "harm avoidance" case referred to above, the opposite.

Another point to note about these theories refers to their proposals for the biological underpinnings of individual differences. Early accounts made use of relatively "static" constructs like arousal or activation (e.g., Eysenck, 1967). However, explanations have become increasingly "dynamic" as some theorists have formulated their models in explicitly motivational terms. There is a hint of that even in labels such as "novelty seeking" and "sensation seeking," but it has become more manifest in cases where the whole theory is cast as having to do with motivation. The trend started with Gray's modification to Eysenck's theory of extraversion and neuroticism: replacing those dimensions with anxiety and impulsivity as alternative continua that have sensitivity to punishment and sensitivity to reward as their respective biological and behavioral correlates. Since then Gray's version of a reinforcement theory of personality—including the idea of interacting behavioral inhibition and behavioral activation motivational systems—has been much elaborated, drawing upon contemporary evidence from experimental psychology and neurobiology (Pickering & Gray, 1999). An early follower of Gray's motivational approach was Fowles (1987), while more recently a similar theme is to be found in the work of Tellegen and his colleagues (Watson, Wiese, Vaidya, & Tellegan, 1999) and in the Depue theory, already referred to.

An advantage of the motivational element introduced into some of these theories is that it provides a useful conceptual bridge between the descriptive dimensions proposed and their putative biological mechanisms. So it becomes easier to envisage how affect laden traits (and states) can drive, say, impulsive acts which result in poor decision making which in turn, in deviance, can translate into behaviors like drug abuse, eating disorders, or self-harm. Another benefit is for advancing the neuropsychology. Thus, continuing our example of impulsivity, the likelihood that frontal and frontolimbic circuitry forms a physiological basis for that trait provides a good rationale for using laboratory paradigms such as executive function and decision making as tools for closing the gap between nervous system differences and variations in motivationally-related personality variations.

This brings us indirectly to what some would say is a serious limitation of the theories under review: that they are theories, not of *personality*, but merely of temperament, capable of explaining only primitive, biologically-based features of human variation. It must be conceded that despite claims to the contrary, notably by Eysenck himself, theories of the kind that he spawned do not capture the full range of psychological attributes that most people would understand as "personality." Among the theorists cited here, Cloninger has been the only one to explicitly recognize the fact and to incorporate it into his model. He has done so by adding to his four temperament dimensions three character dimensions, representing socially learned cognitive sets that help shape temperamental dispositions into a fully formed personality habit structure. The utility of doing so is illustrated by an example that Cloninger himself gives (Cloninger, Przybeck, Svrakic, & Wetzel, 1994). He asks us to compare two individuals with identical degrees of low harm avoidance and high novelty seeking, but differing on the character forming dimensions of Cooperativeness and Self-directedness; one of the two people, Cloninger points out, might develop an impulse disorder although the other might become a daring explorer or a successful businessman. The point being made here is a fairly obvious one, yet it is surprising how rarely biological "temperament" (*sic!*) theorists incorporate the idea into their thinking. Mostly their writings give the impression that individuals are somehow passive victims of their physiology; thus carrying across into the domain of normal personality the reductionism which, as noted earlier, is a cause for concern in explanations of many abnormal behaviors.

However, so long as, like Cloninger, we recognize the true nature of temperament theories and temperament constructs and are prepared to work within their limitations, the narrow focus of the models can be seen as one of their strengths. Their major advantage could be said to stem from precisely those features which critics of the biological approach to personality find wanting. The low-level nature of temperament, conceptually and physiologically, means that *this* aspect of personality at least should be fairly manageable to study; the sources of variation to be revealed relatively few in number and easy to agree upon; and their neurobiology reasonably accessible. In fact, as discussed above, we already know these things to be the case. True, temperament research is still in a somewhat inchoate state, but there are definite signs of a sensible picture beginning to emerge.

Two particular kinds of evidence have contributed to this progress—at the same time as reminding us of the rudimentary nature of "temperament" as compared with "personality." One comes from the finding that much of what can be described as temperamental variation in humans can also be recognized in other animals. Expanding on Pavlov's early observations—from which, after all, the modern theories originated—a great deal of research since then has confirmed individual differences ascribable to temperament in a wide range of nonhuman species, from fish to chimpanzees (Gosling, 2001).

This phylogenetic dimension is duplicated in the ontogenesis of temperament, whereby individual differences in emotional "style" can be observed in children from a very early age. These variations have traditionally been studied under the heading of "temperament," in recognition of the fact that the characteristics studied are fairly uncomplicated and quite biologically based, probably with a strong genetic component. Early pioneers in the area, notably Thomas and Chess (1977) and Buss and Plomin (1984), laid down a solid foundation of evidence suggesting that precursors of some of the adult dimensions of personality (e.g., Neuroticism) are to be found in children. Interestingly, adult theorists themselves have traditionally paid little attention to this work, and developmental psychologists have been slow to make the connection with the adult personality literature. However, in recent years there has been much more convergence between the two streams of research, including (and partly inspired by) the relevance to psychopathology (see Shiner (2005) for a review). An important question here is the degree to which there is overlap—and by implication developmental continuity-between the two domains.

One approach to this has been to see how far descriptors used to characterize temperament differences in infancy and childhood map onto dimensions contained within the adult personality theories. In recent work, at least, a favored template here has been the so-called "Big Five," where a useful similarity of adult and childhood constructs has been reported (Mervielde, De Clercq, De Fruyt, & Van Leeuwen, 2005; Shafer, 2001). It has to be said that the choice of Five-Factor theory in such research does seem rather surprising; however, given all of the theories available, it is the one that has been least developed from a *biological* point of view. Admittedly its two important dimensions, Extraversion and Neuroticism, are highly correlated with similar dimensions in other more biological-based models; and so some extrapolation should be possible. But those workers who have opted for the Big Five do seem to have passed up an opportunity to exploit what could be a more seamless connection between ideas and empirical evidence about the neurobiology of, respectively, adult personality and childhood temperament.

The other important facet of the child/adult overlap in temperament and personality is longitudinal, addressing the continuity and stability of traits across the life span. Evidence of such an effect was demonstrated in early studies of the Emotionality-Activity-Sociability (EAS) triad developed by Buss and Plomin (1984); and research since then, using a variety of measures, has confirmed that there is indeed a significant degree of continuity from childhood through adolescence to adulthood for some personality/temperamental traits (see Roberts & DelVecchio (2000) for a review and meta-analysis). Some of the data lending weight to this conclusion has come from the longitudinal "Dunedin study," referred to earlier (Caspi et al., 2003; Caspi & Silva, 1995; Caspi, Roberts, & Shiner, 2005). That project has also helped with a further question, relevant in the present context, by showing that early temperament can predict certain kinds of later *abnormal* functioning, such as antisocial behavior and mood disorder (Caspi, 2000). The latter evidence dovetails well with the molecular genetic analyses of depression emanating from the same data source, cited in a previous section.

The separation of "temperament" from "personality" therefore proves to be an important distinction for clarifying some of the issues being considered here, emphasizing where the strengths as well as the limitations lie in current theories of individual differences, both normal and abnormal. Temperament merely forms the rough blueprint of tendencies and impulses from which the final product emerges as a fully formed personality. In this sense temperament could be said to be "neutral" with respect to its ultimate expression in adulthood behavior; for example, whether the latter is to be judged healthy or pathological. Here we might recall Cloninger's example about how quite differently adjusted personalities can develop from similar temperamental profiles. And join this to the now self-evident fact, recognized by almost all writers in the area, that personality is always the consequence of genetic/environmental interactions occurring throughout life. Having said that, we might still ask—Cloninger notwithstanding and reminiscent of Foulds' idea of deviant traits—if some temperamental characteristics can be so powerful that they effectively swamp environmental influences and virtually *become* the personality of some persistently maladjusted individuals.[3] Potentially one of the best examples is the primary psychopath.

First described by Cleckley (1976), primary psychopathy is the paradigm case of a form of personality deviance which can find expression in both seriously maladaptive antisocial-disorder or in behavior that is socially effective and sometimes grudgingly admired, though also frequently disliked, by others. (Cleckley writes, convincingly, of the psychopath as businessman, gentlemen, scientist, physician, and psychiatrist—to which, surely, he should have added politician!) In the literature on primary psychopathy

---

[3]We come close here to the dilemma facing the *DSM-V* task force about the Axis I/Axis II distinction: that between chronic illness and long-standing maladaptive personality traits (Widiger, 2003).

there is a sense of a personality so extreme that it is effectively untouched by the world. Of course, this cannot be literally true, but it might be relatively so for some of the basic key tendencies that define primary psychopathy, such as narcissistic and callous-emotional traits, coupled to thoughtless risk-taking. It appears that these tendencies have higher heritability than most other personality characteristics (see Viding, 2004). In this case perhaps family and other social influences act more than usual simply to provide a content and context to the expression of temperamental tendencies that are otherwise difficult to modify. The rich spoilt kid might then grow up with a talent for pulling off dubious business deals, while the unprivileged and emotionally deprived turn to more manifest criminality. But in both cases the basic personality style remains intact.

Perhaps partly because of this element of incorrigibility, primary psychopathy, among the personality disorders, has received the most attention from biologically-orientated investigators. The work was pioneered by Hare and his colleagues who, in a research program spreading over many years, have proposed increasingly sophisticated explanations. Early psychophysiological accounts (summarized by Hare [1986]) drew upon such notions as "arousal deficiency," "poor anticipation of punishment," and "deficient sensory gating." These are still valid as explanations of certain features of psychopathic behavior, but with the availability of new technologies, especially brain-imaging, the focus has now shifted to a more direct investigation of the neural circuitry involved. There is now good evidence to support what Kiehl (in press) calls the "paralimbic hypothesis," *viz.* that psychopaths have some inherent abnormality in a brain circuit implicating the limbic system and parts of the temporal and frontal lobes. This explanation would account well for a range of experimental data demonstrating deficiencies in two areas of neurocognition that underpin salient features of psychopathic behavior: affective processing (Blair et al., 1995; Kiehl et al., 2001) and decision making (Mitchell, Colledge, Leonard, & Blair, 2002). Both of these effects have also been shown in children with psychopathic tendencies (Blair, Colledge, & Mitchell, 2001; Blair, Colledge, Murray, & Mitchell, 2001).

Considering the preceding explanation of the biology of psychopathy it is interesting that, in constructing his argument for the paralimbic hypothesis, Kiehl draws quite heavily on evidence showing that damage to areas of the brain he is implicating can bring about a clinical picture reminiscent of psychologically diagnosed primary psychopathy. However, he is cautious about drawing the conclusion that the latter must therefore involve some structural abnormality; indeed his own neuroimaging data apparently suggest that it does not. The point is worth making because it picks up on a remark made earlier in this chapter about the dangers of extrapolating to functional disorders by analogy with cases of brain injury.

In primary psychopathy—and other personality disorders—we see the clearest instances of dimensionality occurring along a pathway of normal individual differences, even though in maladaptive form the temperamental variation involved, can be so extreme as to contribute to some noticeable discontinuity in behavior. The other meaning of dimensionality introduced here is somewhat different and draws upon the notion of personality/temperament as having the dual function of healthy variation and predisposition to the clinical symptoms of illnesses of the Axis I type. The model is reasonably uncontroversial when applied to mild psychological illness and to the more familiar personality dimensions; for example, anxiety/neuroticism and anxiety disorder. It is more contentious when applied to the serious, psychotic disorders, an issue discussed in the following section.

## Dimensionality of Psychosis

As noted in a previous section, the received wisdom among biologically orientated psychiatrists and abnormal psychologists is that the psychotic illnesses are "broken brain" disorders of a neurological disease type; which effectively means that they can have no true representation in healthy personality functioning. This not to imply that there is no dimensionality; it can still be argued that, like other medical conditions, psychoses can occur as *formes frustes*, or mild variants of the full-blown illnesses. However, the assumption is always that the cause lies in some CNS *defect*, which like all biological processes, can vary in degree.

There has been little serious challenge to this idea from within the kinds of biological/dimensional theories discussed here, though an exception, again, was Eysenck. From the very beginning—inspired by Kretschmer's (1925) notion of schizothymia-cyclothymia as a temperament continuum—Eysenck (1952) proposed "psychoticism" as a third dimension of personality: It was considered to have the same relation to clinical psychosis as neuroticism does to neurosis. Although, the general status of the psychoticism dimension was made plain early on, it was not until the mid-1970s onwards that Eysenck made a serious attempt to weave it properly into the framework of his theory (Eysenck & Eysenck, 1976). It has to be said that the exercise was something of a flop. That stems from the way Eysenck conceptualized psychotic traits, as primarily to do with impulsiveness, aggressiveness, and lack of empathy; a fact strongly reflected in the items in his psychoticism (P) scale (Eysenck & Eysenck, 1991). Eysenck was regularly criticized for this interpretation of "psychoticism" (Claridge, 1981, 1983, 1997b), but continued to insist on its basic correctness (Eysenck, 1992). Meanwhile others preferred to accept what seemed ecologically more valid: that psychoticism, as defined by the P-scale, had little to do with psychosis and could be better aligned with psychopathy and antisocial personality. This has been especially true of Zuckerman (1993) who has explicitly incorporated it into his awkwardly named dimension, P-Impulsive Unsocialised Sensation Seeking (P-ImpUSS).

Some might therefore be tempted to dismiss Eysenck's contribution to a debate about psychotic disorders as too idiosyncratic to be taken seriously. However two important themes in his writings need to be borne in mind; in addition, that is central to his thesis about there being genuine dimensionality in psychosis. One was his proposition that there is a relationship—albeit given too much prominence in his own theory—between psychosis and personality disorder. The other concerns Eysenck's embracing of a unitary theory of psychosis, as against the conventional view of schizophrenia and bipolar illness as etiologically distinct disorders. Both of these points will be touched upon later. First, however, it is necessary to examine the general issue of dimensionality.

Debate about that has mostly been carried on, not in the personality arena *per se*, but in the so-called "schizotypy literature." It has therefore mostly focused on the schizophrenias, rather than psychosis in general, and has been concerned with issues such as vulnerability to that group of disorders and the nature of the schizophrenia spectrum. Coined originally by the psychoanalyst Rado (1953), the concept of schizo-typy was subsequently taken up and is mostly associated with the name of Paul Meehl (1962, 1990). His imaginative theorizing about schizophrenia inspired a vigorous school of researchers to develop questionnaire measures of schizotypy, laboratory procedures for examining it experimentally, and ways of exploring it as a paradigm for schizophrenia risk (Raine, Lencz, & Mednick, 1994; *Schizophrenia Research*, special issue, 2002).

Over the past decade and a half, two differing opinions have imperceptibly emerged about the interpretation of schizotypy as a construct for understanding the dimensionality of schizophrenia. One, more personality based, is in the Eysenckian tradition, just described (see also Claridge, 1997a). The other, favored by the Meehl school, is predicated on the idea of schizotypy as deficit. Figure 6.1 compares these two perspectives diagrammatically, distinguishing between quasi-dimensional and fully dimensional models. The former, although recognizing dimensionality as part of the schizophrenia spectrum, does not extend this into the healthy domain. Instead "normal" schizotypy is perceived as compensation for, and SPD as a *forme fruste*, of the deficit (or deficits) assumed to underlie schizophrenia itself. In contrast, the fully dimensional model takes an open stance on schizotypy, regarding it as neutral with respect to possible outcome, which can be healthy or pathological depending on other moderating effects. The nature of its biology is assumed to follow principles established for other personality dimensions; as implied earlier, anxiety/neuroticism and anxiety disorders make a good analogy.

Table 6.1 lists points of comparison between these two models of schizotypy. Some have already been mentioned, but others deserve further comment. One concerns the psychometric measurement of schizotypy and, allied to that, the underlying assumptions on which that is based. The hub of the issue is the correctness or otherwise of Meehl's view of schizotypy as a discrete taxon and therefore the appropriateness of using taxonometric methods to determine whether an individual does or does not fall within the target group. Here questionnaires made up of strongly worded items of a clinical or semiclinical nature are likely to have the best discriminating power. An example is the commonly used Perceptual Aberration scale (Chapman, Chapman, & Raulin, 1978); as contrasted with, say, the Unusual Experiences scale from the *Oxford-Liverpool Inventory of Feelings and Experiences* (O–LIFE), a questionnaire that was deliberately designed to measure more normally distributed traits in the general population (Mason, Claridge, & Jackson, 1995; Mason & Claridge, in press).

Followers of the quasi-dimensional model consistently argue that taxonometric analyses of questionnaire data support Meehl's view of schizotypy. However, the evidence is not unequivocal, as a recently completed study demonstrated (Haslam, Williams, Rawlings, & Claridge, unpublished)[4]. The authors, who had the advantage of a very large sample of healthy subjects, concluded that important aspects of schizotypy showed no sign of taxonicity, but conformed more to a conventional continuous distribution. They argued that previous claims for the taxon model were based on less than optimal sample sizes for the methods used and skewed questionnaire data (which naturally favor a dichotomous solution). However, they conceded that more evidence of genuine taxonicity is found where subjects come from special groups of individuals already selected as at high risk for schizophrenia (Erlenmeyer-Kimling, Golden, & Cornblatt, 1989; Tyrka,

---

[4]Readers who wish further details of this study should contact Dr. Nick Haslam.

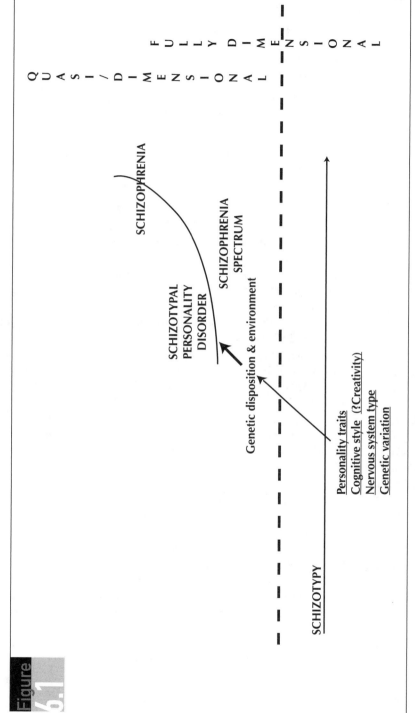

Figure 6.1

Diagrammatic illustration of quasi and fully dimensional models of schizotypy.

| Table 6.1 | Comparison of main features of quasi and fully dimensional models of schizotypy |  |
|---|---|---|
| **Quasi-Dimensional Model** |  | **Fully Dimensional Model** |
| *Forme fruste* of disease | View of Schizotypy | Personality variation |
| Strong (clinical) items | Questionnaire Measurement | More dilute items |
| Discrete taxon | Psychometric Assumptions | Normally distributed trait |
| Compare extreme groups | Experimental Investigation | Correlational analysis |
| CNS deficit | Biological Theory | "Nervous type" |
| Single gene | Genetic Influence | Multigenic |
| Impossible idea | Healthy Form? | Yes |

Haslam, & Cannon, 1995). It is possible, therefore, that at the *descriptive* level, at least, neither the quasi nor the fully dimensional model is entirely accurate; that both are valid, depending on the manner in or degree to which schizotypy is being expressed. Even fully dimensional theory would predict signs of discontinuity (and therefore taxonicity) among persons presumed to be toward the far end of the schizotypy dimension and displaying minimal symptoms of disorder.

Relative preference for the quasi or the fully dimensional model has implications for the way schizotypy differences are examined in the laboratory among nonclinical participants; for example, by comparing their questionnaire scores against some experimental paradigm. As noted in Table 6.1, quasi theorists, almost as a matter of necessity, are forced to identify extremely high questionnaire scorers in order to maximize the possibility that the individuals chosen for study fall within the schizotypy taxon. This is not relevant to the fully dimensional approach, however, because the underlying determinants—biological or otherwise—of the measure in question are always assumed to have a continuous property, making correlational analysis quite appropriate. Space does not permit a detailing of evidence on either side of this methodological point. Suffice it to say that there is plenty of evidence supporting the use of a bivariate approach to the analysis of laboratory data in schizotypy research (see Claridge, 1997a).

The most far-reaching difference, philosophically, between the two models concerns the notion of schizotypy as a potentially healthy personality dimension. For followers of Meehl that is logically impossible; "healthy" schizotypy can only exist as a phenocopy or as result of favorable circumstances preventing the individual decompensating into a schizophrenic state. By contrast, the possibility of genuinely healthy schizotypy is intrinsic to the fully dimensional model. The evidence strongly favors the latter. A high degree of measured schizotypy—without evidence of psychopathology, either overt or masked— has been observed in individuals engaged in a wide range of unusual (or "alternative") activities and belief systems. This has included profound spiritual experiences of a formally "psychotic" quality (Jackson, 1997); out-of-the-body experiences (McCreery & Claridge, 1996); New Age belief (Day & Peters, 1999; Farias, Claridge, & Lalljee, 2005); paranormal belief (Goulding, 2004); and enhanced creativity (Nettle, 2001; *Bulletin of Psychology and the Arts*, special issue, 2000; *Creativity Research Journal*, special issue, 2000; for a review also see Brod, 1997). The creativity connection has been the most widely researched and has offered the strongest support against the argument of schizotypy as neurocognitive deficit; for on occasions, and in the presence of true genius, quite the opposite must be case.[5]

Finally from Table 6.1 there is the question of the genetics of schizotypy. Logically underpinning the taxonomic view was Meehl's proposal for a single gene accounting for "schizotaxia," the discrete neurocognitive deficit presumed responsible for the "schizophrenic phenotype" (schizotype). In fact, single gene explanations of schizophrenia have long been discounted in favor of polygenic theories (e.g., Gottesman & Shields, 1982, and continue to be so Weinberger, 2002). As the latter author points out:

> An argument can be made that schizophrenia is not a genetic illness per se, but a varying combination of component heritable traits (and genes) that comprise susceptibility and that interact with each other, with modifying alleles, and with the environment to produce the complex clinical phenotype.

Admittedly there is something of the magician's sleight of hand in this statement, though in our present state of knowledge it probably represents the reality. But it might also offer another point of reconciliation between the quasi and fully dimensional viewpoints. As in the psychometric domain, perhaps both are true in their own way. Thus, even though the overall picture turns out to be multigenic, particular genes might eventually be found that code for quite specific, especially pathognomic, aspects of schizophrenia risk, or schizotypy. Here the heterogeneous nature of the latter construct is relevant. Although often referred to under a single, shorthand label, it is now well established that "schizotypy" can be deconstructed into several components (Vollema & Hoijtink, 2000; Vollema & van den Bosch, 1995). The usual consensus is that there are three subfactors corresponding to "positive schizotypy" (unusual beliefs and experiences), "negative schizotypy" (anhedonia), and "cognitive disorganization." Some biometrical analysis suggests that these components, though overlapping, might have different genetic architectures (Linney, Murray, Peters, MacDonald, & Rijsdijk, 2003). Further to this, there is a varied range of evidence indicating that it is the negative, anhedonic features that might be particularly "lethal" in defining pathological rather than healthy outcomes for high schizotypes. Thus, it is generally the case that where the outcome is happy it is always the positive, and rarely the negative, component of schizotypy that is raised in subjects. This was emphasized, for example, by McCreery and Claridge (1995) who showed that one aspect of anhedonia—physical anhedonia—was actually significantly *lower* than controls in their cases of out-of-the-body-experience. It is therefore consistent that, in long-term follow-up of the Chapman psychosis-proneness scales in a general population sample, Kwapil (1998) found that it was anhedonia—in this case social anhedonia—that best predicted later schizophrenia-spectrum disorders. Then, in a more clinical context, Cardno, Thomas, & McGuffin (2002) showed that pervasive *negative* symptoms among schizophrenics were the best predictors of risk of schizophrenia in their biological

---

[5]Here it is wrily interesting to note a comment by Bentall (2003), a clinical cognitive behaviorist and therefore someone who should presumably be on the fully dimensional side of the fence. Discussing theories of schizotypy, he notes that the 'revised biomedical model'—by which he explicitly means the fully dimensional theory as described here—is threatened by the madness/genius connection. It seems that in his rush to avoid reference to anything biological in schizophrenia he has missed the point!

relatives. In a complementary paper addressing the heritability of Schneiderian first-rank symptoms, the same group of authors concluded that the latter were unlikely to be a good candidate marker for genetic liability to schizophrenia (Cardno, Sham, Farmer, Murray, & McGuffin, 2002). Drawing these observations together, one could reach the following conclusion: that, though the tendency to have bizarre experiences and formulate strange ideas might be *necessary* for a clinical psychosis to occur, it is by no means a *sufficient* condition because it is clear that so-called "positive symptoms" can occur as a normal part of healthy cognition. Whether they are labeled as clinically significant would then depend on sociocultural and other contextual factors, as well their content, manageability by the person, and the accompanying mood.

Returning to the structure of schizotypy, although a three-factor solution is normally cited in most of the current schizotypy literature, four components were actually identified in the large-scale Oxford–Liverpool analyses that led to the O–LIFE questionnaire referred to earlier (Bentall, Claridge, & Slade, 1989; Claridge et al., 1996). This fourth factor was eventually named "Impulsive Nonconformity," but it has generally been dismissed by others as outside the domain of interest of schizotypy research (e.g., Pickering, 2004). The reason generally given is that the factor loads on the Eysenck P-scale which, as noted earlier, is now largely sidelined more as a measure of antisocial personality. However, the critics fail to mention two points: One is that the Impulsive Nonconformity factor was also defined by scales other than the P-scale; *viz.* borderline personality and, importantly, hypomania.[6] Secondly, in addition to helping to define Impulsive Nonconformity these other scales are also loaded on the more "regular" components of schizotypy, especially the positive schizotypy factor of Unusual Experiences; to a very significant degree in the case of hypomania. In other words, there was much less separation than implied between the different facets of "schizotypy" sampled. Looked at from a purely pragmatic viewpoint, the reason four factors emerged from the Oxford–Liverpool analyses—rather than the three (or even two) reported elsewhere—is merely that the investigators chose to include a large number and a broad range of measures that were considered relevant to the topic.

Dismissing "Impulsive Nonconformity" (or equivalents of it) as irrelevant to the issue of dimensionality in serious mental disorder is therefore probably unwise and forecloses prematurely on another important question: the validity of a unitary model of psychosis. As Berrios (1995) notes, *Einheitpsychose* theory has a long history in psychiatry and in past decades has resurfaced from time to time in the writings of clinicians (e.g., Crow, 1986) wishing to challenge the traditional (Kraepelinian) model of distinct schizophrenic and manic-depressive (bipolar) disorders. In recent years the theory has emerged as a very real alternative, bolstered by evidence from a number of sources. One is simply the overlap of clinical features—actually long commented upon (Kendell & Brockington, 1980) and reflected in the diagnostic category of schizo-affective disorder. Another is genetic and the failure to discover straightforward segregation of susceptibility for schizophrenic and bipolar disorder (Berrettini, 2003; Maier, Rietschel, Lichtermann, & Wildenauer, 1999). The degree of nonspecificity implied there is supported by the observation that bipolar patients resemble schizophrenics and schizotypal individuals when tested on experimental procedures based on paradigms

---

[6]Notably, in an analysis of *items* (rather than scales) Hay and his colleagues also reported a four-factor solution, which similarly included a component they labeled Hypomania-Impulsive Nonconformity (Hay et al., 2001).

often considered crucial to theories about the biology of schizophrenia risk; e.g., sensory gating differences (Perry, Minassian, Feifel, & Braff, 2001). There is also convergence between the two disorders at the questionnaire level. Bipolars score highly on scales ostensibly designed to measure schizotypy (Heron et al., 2003); while, in another of the reports on the long-term follow-up of the Chapman scales referred to above, it appeared that where Magical Ideation (together with Social Anhedonia) could predict later psychosis, this was equally like to be bipolar disorder as schizophrenia (Kwapil, Miller, Zinser, Chapman, & Chapman, 1997).

Can we conclude, then, that the term "schizotypy" is now out of time and would be better replaced by "psychoticism?" The disadvantage (and irony) of doing so is that the latter is strongly associated with Eysenck's use of the descriptor for what turns out to be only a small part of the general domain of personality differences that relate to psychosis. An alternative would be "psychosis-proneness," a label which the Chapman's—originators of the largest number of questionnaires in this area—have used for many years. However named, a broader construct would help to refresh some thinking currently constrained by the traditional nosology of psychotic disorders and so open up for debate and scientific enquiry some issues that remain awkwardly unresolved. For example, harking back to earlier sections of this chapter, there is the association between and among the Axis I and Axis II disorders and how that might be dealt with in future editions of the *DSM*. A particular instance that we mentioned, and which we should return to briefly before closing this section, is the curious status of BPD. Despite the history of the borderline construct—as in some way forming part of the psychosis spectrum—investigators have largely retreated from that position, reflecting the placement of BPD in Axis II as a Cluster B disorder.

The temperamental underpinnings of bipolar disorder have nevertheless been the subject of some debate (Barrantes, Colon, & Claridge, 2002). This has included discussion of a possible link between BPD and bipolar disorder (Akiskal, 1996), though it now looks as though a more likely working model would be a bipolar spectrum that includes some aspects of BPD, but which also takes in obvious features like cyclothymia (Perugi & Akiskal, 2002). However when such a spectrum comes to be defined there is a great deal to be done to catch up on work on the schizophrenia spectrum. A vast effort has gone into laboratory studies of the latter, whereas an equivalent bipolar spectrum has scarcely been explored experimentally. Of course, the idea of a bipolar spectrum is not predicated on a view of it as part of a unitary psychosis; or, at a personality level, as a component of "psychoticism," or, indeed as implicating BPD characteristics as currently defined. But even considered as a stand-alone topic—as personality disorder—"borderline" has received almost no attention from experimentalists: just a handful of studies, compared with the massive interest generated by "schizotypy." It would be interesting to know the reasons for this neglect: whether ideological differences within psychiatry, a distaste for the topic among abnormal psychologists, or merely the whims of fashion.

# Final Remarks

It is tempting to close this chapter by summarizing the themes outlined in the previous sections and discuss how these have changed in the 10 years, since I last reviewed the topic. However, I leave readers to draw their own conclusions, inviting them to do so by consulting the present revision alongside the earlier version written a decade ago. From an author's point of view—and hopefully the reader's—it is more instructive to arrange the conclusions around a different question: how might "psychobiological models and issues" look after another 10 years?

Given the exponential growth in science it is safe to predict that on the biological side the field will be virtually unrecognizable. The genetic architecture of temperament and its associated disorders will have been pretty well worked out, as will the brain systems that mediate individual differences in these two domains. On the nonclinical side of the topic, this exercise will no doubt help and be helped by agreement being reached on what the basic dimensions of temperament are, allowing researchers to escape the confusion currently generated by having theoretical models where half overlapping constructs sometimes have the same, and sometimes a different, name. Differential psychologists should also by then have agreed that Cloninger is right to distinguish temperament from character and decided that the former is where the real strength of their biological modeling lies. As a result, the theories themselves could assume a quality that is more maturely psychobiological than they look at present. Certainly models will need to be devised that help us understand in detail—rather than, as now, in broad generalizations—how different personalities emerge from the interaction between temperamental traits and life experience. Here a vital contribution will come from an increased sharing of data and ideas with developmental psychologists looking at what are the same issues from a longitudinal perspective. This should help to answer some interesting questions. What nongenetic factors influence temperament itself? And what limits does temperament place on the direction in which personalities can develop? Can an individual very high in fearfulness ever properly swap places in the relaxation stakes with his or her counterpart at the other end of that biological dimension? There could here be implications for the treatment of people with extreme varieties of temperament.

In 10 years psychiatry will surely have finally taken dimensionality on board, especially for the personality disorders; though it is conceivable that these will have disappeared altogether as a separate diagnostic axis in a fifth revision of the *DSM*. This will presumably be temporary, because one of the most enduring ideas on the boundary between psychology and psychiatry is that personality can have both healthy and unhealthy expression—and that this can sometimes be understood without recourse to symptom-based explanations. Here the notion of deviant traits remains a useful idea as a way of conceptualizing extreme, maladaptive patterns of behavior and motivations that remain stable throughout life. The distinction between deviant traits and symptoms is also important in highlighting the contribution that personality (or temperament) makes to clinical, Axis I, illnesses; as intrinsic factors of predisposition which may or may not translate into disorder. It should eventually be possible to discover more exactly the rules that determine why vulnerability translates into illness or, alternatively, is masked by a cloak of uneasy coping—or is even turned to good use in the developing personality—as, say, the temperamentally black humored depressive becomes a successful comedian.

Applying this model of alternative healthy or unhealthy outcome to the *serious* mental disorders, like schizophrenia, presents a special problem though. Or does it? Un-apologetically advocating what was called here a fully dimensional model of psychosis, it would be absurdly self-serving to venture a guess about how that particular debate will work itself through. It is safer to say: "watch this space!" But irrespective of the niceties of argument about the nature of schizotypy—or, as I would now prefer to call it, psychoticism or, with the Chapmans, psychosis-proneness—there is a serious issue that will need to be confronted about the psychotic disorders. Currently biological psychiatry is in an upbeat mood about its ability to explain schizophrenia, and one can be confident that over the next decade this optimism will not diminish. Certainly much more will be discovered about the neurobiology, including the genetics, of psychosis; and if, among the issues discussed here, the separation of schizophrenia from bipolar disorder has by then started to look really shaky, or even disappeared, it will be largely because of research in those areas. But—and this is a hope rather than a prediction—maybe greater understanding of the biology will finally put to rest the crude analogy with dementing neurological disease. By the same token, cognitive behavior therapists interested in psychotic disorder will hopefully have seen that there are ways of interpreting the biology that poses no threat to their preference for psychological analysis (and treatment).

As a corollary to the preceding, progress will be expected in the ability to detect from prognostic signs and predisposing traits those likely to develop a psychological disorder, what that disorder might be, and what factors determine breakdown into illness. This will be an invaluable practical application to a clinical problem of knowledge lying at the interface between normal and abnormal personality research. Such high-risk strategies have a long history in psychiatry and abnormal psychology, especially in relation to schizophrenia (for a compilation of early work see Watt, Anthony, Wynne, & Rolf, 1984). It would be a pity, however, if the endeavor became too dominated by a focus on pathological outcomes. We already know that even for serious disorders and even in individuals at maximum risk actual illness is the exception rather than the rule; most people survive their vulnerability. It would be a pity, therefore, if the opportunity were missed to widen the scope of research and more deliberately set out to discover the various factors that protect those at risk from breakdown, or even encourage a healthy expression of apparently deviant traits; work, that is, along the lines presaged by Anthony & Cohler (1987) in their landmark set of readings on so-called "invulnerable children."

Finally, although some contemporary neuroscientists would no doubt vehemently disagree, one topic theme which, in my view, will remain virtually unchanged is the philosophical one: the implications of the material discussed here for understanding mind/brain relationships. It will be a mistake to fall further and further into the common trap of confusing correlation for cause as data pour daily out of genetics, neurochemical, and neuroimaging laboratories, demonstrating relationships between brain process and every conceivable psychological state, trait, or propensity. (My current favorite is the neurobiology of lust and romantic attachment, subtitled "brain systems for love"! [Fisher, Aron, Mashek, Li, & Brown, 2002]) The caveats, presented near the beginning of this chapter, about the dangers of too ready a slide into such reductionism and biological determinism will almost certainly last the next decade—and probably beyond.

## REFERENCES

Akiskal, H. S. (1996). The prevalent clinical spectrum of bipolar disorders beyond DSM-III. *Journal of Clinical Psychopharmacology, 16*(Suppl 1), 4–14.

American Psychiatric Association. (1994). *Diagnostic and statistical manual of mental disorders* (4th ed., pp. 633–634). Washington, DC: American Psychiatric Press.

American Psychiatric Association. (2000). *Diagnostic and statistical manual of mental disorders* (4th ed., text revision). Washington, DC: American Psychiatric Press.

Andreasen, N. (1984). *The broken brain: The biological revolution in psychiatry*. New York: Harper & Row.

Anthony, E. J., & Cohler, B. J. (Eds). (1987). *The invulnerable child*. New York: Guilford Press.

Barrantes, N., Colon, F., & Claridge, G. (2002). Temperament and personality in bipolar affective disorders. In E. Vieta (Ed.), *Bipolar disorders: Clinical and therapeutic progress* (pp. 217–242). Madrid: Panamericana.

Bentall, R. P. (2003). *Madness explained*. London: Allen Lane.

Bentall, R. P., Claridge, G., & Slade, P. (1989). The multidimensional nature of schizotypal traits: A factor analytic study with normal subjects. *British Journal of Clinical Psychology, 28*, 363–375.

Berman, S., Ozkaragoz, Y., Young, R. McD., & Noble. E. P. (2002). D2 dopamine receptor gene polymorphism discriminates two kinds of novelty seeking. *Personality and Individual Differences, 33*, 867–882.

Berrettini, W. H. (2003). Evidence for shared susceptibility in bipolar disorder and schizophrenia. *American Journal of Medical Genetics, 123C*, 59–64.

Berrios, G. E. (1995). Conceptual problems in diagnosing schizophrenic disorders. In J. A. Den Boer, H. G. M. Westenberg, & H. M. van Praag (Eds.), *Advances in the neurobiology of schizophrenia*. Chichester, UK: Wiley.

Berrios, G. E., & Marková, I. S. (2002a). Conceptual issues. In H. D'haenen, J. A. den Boer, & P. Willner (Eds.), *Biological psychiatry*. New York: Wiley.

Berrios, G. E., & Marková, I. S. (2002b). The concept of neuropsychiatry: A historical review. *Journal of Psychosomatic Research, 53*, 629–638.

Blair, R. J. R., Colledge, E., & Mitchell, D. G. V. (2001). Somatic markers and response reversal: Is there orbitofronal cortex dysfunction in boys with psychopathic tendencies? *Journal of Abnormal Child Psychology, 29*, 499–511.

Blair, R. J. R., Colledge, E., Murray, L., & Mitchell, D. G. V. (2001). A selective impairment in the processing of sad and fearful expression in children with psychopathic tendencies. *Journal of Abnormal Child Psychology, 29*, 491–498.

Blair, R. J. R., Sellars, C., Strickland, I., Clark, F., Williams, A. O., Smith, M., & Jones, L. (1995). Emotion attributions in the psychopath. *Personality and Individual Differences, 19*, 431–437.

Brod, J. H. (1997). Creativity and schizotypy. In G. Claridge (Ed.), *Schizotypy: Implications for illness and health* (pp. 274–298). Oxford: Oxford University Press.

Bulletin of Psychology and the Arts. (2000). *Special issue: Creativity and psychopathology. 1*(2).

Buss, A. H., & Plomin, R. (1984). *Temperament: Early developing personality traits*. Hillsdale, NJ Erlbaum.

Cardno, A. G., Sham, P. C., Farmer, A. E., Muray, R. M., & McGuffin, P. (2002). Heritability of Schneider's first-rank symptoms. *British Journal of Psychiatry, 180*, 35–38.

Cardno, A. G., Thomas, K., & McGuffin, P. (2002). Clinical variables and genetic loading for schizophrenia: Analysis of published Danish adoption study data. *Schizophrenia Bulletin, 28*, 393–399.

Caspi, A. (2000). The child is father of the man: Personality continuities from childhood to adulthood. *Journal of Personality and Social Psychology, 78*, 158–172.

Caspi, A., Harrington, H., Milne, B., Amell, J. W., Theodore, R. F., & Moffitt, T. E. (2003). Children's behavioral styles at age 3 are linked to their adult personality traits at age 26. *Journal of Personality, 71*, 495–513.

Caspi, A., Roberts, B. W., & Shiner, R. L. (2005). Personality development: Stability and change. *Annual Review of Psychology, 56*, 453–484.

Caspi, A., & Silva, P. A. (1995). Temperamental qualities at age three predict personality traits in young adulthood: Longitudinal evidence from a birth cohort. *Child Development, 66*, 486–498.

Caspi, A., Sudgen, K., Moffitt, T. E., Taylor, A., Craig, I. W., Harrington, H., McClay, J., Mill, J., Martin, J., Braithwaite, A., & Poulton, R. (2003). Influence of life stress on depression: Moderation by a polymorphism in the 5-HTT gene. *Science, 301*, 386–389.

Chapman, L. J., Chapman, J. P., & Raulin, M. L. (1978). Body image aberration in schizophrenia. *Journal of Abnormal Psychology, 87*, 399–407.

Claridge, G. (1967). *Personality and arousal*. Oxford: Pergamon.

Claridge, G. (1981). Psychoticism. In R. Lynn (Ed.), *Dimensions of personality. Papers in Honour of H. J. Eysenck* (pp. 364–387). Oxford: Pergamon Press.

Claridge, G. (1983). The Eysenck Psychoticism Scale. In J. N. Butcher, & C. D. Spielberger (Eds.), *Advances in personality assessment* (Vol. 2). Hillsdale, NJ: Erlbaum.

Claridge, G. (1995). *Origins of mental illness*. Cambridge, MA: Malor Books.

Claridge, G. (Ed.). (1997a). *Schizotypy: Implications for illness and health*. Oxford: Oxford University Press.

Claridge, G. (1997b). Eysenck's contribution to understanding psychopathology. In H. Nyborg (Ed.), *The scientific study of human nature. Tribute to Hans J Eysenck at eighty* (pp. 364–387). Oxford: Pergamon.

Claridge, G., & Davis, C. (2003). *Personality and psychological disorders*. London: Arnold.

Claridge, G., McCreery, C., Mason, O., Bentall, R., Boyle, G., Slade, P., & Popplewell, D. (1996). The factor structure of 'schizotypal' traits: A large replication study. *British Journal of Clinical Psychology, 35*, 103–115.

Cleckley, H. (1976). *The Mask of Sanity* (5th ed.). St. Louis, MO: The Mosby. Cloninger, C. R. (1998). The genetics and psychobiology of the seven-factor model of personality. In K. R. Silk (Ed.), *Biology of personality disorders*. Washington, DC: American Psychiatric Press.

Cloninger, C. R., Przybeck, T. R., Svrakic, D. M., & Wetzel, R. D. (1994). *The Temperament and Character Inventory (TCI): A guide to its development and use*. Washington, DC: Washington University Center for Psychobiology of Personality.

Cloninger, C. R., Svrakic, D. M., & Przybeck, T. R. (1993). A psychobiological model of temperament and character. *Archives of General Psychiatry, 50*, 975–990.

Conklin, H. M., & Iacono, W. G. (2003). At issue: Assessment of schizophrenia: Getting closer to the cause. *Schizophrenia Bulletin, 29*, 405–411.

Costa, P. T., Jr., & McCrae, R. R. (1992). Four ways five factors are basic. *Personality and Individual Differences, 13*, 653–665.

CreativityResearch Journal. (2000). *Special issue: Creativity and the schizophrenia spectrum, 13*(1).

Crow, T. J. (1986). The continuum of psychosis and its implication for the structure of the gene. *British Journal of Psychiatry, 149*, 419–429.

Day, D., & Peters, E. (1999). The incidence of schizotypy in new religious movements. *Personality and Individual Differences, 27*, 55–67.

Depue, R. A., & Collins, P. F. (1999). Neurobiology of the structure of personality: Dopamine, facilitation of incentive motivation, and extraversion. *Behavioral and Brain Sciences, 22*, 491–569.

Depue, R. A., & Lezenweger, M. (2001). A neurobehavioral dimensional model. In W. J. Livesley (Ed.), *Handbook of personality disorders: Theory, research, and treatment* (pp. 137–176). New York: Guilford Press.

Erlenmeyer-Kimling, L., Golden, R. R., & Cornblatt, B. A. (1989). A taxonometric analysis of cognitive and neuromotor variables in children at risk for schizophrenia. *Journal of Abnormal Psychology, 98*, 203–208.

Eysenck, H. J. (1947). *Dimensions of personality*. London: Routledge and Kegan Paul.

Eysenck, H. J. (1952). Schizothymia-cyclothymia as a dimension of personality. II. Experimental. *Journal of Personality, 20*, 345–384.

Eysenck, H. J. (1957). *Dynamics of anxiety and hysteria*. London: Routledge and Kegan Paul.

Eysenck, H. J. (1960). Classification and the problem of diagnosis. In H. J. Eysenck (Ed.), *Handbook of abnormal psychology* (pp. 1–31). London: Pitman.

Eysenck, H. J. (1967). *The biological basis of personality*. Springfield, IL: Charles C Thomas.

Eysenck, H. J. (1987). The definition of personality disorders and the criteria appropriate for their description. *Journal of Personality Disorders, 1*, 211–219.

Eysenck, H. J. (1992). The definition and measurement of psychoticism. *Personality and Individual Differences, 13*, 757–785.

Eysenck, H. J., & Eysenck, S. B. G. (1976). *Psychoticism as a dimension of personality*. London: Hodder & Stoughton.

Eysenck, H. J., & Eysenck, S. B. G. (1991). *Manual of the eysenck personality scales*. London: Hodder & Stoughton.

Farias, M., Claridge, G., & Lalljee, M. (2005). Personality and cognitive predictors of New Age practices and beliefs. *Personality and Individual Differences, 39*, 979–989.

Farmer, R. E., & Nelson-Gray, R. O. (2005). *Personality-guided Behavior Therapy*. American Psychological Association.

Fisher, H. E., Aron, A., Mashek, D., Li, H., & Brown, L. L. (2002). Defining the brain systems of lust, romantic attraction, and attachment. *Archives of Sexual Behavior, 31*, 413–419.

Foulds, G. A. (1965). *Personality and personal illness*. London: Tavistock.

Foulds, G. A. (1971). Personality deviance and personal symptomatology. *Psychological Medicine, 1*, 222–233.

Fowles, D. C. (1987). Application of a behavioral theory of motivation to the concepts of anxiety and impulsivity. *Journal of Research in Personality, 21*, 417–435.

Fulford, K. W. M., Broome, M., Stanghellini, G., & Thornton, T. (2005). Looking with both eyes open: Fact and value in psychiatric diagnosis. *World Psychiatry, 4*, 78–86.

George, A., & Soloff, P. H. (1986). Schizotypal symptoms in patients with Borderline Personality Disorder. *American Journal of Psychiatry, 143*, 212–215.

Gosling, S. D. (2001). From mice to men: What can we learn about personality from animal research? *Psychological Bulletin, 127*, 45–86.

Gottesman, I. I., & Shields, J. (1982). *Schizophrenia: The epigenetic puzzle*. Cambridge: Cambridge University Press.

Goulding, A. (2004). Schizotypy models in relation to subjective health and paranormal beliefs and experiences. *Personality and Individual Differences, 37*, 157–167.

Gray, J. A. (1981). A critique of Eysenck's theory of personality. In H. J. Eysenck (Ed.), *A model for personality* (pp. 246–276). Berlin: Springer-Verlag.

Hare, R. D. (1986). Twenty years of experience with the Cleckley psychopath. In W. H. Reid, D. Dorr, J. I. Walker, & J. W. Bonner III (Eds.), *Unmasking the psychopath*. New York: W.W. Norton.

Hare, R. D., Harpur, T. J., Hakstian, A. R., Forth, A. E., Hart, S. D., & Newman, J. P. (1990). The revised Psychopathy Checklist: Reliability and factor structure. *Psychological Assessment, 2*, 338–341.

Haslam, N., Williams, B., Rawlings, D., & Claridge, G. (2005). *The latent structure of schizotypy: A taxometric re-*. Unpublished manuscript available from Nick Haslam, Ph.D., Department of Psychology, University of Melbourne, Parkville, VIC 3010, Australia.

Hay, D. A., Martin, N. G., Foley, D., Treloar, S. A., Kirk, K. M., & Heath, A. C. (2001). Phenotypic and genetic analyses of a short measure of psychosis-proneness in a large-scale Australian twin study. *Twin Research, 4*, 30–40.

Heron, J., Jones, I., Williams, J., Owen, M. J., Craddock, N., & Jones, L. A. (2003). Self-reported schizotypy and bipolar disorder: Demonstration of a lack of specificity of the Kings Schizotypy Questionnaire. *Schizophrenia Research, 65*, 153–158.

Jackson, M. C. (1997). Benign schizotypy? The case of spiritual experience. In: G. Claridge (Ed.), *Schizotypy: Implications for illness and health* (pp. 227–250). Oxford: Oxford University Press.

Jackson, M. C., & Fulford, K. W. M. (2003). Psychosis good and bad: Values-based practice and the distinction between pathological and nonpathological forms of psychotic experience. *Philosophy, Psychiatry, & Psychology, 9*, 387–394.

Kendell, R. E., & Brockington, J. F. (1980). The identification of disease entities and the relationship between schizophrenia and affective psychosis. *British Journal of Psychiatry, 137*, 324–331.

Kiehl, K.A. (in press). A cognitive neuroscience perspective on psychopathy: Evidence for paralimbic system dysfunction. *Psychiatry Research*.

Kiehl, K. A., Smith, A. M., Hare, R. D., Mendrek, A., Forster, B. B., Brink, J., & Liddle, P. F. (2001). Limbic abnormalities in affective processing by criminal psychopaths as revealed by functional magnetic resonance imaging. *Biological Psychiatry, 50*, 677–684.

Kretschmer, E. (1925). *Physique and character* (Trans. W. J. H. Sprott). London: Kegan, Trench, & Trubner.

Kwapil, T. R. (1998). Social anhedonia as a predictor of the development of schizophrenia-spectrum disorders. *Journal of Abnormal Psychology, 107*, 558–565.

Kwapil, T. R., Miller, M. B., Zinser, M. C., Chapman, J., & Chapman, L. J. (1997). Magical Ideation and Social Anhedonia as predictors of psychosis proneness: A partial replication. *Journal of Abnormal Psychology, 106*, 491–495.

Laing, R. D. (1960). *The divided self*. London: Tavistock.

Linney, Y., Murray, R., Peters, E., MacDonald, A., & Rijsdijk, S. A. (2003). A quantitative genetic analysis of schizoptypal personality traits. *Psychological Medicine, 33*, 803–816.

Maier, W., Falkei, P., & Wagner, M. (1999). Schizophrenia spectrum disorders: A review. In M. Maj, & N. Sartorius (Eds.), *Schizophrenia*. New York: Wiley.

Maier, W., Rietschel, M., Lichtermann, D., & Wildenauer, D. B. (1999). Family and genetic studies on the relationship of schizophrenia to affective disorders. *European Archives of Psychiatry and Clinical Neuroscience, 249*(Suppl 4), 57–61.

Marinangeli, M. G., Butti, G., Scinto, A., Di Cicco, L., Petruzzi, C., Daneluzzo, E., & Rossi, A. (2000). Patterns of comorbidity among DSM-III-R personality disorders. *Psychopathology, 33*, 69–74.

Mason, O., & Claridge, G. (s2006), TheOxford-Liverpool Inventory of Feelings and Experiences (O-LIFE): Further description and extended norms.

Mason, O., Claridge, G., & Jackson, M. (1995). New scales for the assessment of schizotypy. *Personality and Individual Differences, 18*, 7–13.

McCreery, C., & Claridge, G. (1995). Out-of-the-Body experiences and personality. *Journal of the Society for Psychical Research, 60*, 129–148.

McCreery, C., & Claridge, G. (1996). A study of hallucination in normal subjects—I self-report data. *Personality and Individual Differences, 21*, 739–747.

Meehl, P. E. (1962). Schizotaxia, schizotypy, and schizophrenia. *American Psychologist, 17*, 827–838.

Meehl, P. E. (1990). Toward an integrated theory of schizotaxia, schizotypy, and schizophrenia. *Journal of Personality Disorders, 4*, 1–99.

Mervielde, I., De Clercq, B., De Fruyt, F., & Van Leeuwen, K. (2005). Temperament, personality, and developmental psychopathology as childhood antecedents of personality disorders. *Journal of Personality Disorders, 19*, 171–201.

Mitchell, D. G. V., Colledge, E., Leonard, A., & Blair, R. J. R. (2002). Risky decisions and response reversal: Is there evidence of orbitofrontal cortex dysfunction in psychopathic individuals? *Neuropsychologia, 40*, 2013–2022.

Nettle, D. (2001). *Strong imagination*. Oxford: Oxford University Press.

Parnas, J. (1994). The concept of borderline conditions: A critical comment on validity issues. *Acta Psychiatrica Scandinavica, 89*(Suppl 379), 26–31.

Perry, W., Minassian, A., Feifel, D., & Braff, D. L. (2001). Sensorimotor gating deficits in bipolar disorder patients with acute psychotic mania. *Biological Psychiatry, 50*, 418–424.

Perugi, G., & Akiskal, H. S. (2002). The soft bipolar spectrum redefined: Focus on the cyclothymic, anxious-sensitive, impulse-dyscontrol, and binge-eating connection in bipolar II and related conditions. *Psychiatric Clinics of North America, 25*, 713–737.

Pickering, A. D. (2004). The neuropsychology of impulsive antisocial sensation seeking personality traits: From dopamine to hippocampal function? In R. M. Stelmack (Ed.), *On the psychobiology of personality: Essays in honor of Marvin Zuckerman* (pp. 455–478). Oxford: Elsevier.

Pickering, A. D., & Gray, J. A. (1999). The neuroscience of personality. In L. A. Pervin, & O. P. John (Eds.), *Handbook of personality: Theory and research*. New York: The Guilford Press.

Rado, S. (1953). Dynamics and classification of disordered behaviour. *American Journal of Psychiatry, 110*, 406–416.

Raine, A., Lencz, T., & Mednick, S. (Eds.). (1994). *Schizotypal personality*. Cambridge: Cambridge University Press.

Rasmussen, P. R. (2005). *Personality-guided cognitive-behavioral therapy*. Washington, DC: American Psychological Association.

Revelle, W. (1997). Extraversion and impulsivity: The lost dimension. In H. Nyborg (Ed.), *The scientific study of human nature. Tribute to Hans J. Eysenck at eighty* (pp. 189–212). Oxford: Pergamon.

Roberts, B. W., & DelVecchio, W. F. (2000). The rank-order consistency of personality traits from childhood to old age: A quantitative review of longitudinal studies. *Psychological Bulletin, 126*, 3–25.

Salkovskis, P. M. (1999). Understanding and treating obsessive-compulsive disorder. *Behaviour Research and Therapy, 37*(Suppl 1), 529–552.

Sass, L. A. (1992). *Madness and modernism* (p. 375). New York: Basic Books.

Sass, .L.A., & Parnas, J. (2003) Schizophrenia, consciousness, and the self. *Schizophrenia Bulletin, 29*, 427–444.

Saxena, S., Brody, A. L., Schwartz, J. M., & Baxter, L. R. (1998). Neuroimaging and frontl-subcortical circuitry in obsessive-compulsive disorder. *British Journal of Psychiatry, 173*(Suppl 35), 26–37.

Shafer, A. B. (2001). Relation of the Big Five to the EASI scales and the Thurstone Temperament Schedule. *Personality and Individual Differences, 31*, 193–204.

Schizophrenia Bulletin (1989). *Issue theme: Subjective experiences of schizophrenia and related disorders, 15*, 177–337.

Schizophrenia Research. (2002). *Special issue: NATO advanced workshop on schizophrenia and schizotypy, 54*(1–2).

Shiner, R. L. (2005). A developmental perspective on personality disorders: Lessons from research on normal personality development in childhood and adolescence. *Journal of Personality Disorders, 19*, 202–210.

Spitzer, R. L., Endicott, J., & Gibbon, M. (1979). Crossing the border into borderline personality and borderline schizophrenia: The development of criteria. *Archives of General Psychiatry, 36*, 17–34.

Thomas, A., & Chess, S. (1977). *Temperament and development*. New York: Brunner/Mazel.

Tyrka, A., Haslam, N., & Cannon, T. D. (1995). In A. Raine, T. Lencz, & S. Mednick (Eds.), (1994) *Schizotypal personality* (pp. 168–191). Cambridge: Cambridge University Press.

Viding, E. (2004). Annotation: Understanding the development of psychopathy. *Journal of Child Psychology and Psychiatry, 45*, 1329–1337.

Vollema, M. G., & Hoijtink, H. (2000). The multidimensionality of self-report schizotypy in a psychiatric population. *Schizophrenia Bulletin, 26*, 565–575.

Vollema, M. G., & van den Bosch, R. J. (1995). The multidimensionality of schizotypy. *Schizophrenia Bulletin, 21*, 19–31.

Watson, D., Wiese, D., Vaidya, J., & Tellegen, A. (1999). The two general activation systems of affect: Structural findings, evolutionary considerations, and psychobiological evidence. *Journal of Personality and Social Psychology, 76*, 820–838.

Watt, N. F., Anthony, E. J., Wynne, L. C., & Rolf, J. E. (Eds.). (1984). *Children at risk for schizophrenia. A longitudinal perspective*. Cambridge: Cambridge University Press.

Weinberger, D. R. (2002). Biological phenotypes and genetic research on schizophrenia. *World Psychiatry, 53*, 5–13.

Widiger, T. A. (2003). Personality disorder and Axis I psychopathology: The problematic boundary of Axis I and Axis II. *Journal of Personality Disorders, 17*, 90–108.

Widiger, T. A., & Costa, P. T. (1994). Personality and personality disorders. *Journal of Abnormal Psychology, 103*, 78–91.

Widiger, T. A., & Simonsen, E. (2005a). Alternative models of personality disorder: Finding a common ground. *Journal of Personality Disorders, 19*, 110–130.

Widiger, T. A., & Simonsen, E. (2005b). Introduction to the special section: The American Psychiatric Association's research agenda for the DSM-V. *Journal of Personality Disorders, 19*, 103–109.

Willner, P. (1985). *Depression*. New York: John Wiley.

World Health Organization. (1992). *ICD-10 Classification of mental and behavioural disorders*. Geneva, Switzerland: Author.

Zuckerman, M. (1993). P-impulsive sensation seeking and its behavioural, psychophysiological, and biochemical correlates. *Neuropsychobiology, 28*, 30–36.

Zuckerman, M. (1994). *Behavioral expressions and biosocial bases of sensation seeking*. New York: Cambridge University Press.

Douglas B. Samuel

Thomas A. Widiger

I he purpose of this chapter is to present and discuss how normal and abnormal personality is distinguished in the American Psychiatric Association's (APA) *Diagnostic and Statistical Manual of Mental Disorders* (*DSM-IV-TR*; American Psychiatric Association, 2000). We begin the chapter with a description of how personality disorders are diagnosed via *DSM-IV*, as well as provide several competing definitions that have been proposed. We then relate these procedures to the more general definitions of personality and mental disorder provided within the diagnostic manual, delineating the fundamental components of the definition, such as deviation from one's culture, dysfunction, inflexibility/dyscontrol and clinical significance/impairment. Finally, we end the chapter with several critiques of the current system and conclude that ultimately the distinction between normal and abnormal personalities should be drawn in a manner, which maximizes both validity and clinical utility.

## Personality Disorder Diagnoses via *DSM-IV*

*DSM-IV* provides a number of options for recording the presence of maladaptive personality traits. The most familiar is to provide one or more of the 10 officially recognized individual diagnoses (e.g., borderline, histrionic, antisocial, or paranoid). However, it is useful to recognize that there are additional options, including a diagnosis of personality disorder not otherwise specified and the recording of maladaptive personality traits that are below the threshold for a mental disorder diagnosis. We will discuss each of these.

The option used by all clinicians is to provide one or more of the 10 officially recognized diagnoses. For example, the schizoid personality disorder is diagnosed by determining whether four of the set of seven diagnostic criteria are present (as well as ruling out the presence of a mood disorder with psychotic features, a pervasive developmental disorder, and other Axis I mental disorders). If four or more of the diagnostic criteria are present, then the person is diagnosed as having a schizoid personality disorder; if three or less of the criteria are present, then the diagnostic judgment is that the person does not have this personality disorder.

Identifying the presence of a schizoid personality disorder does not rule out the presence of additional personality disorder diagnoses. "When (as is often the case) an individual's pattern of behavior meets criteria for more than one Personality Disorder, the clinician should list all relevant Personality Disorder diagnoses in order of importance" (American Psychiatric Association, 2000, p. 686). Many patients will meet diagnostic criteria for more than one *DSM-IV* personality disorder (Bornstein, 1998; Lilienfeld, Waldman, & Israel, 1994; Livesley, 2003; Widiger & Trull, 1998). Determining which of the many personality disorder diagnoses should be provided requires an assessment of at least most of the diagnostic criteria for each of them; therefore, the standard procedure used by most researchers is to assess all of the diagnostic criteria using semistructured interviews. Semistructured interviews for personality disorders typically consist of a series of questions posed by a clinician to a patient whose responses are then judged and coded by the clinician. Semistructured interviews have a number of advantages over unstructured interviews in that they ensure and document that a systematic and comprehensive assessment of each personality disorder diagnostic criterion has in fact occurred; an aspect which can be particularly useful in clinical settings where credibility or reliability are crucial, such as forensic or disability evaluations. A further discussion of semistructured interviews for personality disorders is beyond the scope of this chapter, but is readily available from other sources (e.g., Widiger & Samuel, 2005).

In any case, the assessment of all 80 *DSM-IV* personality disorder diagnostic criteria (94 if the depressive and passive-aggressive disorders are assessed) typically requires 2–4 h, if each diagnostic criterion is indeed systematically assessed (Rogers, 2003; Widiger, 2002; Widiger & Samuel, 2005). Clinicians typically provide only one diagnosis within a patient's medical record (Gunderson, 1992; Zimmerman & Mattia, 1999), perhaps because a systematic and comprehensive assessment of all of the diagnostic criteria is simply not feasible in general clinical practice (Widiger & Coker, 2002). However, studies have indicated that the failure to provide a comprehensive assessment of the full range of personality disorder symptomatology results in a substantial loss of clinically important information, notably the presence of additional maladaptivity that is likely to have an important impact on the understanding and treatment of the patient (Zimmerman & Mattia, 1999).

Another option is to provide the diagnosis of personality disorder not otherwise specified (PDNOS). However, most semistructured interviews and systematic empirical studies fail to even consider the presence of PDNOS (Verheul & Widiger, 2004) even though it is perhaps the most common diagnosis in clinical practice (e.g., Fabrega, Ulrich, Pilkonis, & Mezzich, 1991; Koenigsberg, Kaplan, Gilmore, & Cooper, 1985; Loranger, 1990) and the most frequent diagnosis when it is considered in empirical studies (e.g., Kass, Skodol, Charles, Spitzer, & Williams, 1985; Morey, 1988; Zimmerman & Coryell,

1989). The diagnosis of PDNOS can be used in a variety of ways. PDNOS probably should not be used to diagnose subthreshold cases for any one of the 10 officially recognized personality disorders (i.e., failing to meet the respective diagnostic threshold should suggest that the disorder is not present) but it can be used to diagnose persons who have enough of the features from more than one of them "that together cause clinically significant distress or impairment in one or more important areas of functioning (e.g., social or occupational)" (American Psychiatric Association, 2000, p. 729). After all, it is likely that a person with only three borderline criteria, but also three avoidant, two histrionic, and three dependent, would probably have as much clinically significant impairment or distress as a person with five borderline diagnostic criteria. The specific title for this PDNOS diagnosis is often given as "mixed," followed by a specification of the particular features that were present (e.g., 301.9, PDNOS, mixed, with borderline, avoidant, and dependent features).

A second option for PDNOS is "when the clinician judges that a specific Personality Disorder that is not included in the Classification is appropriate" (American Psychiatric Association, 2000, p. 729). This could include diagnoses that had previously received official or unofficial recognition (e.g., sadistic or self-defeating), that currently receive unofficial recognition (i.e., depressive or passive-aggressive), or even those that have never received any official or unofficial recognition (e.g., alexithymic, delusional dominating, pleonexic, abusive, or aggressive). The availability of this option is in recognition of the fact that *DSM-IV* fails to cover all of the possible ways in which one might have a personality disorder (Westen & Arkowitz-Westen, 1998). If one has a diagnostic term that adequately describes the particular constellation of personality traits, then this term could be provided (e.g., 301.9, PDNOS, sadistic). However, if there is no specific term available for that particular constellation of maladaptive personality traits, then a generic, nondescript term is typically provided (e.g., 301.9, PDNOS, atypical).

Note that clinicians can also diagnose PDNOS along with one or more of the 10 officially recognized personality disorders. For example, a patient could be given the diagnoses of antisocial (301.7) and abusive (301.9); antisocial (301.7) and mixed (301.9, with borderline, paranoid, and narcissistic features); or antisocial (301.7) and mixed (301.9, with borderline and abusive features). It is stated in the *DSM-IV* text that PDNOS "is for disorders of personality functioning that do not meet criteria for any specific Personality Disorder" (American Psychiatric Association, 2000, p. 729). This statement has been interpreted by some clinicians and researchers to mean that PDNOS is only to be used when a person fails to meet the criteria for any one of the 10 officially recognized personality disorders (Widiger, Mangine, Corbitt, Ellis, and Thomas 1995) but PDNOS could be used to diagnose personality disorder symptoms in addition to one of the 10 officially recognized disorders.

Personality disorder semi-structured interviews vary substantially in the extent and manner in which they consider a PDNOS diagnosis (Verheul & Widiger, 2004). The IPDE (Loranger, 1999) confines its assessment to the mixed case, with a minimum requirement of 10 diagnostic criteria from at least two different personality disorders. The SIDP-IV (Pfohl, Blum, & Zimmerman, 1997) also confines its assessment to the mixed case and recommends using PDNOS only when two or more personality disorder diagnoses are just one diagnostic criterion short. The PDI-IV (Widiger et al., 1995) allows for a more extended application of this diagnosis, as it requires only that the patient meet the general diagnostic criteria for a personality disorder (discussed further below).

An additional option beyond the provision of an officially recognized diagnosis, or PDNOS, is to indicate the presence of specific maladaptive personality traits that together are below the threshold for an officially recognized, mixed, or atypical diagnosis. "Specific maladaptive personality traits that do not meet the threshold for a Personality Disorder may also be listed on Axis II" (American Psychiatric Association, 2000, p. 687). These are instances in which the clinician has determined that the person does not have a personality disorder, but does have maladaptive personality traits. "In such instances, no specific code should be used" (American Psychiatric Association, 2000, p. 687) because the judgment is that there are maladaptive personality traits but no personality disorder is present. One instance in which this occurs is when a person has features of one or more personality disorders that are below the threshold for any one of them and are also below the threshold for a mixed personality disorder. In this instance, the clinician might record (for example) "V71.09, no diagnosis on Axis II, histrionic and dependent personality traits" (American Psychiatric Association, 2000, p. 687). A second possibility is when the clinician observes the presence of personality traits that are not included within the 10 officially recognized diagnoses. One might record in such an instance, V71.9, no diagnosis on Axis II, introverted and overcontrolled personality traits. How a clinician would distinguish between maladaptive personality traits and a personality disorder will be discussed further below.

## Personality Disorder Diagnostic Thresholds

*DSM-IV-TR* provides specific rules for distinguishing between the presence versus absence of each of the 10 officially recognized personality disorders. For example, at least four of the seven features must be present in order to diagnose schizoid personality disorder (American Psychiatric Association, 2000). The provision of a specific rule is tremendously helpful in decreasing inter-rater unreliability, as clinicians will disagree substantially in their thresholds for a personality disorder diagnosis (Mellsop, Varghese, Joshua, & Hicks, 1982; Morey, 1988). However, the bases for these diagnostic thresholds are largely unexplained or, at best, are weakly justified (Clark, 1992; Kass et al., 1985; Tyrer & Johnson, 1996).

The *DSM-III* schizotypal and borderline diagnoses were the only two for which a published rationale has ever been provided, and the bases for their diagnostic thresholds may not even be sufficiently compelling to use as a model for other disorders. The *DSM-III* requirement that the patient have five of the eight features for the borderline diagnosis (American Psychiatric Association, 1980) was determined on the basis of maximizing agreement with diagnoses provided by clinicians (Spitzer, Forman, & Nee, 1979). However, the borderline and schizotypal criterion sets have been revised substantially since *DSM-III* and no cross-validation of the diagnostic thresholds has been conducted, despite the substantial effects the subsequent revisions have had on clinical diagnosis. For example, Blashfield, Blum, and Pfohl (1992) reported a kappa of only $-0.025$ for the agreement between the *DSM-III* and *DSM-III-R* schizotypal personality disorder diagnoses, with a reduction in prevalence rate from 11% to 1% across the two editions of the diagnostic manual (Morey, 1988, reported a comparable decrease in prevalence from 17% to 9%).

There has not been any comparable effort to develop a rationale for the establishment of the thresholds for any of the other personality disorder diagnoses. The decision to require four of the seven features for the diagnosis of schizoid personality disorder was not based on any data indicating that this threshold had some relevance or meaning to an outcome variable, clinical decision, or expected prevalence rate. It just seemed to the authors of the criterion sets that this was probably the best place to make the cut. In the absence of any data or rationale to guide the decision of where to set the thresholds, it is hardly surprising to find substantial variation across each edition of the diagnostic manual (Frances, 1998). For example, Morey (1988) reported an 800% increase in the number of persons beyond the threshold for a schizoid diagnosis in *DSM-III-R* as compared to *DSM-III*, and a 350% increase for the narcissistic diagnosis. Some of this shift in prevalence might have been intentional (Widiger, Frances, Spitzer, & Williams, 1988), but much of it has been unanticipated (Blashfield et al., 1992).

## Conceptual Distinction Between Normal and Abnormal Personality

A rationale for the personality disorder diagnostic thresholds might be obtained through a consideration of the conceptualization of both mental disorders in general and personality disorders provided in *DSM-IV*. *DSM-IV* does provide a definition of mental disorder, a definition of personality disorder, and even diagnostic criteria for the presence of a personality disorder, all three of which are useful for differentiating between normal and abnormal personality. The diagnostic criteria for a personality disorder were in fact included specifically with the intention that they be used by clinicians when providing the PDNOS diagnoses and for distinguishing between maladaptive personality traits and a personality disorder (Frances, First, & Pincus, 1995).

The general diagnostic criteria include the determination of whether there is an enduring pattern of inner experience and behavior that deviates markedly from the expectations of the individual's culture, and whether this enduring pattern is manifested in two or more of the following ways: (a) cognitively; (b) affectively; (c) interpersonally; and/or (d) through impulse dyscontrol. One must also determine whether the enduring pattern is inflexible and pervasive across a broad range of personal and social situations; whether the enduring pattern leads to clinically significant distress or impairment in social, occupational, or other important areas of functioning; whether the enduring pattern is indeed stable, of long duration, and can be traced back at least to adolescence or early adulthood; whether the enduring pattern is not better accounted for as a manifestation or consequence of another mental disorder; and, finally, whether the enduring pattern is due to the direct physiological effects of a substance or a medical condition, such as head trauma. If all of these criteria are met, then a personality disorder diagnosis can be provided.

It is evident from a consideration of the general diagnostic criteria for a personality disorder that they concern, for the most part, the determination of whether there are pervasive and enduring personality traits rather than the presence of disorder. The aspects of the general diagnostic criteria that address whether there is a disorder of personality are the references to a marked deviation from the expectations of the person's culture, inflexibility, and clinically significant distress or impairment in social, occupational, or another important area of functioning.

The general diagnostic criteria are consistent with the conceptual definition of a personality disorder. As stated in *DSM-IV-TR*, a personality disorder is "an enduring pattern of inner experience and behavior that deviates markedly from the expectations of the individual's culture, is pervasive and inflexible, has an onset in adolescence or early adulthood, is stable over time, and leads to distress or impairment" (American Psychiatric Association, 2000, p. 685). Much of this definition again refers to features of general personality functioning (e.g., enduring pattern, early onset, and stable), but embedded within this definition also are features that suggest the presence of a disorder of personality (e.g., marked deviation from expectations of culture, inflexibility, and impairment or distress). The broader definition of a mental disorder is as follows:

> A clinically significant behavioral or psychological syndrome that is associated with present distress (e.g., a painful symptom) or disability (i.e., impairment in one or more important areas of functioning) or with a significantly increased risk of suffering death, pain, disability, or an important loss of freedom. In addition, this syndrome or pattern must not be merely an expectable and culturally sanctioned response to a particular event, for example, the death of a loved one. Whatever its original cause, it must currently be considered a manifestation of a behavioral, psychological, or biological dysfunction in the individual. Neither deviant behavior (e.g., political, religious, or sexual) nor conflicts that are primarily between the individual and society are mental disorders unless the deviance or conflict is a symptom of a dysfunction in the individual, as described above. (American Psychiatric Association, 2000, p. xxxi)

Note that the definition of a mental disorder again refers to clinically significant impairment (i.e., disability or impairment in one or more important areas of functioning, including increased risk of suffering, pain, or death), personal distress, and inflexibility (i.e., loss of freedom). On the other hand, there is no reference to deviation from cultural expectations, and it also refers explicitly to the presence of a dysfunction within the individual. We will discuss below each of these major components: deviation from cultural expectations, dysfunction within the individual, inflexibility or dyscontrol, and impairment.

# Deviation from Cultural Expectations

It is stated within the definition of and diagnostic criteria for a personality disorder that the behavior pattern "deviates markedly from the expectations of the individual's culture" (American Psychiatric Association, 2000, p. 689). This requirement is useful in emphasizing that some behavior patterns that appear to be abnormal from one cultural perspective might be considered to be normative from the perspective of a different culture (Alarcon, 1996). One would not want to diagnose immigrants to a new culture with a mental disorder simply because they brought with them behavior patterns that were normative within their original culture but are considered to be deviant or unusual within the new culture. What is considered to be excessively inhibited in one culture may be courteously dignified within another.

This requirement, however, is also readily misunderstood. It could imply to some that cultural deviation is fundamental to the conceptualization of a personality disorder, even though deviation from cultural expectations has long been recognized to be a fallible and problematic basis for the diagnosis of a mental disorder (Gorenstein, 1984). In fact, the general definition of a mental disorder makes it quite clear that "neither deviant behavior (e.g., political, religious, or sexual) nor conflicts that are primarily between the individual and society are mental disorders unless the deviance or conflict is a symptom of a dysfunction in the individual, as described above" (American Psychiatric Association, 2000, p. xxxi).

In addition, it is also useful to recognize that a cultural expectation could impart upon a person clinically significant maladaptive behavior patterns, such as excessive submissiveness (Brown, 1992; Kaplan, 1983) or excessive achievement striving (Garamoni & Schwartz, 1986). Optimal functioning does not necessarily involve adaptation to cultural expectations, and adaptation to cultural expectations does not necessarily ensure the absence of maladaptive personality traits. Many maladaptive behavior patterns will represent excessive or exaggerated expressions of traits that the culture values or encourages. For example, it is within cultural expectations to be conscientious, responsible, diligent, and dedicated to one's work or career, but not to the point that one sacrifices one's physical health, friendships, or family. It is within cultural expectations to be agreeable but not to be docile, meek, and submissive. It is within cultural expectations to be assertive, but not to be domineering, or to be confident but not to be conceited and arrogant. In sum, deviation from cultural expectations does not necessarily imply that the maladaptive behavior patterns were not at some level supported, reinforced, or encouraged by cultural expectations or values.

The reference to a cultural deviation within the definition of and criteria for a personality disorder was obtained from the World Health Organization's (WHO) criteria for a personality disorder. The ICD-10 version of this requirement is perhaps preferable to the version provided in DSM-IV because ICD-10 does not imply that cultural deviation is actually necessary for the diagnosis or that personality disorders must represent culturally deviant behavior. The ICD-10 simply states that "for different cultures it may be necessary to develop specific sets of criteria with regard to social norms, rules, and obligations" (WHO, 1992, p. 202) in order to discourage clinicians from imposing the cultural values or expectations of one culture onto another.

# Behavioral, Psychological, or Biological Dysfunction

Neither the *DSM-IV* definition of a personality disorder nor the diagnostic criterion set for personality disorder refer to or require the presence of any dysfunction within the individual. However, a reference to pathology is explicit within the general definition of a mental disorder, stating that the condition "must currently be considered a manifestation of a behavioral, psychological, or biological dysfunction in the individual" (American Psychiatric Association 2000; p xxxi). Some suggest that an underlying pathology should in fact be included within the criterion sets for each mental disorder, including the personality disorders, because these criterion sets may currently be unsuccessful in differentiating normal and abnormal psychological functioning due to their reliance on a clinically significant impairment for providing the distinction (Wakefield & Spitzer, 2002).

Consider, for example, the diagnosis of pedophilia. In order to be diagnosed with pedophilia, *DSM-III-R* (American Psychiatric Association, 1987) required only that an adult have recurrent intense urges and fantasies involving sexual activity with a prepubescent child over a period of at least 6 months and have acted on them or be markedly distressed by them. However, virtually every adult who has engaged in a sexual activity with a child would probably have met this diagnostic threshold (the only additional requirement was a duration of at least 6 months of the behavior, urges, or fantasies). The *DSM-III-R* diagnosis in essence presumed that no adult was capable of willfully engaging in this deviant sexual act or fantasy for longer than 6 months without being compelled to do so by the presence of a mental disorder. No effective distinction was being made between a willful (criminal) sexual exploitation of a child and a pathologically compelled sexual exploitation of a child. The authors of *DSM-IV*, therefore, added the requirement that "the behavior, sexual urges, or fantasies cause clinically significant distress or impairment in social, occupational, or other important areas of functioning" (American Psychiatric Association, 1994, p. 523).

Spitzer and Wakefield (1999), however, argued that these impairment criteria were inadequate. They concurred with a concern raised by the National Law Center for Children and Families that *DSM-IV* might contribute to a normalization of pedophilic and other paraphilic behavior by allowing these diagnoses not to be applied if the persons who had engaged in these acts were not distressed by their behavior or were not otherwise experiencing any impairment in their social or role functioning. In response, Frances et al. (1995) argued that pedophilic sexual "behaviors are inherently problematic because they involved a nonconsenting person (exhibitionism, voyeurism, frotteurism) or a child (pedophilia) and may lead to arrest and incarceration" (p. 319). They suggested, therefore, that any person who engaged in an illegal sexual act for longer than 6 months would be exhibiting a clinically significant social impairment and would then meet the *DSM-IV* threshold for the diagnosis of a mental disorder. However, falling back onto the illegality of the behavior to justify a diagnosis undermines the original rationale for the inclusion of the impairment criterion, it provides no meaningful basis for determining when deviant sexual acts or fantasies are or are not due to a mental disorder, and it is inconsistent with the stated definition of a mental disorder, which indicates that neither deviance nor conflicts with the law are sufficient to warrant a diagnosis.

Wakefield (1997) has provided additional examples of *DSM-IV* criterion sets that might be failing to make necessary distinctions between normal problems in living and true psychopathology due to the reliance in *DSM-IV* on indicators of distress or impairment rather than an underlying internal dysfunction or pathology. For example, the *DSM-IV* criterion set for major depressive disorder excludes uncomplicated bereavement, presumably because depressive reactions to the loss of a loved one are normal (nonpathological) problems in living. Depression after the loss of a loved one is considered to be a mental disorder if the symptoms are characterized by "guilt about things other than actions taken or not taken by the survivor at the time of the death, thoughts of death other than the survivor feeling that he or she would be better off dead or should have died with the deceased person, morbid preoccupation with worthlessness, marked psychomotor retardation, prolonged and marked functional impairment, and hallucinatory experiences other than thinking that he or she hears the voice of, or transiently sees the image of the deceased person, (American Psychiatric Association, 2000, p. 741) or if 'the symptoms are still present 2 months after the loss'" (American Psychiatric Association, 2000, p. 741). Allowing 2 months to grieve before one is diagnosed with a mental disorder might be as arbitrary and meaningful as allowing a person to engage in a sexually deviant act for 6 months before the behavior is diagnosed as a paraphilic. Spitzer and Wakefield (1999) therefore argue that the diagnostic criterion sets should require, or at least include, specific references to pathology, consistent with the *DSM-IV* definition of a mental disorder.

Lehman, Alexopoulos, Goldman, Jeste, and Ustun. (2002) go further to suggest that future editions of the diagnostic manual remove all references to impairment, thereby allowing a clinician to diagnose a disorder even when there is no discernible impairment. "The diagnosis of mental disorders [should] be uncoupled from disability in order to foster a more vigorous research agenda on the etiologies, courses, and treatments of mental disorders" (Lehman et al., 2002, p. 203). A number of physical disorders are currently diagnosed in the absence of any notable impairment (e.g., hypertension & diabetes), and this early detection can be of considerable benefit in providing effective treatment prior to the occurrence of the harmful effects of the disorder. "Once it is possible to define a mental disorder based on the identification of its underlying pathology, then it would surely make sense to follow the course of other medical conditions and have the presence of disorder be based solely on pathology and not on the effect this pathology exerts on the individual's functioning" (Lehman et al., 2002; p. 208). Lehman et al. (2002), however, acknowledge that applying this approach to mental disorders would be extremely difficult because "their causes and pathophysiological mechanisms remain largely unknown" (p. 208).

The *DSM-IV* personality disorder criterion sets do at times refer to phenomena that could imply an internal pathology (e.g., feelings of inadequacy for the avoidant, a need for admiration for the narcissistic, and a need to be taken care of for the dependent). However, these are perhaps better understood as references to particular cognitive, affective, or interpersonal impairments in functioning that would in turn be due to either a neurochemical dysregulation (Depue, 1996), an unconscious conflict (Kernberg, 1996), an irrational cognitive schema (Beck & Freeman, 1990) or a pathological interpersonal introject (Benjamin, 1996. Pathologies are not currently specified within *DSM-IV* criterion sets in part, because there is insufficient empirical support to give preference to one cognitive, interpersonal, neurochemical, psychodynamic or other theoretical model in preference to another, and there is unlikely to be much agreement regarding the fundamental pathology that should be required for most of the disorders included within *DSM-IV*. The authors of the diagnostic manual have preferred to remain neutral with respect to these alternative theoretical perspectives (Frances et al., 1995; Spitzer, Williams, & Skodol, 1980).

For example, Wakefield (1997) suggested that for the diagnosis of major depressive disorder (vs. normal bereavement) it should be "necessary to formulate some account of the evolutionary programming of the mechanisms with respect to what kinds of triggering circumstances are supposed to cause which kinds of responses (e.g., loss–response mechanisms are designed so that perceptions of major losses trigger roughly proportional sadness responses)" (p. 647). Evolutionary theory has enriched our understanding of the etiology and pathology of many mental disorders, but evolutionary theory is unable to provide adequate guidance as to the "natural functions" of specific behavioral and psychological response mechanisms. Given that, it is itself a particular theoretical model for the etiology and pathology of psychopathology, evolutionary theory might not be capable of serving as a general definition of mental disorder that is compatible with alternative theoretical perspectives (Bergner, 1997; Kirmayer & Young, 1999; Lilienfeld & Marino, 1995, 1999; Widiger & Sankis, 2000).

# Inflexibility and Dyscontrol

Also included within the *DSM-IV* definitions of personality and mental disorder are references to being "inflexible" (American Psychiatric Association, 2000, p. 685) or experiencing an "important loss of freedom" (American Psychiatric Association, 2000, p. xxxi). Inherent to the concept of a mental disorder is the inability to exercise one's free will. The presence of a mental disorder compels the person to behave in manner that is usually harmful or impairing to themselves or to other persons. This fundamental component of a mental disorder is missing entirely from Wakefield's (1999) harmful dysfunction conceptualization. The component of harm within his conceptualization is concerned with the presence of impairment; the component of dysfunction with the presence of pathology. Mental disorders, however, could also be understood as dyscontrolled organismic impairments in psychological functioning (Kirmayer & Young, 1999; Klein, 1999; Widiger & Trull, 1991). "Involuntary impairment remains the key inference" (Klein, 1999, p. 424, our emphasis). Dyscontrol is one of the fundamental features of a mental disorder emphasized in Bergner's (1997) "significant restriction" and Widiger and Sankis' (2000) "dyscontrolled maladaptivity" definitions of mental disorder.

Lacking adequate control over distressing or harmful feelings, thoughts, or behaviors is fundamental to the concept of a mental disorder. To the extent that a person is willfully, intentionally, freely, voluntarily, or with adequate self-control engaging in harmful sexual acts, drug usage, gambling, or child abuse, the person would not be considered to have a mental disorder. Current diagnostic criteria are indicators of impairment, but they are also indicators of dyscontrol (e.g., continued usage of a drug despite social, legal, financial, physical, or other significant negative consequences). Distress is a fallible but valid indicator for the presence of a mental disorder in part because it suggests that the person lacks adequate ability to simply change the problematic symptom or behavior. Fundamental to a judgment of mental disorder is the inadequate ability of the person to be able to willfully or freely correct his or her own maladaptive functioning (Bergner, 1997). Persons seek professional intervention in large part to obtain the insights, techniques, skills or other tools (e.g., medications) that increase their ability to better control their mood, thoughts, or behavior.

Persons with a personality disorder lack adequate control of their behavior. Persons with a dependent personality disorder are not simply choosing to feel uncomfortable or helpless when they are alone; they are not simply deciding to urgently seek another relationship when a close relationship ends; and they are not freely or willfully wanting others to assume responsibility for major areas of their lives. They are compelled to have these feelings, to make these poor decisions, or to engage in these behaviors. They may at times perceive themselves as making a willful, free decision but this self-perception would be considered by most clinicians to be largely illusory. If it were a matter of voluntary or free choice, they would not need professional interventions to change their behavior patterns. They would simply decide or willfully choose to behave otherwise.

Inflexibility and dyscontrol, however, are very difficult constructs to operationalize. In addition, inflexibility is unlikely to be an absolute, black–white distinction and the point at which a person lacks adequate self-control to warrant a diagnosis of a mental disorder (independent of impairment) would be difficult to demarcate. Some of the *DSM-IV* personality disorder diagnostic criteria imply an absolute inflexibility. A person with a schizoid personality disorder "neither desires nor enjoys close relationships, including being part of a family" (American Psychiatric Association, 2000, p. 697); a person with a narcissistic personality disorder "lacks empathy" (American Psychiatric Association, 2000, p. 717); and a person with an obsessive-compulsive personality disorder "is unable to discard worn-out or worthless objects even when they have no sentimental value" (American Psychiatric Association, 2000, p. 729). Neither desiring nor enjoying close relationships implies that there is not one single relationship that one desires or enjoys (if there was, then apparently the person is able to experience a desire or an enjoyment); lacking empathy means that the narcissistic person never expresses any empathy under any circumstances or any time (if they did, then apparently they were not lacking in empathy); and obsessive-compulsive persons must never have discarded any worn-out or worthless objects (if they had, then apparently there are times in which they are able to do so).

However, most of the diagnostic criteria provide room for some degree of flexibility. For example, the schizoid person "almost always chooses solitary activities," "takes pleasure in few, if any activities," and "has little, if any, interest in having sexual experiences with another person" (American Psychiatric Association, 2000, p. 697). One can meet the *DSM-IV* criteria for schizoid personality disorder and "choose" a nonsolitary activity, take pleasure in a few activities, and have at least a little interest in having sexual experiences with another person. Even the diagnostic criteria that appear to provide no room for variation or exception are modified or softened within the text discussion. For example, although the diagnostic criterion states that a schizoid person "neither desire nor enjoys close relationships, including being part of a family" (American Psychiatric Association, 2000, p. 697), in the text it is stated that persons with this disorder "appear to lack a desire for intimacy, seem indifferent to opportunities to develop close relationships, and do not seem to derive much satisfaction from being part of a family or other social group" (American Psychiatric Association, 2000, p. 694). According to the text discussion of the diagnostic criteria, giving the appearance of lacking a desire for intimacy does not necessarily mean actually lacking any desire whatsoever, and not seeming to derive much satisfaction from being part of a family does suggest that schizoid persons might in fact derive at least some amount of satisfaction.

The boundary between normal and inadequate self-control is itself difficult to define and demarcate. It is not even clear whether normal psychological functioning is within any person's willful, voluntary control (Bargh & Chartrand, 2000; Howard & Conway, 1986; Wegner & Wheatley, 1999). Inflexibility is a fundamental feature of a personality disorder (American Psychiatric Association, 2000) but normal personality traits are themselves characterized by a cross-situational consistency that is considered by many to reflect innate biological dispositions and environmental experiences that largely compel normal persons to have a characteristic manner of thinking, feeling, and relating to others (McCrae & Costa, 2003). Persons are not generally said to have freely, willfully, or voluntarily created their normal personality traits.

One could perhaps distinguish between different degrees of inflexibility with respect to access to alternative cognitive, behavioral, affective, and interpersonal styles (e.g., Wiggins, Phillips, & Trapnell, 1989). For example, persons may have a characteristic manner of thinking, feeling, or relating to others, but have available to them alternative means of thinking, feeling, and relating that can be accessed within some situational contexts in which they would be adaptive or advantageous. From this perspective, dyscontrol is not necessarily a matter of lacking free will; it is perhaps lacking access to the cognitive, affective, or behavioral "programs" that should be implemented within particular situations. Nevertheless, the assessment of the boundary between adequate versus inadequate access to such will likely be highly problematic (Golding, Skeem, Roesch, & Zapf, 1999; Webster & Jackson, 1997) and often controversial (Alper, 1998).

## Clinically Significant Impairment

*DSM-IV* does rely substantially on the determination of a clinically significant level of impairment for distinguishing between normal and abnormal psychological functioning. The clinically significant impairment criterion "helps establish the threshold for the diagnosis of a disorder in those situations in which the symptomatic presentation by itself (particularly in its milder forms) is not inherently pathological and may be encountered in individuals for whom a diagnosis of 'mental disorder' would be inappropriate" (American Psychiatric Association, 2000, p. 8). However, currently no guidelines are provided in *DSM-IV* for what is meant by a clinically significant level of impairment. *DSM-IV* only states that "assessing whether this criterion is met, especially in terms of role function, is an inherently difficult clinical judgment" (American Psychiatric Association, 2000, p. 8) and that consideration should be given to information provided by family members and other third parties. An important and difficult task for the authors of future editions of the diagnostic manual will be to provide a clearer or more explicit definition of what would be clinically significant impairment that could be used as a common threshold for diagnosis across all of the disorders within the diagnostic manual (Regier & Narrow, 2002; Spitzer & Williams, 1982).

A relatively stringent threshold for the diagnosis of a personality disorder would be when the individual's personality functioning prevents him or her from functioning at an adequate level. A precedent for this point of demarcation is perhaps provided by the diagnosis of mental retardation. Mental retardation is not diagnosed at the point at which there is any personally meaningful impairment in intellectual functioning. It is diagnosed at that point at which there are "deficits or impairments in present adaptive functioning (i.e., the person's effectiveness in meeting the standards expected for his or her age by his or her cultural group) in at least two of the following areas: communication, self-care, home living, social/interpersonal skills, use of community resources, self-direction, functional academic skills, work, leisure, health, and safety" (American Psychiatric Association, 2000, p. 49). Persons with IQs above 70 (the cutoff point for diagnosis) can find their level of intelligence to be associated with meaningful impairment. For example, persons with an IQ of 75 would likely find their level of intelligence to be quite impairing if they wanted to pursue a career in which intelligence is integral to success. They would likely fail, or at least struggle substantially, in their effort to become a lawyer, doctor, scientist, dentist, architect, engineer, or business leader. "The IQ level of 70 was chosen as the upper limit for mental retardation because most people with IQs below 70 are so limited in their adaptive functioning that they require special services and protection, particularly during the school-age years" (American Psychiatric Association, 1980, p. 37). Even persons with a mild degree of mental retardation are said to "need supervision, guidance, and assistance, especially when under unusual social or economic stress" (American Psychiatric Association, 2000, p. 43).

The diagnosis of a personality disorder should perhaps be at a comparably stringent level. Widiger and Trull (1991) had suggested "persons who are hindered in their ability to adapt flexibly to stress, to make optimal life decisions, to fulfill desired potentials, or to sustain meaningful for satisfying relationships have a mental disorder" (p. 113). However, is it really necessary to always be making optimal life decisions or to fulfill all of one's potentials? Clinical psychologists and psychiatrists should perhaps not be in the business of helping persons realize their potentials in life, but simply helping them survive and function at an adequate level. It is common to have a patient ask if it is necessary to continue treatment beyond a certain point, and there is never a certain or absolute answer to this question. There is always room for improvement and for additional progress (Freud, 1957). Becoming even more open, less passive, or less antagonistic might be beneficial, but perhaps a diagnosis of a mental disorder should be confined to persons for whom change is necessary for an adequate level of functioning.

This point of demarcation, however, is highly judgmental and would clearly fail to distinguish between presence versus absence of personality disorder. Perhaps clinicians should in fact be in the business of promoting optimal psychological health, even though the ideal is not in fact attainable. The obtainment of just an adequate level of functioning is a goal that is generally below what is desired by most persons. A threshold for diagnosis that is more consistent with existing clinical practice is whether change would be beneficial toward achieving a desired level of functioning. It is perhaps reasonable to suggest that a level of impairment that warrants clinical attention is one for which treatment would be beneficial (whether judged by the patient or clinician). When this decision is being made by the patient (which does appear to be the case in most instances), it becomes closely aligned with the distress criterion for the diagnosis of a personality disorder. Persons seek treatment for their personality disorder when they perceive their characteristic manner of thinking, feeling, or relating to others to be problematic and they are unable to exert their free will to simply think, feel, or do otherwise; as a result, they become distressed and seek the assistance of a professional clinician to help them make changes to their personality.

Personal distress, however, is a very fallible threshold for the diagnosis of a personality disorder. For example, a woman might seek professional assistance because her assertiveness results in violent anger and abuse from her husband (Simola, 1992; Walker, 1994). She may already be excessively submissive and deferential, and yet wants the clinician to help her become an even more tolerant and forgiving spouse. In such a case, optimal psychological functioning is perhaps more likely to be achieved by helping her become more assertive rather than less assertive. One of the more controversial diagnoses in psychiatry has been homosexuality (Bayer & Spitzer, 1982). All instances of homosexuality were considered to be psychopathological in *DSM-II* (American Psychiatric Association, 1968). However, a referendum was passed by the APA in 1973 and continued into *DSM-III* (American Psychiatric Association, 1980) that deemed that homosexuality was a mental disorder only when it was "ego-dystonic," (Spitzer, 1981). "This category is reserved for homosexuals for whom changing sexual orientations is a persistent concern" (American Psychiatric Association, 1980, p. 282). The diagnosis was not to be applied when the distress over one's homosexuality was due largely to a social or moral condemnation of the behavior. "Distress resulting simply from a conflict between a homosexual and society should not be classified here" (American Psychiatric Association, 1980, p. 282). However, it soon became apparent that much of the distress over one's sexual orientation did appear to reflect stigmatization, discrimination, and social condemnation. The diagnosis as a specific form of paraphilia was deleted in *DSM-III-R* (American Psychiatric Association, 1987).

The absence of distress can also be quite fallible in suggesting the absence of any clinically significant impairment. Persons might be significantly impaired by particular personality traits (e.g., mistrust, low empathy, antagonism, callousness, or anhedonia) but not find them distressing. They may only notice the advantages that come from these traits (e.g., freedom from guilt and concern for others) and not the disadvantages (e.g., failure to sustain lasting relationships). Very few persons seek treatment for an antisocial or psychopathic personality disorder. They might be distressed by the cost of their personality disorder (e.g., loss of job or arrest) but they will often lack the insight that it is their personality that is largely at fault.

The decision that change would be beneficial might then be more appropriately or accurately provided by a professional clinician. Clinicians will likely vary substantially in such judgments, and there is little guarantee that their judgments would not be influenced by social, cultural, or personal biases or would in fact be informed by a sophisticated or even competent understanding of psychological functioning. Nevertheless, it is reasonable to suggest that an important responsibility of a clinician is to offer informed guidance as to when change would be beneficial. However, a further difficulty with a beneficial change threshold is that it would apply to just about any maladaptive personality trait. It is doubtful that there is any trait within any person that leads to adaptive functioning in all instances, or at the very least could not be improved. In fact, it would be difficult to find a person who would not benefit from some form of psychotherapy or even pharmacotherapy.

Knutson et al. (1998) "examined the effects of a serotonergic reuptake blockade on personality and social behavior in a double-blind protocol by randomly assigning 51 medically and psychiatrically healthy volunteers to treatment with a selective serotonin reuptake inhibitor (SSRI), paroxetine—($N = 25$), or placebo ($N = 26$)" (p. 374). Volunteers were recruited through local newspapers. None of them currently met, or had throughout their lifetime met, the *DSM-IV* diagnostic criteria for any mental disorder, including personality disorders (assessed with a semistructured interview). None of them had ever received a psychotropic medication, had ever abused drugs, or had ever been in treatment for a mental disorder, nor were any of them currently seeking or desiring treatment for a mental disorder (including social phobia). In other words, they were probably, in many respects, above normal in psychological functioning. The paroxetine (and placebo) treatment continued for four weeks. Knutson et al. reported that the SSRI administration (relative to placebo) significantly reduced their scores on a self-report measure of the personality trait of neuroticism and increased scores on a laboratory measure of social affiliation (i.e., a cooperative, dyadic puzzle-solving task that was observed and coded by raters blind to personality measures and treatment condition). The magnitude of changes on the self-report and laboratory measures of neuroticism and social affiliation were even correlated with plasma levels of SSRI within the treatment group. As concluded by Knutson et al. (1998), this was a clear "empirical demonstration that chronic administration of a selective serotonin reuptake blockade can have significant personality and behavioral effects in normal humans in the absence of baseline depression or other psychopathology" (p. 378).

The APA is unlikely to take the position that virtually everybody is mentally ill, although this is perhaps not as radical of a proposal as it might first appear. Nobody goes through life without suffering a physical disease or clinically significant impairment in medical functioning. Perfectly healthy bodies are rare, or are at least rarely sustained, achievements. The same realization should perhaps be accepted for mental health. Prevalence estimates of psychopathology reported by NIMH have at times been so high that the APA has questioned whether existing diagnostic criteria sets are in fact identifying instances of "true psychopathologic disorder" (Regier et al., 1998, p. 114). "In the current US climate of determining the medical necessity for care in managed health care plans, it is doubtful that 28% or 29% of the population would be judged to need mental-health treatment in a year. Hence, additional impairment and other criteria should be developed" (Regier et al., 1998, p. 114). The failure of governmental and insurance agencies to adequately fund research and treatment of mental disorders is of substantial social and clinical importance, but perhaps these concerns should not affect the answer to scientific questions regarding the actual prevalence rate of psychopathology (Spitzer, 1998).

Critics of the *DSM* have questioned the increasing number of diagnoses within each edition, suggesting that the expansion is more political than scientific (e.g., Follette & Houts 1996; Rogler 1997). However, it might have been more surprising to find that scientific research and increased knowledge have led to the recognition of fewer instances of psychopathology (Wakefield, 1998). It is also unclear why the prevalence rate of mental disorders should be so much lower than the prevalence rate of physical disorders. For example, in the 2001 National Health Interview Study, 83.5% of the adult respondents indicated that they had at least one health care visit within the past 12 months (Center for Disease Control and Prevention, 2003). These numbers evidence the fact that seeking treatment for physical disorders is a common and accepted part of our culture. In fact, the reader is asked to consider whether they have ever experienced a 12-month period that was completely devoid of any physical illness, injury, or disease. Optimal psychological functioning, as in the case of optimal physical functioning, might represent an ideal that is achieved by no one (Frances, Widiger, & Sabshin, 1991). The rejection of a high prevalence rate of psychopathology may reflect the best of intentions, such as concerns regarding the stigmatization of mental disorder diagnoses (Kutchins & Kirk, 1997) or the inadequate funding of their research and treatment (Regier et al., 1998), but these social and political concerns might be hindering a recognition of a more realistic and accurate estimate of the true rate of psychopathology.

# Conclusions

To the extent that personality functioning (and dysfunction) exists on a continuum ranging from adaptive to maladaptive, the ultimate distinction between normal and abnormal functioning is a matter of degree. The current *DSM-IV* makes the distinction in a categorical manner whereby personality functioning is determined to be either normal or abnormal by counting how many diagnostic criteria an individual meets for each of 10 personality disorders. Although this distinction is somewhat arbitrary and devised on a purely rational (and often nonempirical) basis, this cutoff serves as an explicit proxy by which to determine the presence or absence of a personality disorder. The challenge faced by authors of future editions of the *DSM* series is to better elucidate the meaning and measurement of the constructs of clinically significant impairment, dysfunction, inflexibility, and cultural deviation. Although it is likely that any proposed boundary between normal and abnormal personalities will ultimately prove to be imperfect, it is probable that a data-driven solution can be reached which will draw this boundary in a manner and fashion that will maximize the validity and clinical utility of the diagnoses. Work toward this goal for *DSM-V* has already begun with the publication of a series of "white papers" laid out in *A Research Agenda for DSM-V* (Kupfer, First, & Regier, 2002). As the title of this volume indicates, its primary purpose is to outline the areas of the manual that deserve the most rigorous research attention. As covered throughout this chapter, a primary part of DSM-V's development will be the task of refining and clarifying the definition of mental disorder in general as well as the overall diagnostic system. The *DSM-V* Research Planning Nomenclature Work Group recommended explicitly that attention be again given to the definition of mental disorder. The authors of *DSM-IV* made no changes to the definition that was provided in *DSM-III* (Frances et al., 1995), arguing that it was premature to try to make any significant improvements. This is unlikely to be the case for *DSM-V*. As suggested by the Nomenclature Work Group, more attention needs to be provided to the clarification and meaning of the fundamental concepts. For example, "the [current] definition fails to define or explain the crucial term 'dysfunction,' except to say that it may be 'behavioral, psychological, or biological,'" (Rounsaville et al., 2002, p. 3). With respect to the diagnosis of personality disorders, there will likely be explicit attention provided to whether the threshold for diagnosis should be in terms of a specific pathology or, alternatively, a uniform, consistently applied level of impairment (social or occupational) and personal distress.

## REFERENCES

Alarcon, R. D. (1996). Personality disorders and culture in DSM-IV: A critique. *Journal of Personality Disorders, 10*, 260–270.

Alper, J. S. (1998). Genes, free will, and criminal responsibility. *Social Science and Medicine, 46*, 1599–1611.

American Psychiatric Association. (1968*). Diagnostic and statistical manual of mental disorders* (2nd ed.). Washington, DC: Author.

American Psychiatric Association. (1980). *Diagnostic and statistical manual of mental disorders* (3rd ed.). Washington, DC: Author.

American Psychiatric Association. (1987). *Diagnostic and statistical manual of mental disorders: Text revision* (3rd ed., revised). Washington, DC: Author.

American Psychiatric Association. (1994). *Diagnostic and statistical manual of mental disorders* (4th ed.). Washington, DC: Author.

American Psychiatric Association. (2000). *Diagnostic and statistical manual of mental disorders: Text revision* (4th ed, revised). Washington, DC: Author.

Bargh, J. A., & Chartrand, T. L. (2000). The mind in the middle: A practical guide to priming and automaticity research. In C. M. Judd, & H. T. Reis (Eds.). *Handbook of research methods in social and personality psychology.* New York: Cambridge University Press.

Bayer, R., & Spitzer, R. L. (1982). Edited correspondence on the status of homosexuality in DSM-III. *Journal of the History of the Behavioral Sciences, 18,* 32–52.

Beck, A. T., & Freeman, A. M. (1990). *Cognitive therapy of personality disorders.* New York: Guilford Press.

Benjamin, L. S. (1996). *Interpersonal diagnosis and treatment of personality disorders* (2nd ed.). New York: Guilford Press

Bergner, R. M. (1997). What is psychopathology? And so what? *Clinical Psychology: Science and Practice, 4,* 235–248.

Blashfield, R., Blum, N., Pfohl, B. (1992). The effects of changing Axis II diagnostic criteria. *Comprehensive Psychiatry, 33,* 245–252.

Bornstein, R. F. (1998). Reconceptualizing personality disorder diagnosis in the DSM-V: The discriminant validity challenge. *Clinical Psychology: Science and Practice, 5,* 333–343.

Brown, L. S. (1992). A feminist critique of the personality disorders. In L. S. Brown, & M. Ballou (Eds.), *Personality and psychopathology. Feminist reappraisals* (pp. 206–228). New York: Guilford Press.

Center for Disease Control and Prevention. (2003). *Health, United States, 2003.* Washington, DC: Center for Disease Control and Prevention.

Clark, L. A. (1992). Resolving taxonomic issues in personality disorders: The value of large-scale analyses of symptom data. *Journal of Personality Disorders, 6,* 360–376.

Depue, R. A. (1996). A neurobiological framework for the structure of personality and emotion: Implications for personality disorders. In M. F. Lenzenweger, & J. F. Clarkin (Eds.), *Major theories of personality disorder* (pp. 347–390). New York: Guilford Press.

Fabrega, H., Ulrich, R., Pilkonis, P., & Mezzich, J. E (1991). Personality disorders diagnosed at intake at a public psychiatric facility. *Hospital and Community Psychiatry, 44,* 159–162.

Follette, W. C., & Houts, A. C. (1996). Models of scientific progress and the role of theory in taxonomy development: A case study of the DSM. *Journal of Consulting and Clinical Psychology, 64,* 1120–1132.

Frances, A. (1998). Problems in defining clinical significance in epidemiological studies. *Archives of General Psychiatry, 55,* 119.

Frances, A. J., First, M. B., & Pincus, H. A. (1995). *DSM-IV Guidebook.* Washington, DC: American Psychiatric Press.

Frances, A. J., Widiger, T. A., & Sabshin, M. (1991). Psychiatric diagnosis and abnormality. In M. Sabshin, & D. Offer (Eds.), *The diversity of normal behavior: Further contributions to normatology* (pp. 3–38). New York: Basic Books, Inc.

Freud, S. (1957). Analysis terminable and interminable. In J. L. Strachey (Ed.), *Standard edition* (Vol. 23, pp. 209–254). London: Hogarth Press. (Originally published, 1937)

Garamoni, G. L., & Schwartz, R. M. (1986). Type A behavior pattern and compulsive personality: Toward a psychodynamic–behavioral integration. *Clinical Psychology Review, 6,* 311–336.

Golding, S. L., Skeem, J. L., Roesch, R., & Zapf, P. A. (1999). The assessment of criminal responsibility: Current controversies. In I. B. Weiner, & A. K. Hess (Eds.), *The handbook of forensic psychology* (2nd ed., pp. 379–408). New York: Wiley.

Gorenstein, E. E. (1984). Debating mental illness: Implications for science, medicine and social policy. *American Psychologist, 39,* 50–56.

Gunderson, J. G. (1992). Diagnostic controversies. In A. Tasman, & M. B. Riba (Eds.), *Review of psychiatry* (Vol. 11, pp. 9–24). Washington, DC: American Psychiatric Press.

Howard, G. S., & Conway, C. G. (1986). Can there be an empirical science of volitional action? *American Psychologist, 41,* 1241–1251.

Kaplan, M. (1983). A women's view of DSM-III. *American Psychologist, 38,* 786–792.

Kass, F., Skodol, A., Charles, E., Spitzer, R., & Williams, J. (1985). Scaled ratings of DSM-III personality disorders. *American Journal of Psychiatry, 142,* 627–630.

Kernberg, O. F. (1996). A psychoanalytic theory of personality disorders. In M. F. Lenzenweger, & J. F. Clarkin (Eds.), *Major theories of personality disorder* (pp. 106–140). New York: Guilford Press.

Kirmayer, L. J., & Young, A. (1999). Culture and context in the evolutionary concept of mental disorder. *Journal of Abnormal Psychology, 108*, 446–452.

Klein, D. N. (1999). Commentary on Ryder and Bagby's diagnostic viability of depressive personality disorder: Theoretic and conceptual issues. *Journal of Personality Disorders, 13*, 118–127.

Knutson, B., Wolkowitz, O. M., Cole, S. W., Chan, T., Moore, E. A., Johnson, R. C., Terpstra, J., Turner, R. A., & Reus, V. I. (1998). Selective alteration of personality and social behavior by serotonergic intervention. *American Journal of Psychiatry, 155*, 373–379.

Koenigsberg, H. W., Kaplan, R. D., Gilmore, M. M., & Cooper, A. M. (1985). The relationship between syndrome and personality disorders in DSM-III: Experience with 2,462 patients. *American Journal of Psychiatry, 142*, 207–212.

Kupfer, D., First, M. B., & Regier, D. (2002). A research agenda for DSM-V. Washington, DC: American Psychiatric Association.

Kutchins, H., & Kirk, S. A. (1997). *Making us crazy: DSM: Psychiatric bible and the creation of mental disorders.* New York: Free Press.

Lehman, A. F., Alexopoulos, G. S., Goldman, H., Jeste, D., & Ustun, B. (2002). Mental disorders and disability: Time to reevaluate the relationship? In D. Kupfer (Ed.), *A research agenda for DSM-V* (pp. 201–218). Washington, DC: American Psychiatric Association.

Lilienfeld, S. O., & Marino, L. (1995). Mental disorder as a Roschian concept: A critique of Wakefield's "harmful dysfunction" analysis. *Journal of Abnormal Psychology, 104*, 411–420.

Lilienfeld, S. O., & Marino, L. (1999). Essentialism revisited: Evolutionary theory and the concept of mental disorder. *Journal of Abnormal Psychology, 108*, 400–411.

Lilienfeld, S. O., Waldman, I. D., & Israel, A. C. (1994). A critical examination of the use of the term "comorbidity" in psychopathology research. *Clinical Psychology: Science and Practice, 1*, 71–83.

Livesley, W. J. (2003). Diagnostic dilemmas in classifying personality disorder. In K. A. Phillips, M. B. First, & H. A. Pincus (Eds.), *Advancing DSM: Dilemmas in psychiatric diagnosis* (pp. 153–189). Washington, DC: American Psychiatric Association.

Loranger, A. W. (1990). The impact of DSM-III on diagnostic practice at a university hospital: A comparison of DSM-II and DSM-III on 10,914 patients. *Archives of General Psychiatry, 47*, 673–675.

Loranger, A. W. (1999). *International personality disorder examination (IPDE).* Odessa, FL: Psychological Assessment Resources.

McCrae, R. R., & Costa, P. T., Jr. (2003). *Personality in adulthood: A Five-Factor theory perspective.* New York: GuilfordPress.

Mellsop, G., Varghese, F. T. N., Joshua, S., & Hicks, A. (1982). The reliability of Axis II of DSM-III. *American Journal of Psychiatry, 139*, 1360–1361.

Morey, L. C. (1988). Personality disorders under DSM-III and DSM-III-R: An examination of convergence, coverage, and internal consistency. *American Journal of Psychiatry, 145*, 573–577.

Pfohl, B., Blum, N., Zimmerman, M. (1997). *Structured interview for DSM-IV personality.* Washington, DC: American Psychiatric Press.

Regier, D. A., Kaelber, C. T., Rae, D. S., Farmer, M. E., Knauper, B., Kessler, R. C., & Norquist, G. S. (1998). Limitations of diagnostic criteria and assessment instruments for mental disorders: Implications for research and policy. *Archives of General Psychiatry, 55*, 109–115.

Regier, D. A., & Narrow, W. E. (2002). Defining clinically significant psychopathology with epidemiologic data. In J. E. Helzer, & J. J. Hudziak (Eds.), *Defining psychopathology in the21st Century. DSM-V and beyond* (pp. 19–30). Washington: American Psychiatric Press.

Rogers, R. (2003). Standardizing DSM-IV diagnoses: The clinical applications of structured interviews. *Journal of Personality Assessment, 81*, 220–225.

Rogler, L. H. (1997). Making sense of historical changes in the diagnostic and statistical manual of Mental Disorders: Five propositions. *Journal of Health and Social Behavior, 38*, 9–20.

Rounsaville, B. J., Alarcon, R. D., Andrews, G., Jackson, J. S., Kendell, R. E., & Kendler, K. (2002). Basic nomenclature issues for DSM-V. In D. J. Kupfer, M. B. First, D. E. Regier (Eds.), *A research agenda for DSM-V* (pp. 1–29). Washington, DC: American Psychiatric Press.

Simola, S. K. (1992). Differences among sexist, nonsexist, and feminist family therapies. *Professional Psychology: Research and Practice, 23*, 397–403.

Spitzer, R. L. (1981). The diagnostic status of homosexuality in DSM-III: A reformulation of the issues. *American Journal of Psychiatry, 138*, 210–215.

Spitzer, R. L. (1998). Diagnosis and treatment are not the same. *Archives of General Psychiatry, 55*, 119.

Spitzer, R. L., Forman, J. B. W., & Nee, J. (1979). DSM-III field trials: I. Initial interrater diagnostic reliability. *American Journal of Psychiatry, 136*, 815–817.

Spitzer, R. L., & Wakefield, J. C. (1999). DSM-IV diagnostic criteria for clinical significance: Does it help solve the false positives problem? *American Journal of Psychiatry, 156*, 1856–1864.

Spitzer, R. L., & Williams, J. B. (1982). The definition and diagnosis of mental disorder. In W. R. Grove (Ed.), *Deviance and mental illness* (pp. 15–31). Beverly Hills, CA: Sage.

Spitzer, R. L., Williams, J. B., & Skodol, A. E. (1980). DSM-III: The major achievements and an overview. *American Journal of Psychiatry, 137*, 151–164.

Tyrer, P., & Johnson, T. (1996). Establishing the severity of personality disorder. *American Journal of Psychiatry, 153*, 1593–1597.

Verheul, R., & Widiger, T. A. (2004). A meta-analysis of the prevalence and usage of the personality disorder not otherwise specified (PDNOS) diagnosis. *Journal of Personality Disorders, 18*, 309–319.

Wakefield, J. C. (1997). Diagnosing DSM-IV—Part I: DSM-IV and the concept of disorder. *Behaviour, Research and Therapy, 35*, 633–649.

Wakefield, J. C. (1998). The DSM's theory neutral nosology is scientifically progressive: Response to Follette & Houts. *Journal of Consulting and Clinical Psychology, 66*, 846–852.

Wakefield, J. C. (1999). Evolutionary versus Roschian analyses of the concept of disorder. *Journal of Abnormal Psychology, 108*, 374–399.

Wakefield, J. C., & Spitzer, R. L. (2002). Why requiring clinical significance does not solve epidemiology's and DSM's validity problem: Response to Regier and Narrow. In J. J. Hudziak, & J. E. Helzer (Eds.), *Defining psychopathology in the 21st century: DSM-V and beyond* (pp. 31–40). Washington, DC: American Psychiatric Press.

Walker, L. E. A. (1994). Are personality disorders gender biased? In S. A. Kirk, & S. D. Einbinder (Eds.), *Controversial issues in mental health* (pp. 22–29). New York: Allyn & Bacon.

Webster, C., & Jackson, M. A. (1997). *Impulsivity: Theory, assessment & treatment.* New York: Guilford Press.

Wegner, D. M., & Wheatley, T. (1999). Apparent mental causation: Sources of the experience of will. *American Psychologist, 54*, 480–492.

Westen, D., & Arkowitz-Westen, L. (1998). Limitations of Axis II in diagnosing personality pathology in clinical practice. *American Journal of Psychiatry, 155*, 1767–1771.

Widiger, T. A. (2002). Personality disorders. In M. M. Antony, & D. H. Barlow (Eds.), *Handbook of assessment, treatment planning, and outcome for psychological disorders* (pp. 453–480). New York: Guilford Press.

Widiger, T. A., & Coker, L. A. (2002). Assessing personality disorders. In J. N. Butcher (Ed.), *Clinical personality assessment: Practical approaches. Oxford textbooks in clinical psychology* (2nd ed., Vol. 2, pp. 407–434). London, UK: Oxford University Press.

Widiger, T. A., Frances, A., Spitzer, R., & Williams, J. (1988). The DSM-III-R personality disorders: An overview. *American Journal of Psychiatry, 145*, 786–795.

Widiger, T. A., Mangine, S., Corbitt, E. M., Ellis, C. G., & Thomas, G. V. (1995). *Personality disorder interview-IV: A semistructured interview for the assessment of personality disorders.* Odessa, Florida: Psychological Assessment Resources.

Widiger, T. A., & Samuel, D. B. (2005). Evidence based assessment of personality disorders. *Psychological Assessment, 17*, 278–287.

Widiger, T. A., & Sankis, L. (2000). Adult psychopathology: Issues and controversies. *Annual Review of Psychology, 51*, 377–404.

Widiger, T. A., & Trull, T. J. (1991). Assessment of the five-factor model of personality. *Journal of Personality Assessment, 68*, 228–250.

Widiger, T. A., & Trull, T. J. (1998). Performance characteristics of the DSM-III-R personality disorder criteria sets. In T. A. Widiger, A. J., Frances, H. A. Pincus, R. Ross, M. B. First, W. W. Davis, & M. Klein (Eds.), *DSM-IV Sourcebook* (Vol. 4, pp. 357–373). Washington, DC: American Psychiatric Press.

Wiggins, J. S., Phillips, N., & Trapnell, P. (1989). Circular reasoning about interpersonal behavior: Evidence concerning some untested assumptions underlying diagnostic classification. *Journal of Personality and Social Psychology, 56*, 296–305.

World Health Organization. (1992). *The ICD-10 classification of mental and behavioural disorders. Clinical descriptions and diagnostic guidelines.* Geneva, Switzerland: World Health Organization.

Zimmerman, M., & Coryell, W. (1989). The reliability of personality disorder diagnoses in a nonpatient sample. *Journal of Personality Disorders, 3*, 53–57.

Zimmerman, M., & Mattia, J. I. (1999). Differences between clinical and research practices in diagnosing borderline personality disorder. *American Journal of Psychiatry, 156*, 1570–1574.

# 2

## Methodology

# Problems and Pitfalls in Designing Research on Normal–Abnormal Personality

**8**

Stephen Strack

In the first decade of the twenty-first century there are few areas of scientific inquiry as exciting as that of the interface between normal and abnormal personality. In just the last 25 years, theory and research in this area helped steer the American Psychiatric Association (1980, 1987, 1994) toward three revisions of the *Diagnostic and Statistical Manual of Mental Disorders* (i.e., *DSM-III, DSM-III-R, DSM-IV*), and is now shaping a fourth revision (i.e., DSM-V; Kupfer, First, & Regier, 2002; Livesley, 2001b; Widiger, 2003). Not only has research in this area helped to change and improve the official diagnostic manual, it has transformed the way we think about the classification of mental disorders, their definitional boundaries, their etiology, course, and remediation (Endler & Kocovski, 2002; Strack & Lorr, 1994).

At the same time, the study of normal–abnormal personality is still in its infancy. We are in the midst of defining what is normal and abnormal, how best to conceptualize and categorize personality disorders (PDs), how to explain why some people develop psychopathology and others do not, and how to intervene to improve the lives of those who suffer disorders of personality (Livesley, 2001b). Other entries in this volume offer a wealth of possibilities of how to approach the field of normal–abnormal personality in terms of theory, statistical methods, and assessment options. My task is to highlight some of the research design issues that must be considered when planning investigations to answer many important questions in this field. By developing an awareness of these issues, my hope is that students and novice professionals will learn to avoid some of the problems and pitfalls that befall researchers in this area.

My focus will be on pragmatic issues that affect the validity, reliability, and generalizability of research findings. I will touch only briefly on different kinds of experimental designs, as this is a complete topic all by itself. Likewise, I will not cover design problems that are specific to subfields like personality taxomony and assessment, or how to select statistical procedures to test specific hypotheses. For information about these topics, interested readers may consult other chapters in this volume as well as Kazdin (2003) and Reis and Judd (2000) on research designs; Tabachnick and Fidell (2000) on statistics; and Clark and Watson (1995), Lanyon and Goodstein (1997), Morey (2003), and Widiger and Coker (2002), on personality assessment.

When discussing research studies in a general way, and when giving examples, I will hold to three conventions for the sake of simplicity: I will use the term *experiment* for studies of all kinds (whether true experiments or not), Axis II of the *DSM-IV-TR* (American Psychiatric Association, 2000) as a definition for PDs, and assume that personality traits are the object of investigation. Readers should not mistake these conventions as a personal preference for, or endorsement of, experiments, *DSM*-defined PDs, and traits as being better than their alternatives.

# General Design Issues

Before discussing research design problems that are particular to studying the interface between normal and abnormal personality, let us consider some issues that are important for most areas of psychological study. In this section I will cover the nature and purpose of research, define what is meant by *methodology* and *research design*, identify major types of research designs, and discuss the importance of internal and external validity and reliability of measurement.

The goal of scientific research is to help establish knowledge. Although our everyday experience and clinical observations can be useful in answering many kinds of questions, the natural world is so complex that experience alone is not enough to understand the relationships among many variables. As well, we often have ingrained biases that cause us to see certain things but not others. Scientific research attempts to simplify the complexity of nature and to isolate particular phenomena for careful scrutiny. Research also attempts to limit and regulate our natural biases by making us adhere to objective methods and standards for determining cause and effect. Phenomena are examined by manipulating or varying values of the variable of interest while controlling extraneous factors that might otherwise influence the results. By controlling or holding constant sources of influence that might vary under ordinary circumstances, the relation between the variables of interest can be examined with some clarity.

## Methodology and Research Design

Methodology refers to the diverse principles, procedures, and practices that govern research, while research design refers to the plan or arrangement that is used to examine the question(s) of interest. When most people think of designing a research study they focus on the pragmatics of the task; namely, the details of putting together and carrying out an investigation. However, methodology is also a way of thinking: It teaches us about the relations between variables, about cause and effect, and about the conclusions that may be drawn from theory, research, and experience (Kazdin, 2003).

Designing research studies is sometimes conceptually simple, such as having an experimental and control group of subjects. One group is exposed to an experimental manipulation while the other group is not, and measurements are taken to determine any differences between the groups before and after the manipulation. Unfortunately, most research on normal–abnormal personality is not this simple. Few personality studies have true experimental designs with random selection and assignment of subjects (Campbell & Stanley, 1966). As well, personality is so complex that investigators are rarely able to isolate and control extraneous factors to the point that a single interpretation is possible (Reis & Judd, 2000).

The particular methods and research design that one chooses for a study follow from the questions that are asked. Most research questions are posed in the form of *hypotheses*. An example of a hypothesis in personality investigation might be, "Persons diagnosed with antisocial PD are more likely to use illegal drugs than persons who do not meet diagnostic criteria for this disorder." Scientific hypotheses are attempts to explain, predict, and explore specific relations. When hypotheses are formulated, they represent *if–then* statements about a particular phenomenon. The *if* portion usually refers to the independent variable that is manipulated or varied in some way; the *then* portion refers to the dependent variable or resulting data. In our example, antisocial PD diagnosis is the independent variable and illegal drug use is the dependent variable.

Findings consistent with an experimental hypothesis do not necessarily *prove* the hypothesis. Data can be taken as proof of a hypothesis only if no reasonable alternative hypothesis can account for the results, or if the predicted relations would be obtained if and only if the hypothesis were true. Unfortunately, these requirements are more likely to be met by logic and deductive reasoning than by scientific research. Whether another hypothesis could reasonably account for the results may be a matter for future investigators to ascertain. Also, whether a finding would result only from a particular hypothesis cannot be known with certainty. The confidence of certainty provided in logical deductions is not available in science (Kazdin, 2003).

Methods are chosen so as to give investigators the best chance of ruling out or making implausible competing explanations for the results. The better an experiment is designed, the fewer the alternative plausible explanations that can be advanced to account for the findings. Ideally, only the effects of the independent variable will stand alone as the proximal cause of the results, but in personality research this condition is rarely met.

## Types of Research Designs

Three types of designs are frequently used by psychological investigators: *experimental*, *quasiexperimental*, and *case–control* or *correlational*. True *experiments* seek to control as many nonexperimental variables as possible (i.e., the elements not being investigated), and require random assignment of study subjects to the groups that receive an experimental manipulation and those that do not (control groups). These studies are typically conducted in controlled environments in such settings as a laboratory, medical facility, or university office. The goal is to show that a particular outcome or set of outcomes following the introduction of an experimental variable is proximally caused by the experimental variable only.

*Quasiexperimental* designs are those that fail to control for one or more extraneous variables such that certainty cannot be achieved that the outcome of the study is due only to the experimental manipulation. Clinical investigators are frequently unable to randomly assign subjects to the various groups under scrutiny and to have true control groups. This is because hospital and clinic patients often need to receive specific treatments within a short period of time and might be injured if they received an experimental treatment or had to wait unnecessarily for an intervention (as might be true in control groups).

Experimental and quasiexperimental designs are useful when investigators wish to study the effects of a particular manipulation on a group of subjects, for example, the introduction of a new drug or type of psychotherapy. In personality research, investigators are more frequently interested in identifying and understanding the characteristics of people who vary with respect to a particular attribute or trait. An assumption in this research is that the variables under study are relevant to all the subjects in a defined population, and that differences in the variables can be reliably measured. By measuring levels of a particular attribute or trait in a selected group of people and then associating those levels with other attributes or traits possessed by the same group of people, conclusions can be made about particular individual differences associated with the experimental variable. These types of studies are called *case-control* or *correlational* (Kazdin, 2003). Here the investigator does not manipulate a particular variable or variables under controlled conditions, but rather makes observations on how two or more variables behave in relation to one another. An example would be selecting groups of patients with and without a PD and comparing them on other variables like the number of interpersonal problems they report.

As the reader will conclude, the greater control over extraneous variables permitted by experimental designs gives them the greatest chance of producing results where causation can be determined with good certainty. Nevertheless, quasiexperimental and case-control/correlational designs can provide the foundation for strong causal inferences when investigators select subjects wisely, use valid and reliable measuring instruments, take outcome measures at appropriate times, and use powerful statistical procedures for analyzing results.

Whether experimental, quasiexperimental, or case-control/correlational in nature, most research studies concern themselves with the here-and-now, and take measurements at one point in time. Studies that take a single set of measurements are sometimes called *one shot, single sample*, or *single measurement* designs. Some studies take measurements at multiple time points within a relatively small time frame, say several days to a few months. Characteristics of study subjects are usually assessed at specific time intervals but may involve continuous measurements (e.g., ongoing recordings of pulse, heart rate, and temperature). Other studies examine persons over long periods of time—decades and beyond—and take periodic measurements over many years. Studies that take measurements at multiple time points have many names that highlight a central feature of the way measurements are taken, for example *repeated measures, cross-logged, time interval*, etc. (Kazdin, 2003).

A study is called *cross-sectional* when comparisons are made between groups at a given point in time. A study is called *longitudinal* when comparisons are made within a group or between groups over an extended period of time, often several years. Longitudinal studies are usually more complex and expensive than cross-sectional studies, and require a considerable time commitment from both the investigator and subject. In return for this investment longitudinal studies of well-defined groups offer insights into intraindividual changes and age-related developmental issues that cannot be examined in cross-sectional research. For example, a central thesis of personality theory is that trait characteristics of normal persons are stable across the adult life span. A series of cross-sectional studies using subjects of varying ages might be able to demonstrate that levels of a particular trait do not vary as a function of age, but only a longitudinal study can document stability or change *within the same person over time*, and firmly link this to the aging process (McCrae & Costa, 2003).

## Validity

Although many extraneous factors can be recognized and eliminated or controlled in advance of an experiment, others cannot. Human beings are notoriously unreliable and can introduce many sources of systematic and unsystematic error within a given study (e.g., due to carelessness, fatigue, and motivation to dissimulate). Additionally, findings from large groups of studies may be invalidated when a subsequent researcher discovers a "bug" in a method or procedure that was previously believed to be reliable (e.g., a personality measure believed to be valid is later found to be problematic; Block, Block, & Harrington, 1974).

There are a number of well-known threats to the validity of experimental results (see Table 8.1). Some of these are caused by failures to properly control the events that might serve as the basis for competing explanations of why the findings occurred. Others refer to problems that limit reliability and generalizability of study findings. Most readers are already familiar with these issues, so a summary should suffice. Discussions of these issues can be found in many research design texts (e.g., Campbell & Stanley, 1966; Kazdin, 2003; Kirk, 1994).

*Internal validity* refers to whether a research study was designed and conducted in such a way as to permit valid conclusions about the findings. In other words, can we be reasonably sure that the experimental manipulation caused the observed effect on the dependent variable as opposed to some other extraneous effect? *External validity* refers to the extent that an observed finding or set of findings can be generalized to populations, settings, times, and measures not specifically studied in the investigation. For example, can the findings obtained with a particular group of PD subjects be said to apply to other groups of PD subjects who may be of different ages, gender, or come from different cultures?

Given the definitions for internal and external validity it may seem that an investigator should always maximize internal validity by eliminating or holding constant all sources of experimental error. However, doing this comes at the cost of external validity. For example, when human behavior is examined in a precisely controlled laboratory setting it is difficult to say that study findings will generalize to human behavior in the outside world where extraneous factors are not controlled. As a rule, design elements that increase internal validity have an inverse effect on external validity, and vice versa;

### Internal validity threats

Factors that affect the extent to which an experiment rules out alternative explanations of the results

*History:* Any event occurring in the experiment (other than the independent variable) or outside the experiment that may account for the results.

*Maturation:* Changes over time that occur in subjects that are outside the control of the experiment (e.g., becoming fatigued or bored) that may affect outcomes.

*Testing:* The effect that taking a test one time may have on subsequent performance on the test.

*Instrumentation:* Changes in the measurement instruments or procedures that affect the accuracy of measurement.

*Statistical Regression:* The tendency of extreme scores on any measure to revert (regress) toward the mean of a distribution when the measurement device is readministered.

*Selection Biases:* Systematic differences in groups that occur as a result of the selection or assignment of subjects.

*Attrition:* The effect on study findings of the loss of subjects over a period of time.

*Combination of selection and other threats (e.g., selection x history):* This refers to the effects of selection in interaction with other factors. Selection × history interaction occurs when one of the study groups has a historical experience that the other group did not have and that may affect outcomes.

*Diffusion or Imitation of Treatment:* When an intervention given to one group is accidentally given (or exposed) to some or all of the subjects in other groups.

*Special Treatment or Reactions of Controls:* Control groups may react to special treatment or conditions offered to it that are not accounted for in the research design.

### External validity threats

Factors that influence the extent to which the results of an experiment can be generalized beyond the conditions of the experiment to other populations, settings, and condition

*Sample Characteristics:* The extent to which study findings may be generalized to groups that differ with respect to such features as age, race, ethnic background, or education.

*Stimulus Characteristics and Settings:* Features of the study with which the intervention or condition may be associated and include the setting, experimenters, interviewers, etc.

*Reactivity of Experimental Arrangements:* The influence of the subjects' awareness that they are participating in an investigation.

*Multiple-Treatment Interference:* Drawing conclusions about a given treatment when it is evaluated in the context of other treatments. The conclusion drawn about one treatment or intervention might be restricted by the administration of prior treatments.

*Novelty Effects:* Refers to the possibility that the effects of an intervention may in part depend on their innovativeness or novelty in the situation.

*Reactivity of Assessment:* Any condition of assessment that differs from those to which the investigator may wish to generalize. For example, subjects may vary their responses on tests based on their beliefs about what is expected of them.

*Test Sensitization:* The effects of prior testing on later administrations of the same or different tests.

*Timing of Measurement:* Refers to the differences in measurements attributable to the time frame within which they were obtained. For example, outcomes measures taken at 1-month post treatment may not be similar to results of tests given 3 months after the treatment was administered. Different conclusions may obtain from such differences.

*Notes:* Adapted from Kazdin (2003). Although originally developed with true experiments in mind, these validity threats are applicable to the quasiexperimental and nonexperimental (e.g., correlational) studies typically undertaken by personality researchers.

the more internally precise and controlled a study is (high internal validity), the less generalizability there will be (low external validity).

*Construct validity in research design* refers to how we explain the observed effects of an experimental manipulation on the outcome variable(s). What was the causal agent involved? Can we adequately explain the effect by a hypothesized construct? In the study of personality we are typically interested in whether a study's findings support or challenge a particular theoretical perspective. Construct validity also has other meanings. In particular, the *construct validity of a test measure* refers to how accurately and well it assesses the quality or characteristic it was intended to measure. For example, a measure of *DSM-IV-TR* (American Psychiatric Association, 2000) PD would be said to have high construct validity if it could be demonstrated, by independent measures, to fully and accurately assess the diagnostic criteria spelled out in the manual.

*Statistical conclusion validity* addresses our confidence in making a conclusion about an experimental effect using particular statistical tests and procedures. Can the particular statistical tests used by the researchers adequately determine the outcome under investigation? Another important issue is how well a particular investigation can detect the hypothesized effects if they actually exist (i.e., the *power* of a study; see Cohen, 1988, 1992).

## Reliability of Measurement

A measuring instrument may be said to be accurate if it can precisely assay the quality or characteristic it was designed to measure. We expect a weight scale to measure pounds and ounces (or grams) quite accurately, but we do not expect such precision in the measurement of personality characteristics. This is because our definitions for personality variables are usually inexact or *fuzzy*, and our assessment methods are typically indirect and imprecise. For example, although most people agree on what is meant by *sociability* (i.e., the qualities that make a person sociable), theorists usually do not define this characteristic precisely (e.g., state that a person who has $X$ number of friends is high in sociability), and our assessments usually come from self-reports and observer ratings of behavior in circumscribed settings, methods that are known to be vulnerable to error.

Because the definitions of personality variables are expected to be imprecise, investigators place great emphasis on the reliability of the measurements that are taken. In this context *reliability* refers to the repeatability or dependability of measurement. In a hypothetical situation where the measuring procedure is known to be completely reliable (e.g., a well-calibrated weight scale), and where the attribute being measured is stable and unlikely to change over a short period of time (e.g., weight of a person over 1 week), repeated measurement of the attribute over the short time interval will yield highly similar results. Alternately, it would be assumed that any change in the obtained measure over time would reflect a true change in the attribute under study (i.e., not be due to errors in measurement). As an example, a reliable measure of sociability should show that a person has the same or very similar sociability score over a period of a few weeks (because sociability is a stable characteristic). If a person's sociability score increased or decreased significantly over this time interval (e.g., following an experimental manipulation), we should be able to verify that this was caused by a change in sociability (not a flaw of the measure). Reliability is the more generic term; the terms *consistency* and *stability* are employed to describe instrument-related and time-related reliability, respectively (Kazdin, 2003).

Consistency refers to the agreement that is obtained by simultaneously using two or more instruments (e.g., scales, rulers, or tests). Any measuring instrument or set of instruments may be regarded as being drawn from a large population of such instruments (real or hypothetical) that might have been used to measure this particular attribute. Consistency is usually evaluated by simultaneous testing with multiple instruments, preferably selected at random from the available population of such instruments (Lanyon & Goodstein, 1997). Although this can be a fairly easy process in some areas of science (e.g., measures of temperature and physical dimensions such as height and weight), consistency is often difficult to achieve in personality assessment. This will be discussed in subsequent sections of this chapter.

Stability refers to the consistency of the measurement obtained with the same instrument over time. Retesting over time may involve consistency as well as stability, if another instrument is used to make the second measurement. If the same instrument is used on both occasions, a direct assessment of the stability of the measurement can be made. Failure to obtain complete reliability is thus a consequence of the inconsistencies or errors that are a function of changes occurring in the system over time, or of differences associated with the particular instrument used, or both (Lanyon & Goodstein, 1997).

## Summary of General Issues

Scientific methods are used to create knowledge by simplifying and regulating relationships among variables so that a clear understanding of cause and effect can be achieved. In doing this, science helps us overcome personal biases. Researchers focus their efforts on planning experiments in such a way as to rule out or make implausible competing explanations of the results. The better an experiment is designed, the fewer the alternative plausible explanations that can be advanced to explain the findings. Toward this end, they seek methods of investigation that maximize the internal and external validity of their findings, an important feature of which is reliability of measurement.

# Specific Design Issues

Along with the issues just covered, researchers who study the interface between normal and abnormal personality must additionally consider design problems unique to this area of scientific inquiry, for example problems associated with defining and measuring the phenotypic (observed) expression of traits that cannot be observed or measured directly, in populations of disturbed persons who cannot be placed in controlled environments for experimental purposes.

## Defining the Domains of Normality and Psychopathology

A pervasive problem in the study of normal–abnormal personality is how to define the domains of normality and psychopathology. There is no gold standard or widely accepted definition of what makes one person "normal" and another "abnormal." The most widely accepted definition of PD is the one offered by the *DSM* (e.g., *DSM-IV-TR*; American Psychiatric Association, 2000), but even this definition is widely criticized because the diagnostic criteria are sometimes confusing and arbitrary, and diagnosis is categorical rather than dimensional (i.e., present vs. absent as opposed to a cut-off point along a dimensional scale; Samuel & Widiger, this volume, chapter 7). Complicating matters is the research showing that the traits underlying some PDs may be continuous in nature while others are discontinuous (i.e., categorical; see Haslam & Williams, this volume, chapter 12; Markon & Krueger, this volume, chapter 10). Prototype models of PD (see Millon & Grossman, this volume, chapter 1; Pincus, 2005; Westen & Bradley, 2005) offer alternatives to traditional, dimensional and categorical descriptons of PD that may resolve some of the problems we have in definition and trait overlap.

Curiously, there is no counterpart to the *DSM* in the realm of normality. That is, no one is diagnosed as being normal by widely accepted criteria for normality or health. Many see this as a major stumbling block that interferes with progress in the field (Sabshin, 1989, 2005; Strack & Lorr, 1997). In current research, normality is usually *assumed* among persons who (a) do not meet *DSM* criteria for PD or other mental disorder, (b) have no history of psychiatric problems, and (c) are not currently seeking help for mental health reasons.

Although there is no gold standard for either normality or abnormality, there are a number of theories of personality that offer well-reasoned definitions for these domains, and that may be used for research purposes (see Part I of this book). Each theory defines normality and abnormality differently, but the important point is that they have specific definitions that are tied to broad theoretical constructs. For research on normal–abnormal personality to yield valid and reliable findings, the definitions for these domains must be clearly spelled out and faithfully followed by the researcher.

In this context it is important to note that *because* there are many competing definitions of normality and abnormality, when interpreting study results, conclusions and generalizations should be limited to the variable domain(s) within which the study was cast. For example, research on *DSM* PDs (American Psychiatric Association, 2000) can be generalized to other studies that define and measure psychopathology the same way (i.e., use *DSM* criteria), but not directly to studies that define psychopathology differently (e.g., those addressing Eysenck's, 1994, model of PDs). It is a common fault for researchers to ignore the conceptual differences between different models of psychopathology, and to erroneously conclude that one study supports or does not support a particular model when the research does not actually address the model in question. This is akin to comparing apples with oranges and should be avoided.

## Dimensional Models

Most current models of personality and psychopathology view normality and abnormality as end points on a continuum, with no sharp dividing line differentiating the two domains (Livesley, 2001b; Millon, 1996). The assumption in these models is that the same traits underlie normal and abnormal personality. Abnormality is presumed to be caused by too much or too little of a given trait or set of traits. For example, a high level of neuroticism (which includes high sensitivity to unpleasant, negative emotions) may, by itself, place an individual at risk for mood disorders, but more pervasive problems may crop up if the same person has low levels of agreeableness and openness to experience (which, at moderate levels, might help the person cope with his or her emotional sensitivity). Normal persons are presumed to have moderate or high levels of adaptive traits and low levels of maladaptive traits. Each personality model specifies which traits are involved in differentiating normal and abnormal personality, and the levels of specific traits, or profile of multiple traits, that are associated with dysfunctional behavior (see Part I of this book for examples). With research on dimensional models it is important to specify which trait variables are being studied, how these variables are involved in differentiating normal and abnormal personality, and the specific definitions for when normality is presumed and when psychopathology is developed.

## Categorical Models

In this perspective, normal and abnormal personalities are believed to be distinctly different, so much so that they are viewed as being categorically different (apples and oranges). Although virtually all categorical models acknowledge borderline cases (those in the gray area between normality and abnormality), they presume that the vast majority of persons will fall well within their defined boundaries for normality and abnormality. As an example, in the *DSM* (American Psychiatric Association, 2000) approach psychiatric patients with PDs are distinguished from nondisordered cases by meeting the criteria specified in the diagnostic manual. Alternatively, in some biological/neurological models psychopathology is defined by the presence of a particular physiological marker for a trait assayed by blood test (see Claridge, this volume, chapter 6; Haslam & Williams, this volume, chapter 12; Korfine & Lenzenweger, 1995; Lenzenweger & Korfine, 1992; Markon & Krueger, this volume, chapter 10). The class or group of disordered individuals is defined by those who are "positive" for the presence of the marker, while nondisordered persons are those who are "negative" with respect to the marker. Here again, the main issue for prospective researchers is to clearly define which model is being used and how the model differentiates normal and abnormal persons into categories.

## Pragmatic Criteria

Although mainstream models of personality and psychopathology posit the existence of underlying traits as being the proximal cause of observed differences in normality and abnormality, some theorists and researchers have focused their attention on sociocultural variables (Millon, 1996; Paris, 1999, 2005). In this view, normality and abnormality are shaped by factors that are external to the self, and definitions of what is normal and abnormal are determined by what a particular culture or group says is normal and deviant. For example, high levels of a particular trait like dependency may be viewed favorably in one culture and unfavorably in another. Dependent behaviors will be reinforced and shaped differently based on whether members of the culture see these as socially desirable or undesirable. Behaving in a particularly obsequious or submissive manner might be viewed as a sign of PD in one culture, although it may be an indicator of good manners in another. As well, even within the same culture, some behaviors may be viewed as evidence of abnormality in some situations but be viewed as normal in others (e.g., aggressiveness).

The variability of behavior within a particular person (intraindividual variability) is a recent area of interest, particularly among interpersonal theorists and researchers (Moskowitz & Zuroff, 2004; Pincus, 2005; Pincus & Gurtman, this volume, chapter 4). Instead of looking at normality and abnormality as a function of dimensionalized traits or categories, the behavioral flexibility or rigidity of persons is examined in interpersonal interactions where measurements of responses are taken to the same targets (specific people) in the same situations, and across targets and situations. Variables like *spin*, *flux*, and *pulse* (Moskowitz & Zuroff, 2004) are used to define an individual's characteristic interpersonal style. People with PDs presumably demonstrate more stereotyped and narrowly defined sets of behaviors to a variety of people and situations than healthy people, but evidence for this conclusion is still being collected.

When studying personality from a model that specifies socially arbitrary or pragmatic criteria for normality–abnormality, there is a particularly heavy burden on the researcher to clearly define not only which variables differentiate normal from abnormal functioning, but also how the differentiating variables are expected to perform under which conditions.

## Selecting Subjects

The type(s) of subjects used for a particular study are determined primarily by the kinds of research questions being addressed. Psychiatric samples are typically used for determining the structure and stability of personality traits in abnormal populations, the incidence and prevalence of various diagnoses, co-occurrence of PDs and clinical syndromes, and the efficacy of treatment interventions. Samples of nonhelp-seeking normal adults are used to determine the structure and stability of personality traits in normal populations, the incidence and prevalence of various traits and clinical diagnoses in groups that are not seeking psychiatric help, and the experimental effects of various procedures and treatments on presumably healthy people.

Matched samples of psychiatric patients and normal adults are especially useful in studies designed to highlight similarities and differences between the two populations. Researchers first define the characteristics of the patient sample they are working with in terms of variables like sex, age, education, socioeconomic level, ethnicity, and medical and family history. They start with the psychiatric group because they are usually unable to manipulate the characteristics of this sample (i.e., they have to use the people who show up at the clinic or hospital). After this is done, they recruit normal subjects from the surrounding community so that the characteristics of the group as a whole are as closely aligned as possible to the psychiatric group on the matching variables. In these studies, both groups of subjects may be exposed to the same experimental manipulations, and the same measurements would be taken for each group. The statistical procedures employed would target differences between the groups. When executed properly, this kind of study can provide powerful evidence for effects caused by the population differences alone (e.g., personality trait levels that are different in the two groups).

Whatever population is chosen for research it is important to clearly define the target domain and spell out how selection procedures ensure that participants are members of that domain. This is often not an easy task. For example, there is no widely accepted standard for normality, and even when using presumably normal subjects (e.g., nonhelp-seeking college students) research has shown that these samples usually contain individuals with undiagnosed personality disorders, substance abuse problems, and affective disorders. Furthermore, although psychiatric samples are often presumed to be abnormal, individuals within these samples may vary widely in the degree and persistence of their psychopathology (Livesley, 2001a).

When selecting disordered subjects, investigators need to objectively define what is meant by abnormal, specify how the participants were selected, and how they are similar with respect to nontargeted variables (e.g., sex, age, education). Patient samples can be generic (e.g., all persons admitted to a psychiatric clinic) or defined by particular diagnostic criteria (e.g., PD). They can be selected on the basis of a clinical interview (by one or more qualified professionals), by psychometrically sound assessment devices (interviews, self-report forms), and/or laboratory measures (blood tests, DNA). The time frame within which the patients are selected is important. For example, people are typically most distressed when they first present for help. Their level of distress typically goes down within a few days after admission to treatment regardless of the type of treatment offered, or even when no treatment is given. Measurements taken in the first few days of admission may not accurately assess a patient's typical level of functioning (Shea, 1997).

Normal samples are frequently obtained from college campuses and the general community. Selection criteria need to be unambiguous in order to avoid inclusion of people who have non-normal characteristics. Many researchers do selection interviews or give questionnaires that target current and past mental health problems. On the basis of these data they exclude prospective candidates who are currently receiving psychiatric treatment, have a history of substance abuse, or have been previously hospitalized for psychiatric symptoms or treated with psychotropic medication.

In clinical research, psychiatric comparison samples are frequently used instead of normal control groups. Subjects for these samples are typically chosen from among the population of persons admitted for treatment to a particular clinic or hospital, but who (a) do not meet the same diagnostic criteria as the experimental clinical group, or (b) are the same as the experimental group but do not receive the experimental manipulation. When properly selected, psychiatric control groups can be excellent for comparison purposes because they share many of the characteristics of the experimental group. However, generalization to nonpsychiatric (normal) samples is usually tenuous.

Whether normal or psychiatric, random selection and assignment of subjects to experimental conditions are ideal because these procedures help to balance out the effects of nonresearch variables on observed measurements, such as the effects of age, socioeconomic status, and life experience. However, this is often not possible in clinical settings. If random selection is not feasible, researchers should take special care to make sure that the sample obtained is reasonably reflective of the characteristics of the patient population from which it was selected. Common techniques for this purpose are (a) selecting consecutive admissions to a particular clinic or treatment program, (b) sampling patients from multiple settings, and (c) matching sample characteristics to those of the known population.

When random assignment is not possible, it is appropriate to compare the characteristics of the samples assigned to various treatment conditions (e.g., sex, age, education), and to control for observed differences either in the experimental procedures or later, through statistical analysis.

## Diagnosing Personality

Just as there is no standard for defining normality and pathology, there is no standard method for *operationalizing* major variables within these domains (i.e., no best strategy for measuring the attributes and behaviors believed to define normality and abnormality; Livesley, 2001a, 2001b). Investigators may choose from a variety of experimental and commercially available interviews, rating scales, check lists, questionnaires, and behavioral sampling devices to diagnose personality (Clark & Harrison, 2001). When making choices, investigators must be careful to select instruments that actually assess the constructs they wish to study and also have good psychometric properties (e.g., are reliable and valid). This can be difficult because definitions of PD have changed significantly over the last 25 years. For example, to study *DSM-IV-TR* PDs (American Psychological Association, 2000) requires one or more measures that can assess specific diagnostic criteria for individual disorders, the functional impairment or distress in major life areas such as work and relationships, which is presumed to exist in PDs, and be able to verify that the pattern of disturbance in those diagnosed was manifest early in life. A small number of structured interviews cover all of these bases (e.g., *International Personality Disorder Examination*, IPDE, Loranger, 1999, and *Personality Disorder Interview-IV*, PDI-IV, Widiger, Manguine, Corbitt, Ellis, & Thomas, 1995), but because they are relatively new there are almost no data on their validity (Clark & Harrison, 2001). Instruments using criteria from earlier versions of the *DSM* may be better validated than the newer interviews, but caution is advised in using these because even minor changes in the wording of diagnostic criteria can have major effects on patients receiving a PD diagnosis (Blashfield, Blum, & Pfohl, 1992).

Dimensional models of personality, and most models that distinguish normal and abnormal personality on the basis of categories, are concerned with multiple traits that underlie the specific personality types or categories. However, traits are typically not "all or none" (present or absent within a person), they are often viewed as being broad or narrow in their effects on behavior, and they are believed to be hierarchical in nature, with broader traits subsuming more narrow traits (e.g., Eysenck, 1994; Goldberg, 1993; Markon, Krueger, & Watson, 2005). Because of this most personality measurement systems do not assess the presence or absence of traits within an individual, but rather the level of various traits on separate continua. As well, some measures assess aggregate personality types (or styles), whereas others measure broad or narrow traits. For example, *Millon Clinical Multiaxial Inventory-III* (MCMI-III; Millon, 1997) scales measure individual personality styles that are linked to the PDs diagnosed on Axis II of *DSM-IV* (American Psychiatric Association, 2000). This is the broadest (or highest) level of measurement because each personality style is believed to be the expression of (and result of) many traits in interaction with each other. The NEO-PI-R (Costa & McCrae, 1992) measures five broad trait dimensions, and several subtrait dimensions that are nested under each of the five broader traits. Even at the broadest level of measurement, the NEO-PI-R does not offer a personality portrait of an individual until the profile configuration of traits and subtraits is examined as a whole.

The point here is that in addition to specifying the theory or model that is being used to guide an empirical project, researchers need to be mindful of how the theory or model is operationalized by the study measures in terms of such factors as (a) how well the measures define and assess the theoretical constructs under consideration, (b) their reliability and validity, and (c) the level of measurement offered—aggregate personality style, superordinate (higher order) trait, or narrow (lower order) trait.

In this context I want to again emphasize the importance of limiting one's research conclusions and generalizations to the domain of studies that use the same or equivalent definitions. It is a common problem in PD research for investigators to assume the equivalency of operational definitions when no such equivalency has been established. This leads to erroneous conclusions and slows down scientific progress. An example of this is that many studies purport to focus on the *DSM* (American Psychiatric Association, 2000) definition of PD but use measurement techniques that operationalize PDs differently from *DSM* standards, like the MMPI-2 (Butcher et al., 2001) and MCMI-III (Millon, 1997). Investigators of these studies typically discuss their findings as if diagnosing PDs with these self-report instruments is the same as a clinician diagnosing a patient by following the exact *DSM* guidelines. However, these measures do not directly assess many *DSM* diagnostic criteria, and the MCMI-III is arguably a better measure of Millon's (1996) model of psychopathology than the *DSM* model. The outcome in these instances will be research data that do not faithfully represent *DSM*. As a rule, people who conduct studies that diagnose PDs solely on the basis of self-report measures should limit their conclusions and generalizations to other studies that diagnose PDs the same way. When making conclusions and generalizations *across* diagnostic methods (e.g., from self-report to interview or vice versa) these should be labeled as *speculation* until and unless equivalency across methods is demonstrated.

## Clinical Diagnosis of PD

The *DSM* (American Psychiatric Association, 2000) model provides a widely used, clinical standard for determining personality pathology, and because of this research participants may be selected on the basis of a clinical diagnosis of PD. However, clinicians vary greatly in their level of skill in making diagnoses, so care should be taken to assure *reliability* of the diagnoses. This can be established by training clinicians in the proper use of *DSM*, and having multiple persons diagnose the same individuals to demonstrate a high level of agreement using statistics like the *kappa* coefficient (Cohen, 1968; Tabachnick & Fidell, 2000). Ideally, it is best to use multiple clinicians who provide independent diagnoses of the same persons.

## Structured Interviews

In many circumstances reliability of diagnosis can be enhanced by the use of a structured interview (see Widiger, Costa, & Samuel, this volume, chapter 13). These provide a standard set of questions and probing guidelines for the interviewer. Each patient is presented with the same or similar set of questions (based on the particular protocol used), and diagnosis is made based on standardized scoring criteria. This method of assessment often takes more time than a typical clinical interview, but it increases reliability by standardizing the diagnostic procedure. To assure reliability, all interviewers should be trained in the same way, and an estimate of each interviewer's reliability should be calculated. Many structured interviews can be effectively given by nonprofessionals, thereby decreasing the cost of obtaining accurate diagnoses.

## Self-Report Questionnaires

Wide availability, ease of use, and low cost have helped make self-report questionnaires very popular among personality researchers for assessing normality and psychopathology (see Part III of this book). Because many of these instruments were developed using sound psychometric techniques, and have a set of norms with which to compare an individual's scores, some validity and reliability can be assured as long as they are used for their intended purposes. However, self-report questionnaires are susceptible to biased responding and faking (Lanyon & Goodstein, 1997). Additional problems may accrue in trying to get an accurate assessment from individuals who may not understand what they are supposed to do, are uncooperative, confused, tired, distressed, or under the influence of psychotropic medication.

Although not a problem with the method per se, many self-report measures incompletely assess a particular domain. For example, two frequently used inventories, the MMPI-2 (Butcher et al., 2001) and MCMI-III (Millon, 1997), can be scored to measure *DSM* (American Psychiatric Association, 2000) PDs, but neither provides an exact match to *DSM* diagnostic criteria. Among the mismatched areas is that *DSM* diagnosis is categorical whereas measurement of PDs on the MMPI-2 and MCMI-III is by continuous (ordinal) scales. No accepted standard exists for determining when a particular score or sets of scores on these instruments maximizes *DSM* diagnosis.

# Differentiating Personality From Other Qualities and Characteristics

The *DSM* (American Psychiatric Association, 2000) system since 1980 has placed PDs on a separate axis from other psychiatric disorders. The assumption is that personality is a stable feature of psychiatric patients while Axis I disorders are more fleeting, with courses that typically wax and wane based on underlying disease factors and psychosocial stressors. In spite of this conceptual distinction, clinicians often find it difficult to differentiate personality features from other psychiatric disorders. For example, there are many overlapping criteria for depressive PD, dysthymic disorder, and major depressive disorder. When interviewing a depressed psychiatric patient it may be difficult or impossible to get an accurate reading of the symptoms that arise from PD and those that stem from other causes. Except among researchers who diagnose PD according to physiological markers that remain relatively unchanged throughout adulthood, a persistent problem is how to differentiate personality from psychiatric disorders and vice versa. This is because trait expression on a superficial (phenotypic) level can vary greatly across persons, and because most of our current methods for diagnosing PD rely on observation, interview, and self-report.

## Co-occurrence of Personality Style/Disorder and Psychiatric Disorders

As is true with issues of how to define normality and abnormality, it is important to be clear about how one defines diagnostic or grouping criteria, as well as the areas of overlap between personality and psychiatric disorder. The term *comorbidity* was coined by Feinstein (1970) to describe "any distinct additional clinical entity that has existed or that may occur during the clinical course of a patient who has the index disease under study" (pp. 456–457). However, in our current scientific state of fuzzy definitions and shifting boundaries of classification, the term *co-occurrence* seems more appropriate for describing Axis I disorders that occur in people diagnosed with PD:

> Feinstein's definition presupposes that we understand enough about mental disorders that we would feel comfortable describing them as "distinct"—stating with confidence that a specific patient with a specific "index disease" has an "additional," co-occurring disorder. [O]ur understanding of mental disorders has not yet reached the level at which current nosological entities can be described as truly "distinct." (Dolan-Sewell, Krueger, & Shea, 2001, p. 85)

Whether one uses *DSM* (American Psychiatric Association, 2000) criteria for diagnosing personality and clinical syndromes or other criteria (e.g., scores on self-report tests), several issues should be kept in mind about the rate of co-occurrence one will find: (a) The time frame of co-occurrence can influence the results; for example, lifetime co-occurrence will be different from co-occurrence during a single presentation at a hospital or clinic. (b) Rates of co-occurrence will vary by type of sample; for example, psychiatric samples show higher rates of co-occurrence than nonhelp-seeking college students. (c) Different methods of assessment can cause different rates of co-occurrence; for example, higher rates are typically found with self-report measures compared with structured interviews. (d) Whenever diagnostic criteria overlap, co-occurrence rates will be higher because of this overlap; for example, *DSM-IV-TR* (American Psychiatric Association, 2000) depressive PD and dysthymic disorder. (e) Different cut-off criteria for diagnosis will alter rates of occurrence; for example, using a cut-off score of 20 on the BDI-II will yield more "depressed" cases than a cut-off score of 30 (Dolan-Sewell, Krueger, & Shea, 2001).

### State versus Trait Issues

Although by definition personality is a stable and pervasive feature of any individual, personality characteristics can vary within a person depending on a variety of factors, for example, life stress, chronic disease, and presence of a psychiatric disorder (Livesley, 2001b; McCrae & Costa, 2003). As well, some persons by nature are inconsistent, experiencing and expressing variable moods even without the presence of stressors or illness, while some seem to be impervious to strong emotion or outside influences (Millon, 1996). Thus, many outside variables can affect personality expression, while personality can affect the way people handle the same kinds of outside influences.

This bidirectional process is a thorny issue for researchers in the realm of normal–abnormal personality. In many types of cross-sectional research the problem cannot be fully resolved. For example, taking a single measurement of PDs and clinical syndromes in persons who are being admitted to a psychiatric clinic will yield confounded information about how personality traits and emotional states influence each other. Measurement at multiple time points is required to assess change, but success will occur only if appropriate measures and statistical procedures are used. With regard to measurement, personality and symptoms should be assessed separately with different instruments that were designed to minimize overlap between trait and state domains. Concerning statistical procedures, factor analysis, multivariate repeated measures techniques, structural equation modeling, and regression methods that hold constant the effects of variables from each domain are especially useful. Researchers who have employed these techniques have been successful in separating trait and state effects (e.g., Clark, Vittengl, Kraft, & Jarrett, 2003).

The most stable estimates of personality variables are likely to come from psychometrically sound personality assessment devices that are applied to samples of fairly healthy adults (ages 25–64) who are stable in their own lives (i.e., not experiencing a crisis or undergoing a major life event). Longitudinal studies have thus far been most successful in creating a picture of how personality changes and stays the same over long time periods (e.g., Shea & Yen, 2003). The idea here is to let time and natural course determine the outcome, but this is only possible with psychometrically sound measures that assess personality and state effects separately, when measurements are taken at multiple time points and with the use of statistical techniques that can hold constant multiple effects.

## Case Example

Some of the research design issues that are pertinent to the study of normal–abnormal personality can be examined in an unpublished study conducted for the purpose of estimating the prevalence of *DSM-IV-TR* (American Psychiatric Association, 2000) PDs among outpatients with eating disorders. Details of the investigation have been disguised for purposes of confidentiality.

The study was conducted in a large, outpatient mental health facility in the United States. To determine PD diagnoses the investigators used a well-known structured diagnostic interview, the IPDE (Loranger, 1999) and a well-known self-report questionnaire, the MCMI-III (Millon, 1997). Subjects for the study were adult women (ages 21–52) who were admitted to the clinic for treatment of an eating disorder. Admission to the clinic was made on the basis of whether they met *DSM-IV-TR* (American Psychiatric Association, 2000) criteria for anorexia or bulimia, as determined by one of the two experienced clinicians who interviewed each patient independently. Once admitted to the program, patients were approached to participate in the research study. Only those who gave informed consent to participate were included. Approximately 2 weeks after admission subjects were given the questionnaire to complete individually, and were then interviewed by one of the two clinicians who were trained to use the IPDE. Results of the investigation demonstrated that many more patients were diagnosed as having PDs by the self-report measure (75%) than by the interview measure (49%). Furthermore, when the PD diagnoses were compared across instruments, there was poor agreement. In other words, the instruments often came up with different PDs for the same person. By comparing their findings with those of previous investigations using similar samples and measures, the investigators concluded that the interview measure was more accurate in diagnosing PDs in their sample than the questionnaire measure.

The study employed a *single measurement, cross-sectional* design. In evaluating the research design our main question is whether or not we can accept the study's findings and conclusions as valid and reliable. The main finding was that the investigators could not reliably differentiate among the eating disorder patients with and without a diagnosis of PD using their two measures. Their conclusion that the structured interview was better at diagnosing PDs than the questionnaire is spurious because there was no standard against which they could measure accuracy of the diagnoses. To estimate the accuracy of the two measures (IPDE and MCMI-III) they would need to use a *third* measure as a gauge, and no such measure was obtained. Note that the eating disorder patients were not assessed at admission for presence of PDs, and were not independently diagnosed by two raters with the IPDE (Loranger, 1999). Although the raters were apparently trained to use the IPDE, the investigators did not offer a measure of their interrater reliability (e.g., kappa). We do not have a way to determine the number of hits (accurate diagnoses) and misses (errors in diagnosis). Furthermore, the investigators determined PD diagnosis with the MCMI-III (Millon, 1997) by using PD scale score elevations above a certain cut-off point (BR–85). Although the cut-off score they used is fairly stringent based on previous research, no self-report measure can, by itself, diagnose a PD by *DSM* (American Psychiatric Association, 2000) criteria because none of the measures currently available can determine whether a patient has significant problems in several areas of functioning, including work and relationships, that are caused by rigid and maladaptive traits that show up during adolescence or early adulthood. Using a simple cut-off for diagnosis on the MCMI-III surely caused errors in diagnosis, but we do not know how many.

These issues alone would generate skepticism in most people such that they would not be comfortable accepting the findings and conclusions from this study as being valid or reliable. In the future, other investigators might establish the prevalence of PDs in outpatients being treated for eating disorders, and prove that the IPDE (Loranger, 1999) is a better measure of PD diagnosis than the MCMI-III (Millon, 1997), but this particular study does not help us attain this knowledge with any certainty.

What are some other important issues to consider in this research design?

1  The investigators made a common mistake in assuming equivalency between various definitions of PD and measures of PD. A stated goal was to determine the numbers of patients in the eating disorder sample who had concomitant *DSM-IV-TR* (American Psychiatric Association, 2000) PDs. The operational definition of PDs is found in the measures that were used. The IPDE (Loranger, 1999) was developed as a structured interview that follows *DSM-IV* (American Psychiatric Association, 1994) diagnostic criteria. Although the instrument itself is faithful to the *DSM*, the results obtained with a structured interview are likely to be somewhat different from the results obtained with the unstructured interview usually given by a psychiatrist or psychologist in clinical practice (see Widiger, Costa, & Samuel, this volume). The MCMI-III (Millon, 1997) was developed to measure *DSM-IV* PDs, but items on the PD scales measure many personality features that follow Millon's (1996) model of psychopathology rather than the *DSM*. It is important to be aware that there are differences between a clinical diagnosis of PD using *DSM* criteria, a diagnosis made on the basis of a structured interview that operationalizes *DSM* criteria, and a diagnosis made on the basis of a self-report measure of PD (which does not incorporate all *DSM* diagnostic criteria). Substantial errors will accrue due to differences in the way *DSM* diagnosis is operationalized across methods, and by the type of method employed (i.e., unstructured interview, structured interview, self-report).

2  To make study results as generalizable as possible we hope to select patients for our investigations who are representative of not only the population of the

particular hospital or clinic we sample from, but also populations of patients in other psychiatric hospitals and clinics. We are aware that only women were sampled for this study. This limits generalization of study findings to populations of women patients until and unless equivalency is established for samples of men.

Knowing that the patients in this particular study were voluntarily admitted to an outpatient treatment program for eating disorders on the basis of a clinical interview gives us some measure of assurance that these patients are typical of other populations of patients who are seen in outpatient treatment for eating disorders. However, we do not know how this particular sample of patients was selected from the treatment ward other than that everyone read and signed an informed consent form. Were all of the patients admitted to the program over a period of time approached to participate in the study? If not, why not? How many of the patients refused to participate? There could be biases in subject selection that would threaten the validity and generalizability of the findings (Kazdin, 2003).

3  Psychiatric patients are typically in a distressed state when they enter a treatment program, and so our measurements of their traits and symptoms may be influenced by the distress. Greater reliability of measurement is often obtained when subjects are assessed several days after admission, when they are more stable. The investigators in this study did well to wait approximately 2 weeks after the patients were admitted to take their study measurements. Because of this procedure we can be reasonably assured that the results will be relatively stable and, therefore, the results may be generalizable to other populations of patients. It would have been even better if the investigators had informed us that study patients were judged to be stable at the time measurements were taken. The judgments could have been made by the investigators or a clinician on the treatment ward. A more precise method would be to take measurements of the patients' mental state and emotional stability, and offer these data to the reader as proof.

# Conclusions

Science offers methods and procedures for conducting studies that maximize our chances of obtaining unambiguous information about cause and effect, and the complex nature of relationships among variables in the natural world. In the realm of normal–abnormal personality, scientific progress will be enhanced when investigators are aware of, and correct for, problems and pitfalls that are central features of this research domain. Foremost among these are (a) using sound definitions for normality and abnormality, (b) recruiting satisfactory samples of disordered and normal persons, (c) selecting reliable and valid measures, (d) separating personality from other characteristics, and (e) limiting conclusions and comparisons to studies that address the same personality definitions and measures. Creative solutions to these problems are a challenge to the next generation of researchers, and will determine how far we go in answering such important questions as "How are normal and disordered personalities similar and different?" and "How do we intervene to help people with PDs?"

# Acknowledgments

Preparation of this manuscript was supported by the U.S. Department of Veterans Affairs. I am grateful to Aaron Pincus, Michael Gurtman, and Christopher Haddy for their consultation and advice.

## REFERENCES

American Psychiatric Association. (1980). *Diagnostic and statistical manual of mental disorders* (3rd ed.). Washington, DC: Author.

American Psychiatric Association. (1987). *Diagnostic and statistical manual of mental disorders* (3rd ed., rev.). Washington, DC: Author.

American Psychiatric Association. (1994). *Diagnostic and statistical manual of mental disorders* (4th ed.). Washington, DC: Author.

American Psychiatric Association. (2000). *Diagnostic and statistical manual of mental disorders* (4th ed., text revision). Washington, DC: Author.

Blashfield, R. K., Blum, N., & Pfohl, B. (1992). The effect of changing Axis II diagnostic criteria. *Comprehensive Psychiatry, 33,* 245–252.

Block, J., Block, J. H., & Harrington, D. M. (1974). Some misgivings about the Matching Familiar Figures Test as a measure of reflectivity-impulsivity. *Developmental Psychology, 10,* 611–632.

Butcher, J. N., Graham, J. R., Ben-Porath, Y. S., Tellegen, A., Dahlstrom, W. G., & Kaemmer, B. (2001). *The Minnesota Multiphasic Personality Inventory-2 (MMPI-2): Manual for administration and scoring* (rev. ed.). Minneapolis, MN: University of Minnesota Press.

Campbell, D. T., & Stanley, J. C. (1966). *Experimental and quasiexperimental designs for research.* New York: Houghton-Mifflin.

Clark, L. A., & Harrison, J. A. (2001). Assessment instruments. In W. J. Livesley (Ed.), *Handbook of personality disorders* (pp. 277–306). New York: Guilford Press.

Clark, L. A., Vittengl, J., Kraft, D., & Jarrett, R. B. (2003). Separate personality traits from states to predict depression. *Journal of Personality Disorders, 17,* 152–172.

Clark, L. A., & Watson, D. (1995). Constructing validity: Basic issues in objective scale development. *Psychological Assessment, 7,* 309–319.

Cohen, J. (1968). Weighted kappa: Nominal scale agreement provision for scaled disagreement or partial credit. *Psychological Bulletin, 70,* 213–220.

Cohen, J. (1988). *Statistical power analysis in the behavioral sciences* (2nd ed.). Hillsdale, NJ: Erlbaum.

Cohen, J. (1992). A power primer. *Psychological Bulletin, 112,* 155–159.

Costa, P. T., Jr., & McCrae, R. R. (1992). *Revised NEO Personality Inventory (NEO-PI-R) and NEO Five-Factor Inventory (NEO-FFI) professional manual.* Odessa, FL: Psychological Assessment Resources.

Dolan-Sewell, R. T., Krueger, R. F., Shea, M. T. (2001). Co-occurrence with syndrome disorders. In W. J. Livesley (Ed.), *Handbook of personality disorders* (pp. 84–104). New York: Guilford Press.

Endler, N. S., & Kocovski, N. L. (2002). Personality disorders at the crossroads. *Journal of Personality Disorders, 16,* 487–502.

Eysenck, H. J. (1994). Normality-abnormality and the three-factor model of personality. In S. Strack, & M. Lorr (Eds.), *Differentiating normal and abnormal personality* (pp. 3–25). New York: Springer.

Feinstein, A. R. (1970). The pre-therapeutic classification of comorbidity in chronic disease. *Journal of Chronic Diseases, 23,* 455–468.

Goldberg, L. R. (1993). The structure of phenotypic personality traits. *American Psychologist, 48,* 26–34.

Kazdin, A. E. (2003). *Research design in clinical psychology* (4th ed.). Boston, MA: Allyn & Bacon.

Kirk, R. E. (1994*). Experimental design: Procedures for behavioral sciences* (3rd ed.). Belmont, CA: Wadsworth.

Korfine, L., & Lenzenweger, M. F. (1995). The taxonicity of schizotypy: A replication. *Journal of Abnormal Psychology, 104,* 26–31.

Kupfer, D. J., First, M. B., & Regier, D. A. (Eds.). (2002). *A research agenda for DSM-V.* Washington, DC: American Psychiatric Association.

Lanyon, R. I., & Goodstein, L. D. (1997). *Personality assessment* (3rd ed.). New York: Wiley.

Lenzenweger, M. F., & Korfine, L. (1992). Confirming the latent structure and base rate of schizotypy: A taxometric analysis. *Journal of Abnormal Psychology, 101*, 567–571.

Livesley, W. J. (2001a). Conceptual and taxonomic issues. In W. J. Livesley (Ed.), *Handbook of personality disorders* (pp. 3–38). New York: Guilford Press.

Livesley, W. J. (Ed.). (2001b). *Handbook of personality disorders*. New York: Guilford Press.

Loranger, A. W. (1999). International Personality Disorder Examination (IPDE). Odessa, FL: Psychological Assessment Resources.

Markon, K. E., Krueger, R. F., & Watson, D. (2005). Delineating the structure of normal and abnormal personality: An integrative hierarchical appraisal. *Journal of Personality and Social Psychology, 88*, 139–157.

McCrae, R. R., & Costa, P. T., Jr. (2003). *Personality in adulthood* (2nd ed.). New York: Guilford.

Millon, T. (1996). *Disorders of personality* (2nd ed.). New York: Wiley.

Millon, T. (1997). *Millon Clinical Multiaxial Inventory-III manual* (2nd ed.). Minneapolis, MN: National Computer Systems.

Morey, L. C. (2003). Measuring personality and psychopathology. In J. Schinka, & W. Velicer (Eds.), *Handbook of psychology, research methods in psychology* (Vol. 2, pp. 377–406). New York: Wiley.

Moskowitz, D. S., & Zuroff, D. C. (2004). Flux, pulse, and spin: Dynamic additions to the personality lexicon. *Journal of Personality and Social Psychology, 86*, 880–893.

Paris, J. (1999). *Nature and nurture in psychiatry*. Washington, DC: American Psychiatric Press.

Paris, J. (2005). Nature and nurture in personality disorders. In S. Strack (Ed.), *Handbook of personology and psychopathology* (pp. 24–38). Hoboken, NJ: Wiley.

Pincus, A. L. (2005). The interpersonal nexus of personality disorders. In S. Strack (Ed.), *Handbook of personology and psychopathology* (pp. 120–139). Hoboken, NJ: Wiley.

Reis, H. T., & Judd, C. M. (2000). *Handbook of research methods in social and personality psychology*. New York: Cambridge University Press.

Sabshin, M. (1989). Normality and the boundaries of psychopathology. *Journal of Personality Disorders, 3*, 259–273.

Sabshin, M. (2005). Concepts of normality and the classification of psychopathology. In S. Strack (Ed.), *Handbook of personology and psychopathology* (pp. 229–237). Hoboken, NJ: Wiley.

Shea, M. T. (1997). Core battery conference: Assessment of change in personality disorders. In H. H. Strupp, L. M. Horowitz, & M. J. Lambert (Eds.), *Measuring patient changes in mood, anxiety, and personality disorders* (pp. 389–400). Washington, DC: American Psychological Association.

Shea, M. T., & Yen, S. (2003). Stability as a distinction between Axis I and Axis II disorders. *Journal of Personality Disorders, 17*, 373–386.

Strack, S., & Lorr, M. (Eds.). (1994). *Differentiating normal and abnormal personality*. New York: Springer.

Strack, S., & Lorr, M. (1997). Invited essay: The challenge of differentiating normal and disordered personality. *Journal of Personality Disorders, 11*, 105–122.

Tabachnick, B. G., & Fidell, L. S. (2000). *Using multivariate statistics* (4th ed.). Boston: Allyn & Bacon.

Westen, D., & Bradley, R. (2005). Prototype diagnosis of personality. In S. Strack (Ed.), *Handbook of personology and psychopathology* (pp. 238–256). Hoboken, NJ: Wiley.

Widiger, T. A. (2003). Personality disorder and Axis I psychopathology: The problematic boundary of Axis I and Axis II. *Journal of Personality Disorders, 17*, 90–108.

Widiger, T. A., & Coker, L. A. (2002). Assessing personality disorders. In J. N. Butcher (Ed.), *Clinical personality assessment: Practical approaches* (2nd ed., pp. 407–434). New York: Oxford University Press.

Widiger, T. A., Manguine, S., Corbitt, E. M., Ellis, C. G., & Thomas, G. V. (1995). *Personality disorder interview-IV: A semistructured interview for the assessment of personality disorders*. Odessa, FL: Psychological Assessment Resources, Inc.

# Principles of Exploratory Factor Analysis

**9**

**Lewis R. Goldberg**
**Wayne F. Velicer**

One goal of science is to understand the relations among variables, and the object of factor analysis is to aid scientists in this quest. Factor analysis can be thought of as a variable-reduction procedure, in which many variables are replaced by a few factors that summarize the relations among the variables. Consequently, in its broadest sense factor analysis is a procedure for identifying summary constructs. If one already has a theory about the structure of a set of variables, one can investigate the extent to which that theory accounts for the relations among the variables in a sample of data; "confirmatory" factor procedures are used for this purpose. "Exploratory" factor procedures, the subject of this chapter, are used to discover summary constructs when their nature is still unknown.

Over the years since its development, factor analysis has been used for a wide variety of purposes, and investigators have differed enormously in their views about the scientific status of factors. In the context of personality and psychopathology (the focus of the present chapter), the most "realist" position has been taken by Cattell (1957), who explicitly equated factors with motivational "causes" (neuropsychological structures that produce behavioral patterns). At the other end of this continuum are those investigators who use factor analysis merely as a means of organizing a large number of observed variables into a more parsimonious representation, and thus who make no assumptions that factors have any meaning beyond a particular data set.

Factor analysis and its near relative, component analysis, are statistical techniques that were first introduced by Pearson (1901) and Spearman (1904) and later refined by Thurstone (1931, 1947) and Hotelling (1933). For many years after their introduction, their intense computational demands virtually prohibited their widespread use; the prospect of spending months on hand-calculations was certainly discouraging, if not completely disheartening, to most investigators. As time passed and the mathematical foundations of the techniques became more securely established, textbooks such as those by Mulaik (1972), Harman (1976), and McDonald (1985), linking the basic concepts of factor analysis to matrix algebra and the geometry of hyperspace, made these concepts accessible to the mathematically adept. The typical researcher, however, struggling with the mathematical complexity of the concepts and the intensive computational demands of the procedures, had to await the arrival of the packaged statistical computer programs. Today, with programs for factor analysis available even for notebook computers, anyone with a large, complex, or bemusing set of variables can consider using these techniques, in the hope that they will provide some insight and order to his or her data.

However, in consulting the manual for one's statistical package and finding the chapter on factor analysis, the user is likely to be confronted with several anxiety-arousing decision options, such as: (a) Should one conduct a factor analysis or a components analysis? (b) How does one decide on the number of factors to extract? (c) Should the factors be rotated, and if so should the rotation be an orthogonal or an oblique one? (d) Should one obtain factor scores, and if so, by which procedure? (e) How big a sample size is needed for the analysis? (f) How many variables, and of what type, should be included? Such questions may be puzzling to the first-time user, and even to the experienced researcher. Fortunately, there is an emerging empirical and theoretical basis for making these decisions.

In this chapter, we will present some of the major features of exploratory factor analysis as it is used in the context of personality research. In so doing, we hope to answer some of the questions faced by the user when considering the various options commonly available in factor programs, such as those found in the SPSS, SAS, and SYSTAT statistical packages. As we describe these decisions, we shall comment on the choices faced by the researcher, pointing out the available empirical studies that have evaluated the procedures and our own personal preferences. Obviously, this chapter is not intended as a comprehensive course in factor analysis, nor can it be regarded as a substitute for the major textbooks in the field, such as Gorsuch (1983) and McDonald (1985).

We have included a short numerical example to illustrate the procedures that we are describing. This data set is based on a sample of 273 individuals responding to the 8-item short form of the Decisional Balance Inventory (DBI: Velicer, DiClemente, Prochaska, & Brandenberg, 1985), a measure of individuals' decision-making about a health-related behavior, in this case smoking cessation. The DBI has been used in multiple studies with a variety of different behaviors (Prochaska, et al., 1994), and its factor structure has been found to be robust across different subject samples (Ward, Velicer, Rossi, Fava, & Prochaska, 2004). In most applications, there are two factors—in this case the Pros of Smoking and the Cons of Smoking—each measured by four items.[1] To replicate the analyses presented in this chapter, the interested reader can enter the 8 by 8 correlation matrix provided in Part I of Figure 9.1 in any of the widely available factor-analysis programs, and then compare his or her results with ours.

---

[1] Items: 1, Smoking cigarettes relieves tension; 2, I am embarrassed to have to smoke; 3, Smoking helps me concentrate and do better work; 4, My cigarette smoking bothers other people; 5, I am more relaxed and therefore more pleasant when smoking; 6, People think that I am foolish for ignoring the warnings about cigarette smoking; 7, Smoking cigarettes is pleasurable; 8, Smoking cigarettes is hazardous to my health.

**Part I. Example Correlation Matrix**

$$R = \begin{bmatrix} 1.000 & .280 & .350 & .159 & .512 & .210 & .335 & .114 \\ .280 & 1.000 & .217 & .395 & .204 & .361 & .039 & .280 \\ .350 & .217 & 1.000 & .128 & .482 & .166 & .215 & .078 \\ .159 & .395 & .128 & 1.000 & .176 & .474 & .045 & .292 \\ .512 & .204 & .482 & .176 & 1.000 & .264 & .369 & .172 \\ .210 & .361 & .166 & .474 & .264 & 1.000 & .099 & .500 \\ .335 & .039 & .215 & .045 & .369 & .099 & 1.000 & .073 \\ .114 & .280 & .078 & .292 & .172 & .500 & .073 & 1.000 \end{bmatrix}$$

**Part II. The Eigenvalues of the Example Correlation Matrix**

$$D = \begin{bmatrix} 2.794 & 1.553 & .866 & .721 & .638 & .569 & .434 & .424 \end{bmatrix}$$

**Part III. Unrotated Pattern Matrix**  **Part IV. Varimax Pattern Matrix**  **Part V. Oblimin Pattern Matrix**

$$A = \begin{bmatrix} .65 & .41 \\ .60 & -.31 \\ .56 & .41 \\ .57 & -.48 \\ .69 & .44 \\ .67 & -.47 \\ .42 & .50 \\ .52 & -.48 \end{bmatrix} \quad A^* = \begin{bmatrix} .59 & .18 & .75 \\ .46 & .65 & .19 \\ .48 & .12 & .69 \\ .56 & .74 & .06 \\ .67 & .19 & .80 \\ .67 & .80 & .14 \\ .43 & -.05 & .65 \\ .50 & .71 & .02 \end{bmatrix} \quad A^{**} = \begin{bmatrix} .08 & .74 \\ .64 & .12 \\ .03 & .69 \\ .75 & -.03 \\ .09 & .80 \\ .80 & .04 \\ -.13 & .67 \\ .72 & -.07 \end{bmatrix}$$

**Part VI. First 7 Values for the MAP Function**

**MAP** = .0591  .0535  .0963  .1612  .2650  .4385  .9999

**Part VII. Mean Eigenvalues for 100 Random 8-Variable Matrices**

$$D \text{ [Chance]} = \begin{bmatrix} 1.253 & 1.152 & 1.085 & 1.027 & .966 & .909 & .843 & .765 \end{bmatrix}$$

Numerical example (Decisional Balance Inventory for Smoking Cessation, $k = 8$. $N = 273$). Response format: 1, not mentioned; 2, slightly important; 3, moderately important; 4, very important; 5, extremely important.

There are many decisions that have to be made when carrying out a factor analysis. We will identify each of the relevant decision points, and some of the major options available at each decision point. Moreover, we will indicate which of the decisions we think are important (very few) and which are unimportant (all the rest). We assume the following fundamental principle: In general, the more highly structured are one's data, the less it matters what decisions one makes. The best way to assure oneself about a factor structure is to analyze the data in several different ways. If one's conclusions are robust across alternative procedures, one may be on to something. However, if one's conclusions vary with the procedures that are used, we urge the investigator to collect another data set, or to think of some alternative procedures for studying that scientific problem.

# Decisions to Be Made Prior to Collecting the Data

## Selection of Variables

*This is by far the single most important decision in any investigation, and it should be guided by theory or the findings from past research.* Although the particular strategy for variable selection should be a function of the purpose of the investigation, it will often be the case that one seeks a *representative* selection of variables from the domain of scientific interest. One extremely powerful strategy to attain representativeness rests on the "lexical hypothesis" (Goldberg, 1981), which assumes that the most important variables in a domain are those used frequently in human communication, thus eventually becoming part of our natural language. For example, personality-descriptive terms culled from the dictionaries of various languages have been shown to be a reasonable starting-place for selecting personality traits for individuals to use to describe themselves and others; factor-analyses of these terms have led to current models of personality structure (Saucier & Goldberg, 2003).

Nor is the lexical hypothesis limited solely to commonly used terms. In an attempt to define a representative set of variables related to social attitudes and ideologies, Saucier (2000) extracted all of the terms with the suffix "-ism" from an English dictionary, and then used the dictionary *definitions* of those world-views as items in an attitude survey; when individuals indicated the extent of their agreement with each of these items, the factors derived from their responses turned out to provide a highly replicable hierarchical structure for the social-attitude domain. And in the realm of psychopathology, analyses of the symptoms associated with abnormal traits lexicalized by suffixes such as "-mania," "-philia," and "-phobia" may provide the grist for new factors to supplement current models of the personality disorders.

At a more technical level, simulation studies (Velicer & Fava, 1987, 1998) have investigated this topic in the context of variable sampling. The findings from these studies suggest that: (a) The number of variables per factor is far more important than the total number of variables; (b) if the variables are good measures of the factors (i.e., they have high factor loadings), then fewer variables are needed to produce robust solutions; (c) variable and subject sampling interact so that a well-selected variable set can produce robust results even with smaller sample sizes (Velicer & Fava, 1998); and (d) even with the best variables for measuring a factor, a minimum of three variables for each factor is needed for its identification. (A factor loading is the correlation between the observed variable and the factor for the varimax pattern matrix. In Part IV of Figure 9.1, the first variable correlates 0.18 with the first factor and 0.75 with the second factor. Correlations of 0.50 or above are what we mean by "high" factor loadings.)

In practice, one should include at least a half dozen variables for each of the factors one is likely to obtain, which means that in the personality realm, where there are at least five broad factors, it will rarely be useful to apply exploratory factor analysis to sets of less than 30 variables. Later in this chapter we will discuss other aspects of this problem as they relate to such issues as the hierarchical nature of personality-trait representations.

## Selection of Subjects

Although, this is a less important decision than that involving the selection of variables, it is not trivial. Among the issues involved: (a) Should the investigator try to increase sample heterogeneity, and if so, on what variables (e.g., ethnic group, social class)? (b) Alternatively, or in addition, should one select subjects who are relatively homogenous on some variables (e.g., reading ability, general verbal facility, absence or presence of psychopathology), so as to discover relations that may be obscured in heterogenous samples? These questions are not specific to factor analysis, of course; for example, the first question is directly related to the ever-present problem of generalizing from a sample to a population.

Of particular importance for readers of this volume are issues related to the inclusion of abnormal versus normal subject samples and the use of self-reports versus reports from knowledgeable others. Because most clinical samples are so heterogenous, it should come as no surprise that studies show no systematic differences in factor structures between general clinical samples and normal ones (O'Connor, 2002). On the other hand, the more restricted is the clinical sample to one particular diagnostic group (e.g., a sample composed solely of depressed patients), the more likely is there to be restriction of range on some crucial variables (in this case, variables assessing aspects of depression), and consequently the more likely will the findings differ from those in normal samples.

Any differences in factor structures between self-reports and observer or peer reports are likely to be quite subtle. Thomas, Turkheimer, and Oltmanns (2003) demonstrated the similarity in the factor structures derived from self-reports and reports from knowledgeable peers using variables related to personality disorders, even though there was only a modest consensus between individual self-descriptions and peer descriptions on those highly sensitive variables. In regard to normal personality traits, there seems to be no strong systematic differences in factor structures between the use of self or peer samples.

Among the most vexing problems involved in subject selection is the decision about the *number* of subjects to be included in the investigation. This problem is unusually thought-provoking because it always involves a trade-off between (a) the use of many subjects so as to increase the likely generalizability of one's findings from the sample to the population and (b) the use of few subjects so as to decrease the cost of collecting the data. An additional problem is that the guidance provided by many of the early textbooks recommended rules relating sample size to the number of variables. These rules turned out to be incorrect when evaluated empirically (e.g., Guadagnoli & Velicer, 1988).

**Table 9.1**

The Average Difference Between the Factor Loading in an Observed Sample and the Corresponding Value in the Population, as a Function of the Sample Size (*N*) and the Mean Factor Loading of the Salient Variables on Each Factor (0.40, 0.60, and 0.80)

| N | Mean 0.40 | Factor 0.60 | Loading 0.80 |
|---|---|---|---|
| 50 | 0.174 | 0.150 | 0.126 |
| 70 | 0.149 | 0.125 | 0.101 |
| 100 | 0.128 | 0.104 | 0.080 |
| 125 | 0.116 | 0.092 | 0.068 |
| 150 | 0.108 | 0.084 | 0.060 |
| 175 | 0.101 | 0.077 | 0.053 |
| 200 | 0.096 | 0.072 | 0.048 |
| 225 | 0.091 | 0.067 | 0.043 |
| 250 | 0.088 | 0.064 | 0.040 |
| 300 | 0.082 | 0.058 | 0.034 |
| 350 | 0.077 | 0.053 | 0.029 |
| 400 | 0.073 | 0.049 | 0.025 |
| 500 | 0.067 | 0.043 | 0.019 |
| 600 | 0.063 | 0.039 | 0.015 |
| 750 | 0.058 | 0.034 | 0.010 |
| 1,000 | 0.053 | 0.029 | 0.005 |

Fortunately, we do have some empirically based guidance on this topic that will allow researchers to perform the equivalent of a power analysis for determining a reasonable sample size.

As already noted, the issue of determining an optimal sample size is complicated by the fact that there is an interaction between sample size and the quality of the variables representing each factor (Guadagnoli & Velicer, 1988; MacCallum, Widaman, Zhang, & Hong, 1999; Velicer & Fava, 1998). Table 9.1 illustrates the impact of sample size and the average factor loadings. The entries in Table 9.1 are the predicted mean differences between the observed loadings and the actual population loadings (Guadagnoli & Velicer, 1988). A value of 0.05 means that the differences between the sample and the population loading is likely to be found only in the second decimal place. If an investigator anticipates factor loadings around 0.75, then a sample size as small as 200 persons should be adequate. However, if one anticipates factor loadings around 0.40, a sample of 1,000 is barely adequate. Because a set of factor-univocal variables is unusual for an exploratory study, factor analysis should be viewed as inherently a subject-intensive enterprise; robust findings are only likely when based on samples of at least a few hundred subjects, and samples in the 500–1,000 range are preferred.

## Selection of the Measurement Format

In personality research, subjects' responses can be obtained using a variety of item formats, including multi-step scales (e.g., rating scales with options from 1 to 5 or from 1 to 7), dichotomous choices (e.g., True vs. False, Agree vs. Disagree, Like vs. Dislike), or checklists (defined by instructions to check those items that apply). From the subject's point of view, the last of these is the most user-friendly, and the first is the most demanding. However, from a psychometric point of view, rating scales have substantial advantages over both of the other formats. In general, multi-step scales produce higher factor loadings than dichotomous items and checklists. Dichotomous items are characterized by large differences in their response distributions, which affect the size of the correlations among them, and thus the nature of any factors derived from those correlations. Moreover, scores derived from checklists are greatly influenced by individuals' carefulness in considering each of the items (as compared to racing through the list), reflected in an enormous range of individual differences in the number of items that are checked. In general, we recommend the use of rating scales (with five to seven response categories) over the use of dichotomous items. About one thing, however, we are adamant: Never use a checklist response format.[2]

# Decisions to Be Made After the Data Have Been Obtained

## Cleaning the Data

### Examining the Distributions of Each of the Variables

We strongly recommend that investigators always examine each of the univariate frequency distributions to assure themselves that all variables are distributed in a reasonable manner, and that there are no outliers. The distribution of the variables should be approximately normal or at least uniform (rectangular). If there are one or more extreme values, are they coding errors, or genuine freaks of nature? Clearly all of the errors should be corrected, and the few subjects who produced the freakish values should probably be omitted.

---

[2]Even for multi-step rating scales, when subjects respond to hundreds of items on the same occasion, there are typically large individual differences in the means and the variances of the subjects' response distributions across the items. Some of these differences may stem from such response biases as Extremeness Response Style (a tendency to use the polar categories of the rating scale versus the middle ones) and Acquiescence Response Set (a tendency to agree rather than to disagree with items, regardless of their content). To attenuate individual differences in such response biases, investigators may elect to standard (Z) score each subject's responses separately across the total set of items. Standard scoring can be useful for items rated on continuous scales, for dichotomous response formats, and even for items administered in a checklist. However, standard scoring may also serve to remove important individual differences when the item pool includes more items keyed in one direction than the other on any of the underlying dimensions. Under those conditions, one might consider more complex procedures, such as those developed by ten Berge (1999).

In addition, it is sometimes assumed that the correlation coefficient is free to vary between −1.00 and +1.00. *However, this is true only when the shapes of the distributions of both variables are the same and they are both symmetric around their means.* Two variables with distributions of different shapes can correlate neither +1.00 nor −1.00. Two variables with distributions of the same shape that are skewed in the same direction can correlate +1.00, but not −1.00; whereas two variables with distributions of the same shape but skewed in the opposite directions can correlate −1.00, but not +1.00. In general, differences in distributions serve to decrease the size of the correlations between variables, and this will affect any factors derived from such correlations.

### Handling Missing Data

Much has been written about this problem in the statistical and psychometric literature (e.g., Graham, Cumsille, & Elek-Fisk, 2003; Little & Rubin, 1987; Schafer, 1997; Schafer & Graham, 2002), so we will not cover the proposed solutions in this chapter. Small amounts of missing data can be handled elegantly by such recently developed statistical procedures as multiple imputation and maximum likelihood estimation, which are becoming widely available in computer software packages. When older procedures such as substituting mean values, list-wise deletion, or pair-wise deletion are used, one should compare the findings from different methods so as to assure oneself that the results are not dependent on a particular methodological choice.

However, the presence of substantial amounts of missing data should alert the investigator to deficiencies in the procedures used to collect the data, including such problems as a lack of clarity in the instructions or in the response format. Stimuli that elicit extensive missing data may have been phrased ambiguously, and subjects who have omitted many responses may have found the task too difficult or demanding or they may have been unwilling to cooperate with the investigator. In general, such problematic variables and subjects should not be included in the analyses.

### Checking to Make Sure that the Relations Among All Pairs of Variables Are Monotonic

We recommend that each of the bivariate frequency distributions (scatter-plots) be examined to make sure that there are no U-shaped or inverted U-shaped distributions. Such nonmonotonic relations, which are extremely rare with personality variables, result in an underestimate of the degree of association between the variables; for example, in the case of a perfectly U-shaped distribution, the linear correlation could be zero. In some such cases, one variable might be rescaled as a deviation from its mid-point.

## Selecting an Index of Association

There are four major varieties of association indices for continuous variables (Zegers & ten Berge, 1985), each type being a mean value based upon one of the following indices: (a) *Raw cross-products*, where the measures of the association between the variables can be affected by their means, their standard deviations, and the correlation between them; (b) *proportionality coefficients*, or the raw cross-products divided by the two standard deviations, where the measures of association can be affected by their means and correlations but not by their standard deviations; (c) *covariances*, or the cross-products of deviation scores, where the measures of association can be affected by their standard deviations and their correlation but not by their means; and finally (d) *correlations*, or the cross-products of standard scores, where the measures of association are not affected by differences in either the means or the standard deviations.

Neither raw cross-products nor proportionality coefficients have been employed extensively as indices of association among the variables included in exploratory factor analyses, although the latter (referred to as congruence coefficients) are widely used to assess the similarity between factors derived from different samples of subjects. Covariances have been often employed in confirmatory factor analyses, whereas most applications of exploratory factor analysis have relied upon the correlation as an index of relation between variables. The rationale for the use of correlations is based on the assumption that the means and standard deviations of the observed variables are typically arbitrary, and easily changed by even small changes in the wording of the variables or the instructions. The scale of the variables is, therefore, not viewed as meaningful and the correlation coefficient represents a common metric for all the variables. Thus, although this is a decision that should be guided by one's theoretical concerns, for the remainder of this chapter we will assume that the reader has selected the correlation as an index of association.

In preparation for a factor analysis, then, one has a *data matrix*, which consists of N rows (one for each subject in the study) by K columns (one for each of the variables). From the data matrix, one begins by computing a *correlation matrix*, which consists of K rows and K columns. (Part I of Figure 9.1 illustrates a correlation matrix.) This matrix is square and symmetric, which means that it can be folded into two triangles along its main diagonal, with each of the values in one triangle equal to the corresponding value in the other triangle. Excluding the entries that lie along the main diagonal, there are $K \times (K-1)/2$ distinctive entries in the correlation matrix.

# Decisions Directly Related to Factor Analysis

## Deciding Whether to Use the "Component" or the "Factor" Model

Much has been written about this decision, and some factor-analytic theorists consider it the most important decision of all. Others, however, have argued that the decision is not very important because the results from both methods will usually be much the same (e.g., Fava & Velicer, 1992). We agree with the latter position. Readers who wish to make up their own minds should consult the special issue of the journal *Multivariate Behavioral Research* on this topic (January 1990, Volume 25, Number 1) in which Velicer and Jackson discuss the pros and cons of the two approaches and argue in favor of the use of component analysis in most applications. A number of other factor theorists provide extensive commentaries on this target article.

*We would argue that if this decision makes any substantial difference with personality data, the data are not well-structured enough for either type of analysis.* At a theoretical level, the models are different, but in actual practice the difference lies in the values that are used in the main diagonal of the correlation matrix: In the component model, values of 1.00 (i.e., the variances of the standardized variables) are included in each cell of the main diagonal. In the factor model, the diagonal values are replaced by each variable's "communality" (the proportion of its variance that it shares with the factors). In most cases any differences between the two procedures will be quite minor, and will virtually disappear when the number of variables per factor is large and when many of the correlations are of substantial size. Component loadings will typically be larger than the corresponding factor loadings, and this difference will be more marked if the number of variables per factor is small and the loadings are small. A compromise is to analyze one's data by both procedures so as to ascertain the robustness of the structure to procedural variations (e.g., Goldberg, 1990). For the remainder of this chapter, we will use the term "factor" to refer to either a factor or a component.

### The General Component Model

Figure 9.2 presents a schematic flowchart of the factor-analytic process, beginning with the correlation matrix. Such a matrix of K by K elements can be approximated by multiplying a smaller matrix of K rows by L columns, called a *factor matrix*, by its "transpose," which is the identical matrix with its rows and columns reoriented and thus turned into a matrix of L rows by K columns. (Parts III, IV, and V of Figure 9.1 illustrate the factor matrix in three different rotational positions. Rotation is discussed below.) If the index

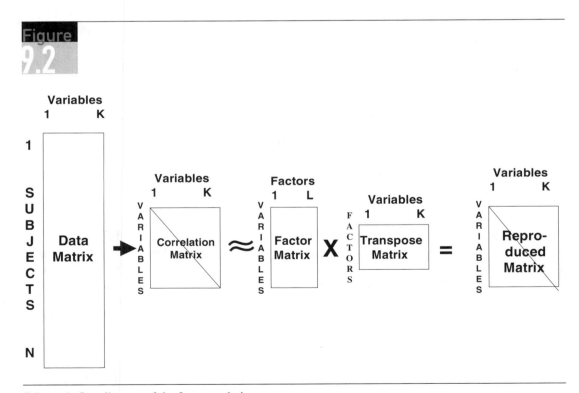

Schematic flow diagram of the factor-analytic process.

of association one has selected is the correlation coefficient, then the entries in the factor matrix are also correlation coefficients, specifically the correlations between each particular variable and each of the factors.[3]

In the procedures referred to as principal components or principal factors, the loadings on the first factor are those that serve to best recreate the values in the correlation matrix when that factor matrix is multiplied by its transpose. *Thus, the first principal factor provides a measure of whatever is most in common to the variables that have been included in the analysis.* In the case of measures of aptitude or knowledge, the first principal factor has sometimes been considered to be an index of general ability or intelligence. In the case of personality variables, the first principal factor will typically be a blend of general evaluation (contrasting good vs. bad attributes) and whatever particular content domain is most highly represented within the set of variables.

Moreover, each successive principal factor serves to best recreate the values in the correlation matrix *after taking into account the factors extracted before it.* Said in another way, as each factor is extracted, the influence of that factor is partialed out of the correlations, leaving residual values that are independent of all factors that have been extracted. Thus, each factor is independent of all others; the intercorrelations among all pairs of factors are zero. (As noted below, this will no longer be true after an oblique rotation).

When factor analysis is used instead of component analysis, a researcher may encounter "improper" solutions (Thurstone, 1947), which are uninterpretable theoretically. For example, the estimate of the unique variance for one of the observed variables might be negative or zero. Some computer programs provide warnings and offer methods to "fix" the problem, such as constraining the estimates of the unique variances to be greater than zero (Joreskog, 1967). However, instead of correcting this problem with an *ad hoc* procedure, it would be better to diagnose the source of the problem. Van Driel (1978) described some of the causes of improper solutions. In simulation studies (Velicer & Fava, 1987, 1998), the probability of an improper solution increases when the number of variables per factor decreases, the sample size is small, or the factor leadings are small. In some cases, reducing the number of factors retained will solve the problem. In other cases, improving the selection of variables and/or the sample of subjects might be necessary.

## Determining the Optimal Number of Factors

After the factors have been extracted, one can multiply the factor matrix by its transpose to form a new K by K matrix, which is typically called a reproduced correlation matrix. As more factors are extracted, the differences between the values in the original and the reproduced matrices become smaller and smaller. If each value in the reproduced matrix is subtracted from its corresponding value in the original correlation matrix, the result is a K by K "residual" matrix, as shown in Figure 9.3. The more factors that are extracted, the better approximation of the original correlation matrix is provided by those factors, and thus the smaller are the values in the residual matrix. Consequently, if one's goal is to reproduce the original correlation matrix as precisely as possible, one will tend to

---

[3]The explanations in this section only apply to the original matrix of principal factors, which are "orthogonal," and not to the subsequent "rotated" matrices, which may be "oblique."

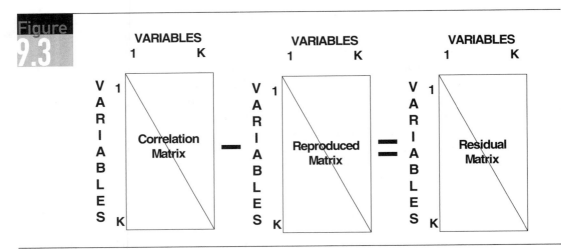

Schematic flow diagram of the relation between the correlation matrix, the reproduced matrix based on the first $K$ factors, and the residual matrix.

extract many factors. On the other hand, the scientific principle of parsimony suggests that, other things being equal, fewer factors are better than many factors. *One of the major decisions in factor analysis is the selection of the optimal number of factors, and this always involves a trade-off between extracting as few factors as possible versus recreating the original correlation matrix as completely as possible.*

Over the years, many rules have been proposed to provide guidance on the number of factors to extract (e.g., Zwick & Velicer, 1986). Unfortunately, none of these rules will invariably guide the researcher to the scientifically most satisfactory decision. Perhaps even more unfortunately, one of the least satisfactory rules (the "eigenvalues greater than one" criterion, which will be explained later) is so easy to implement that it has been incorporated as the standard "default" option in some of the major statistical packages.

Figure 9.4 shows two indices that are typically derived from the factor matrix: "communalities" and "eigenvalues." *A variable's communality is equal to the sum of the squared factor loadings in its row of the unrotated or varimax rotated factor matrix.* Thus, there are as many communality values as there are variables, and these values are normally provided as the final column of a factor matrix. In Part III of Figure 9.1, we include the communalities for all eight variables. The first variable (i.e., the first row) has a communality of $(0.65)^2 + (0.41)^2 = 0.59$. The communalities for the factor pattern presented in Part IV of Figure 9.1 are the same, except for rounding error.

The communality of a variable is the proportion of its variance that is associated with the total set of factors that have been extracted. That proportion can vary from zero to one. A variable with a communality of zero is completely independent of each of the factors. A variable with a communality of 1.00 can be perfectly predicted by the set of factors, when the factors are used as the predictors in a multiple regression equation and the variable itself is the criterion. In the "factor" model, these communalities are used to replace the original values of unity in the main diagonal of the correlation matrix.

*The sums of the squared factor loadings down the columns of the principal component matrix are equal to the first of the "eigenvalues" (or "latent roots") of the correlation matrix*

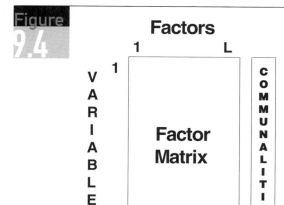

Schematic flow diagram of the factor pattern, the eigenvalues, and communalities.

*from which the factors were derived.* These values are normally provided in the bottom row in a factor matrix. In Figure 9.1, the eigenvalues are presented in Part II. In Part III of that figure, the sum of the squared loadings in the first two columns (2.79 and 1.55) is the same as the first two entries in the vector of eigenvalues. The eigenvalue associated with a factor is an index of its relative size: The eigenvalue associated with the first factor will always be at least as large, and normally much larger than, any of the others; and the eigenvalues of successive factors can never be larger, and will typically be smaller, than those that precede them.

A plot of the size of the eigenvalues as a function of their factor number will appear as a rapidly descending concave curve that eventually becomes a nearly horizontal line. An example of such an eigenvalue plot (sometimes referred to as a "scree" plot, after Cattell, 1966) is provided in Figure 9.5. Included in that figure are the eigenvalues from a principal components analysis of 100 personality-descriptive adjectives, selected by Goldberg (1992) as markers of the Big Five factor structure, in a sample of 636 self and peer ratings. This represents a better illustration than the eight-variable example in Figure 9.1 but the reader may want to graph the values in Part II of Figure 9.1 as a second example.

Some of the rules for deciding on the optimal number of factors are based on the characteristics of such eigenvalue plots (e.g., Cattell, 1966). *For example, if there is a very sharp break in the curve, with earlier eigenvalues all quite large relative to later ones that are all of similar size, then there is presumptive evidence that only the factors above the break should be retained.* However, as indicated in Figure 9.5, although this highly selected set of variables provides an extremely clear Five-factor structure, subjective interpretations of this eigenvalue plot could lead to decisions to extract 2, 5, 7, 8, 10, or 16 factors, depending on the preconceptions of the investigator. Indeed, it is quite rare for a plot of the eigenvalues to reveal unambiguous evidence of factor specification, and therefore alternative rules must be invoked.

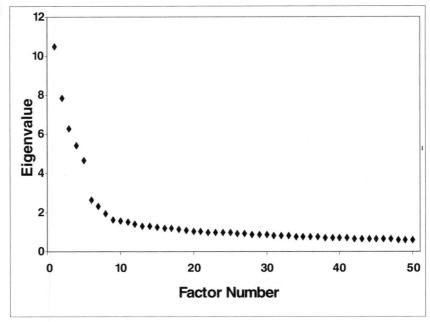

Plot of the first 50 eigenvalues from an analysis of 100 personality adjectives.

One simple procedure is to examine the numerical value of each eigenvalue and to retain those above some arbitrary cutting point. *Kaiser (1960) proposed that principal components with eigenvalues of 1.00 or above should be retained, and it is this quick-and-dirty heuristic that has been incorporated as the default option for factor extraction in some of the major statistical packages.* In fact, however, the number of components with eigenvalues greater than one is highly related to the number of variables included in the analysis. Specifically, the number of eigenvalues greater than one will typically be in the range between one-quarter to one-third of the number of variables—no matter what the actual factor structure (the number of factors with eigenvalues of 1.00 or above is 24 in the data displayed in Figure 9.5). Simulation studies have consistently found this method to be very inaccurate (Velicer, Eaton, & Fava, 2000; Zwick & Velicer, 1982, 1986), and therefore the "eigenvalues greater than one" rule is not a reasonable procedure for deciding on the number of factors to extract.

*Another method based on the eigenvalues is parallel analysis, introduced by Horn (1965).* This method was originally proposed as a means of improving the Kaiser rule by taking sampling error into account. In this method, a set of random data correlation matrices is generated, with the same number of variables and subjects as in the actual data matrix. The means of the eigenvalues across the set of random data matrices is calculated. The eigenvalues from the actual data are then compared to the mean eigenvalues of the random data. Components are retained as long as the eigenvalue from the actual data exceeds the eigenvalue from the random data. Figure 9.6 illustrates this procedure for the

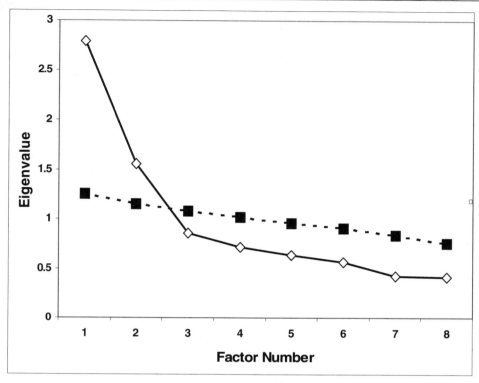

Illustration of the parallel analysis procedure applied to the numerical example in Figure 9.1.

correlation matrix in Figure 9.1. The eigenvalues in Part II of Figure 9.1 are compared to the average eigenvalues from eight random variables, with a sample size of 273. When the two eigenvalue sets are compared, this rule suggests the extraction of two factors. Simulation studies (Velicer et al., 2000; Zwick & Velicer, 1986) have found that parallel analysis is one of the most accurate methods.

*An alternative procedure is a statistical test associated with maximum-likelihood factor analysis* (there is a similar test for component analysis called the Bartlett test.). An asymptotic Chi-square test is calculated for each increase in the number of factors retained; the statistic becomes nonsignificant when the eigenvalues associated with the remaining factors do not differ significantly with each other, at which point it is assumed that the correct number of factors has been discovered. This test has not performed well in evaluative studies (Velicer et al., 2000), in part because it is so highly sensitive to the sample size. When the number of subjects becomes even moderately large or the observed variables depart even moderately from the assumption of multivariate normalacy, it will result in retaining too many factors.

*The minimum average partial-correlation (MAP: Velicer, 1976) method for finding the number of factors was developed for use with principal components analysis.* Each component is partialed out of the original correlation matrix and a partial correlation matrix is

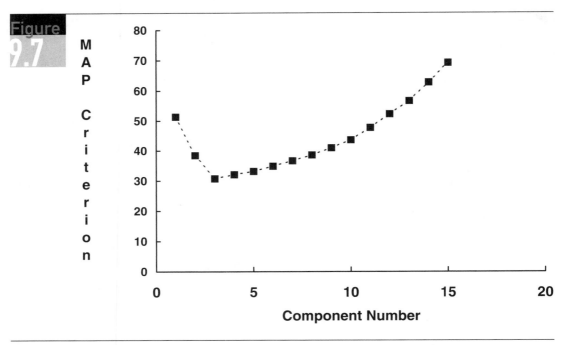

An illustration of the MAP procedure from an analysis of the Situational Temptations Inventory.

calculated. The average of the squared partial correlations is computed again after each additional factor is extracted. The MAP function will decrease as long as the components are removing common variance but will begin to increase when the components are removing unique variance (i.e., variance specific to only one variable). The correct number of components to retain is indicated at the point where the average squared partial correlation reaches a minimum. Figure 9.7 illustrates the MAP procedure with a 24-variable example with three factors from the Situational Temptations Inventory (Velicer, DiClemente, Rossi, & Prochaska, 1990). The MAP function for Figure 9.1 is presented in Part VII of that figure. Simulation studies (Velicer et al., 2000; Zwick & Velicer, 1982, 1986) have found that the MAP procedure is one of the most accurate methods.[4]

However, all of these methods should be viewed as providing guidance rather than an absolute answer. In recommending procedures for deciding on the optimum number of factors, we are necessarily guided by our criteria for a useful structural model. *Such a structure, in our view, is one that (a) incorporates the distinction between higher-level and lower-level factors, and (b) is robust across variations in the selection of variables, subject samples, and measurement procedures.* We will have more to say later in this chapter about the first criterion when we discuss the hierarchical nature of factor structures. For the

---

[4]Although many popular computer programs do not include the parallel analysis or MAP procedures, readers can obtain SPSS and SAS programs to compute them at the following Website: http://flash.lakeheadu.ca/~boconno2/boconnor.html

present, we will point out that an optimal model differentiates between narrow oblique *clusters* of variables at the lower level of the trait hierarchy and the necessarily quite broad *factors* at the highest level of the structure.

In studies of personality traits, there appear to be at least five broad higher-level factors (Digman, 1990; Goldberg, 1990; John, 1990; McCrae & John, 1992; Wiggins & Pincus, 1992), whereas at levels that are lower in the hierarchy the number of such factors varies enormously, reflecting the theoretical predilections of different investigators. In the explicitly hierarchical models of Cattell (1957) and of McCrae and Costa (1985, 1987), Cattell argued for 16 lower-level factors in analyses of the items in his Sixteen Personality Factors Questionnaire, whereas Costa and McCrae (1992) provide scales to measure 30 lower-level factors in the revised version of their NEO Personality Inventory. Both Cattell and Costa and McCrae have claimed substantial evidence of factor robustness across subject samples (although not of course across differing selections of variables), and their disagreements could simply reflect differences in the vertical locations of their factors (clusters) within the overall hierarchical structure.

In any case, there seems to be widespread agreement that *an optimal factor structure is one that is comparable over independent studies*, and we advocate the incorporation of this principle into any procedure for deciding on the number of factors to extract (see Everett, 1983; Nunnally, 1978). What this means is that no single analysis is powerful enough to provide evidence of the viability of a factor structure; *what is needed are two or more (preferably many more) analyses of at least somewhat different variables in different subject samples.*

## Rotating the Factors

The factor matrix displayed in Figure 9.2 includes K rows (one row for each variable) and L columns (one column for each of the L factors that have been extracted). Multiplying the factor matrix by its transpose produces the K by K reproduced matrix. *However, there are an infinite number of K by L matrices which when multiplied by their transposes will produce that identical reproduced matrix.* Each of these "rotations" of the original factor matrix has the same set of communality values (the sums of the squared factor loadings within each row). Matrices included in this family of factor rotations differ from one another in the relative sizes of their factors, as indexed by the sums of squared factor loadings down the columns. Given any particular set of data, the unrotated principal factors have the steepest possible descending pattern of factor variances (i.e., eigenvalues). At the other extreme, it is possible to obtain a factor matrix in which each factor is of approximately the same size.

Figure 9.8 illustrates the original unrotated factor pattern presented in Part III of Figure 9.1. The factor loadings in Part III correspond to the projection of the eight points (the items) onto the two axes (the factors). The sum of the squared loadings in each column of the factor pattern correspond to the first two eigenvalues (2.79 and 1.55). The first unrotated factor is located in the position that maximizes its variance across all eight variables, and the second unrotated factor is orthogonal to the first. As is usually the case, however, these two unrotated factors do not pass through any of the dense clusters of variables.

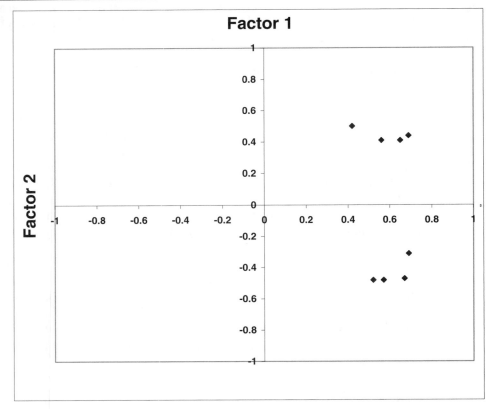

Plot of the unrotated factor pattern from Part III of Figure 9.1.

Indeed, the unrotated factors do not normally have much scientific utility, except in a few quite limited contexts.[5] Instead, the criterion usually invoked for selecting the optimal rotation is that of "simple structure," which informally can be defined as a pattern of factor loadings that contains a few high values in each column, with the rest

---

[5]The first unrotated principal component has some properties that make it useful when all of the variables under analysis have been selected as measures of the exact same construct. Given that it provides an index of whatever is most in common to the variables, it can sometimes be used as a surrogate for the underlying "latent" construct, and its loadings then can be viewed as reflecting the correlations of each variable with that construct. In our experience, however, the most useful application of the first unrotated component is with tasks in which judges rate a common set of stimuli on some attribute. In such a situation, one can correlate the judges' ratings across the set of stimuli to index the extent to which pairs of raters agree with one another. The first unrotated principal component of this matrix of interjudge agreement correlations reflects the group consensus, and the factor loadings of each judge on this first component indicates that judge's correlation with the consensus. The factor scores for each stimulus on this component are the optimal scale values for that stimulus, when judges are weighted by their contribution to the group consensus. The coefficient alpha reliability of these factor scores is equal to $N/(N - 1) \times (E - 1)/E$, where E is the eigenvalue of the component and N is the number of judges (Serlin & Kaiser, 1976).

mostly around zero. Such a factor pattern is "simple" in the sense that most variables have high loadings on only one factor and each of the factors is defined by only a few variables, thus facilitating its interpretation. In practice, the various procedures for factor rotation search for a pattern of near zero and very high factor loadings, typically by maximizing the variance of the squared factor loadings and thereby maximizing the number of factor loadings that are approximately zero. Geometrically, one characteristic of such "simple-structured" factor patterns is that each of the factors is located near a dense cluster of variables. In such a factor pattern, there are relatively few variables that are located between the clusters, and which therefore would be interpreted as blends of two or more factors.

If one's aim is solely to maximize simple structure, one would locate the factors as close to the clusters as possible. In such a solution, however, the factors would no longer be unrelated to one another, but would be "oblique" (correlated with each other). If one desires "orthogonal" factors (each of which has a correlation of exactly zero with all of the other factors), the locations of the rotated factors are selected to be as close as possible to the positions that maximize simple structure, given the orthogonality constraint. As a consequence, oblique solutions are always at least as close if not closer to a simple-structure pattern than are their orthogonal counterparts. Thus, the decision to employ an oblique or an orthogonal rotational algorithm always involves a trade-off between the better fit of a more simple structure (oblique) and the parsimony of uncorrelated factors (orthogonal). In our view, the relative advantages of each kind of rotation depend on the vertical location of one's factors in the hierarchical representation; if one seeks lower-level factors within a single domain, we recommend the use of an oblique rotation. On the other hand, if one seeks broad higher-level factors, we recommend the use of an orthogonal rotation.

By far the most commonly used procedure for *orthogonal* factor rotation is the "varimax" algorithm of Kaiser (1958), which is available in all of the statistical packages. The numeric values for the orthogonal (varimax) rotated pattern are presented in Part IV of Figure 9.1. Figure 9.9 illustrates the orthogonal rotation for this data. Note that the two axes are now more closely aligned with the two item clusters.

The problem of providing an optimal algorithm for *oblique* rotations is more complex than that for the orthogonal case, and there is less uniformity in the oblique rotational options provided by the major statistical packages. Indeed, the particular algorithm that we prefer, one called "promax" (Hendrickson & White, 1964), is not included in all of the popular factor programs. We will use the readily available oblimin rotation to illustrate the method. The numeric values for the oblique (oblimin) rotated pattern are listed in Part V of Figure 9.1. Figure 9.10 illustrates the oblique rotation for these data. The two axes are now almost perfectly aligned with the two item clusters but they are no longer at right angles to each other.

After an *orthogonal* rotation, the resulting factor matrix of K rows by L columns can be interpreted in the same way as the original unrotated matrix: Its entries are the correlations between each of the variables and each of the factors. The relative size of a particular unrotated or rotated factor can be indexed by the sum of its squared factor loadings down the column, but for the rotated factors these sums can no longer be referred to as eigenvalues, which have distinct mathematical properties based on the original correlation matrix. When each of the sums of squared factor loadings down a column of a factor matrix is divided by the number of variables in the analysis, the

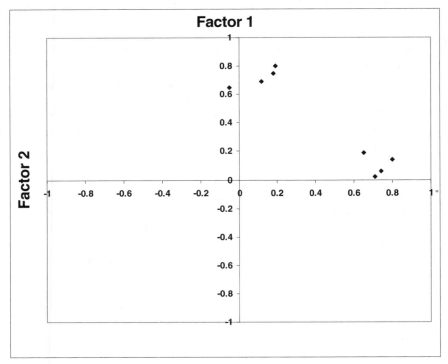

Plot of the orthogonal (varimax) rotated factor pattern from Part IV of Figure 9.1.

resulting ratio indicates the proportion of the total variance from all variables that is provided by that factor.

In the case of an oblique rotation, there are three meaningful sets of factor-loading coefficients that can be interpreted: (a) The *factor pattern*, or the regression coefficients linking the factors to the variables; (b) the *factor structure*, or the correlations between the variables and each of the factors; and (c) the *reference vectors*, or the semipartial (also called part) correlations between the variables and each of the factors, after the contributions of the other factors have been partialed out. In addition, it is necessary to obtain the correlations among the factors. With orthogonal factors, all three sets of factor-loading coefficients are the same, and the correlations among all pairs of factors are zero.

## Calculating Factor Scores

One important use of factor analysis is to discover the relations between factors in one domain and variables from other domains (which in turn might be other sets of rotated factors). One way to obtain such relations is to score each subject in the sample on each of the factors, and then to correlate these "factor scores" with the other variables included in the study. The major statistical computing packages provide such factor scores upon request. In component analyses, the component scores are calculated directly, whereas in factor analysis they must be estimated. The best methods of factor-score

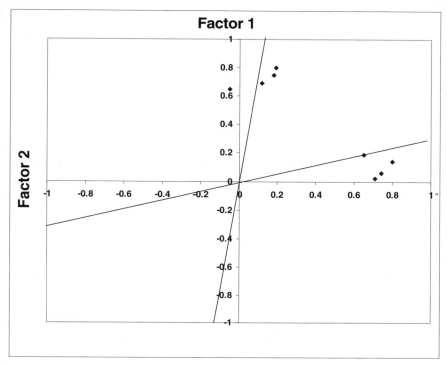

Plot of the oblique (oblimin) rotated factor pattern from Part V of Figure 9.1.

estimation (McDonald & Burr, 1967) include the Thurstone (1935) regression estimate, the Bartlett (1937) residual minimization estimate, and the Anderson and Rubin (1956) constrained residual minimization method.

All three of these methods are based on the data from a single sample, and when that sample is small in size, these values may not be particularly robust across different subject samples (Dawes, 1979). More robust should be less sample-dependent coefficients such as a simple weighting of the variables by 1.00, 0.0, and −1.00 corresponding to the size and direction of their factor loadings. This type of procedure is typically referred to as providing "scale" scores. However, the choice of method does not represent a critical decision in factor analysis. Simulation studies have found that the correlation between component scores, factor score estimates, and the simpler scale scores calculated on the same data typically exceed 0.96 (Fava & Velicer, 1992).

Finally, a number of factor theorists eschew the use of factor scores altogether, preferring to use alternative "extension" methods of relating factors to other variables (McDonald, 1978). When one requests factor scores from one of the major statistical packages, orthogonal components lead to orthogonal factor scores (unfortunately, this is not necessarily the case with orthogonal factors). *However, even with orthogonal components, if one develops scales by selecting items with high factor loadings on each of those components, it is likely that these scales will be related to each other.* In general, the reason for the sizeable correlations among scales derived from orthogonal factors is that (a) there are few factor-univocal items, most items having secondary factor loadings of substantial size, and (b) if one selects items solely on the basis of their highest factor loading, it is extremely unlikely that the secondary loadings will completely balance out. To decrease the intercorrelations among such scales, one needs to take secondary loadings into account (Saucier, 2002; Saucier & Goldberg, 2002), for which purpose one may want to use a procedure such as the AB5C model of Hofstee, de Raad, and Goldberg (1992), which will be described later.

# Vertical and Horizontal Aspects of Factor Structures in Personality

Like most concepts, personality-trait constructs include both vertical and horizontal features. The vertical aspect refers to the hierarchical relations among traits (e.g., "Reliability" is a more abstract and general concept than "Punctuality"), whereas the horizontal aspect refers to the degree of similarity among traits at the same hierarchical level (e.g., 'Sociability' involves aspects of both Warmth and Activity Level). Scientists who emphasize the vertical aspect of trait structure could employ multivariate techniques such as hierarchical cluster analysis, or they could employ oblique rotations in factor analysis, and then factor the correlations among the primary dimensions, thus constructing a hierarchical structure. Scientists who emphasize the horizontal aspect of trait structure could employ discrete cluster solutions or orthogonal factor rotations.

Historically, however, there has been no simple relation between the emphases of investigators and their methodological preferences. For example, both Eysenck (1970) and Cattell (1947) have developed explicitly hierarchical representations, Eysenck's leading to three highest-level factors, Cattell's to eight or nine. However, whereas Cattell has always advocated and used oblique factor procedures, Eysenck has typically preferred orthogonal methods. In the case of the more recent five-factor model, some of its proponents construe the model in an expressly hierarchical fashion (e.g., Costa, McCrae, & Dye, 1991; McCrae & Costa, 1992), whereas others emphasize its horizontal aspects (e.g., Hofstee et al., 1992; Peabody & Goldberg, 1989).

## Vertical Approaches to Trait Structure

The defining feature of hierarchical models of personality traits is that they emphasize the vertical relations among variables (e.g., from the most specific to the most abstract), to the exclusion of the relations among variables at the same level. One of the most famous hierarchical models of individual differences is the classic Vernon-Burt hierarchical model of abilities (e.g., Vernon, 1950); specific test items are combined to form ability tests, which are the basis of specific factors, which in turn are the basis of the minor group factors, which in turn lead to the major group factors, which at their apex form the most general factor, "g" for general intelligence.

Another classic example of a hierarchical structure is Eysenck's (1970) model of Extraversion; specific responses in particular situations (e.g., telling a joke, buying a new car) are considered as subordinate categories to habitual responses (e.g., entertaining strangers, making rapid decisions), which in turn make up such traits as Sociability and Impulsiveness, which finally form the superordinate attribute of Extraversion.

## Horizontal Approaches to Trait Structure

The defining feature of horizontal models is that the relations among the variables are specified by the variables' locations in multidimensional factor space. When that space is limited to only two dimensions, and the locations of the variables are projected to some uniform distance from the origin, the resulting structures are referred to as "circumplex" representations. The most famous example of such models is the Interpersonal Circle (e.g., Kiesler, 1983; Wiggins, 1979, 1980), which is based on Factors I (Surgency) and II (Agreeableness) in the Big Five model. Other examples of circumplex models involve more than a single plane, including the three-dimensional structures that incorporate Big Five Factors I, II, and III (Peabody & Goldberg, 1989; Stern, 1970), and Factors I, II, and IV (Saucier, 1992). A more comprehensive circumplex representation has been proposed by Hofstee et al. (1992). Dubbed the "AB5C" model, for Abridged Big Five-dimensional Circumplex, this representation includes the ten bivariate planes formed from all pairs of the Big Five factors.

## Comparing Vertical and Horizontal Perspectives

All structural representations based on factor-analytic methodology can be viewed from either vertical or horizontal perspectives. Factor analysis can be used to construct hierarchical models *explicitly* with oblique rotational procedures and *implicitly* even with orthogonal solutions, because any factor can be viewed as being located at a level above that of the variables being factored; that is, even orthogonal factors separate the common variance (the factors) from the total (common plus unique) variance of the measures. One could therefore emphasize the vertical aspect by grouping the variables by the factor with which they are most highly associated, thereby disregarding information about factorial blends. Alternatively, one could concentrate on the horizontal features of the representation, as in the AB5C model. What are the advantages associated with each perspective?

McCrae and Costa (1992) have argued that hierarchical structures are to be preferred to the extent to which the variances of the lower-level traits are trait-specific, as compared to the extent that they are related to the five broad factors. These investigators demonstrated that, after partialing out the five-factor common variance from both self and other ratings on the facet scales from the revised NEO Personality Inventory (Costa & McCrae, 1992), the residual variance in these scales was still substantial enough to elicit strong correlations among self-ratings, spouse ratings, and peer ratings of the same lower-level trait. From this finding, they argued in favor of hierarchical representations, in which relatively small amounts of common variance produce the higher-level factors, with ample amounts of unique variance still available for predictive purposes.

This argument has powerful implications for the role of trait measures when used in multiple regression analyses in applied contexts, such as personnel selection and classification. When thinking about items, scales, and factors, it is important to distinguish between the common and the unique variance of the variables at each hierarchical level. Any time that two or more variables are amalgamated, the variance that is unique to each of them is lost, and only their common variance is available at the higher amalgamated level. That is, most of the variance of individual items is lost when items are averaged into scale scores, and most of the variance of personality scales is lost when they are combined in factors. Indeed, most of the variance of personality scales is specific variance, not the common variance that is associated with the higher-level factor domains. And, therefore, for purposes of optimal prediction in applied contexts one should descend the hierarchical structure as far as sample size (and thus statistical power) permits. Other things being equal, the optimal number of predictors to be included in a regression analysis varies directly with the size of the subject sample; for large samples, one can include more variables than can be included in small samples, where one can more easily capitalize on the chance characteristics of the sample and thus lose predictive robustness when one applies the regression weights in new samples.

## Summary and Conclusions

Over more years than we'd like to admit, each of the two authors of this chapter has independently carried out hundreds of factor analyses. Although our intellectual roots differ substantially, we tend to agree on most of the controversial issues in the field. For example, with regard to two of the most vexing decisions—the use of factor analysis versus component analysis and the use of orthogonal versus oblique rotations—our experience suggests that in the realms of personality and psychopathology these choices are not very important, at least with well-structured data sets. In general, the more highly structured are the data, the less it matters *which* factor-analytic decisions one makes. Indeed, the best way to assure oneself about a factor structure is to analyze the data in different ways, and thereby test the robustness of one's solution across alternative procedures.

On the other hand, two decisions are of considerable importance—the initial selection of variables and the number of factors to extract. The selection of variables should be guided by theory and/or the findings from past research. Because we believe that an optimal factor structure is one that is comparable over independent studies, we advocate the incorporation of this principle into any procedure for deciding on the number of factors to extract. What this means is that no single analysis is powerful enough to provide definitive evidence of the viability of a factor structure; what is needed are multiple analyses of at least somewhat different variables in different subject samples.

Moreover, the comparison of solutions from different subject samples will almost always be more useful when the complete hierarchical structures are available. To do this requires the analysis at differing hierarchical levels, which in practice means the repeated analyses of the same data set extracting different numbers of factors. One can begin with the first unrotated component, then examine the two-factor varimax-rotated solution, then the three-factor representation, stopping only when a new factor does not include at least two variables with their highest loadings on it. If one rotates the factors at each level, and computes orthogonal factor scores on these rotated factors, then one can intercorrelate the set of all factor scores, and thus discover the relations between the factors at differing levels. For examples of such hierarchical representations, see Goldberg (1999), Goldberg and Somer (2000), Goldberg and Strycker (2002), and Saucier (1997, 2000, 2003).

A hierarchical perspective has powerful implications for the role of trait measures when used in multiple regression analyses in applied contexts, such as personnel selection and classification. Because one loses some unique variance as one amalgamates measures, the optimal level of prediction is a function of statistical power, and thus of sample size. Other things being equal, the optimal number of predictors to be included in a regression analysis varies directly with the size of the subject sample; for large samples, one can include more variables than can be included in small samples, which more easily capitalizes on chance characteristics and thus lose predictive robustness when one applies the regression weights in new samples.

However, a horizontal perspective is necessary for basic research on trait structure, because trait variables are not clustered tightly in five-dimensional space; rather, most variables share some features with one set of variables while they share other features with another set. Thus, even after rotation of the factors to a criterion of simple structure such as varimax, most variables have substantial secondary loadings, and thus must be viewed as blends of two or more factors. Because hierarchical models de-emphasize these horizontal aspects of trait relations, they provide no information about the nature of such factorial blends. For purposes of basic research on the structure of traits, therefore, models that emphasize horizontal relations such as the AB5C model will typically be more informative.

In concluding this chapter, we acknowledge the fact that many investigators are now turning away from exploratory factor analysis altogether in favor of confirmatory models and procedures; indeed, a spate of new textbooks deal exclusively with confirmatory models, whereas the most recent of the major textbooks that focus primarily on exploratory techniques were published over two decades ago (Gorsuch, 1983). For readers who may be curious about our continued use of exploratory factor analysis in the face of the emerging consensus against it, we will now try to provide some justification for our beliefs.

First of all, it is important to realize that most applications of confirmatory models involve, by our standards, extremely small sets of variables; a typical confirmatory analysis includes only a dozen or two dozen variables, and applications of these models to variable sets of the sizes we work with (e.g., Goldberg, 1990, 1992) are still computationally prohibitive. Second, an increase in the number of factors can result in a reduction in the size of some fit indices (Marsh, Hau, Balla, & Grayson, 1998). Applied researchers often substitute arbitrary sums of subsets of the observed variables called "item parcels" to address this problem. Third, as much as we support theory-driven research, we recognize that most work in personality and psychopathology often falls on a continuum between the testing of a well-established theory and the development of a new theoretical model. Very few studies represent pure examples of theory testing.

Moreover, we view exploratory and confirmatory procedures as complementary rather than as competing. From this viewpoint, it is more appropriate to talk about a program of research rather than a single study and use both methods at different times during the planned set of studies. In addition, we have a concern about the problem of a confirmatory bias. Greenwald, Pratkanis, Leippe, and Baumgardner (1986) distinguish between theory-oriented and result-centered research. These two types of investigations roughly correspond to confirmatory and exploratory approaches. In their criticism of theory-oriented research, Greenwald et al. warn about the tendency to persevere by modifying procedures and not reporting results that are inconsistent with the theory. There are numerous examples in the literature where an initial failure to confirm was followed by a reliance on modification indices such as the use of correlated error terms.

In contrast, repeated independent discoveries of the same factor structure derived from exploratory techniques provide stronger evidence for that structure than would be provided by the same number of confirmatory analyses. In other words, if results replicate and the analysis does not involve a target, the results can be viewed as more independently tested than if the data are fitted to a specified model. Indeed, when a confirmatory analysis is used to reject a model (which will virtually always occur if the sample is large enough), the investigator's subsequent tinkering with the model can be viewed as a return to exploratory analysis procedures.

Although we have not been impressed with the substantive knowledge of personality structure that has yet accrued from findings based on confirmatory techniques, we applaud their development, and we encourage their use. We suspect that when theories of personality structure become specified more precisely, perhaps on the basis of findings from exploratory analyses, we will see the advantages of confirmatory factor models over exploratory ones. In the interim, we believe that there is a substantial role for both types of methodologies.

# Acknowledgments

The writing of this chapter was supported by Grant MH49227 from the National Institute of Mental Health to Lewis R. Goldberg and Grants CA50087, CA71356, and CA27821 from the National Cancer Institute to Wayne F. Velicer. Substantial portions of the text have been adapted from Goldberg and Digman (1994). The authors are indebted to Michael C. Ashton, Bettina Hoeppner, Willem K. B. Hofstee, John J. McArdle, Roderick P. McDonald, Stanley A. Mulaik, Fritz Ostendorf, Racheal Reavy, Gerard Saucier, Christopher Soto, Stephen Strack, Robert M. Thorndike, and Richard E. Zinbarg for their many thoughtful editorial suggestions.

## REFERENCES

Anderson, T. W., & Rubin, H. (1956). Statistical inference in factor analysis. In J. Neyman (Ed.), *Proceedings of the third Berkeley symposium on mathematical statistics and probability* (pp. 111–150). Berkeley, CA: University of California Press.

Bartlett, M. S. (1937). The statistical conception of mental factors. *British Journal of Psychology, 28,* 97–104.

Cattell, R. B. (1947). Confirmation and clarification of primary personality factors. *Psychometrika, 12,* 197–220.

Cattell, R. B. (1957). *Personality and motivation structure and measurement.* Yonkers-on-Hudson, NY: World Book.

Cattell, R. B. (1966). The scree test for the number of factors. *Multivariate Behavioral Research, 1,* 245–276.

Costa, P. T., Jr., & McCrae, R. R. (1992). *Revised NEO Personality Inventory (NEO-PI-R) and NEO Five-Factor Inventory (NEO-FFI) professional manual.* Odessa, FL: Psychological Assessment Resources.

Costa, P. T., Jr., McCrae, R. R., & Dye, D. A. (1991). Facet scales for agreeableness and conscientiousness: A revision of the NEO Personality Inventory. *Personality and Individual Differences, 12,* 887–898.

Dawes, R. M. (1979). The robust beauty of improper linear models in decision making. *American Psychologist, 34,* 571–582.

Digman, J. M. (1990). Personality structure: Emergence of the five-factor model. In M. R. Rosenzweig, & L. W. Porter (Eds.), *Annual review of psychology* (Vol. 41, pp. 417–440). Palo Alto, CA: Annual Reviews.

Everett, J. E. (1983). Factor comparability as a means of determining the number of factors and their rotation. *Multivariate Behavioral Research, 18*, 197–218.

Eysenck, H. J. (1970). *The structure of human personality* (3rd ed.). London: Methuen.

Fava, J. L., & Velicer, W. F. (1992). An empirical comparison of factor, image, component, and scale scores. *Multivariate Behavioral Research, 27*, 301–322.

Goldberg, L. R. (1981). Language and individual differences: The search for universals in personality lexicons. In L. Wheeler (Ed.), *Review of personality and social psychology* (Vol. 2, pp. 141–165). Beverly Hills, CA: Sage.

Goldberg, L. R. (1990). An alternative "Description of personality": The Big-Five factor structure. *Journal of Personality and Social Psychology, 59*, 1216–1229.

Goldberg, L. R. (1992). The development of markers for the Big-Five factor structure. *Psychological Assessment, 4*, 26–42.

Goldberg, L. R. (1999). The Curious Experiences Survey, a revised version of the Dissociative Experiences Scale: Factor structure, reliability, and relations to demographic and personality variables. *Psychological Assessment, 11*, 134–145.

Goldberg, L. R., & Digman, J. M. (1994). Revealing structure in the data: Principles of exploratory factor analysis. In S. Strack & M. Lorr (Eds.), *Differentiating normal and abnormal personality* (pp. 216–242). New York: Springer.

Goldberg, L. R., & Somer, O. (2000). The hierarchical structure of common Turkish person-descriptive adjectives. *European Journal of Personality, 14*, 497–531.

Goldberg, L. R., & Strycker, L. A. (2002). Personality traits and eating habits: The assessment of food preferences in a large community sample. *Personality and Individual Differences, 32*, 49–65.

Gorsuch, R. L. (1983). Factor analysis (2nd ed.). Hillsdale, NJ: Erlbaum.

Graham, J. W., Cumsille, P. E., & Elek-Fisk, E. (2003). Methods for handling missing data. In J. A. Schinka, & W. F. Velicer (Eds.), *Research methods in psychology: Handbook of psychology* (Vol. 2, pp. 87–114). New York: Wiley.

Greenwald, A. G., Pratkanis, A. R., Leippe, M. R., & Baumgardner, M. H. (1986). Under what conditions does theory obstruct research progress? *Psychological Review, 93*, 216–229.

Guadagnoli, E., & Velicer, W. F. (1988). Relation of sample size to the stability of component patterns. *Psychological Bulletin, 103*, 265–275.

Harman, H. H. (1976). *Modern factor analysis* (3rd ed.). Chicago, IL: University of Chicago.

Hendrickson, A. E., & White, P. O. (1964). Promax: A quick method of rotation to oblique simple structure. *British Journal of Statistical Psychology, 17*, 65–70.

Hofstee, W. K. B., de Raad, B., & Goldberg, L. R. (1992). Integration of the Big Five and circumplex taxonomies of traits. *Journal of Personality and Social Psychology, 63*, 146–163.

Horn, J. L. (1965). A rationale and test for the number of factors in factor analysis. *Psychometrika, 30*, 179–185.

Hotelling, H. (1933). Analysis of a complex of statistical variables into principal components. *Journal of Educational Psychology, 24*, 417–441, 498–520.

John, O. P. (1990). The "Big-Five" factor taxonomy: Dimensions of personality in the natural language and in questionnaires. In L. A. Pervin (Ed.), *Handbook of personality theory and research* (pp. 66–100). New York: Guilford Press.

Joreskog, K. G. (1967). Some contributions to maximum likelihood factor analysis. *Psychometrika, 32*, 443–482.

Kaiser, H. F. (1958). The varimax criterion for analytic rotation in factor analysis. *Psychometrika, 23*, 187–200.

Kaiser, H. F. (1960). The application of electronic computers to factor analysis. *Educational and Psychological Measurement, 20*, 141–151.

Kiesler, D. J. (1983). The 1982 interpersonal circle: A taxonomy for complementarity in human transactions. *Psychological Review, 90*, 185–214.

Little, R. J. A., & Rubin, D. B. (1987). Statistical analysis with missing data. New York: Wiley.

MacCallum, R. C., Widaman, K. F., Zhang, S., & Hong, S. (1999). Sample size in factor analysis. *Psychological Methods, 4*, 84–99.

Marsh, H. W., Hau, K.-T., Balla, J. R., & Grayson, D. (1998). Is more ever too much? The number of indicators per factor in confirmatory factor analysis. *Multivariate Behavioral Research, 33*, 181–220.

McCrae, R. R., & Costa, P. T., Jr. (1985). Updating Norman's "adequate taxonomy": Intelligence and personality dimensions in natural language and in questionnaires. *Journal of Personality and Social Psychology, 49*, 710–721.

McCrae, R. R., & Costa, P. T., Jr. (1987). Validation of the five-factor model of personality across instruments and observers. *Journal of Personality and Social Psychology, 52*, 81–90.

McCrae, R. R., & Costa, P. T., Jr. (1992). Discriminant validity of NEO-PIR facet scales. *Educational and Psychological Measurement, 52*, 229–237.

McCrae, R. R., & John, O. P. (1992). An introduction to the five-factor model and its applications. *Journal of Personality, 60*, 175–215.

McDonald, R. P. (1978). Some checking procedures for extension analysis. *Multivariate Behavioral Research, 13*, 319–325.

McDonald, R. P. (1985). *Factor analysis and related methods.* Hillsdale, NJ: Erlbaum.

McDonald, R. P., & Burr, E. J. (1967). A comparison of four methods of constructing factor scores. *Psychometrika, 32*, 381–401.

Mulaik, S. A. (1972). *The foundations of factor analysis.* New York: McGraw-Hill.

Nunnally, J. (1978). *Psychometric theory* (2nd ed.). New York: McGraw-Hill.

O'Connor, B. P. (2002). The search for dimensional structure differences between normality and abnormality: A statistical review of published data on personality and psychopathology. *Journal of Personality and Social Psychology, 83*, 962–982.

Peabody, D., & Goldberg, L. R. (1989). Some determinants of factor structures from personality-trait descriptors. *Journal of Personality and Social Psychology, 57*, 552–567.

Pearson, K. (1901). On lines and planes of closest fit to systems of points in space. *Philosophical Magazine, Series B, 2*, 559–572.

Prochaska, J. O., Velicer, W. F., Rossi, J. S., Goldstein, M. G., Marcus, B. H., Rakowski, W., Fiore, C., Harlow, L. L., Redding, C. A., Rosenbloom, D., & Rossi, S. R. (1994). Stages of change and decisional balance for twelve problem behaviors. *Health Psychology, 13*, 39–46.

Saucier, G. (1992). Benchmarks: Integrating affective and interpersonal circles with the Big-Five personality factors. *Journal of Personality and Social Psychology, 62*, 1025–1035.

Saucier, G. (1997). Effects of variable selection on the factor structure of person descriptors. *Journal of Personality and Social Psychology, 73*, 1296–1312.

Saucier, G. (2000). Isms and the structure of social attitudes. *Journal of Personality and Social Psychology, 78*, 366–385.

Saucier, G. (2002). Orthogonal markers for orthogonal factors: The case of the Big Five. *Journal of Research in Personality, 36*, 1–31.

Saucier, G. (2003). Factor structure of English-language personality type-nouns. *Journal of Personality and Social Psychology, 85*, 695–708.

Saucier, G., & Goldberg, L. R. (2002). Assessing the Big Five: Applications of 10 psychometric criteria to the development of marker scales. In B. de Raad & M. Perugini (Eds.), *Big Five assessment* (pp. 29–58). Goettingen, Germany: Hogrefe & Huber.

Saucier, G., & Goldberg, L. R. (2003). The structure of personality attributes. In M. R. Barrick, & A. M. Ryan (Eds.), *Personality and work: Reconsidering the role of personality in organizations* (pp. 1–29). San Francisco, CA: Jossey-Bass.

Schafer, J. L. (1997). *Analysis of incomplete multivariate data.* New York: Wiley.

Schafer, J. L., & Graham, J. W. (2002). Missing data: Our view of the state of the art. *Psychological Methods, 7*, 147–177.

Serlin, R. C., & Kaiser, H. F. (1976). A computer program for item selection based on maximum internal consistency. *Educational and Psychological Measurement, 36*, 757–759.

Spearman, C. (1904). General intelligence, objectively determined and measured. *American Journal of Psychology, 15*, 201–293.

Stern, G. G. (1970). *People in context: Measuring person-environment congruence in education and industry.* New York: Wiley.

ten Berge, J. M. F. (1999). A legitimate case of component analysis of ipsative measures, and partialing the mean as an alternative to ipsatization. *Multivariate Behavioral Research, 34*, 89–102.

Thomas, C., Turkheimer, E., & Oltmanns, T. F. (2003). Factorial structure of pathological personality as evaluated by peers. *Journal of Abnormal Psychology, 112*, 81–91.

Thurstone, L. L. (1931). Multiple factor analysis. *Psychological Review, 38*, 406–427.

Thurstone, L. L. (1935). *The vectors of the mind.* Chicago, IL: University of Chicago.

Thurstone, L. L. (1947). *Multiple factor analysis.* Chicago, IL: University of Chicago.

Van Driel, O. P. (1978). On various causes of improper solutions in maximum likelihood factor analysis. *Psychometrika, 43*, 225–243.

Velicer, W. F. (1976). Determining the number of components from the matrix of partial correlations. Psychometrika, 41, 321–327.

Velicer, W. F., DiClemente, C. C., Prochaska, J. O., & Brandenberg, N. (1985). A decisional balance measure for assessing and predicting smoking status. *Journal of Personality and Social Psychology, 48,* 1279–1289.

Velicer, W. F., DiClemente, C., Rossi, J. S., & Prochaska, J. O. (1990). Relapse situations and self-efficacy: An integrative model. *Addictive Behaviors, 15,* 271–283.

Velicer, W. F., Eaton, C. A., & Fava, J. L. (2000). Construct explication through factor or component analysis: A review and evaluation of alternative procedures for determining the number of factors or components. In R. D. Goffin, & E. Helmes (Eds.), *Problems and solutions in human assessment: Honoring Douglas Jackson at seventy* (pp. 41–71). Boston, MA: Kluwer.

Velicer, W. F., & Fava, J. L. (1987). An evaluation of the effects of variable sampling on component, image, and factor analysis. *Multivariate Behavioral Research, 22,* 193–210.

Velicer, W. F., & Fava, J. L. (1998). The effects of variable and subject sampling on factor pattern recovery. *Psychological Methods, 3,* 231–251.

Velicer, W. F., & Jackson, D. N. (1990). Component analysis versus common factor analysis: Some issues in selecting an appropriate procedure. *Multivariate Behavioral Research, 25,* 1–28.

Vernon, P. E. (1950). *The structure of human abilities.* London: Methuen.

Ward, R. M., Velicer, W. F., Rossi, J. S., Fava, J. L., & Prochaska, J. O. (2004). Factorial invariance and internal consistency for the Decisional Balance Inventory—Short form. *Addictive Behaviors, 29,* 953–958.

Wiggins, J. S. (1979). A psychological taxonomy of trait-descriptive terms: The interpersonal domain. *Journal of Personality and Social Psychology, 37,* 395–412.

Wiggins, J. S. (1980). Circumplex models of interpersonal behavior. In L. Wheeler (Ed.), *Review of personality and social psychology* (Vol. 1, pp. 265–294). Beverly Hills, CA: Sage.

Wiggins, J. S., & Pincus, A. L. (1992). Personality: Structure and assessment. In M. R. Rosenzweig, & L. W. Porter (Eds.), *Annual review of psychology* (Vol. 43, pp. 473–504). Palo Alto, CA: Annual Reviews.

Zegers, F. E., & ten Berge, J. M. F. (1985). A family of association coefficients for metric scales. *Psychometrika, 50,* 17–24.

Zwick, W. R., & Velicer, W. F. (1982). Factors influencing four rules for determining the number of components to retain. *Multivariate Behavioral Research, 17,* 253–269.

Zwick, W. R., & Velicer, W. F. (1986). Comparison of five rules for determining the number of components to retain. *Psychological Bulletin, 99,* 432–442.

# Latent Variable Modeling
## Representing the Structural Continuity and Discontinuity of Normal and Abnormal Personality

10

Kristian E. Markon
Robert F. Krueger

Latent variable modeling—the statistical modeling of variables that are not directly observed—is critical to normal and abnormal personality measurement and theory. Personality traits such as Neuroticism or Disinhibition, like other psychological constructs, are "fuzzy," and it is difficult or impossible to measure them directly. Because personality traits are themselves not directly measured, they must be measured indirectly, which poses challenges to empirical study and theory of personality. How to best measure, model, and conceptualize personality traits and other latent variables is, therefore, fundamental to understanding normal and abnormal personality.

In this chapter, we briefly review general latent variable models. Using a common type of latent variable model, we illustrate how to explore different hypotheses regarding personality traits and measures. We discuss the use of latent variable models in comparing and distinguishing between different personality trait distributions, such as continuous and categorical personality trait distributions. We also discuss the use of latent variable models in determining how well personality measures assess personality traits.

## Generalized Linear Latent Variable Models

Although numerous latent variable models have been proposed, many of them can be formulated within a single, unified framework. Under this framework, each model can be thought of as a specific form of a single, more general model known as the general-ized linear latent variable model (GLLVM; Bartholomew & Knott, 1999; Skrondal & Rabe-Hesketh, 2004). The GLLVM has the general form

$$f(X|\theta) = A\theta + B + e \tag{1}$$

where $X$ is a vector of numbers arranged in a column, corresponding to a pattern of ob-served responses. $\theta$ is a vector of unobserved latent trait values. $A$ is a matrix of numbers arranged in a grid, containing a set of coefficients associating latent trait values with observed response values. $B$ is a vector of coefficients associated with observed response values alone. The final term, $e$ is a vector of random errors and reflects random noise.

The GLLVM is extremely similar to models such as the generalized linear model (GLM) and the standard linear regression model. In the GLLVM, just as in the GLM and regression model, a set of outcome variables is being regressed on, or correlated with, a set of predictor variables. In the GLLVM, just as in the GLM and the regres-sion model, the outcome variables are observed. The difference between the GLLVM and models such as the GLM and linear regression model is that in the GLLVM, the predictor variables are latent and not observed directly. The modeling problem at hand in the GLLVM is to estimate $A$ and $B$ even though the predictor variables $\theta$ are not observed.

Just as the GLLVM parallels the standard regression model, $A$ can be interpreted as a slope or regression coefficient, relating the observed values $X$ to the latent trait values $\theta$. Similarly, $B$ can be interpreted as an observed variable intercept, reflecting the tendency of observed values $X$ to be greater or lower regardless of the latent trait value. The slope $A$ is proportional to the strength of relationship between the observed vari-ables and the latent variables—in other words, how well the observed variables measure the latent variables. The intercept $B$, in contrast, is proportional to how difficult it is to obtain large values of the observed variable—in other words, the severity or abnormality represented by the observed variables.

As an example, consider a situation where an individual's observed scores on four measures are being predicted from their levels of trait anxiety and depression:

$$\begin{bmatrix} 0.26 \\ 1.4 \\ 0.60 \\ 2.8 \end{bmatrix} = \begin{bmatrix} 0.85 & 0.50 \\ 0.75 & 0.45 \\ 0.47 & 0.89 \\ 0.51 & 0.91 \end{bmatrix} \begin{bmatrix} 1.0 \\ 0.78 \end{bmatrix} + \begin{bmatrix} -1.1 \\ 0.50 \\ -0.65 \\ 1.6 \end{bmatrix} + \begin{bmatrix} 0.12 \\ -0.25 \\ 0.09 \\ -0.05 \end{bmatrix}$$

The two values in the second matrix on the right side of the equation, 1.0, and 0.78, are the individual's anxiety and depression scores, respectively. They can be interpreted much in the same way as standardized scores (i.e., z scores). Normally, these values would not be observed—they would be latent variables with unknown values. However, for the sake of the example, we assume that they are known. These values are both above zero, indicating that this individual is more anxious and depressed than the average person.

Values in the first matrix on the right side of the equation represent the slopes relat-ing individual's anxiety and depression scores to the observed measures. For example, in the first column of the first row is the slope (0.85) relating the first latent variable, anxiety, to the first measure. Similarly, in the second column of the third row is the slope (0.89) relating the second latent variable, depression, to the third measure. The rows indicate which observed measure the slopes correspond to, and the columns indicate which latent variable, anxiety, or depression, the slopes correspond to. The larger the slope, the stronger the measure. For example, the first and the second measures measure anxiety better than depression, and the third and the fourth measure measures depression better than anxiety.

The third matrix on the right side of the equation reflects the severity of each measure, or how "easy" it is for an individual to have a large value on each measure. The smaller the value, the more severe the measure, and the more difficult it is to obtain a large value. The first measure, for example, has a severity of $-1.1$, indicating that this item is relatively severe, and few individuals have large scores. An individual must have a relatively large anxiety score to overcome the $-1.1$ intercept that is added. Similarly, the second measure has a severity of 0.50, indicating that this item is less severe, and many individuals have large scores. The first measure, which is more severe, might be an item such as "I am in constant fear of many things." The second measure, which is less severe, might be an item such as "I get anxious sometimes."

The last matrix on the right side of the equation contains values that reflect random noise. These values reflect random factors influencing scores, such as noises in the room, fluctuations in mood, and other similar variables. For example, the first value, 0.12, adjusts the predicted response to the first measure upwards, in the direction of higher anxiety. Perhaps when the first measure was responded to, there was a loud noise in the next room that made the individual feel somewhat more anxious when responding. The second value, $-0.25$, indicates that the individual felt less anxious when responding to the second measure, for random reasons. For example, perhaps they remembered a date they have been looking forward to with a longterm romantic partner. The values in the final matrix reflect all of the random, minor influences on responses to observed measures that are not explained by the traits of interest, which in this case are anxiety and depression.

The observed scores are obtained by multiplying and adding the matrices as appropriate (see, e.g., Loehlin, 2004 for a more detailed explanation of matrix algebra). For example, the individual's score on the first measure is obtained as:

$$0.26 = [(0.85 \times 1.0) + (0.5 \times 0.78)] + -1.1 + 0.12$$

The individual's score on the last measure, similarly, is obtained as:

$$2.8 = [(0.51 \times 1.0) + (0.91 \times 0.78)] + 1.6 + -0.05$$

The scores on the second and third measures can be obtained in the same way.

Many common latent variable models can be derived from the GLLVM. For example, if the observed variables $X$ are assumed to be continuous and normally distributed, $A$ and $B$ can be estimated from the means and covariances between the observed variables. The problem then becomes one of modeling the means and covariances between the observed variables, rather than the observed variables directly. That is, the slopes $A$ and intercepts $B$ are estimated from the means and covariances of $X$, rather than from the $X$ values themselves.

Models where the slopes $A$ and intercepts $B$ are estimated indirectly through modeling of means and covariances are known as a structural equation models or mean and covariance structure models. The exploratory factor model discussed elsewhere in this volume is an important and commonly used type of covariance structure model. In the exploratory factor model, the slopes $A$—typically referred to as factor loadings—are not assumed to have any particular form. The slopes are "freely estimated" from the observed data, with all the latent variables being associated at some level with all the observed variables. In other types of mean and covariance structure models, the slopes and intercepts are modeled as having particular forms. In those mean and covariance structure models, some associations between latent variables and observed variables are estimated, but others are not, because they are assumed to have a certain value (e.g., 0).

Other common latent variable models can also be described using the GLLVM. For example, if an observed variable $X$ is ordinal or nominal in scale (e.g., with response categories of "disagree," "maybe," "agree," or response categories of "yes" versus "no"), the logistic latent trait model, commonly encountered in item response theory (IRT), can be used to model responses to each item category:

$$\ln\left[\frac{P(X_1|\theta)}{P(X_0|\theta)}\right] = A\theta + B \tag{2}$$

where $X_0$ is some baseline response category (e.g., "disagree"), and $X_1$ is the next category in order (e.g., "agree"). $P(X_j|\theta)$ is the probability of responding in category $X_j$ given the value of the latent traits $\theta$, and ln is the natural logarithm function. $A$ and $B$ are regression coefficients and intercepts as before.

The logistic model can be seen as a specific form of the GLLVM where the logarithm of the odds of responding in one category versus another is predicted from the latent trait. Specifically, the $f(X|\theta)$ term on the left side of the GLLVM in Equation 1 becomes the logistic term on the left side of Equation 2. As before, the model is linear, and the right side of the model involves slope and intercept terms. In the GLLVM (Eq. 1), increases in the observed variables are explained in terms of linear increases in latent variables; in the more specific logistic form of the GLLVM (Eq. 2), increases in the probability of responding in a more extreme category are explained in terms of linear increases in latent variables.

Many latent variable models are subsumed by the logistic model represented by Equation 2. Logistic latent variable models with continuous latent traits, for example, are equivalent to many models used in item response theory (IRT) modeling. Similarly, logistic latent variable models with categorical latent traits are equivalent to varieties of latent class models (Bartholomew & Knott, 1999; Heinen, 1996). As latent trait and latent class models can both be formulated within the same logistic model framework (Eq. 2), continuous and categorical latent trait models can be compared (Heinen, 1996; Vermunt, 2001). This allows for comparisons between models of personality structure that differ in the assumption that latent traits are either continuous or discrete. Comparisons between continuous and discrete latent trait models allow for exploration of how normal and abnormal personality differ. In particular, they provide evidence as to whether normal and abnormal forms of personality are quantitatively or qualitatively different (see Haslam & Williams, this volume, Chapter 12 for a thorough discussion of discrete accounts of personality and their implication for personality theory).

Many issues relating to differentiation between and description of normality and abnormality have been elaborated in greater detail for logistic latent variable models than mean and covariance structure models. For example, comparisons between continuous and discrete latent trait models have been elaborated in greater detail for the logistic latent variable model (Eq. 2) than mean and covariance structure models (Bauer & Curran, 2004; Heinen, 1996; Vermunt, 2001). For these reasons, we will focus on the logistic model throughout the remainder of the chapter. Many of the general principles described here using the logistic model, however, also apply to other variants of the GLLVM, including the normal mean and covariance structure model.

# Estimating Latent Variable Models

Just as there are numerous latent variable models, there are also numerous methods for estimating them—that is, for inferring the most likely values of the unobserved quantities in the equations (e.g., $A$ and $B$) from the observed data. One method—the maximum likelihood method—is particularly useful however. Maximum likelihood estimators have a variety of desirable statistical properties, and have been shown to perform well, relative to other estimators. Moreover, as will be discussed, maximum likelihood estimation is related to other areas of statistical theory in such a way so as to allow methods developed in those other areas to be applicable to model selection.

The basic premise of maximum likelihood estimation is relatively simple: One chooses model estimates in such a way as to maximize the probability of a dataset. That is, maximum likelihood estimates are based on the probability of a given dataset given a particular model. Different model estimates imply different probabilities of a given dataset; the goal in maximum likelihood estimation is to find model estimates that maximize the probability—that is, likelihood—of the data.

An important step in maximum likelihood estimation is to determine the probability of the data as a function of the model estimates. In the logistic latent variable model of Equation 2, this is relatively simple, as the probability of the data—that is, $P(X)$—is explicitly included in the model. With algebraic manipulation, Equation 2 can be rewritten as:

$$P(X_{ij}|\theta) = \frac{\exp(A_{ij}\theta + B_{ij})}{\sum_{J} \exp(A_{ij}\theta + B_{ij})} \tag{3}$$

where $i$ is the item number, $j$ is an index of response category (e.g., 0, 1, . . . for "true," "somewhat true," and so forth), $J$ is the total number of categories, $\Sigma$ is the summation operator, and $exp$ is the exponential function. As in Equation 2, $P(X_{ij}|\theta)$ is the probability of responding to item $i$ in response category $j$ given the level of the latent traits $\theta$.

It is important to note that the slope $A$ and intercept $B$ in Equations 1 and 2 are now subscripted as $A_{ij}$ and $B_{ij}$ in Equation 3. This is emphasized because Equation 3 is modeling the probability of responding in a specific category of a specific item. Because an item may have two or more response categories, there will be one slope and intercept for each category, and thus, two or more slopes and intercepts for each item. Each item category has its own slope and intercept.

Equation 3 indicates that the likelihood of responding in a given item category can be expressed as a proportion of some total possible value. This value—given in the exponential term—can be thought of as something like an exponential effect of the latent variable on the observed variable. The numerator of Equation 3 gives the latent effect associated with a particular category; the denominator gives the total latent effect associated with all the categories. The probability of responding in a given category, then, is equal to the proportion of the total latent effect associated with the category. It is for this reason that the logistic latent trait model, as reflected in Equations 2 and 3, is sometimes called the "divide-by-total" model (Thissen & Steinberg, 1986).

In examining Equation 3, it is clear that the probability of responding to an item in a given category varies as a function of three types of parameters: item category slopes, item category intercepts, and latent trait values. These are the three values that determine the likelihood of responding in a certain way to a certain item; the goal of maximum likelihood estimation in this case is to find the values of the slope, intercept, and trait parameters that maximize the probability of the observed response to the items.

Generally, one is interested in the probability of an entire dataset of responses, and not a single response to a single item. To find the probability or likelihood of the entire dataset, one finds the joint probability of all the individuals' responses to all of the items. Moreover, one uses the log-likelihood of the dataset rather than the likelihood to simplify computation. The log-likelihood of the dataset is given by

$$
\begin{aligned}
\ln(L) &= \sum_N \ln P(X_n) \\
&= \sum_N \ln \sum_K [P(X_n|\theta_k)P(\theta_k)] \\
&\quad \sum_N \ln \sum_K \left[ \left\{ \prod_I \prod_J P(X_{ij}|\theta_k) \right\} P(\theta_k) \right]
\end{aligned}
\tag{4}
$$

where $N$ is the total sample size, and $X$ is the response pattern of individual $n$. $\prod$ is the multiplication operator, $i$ is an index of item number, $j$ is an index of category number as in Equation 3, and $k$ is an index of latent trait value. There are as many values of $k$ as there are latent trait values, and the total number of latent trait values is $K$. Multiplication is done over all the items $i$ and all the categories $j$ that individuals respond to.

Equation 3 indicates that the log-likelihood for an entire dataset is equal to the sum of the log-likelihoods of each person's response pattern $X$. The probability of each person's response pattern $X$ under the model can be written, in turn, in terms of the product of the conditional probability of $X$ given $\theta$, and the probability of $\theta$. Finally, the conditional probability of response pattern $X$ given $\theta$ is given by multiplying the conditional probabilities of individual responses to individual categories of individual items $X_{ij}$. The conditional probability of $X_{ij}$ given $\theta$, $P(X_{ij}|\theta)$, is given by Equation 3 (in Eq. 3 the latent trait value subscript $k$ is omitted).

In considering Equation 3 together with Equation 4, it is important to note that the likelihood of the dataset depends on $\theta$ not directly, but through its probability $P(\theta)$. As was emphasized, the likelihood of the data depends on three types of parameters—slope, intercept, and trait parameters. Equation 4 illustrates that the likelihood of the data depends on the distribution of the latent trait values, rather than latent trait values per se. In this regard, what is being estimated in the logistic latent variable model—in addition to the slope and intercepts—are the latent variable distributions.

# Modeling Latent Distributions

Given that the likelihood of a dataset depends on the latent trait distribution, different hypotheses about the latent trait distribution can be tested. For example, one might hypothesize that Neuroticism is normally distributed in the population, and that abnormal personality represents an extreme of this normal distribution. Alternatively, one might hypothesize that Neuroticism is skewed, and that abnormal personality represents the tail of this skewed distribution. Finally, one might hypothesize that there are two populations of individuals, one with lower levels of Neuroticism, and the other with greater levels of Neuroticism. Each of these hypotheses regarding the latent distribution can be statistically tested under the logistic form of the GLLVM in Equation 3.

Figures 10.1 to 10.3 represent distributions under these three hypotheses. Figure 10.1 represents a latent Neuroticism distribution that is normal; Figure 10.2 represents a latent Neuroticism distribution that is skewed; Figure 10.3 represents a latent Neuroticism distribution that comprises two discrete groups. Each figure is essentially a histogram presenting the probability of having each latent value. The number of bars in each figure represents the number of latent trait values—that is, $K$. The height of each bar represents the probability of having each latent trait value—that is, $P(\theta_k)$.

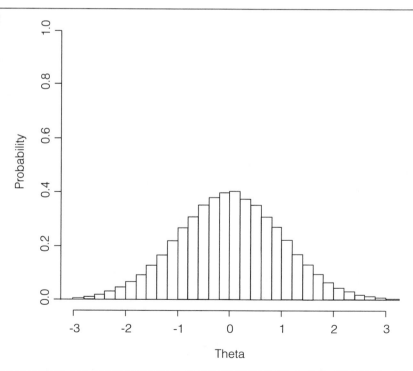

Normal distribution.

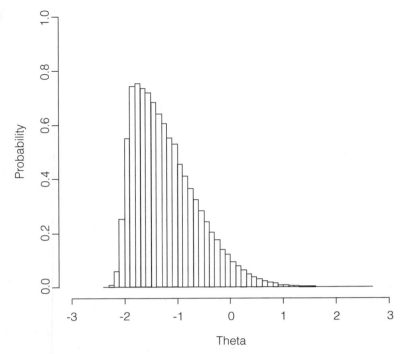

Nonnormal distribution.

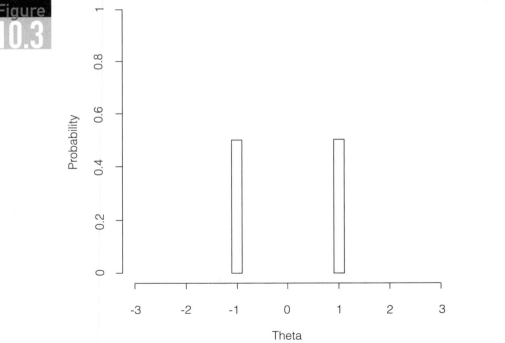

Discrete distribution.

In modeling observed distributions, the number of values whose probabilities are being estimated—that is, the number of bars in a histogram—is often somewhat arbitrary. In modeling latent distributions, however, the number of latent values is not necessarily arbitrary. Various theories have proposed that latent distributions are discontinuous or discrete (i.e., typological, taxonic; Haslam & Williams, this volume, chapter 12). These theories typically propose that a limited number of latent values exist, often very few latent values, as in Figure 10.3. These models contrast with other models that propose that latent distributions are continuous, often normal, having many values, as in Figure 10.1 and 10.2. These two accounts of a latent distribution differ specifically in the number of latent values and how they are distributed.

Models in which latent traits are continuous and have many values can be compared to models in which latent traits are discontinuous and have few values, by setting the number of latent trait values $K$ and possibly their probabilities $P(\theta_k)$, and comparing the resulting likelihoods of the data. One can statistically evaluate these different hypotheses by evaluating the probability of the observed data as a function of the hypothesized latent distribution.

For example, a model of a latent continuous normal distribution can be tested by fixing the number of latent values $K$ to some very large number—for example, 100—and fixing the probability of those latent values $P(\theta_k)$ to equal those of a normal distribution. Similarly, a model of a latent continuous skewed distribution can be tested by fixing the number of latent values $K$ to some very large number—for example, 100—and fixing the probability of those latent values $P(\theta_k)$ to equal those of some skewed distribution. Alternatively, rather than fixing the probability of the latent values $P(\theta_k)$ to a normal or skewed distribution, the $P(\theta_k)$ can be freely estimated. Finally, a model of a discrete latent distribution comprising two types can be tested by fixing the number of latent values $K$ to 2, and freely estimating the probability of each latent value $P(\theta_1)$ and $P(\theta_2)$.

Generally, the latent trait values themselves are fixed in advance, and are equally spaced. For example, in a discrete latent trait model, in which the latent trait only has two values, those latent values might be set at $-1$ and 1. Similarly, in a continuous normal latent trait model, in which the latent trait has 100 values and a mean of zero and standard deviation of one, those values might be set at $-3.0$, $-2.94$, $-2.88$, and so forth, to 3. Thus, in modeling the latent distributions, it is the probabilities of each latent value, that is, the $P(\theta_k)$, that are being modeled or estimated, not the latent values per se.

# Comparing Models

Each of these latent variable models—for example, a continuous normal model, a continuous skewed model, and a discrete model—will produce different data likelihoods. That is, any given dataset will be more or less probable under each of the models. These differences in likelihoods form the basis for choosing between different models and testing various hypotheses about the latent distribution.

One approach to choosing between models is to choose the model that produces the greatest likelihood. The principle of maximum likelihood estimation, after all, emphasizes selection of models that result in the greatest likelihood of the data. Under this approach, if one model—for example, the normal distribution model—results in a greater likelihood than another model—for example, a discrete distribution model, the former model should be preferred.

A problem arises in using the likelihood alone to choose between different models, however. Generally speaking, as the number of latent trait values $K$ in a model increases, the likelihood will increase, simply because the model has greater flexibility in accounting for observed data. This phenomenon is similar to problems in linear regression arising from spurious increases in fit with increases in the number of predictors. In both cases, the likelihood is increasing simply because there are more parameters in the model to account for random features of a particular dataset.

In modeling latent distributions, as in many other modeling problems, the question is not simply whether or not a given model results in greater likelihood of the data. Rather, the question is whether or not increases in the likelihood of the data are large, relative to increases in the complexity of the model. When a small change in a model produces a large change in the likelihood of the data, the change is arguably important to understanding the data. Conversely, when a large change in a model produces a small change in the likelihood of the data, the change is arguably less important to understanding the data.

Balancing increases in likelihood against increases in model complexity is central to the principle of parsimony. As such, parsimony provides an important basis for selecting between models. The principle of parsimony suggests that we should choose models that provide the greatest ratio of likelihood to model complexity. This can be quantified as:

$$\frac{\text{Likelihood}}{\text{Complexity}} \tag{5}$$

Parsimony forms the basis of an entire class of statistics that can be used to choose between different latent variable models. These statistics, known as information-theoretic criteria, are often formulated in terms of the inverse of parsimony, and in particular in terms of the negative logarithm of parsimony as defined in Equation 5. They generally have the form

$$-\ln(L) + C \tag{6}$$

where $\ln(L)$ is the log-likelihood of the data at the maximum likelihood estimates, and $C$ reflects the complexity of the model.

In using information-theoretic statistics, one chooses the model that is "least unparsimonious," which is equivalent to choosing the model that has the greatest parsimony. This is equivalent to choosing the model with the smallest value of the criterion given in Equation 6. In doing so, one chooses the model that achieves the most efficient balance of data likelihood and model complexity.

The formula for complexity in Equation 6 contains two terms, one reflecting the likelihood, the other reflecting model complexity. In general, the log-likelihood of the data given a model—that is, $\ln(L)$—is known, as in Equation 4. However, the complexity of the model—that is, $C$—can be defined in different ways. Different information-theoretic criteria arise from different ways of defining model complexity.

For example, one simple way to define model complexity is in terms of the number of parameters in the model—that is, the number of unique features of the model that are being estimated. This is the definition of model complexity used in one prominent criterion, Aikaike's Information Criterion (AIC). AIC is defined as:

$$AIC = -\ln(L) + p \tag{7}$$

where $\ln(L)$ is the log-likelihood, and $p$ is the number of parameters in the model. In the example of the normal distribution model illustrated in Figure 10.1, $p$ would be equal to the total number of slopes and intercepts in the model, which would be proportional to the number of items and item categories. There would be no $P(\theta_k)$ parameters for the latent trait distribution, because the $P(\theta_k)$ would be fixed to those of the normal distribution. In the example of the discrete distribution model, $p$ would again be equal to the number of slopes and intercepts, but there would additionally be two $P(\theta_k)$ parameters, one for each of the latent trait values. This is because $P(\theta_1)$ and $P(\theta_2)$ are both being estimated, rather than being fixed to some arbitrary distribution.

Another possible definition of model complexity is given by the Bayesian Information Criterion (BIC). BIC defines model complexity as being dependent on the sample size, so that the number of parameters in the model is given more weight as the sample size increases. BIC is defined as:

$$BIC = -\ln(L) + \frac{p}{2}\ln(N) \tag{8}$$

where $p$ is again the number of parameters, and $N$ is the sample size. BIC penalizes relatively complex models more as sample size increases.

Information-theoretic criteria provide an attractive basis for selecting between different latent variable models. By selecting models that are the least unparsimonious—or, equivalently, the most parsimonious—information-theoretic criteria encourage the development of models that provide succinct accounts of observed phenomena. Parsimony represents an important criterion in the development of scientific theory; information-theoretic criteria help quantify the relative parsimony of competing theories.

## Example

As an example, consider a hypothetical study designed to distinguish between two accounts of the Neuroticism distribution, reflected in Figures 10.1 and 10.3 (the normal and discrete models). In this study, data on 2000 subjects, representative of the population, are collected on a hypothetical Neuroticism measure containing 20 items. Each item is polytomous, with four response options (e.g., "strongly disagree," "disagree," "agree," and "strongly agree").

In this hypothetical example, both models of the latent Neuroticism distribution were examined. In the first model, the number of latent trait values $K$ was arbitrarily set to 100, with the latent values themselves ranging from $-3$ to 3. The probability of each latent value $k$, $P(\theta_k)$, was set to equal the probability of observing the latent value under the standard normal distribution. In the second model, however, the number of latent trait values $K$ was set to 2, with one latent trait value equal to $-1$ and the

| Model Fit Statistics for Hypothetical Neuroticism Inventory | | | | |
| --- | --- | --- | --- | --- |
| Model | p | ln(L) | AIC | BIC |
| Normal | 80 | −36264.05 | 36344.05 | 36568.09 |
| Discrete | 81 | −41417.55 | 41498.55 | 41725.39 |

*Note:* Table includes number of parameters $p$, log-likelihood $ln(L)$, AIC, and BIC for normal and discrete latent distribution models.

other value equal to 1. The probabilities of those two latent trait values were freely estimated.

Results for this hypothetical study are presented in Table 10.1. The number of parameters $p$, log-likelihood $ln(L)$, AIC, and BIC for each model are presented in the table. As is shown in the table, the normal distribution model had 80 parameters that were estimated. Each item had a total of four parameters: one slope and three intercepts (one for each of the nonbaseline response categories; the first, or baseline response category, was arbitrarily set to 0). Because the latent trait distribution was assumed to be normal, the probabilities of each of the 100 latent values, $P(\theta_k)$, were set to equal the probabilities of the normal distribution and were not estimated. Therefore, with 20 items, each item having 4 parameters, the total number of parameters was $4(20) = 80$.

The discrete latent distribution model, in contrast, had 81 parameters. The item response model in the discrete distribution model was not different from the continuous distribution model. Therefore, each item again had one slope and three intercepts, and the total number of parameters associated with the items was again $4(20) = 80$. However, because the probabilities of the latent values $P(\theta_k)$ were not set to any particular distribution, additional latent probability parameters were estimated. Because there were two latent values $K$, one additional latent probability was estimated (the other was not estimated because the probabilities of a distribution must sum to one; i.e., $P(\theta_1) + P(\theta_2) = 1$, and therefore, $1 - P(\theta_1) = P(\theta_2)$). Therefore, the total number of parameters in the discrete distribution model was equal to the number of item parameters plus latent probability parameters, $80 + 1 = 81$.

As is shown in Table 10.1, the log-likelihood of the data was larger for the normal distribution model than the discrete distribution model (i.e., the log-likelihood was less negative for the former than the latter model). In other words, the probability of the data was greater for the normal distribution model than the discrete distribution model. AIC and BIC, moreover, were smaller for the normal distribution model than the discrete distribution model. The smaller AIC and BIC values for the normal distribution model indicate that the normal distribution model is less complex— that is, it provides a less complex, simpler, more parsimonious explanation of the data.

These two considerations—the data are more probable or likely under the normal distribution model, and the normal distribution model provides a less complex, simpler,

**Table 10.2** **Item Parameter Estimates for Hypothetical Neuroticism Inventory**

| Item | a | $b_1$ | $b_2$ | $b_3$ |
|------|------|-------|-------|-------|
| 1 | 1.726 | 3.544 | 1.803 | −0.005 |
| 2 | 1.834 | 3.520 | 1.575 | −0.456 |
| 3 | 1.813 | 2.844 | 1.167 | −0.872 |
| 4 | 2.136 | 2.968 | 0.713 | −1.481 |
| 5 | 2.853 | 3.242 | 0.388 | −2.590 |
| 6 | 2.330 | 2.158 | −0.314 | −2.761 |
| 7 | 2.328 | 1.641 | −0.722 | −3.248 |
| 8 | 2.066 | 0.916 | −1.185 | −3.382 |
| 9 | 1.751 | 0.366 | −1.312 | −3.238 |
| 10 | 1.483 | −0.013 | −1.520 | −3.107 |
| 11 | 1.871 | 3.724 | 1.945 | 0.074 |
| 12 | 1.768 | 3.273 | 1.543 | −0.491 |
| 13 | 1.850 | 3.143 | 0.950 | −0.825 |
| 14 | 2.171 | 3.105 | 0.824 | −1.474 |
| 15 | 2.901 | 3.548 | 0.313 | −2.648 |
| 16 | 2.425 | 2.216 | −0.266 | −2.756 |
| 17 | 2.241 | 1.544 | −0.830 | −2.958 |
| 18 | 1.932 | 0.906 | −1.024 | −3.234 |
| 19 | 1.749 | 0.376 | −1.526 | −3.187 |
| 20 | 1.308 | −0.041 | −1.301 | −2.858 |

*Note:* Values in table are slopes *A* for each item and intercepts *b* for each item response category.

more parsimonious explanation of the data—both suggest that the normal distribution model is most appropriate for the data. That is, the results indicate that the best model for the data is one where the Neuroticism distribution is continuous and normally distributed.

Given that the hypothetical Neuroticism data are best modeled by a normal distribution, one can next examine how well individual items measure this distribution. Estimates of item parameters are given in Table 10.2. The second column in Table 10.2 includes the slopes for each item, and the third, fourth, and fifth columns include the intercepts for each nonbaseline response category for each item.

Table 10.2 indicates that items differ substantially in their characteristics. Item 15, for example, has the largest slope (2.901), indicating that the item provides the most precise measurement of the overall latent Neuroticism distribution. Item 20, in contrast, has the

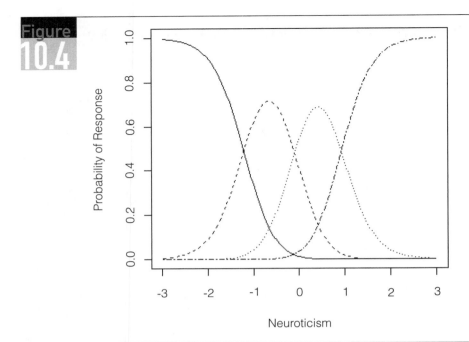

Probability of responding in each response category of Item 15 as a function of latent Neuroticism score. Solid line, "disagree"; dashed line, "somewhat disagree"; dotted line, "somewhat agree"; dashed and dotted line, "agree."

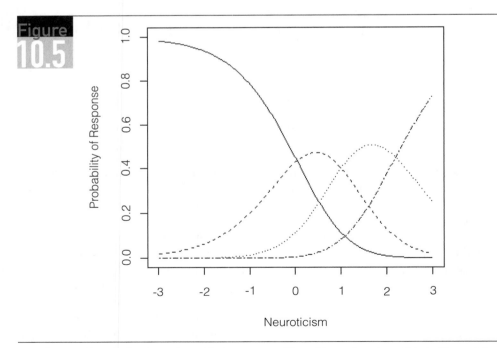

Probability of responding in each response category of Item 20 as a function of latent Neuroticism score. Solid line, "disagree"; dashed line, "somewhat disagree"; dotted line, "somewhat agree"; dashed and dotted line, "agree."

smallest slope (1.308), indicating that the item provides the least precise measurement of the overall latent Neuroticism distribution. Items also differ in their response category intercepts; Item 1, for example, has very positive intercepts, indicating that individuals relatively low in Neuroticism obtain large scores on the item, and that the item reflects less severe manifestations of Neuroticism. Item 20, in contrast, has very negative intercepts, indicating that only individuals relatively high in Neuroticism obtain large scores on the item, and that the item reflects more severe manifestations of Neuroticism. Item 15, being less severe, may be an item such as "I get nervous sometimes." Item 20, in contrast, being more severe, may be an item such as "I am much more anxious than most people."

Example item response functions for items 15 and 20 are shown in Figure 10.4 and 10.5. Each figure presents the probability of responding in each response category as a function of the Neuroticism distribution. These curves illustrate the characteristics of each item. Items with greater slopes, which are more precise in their measurement, have more sharply peaked curves. The item response curves for Item 15, for instance, are more sharply peaked than those for Item 20, reflecting the greater slope and measurement precision of Item 15 relative to Item 20.

The intercepts for each item are reflected in Figure 10.4 and 10.5 in the points where adjacent response category curves intersect. The points where adjacent response category curves intersect are equal to the negative of the intercepts divided by the slopes. For example, the first response category intercept for Item 15 is 3.548; in Figure 10.4 the point on the x axis where the first and second response category curves intersect is equal to $-(3.548/2.901) = -1.223$. The second response category intercept for Item 15 is 0.313; in Figure 10.4 the point on the $x$ axis where the second and third response category curves intersect is $-(0.313/2.901) = -0.108$. In Figure 10.5, the point on the $x$ axis where the first and second response category curves intersect is equal to $-(-0.041/1.308) = 0.031$. Thus, indirectly, the item intercepts reflect where item response category curves intersect.

A particularly efficient way of representing how well an item measures a latent trait is through the use of item information. The greater the item information, the better the measurement. Item information is directly related to the standard error of the trait estimates, in that item information is related to the inverse of the standard error of the trait estimates. When the item information is large, the standard error is small, and when the standard error is large, the item information is small. Item information can differ across a latent trait distribution; an item may measure one region of the trait distribution better than other regions, and thus may have greater information in one region than in others. This is the case, for example, when an item measures people who are high on a trait better than those who are low on the trait.

Figure 10.6 presents the item information and standard error as a function of the latent Neuroticism distribution, for Item 20. The item information is greater—and the standard error is lower—at the upper end of the Neuroticism distribution than at the lower end, indicating that Item 20 measures the upper end of the Neuroticism distribution better than the lower end. This is consistent with the conclusion that Item 20 measures relatively severe Neuroticism. The item information reaches a maximum just below a latent Neuroticism score of 1, indicating that Item 20 best measures individuals who are almost 1 standard deviation above the mean of the Neuroticism distribution.

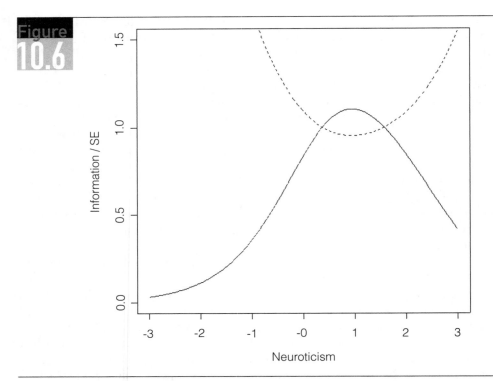

Item information and standard error for Item 20. Solid line, information; dashed line, standard error.

# Summary

Here, we have illustrated how latent variable models can be used to evaluate hypotheses about the distribution of a personality trait, and to evaluate how well individual items measure that trait. Latent variable models include parameters representing item as well as person characteristics, and by comparing models that differ in those characteristics, hypotheses regarding items and persons can be evaluated. Numerous hypotheses regarding personality structure and measure characteristics can be tested through constraints on item and person parameters.

The approach to distinguishing continuous and discrete latent distributions described here is relatively novel. The approach described here was used in recent papers to distinguish between continuous and discrete models of externalizing psychopathology in adults (Krueger, Markon, Patrick, & Iacono, in press; Markon & Krueger, in press). In those papers, comparison of discrete and continuous models of externalizing psychopathology have indicated that externalizing phenomena are best described by a continuous normal distribution.

Other related methods, however, have also been used to model latent distributions in personality and psychopathology. Ferrando (2003), for example, used an approach similar to that described here to model the latent distributions of Extraversion, Neuroticism, and

Psychoticism as measured by the EPQ-R (Eysenck Personality Questionnaire-Revised; Eysenck & Eysenck, 1975; Eysenck, Eysenck, & Barrett, 1985). It was demonstrated that the three traits have distributions resembling a normal curve. Using similar methods, van den Oord and colleagues (van den Oord, Pickles, & Waldman, 2003) have demonstrated that depression and delinquency in childhood are each best described by a continuous normal distribution. van den Oord and colleagues (2003) argued that the skewed nature of measures of depression and delinquency is likely due to measurement artifacts, rather than the distribution of the constructs themselves.

In addition to evaluating hypotheses regarding the shape of a trait distribution, the approach taken here can be extended to other hypotheses regarding person characteristics and personality structure. Models differing in the number of latent traits, or the hierarchical arrangement of those traits, could be compared, for example. Hypotheses regarding differences in personality across different populations could be evaluated by comparing models that differ in trait structure or mean level across samples. Models in which mean levels of a personality trait differ between clinic and community samples could be compared to models in which mean levels do not differ, for example.

Although models differing in item characteristics were not explicitly considered here, the approach described here could be extended to such comparisons, as well. Models in which personality measures differ in their measurement precision across groups (e.g., racial or gender groups) could be evaluated (see, Smith & Reise, 1998, or Waller, Thompson, & Wenk, 2000 for examples). It is also possible to evaluate the hypotheses that different items measure a single latent trait, but differ in the level of the trait they measure. For example, one might hypothesize that measures of normal and abnormal personality assess the same personality traits, but that measures of abnormal personality provide information about the extremes of those traits.

Emerging evidence from meta-analyses indicates that normal and abnormal personality share a common trait structure (Markon, Krueger, & Watson, in press; O'Connor, 2002). Traits characterizing abnormal personality generally tend to be the same as those characterizing normal personality (O'Connor, 2002), and at an abstract level, those traits tend to resemble Big Traits frequently identified in the literature (e.g., the Big Three and the Big Five; Clark & Watson, 1999; Goldberg, 1993; Markon, et al., in press). That is, the traits of normal and abnormal personality are largely the same, and can be thought of at an abstract level in terms of constructs such as Negative Emotionality, Disinhibition, and Positive Emotionality, or constructs such as Neuroticism, Extraversion, Agreeableness, Conscientiousness, and Openness.

Latent variable analyses such as those described here could be used to further elaborate relationships between measures of normal and abnormal personality. For example, the techniques applied here could be used to elucidate the latent distribution of traits related to Agreeableness—to determine whether such traits tend to be normally distributed, skewed, or discrete in nature. These techniques could also be used to clarify the severity of phenomena assessed by different measures of these traits. For example, one measure of aggression might tend to assess relatively severe forms of aggression, such as physical violence. Another measure might assess relatively less severe forms, such as relational aggression.

These analyses have important implications for theory as well as clinical practice. By elucidating the distributions of normal and abnormal personality traits, the boundaries between normality and abnormality might better be understood. Determining that a trait is continuous in its distribution might suggest that the boundary between normality and abnormality is not clear; conversely, determining that the trait is discrete in its distribution would delineate the boundaries of normality and abnormality. Determining where specific measures assess a trait in relation to those boundaries is also important, for understanding the nature of a trait as well as where individuals are located on it.

## REFERENCES

Bartholomew, D. J., & Knott, M. (1999). *Latent variable models and factor analysis.* London: Arnold.

Bauer, D. J., & Curran, P. J. (2004). The integration of continuous and discrete latent variable models: Potential problems and promising opportunities. *Psychological Methods, 9,* 3–29.

Clark, L. A., & Watson, D. (1999). Temperament: A new paradigm for trait psychology. In L. A. Pervin, & O. P. John (Eds.), *Handbook of personality: Theory and research* (2nd ed., pp. 399–423). New York: Guilford Press.

Eysenck, H. J., & Eysenck, S. B. G. (1975). *Manual of the Eysenck Personality Questionnaire.* London: Hodder & Stoughton.

Eysenck, S. B. G., Eysenck, H. J., & Barrett, P. (1985). A revised version of the Psychoticism scale. *Personality and Individual Differences, 6,* 21–29.

Ferrando, P. J. (2003). The accuracy of the E, N and P trait estimates: An empirical study using the EPQ-R. *Personality and Individual Differences, 34,* 665–679.

Goldberg, L. R. (1993). The structure of phenotypic personality traits. *American Psychologist, 48,* 26–34.

Heinen, T. (1996). *Latent class and discrete latent trait models.* Thousand Oaks, CA: Sage.

Krueger, R. F., Markon, K. E., Patrick, C. J., & Iacono, W. G. (in press). Externalizing psychopathology in adulthood: A dimensional-spectrum conceptualization and its implications for DSM-V. *Journal of Abnormal Psychology.*

Loehlin, J. C. (2004). *Latent variable models: An introduction to factor, path, and structural equation analysis.* Hillsdale, NJ: Erlbaum.

Markon, K. E., & Krueger, R. F. (in press). Categorical and continuous models of liability to externalizing disorders: A direct comparison in NESARC. *Archives of General Psychiatry.*

Markon, K. E., Krueger, R. F., & Watson, D. (in press). Delineating the structure of normal and abnormal personality: An integrative hierarchical approach. *Journal of Personality and Social Psychology.*

O'Connor, B. P. (2002). The search for dimensional structure differences between normality and abnormality: A statistical review of published data on personality and psychopathology. *Journal of Personality and Social Psychology, 83,* 962–982.

Skrondal, A., & Rabe-Hesketh, S. (2004). *Generalized latent variable modeling.* Boca Raton: Chapman & Hall.

Smith, L. L., & Reise, S. P. (1998). Gender differences on negative affectivity: An IRT study of differential item functioning on the Multidimensional Personality Questionnaire Stress Reaction scale. *Journal of Personality and Social Psychology, 75,* 1350–1362.

Thissen, D., & Steinberg, L. (1986). A taxonomy of item response models. *Psychometrika, 51,* 567–577.

van den Oord, E. J. C. G., Pickles, A., & Waldman, I. D. (2003). Normal variation and abnormality: An empirical study of the liability distributions underlying depression and delinquency. *Journal of Child Psychology and Psychiatry and Allied Disciplines, 44,* 180–192.

Vermunt, J. K. (2001). The use of restricted latent class models for defining and testing nonparametric and parametric item response theory models. *Applied Psychological Measurement, 25,* 283–294.

Waller, N. G., Thompson, J. S., & Wenk, E. (2000). Using IRT to separate measurement bias from true group differences on homogeneous and heterogeneous scales: An illustration with the MMPI. *Psychological Methods, 5,* 125–146.

# Methods for Understanding Genetic and Environmental Influences in Normal and Abnormal Personality

**Laura A. Baker**

The relative contributions of genetic and environmental influences on normal personality traits were well known in 1994, at the time of publication of the first edition of this book. Nearly half of the observable (phenotypic) variance for each of the major dimensions of adult personality was explained by heritable (genetic) differences between individuals. Of the remaining environmental influences, unique experiences of individuals within the same family appeared of far greater importance than shared family environmental factors. Although more twin and adoption studies have been conducted using more recently developed personality instruments (e.g., Heath, Madden, Cloninger & Martin, 1999), these results have not changed in the last decade of research in this area.

Likewise, what was known over a decade ago about genetics of psychopathology during adulthood, including personality disorders, remains true today. Genetic influences are at least moderate for clinical diagnoses for the major Axis I disorders, including schizophrenia, unipolar and bipolar depression, as well as for many Axis II disorders, including antisocial and schizotypal personality disorders (McGuffin, Moffitt, & Thapar, 2002), even with more recent definitions provided in the fourth edition of the *Diagnostic and Statistical Manual for Mental Disorders* (*DSM-IV*; American Psychiatric Association [APA], 1994). More important, there has been *no major gene found for any of these mental disorders*. Instead, most clinical mental disorders appear to be polygenic (i.e., influenced by many different genetic loci).

Are there any new findings in genetic studies of normal and abnormal personality? The answer is most certainly, yes. Although the big picture of genetic and environmental effects has not changed, there have been several important developments in behavioral genetic studies of personality and psychopathology, which have helped to flesh out the details of both genetic and environmental effects. First, multivariate genetic analyses have helped shed light on inter-relationships among different facets of personality, comorbidities among personality disorders, and to a lesser extent, relationships between normal personality and certain forms of psychopathology. Second, longitudinal studies have contributed to our understanding of the developmental course of the genetic and environmental processes. Finally, and perhaps most important, molecular genetic methods have begun the arduous path leading to identification of specific genetic influences for both normal personality and personality disorders.

The purpose of this chapter is to provide a basic overview of the genetic methods used to investigate normal and abnormal personality, in terms accessible to students and researchers with no prior background in behavioral genetics. The chapter provides an introduction to the two primary approaches in behavioral and psychiatric genetics, namely quantitative genetic and molecular genetic methods. Given that none of the major *DSM* disorders have been shown to follow Mendelian patterns of inheritance (i.e., no major gene is involved in any mental disorder), the methods of segregation and commingling analysis are not reviewed here, although the chapter by Moldin (1991) in the first edition of this book provides an excellent account of these methods. More detailed coverage of the methods presented here can be found in other recent sources (e.g., see Cardno & McGuffin, 2002; Evans, Gillespie & Martin, 2002, and the appendix of the Behavioral Genetics [4th edition] textbook by Plomin, DeFries, McClearn, & McGuffin, 2000 for excellent and more in-depth overviews of quantitative genetics; see Sham, 2003, and Sham & McGuffin, 2002, for molecular genetic methods). Those challenged to pursue statistical genetics (both quantitative and molecular methods) in much greater depth should carefully read Sham (1997).

# Quantitative Genetic Methods

There are several classic research designs for estimating the relative contributions of genetic and environmental influences in phenotypic traits. These include family, adoption, and twin designs, in which the basic strategy is to examine phenotypic resemblance among relatives who vary in their degree of genetic relatedness and extent to which they share environments. Each of these basic designs is outlined here, although combinations of these designs are often used (e.g., twins separated at birth and reared by different adoptive families; twins and their parents, spouses or offspring). As a general rule, greater information about genetic and environmental effects is provided in extended designs in which additional relatives are included.

## Categorical versus Continuous Traits

One important issue that must be considered before delving into these various designs concerns the level of measurement in the phenotypic trait, i.e. whether the characteristic is categorical (e.g., discrete, all-or-none clinical diagnoses) or continuous (e.g., quantitative personality traits) because this determines the sampling and statistical methods employed to examine patterns of resemblance among relatives. For continuous traits, unselected samples of the various types of relatives are examined, using correlations or covariances (unstandardized correlations) between pairs of relatives to examine their resemblance to one another. Model-fitting procedures (see Loehlin, 2004) are then used to estimate the relative contributions of genetic and environmental influences on these correlations.

For categorical traits, there are a variety of methods that may be employed. One approach is to study selected samples in which family members of probands or index cases (i.e., individuals affected with a disorder) are examined. Risk rates of the disorder being studied, or other disorders that may be comorbid, are compared for various relatives of probands. For twins and siblings, concordance rates may be computed and compared for different twin (monozygotic or dizygotic) or sibling types (full or half-siblings). An alternative to comparing risk rates, however, is to employ correlational methods, assuming that the categorical disorder is influenced by an underlying continuum, or "liability," which is quantitative in nature. Affected individuals are those whose liability exceeds a given threshold ($\tau$) and hence the disorder is considered to be a "threshold characteristic." In such cases tetrachoric or polychoric correlations may be computed from the frequencies of affected and unaffected relatives, and these correlations may be subjected to similar model-fitting procedures as in the case of continuous phenotypic traits. Comparison of these different statistical approaches to categorical variables has indicated that the threshold model-fitting approach is more powerful and more likely to yield accurate estimates of genetic and environmental effects than the risk-rate approach (Rhee, Hewitt, Corley, & Stallings, 2003). Only the model-fitting approach is thus described in detail here, although readers may find a thorough presentation of both approaches (Rhee et al., 2003).

These liability threshold models also allow the specification of multiple thresholds ($\tau_1$ and $\tau_2$) representing different degrees of severity (see Figure 11.1). Support for such a model has been found for unipolar and bipolar depressions (see review in Plomin et al., 2000), in which a single liability distribution is purported to underlie both disorders, with bipolar depression resulting from the more extreme threshold.

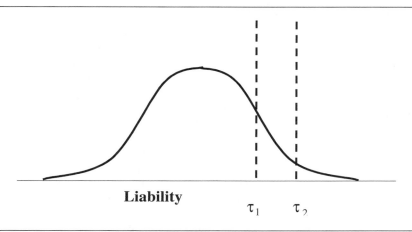

**Liability**

$\tau_1$      $\tau_2$

Liability threshold model for qualitative trait.

The quantitative genetic model is essentially the same for continuously measured traits or qualitative (threshold) traits that are assumed to have an underlying continuous liability distribution. This model is presented here in its basic univariate form first, followed by a discussion of various complications to the model, including multivariate extensions to investigate relationships between two or more traits.

## The Basic Gene-Environment Model

The relative contributions of genes (G) and environment (E) to an observable phenotype (P) in one individual may be represented in a simple mathematical equation:

$$P = G + E \tag{1}$$

Of interest to behavioral geneticists, however, are the individual differences in $P$ in a population, and how these may be explained by variations in $G$ and $E$ across individuals. In a similar equation, the phenotypic variance for a given trait ($V_p$) may be considered as a function of variance in both genetic ($V_G$) and environmental ($V_E$) factors:

$$V_P = V_G + V_E \tag{2}$$

and dividing both sides of Equation 2 by $V_P$ shows the relative contributions of genes and environment to phenotypic variance:

$$\begin{aligned} 1 &= V_G/V_P + V_E/V_P \\ &= h^2 + e^2 \end{aligned} \tag{3}$$

Thus, heritability ($h^2$) is simply the ratio of genetic to phenotypic variance, or the proportion of phenotypic variance explained by genetic factors. Correspondingly, $e^2$ (sometimes called "environmentality") refers to the proportion of phenotypic variance explained by environmental (nongenetic) factors. Heritability and environmentality may also be expressed as the squared correlation between genotype and phenotype ($h^2 = r^2_{GP}$) or between environment and phenotype ($h^2 = r^2_{EP}$), respectively. Regardless, the proportional effects of genes and environment are considered mutually exclusive and exhaustive in explaining individual differences in an observable phenotype.

Environmental effects are routinely divided into two general classes: those shared ($e^2_S$) and not shared ($e^2_{NS}$) by family members. The total environmental effects are a linear composite of these shared and nonshared influences:

$$e^2 = e^2_S + e^2_{NS} \tag{4}$$

Shared environmental influences may stem from common variables such as socioeconomic level of the home or neighborhood, or characteristics of the parents or teachers that systematically influence multiple offspring within a family. These shared influences make family members more similar to one another. Conversely, nonshared environmental factors are specific to each person within a family, and may include unique events, differential parental treatment, peer relationships, or idiosyncratic experiences. Non-shared environmental influences make family members different from one another. Environmental influences in most normal personality traits are almost entirely of the nonshared variety (Plomin et al., 2000).

Genetic influences may also be decomposed into two types of effect—additive and nonadditive—although studies vary in their ability to estimate these different effects separately. Additive genetic influences (A) reflect the incremental effects of multiple alleles on a given phenotype, although nonadditive genetic influences include effects of genetic dominance (D, which involves the interaction between genes at one locus). To the extent that dominant or recessive genes may influence a given trait, for example, there may be both additive and nonadditive genetic effects.[1]

Extending the basic genetic model to include these effects results in a modification to Equation 1 as follows:

$$P = A + D + E_S + E_{NS} \tag{5}$$

with a corresponding modification of the variance decomposition:

$$V_P = V_A + V_D + V_{ES} + V_{ENS} \tag{6}$$

and dividing both sides of the equation by $V_P$ yields the proportional effects:

$$1 = a^2 + d^2 + e^2_S + e^2_{NS} \tag{7}$$

Genetic researchers distinguish between two forms of heritability, depending on whether additive or nonadditive effects are taken into account. Narrow heritability ($h^2_N$) reflects only the additive genetic influences:

$$h^2_N = V_A/V_P = a^2 \tag{8}$$

although broad heritability ($h^2_B$) considers all genetic influences, including both additive and nonadditive effects:

$$h^2_B = V_G/V_P = (V_A + V_D)/V_P = a^2 + d^2 \tag{9}$$

Estimating the effects in Equation 7 is generally achieved through information about phenotypic resemblance between relatives of varying degrees of genetic and environmental relatedness. Sir Ronald Fisher originally laid out these quantitative genetic methods in his classic paper (Fisher, 1918). Figure 11.2 shows a graphic representation ("path diagram") of A, D, $E_S$, and $E_{NS}$ in a pair of relatives. The observable phenotype in each of these two related individuals ($P_1$ and $P_2$) is influenced by both unobservable

---

[1] Nonadditive genetic influences may also include those due to epistasis (the interaction between genes at different loci), although these effects tend to be quite small in comparison to A and D genetic effects. Thus, epistatic genetic influences are not considered in these equations. A more detailed discussion of epistatis and its effects on genetic analyses may be found in Sham ( 1997).

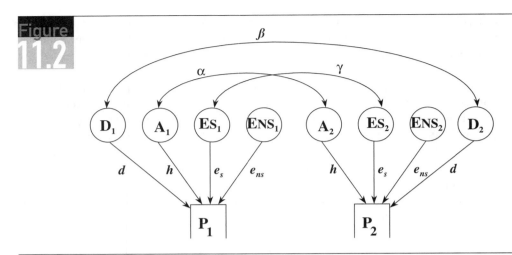

Basic gene–environment model in a pair of relatives ($P_1$ and $P_2$).

(latent) genetic (A, D) and environmental ($E_S$, $E_{NS}$) factors. The correlations between these latent factors for two individuals depend on their genetic and environmental relatedness (see Table 11.1). The coefficient $\alpha$ represents the correlation between additive genetic values for the two individuals ($A_1$ and $A_2$), which has been shown to be 0.5 between parent and offspring, between dizygotic (DZ) twins, or between nontwin siblings, 1.0 between monozygotic (MZ) twins, and 0.25 between half-siblings and 0.125 between first cousins. The correlation between dominant genetic values ($D_1$ and $D_2$) is represented by $\beta$, which ranges from 1.0 for MZ twins, to 0.25 for DZ twins and nontwin siblings, to 0.0 for parents and offspring. Thus, nonadditive genetic influences affect sibling but not parent–offspring resemblance. Shared environmental influences ($E_S$) affect both individuals equally, increasing their similarity, although its relative effect ($e^2_S$) may depend on the type of relatives (e.g., twins may have greater shared environments than nontwin siblings, although parents and offspring or other pairings from different generations may have less shared environment). The correlation between the shared environmental factors for two individuals is represented by $\gamma$ in Figure 11.2, which may vary from 0 (for genetically related siblings raised in separate, uncorrelated environments) to 1 (for two individuals living in the same home, such as twins, other siblings, or parents and offspring).

Expected correlations for various pairings of relatives may be derived from the basic model (Figure 11.2) and the corresponding coefficients of relatedness (Table 11.1), using simple tracing rules for path diagrams (see Loehlin, 2004). For example, the expected correlation between parents and adopted-away offspring on a given personality trait is $0.5a^2$, and for MZ twins raised apart the expected correlation is $a^2 + d^2$. Heritability may thus be estimated through algebraic manipulations of observed correlations for certain kinds of relatives, or combinations thereof. For example, broad-sense heritability is estimated directly from the correlation between MZ twins raised apart ($h^2_B = r_{MZ\text{-}Apart}$, although narrow-sense heritability is estimated by doubling the observed correlation between adopted children and their biological parents ($h^2_N = 2\,r_{PO}$).

| Table 11.1 | Coefficients of Genetic ($\alpha$, $\beta$) and Environmental ($\gamma$) Relatedness in Pairs of Relatives | | |
|---|---|---|---|
| Relatives | $\alpha$ | $\beta$ | $\gamma$ |
| MZ twins reared apart | 1.0 | 1.0 | 0 |
| DZ twins reared apart | 0.5 | 0.25 | 0 |
| MZ twins reared together | 1.0 | 1.0 | 1.0 |
| DZ twins reared together | 0.5 | 0.25 | 1.0 |
| Full siblings reared together | 0.5 | 0.25 | 1.0 |
| Biological parents and offspring (separated at birth) | 0.5 | 0 | 0 |
| Biological parents and offspring (living together) | 0.5 | 0 | 1.0 |
| Adoptive parents and offspring (living together) | 0 | 0 | 1.0 |
| Adoptive siblings (living together) | 0 | 0 | 1.0 |

Various expected correlations among different pairings of relatives are provided in the center column of Table 11.2 for the basic gene–environment model in which both additive and nonadditive genetic effects are allowed. Several methods for estimating heritability from these correlations are discussed in sections below, including from twin and adoption studies. It should be noted that these expectations for the additive and nonadditive models assume a system of random mating for the trait. For many psychological traits, including personality, this assumption may not be true. Thus, the issue of nonrandom mating must be considered.

## Nonrandom Mating

There is, in fact, evidence for nonrandom mating for both normal personality traits (Lykken & Tellegen, 1993) and several areas of psychopathology, including antisocial personality (Galbaud du Fort, Boothroyd, Bland, Newman, & Kakuma, 2002; Krueger, Moffitt, Caspi, Bleske, & Silva, 1998). The extent that spouses resemble one another (called *assortative mating*) for one or more personality traits may influence the genetic and environmental variances themselves, as well as estimates of heritability and environmentality from observed correlations among relatives. Moreover, the mechanisms through which assortative mating occurs (e.g., phenotypic assortment, whereby individuals select a mate based on phenotypic characteristics, vs. social homogamy, whereby mate similarity arises due to geographic proximity or shared cultural background) can influence these estimates in different ways (Reynolds, Baker, Pedersen, 1996). Under phenotypic assortative mating, for example, genotypes of the mother and father become correlated and both parent–offspring and sibling resemblance are subsequently increased. The last column of Table 11.2 shows the expected correlations

| **Table 11.2** | **Expected Correlations Between Relatives** | |
| --- | --- | --- |

| | Expected Correlation | |
| --- | --- | --- |
| Relationship | Additive and Nonadditive Genetic Effects/ Random Mating | Additive Genetic Effects/Phenotypic Assortative Mating |
| Mother–father | 0 | $\mu$ |
| MZ twins reared apart | $a^2 + d^2$ | $h^2$ |
| DZ twins reared apart | $0.5\,a^2 + 0.25\,d^2$ | $0.5\,h^2\,(1 + \mu\,h^2)$ |
| MZ twins reared together | $a^2 + d^2 + e^2_s$ | $h^2 + e^2_s$ |
| DZ twins reared together | $0.5\,a^2 + 0.25\,d^2 + e^2_s$ | $0.5\,h^2(1 + \mu\,h^2) + e^2_s$ |
| Full siblings reared together | $0.5\,a^2 + 0.25\,d^2 + e^2_s$ | $0.5\,h^2(1 + \mu\,h^2) + e^2_s$ |
| Biological parents and offspring (separated at birth) | $0.5\,a^2$ | $0.5\,h^2(1 + \mu)$ |
| Biological parents and offspring (living together) | $0.5\,a^2 + e^2_s$ | $0.5\,h^2(1 + \mu) + e^2_s$ |
| Adoptive parents and offspring (living together) | $e^2_s$ | $e^2_s$ |
| Adoptive siblings (living together) | $e^2_s$ | $e^2_s$ |
| Constraints | $a^2 + d^2 + e^2 = 1.0$ $a^2 + d^2 + e^2_s + e^2_{ns} = 1.0$ | $h^2 + e^2 = 1.0$ $h^2 + e^2_s + e^2_{ns} = 1.0$ |
| Notes | $a^2 = V_A / V_P$ $d^2 = V_D / V_P$ $h_B^2 = a^2 + d^2$ | $h_N^2 = V_A / V_P$ |

among various relatives in an additive genetic model with phenotypic assortment, in which the observed correlation between spouses is $\mu$. Nonadditive genetic effects are presumed to be negligible for simplicity in Table 11.2. Phenotypic assortment thus increases parent–offspring and sibling resemblance, but to differing degrees, by effectively making them each more genetically related. The process of mate selection (phenotypic vs. social homogamy) for personality traits remains an open question, which may be resolved through studies of twins and their parents (Reynolds, Baker, & Pedersen, 2000).

Although assortative mating for personality and personality disorders is known to occur, spouse correlations are typically low or negligible ($r = 0.10 - 0.15$) for most major personality traits (Lykken & Tellegen, 1993), with somewhat higher correlations for some specific factors (e.g., sensation-seeking; see Glicksohn & Golan, 2001) and abnormal traits (e.g., antisocial behavior; see Galbaud du Fort et al., 2002; Krueger et al., 1998). Although it is desirable to account for assortative mating in genetic analyses, its effects may be negligible in many cases. Nonetheless, the implications of assortative mating (or ignoring its effects) are discussed below for each design. When assortative mating is not taken into account, for example, effects of common environment may be overestimated and genetic effects underestimated in twin studies.

## Complications of the Basic Model

The most basic model (Eq 1) assumes no correlation between $G$ and $E$, and that the effects of $G$ and $E$ are linear and independent of one another. These assumptions may be relaxed in more complex models. For example, to the extent that certain environments may be systematically associated with some genotypes more than others, a *gene-environment correlation* ($r_{GE}$) will arise and consequently lead to greater variance in P, as well as influence correlations between relatives, albeit to different degrees. The different mechanisms that may lead to $r_{GE}$ (e.g., passive, active, or evocative processes) have been discussed in the classic papers by Plomin, DeFries and Loehlin (1977) and Scarr and McCartney (1983), and several methods for estimating various types of $r_{GE}$ are described in Plomin et al. (2000) and Evans et al. (2002). In general, adoption studies are the most useful for detecting $r_{GE}$ (especially passive forms), and its effects would tend to lead to overestimation of both *absolute* genetic and environmental variance ($V_G$ and $V_E$) if not taken into account explicitly in twin or adoption studies. However, *relative* effects of genes and environment ($h^2$ and $e^2$) are not necessarily affected in these studies.

The extent to which the magnitude of genetic influences may be greater in some environments over others suggests the presence of a statistical interaction between genes and environment—a $G \times E$ *interaction*. One psychological domain in which $G \times E$ interactions have been repeatedly found is antisocial behavior (ASB), e.g., where genetic risk for criminal offending appears to be amplified by adverse environmental factors (see Baker, 2003 for a review). In addition to these $G \times E$ interactions for ASB at a global level, recent studies have also demonstrated similar effects at the level of specific genes and environment. ASB (especially violence) during adulthood has been shown to be associated with a gene resulting in monoamine oxidase (MAO) deficiency (Brunner, Nelen, Breakefield, Ropers, & van Oost, 1993), but these effects may be most deleterious under adverse rearing conditions in which children at genetic risk have experienced harsh discipline or child abuse (Caspi et al., 2002). Adoption studies are also the most powerful method for identifying $G \times E$ interactions. If not explicitly taken into account in genetic analyses of a trait, $G \times E$ interaction effects would tend to fall into the absolute values of both $V_E$ and $V_G$. As in the case of $r_{GE}$, however, the relative effects of $G$ and $E$ on $P$ are not necessarily affected by $G \times E$ interactions.

In general, $G \times E$ interactions and GE correlations have typically been difficult to detect using traditional quantitative genetic methods. Rapidly advancing methods in molecular genetics, however, are now providing unparalleled opportunities for researchers in behavioral and psychiatric genetics to investigate the more complex and interesting effects of $G \times E$ interactions and GE correlations in human behavior. These effects will almost certainly become the focus in investigations of both normal and abnormal personality during the coming decades.

Sex differences in genetic and environmental influences may also be tested in these models. Such differences may be found in the relative importance of genes and environment (i.e., differential heritability) between males and females, or in the specific genes and environment themselves (e.g., different genes may operate in the two sexes). Genetic models of *sex limitation* investigate both kinds of differences. Studies of twins that include opposite-sex pairs are especially useful for examining sex-limited genetic and environmental effects.

A review of the basic designs is provided here, followed by a discussion of multivariate and longitudinal extensions. The methods in quantitative genetics are an excellent starting point in understanding genetic and environmental influences in personality and personality disorders, because they provide the "big picture" of heritable and nonheritable (environmental) effects. These studies then give way to molecular genetic studies, in which the effects of specific genes are investigated more closely.

## Family Study Designs

Studies of nuclear (in tact) family members have traditionally been considered a first step in behavioral genetic research. These may include a single generation (e.g., siblings, half-siblings, cousins) or multiple generations (children, parents, grandparents, etc.). Family studies are generally less informative than twin or adoption studies, because the effects of genes and shared family environment are confounded and cannot be estimated separately from phenotypic correlations among genetically-related individuals living in the same environment. Comparing the expected correlations for parent–offspring and full sibling pairs in Table 11.2 (for the model with random mating, additive and nonadditive effects) readily shows this—together these two correlations are functions of four parameters ($a^2$, $d^2$, $e_s^2$ for siblings, and $e_s^2$ for parents and offspring). The two observed correlations are mathematically insufficient for estimating four different underlying parameters. Nonetheless, nuclear families are more readily available for study than either twins or adopted children, and may be useful in establishing whether any familial resemblance for a given trait exists, warranting further investigation in a more genetically-informative design. Lack of any family resemblance would, of course, rule out the importance of both shared genes and shared environment in the trait.

Family studies are also particularly useful in establishing the degree of *assortative mating* for a given trait (i.e., resemblance between spouses), which may be taken into account in genetic analyses in other studies (e.g., twins).

A path diagram depicting relationships among four family members (M = mother, F = father, and two siblings, $S_1$ and $S_2$) is provided in Figure 11.3. Only additive genetic influences (A) are included in this model, along with both shared and non-shared environment (shown as C and E, respectively, in Figure 11.3). A more complex model of cultural transmission is also included in this diagram, whereby the parents' phenotypes have a direct influence (via m and f) on the offspring's shared environment (shown as C in Figure 11.3). One interesting feature of this model is that a passive gene-environment correlation ($r_{GE}$, or s in Figure 11.3) arises from the phenotypic cultural transmission. Expected correlations for parents and their two offsprings under this model may be found in Abrahamson, Baker and Caspi (2002), in an investigation of family resemblance for conservative and religious social attitudes. Although information from intact nuclear families is not sufficient to estimate the genetic and environmental parameters in this model, inclusion of adopted children and their family members provides the opportunity to disentangle these genetic and environmental effects.

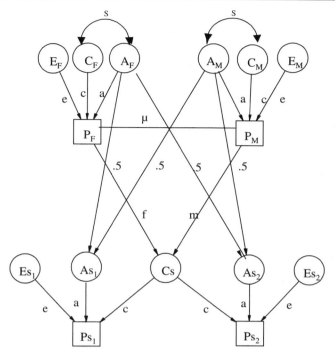

Path model for nuclear families.

## Adoption Study Designs

Adoption studies are considered the most powerful design for separating the effects of genes and environment on behavior. There are three basic designs in which adopted children may be studied. The first examines the rearing family members, and any resemblance they may have to the adopted child. Such designs are clearly able to estimate the role of shared family environment. The second design involves the biological relatives (usually the parents) of the adopted child, which provides information about the genetic influences. The third design combines both biological and adoptive relatives.

The two variations of the adoption design are presented in path diagrams in Figures 11.4 (for one adopted child and biological parents) and 11.5 (for two adopted children and their adoptive parents). The correlation between biological parent and child (exactly the same as in Table 11.2) provides information about the additive genetic influences in the trait, although the effects of shared environment between siblings (c) is indicated by the correlation between adopted siblings. Combining data from families of both adopted (Figures 11.4 and 11.5) and nonadopted children (Figure 11.3) provides sufficient information to separate the influences of genetic influence, shared environment between siblings, and cultural transmission from parents to offspring, while taking phenotypic assortative mating into account (see Abrahamson et al., 2001; Fulker, 1988). Inclusion of nuclear families is particularly important for resolving the effects of cultural transmission and the resulting gene–environment correlation (s) because the model

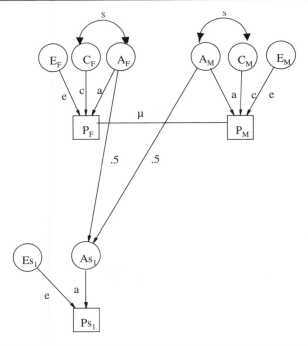

Path model for one adopted child and biological parents.

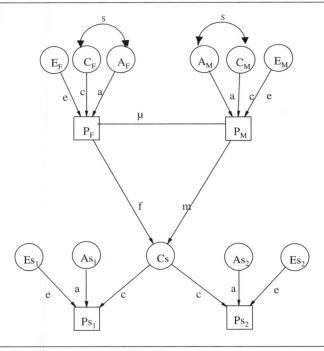

Path model for two adopted children and adoptive parents.

predicts smaller phenotypic trait variance in adopted children compared to nonadopted children (Fulker, 1988).

Perhaps the most critical issue in adoption studies is whether the adopted children were randomly or selectively placed into adoptive homes. When *selective placement* occurs (i.e., biological and adoptive parents are matched for certain characteristics), correlations between adopted children with both biological and adoptive parents may be inflated, leading to biased estimates in genetic and environmental parameters (Plomin, et al., 2000). However, it must be emphasized that placement effects will only occur for a given trait if placement for that trait itself has occurred. For example, matching children into homes in which their physical characteristics (such as skin, eye, or hair color) will not necessarily influence their similarity for personality or psychopathology. Nonetheless, the most powerful adoption designs are those in which both biological and adoptive parents are studied, so that selective placement for various characteristics may be evaluated and taken into account in genetic analyses.

## Twin Study Designs

Studies of twins are by far the most common design employed for disentangling genetic and environmental influences in both normal and abnormal personality. Although studies of twins reared apart—a special kind of adoption design—are extremely powerful behavioral genetic designs, the rarity of twins separated at birth makes them a difficult population to study. Given the relatively high twinning rate (about 1 of 80 live births are twins or higher multiples), studies of twins raised together are much more common than twins raised apart.

The path model for twins reared together may be easily deduced from the general model in Figure 11.2, in which the $\alpha$, $\beta$, and $\gamma$ values are set according to those provided in Table 11.1. The genetic correlation between two monozygotic (MZ) twins (who develop as two individuals from a single fertilized egg) is exactly 1.0 for both additive and nonadditive influences, due to their genetic identity. Dizygotic (DZ) twins (who develop from two eggs fertilized by two different sperm) share only about half their genes, on an average, and thus have less correlated genotypes (0.50 for additive and 0.25 for dominant effects). Having contemporaneously shared the same womb and much of their childhood experiences, both MZ and DZ cotwins have correlated environments ($\gamma = 1.0$ for both types of twins). The key assumption in studies of twins raised together is, in fact, that environments are shared by cotwins to approximately equal degrees for MZ and DZ pairs. Thus, under random mating ($\mu = 0$), if $e^2_S$ (for MZ pairs) $= e^2_S$ (for DZ pairs), narrow-sense heritability may be estimated by doubling the difference between the two observed correlations for MZ and DZ pairs: $h^2_N = 2(r_{MZ} - r_{DZ})$.

How might violations of assumptions of random mating and additive genetic influence affect this heritability estimate in studies of personality? Assortative mating (positive correlation between parents' personality trait) will lead to greater $r_{DZ}$, and thus $h^2_N$ will be *under*estimated and $e^2_S$ will be overestimated for that trait. Ideally, assortative mating should be empirically tested and taken into account when calculating genetic and environmental effects in twin studies. Nonadditive genetic influences will lead to greater increases in $r_{MZ}$ compared to $r_{DZ}$; hence, the narrow heritability will be overestimated. One way to check for nonadditive genetic effects is by examining the magnitude of difference in MZ and DZ twin correlations for a given trait. When nonadditive genetic effects are important, the MZ twin correlation may exceed twice the value of the DZ twin correlation (i.e., $r_{MZ} > 2r$DZ). Other factors might also produce a larger than expected MZ correlation, including violation of the equal environments assumption, and rater bias (e.g., when childhood personality trait differences between DZ pairs are more exaggerated in ratings provided by parents or teachers). Thus, genetic and environmental parameters are not unequivocally estimated from studies of twins alone. Although replication of findings across multiple twin studies may be desirable, the most powerful investigations include additional relatives besides the twins themselves.

Twin studies may include other relatives, such as parents, siblings, or offspring of the twins. These extended twin designs are effectively a combination of family and twin study designs, and provide additional information about various effects. For example, assortative mating may be tested and taken into account when parents of twin children or spouses of adult-twins are included. Different aspects of shared family environment may also be estimated, such as between twins, parents and offspring, or nontwin siblings.

## Multivariate Genetic Models

Individual differences in normal personality trait variation as well as abnormal personality disorders have been investigated extensively using the basic gene-environment model and its various extensions. Until the mid 1980s, most of these investigations were based on univariate analyses, comparing relative genetic and environmental influences across a variety of personality traits. Multivariate extensions of the basic gene-environment model became the focus of behavioral genetic research toward the end of that decade, shortly before the publication of the first edition of this book. Since then, multivariate models have become common in quantitative genetic studies of human behavior, including personality and psychopathology. These models have provided the opportunity to move beyond simple heritability estimates, toward understanding of the structure of personality traits. In addition to investigating sources of variation for various traits, multivariate models provide information about the relationships (covariation) among several dimensions of personality, both normal and abnormal (e.g., Markon, Krueger, Bouchard, Gottesman., 2002).

Figure 11.6 shows the extension of the basic gene-environment model for a single phenotype to examine two or more phenotypes (X and Y) jointly. In addition to estimating genetic and environmental components of variance for X and Y, multivariate analyses investigate the extent to which genetic or environmental influences may be correlated between two or more traits. It is commonly understood that specific genes do not influence a single trait, but instead may have *pleiotropic* effects, whereby many traits are influenced. For example, serotonin-related genes appear to be associated with a range of behaviors, including mood, anxiety, impulsivity and aggression (see Ebstein, Benjamin, & Belmaker, 2003). The genetic correlation between two traits ($r_{AxAy}$) may result from such pleiotropic effects, or from linkage disequilibrium, which may arise if one or more genes influencing X are in close proximity (i.e., near each other on the same chromosome) to genes which influence trait Y.

## Longitudinal Genetic Models

Considerable developments have also been made in the past 15 years in longitudinal genetic models, which may be considered as a special case of the more general

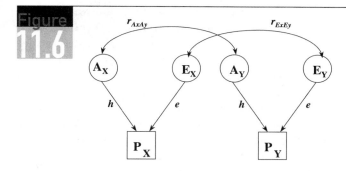

Bivariate gene-environment model (within persons).

multivariate models. Phenotypes X and Y in Figure 11.6, for example, might be the same trait measured at two different points in development (Time 1 and Time 2) in a longitudinal study. In addition to providing information about the changes in relative influences of genes and environment over time, longitudinal genetic models also estimate correlations between genetic influences ($r_{A1A2}$) and between environmental influences ($r_{E1E2}$) at different ages. More complex models may be employed to examine the patterns of continuity and change in genetic and environmental influences, such as the model of three time points shown in Figure 11.7.

Numerous longitudinal twin and adoption studies have been initiated in the past two decades, and several of these are still ongoing. Many of these studies encompass a wide range of behaviors, including cognitive and personality domains (e.g., the Colorado Adoption Project—see Petrill, Plomin, DeFries, & Hewitt, 2002 for a review of recent results), as well as psychopathology (e.g., Hewitt et al., 1997). Some studies focus more specifically on the development of social or emotion-related processes (e.g., Baker, Barton, & Raine, 2002; Goldsmith, Buss, & Lemery, 1997).

## DF Extremes Analysis

Most twin, family, and adoption studies that investigate normal trait variation (e.g., personality) are based on unselected samples, meant to be representative of the general population. It is also possible, however, to study samples of twins or families selected in which one or more family members are affected with a given disorder or fall beyond a

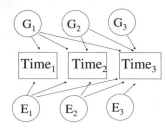

Longitudinal gene-environment model.

certain threshold of a normal varying trait. One example from the cognitive domain is reading disability, which is defined as lower reading scores than would be expected given the individual's general intellectual functioning. Alternative methods for genetic analyses of quantitative traits in such selected samples are also available. DeFries and Fulker (1985, 1988) presented a multiple regression approach for analyzing individuals sampled from the extremes of a normal distribution (called *probands*), along with their relatives. When genetic influences are important in the underlying trait, mean levels of the trait in relatives of affected individuals are predicted to regress toward the mean of the general population, but to differing degrees depending on the genetic relatedness between the proband and relatives. The DF extremes method is conceptually similar to the liability threshold model described earlier in this chapter, but regression coefficients are used instead of correlations to estimate heritability. In twin studies, for example, the regression equation for predicting the one twin's trait $(T_2)$ from the affected twin $(T_1)$ is:

$$T_2 = b_0 + b_1 T_1 + b_2 R \qquad (10)$$

in which the variable $R$ indicates the coefficient of genetic relatedness (1.0 for MZ twins; 0.50 for DZ twins). The partial regression of the score for co-twin on the proband's score $(b_1)$ indicates the degree of twin resemblance independent of zygosity (MZ or DZ). The $b_2$ coefficient is a function of the differential regression of MZ and DZ co-twins to the population mean, and if significant, indicates heritability of the group difference. DF extremes analysis is particularly useful in determining whether the trait heritability differs for the extremes of a trait (e.g., in selected samples) compared to heritability in the general population (e.g., in unselected samples). These regression methods have also been useful in development of linkage and association methods used to identify specific genes for behavior, as described in the Molecular Genetics Methods section later in this chapter.

## Summary of Quantitative Genetic Studies of Personality and Personality Disorders

Quantitative genetic methods based on family, adoption, and twin designs have been extremely useful in establishing whether and how much genetic and environmental influences impact normal personality trait variation. Genetic influences appear substantial (with heritabilities ranging from 0.30 to 0.50) and include both additive and nonadditive effects (e.g., due to genetic dominance and/or epistasis) for many personality traits, such as those measured by Cloninger's Tridimensional Personality Questionnaire (TPQ) (see Heath et al., 1999), Eysenck's Personality Questionnaire (EPQ) (see Eaves, Heath, Neale, Hewitt, & Martin, 1998; Plomin et al., 2000), and the Big Five factors of personality (Jang, Livesley, & Vernon, 1996). These same studies, like others both prior to and since the first edition of DNAP, have found nonshared environmental influences to be substantial for most personality traits, although shared family environmental effects are small or negligible. Moreover, multivariate analyses have suggested a multidimensional factor structure of most major personality traits ( Eaves, Eysenck, & Martin, 1989; Heath et al., 1999). Much of the genetic and environmental variance appears specific to each trait, although some overlapping influences are also found. Unlike cognitive abilities (Plomin, et al., 2000), personality traits do not appear to be influenced by a common "g" factor. It may also be possible that even the broad personality factors captured in many of these instruments may have multidimensional genetic and environmental structures.

These same quantitative genetic methods have also demonstrated the relative effects of genetic and environmental factors in abnormal personality traits and personality disorders. Only a small handful of the 10 DSM-IV personality disorders, however, have been investigated extensively using quantitative genetic methods. There is consistent evidence from twin, family, and adoption studies for moderate genetic influence on antisocial behavior in general, including antisocial personality disorder, with both additive and nonadditive genetic effects being important (McGuffin, et al., 2002). Twin and family studies have suggested that the liability toward schizotypal personality disorder is also influenced by genetic factors, with significant overlap for genetic influences in liability toward schizophrenia (McGuffin, et al., 2002; Plomin, et al., 2000). Significant family resemblance has also been shown for disorders in the anxious/avoidant cluster of personality disorders, including obsessive-compulsive disorder, although genetic and shared environmental effects have not yet been resolved using twin and adoption studies (McGuffin, et al., 2002; Plomin et al., 2000).

Multivariate genetic analyses have also been useful for investigating the relationships between normal and abnormal personality dimensions. For example, Markon, Krueger, Bouchard, and Gottesman (2002) demonstrated significant genetic correlations between normal varying personality traits measured through the MPQ and deviant personality dimensions measured by the MMPI. Considerable genetic overlap has also been found between Big Five personality traits and personality dysfunction (Jang & Livesley, 1999). Longitudinal and crosssectional analyses of the EPQ in Australian twins suggest that heritabilities for extraversion, neuroticism, and psychoticism are reasonably stable throughout much of the adult life span (i.e., 23–62 years old; Loehlin & Martin, 2001).

At this point, however, both genetic and environmental influences for both normal and abnormal personality remain "black boxes"—knowing that substantial genetic variation exists for normal and abnormal personality does not shed light on the biological mechanisms, specific aspects of the environment, or how these factors may moderate each other's effects in behavior. The next challenge is to understand the specific nature of both genetic and environmental influences. Researchers have recently turned to molecular genetic methods to search for these answers.

# Molecular Genetic Methods

Rapid advances in methods for identifying specific genes which contribute to both normal variation and extremes have been made in the last two decades, with the merging of classical quantitative genetic methods and more recent developments in molecular genetics. There are two primary designs in molecular genetic studies: (a) Linkage designs, in which the major goal is to detect chromosomal regions of significance in a given phenotype—that is, which areas of which chromosomes appear to hold genes that are transmitted along with the phenotype of interest; and (b) association designs, in which specific alleles (variations of a gene) are shown to be inherited along with the phenotypic trait. A distinction is made between major genes that may entirely or primarily account for a qualitative trait (disorder), and quantitative trait loci (QTLs), which may explain small amounts of variance in a continuously distributed (quantitative) trait. Linkage studies test for cosegregation using a number of markers that "hitchhike" with a trait locus but do not contribute to the trait—that is, markers are genes unimportant to the trait or disorder, which are near and inherited along with a gene which is influential. Association studies test actual genes that either empirically or theoretically have a probability of contributing to the disorder.

Linkage designs may use a few large pedigrees to detect locations of major genes, or may use many small families (usually siblings) to detect locations of genes that account for small amounts (10% or less) of the phenotypic variance. Association designs, on the other hand, may use large samples of unrelated individuals (a population approach) or pairs of relatives such as siblings (a within-family approach) to identify genes that account for much smaller amounts of variance (<1%). No study has yet broken the 1% QTL barrier (Plomin et al., 2003)—that is, genes that have been identified as contributing to psychological traits or disorders so far explain very little of the total phenotypic variance.

## Linkage Designs

Two important discoveries by Thomas Hunt Morgan early in the 20th century provided the basis for methods to detect specific regions of the chromosomes that may contain genes important to a given phenotype. Through his experiments with Drosophila, Hunt determined that (a) genes are ordered on the chromosomes in a linear fashion and (b) that chromosomes recombine during meiosis and exchange genetic material (see Chapter 10 in Carey, 2003, for a basic review of linkage). The probability of recombination of genes at two loci depends on their physical distance from one another on the chromosome. This probability is quantified using the recombination fraction ($\theta$), which represents the proportion of gametes (sex cells) with recombined alleles out of the total number of gametes. For two loci each with two allele variations of equal frequency in the population (A and a at one locus and B and b at the second locus), there are four possible gametes (AB, aB, Ab, and ab). If the two loci are on different chromosomes or far enough apart on the same chromosome, these four gametes will appear in equal frequency and their recombination fraction ($\theta$) will equal 0.5. If the two loci are physically close together on the same chromosome (i.e., are tightly "linked"), then some combinations will be more frequent than others (e.g., if A and B are physically adjacent on a chromosome, they will almost always be inherited together, appearing in far greater frequency than the Ab or aB in gametes), and a recombination fraction close to 0.0 will result.

Linkage studies typically include a large number of genetic markers that are measured in each participant. Early studies used markers based on gene products such as blood types (measured by testing the presence of certain antigens in each person's red blood cells to infer each person's genotype), although more recent developments use actual DNA samples to determine the specific genes or variations (*polymorphisms*) in DNA segments for each person. In addition to measures of genetic markers, each person's phenotype (a quantitative trait or qualitative disorder) is also measured. Linkage studies then test for cosegregation of the phenotype with these various genetic markers, by estimating the $\theta$ values between the trait and each marker. Markers with small values of $\theta$ are indicative of "regions of significance." It is important to keep in mind that linkage between a trait and marker does not necessarily mean that the locus has a causal effect on the trait.

Early linkage analyses were based on large pedigrees. These used a parametric approach, which estimates $\theta$ and uses likelihood of difference (LOD) scores as a statistical test to identify "regions of significance" (see Sham 2003). The large pedigree approach is favored for Mendelian (single gene) disorders, which are usually rare. Such arametric (model-based) linkage analysis requires an explicit model of the disease locus—e.g., knowing whether the disease gene resides on the X or Y sex chromosome or one of the autosomes, and whether it is dominant or recessive to other alleles. Many large pedigrees are also required for parametric linkage analyses. Although parametric approaches have been successful for studying rare Mendelian diseases (e.g., Huntington's disease), it has been less successful in studies of more common disorders which do not follow Mendelian patterns of inheritance and only are only moderately familial (e.g., most forms of psychopathology).

In response to the shortcomings of parametric linkage approaches, other nonparametric approaches (i.e., in which $\theta$ is not estimated) were developed more recently. Nonparametric linkage analyses are currently the favored approach for "complex genetic disorders" which are typically more frequent in the population. Rather than requiring large pedigrees, these methods may rely on information from only a few family members from a large number of families. For example, in "affected sib-pair designs" large number of sibling pairs affected with a given disorder are genotyped for a marker locus. A comparison is made between the number of sibling pairs who are (a) concordant for the marker locus and (b) discordant for the marker locus. If the marker is linked to the disease, there should be more sib pairs in the first group. Other designs may study both affected and nonaffected siblings, although it has been shown that extremely discordant sib pairs are the most informative in such linkage analyses (see Sham, 2003). These methods have also been extended to study general pedigrees in last two decades. Although studies using nonparametric approaches have become popular in recent years, their results have also been largely disappointing because regions of significance often fail to replicate across different studies (see Bishop & Sham, 2000, for review).

The lack of success of parametric and nonparametric linkage approaches in the study of qualitative disorders led to development of *variance components linkage analysis* (see Sham, 2003). These methods analyze quantitatively defined phenotypes, rather than all-or-none disease categories. It thus may be particularly useful in studying continuously distributed personality traits. The variance components model uses methods most similar to those described in the quantitative genetics section of this chapter. Essentially, information about the correlation between relatives derived by Fisher (1918) has been extended to the analysis of QTLs (Almasy & Blangero 1998; Eaves, Neale, Maes, 1996; Fulker & Cherny, 1996). Instead of using the overall genetic correlations between relatives (as shown in Table 11.1), variance components linkage analysis uses specific measures of genetic relatedness obtained through DNA markers. Specifically, the number of alleles shared (*identical by descent*, or IBD) by two relatives is used as a direct measure of their genetic relatedness. The statistical analyses thus involve methods similar to those in the twin design described earlier in this chapter. Instead of dividing twins into groups of MZ and DZ pairs, variance components linkage analysis examines groups of siblings with 0, 1, or 2 IBD alleles for a marker locus. Group differences in quantitative traits would be evidence of linkage between the marker and the trait.

Linkage studies often use a whole genome scan (the "shotgun approach") in which hundreds of genetic markers throughout the genome are studied in one sample. In such studies, a "region of interest" may include several million nucleotides with several different genes. Additional genetic analyses are required to pinpoint the exact location and, eventually, the function of the gene. Association studies can be especially useful in these next steps.

## Association Designs

Although linkage studies typically examine large regions of the genome to identify the *location* of genes that may contribute to a given phenotype, association studies generally focus on a narrower region of the genome in an attempt to find genes that actually have some *functional significance* to the trait. The difference between the two approaches is analogous to finding the address of a gene, versus understanding the specific contents at that address. Association studies may have one of two primary goals: (a) pinpoint the exact location of a gene in a region of interest previously identified in linkage analyses (called *fine point mapping*) or (b) determine whether a known polymorphism in a protein-coding gene is related to the trait. In fine-point mapping, many DNA markers within the region of significance are examined for linkage with the trait or disorder, in an attempt to hone in on possible genes of functional significance. Association studies test actual genes that either empirically or theoretically have a probability of contributing to the disorder. Thus, "candidate" genes may be selected for study to determine whether and to what extent they may explain variance in a given trait.

In studies of personality, for example, genes related to dopamine or serotonin might be purported to relate to disorders involving faulty systems of reward dependence or impulsive behaviors, such as attention deficit hyperactivity disorder (ADHD). Thus, association studies may begin with a polymorphic gene (e.g., DRD4) that has clear relevance for a trait (e.g., ADHD) and tests individuals on the gene to determine whether the gene is of greater frequency in affected versus nonaffected individuals.

There are two major designs for investigating associations: (a) a population-based (between-family) designs; and (b) family-based (within-family) designs. Population-based association designs do not require multiple members from a given family, but may examine large samples of unrelated individuals. These individuals are genotyped for one or more DNA markers, and phenotypic assessments are made for the traits or disorders of interest. Higher frequency of a given allele in a high-risk or affected group of individuals (compared to a nonaffected control group) may indicate an association between the allele and trait (or underlying liability toward a disorder). One drawback of population-based association studies is that population stratification can lead to spurious associations. For example, the affected and control groups may differ in their ethnic backgrounds, and the gene of interest may differ in frequency between these ethnic groups; thus, the gene may not be related to the trait at all, even though it shows an association. Consider skin color and sickle cell anemia as an example. One could genotype those with and without sickle cell anemia for the gene that codes for melanin, which results in variations of skin pigmentation. Because sickle cell anemia is more frequent in (more dark skinned) African descendants, the melanin gene would be more frequent in the affected group, even though this gene has nothing to do with the disease.

Within-family association designs provide a powerful alternative to population-based designs because they are not subject to spurious associations due to population stratification. These designs use genetic relatives as controls, e.g., by comparing phenotypic trait values for family members with different genotypes. Transmission disequilibrium tests (TDT) have been developed for testing gene associations in within-family designs. For example, studies may examine offspring of heterozygous parents (e.g., genotype Aa) for a candidate gene. Siblings who inherit different forms of the allele are expected to show mean differences in a quantitative (personality) trait, or greater incidence of a (personality) disorder. Association studies such as case control comparisons make it possible to detect genes that account for much smaller amounts of variance compared to linkage designs (Risch, 2000; Risch & Merikangas, 1996).

## Summary of Molecular Genetic Studies of Normal and Abnormal Personality

The rapid advances in statistical methods for studying genes at the molecular level, and the merging of molecular and quantitative genetic approaches has led to a flurry of studies attempting to identify specific genes, especially QTLs, in human behavior. These studies include both normal personality and psychopathology. This research is still in its infancy because large samples and replication of results across studies are required to confirm linkage and association between genes and behavior, and further research is needed to understand the functional significance of these QTLs.

A few candidate genes do appear promising, however, in explaining both personality-trait variation and some personality disorders or other forms of psychopathology. These include genes related to dopamine or serotonin, both of which are neurotransmitters with known relationships to behavior. A polymorphism in the dopamine D4 receptor (DRD4) was the first demonstrated to have an association with normal personality variation. The DRD4 gene involves multiple repeats (from 2 to 8) of a 48-base pair DNA sequence. The number of repeats in a person's DRD4 allele (from 2 to 8) changes the structure of the dopamine receptor, and hence the efficiency of dopamine function. "Short" versions of this allele (2–5 repeats) are more frequent (about 85%) in most populations, compared to "long" versions of the allele (6–8 repeats).

An association between DRD4 and novelty seeking was first demonstrated in two independent studies (Benjamin et al., 1996; Ebstein et al., 1996). Individuals with the longer DRD4 allele had significantly higher novelty seeking scores than individuals with shorter alleles, and this association has been found using both population and within-family approaches. Some studies have failed to replicate the association, but in about a dozen studies so far there appears to be an association of small effect size (for reviews, see Prolo & Licinio 2002; Plomin & Caspi 1999).

The DRD4 long allele has also shown associations with ADHD in children, but it is yet not clear whether this allele increases risk for any personality disorder. It has been proposed, however, that there may be a reward mechanism whereby novelty or sensation seeking promotes dopamine release, and that individuals with the less efficient long-repeat DRD4 allele must "work harder" to seek novelty and increase dopamine release (Blum, et al., 1996). The DRD4 polymorphism is therefore a good candidate gene for investigations of disorders related to reward dependency, such as substance use.

Serotonin-related genes have shown associations with personality, as well as components of personality disorders. A functional polymorphism in the serotonin transporter gene (5-HTTLPR) also involves a repeating section, with "short" and "long" variations of the allele. Higher levels of neuroticism, or harm avoidance, as well as depression have been found in individuals carrying the "short" allele in some (e.g., Lesch et al., 1996) but not all studies (for a review see Ebstein, Benjamin, & Belmaker, 2003). Somewhat greater consistency of results has been found in studies of impulsivity, which has also demonstrated relationships to serotonin function. The short serotonin transporter allele has also been found to be associated with increased risk of Type 2 alcoholism, which includes antisocial, impulsive, and violent behavior (Hallikainen et al. 1999).

An excellent review of both DRD4 and 5-HTTLPR polymorphisms and their contribution to personality traits may be found in Ebstein et al., (2003). More recently, Hennig, Reuter, Netter, Burk, and Landt (2005) reported evidence for another serotonin-related gene (A779C TPH polymorphism) and its relationship to aggressive hostility using a population approach. Undoubtedly, many more genetic associations with personality traits and disorders will be identified in the near future, although replication of these findings across samples will be essential.

## Relationship Between Normal and Abnormal Personality

How might personality *disorders* be considered in light of the multifactorial model of normal personality trait variation? One view is that disorders may be a function of rare, single gene effects that do not contribute to normal personality variation. However, effects (called "major gene effects") have not been found for any mental disorder to date. Another view is that common disorders are simply the extremes of these continuous distributions. Hence, abnormal personality may be defined as being in the tails of some normal distribution of personality trait, or some combination of several traits. Exceeding some threshold value on one or more traits thus requires unusually extreme genetic and/or environmental risk. Support for such a model would be found if unusually high levels of normal varying personality traits (e.g., neuroticism) were found in relatives of individuals diagnosed with a given disorder (e.g., anxious/avoidant personality disorder).

Alternatively, the underlying continuum for a given disorder may not necessarily be one of the major personality traits (e.g., one of the Big Five traits), but may reflect another dimension more specific to the given disorder. For example, schizotypical personality disorder (SPD) may stem from extreme values on a continuously distributed "schizotypy" trait, which exists in shades of gray in the population. Multivariate genetic analyses in which normal personality traits and dimensional components of disorders are studied jointly can certainly shed light on their interrelationships.

# Future Directions

In spite of the well-accepted finding that genetic influences are important in both normal and abnormal personality, we have only begun to scratch the surface in our understanding of the specific genes and environmental factors, and the underlying mechanisms in producing observable outcomes in behavior. Many questions remain open in our attempt to understand the genetic and environmental bases of both normal and abnormal personality and their links. Among these questions are the following:

1 Identification of specific genetic associations in both normal and abnormal personality is perhaps the most immediate goal in studies of normal variation and the extremes. Moreover, these genetic effects must be replicated to establish whether they are true associations.

2 A greater understanding of the genetic overlap among dimensions and disorders is needed. Multivariate quantitative genetic analyses will help shed light on this area, but linkage and association studies may also help resolve whether QTLs for dimensions also explain variation in disorders.

3 Further understanding of underlying mechanisms in the gene-behavior associations is needed. This question is being addressed by researchers in the area of "functional genomics," in which the biochemical pathways between gene and phenotype are the focus.

4 Understanding of environmental influences and how they may moderate genetic influences (i.e., $G \times E$ interactions) is also one of the most interesting and important questions. Subsequent to identification of QTLs, it is essential to investigate the circumstances under which genes are actually expressed in an individual. Although $G \times E$ interactions have traditionally been difficult to detect in quantitative genetic studies, recent developments in molecular approaches will increase opportunities to investigate these important interactions.

Our ability to address these questions about the genetic bases of normal and deviant personality and their relationships rest upon the resolution of phenotypic definitions. There continues to be a debate, for example, whether personality disorders should be viewed as categorical or dimensional. Although the dimensional approach has the advantage of greater statistical power, it is unclear whether extreme forms (i.e., categories) have the same etiologies as clinical diagnoses. Proponents of the categorical approach often emphasize that meaningful categories are rarely defined in terms of severity. Both approaches may have advantages and disadvantages in the study of personality disorders, although the dimensional approach tends to be favored in genetic studies to date. Finding QTL associations and understanding their functional significance in disorders, as well as dimensions may lead to several outcomes. Classification methods for disorders themselves may become gene-based diagnoses, which may or may not resemble symptom-based approaches as in the *DSM-IV*. Ultimately, effective treatment programs for disorders may be developed as a result of our understanding of the genetic and environmental mechanisms involved in personality traits and disorders. This is perhaps the most exciting potential of this research.

# REFERENCES

Abrahamson, A. C., Baker, L. A., & Caspi, A. (2002). Rebellious teens? Familial influences on the social attitudes of adolescents. *Journal of Personality and Social Psychology, 83*, 1392–1408.

Almasy, L., & Blangero, J. (1998). Multipoint quantitative-trait linkage analysis in general pedigrees. *American Journal of Human Genetics, 62*, 1198–1211.

American Psychiatric Association. (1994). Diagnostic and statistical manual *for mental disorders*(ed. 4). Washington, DC: Author.Amos, C. I. (1994). Robust variance-components approach for assessing genetic linkage in pedigrees. *American Journal of Human Genetics, 54*, 535–543.

Baker, L. A. (2003). The nature-nurture problem in violence. In W. Heitmeyer & J. Hagan (Eds.), *International handbook of violence* (pp. 735–762). Dordrecht, The Netherlands: Kluwer.

Baker, L. A., Barton, M., & Raine, A. (2002). The Southern California Twin Register. *Twin Research, 5*, 456–459.

Benjamin, J., Li, L., Patterson, C., Greenberg, B. D., Murphy, D. L., & Hamer, D. H. (1996). Population and familial association between the D4 dopamine receptor gene and measures of novelty seeking. *Nature Genetics, 12*, 81–84.

Bishop, T., & Sham, P. (Eds.). (2000). *Analysis of multifactorial disease*. Oxford: BIOS Scientific.

Blum, K., Cull, J., Braverman, E., Comings, D. (1996). Reward deficiency syndrome. *American Scientist, 84*, 132–145.

Brunner, H. G., Nelen, M., Breakefield, X. O., Ropers, H. H., & van Oost, B. A. (1993). Abnormal behavior associated with a point mutation in the structural gene for monoamine oxidase A. *Science, 262*, 578–580.

Cardno, A., & McGuffin, P. (2002). Quantitative genetics. In P. McGuffin, M. J. Owen, & I. I. Gottesman (Eds.), *Psychiatric genetics and genomics*. New York: Oxford University Press.

Carey, G. (2003). *Human genetics for the social sciences* (pp. 161–180). Thousand Oaks, CA: Sage.

Caspi, A., McClay, J., Moffitt, T., Mill, J., Martin, J., Craig, I. W., Taylor, A., & Poulton, R. (2002). Role of genotype in the cycle of violence in maltreated children. *Science, 297*, 851–854.

DeFries, J. C., & Fulker, D. W. (1985). Multiple regression analysis of twin data. *Behavior Genetics, 15*, 467–473.

DeFries, J. C., & Fulker, D. W. (1988). Multiple regression analysis of twin data: Etiology of deviant scores versus individual differences. *Acta Geneticae Medicae Gemellologine, 37*, 205–216.

Eaves, L. J., Eysenck, H., & Martin, N. G. (1989). *Genes, culture, and personality: An empirical approach*. London: Academic Press.

Eaves, L. J., Heath, A. C., Neale, M. C., Hewitt, J. K., & Martin, N. G. (1998). Sex differences and non-additivity in the effects of genes in personality. *Twin Research, 2*, 131–137.

Eaves, L. J., Neale, M. C., & Maes, H. (1996). Multivariate multipoint linkage analysis of quantitative trait loci. *Behavior Genetics, 26*, 519–525.

Ebstein, R. P., Benjamin, J., & Belmaker, R. H. (2003). Behavioral genetics, genomics, and personality. In R. Plomin, J. C. DeFries, I. W. Craig, & P. McGuffin (Eds.), *Behavioral genetics in the postgenomic era* (pp. 365–388). Washington, DC: American Psychological Association.

Ebstein, R.P., Novick, O., Umansky, R., Priel, B., Osher, Y. Blaine, D., et al. (1996). Dopamine D4 receptor (D4DR) exon III polymorphism associated with the human personality trait of novelty seeking. *Nature Genetics, 12*, 78–80.

Evans, D. M., Gillespie, N. A., & Martin, N. G. (2002). Biometrical genetics. *Biological Psychology, 61*, 33–51.

Fisher, R. A. (1918). The correlation between relatives on the supposition of Mendelian inheritance. *Philosophical Transactions of the Royal Society of Edinburgh, 52*, 399–433.

Fulker, D. W. (1988). Genetic and cultural transmission in human behavior. In B. S. Wei, J. Eisen, M. Goodman, & G. Namkoong (Eds.), *Proceedings of the second international conference on quantitative genetics* (pp. 318–340). Massachusetts: Sinaur Associates.

Fulker D. W., Cherny S. S. (1996). An improved multipoint sib-pair analysis of quantitative traits. *Behavior Genetics, 26*, 527–532.

Galbaud du Fort, G., Boothroyd, L. J., Bland, R. C., Newman, S. C., and Kakuma, R. (2002). Spouse similarity for antisocial behaviour in the general population. *Psychological Medicine, 32*, 1407–1416.

Glicksohn, J., & Golan, H. (2001). Personality, cognitive style and assortative mating. *Personality and Individual Differences, 30*, 1199–1209.

Goldsmith, H. H., Buss, K. A., & Lemery, K. S. (1997). Toddler and childhood temperament: Expanded content, stronger genetic evidence, new evidence for the importance of environment. *Developmental Psychology, 33*, 891–905.

Hallikainen, T., Saito, t., Lachman, H. M., Volavka, J., Pohjalainen, T., Ryynanen, O. P., et al. (1999). Association between low activity serotonin transporter promoter genotype and early onset alcoholism with habitual impulsive violent behavior. *Molecular Psychiatry, 4*, 385–388.

Heath, A. C., Madden, P. A., Cloninger, C. R., & Martin, N. G. (1999). Genetic and environmental structure of personality. In C. R. Cloninger (Ed.), *Personality and psychopathology*. Washington, DC: American Psychiatric Press.

Hennig, J., Reuter, M., Netter, P., Burk, C., & Landt, O. (2005). Two types of aggression are differentially related to serotonergic activity and the A779C TPH polymorphism. *Behavioral Neuroscience, 119*, 16–25.

Hewitt, J. K., Rutter, M., Simonoff, E., Pickles, A., Loeber, R., Heath, A. C., Reynolds, C. A., Silberg, J. L., Meyer, J. M., Maes, H., Neale, M. C., Erickson, M. T., Kendler, K. S., Truett, K. R., & Eaves, L. J. (1997). Genetics and developmental psychopathology: 1. Phenotypic assessment in the Virginia twin study of adolescent behavioral development. *Journal of Child Psychology and Psychiatry, 38*, 943–963.

Jang, K., & Livesley, W. J. (1999). Why do measures of normal and disordered personality correlate? A study of genetic comorbidity. *Journal of Personality Disorders, 13*, 10–17.

Jang, K., Livesley, W. J., & Vernon, P. A. (1996). Heritability of the Big Five dimensions and their facets: A twin study. *Journal of Personality, 64*, 577–591.

Krueger, R. F., Moffitt, T. E., Caspi, A., Bleske, A., & Silva, P. A. (1998). Assortative mating for antisocial behavior: Developmental and methodological implications. *Behavior Genetics, 28*, 173–186.

Lesch, K. P., Bengel, D., Heils, A., Sabol, S., Greenberg, B. D., Petri, S., et al. (1996). Association of anxiety-related traits with a polymorphism in the serotonin transporter gene regulatory region. *Science, 274*, 1527–1531.

Loehlin, J. C. (2004). *Latent variable models: An introduction to factor, path, and structural equation analysis* (4th ed.). Hillsdale, NJ: Erlbaum.

Loehlin, J. C., & Martin, N. G. (2001). Age changes in personality traits and their heritabilities during the adult years: Evidence from Australian twin registry samples. *Personality and Individual Differences, 30*, 1147–1160.

Lykken, D., & Tellegen, A. (1993). Is human mating adventitious or the result of lawful choice? A twin study of mate selection. *Journal of Personality and Social Psychology, 65*, 56–68.

Markon, K., Krueger, R. F., Bouchard, T. J., Jr., Gottesman, I. I. (2002). Normal and abnormal personality traits: Evidence for genetic and environmental relationships in the Minnesota Study of Twins Reared Apart. *Journal of Personality, 70*, 661–692.

McGuffin, P., Moffitt, T., & Thapar, A. (2002). Personality disorders. In P. McGuffin, M. J. Owen, I. I. Gottesman (Eds.), *Psychiatric genetics and genomics* ( pp. 183–210). New York: Oxford University Press.

Moldin, S. O. (1991). Quantitative genetic methods for the study of abnormal and normal personality. In S. Strack, & M. Lorr (Eds.), *Differentiating normal and abnormal personality*. New York: Springer.

Petrill, S., Plomin, R., DeFries, J. C., & Hewitt, J. (Eds.). (2002). *Transitions to adolescence in the Colorado Adoption Project*. Oxford, UK: Oxford University Press.

Plomin, R., & Caspi, A. (1999). Behavioral genetics and personality. In L.A. Pervin & O. John (Eds), *Handbook of personality: Theory and research* (2nd ed., pp. 251–276). New York: Guilford Press.

Plomin, R., DeFries, J. C., Craig, I. W., & McGuffin, P. (2003). Behavioral genetics. In R. Plomin, J. C., DeFries, I. W. Craig, & P. McGuffin (Eds.), *Behavioral genetics in the postgenomic era* (pp. 3-15). Washington, DC: American Psychological Association.

Plomin, R., DeFries, J. C., & Loehlin, J. C. (1977). Genotype-environment interaction and correlation in the analysis of human behavior. *Psychological Bulletin, 84*, 309–322.

Plomin, R., DeFries, J. C., McClearn, G. E., & McGuffin, P. (2000). *Behavioral genetics* (4th ed.). New York: Worth Publishers.

Prolo, P., & Licinio, J. (2002). DRD4 and novelty seeking. In J. Benjamin, R.P. Ebstein, & H. R. Belmaker (Eds.), *Molecular genetics and the human personality*. (pp. 91–107). Washington, DC: American Psychiatric Press.

Reynolds, C. A., Baker, L. A., & Pedersen, N. L. (1996). Models of spouse similarity: Applications to fluid ability measured in twins and their spouses. *Behavior Genetics, 26*, 73–88.

Reynolds, C. A., Baker, L. A., & Pedersen, N. L. (2000). Mechanisms of bivariate assortment for educational attainment and fluid intelligence. *Behavior Genetics, 30*, 455–476.

Rhee, S. H., Hewitt, J. K., Corley, R. P., & Stallings, M. C. (2003). The validity of analyses testing the etiology of comorbidity between two disorders: A review of family studies. *Journal of Child Psychology and Psychiatry, 44*, 612–636.

Risch, N. J. (2000). Searching for genetic determinants in the new millennium. *Nature, 405*, 847–856.

Risch, N. J., & Merikangas, K. R. (1996). The future of genetic studies of complex human diseases. *Science, 273*, 1516–1517.

Scarr, S., & McCartney, K. (1983). How people make their own environments: A theory of genotype—Environment effects. *Child Development, 54*, 424–435.

Sham, P. (1997). *Statistics in human genetics*. London: Arnold.

Sham, P. (2003). Recent developments in quantitative trait loci analysis. In R. Plomin, & J. C. DeFries, I. W. Craig, & P. McGuffin (Eds.), *Behavioral genetics in the postgenomic era*. Washington, DC: American Psychological Association.

Sham, P., & McGuffin, P. (2002). Linkage and association. In P. McGuffin, M. J. Owen, I. I. Gottesman (Eds.), *Psychiatric genetics and genomics* ( pp. 55–73). New York: Oxford University Press.

Nick Haslam
Ben Williams

I he theme of this book is the difference between normal and abnormal personality. Like all interesting issues this one can be approached from many angles. We can ask which theoretical models of personality make the best sense of normal and abnormal personality, which research methods best illuminate them, or which measurement tools and techniques best capture them. In this chapter we ask something different. What is the *nature* of the difference between normal and abnormal personality?

Not all differences are alike. The difference between cats and dogs is not the same as the difference between tall people and short people. Gold differs from silver in a way that boulders do not differ from pebbles. Differences between biological species and between chemical elements are differences in kind, whereas differences of height between people or of size between pieces of rock are differences of degree. Some things in the world seem to fall into discrete kinds. A furry domestic pet, the size of an upturned wastepaper basket, is likely to be a cat or a dog, but it is very unlikely to be both to some degree. Other things fall along a continuum, differing only in magnitude. A line can be drawn that distinguishes tall people from others, but no one imagines that it will be anything but an arbitrary place to slice what is really a continuous dimension. What sort of differences are differences in personality? Do people fall into discrete types, or do they differ only by degree?

Paul Meehl is largely responsible for bringing this distinction between differences in kind and differences of degree to the attention of psychologists, although it had been floating around the discipline in several different guises. Sometimes the distinction has been framed as one of categories versus dimensions, sometimes as one of types versus traits, and sometimes as one of qualitative versus quantitative variations. Meehl's preferred terminology was different. He referred to certain categories as "taxa" (singular "taxon"), and their condition as one of "taxonicity." Categories that qualify as taxa are nonarbitrary, based on a boundary between category members and others (the "complement class") that is objective and naturally occurring rather than imposed by human judgment or convention. "Cat" is a taxon because there is an objective category boundary separating all cats from all other things, a distinction that is one of kind. "Tall people" is not, because there is no discoverable boundary that cleaves the height continuum.

What makes Meehl's contribution particularly important for personality psychologists is its breadth. He did important conceptual research on the difference between taxonic and dimensional variation, placed this distinction in historical context, explored its implications for psychological theory and practice, developed quantitative methods for testing between taxa and dimensions, and pioneered the application of these "taxometric" methods. Meehl's work on taxometrics (e.g., Meehl, 1992) is valuable not only because it supplies a method for investigating the structure of personality, but also because it shows why doing so is important. The distinction between matters of kind and matters of degree is not a clever conceptual division that personality psychologists can safely leave to the philosophers, but one with real implications for how we think about, explain, and assess personality.

For a start, personality is usually conceptualized in a purely dimensional fashion. For a variety of reasons that Meehl (1992) and Gangestad and Snyder (1985) adduce, personality psychologists have tended to dismiss talk of personality "types" as coarse and unrigorous, largely confined to scientifically dubious historical figures (e.g., Jung) and modern-day popular writers. The dimensional view of personality carries the prestige of quantitative measurement, and it is consistent with the basic assumptions of widely used statistical procedures such as factor analysis. If the existence of personality taxa can be demonstrated empirically, the way personality psychologists think about individual differences would consequently have to change and perhaps become open to previously neglected viewpoints.

One way in which personality theory would have to be modified if personal taxa were shown to exist involves the explanation of individual differences. Differences of degree are relatively easy to explain: if people differ along a continuum, their position on that dimension is likely to represent the additive contribution of many small influences (e.g., multiple genes and environmental effects). The normal distribution, for example, arises from precisely such an accumulation of small effects. Differences in kind require somewhat different explanations. If an objective boundary separates some people from others, we need to be able to account for this discontinuity. What do taxon members have, or what have they undergone, that nonmembers have not? One possible kind of explanation is that there is a specific dichotomous causal factor that all taxon members share, such as a particular gene or a particular life experience. Another possibility is a threshold model: taxon members may have initially differed from nonmembers along a dimension, but they alone exceeded some critical value, triggering the emergence of a qualitatively different personality variant. A third possibility is that people are channeled into divergent ways of behaving by some complex environmental shaping process. If personality taxa could be demonstrated, they would require explanation along these lines and thus present scientific challenges in ways that personality dimensions do not.

The distinction between matters of kind and matters of degree also matters for personality assessment. The usual way to assess personality—so usual that people rarely question it—is to rate individuals on a number of items pertinent to the construct of interest and add these ratings to yield a score. This score is taken to operationalize a person's position on an underlying trait dimension, ideally with high measurement precision. When we construct personality measures, we want them to discriminate among people along the entire range of this dimension, distinguishing validly between the low and the very low and between the high and the very high. It should be obvious by now that this commonsense way of assessing personality assumes a dimensional or "nontaxonic" model of personality variation.

But what if at least some personality characteristics are taxonic? Given that it is desirable for an assessment tool to match the underlying structure of the variable that it measures (Ruscio & Ruscio, 2002), a tool for measuring a taxonic variable might look different from one for measuring a dimension. Such a tool's purpose would be to assign people to classes rather than to quantify their levels on a trait. It would therefore need to deliver a class assignment as output rather than a numerical score, and it would be designed to discriminate optimally at the taxon boundary rather than along the entire length of a dimension. The resulting instrument might look quite different from a standard personality scale. It might be briefer, more focused, and "scored" using more complex methods (e.g., Bayesian statistics) than simply summing items. If evidence were found for personality taxa, the complexion of personality assessment might change.

A related implication of the distinction between taxa and dimensions relates especially to research. If a personality characteristic is dimensional, then it is entirely appropriate to use quantitative scores on its measures in statistical analyses. It is generally quite inappropriate, however, to dichotomize these scores (e.g., by median split) as if the variable was well represented in categorical, either-or fashion. Not only would this represent a misrepresentation of the variable, but also it would produce a substantial loss of statistical power. If, on the other hand, the variable is taxonic, it may not be inappropriate to dichotomize its measures, so long as the dichotomy approximates the actual category boundary, accurately distinguishing between taxon members and nonmembers.

In this chapter we present an introductory review of taxometrics as an approach to the study of normal and abnormal personality, and to understanding the nature of the distinction between them. First, in the Overview of Taxometric Methods section, we give a conceptual overview of taxometric methodology, and describe the main ways in which it differs from some of its better-known alternatives. We argue that the taxometric approach is especially well-suited to addressing the latent structure of personality, and that is has several statistical and conceptual advantages. In the Taxometric Studies of Personality section, we then lay out an extended review of taxometric research on personality. We discuss research on normal personality variation, proceed to research on personality characteristics that are abnormal in the sense of being diatheses for major mental disorders, and then review taxometric studies of personality disorders (PDs). After some concluding comments about what this rapidly expanding body of research tells us about the structure of personality, we describe in the How To Do It section the main forms of taxometric analysis, and the requirements and desiderata for conducting ataxometric study. This section does not supply a technical user manual for budding taxometricians, but offers a basic understanding of how the method operates. In The Future of Taxometrics section, we propose some directions and goals for future taxometric research on personality, both in the variables that it targets and in the way in which it does so. We finish with some concluding comments, and an invitation to contribute to the taxometric enterprise.

# Overview of Taxometric Methods

We have argued that taxometric methodology is an especially promising means of examining the latent structure of personality. But exactly what does it entail? In this section of the chapter, we will describe the basic elements of the taxometric approach, and what sets it apart from some of its alternatives. We will not review the technical details of taxometric analyses—several taxometric procedures are discussed in the How To Do It section—but rather the conceptual underpinnings of these analyses. These core features of the taxometric approach can be summarized in four statements, listed and fleshed out in the text that follows.

## Taxometric Methodology Is Concerned with Latent, not Manifest, Structure

When the distinction between categories and dimensions was first raised, many psychologists' first thought was that categories should be quite easy to detect. Simply examine the distribution of people on some characteristic and look for obvious lumps, they suggest. This intuitively plausible idea has had influential advocates in psychiatry. Kendell (1975), for example, proposed that categories can be inferred when scores on a symptom measure are bimodally distributed, so that a "point of rarity" exists between the modes. Unfortunately, the lumpiness of observed variation is an unreliable basis for inferring the existence of a taxon (Murphy, 1964) for two main reasons. First, the absence of bimodality in a distribution is perfectly compatible with the existence of a taxon. Even if a taxon is separated from its complement by 2 standard deviation units ($SD$)—and remember here that a 0.8 $SD$ difference is conventionally considered to represent a "large" effect in psychology—the distribution of taxon and complement combined will not usually be bimodal. For example, the height difference between men and women is substantial, but the distribution of height in mixed samples is usually unimodal. It takes a very large difference between taxon and complement, a difference that is unlikely given the nature of psychological variation and measurement imprecision, to show up as a bimodal distribution. Second, the presence of bimodality does not reliably point to the existence of a taxon. Bimodal distributions can arise for many other reasons. Especially with small samples, bimodalities can represent random clumping of cases. They can occur when observers rate behavior in a polarized fashion, and as a result of certain statistical artifacts. In short, bimodal distributions do not strongly indicate the presence of taxa, nor unimodal distributions their absence.

The inadequacy of bimodality as a criterion for inferring taxa brings us to a fundamental point. A taxon is a latent structure, a structure that underlies observed variation in behavior and experience and that is only imperfectly revealed in such "manifest" variation. A taxon is not simply a collection of superficially similar observations, but a class whose members share a deep, categorical equivalence (i.e., they are of the same kind). Because a bimodal distribution represents a pattern of observed variation—the presence of two "densities" of observations—it does not necessarily reflect the latent structure of this variation. Any statistical procedures that find patterns in the distributions or densities of manifest variation will therefore be unreliable guides to latent structure. Many forms of cluster analysis are pattern-finding procedures of this sort, seeking patterns of clumped cases rather than examining whether these manifest clusters correspond to taxa. Instead of examining the distribution of cases for the existence of manifest clumps, taxometric analysis seeks evidence of latent category boundaries. Taxometric procedures are, in essence, methods for deciding whether manifest variations represent underlying differences in kind or differences of degree.

## Taxometric Methodology Is Not Structure-Imposing

The latent structure of a personality characteristic can be examined in many ways, using many different forms of statistical analysis. The most popular in the study of normal personality has of course been factor analysis, the midwife of all the major trait taxonomies, including the systems of Cattell and Eysenck and the Five-Factor Model. One of the more popular forms of analysis in the study of psychiatric classification has been cluster analysis. Both of these statistical methods differ from taxometrics in that they impose particular kinds of structure on the data that they analyze. Factor analysis generally assumes that data are appropriately modeled by one or more dimensions, and cluster analysis similarly assumes that a data set can be partitioned into two or more discrete classes. Consequently, factor analyses invariably yield dimensions and cluster analyses invariably yield clusters, whether or not the latent structure of the data is dimensional or categorical. Taxometric analysis is fundamentally different. Rather than presuming that a particular view of latent structure is suitable, it examines which view—dimensional or categorical—is empirically justified in a particular case. In short, taxometric analysis derives rather than imposes structure. This is not to deny the importance of structure-imposing analyses, which are valuable modeling tools, but it shows how they address different problems from taxometric analyses.

## Taxometric Methodology Is a Family of Procedures

Unlike most statistical approaches to examining the structure of personality, taxometric analysis involves the use of several independent procedures. Taxometric methodology encompasses a number of statistically distinct procedures; for example, L-Mode, MAMBAC, MAXCOV, MAXEIG, MAXSLOPE, and taxometric studies generally employ two or more of these procedures. In contrast, it is not a standard feature of cluster, factor, or latent class analysis, for example, to examine data sets using more than one procedure (e.g., to use multiple clustering algorithms). Most taxometric procedures examine patterns of covariation among multiple indicators of the latent variable of interest (e.g., responses on self-report scales), and most present these patterns as graphical plots. The shape of these plots varies as a function of taxonicity and of various data parameters. Decisions about taxonicity are generally made by visual inspection of plots rather than by null hypothesis significance testing or the use of fit statistics, as in other statistical approaches.[1]

---

[1]For one promising approach using fit statistics see Markon and Krueger in this volume, chapter 10.

## Taxometric Methodology Seeks Consistency

The reason for the use of multiple procedures in taxometric analysis should be fairly obvious. Clearly, evidence for a particular latent structure—taxonic or dimensional—is stronger when multiple procedures support it. The convergence of inferences about latent structure across multiple procedures is a hallmark of taxometric methodology: When procedures agree conclusions are more likely to be robust than when they do not. Meehl was a strong advocate of this kind of "consistency testing," and argued that it should go beyond simple agreement about taxonicity. Not only should procedures favor the same model of latent structures, but also they should yield consistent estimates of parameters of these structures. For example, if one procedure finds evidence of a taxon, the various estimates of the taxon base rate (i.e., sample prevalence) that it generates should tend to converge on a particular value, and the estimates generated by other procedures should also converge on this value. If these estimates do not agree closely, then the existence of the taxon must be called into question. Thus, taxometric analysis places a premium on the consistency of findings.

# Taxometric Studies of Personality

Up to this point, we have argued that the distinction between taxonic and dimensional latent structure is a fundamentally important one for the study of personality, and that taxometric methods offer a particularly useful way of distinguishing between them. Over the past three decades a substantial body of taxometric research on personality has appeared, and its volume has grown rapidly in the last few years. In this section of the chapter, we review this work. A more comprehensive review, which also covers studies of mental disorders and other latent variables (e.g., social relationships, emotion), is provided in Haslam and Kim (2002). We begin here by laying out research on normal personality, and then move on to personality characteristics that are conceptualized as vulnerability factors for mental disorders. Finally, we discuss taxometric studies of abnormal personality, and PDs in particular.

## Normal Personality

An appropriate place to begin a review of taxometric research on individual differences is with a discussion of the status of normal personality. Most arguments about latent structure arise in the domain of abnormality and whether it is different in kind or degree from normality. However, psychologists tend to assume that a purely dimensional understanding of normality is appropriate, and take latent continuity as the default assumption in their research, measurement, and conceptualization of traits. So deep and tenacious is this default assumption about the nature of normal personality variation that Gangestad and Snyder (1985) claimed that there is among personality psychologists a "prejudice" against categories. However, as Meehl (1992) maintained, the structure of personality is an empirical matter, and taxometric research has played a major role in determining whether this prejudice has a grain, or more, of truth. Knowing whether normal personality variation is lumpy or smooth—whether discrete types or categories are widespread, rare, or non-existent—should therefore serve as a useful reference point for judging research on the latent structure of abnormal personality.

Taxometric research on normal personality characteristics has been relatively diffuse, in the sense that many characteristics have been investigated, but usually only in one or two studies. Ideally, of course, taxometric findings would be replicated by different researchers, using different samples, assessment instruments, and statistical methods. However, replication has been more common in studies of psychopathology than normal personality, so our review of the latter must be somewhat jumpy. Even so, this review should provide an overview of the latent structure of normal personality.

The most obvious personality characteristics to put to the taxometric test are broad personality dimensions. In theory, these dimensions should not be taxonic: They are explicitly conceptualized as dimensions and their breadth implies that many causal influences contribute to them. Perhaps because taxonic models are so implausible for these broad dimensions, few taxometric studies have been conducted, although these have all predictably favored the nontaxonic alternative. Unpublished studies of Five-Factor Model traits by Arnau, Green, and Tubre (1999) and Green, Arnau, and Gleaves (1999) both supported nontaxonic models of Extraversion, Neuroticism, and Agreeableness, although the former obtained somewhat ambiguous findings for Conscientiousness and Openness to Experience. More recently, Arnau, Green, Rosen, Gleaves, and Melancon (2003) investigated the latent structure of Jungian "preferences" (extraversion vs. introversion, thinking vs. feeling, sensing vs. intuiting, and judging vs. perceiving). These preferences, which map onto Five-Factor Model dimensions (Extraversion, Agreeableness, Openness to Experience, and Conscientiousness, respectively), were conceptualized by Jung as dichotomous "type" constructs. However, Arnau et al. (2003) found them all to be nontaxonic, consistent with their earlier work.

Most other taxometric research on normal personality characteristics has focused on more specific, "narrow-band" traits. Because it is more plausible that such traits represent the outcome of a single dominant causal influence, the likelihood that taxonic models apply to them is higher than for broad traits. For many of the characteristics that have been examined taxometrically, there has also been active disagreement within the literature about their latent structure or explicit theoretical claims that the characteristics are taxonic. Such claims underpinned the first two taxometric studies of normal personality. Gangestad and Snyder (1985) conducted a seminal analysis of self-monitoring, the dispositional monitoring and regulation of expressive behavior and self-presentation, in a large undergraduate sample. They obtained a clearly taxonic finding and speculated on the processes of divergent causality operating over the course of social development that might account for it. Soon after, Strube (1989) investigated type A personality, a construct proposed to be typological by its originators. Consistent with this proposal Strube obtained taxonic findings. These two early studies have not been replicated, and must therefore remain somewhat tentative, but they raise the credibility of taxonic models in the domain of normal personality, and imply that the default assumption of dimensionality might sometimes be in error.

Another component of normal personality that has received taxometric scrutiny is sexual orientation (i.e., the disposition to be sexually aroused by and attracted to people of a particular gender). The latent structure of this variable has been contentious, well beyond the boundaries of psychology. Indeed, whereas many scholars have understood heterosexuals and homosexuals to represent discrete types of people, several others have argued that sexual orientation varies in a continuous fashion, and that the idea of sexual categories is a socially-constructed reification. Two taxometric studies have stepped into this contentious territory. Haslam (1997) examined responses of a nationally representative sample of American men on the MMPI-2's $Mf$ (masculinity–femininity) scale, which strongly differentiates self-identified gay and straight men without explicitly referring to sexuality or gender. Taxometric analyses conducted with these responses yielded no evidence of heterosexual or homosexual taxa. The second study, by Gangestad, Bailey, and Martin (2000), examined female as well as male sexual orientation, using measures of sexual preference, childhood gender nonconformity, and adult gender identity, and obtained taxonic findings for both sexes. The estimated base rate of the taxon associated with homosexuality in men (0.15) exceeded that of women (0.09), and both exceeded the base rates of self-identification as predominantly homosexual.

As the larger and more comprehensive study, Gangestad et al. (2000) may carry more weight than Haslam (1997), and its taxonic conclusion should be favored. However, it is also possible that its more direct assessment of sexual preference may account for the discrepant findings of the two studies where men are concerned, and that taxonic and nontaxonic models each have their merits. At a behavioral or phenotypic level, male sexual orientation may indeed be taxonic, polarized by the dichotomous "choice" of preferred sexual object, the process of sexual taste formation, and the taboo within gay and straight communities alike against bisexuality. At a latent level, male sexual orientation may be underpinned by a nontaxonic variable, perhaps represented by gender atypicality rather than sexuality. Categorical sexual identities and behavioral preferences might emerge out of such continuous variation over the course of sexual development. Further research is needed to clarify this possibility.

Attachment styles are personality characteristics that have been studied intensely in recent years, and they have also attracted the attention of taxometric researchers. Derived from research on infant attachment, where distinct variants were generally conceptualized as discrete types, attachment styles are now used to characterize the ways in which adults conduct and construe their close relationships. Responding to the typological assumptions prevailing in infant attachment research, Fraley and Waller (1998) conducted a taxometric analysis of adult attachment styles, and found that they are nontaxonic. This finding implies that adult attachment researchers should conceptualize attachment styles in terms of underlying dimensions, measure them quantitatively rather sorting people into groups, and search for general rather than style-specific attachment mechanisms. In an interesting follow-up study, Fraley and Spieker (2003) obtained nontaxonic findings in a study of attachment behavior in infancy, challenging more directly the typological view of some attachment theorists. In short, the continuity of adult attachment styles also applies early in life.

Fraley and Spieker's (2003) study is one of only two studies that have addressed behavioral tendencies in children. The other, by Woodward, Lenzenweger, Kagan, Snidman and Arcus (2000), tested Kagan's (1994) prediction that there is a highly reactive class of infants, characterized by high levels of distress and motor activity, who tend to grow up into behaviorally inhibited children. Using systematic observational ratings of 4-month-old infants, Woodward et al. (2000). found evidence of taxonicity with a base rate of 0.10. This finding replicated a mixture model analysis of older children by the same research group (Stern, Arcus, Kagan, Rubin, & Snidman, 1995). It also suggests that personality or temperamental taxa are not restricted to adults, and may not invariably be outcomes of prolonged environmental or developmental processes.

All of the research on normal personality reviewed thus far relates to substantive traits. Two recent innovative studies have focused instead on the response sets or styles that people employ when responding to personality inventories. In one study of child custody litigants, Strong, Greene, Hoppe, Johnston, and Olesen (1999) obtained a taxonic finding for validity scales assessing impression management, the deliberate attempt to present a positive social image, but a nontaxonic finding for scales assessing unintentional or self-deceptive positivity. In a second study, Strong, Greene, and Schinka (2000) found that symptom over-reporting was taxonic with a relatively high base rate in two clinical samples. Some response sets may therefore be discrete, and although they may not reflect enduring or cross-situational tendencies, they are nevertheless of real importance for personality psychologists. In addition, they have the potential to enhance the practical identification and assessment of invalid profiles in personality assessment.

Two additional personality characteristics—impulsivity (Gangestad & Snyder, 1985) and femininity (Korfine & Lenzenweger, 1995)—have been examined taxometrically, but only incidentally as control variables in analyses that focused on other latent variables. Both were found to be nontaxonic.

Overall, our review of taxometric studies of normal personality indicates that the continuity assumption that most personality psychologists hold is usually justified. Nontaxonic findings predominate over taxonic findings. Even so, taxometric studies have obtained evidence of several normal personality taxa: self-monitoring, type A, infant reactivity, and sexual orientation. These taxonic findings are all unreplicated, and arguably taxa have been found so commonly because investigators have selected characteristics for which taxonic models are especially plausible. Nevertheless, the fact that taxonic findings have been obtained suggests that the existence of personality taxa needs to be entertained and acknowledged by personality psychologists, rather than dismissed (cf. Meehl, 1992). Such taxa would appear to be more common among relatively specific or narrow traits than among broad dimensions. Needless to say, more taxometric studies of normal personality are needed both to expand the range of characteristics that are investigated, and to remedy the low levels of replication that limit our confidence in existing findings.

## Personality Diatheses

Dimensions of normal personality often shade into abnormality or at least social undesirability at one pole. However, only a few of these dimensions are explicitly conceptualized as vulnerabilities for psychopathology. These "diatheses" are particularly important constructs in the study of abnormal personality. If they are shown to be precursors of mental disorders, they may supply valuable etiological clues, may enable early detection of those at risk, and may serve as targets for preventive interventions.

Personality diatheses are usually conceptualized as continuous dimensions that precipitate a mental disorder when a sufficient quantity of stress bears on the person. In short, both the vulnerability and the stress that triggers it are understood as quantitative factors, but the disorder itself is understood to be a discrete phenomenon produced by a kind of threshold effect. Each person has a unique threshold, set by his or her position on the vulnerability continuum; and if it is reached, then the clinical syndrome emerges.

Although this continuum view of personality diatheses is widespread, it is entirely plausible that diatheses could be taxonic. Only a discrete class of people might be vulnerable to a particular mental disorder, and no amount of stress could trigger the disorder in people who do not fall within the class. This model of personality vulnerability has importantly different clinical and research implications. It would imply that the assessment of vulnerability should involve assigning individuals to categories rather than distributing them along a quantitative scale. Psychological assessments might need to be calibrated to distinguish optimally between taxon members and nonmembers. The refinement of such identification procedures would have a major bearing on efforts at early detection and the prevention. Similarly, a categorical model would imply that a specific causal factor might underlie the vulnerability (e.g., a particular environmental condition, a major gene, or a particular neurochemical aberration), and that this causal factor might be an appropriate target for research. Understanding the latent structure of personality diatheses clearly has considerable importance.

To date, only a few potential personality diatheses have been investigated taxometrically. Most of this work is very recent, reflecting an upswing of taxometric interest in vulnerability. The evidence that has emerged is interestingly discrepant for two diatheses, providing another rationale for further taxometric work. Clarifying the nature of vulnerability for major mental disorders should be a major focus of future research.

Vulnerability to mood disorders has been examined in only three studies, a neglect that is surprising given the massive investment of research into vulnerability to unipolar depression. The first study actually investigated vulnerability to bipolar disorder, examining the latent structure of hypomanic temperament (i.e., dispositional cheerfulness, energy, gregariousness, recklessness, and irritability). Meyer and Keller (2003) investigated this temperament in large samples of adolescents and young adults and found no evidence of a hypothesized taxon. Vulnerability for bipolar mood disorders would appear to fall on a continuum, pending further work.

Two recent studies have addressed vulnerability to major depression, coinciding with a renewed interest among taxometric researchers in the latent structure of depression itself. Gibb, Alloy, Abramson, Beevers, and Miller (2004) conducted analyses of measures of depressogenic attributional style and dysfunctional attitudes in a very large sample of undergraduates, and obtained nontaxonic findings using three distinct taxometric procedures. However, Strong, Brown, Kahler, Lloyd-Richardson, and Niaura (2004) obtained a taxonic result in a study of treatment-seeking smokers assessed on a depression proneness inventory. The differences between the samples and measures employed in these studies may account for their discrepant conclusions, which indicate that further work on vulnerability to depression is urgently needed.

Two additional vulnerability factors have received similarly limited taxometric attention. The structure of anxiety sensitivity, a diathesis for panic disorder that involves the fear of anxiety and anxiety-related sensations, has been examined in two published studies. Taylor, Rabian, and Fedoroff (1999) obtained a nontaxonic finding, whereas Schmidt, Kotov, Lerew, Joiner, and Ialongo (in press) found evidence of taxonicity. As with unipolar depression, then, there is mixed evidence on the structure of this diathesis. Vulnerability to dissociative disorders has arguably been examined by Oakman and Woody (1996), who obtained a taxonic finding for hypnotic susceptibility, a characteristic that is elevated among dissociators.

The diatheses reviewed to this point have only begun to be studied taxometrically. The same cannot be said for the vulnerability to schizophrenia, which has received more taxometric attention than any other latent variable. Indeed, taxometric procedures were developed in an attempt to test Meehl's theory of schizophrenia (Meehl, 1962, 1990), which holds that the genetic liability to the disorder ("schizotaxia") is confined to a discrete class of people, dubbed "schizotypes." In the first published taxometric study, Golden and Meehl (1979) found evidence for the hypothesized schizoid taxon using MMPI indicators in a nonpsychotic clinical sample. Erlenmeyer-Kimling, Golden, and Cornblatt (1989) later found that a similar taxon could be identified in children, using standardized cognitive and neuromotor assessments. Forty seven percent of children who had a parent with schizophrenia were identified as taxon members compared to 4% of normal controls, and taxon membership was strongly associated with subsequent admission to a psychiatric hospital by young adulthood. In a similar vein, and again using a high-risk sample, Tyrka and her colleagues (1995a,b) found evidence of a Schizo-typal taxon of stable prevalence and composition at three waves of a longitudinal study. Schizotypal features were assessed by a variety of methods, included self-report questionnaires, teacher ratings, and structured interviews. Taxon membership was strongly associated with a lifetime schizophrenia spectrum diagnosis, confirming the taxon's status as a vulnerability factor.

Another productive line of taxometric research on the latent structure of schizotypy has employed self-report scales in large undergraduate samples. Most work has focused on measures of "positive" features of schizotypy, such as perceptual aberration (i.e., perceptual distortions and disturbances of body image) and magical ideation, and "negative" features such as social and physical anhedonia. Lenzenweger and Korfine (1992) conducted the first published study of this sort, and found evidence of a taxon defined by high levels of perceptual aberration with a base rate of 0.10. Korfine and Lenzenweger (1995) replicated this taxonic finding (base rate 0.03) in another study of perceptual aberration, and Lenzenweger (1999) broadened the range of indicators to include magical and referential thinking, obtaining a taxonic result (base rate 0.13).

More recently, Blanchard, Gangestad, Brown, and Horan (2000) redirected taxometric researchers toward the negative features of schizotypy, obtaining a taxonic finding for social anhedonia (base rate 0.05). Meyer and Keller (2001) examined both positive and negative features, supporting taxonic models for perceptual aberration and physical anhedonia, with base rates of around 0.12, but not for magical thinking. Keller, Jahn, and Klein (2001) offered further support for the taxonicity of negative components of schizotypy (i.e., constricted affect, lack of close friends, and social anxiety; base rate 0.13), but obtained nontaxonic results for positive features including odd speech, ideas of reference, and perceptual abnormalities. Predominantly taxonic findings, using several self-report measures of positive and negative features of schizotypy and repeatedly yielding comparable base rate estimates, have also been obtained in unpublished work by Raulin and his colleagues (e.g., Lowrie & Raulin, 1990).

This brief review provides quite consistent support for a taxonic model of the diathesis for schizophrenia. Many taxometric procedures, employed in diverse samples by many research teams, have yielded taxonic findings using a variety of measures. The taxon appears to be longitudinally stable, strongly and prospectively associated with clinical outcome, and about equally well identified by positive and negative personality features. In addition, the base rate estimates across numerous studies of normal individuals converge strikingly on the 0.10 value that Meehl (1990) predicted. Support for a schizotypal taxon is therefore both empirically and theoretically robust.

To summarize, personality vulnerabilities have received relatively scant taxometric scrutiny, with the exception of schizotypy. The evidence of the existing studies is intriguing. Whereas taxometric examinations of normal personality have rarely yielded taxonic findings, such findings have been common in studies of diatheses, directly challenging the default assumption that personality vulnerabilities are continua. More replication and extension to additional diatheses is required before this conclusion can be drawn with confidence, but work conducted thus far clearly increases the plausibility of taxonic models of vulnerability. Most research on schizotypy supports a taxonic model, and some limited evidence of taxonicity has been obtained for vulnerabilities to panic disorder, dissociation, and depression. Continuing this work should be a priority.

## Personality Disorders

The categorical versus dimensional status of the *Diagnostic and Statistical Manual of Mental Disorders*'s *(DSM-IV*; APA, 1994) axis II is a particularly important question, which taxometric research should play a major role in resolving. Although the *DSM-IV* represents PDs as distinct categories and diagnoses them as simply present or absent, dimensional models of PDs are popular among theorists and researchers, much as they are popular in the study of normal personality. Thus, there have been a number of proposals to overhaul the classification of PDs in a dimensional fashion (Livesley, Schroeder, Jackson, & Jang, 1994; McCrae, 1994; Widiger & Clark, 2000). Consequently, the latent structure of PDs is not simply an abstract issue for theorists, but a very practical matter with implications for the shape of future psychiatric classifications.

Several considerations argue in favor of the dimensional view of PDs (Haslam, 2003). First, many disorders are strongly associated with dimensions of normal personality, such as the Five-Factor Model (Costa & Widiger, 2002), and most appear to shade imperceptibly into normal personality variation. Second, dimensional measures of PD symptomatology often predict clinical phenomena better than categorical diagnoses (Nakao et al., 1992). Third, the troublingly high levels of "comorbidity" among some PDs—the fact that several PDs are often diagnosed together—might be understood better if the disorders are not discrete categories. Apparent comorbidity might not reflect the co-occurrence of two or more discrete disorders, but only the ways in which features associated with different diagnoses share associations with underlying dimensions of abnormal personality. These arguments against the prevailing system of categorical diagnosis provide a strong rationale for taxometric analyses of PDs.

Given the profound theoretical and practical implications of the categorical versus dimensional issue in the study of PDs, it is surprising how little relevant taxometric research has been conducted. One reason for this neglect may be the taken-for-grantedness of the dimensional view among most research psychologists. Whatever the reasons, taxometric attention has only been paid to three of the ten *DSM-IV* PDs, and some of this work has only an indirect relevance to PDs. We will review the work conducted to date that bears on the latent structure of schizotypal, antisocial, and borderline PDs, and conclude this section of the chapter with some integrating remarks and a plea for further research in this area.

Taxometric research on schizotypy has obvious relevance for the latent structure of personality pathology, and as we note above no latent variable has received more taxometric scrutiny. However, these studies have not usually directly addressed schizo-typal PD (SPD), and the taxon that they point to does not correspond to the disorder straightforwardly. The Tyrka et al. (1995b) study comes closest to being an analysis of SPD, using indicators that corresponded to *DSM-III* (APA, 1980) symptoms of the dis-order, but most studies have addressed particular schizotypal traits rather than the entire syndrome. Moreover, the taxon that has been identified does not correspond precisely with SPD as it is defined within the *DSM* system. Most important, the population prev-alence of SPD (about 3%) is substantially below the 10% taxon base rate that repeat-edly emerges in taxometric studies of normal undergraduates. Similarly, the base rates derived in research on psychiatric inpatient and high-risk (offspring of one parent with schizophrenia) samples—41% (Golden & Meehl, 1979) and 47% or 46% (Erlenmeyer-Kimling et al., 1989; Tyrka et al., 1995a,b), respectively—easily exceed plausible rates of SPD.

One interpretation of these findings is that schizotypy is taxonic, and SPD is a relatively severe and impairing variant of it. The schizotypal traits that have been investi-gated taxometrically are elevated in SPD, and both the taxon and the disorder have been shown to confer increased risk of schizophrenia spectrum disorders. It is therefore plau-sible to view SPD as nested within the broader taxon. Current research does not allow us to determine whether SPD is a discrete variant of schizotypy (i.e., a taxon within a taxon) or simply a quantitative variant. To answer this question a taxometric analysis restricted to a large sample of taxon members would have to be conducted. However, this issue is perhaps not of great importance for larger question of the categorical versus dimensional status of PDs. If SPD is nested within a taxon, whether or not it is itself taxonic, the categorical view of PDs becomes more plausible and any conceptualization of SPD must take the existence of a category boundary into account.

Another issue germane to SPD must also be mentioned. If the disorder is rooted in a significantly more prevalent taxon, then it could be argued that *DSM-IV* draws the diagnostic boundary incorrectly, excluding a large proportion of schizotypes from the diagnosis. Perhaps, if diagnostic systems should "carve nature at the joints" and the joint in this case defines 10% of humanity as taxon members, then the *DSM-IV*'s diagnostic rule should be relaxed to become more inclusive (e.g., by requiring that only four of the nine symptoms be present). Although we are generally sympathetic to the idea that taxo-metric findings should be used to revise diagnostic systems, we believe that this proposal would be a mistake. The existence of a psychopathology-related taxon does not require that a clinical diagnosis should map its boundary. Diagnosis should always be sensitive to practical issues of clinical severity and impairment, rather than simply reflecting struc-tural realities, and if it is only the most severe fraction of schizotypal taxon members who suffer significant impairment then there is little reason to recalibrate the SPD di-agnosis. In this situation there is also a very real concern that relaxing the requirements for SPD diagnosis would amount to a needless and perhaps destructive pathologizing of ordinary eccentricity, a charge that the *DSM* system already faces from its critics.

Antisocial PD (APD) has also been the subject of a limited amount of taxometric research, although as with SPD most of it has had only a glancing relevance to the dis-order as it is defined in *DSM-IV*. Most studies have examined psychopathy rather than APD, or have investigated antisociality in children, in whom PDs cannot be diagnosed, rather than adults. Nevertheless, these studies have yielded quite consistent results, which again tend to favor taxonic models. In the first published study, Harris, Rice, and

Quinsey (1994) found convergent evidence for taxonicity using a variety of psychopathy indicators. However, only some aspects of the psychopathy construct—those representing chronic antisocial behavior beginning in childhood—were taxonic, and a nontaxonic model seemed more appropriate for the interpersonal and affective aspects of psychopathy and for adult criminality per se. Ayers, Haslam, Bernstein, Tryon, and Handelsman (1999) replicated this taxonic finding in a study of antisocial PD features among polysubstance-abusing adults. Similarly, Skilling, Harris, Rice, and Quinsey (2001) found evidence of a taxon using measures of psychopathic tendencies and *DSM-IV* antisocial PD indicators in a study of persistently antisocial adult offenders. Finally, Skilling, Quinsey, and Craig (2001) detected a taxon of antisocial boys of middle-school age in a community sample, consistent with Harris et al.'s finding regarding the discreteness of chronic antisociality.

These four studies consistently support a taxonic model of antisociality, which is characterized by a variety of features associated with psychopathy and APD. The evidence for this taxon is less extensive than for schizotypy, but it has at least addressed diagnostic criteria to a greater degree. The antisocial taxon does not appear to be reducible to criminality and is detectable relatively early in life, implying that it does not originate in adult criminal careers or simply reflect a social role or niche. It is interesting that evidence for the taxon is strongest precisely in those aspects of the psychopathy construct (i.e., chronic antisocial conduct) that are captured by the *DSM-IV* APD diagnosis.

The third and final PD that has submitted to taxometric inquiry is borderline PD (BPD), the most well-researched member of the Axis II family. Trull, Widiger, and Guthrie (1990) conducted the first taxometric analysis of any PD in an investigation of BPD features judged from a chart review of a large sample of psychiatric outpatients. Their findings were somewhat ambiguous, but Trull et al. (1990) inferred support for a nontaxonic model. Several writers (e.g., Korfine & Lenzenweger, 1995) later disputed this interpretation, and suggested that the analysis probably revealed a low base rate taxon.

Although Trull et al.'s (1990) findings proved controversial, their interpretation has been borne out by three more recent studies. Two unpublished investigations by Simpson (1994) and Ayers et al. (1999) also yielded nontaxonic findings for borderline PD in clinical samples, although they were based on a less reliable self-report assessment of BPD symptoms. More recently, Rothschild, Cleland, Haslam, and Zimmerman (2003) conducted a more complete taxometric analysis of BPD features assessed by structured interview, in a large outpatient sample. Obtaining similar results to Trull et al. (1990), they showed that these were more consistent with a nontaxonic model than with a borderline taxon, and that the source of the original ambiguity was most likely the positive skew of BPD indicators. We return to the issue of skewness later, but now it seems reasonable to conclude that BPD is probably not taxonic.

What, then, can we learn about the latent structure of PDs from taxometric research? Most simply, it can be argued that SPD may or may not be taxonic but it is probably rooted in a broader schizotypal taxon, that APD is probably taxonic, and that BPD is probably nontaxonic. By implication, PDs are likely to be a mixed bag when it comes to fundamental questions of latent structure. For some disorders a categorical approach may be most warranted, and for others a purely dimensional approach may be preferable. Consequently, taxometric research argues against any dogmatic preference for categorical or dimensional understandings of Axis II. Equally, it does not support a universal, one-size-fits-all approach to the classification of PDs, whether it be the categorical *status quo* or the dimensional alternative.

Perhaps the most important contribution of taxometric research on PDs, however, is raising the plausibility of taxonic models in this domain. Although it has been claimed that the evidence for the dimensional view of PDs is "overwhelming" (Livesley, 1996, p. 224), taxometric research now makes it unreasonable to dismiss categorical models as questionable in principle. Entertaining the possibility that a PD may have taxonic components does not mean that it can no longer be measured quantitatively, given complex causal explanations, or modeled in terms of established dimensional systems of personality description (Haslam, 2003). It does mean that nonarbitrary distinctions between normal and abnormal personalitymust be admitted as possibilities and given proper theoretical attention. Determining how many PDs are best understood as categories or as dimensions remains an urgent scientific question, given that only three of the ten disorders have been studied taxometrically to date.

# How to Do It

In a chapter like this there is not sufficient space to discuss the nuts and bolts of taxometric methodology in great detail. Thankfully there are a number of publications that offer practical guidance (e.g., Beauchaine, 2003; Ruscio, Haslam & Ruscio, 2006; Ruscio & Ruscio, 2004; Waller & Meehl, 1998). However, in this section we will lay out basic information about the most widely employed taxometric procedures, and discuss the considerations that researchers need to be aware of in conducting a sound taxometric investigation. We hope that this will spur some potential researchers to consider learning more about, and using, this flexible set of procedures.

As in all statistical procedures, taxometrics begin with a set of observed variables, called *indicators*. Indicators are valid, but imperfect, measures of the theoretical construct under investigation, having the potential to distinguish between the members of the putative types under study. The taxometric methods described here are the products and descendents of the *coherent cut kinetics* procedures pioneered by Meehl and colleagues (e.g., Meehl, 1995). To date, at least a dozen different procedures have been described in the literature, but only a relatively small subset of these are routinely applied in research. The statistical underpinnings of these procedures are extremely general, so that they are quite tolerant of some degree of skewness, nuisance covariance (i.e., correlations between indicators within taxon and/or complement), and non-normal kurtosis. The procedures generally begin by sorting one variable (termed the input indicator) in ascending order. The groupings of values for the other variables (i.e., output indicators) conditional on this sorting will depend on the structural relationship between the variables, one aspect of which is their taxonicity or dimensionality. Summaries of the output variables are computed at sliding cut points along the sorted variable, and are often presented as graphs. These graphs provide a readily interpretable summary of evidence for or against taxonicity. If taxonicity is supported, further calculations provide the optimal score for distinguishing the two latent classes, estimates of the base rate and summary information about the taxon and complement members, and of the indicator validities (i.e., how powerfully they separates the classes). The most commonly used taxometric procedures are described in the next section.

## MAXCOV/MAXEIG

MAXCOV (MAXimum COVariance) is one of the earliest taxometric procedures described in the literature, and is the most widely applied and reported in published research (Haslam & Kim, 2002). It requires a minimum of three indicator variables. One variable serves as an input indicator and two other variables serve as output indicators. The input variable is sorted in increasing order and cut into a series of intervals. The covariance of the output indicator pair is computed for each interval, and this covariance value is plotted as a function of the input indicator. This process is repeated so that all indicators serve in every possible input/output combination (i.e., three indicators yield three curves, four indicators yield six, etc.). A statistical result called the generalized mixture covariance theorem (Waller & Meehl, 1998) makes a useful prediction about the outcome of this process. Assuming that the indicator is designed so that taxon members generally score higher than complement members, as the computational process moves up from the region of intervals dominated by low-scoring complement members into the region dominated by taxon members, the covariance of the output indicators will rise, reaching a maximum in the interval where the taxon and complement distributions intersect. This leads to curves with distinct peaks, or rises in the case of low-base rate taxa. This is shown in panel 1 of Figure 12.1, where a taxonic sample with a base rate of 0.5 is shown. If the underlying structure is dimensional, then the covariance will change little from block to block, resulting in a flattish curve. This is shown in the third panel of Figure 12.1, which is a simulated data set matching the original data, but having a dimensional underlying structure. Traditionally intervals were defined so that adjacent windows shared no cases. However, it has been shown effective to use overlapping "windows" (i.e., each window contains some of the cases from the end of the previous window), with overlaps of up to 90% proving useful.

MAXEIG (MAXimum EIGenvalue; Waller & Meehl, 1998) is a logical extension of the MAXCOV procedure, although it is yet to gain such widespread use. MAXEIG

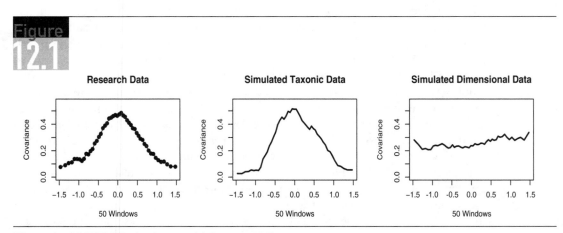

**Figure 12.1**

Illustrative MAXCOV plot (taxon with base rate 0.5).

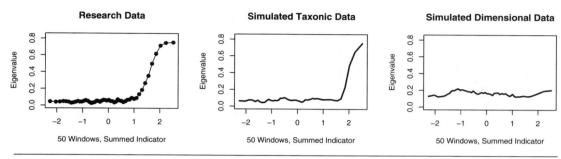

Illustrative MAXEIG plot (taxon with base rate 0.1).

proceeds in exactly the same way as MAXCOV except instead of computing the covariance of an output pair, the first eigenvalue of *all* variables not serving as the input indicator is computed. Figure 12.2 shows a MAXEIG analysis of a taxonic sample with a base rate of 0.1. A clear peak is seen toward the right of the curve. Because there is only MAXEIG curve per indicator, this procedure results in fewer curves than MAXCOV, although it is some respects more powerful. To take advantage of any extra power associated with MAXEIG at least four indicators are required.

## MAMBAC

In a MAMBAC (Mean Above Minus Mean Below A Cut; Meehl and Yonce, 1994) analysis one indicator serves as an input and another single indicator as output. Thus MAMBAC requires a minimum of only two indicators. Each of these can serve as input and output resulting in two curves. If more indicators are available, every possible input–output combination can be employed. MAMBAC begins by sorting an input indicator from smallest to largest value and then performing step-wise calculations on the output indicator. A single cut-point is moved along the sorted input indicator, and at each cut-point the mean of the output indicator cases below the cut-point is subtracted from the mean of output indicator cases above the cut-point. A cut-point that bisects the data near the midpoint of the overlap between the taxon and complement distributions on the input indicator will produce a maximal separation of taxon and complement on the output variable. Either side of this point the mean differences will decrease, so taxonic structures give rise to curves that have distinct peaks (or rises at one end of the graph for low base rate taxa). By contrast, dimensional data sets produce concave graphs. Figure 12.3 shows a MAMBAC analysis of a taxonic data set with a base rate of 0.3. A clear round peaking at the upper third of the curve can be seen. The dimensional simulation, by contrast, has the characteristic bowl shape of a dimensional structure. MAMBAC involves far fewer computations than other methods, produces a moderate number of curves and is apparently quite robust to violations of normality. These qualities make it a good "first pass" procedure for exploring a dataset, with another procedure such as MAXEIG serving as a secondary convergent or confirmatory analysis.

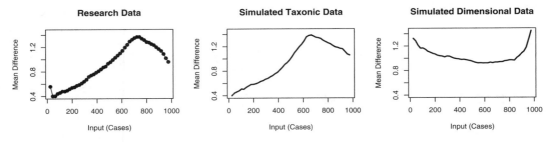

Illustrative MAMBAC plot (taxon with base rate 0.3).

## MAXSLOPE

MAXSLOPE (Grove & Meehl, 1993) is conceptually similar to MAXCOV, but can be performed with only two variables. In MAXSLOPE a sorted input indicator is cut into windows or blocks, and the regression slope of the input indicator onto the output indicator is computed for each block. Contiguous windows containing predominantly taxon or predominantly complement members will produce similar slopes and result in a flat curve. As the windows move from a predominantly complement region to a predominantly taxon region, the steepness of the regression line will increase owing to the "slope" between the taxon and complement members. This is seen in Figure 12.4 for a taxonic data set with a base rate of 0.5. The matching dimensional simulation shows a flat curve, indicating that the regression slope does not change radically over the range of the input indicator.

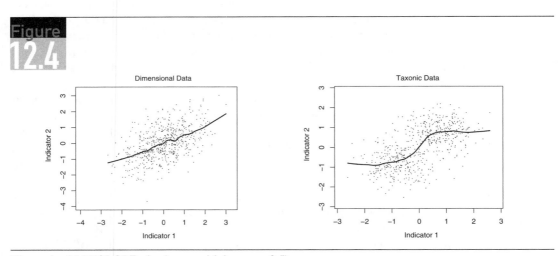

Illustrative MAXSLOPE plot (taxon with base rate 0.5).

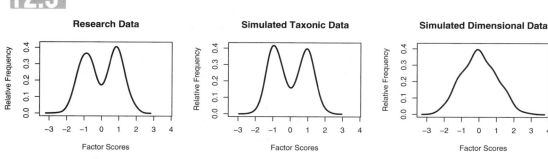

Illustrative L–Mode plot for taxonic data.

### L–Mode

L–Mode (Waller & Meehl, 1998) differs somewhat from the other methods described here, in that it does not use a moving cut procedure but is a special case of nonlinear factor analysis. Also unlike the other methods, L–Mode requires both the latent distributions to be symmetric and produces a single plot in which the distribution of the estimated factor scores for the first factor of the sample is plotted. Plots of taxonic data structures will show two distinct peaks corresponding to the two *latent modes* (hence the procedure's name) in the factor score distribution, whereas dimensional data show only a single peak (see Figure 12.5). Although it only yields a single curve, L–Mode provides its own consistency check: a taxonic curve, which will be bimodal, provides two statistically independent base rate estimates—for taxon and complement—and these rates should sum to unity.

## Consistency Checking and Convergent Evidence

Taxometrics seeks convergent evidence from multiple information sources to support its conclusions. First, taxometric procedures draw support for the existence of a taxon by checking for parameter estimate consistency within procedures (e.g., base rate estimates from individual MAMBAC curves should be consistent). Second, taxometric researchers seek convergent validity by "replicating" a result using multiple procedures, seeking consistent conclusions from different techniques. For example MAMBAC and MAXCOV are often used in tandem, and confidence in a conclusion is gained by agreement in structure (i.e., both agree on the taxonic status of the data) and parameter estimates (e.g., base rate) across the two procedures. Such convergent analyses afford semi-independent tests of taxonicity.

## Data and Research Considerations for Taxometric Studies

There is no hard and fast rule or general mathematical theory that gives an optimal figure for the total number of cases required in a taxometric analysis, but there is a widely held view that a minimum of 300 cases is needed with 600 or more being desirable. This rule of thumb is based on results from simulations and past research, and from the fact that enough cuts (e.g., MAMBAC) must be made to allow the shape of the curve to show itself fully, and enough cases must fall within intervals (e.g., MAXCOV) to get a good estimate of the output statistic. There should also be a sufficient number of cases such that there are at least a few windows or cuts which are relatively "pure" (e.g., containing only taxon members). For taxa anticipated to have very low base rates this consideration implies large samples. Indicator validity, quality, and distribution are also likely to have an impact on the required sample size, such that less valid, coarse, and highly skewed indicators require relatively large samples.

How samples should be drawn from populations is also an issue for taxometric research. Exponents of taxometrics have repeatedly admonished researchers not to deliberately oversample the (putative) type whose existence they hope to demonstrate. Obviously, sampling only cases at high and low extremes of a continuum will produce an artificially taxonic result. Samples should therefore be drawn such that the full range of naturally occurring variation on a measure is observed. This does not mean that taxometrics cannot be used for "at-risk" or other selective sampling studies. The methods are equally applicable here so long as the normal range of the target population is sampled. For example, if a researcher were interested in searching for subtypes of a condition (e.g., schizophrenia) the sample need only be representative of the target group (i.e., patients with schizophrenia).

Different taxometric procedures have different requirements for the minimum number of indicators. The minimum number of indicators for a MAMBAC or a MAXSLOPE analysis is two, MAXEIG properly requires four, and MAXCOV and Lmode require three. However, more than the bare minimum is preferable, larger numbers of indicators giving more power, producing more curves for consistency checking, and allowing the use of summed indicators. Large numbers of indicators, however, can present heavy computational loads, and the modal number of indicators in most studies is between 4 and 8. Taxometric methods require at least ordinal data, to permit sorting of cases, and they work best with pseudo-continuous indicators that vary smoothly. In practice, variables with five or more levels seem to work acceptably with larger numbers of scale divisions producing generally better results. Coarser scales often lead to jagged curves that are difficult to interpret. If more than the bare minimum number of indicators is available, input coarseness can be partially overcome by using "sum" indicators. For example, the required minimum number of output indicators (e.g. one for MAMBAC, two for MAXCOV) is held aside and the remaining pool of variables is summed to produce a new input indicator which will vary more smoothly, and have greater validity, than the individual indicators. This is one way to avoid the problems for taxometric analysis that are posed by dichotomous indicators.

Indicators should be chosen so that they are valid measures of the construct under investigation. Several nonredundant measures are required. Ideally, these should powerfully separate the putative axon and complement but have little covariation (nuisance covariance) within each. Measurements can be of any kind, questionnaire, physiological, observation, interview, or otherwise. However, it has been suggested that multiple independent sources of measurement are preferred to solely self-report measures (Beauchaine, 2003). Self-raters may strive for consistency in their responses, yielding indicators that intercorrelate more strongly than they otherwise should (i.e., nuisance covariance), and it has been shown that raters' expectations can bias taxometric findings

(Beauchaine & Waters, 2003). Objective measures (e.g., behavioral, physiological) and different reporting sources (e.g., patient, professional) are ideal, although carefully designed questionnaire items should serve adequately in most cases.

In taxometrics, validity refers to how well indicators separate the putative taxon and complement classes. Indicators should therefore be constructed to maximize this separation. A minimum separation of 1.25 within-group standard deviations is needed to detect a taxon, with higher values yielding clearer findings and lower ones making "pseudo-dimensional" findings more likely. Taxometric software allows indicator validities to be estimated, so that their adequacy can be checked.

## Caveats

Past work has shown that some taxometric procedures are generally robust for skewed data and moderate levels of nuisance covariance (e.g., Haslam & Cleland, 1996). However, skewed indicators of latent dimensions can produce rising curves that resemble those generated by low base rate taxa (Ruscio, Ruscio & Keane, 2004). This can be a serious problem in taxometric research because most measures of clinical phenomena are skewed. Skew-reducing transformations and data simulation procedures (see below) can at least partially alleviate this problem. Even when a true taxonic structure is present, indicator skew, as well as nuisance covariance, can also bias base rate estimates, so it is an issue that no taxometric researcher can ignore.

## Developments in Taxometrics

Taxometric researchers are continually trying to improve the utility and robustness of the techniques. A recent addition is the use of simulated data to help disambiguate difficult curves. For example, Ruscio et al. (2004) have developed a procedure which produces two simulated data sets which mimic all the parameters of the input research data, except that one matches the correlation matrix using a two group latent structure derived from the best estimate of the base rate, and the other simulates the matrix with a latent dimension (i.e., factor). These simulated taxonic and dimensional structures can be examined, first to see if the two structures can be distinguished by the available indicators and second to see which one the research data more closely resembles. This technique seems to be particularly helpful with skewed data sets. We have used versions of this procedure in preparing this chapter.

## Software

At present there no commercial packages that perform taxometric analyses. There are, however, ready of sources of program code in print or freely downloadable from the web. All of these programs run under the S-Plus program or the public domain statistical language R. S-Plus and R are very similar in most respects, and it is usually possible to adapt programs for one to run under the other with minimum effort. The monograph by Waller and Meehl (1996) contains S-Plus source for all the procedures describe in their book. Ruscio has made S-Plus and R versions of his software, including his simulation procedures, freely available through the Elizabethtown college website (insert Elizabethtown college address). Similarly Waller has produced MAXCOV, MAXEIG L–mode and MAMBAC routines for R. The R language is a freely available open-source package. The latest version can be downloaded from http://cran.r-project.org/mirrors.htm or a local mirror site. S-Plus is a trademark of Statsoft Inc.

# The Future of Taxometrics

Our review of taxometric research shows that many important contributions have already been made, some of which challenge widely held beliefs about personality structure. Our brief discussion of taxometric methodology similarly shows that taxometric practice has continued to advance over the past decades, and that taxometric methods have performed well in simulation studies. For these reasons we are confident that taxometric research has a rosy future in the study of personality and psychopathology. We hope that researchers will continue to explore new personality variables, to replicate past findings with more sophisticated analyses, to test the performance of taxometric methods under a variety of statistical conditions and against a variety of alternative statistical methods, and to refine taxometric procedures. There is certainly a great deal of work to be done. In this section, we will briefly mention a few directions in which future taxometric research on personality might grow.

First, several domains of personality cry out for taxometric study. Perhaps the most important of these is the PDs. Although the categorical versus dimensional issue has been especially fraught in this domain, and has very real implications for the revision of diagnostic classification, only three of the ten recognized PDs have received any taxometric attention at all. Of these, there have been no studies of SPD itself, as distinct from schizotypy more broadly, and hence no direct investigation of whether the disorder, as identified by *DSM-IV*, is or is not taxonic. Only three published studies relevant to APD have appeared, and they have all been conducted by a single research group whose focus has been more on psychopathy or antisociality in general than on the PD. Only two studies have addressed BPD. Before any confident conclusions can be drawn about the latent structure of *DSM*'s Axis II, the seven remaining PDs must be examined, and studies of the three already investigated disorders thoroughly replicated. In all of this work, researchers will need to be heedful of indicator skewness and its effects.

Additional taxometric research on personality diatheses is also a priority. Precious little work has been done, and none at all for diatheses germane to disorders other than major depression, panic disorder, bipolar disorder, dissociative disorders, and schizophrenia. Much of the existing work is unreplicated or, in the case of anxiety sensitivity and depression-proneness, yields conflicting findings.

Within the domain of normal personality it is difficult to know where research priorities should be set. So much territory remains to be investigated, and so few existing findings have been replicated. Some of the early findings—self-monitoring and type A, for example—have not been revisited, although taxometric practice has advanced substantially since they were published. It remains to be seen whether some early findings stand up to scrutiny when more comprehensive analyses are conducted. In regard to new areas to explore, no one has yet conducted taxometric research on bridging constructs between cognition and personality—such as cognitive styles, coping or defense mechanisms, implicit theories, creativity, cognitive strategies, learning styles—that might attract the interest of a broader assortment of cognition, personality, and education researchers. Personality characteristics such as these deserve attention, particularly when there is a disagreement about how their latent structure should be conceptualized, or if questionable assessment practices are used to measure them (e.g., sorting people into classes where no taxon may exist). Finally, claims that three broad personality types—resilients, overcontrollers, and undercontrollers (Asendorpf, 2002)—can be derived from measures of the five-factor model by cluster analysis deserve taxometric attention.

However, the future of taxometric research should not simply involve the colonization of an ever-expanding range of personality variables. We need not only do more research, but better research. One aspect of better research, to which we have just nodded, is having a strong theoretical rationale. Just about any psychological variable can yield to taxometric analysis, but such analyses have little value if very little hinges on them, whether theoretically or practically. It is important for researchers to become more explicit about why it matters for the latent structure of personality to be investigated taxometrically. Unless clear implications for theory or assessment are laid out, it is hard to see why personality theorists and researchers should pay any heed to taxometric findings.

Another aspect of better research involves the use of better measures and better quantitative methods. Some taxometric analyses have been done using single self-report scales, with little concern for their limitations. Although self-report scales are important sources of information, they hardly exhaust the options available to personality researchers, and if they are to be used, efforts should be made to ensure that findings are not distorted by the particularities of a single scale. The failure to used interview-based assessments in most taxometric research on PDs is especially concerning, given the well-known limitations of self-report measures in this domain. With respect to quantitative methods, all researchers need to employ a number of distinct taxometric procedures in the spirit of Meehl's "consistency testing," a requirement that was often not honored in early studies. In addition, researchers need to ensure that the indicators that they use in their analyses are sufficiently valid to allow a powerful test of the latent structure of interest. Insufficient attention has been paid to this issue in some studies, and given that low-indicator validity sharply reduces the reliability of taxometric inference and biases analyses against finding taxa, it needs to be taken more seriously.

# Conclusions

The taxometric approach to the study of normal and abnormal personality is a powerful and exciting one. Taxometric studies have the capacity to support or challenge our basic assumptions about the nature of individual differences, and their findings have very real implications for personality theory and assessment. Knowing whether people differ in kind or by degree matters: it affects how we conceptualize what they are like, how they came to be that way, and how their differences should be registered by our measurement instruments. Taxometric methods offer a versatile toolkit for resolving this fundamental issue, and their use is growing steadily. Taxometrics is no longer a new approach, but it is increasingly influential and it has built up a large body of evidence about normal and abnormal personality. We hope that a new generation of taxometric researchers will continue to extend and deepen this work.

## REFERENCES

*American Psychiatric Association. (1994). Diagnostic and statistical manual of mental disorders* (4th ed.). Washington, DC: Author.

Arnau, R. C., Green, B. A., Rosen, D. H., Gleaves, D. H., & Melancon, J. G. (2003). Are Jungian preferences really categorical? An empirical investigation using taxometric analysis. *Personality and Individual Differences, 34*, 233–251.

Arnau, R. C., Green, B. A., & Tubre, T. (1999). *Taxometric analysis of Goldberg's five-factor markers.* Poster presented at the annual meeting of the Eastern Psychological Association, Providence, RI.

Asendorpf, J. (2002). Editorial: The puzzle of personality types. *European Journal of Personality, 16*, S1–S5.

Ayers, W., Haslam, N., Bernstein, D., Tryon, W. T., & Handelsman, L. (1999). *Categorical vs. dimensional models of personality disorder in substance abusers: A taxometric analysis.* Poster presented at the annual meeting of the American Psychiatric Association.

Beauchaine, T. P. (2003). Taxometrics and developmental psychopathology. *Development and Psychopathology, 15*, 501–527.

Beauchaine, T. P., & Waters, E. (2003). Pseudotaxonicity in MAMBAC and MAXCOV analyses of rating scale data: Turning continua into classes by manipulating observers' expectations. *Psychological Methods, 8*, 3-15.

Blanchard, J. J., Gangestad, S. W., Brown, S. A., & Horan, W. P. (2000). Hedonic capacity and schizotypy revisited: A taxometric analysis of social anhedonia. *Journal of Abnormal Psychology, 109*, 87–95.

Costa, P. T., & Widiger, T. A. (Eds). (2002). *Personality disorders and the five factor model of personality* (2nd ed.). Washington, DC: American Psychological Association.

Erlenmeyer-Kimling, L., Golden, R. R., & Cornblatt, B. A. (1989). A taxonometric analysis of cognitive and neuromotor variables in children at risk for schizophrenia. *Journal of Abnormal Psychology, 98*, 203–208.

Fraley, R. C., & Spieker, S. J. (2003). Are infant attachment patterns continuously or categorically distributed? A taxometric analysis of strange situation behavior. *Developmental Psychology, 39*, 387–404.

Fraley, R. C., & Waller, N. G. (1998). Adult attachment patterns: A test of the typological model. In J. A. Simpson, & W. S. Rholes (Eds.), *Attachment theory and close relationships* (pp. 77–114). New York: Guilford Press.

Gangestad, S. W., Bailey, J. M., & Martin, N. G. (2000). Taxometric analyses of sexual orientation and gender identity. *Journal of Personality and Social Psychology, 78*, 1109–1121.

Gangestad, S. W., & Snyder, M. (1985). "To carve nature at its joints": On the existence of discrete classes in personality. *Psychological Review, 92*, 317–349.

Gibb, B. E., Alloy, L. B., Abramson, L. Y., Beevers, C. G., & Miller, I. W. (2004). Cognitive vulnerability to depression: A taxometric analysis. *Journal of Abnormal Psychology, 113*, 81–89.

Golden, R. R., & Meehl, P. E. (1979). Detection of the schizoid taxon with MMPI indicators. *Journal of Abnormal Psychology, 88*, 217–233.

Green, B. A., Arnau, R. C., & Gleaves, D. H. (1999). *Taxometric analysis of the five-factor model constructs.* Poster presented at the annual meeting of the American Psychological Association, Boston, MA.

Grove, W. M., & Meehl, P. E. (1993). Simple regression-based procedures for taxometric investigations. *Psychological Reports, 73*, 707–737.

Harris, G. T., Rice, M. E., & Quinsey, V. L. (1994). Psychopathy as a taxon: Evidence that psychopaths are a discrete class. *Journal of Consulting and Clinical Psychology, 62*, 387–397.

Haslam, N. (1997). Evidence that male sexual orientation is a matter of degree. *Journal of Personality and Social Psychology, 73*, 862–870.

Haslam, N. (2003). The dimensional view of personality disorders: A review of the taxometric evidence. *Clinical Psychology Review, 23*, 75–93.

Haslam, N., & Cleland, C. (1996). Robustness of taxometric analysis with skewed indicators: II. A Monte Carlo study of the MAXCOV procedure. *Psychological Reports, 79*, 1035–1039.

Haslam, N., & Kim, H. (2002). Categories and continua: A review of taxometric research. *Genetic, Social and General Psychology Monographs, 128,* 271–320.

Kagan, J. (1994). *Galen's prophecy.* New York: Basic.

Keller, F., Jahn, T., & Klein, C. (2001). Applications of taxometric methods and mixture distribution models for the assessment of schizotypy. In B. Andresen & R. Mass (Eds.), *Schizotypie: Psychometrische entwicklungen und biopsychologische forschungsatze schizotypy* (pp. 391–412). Gottingen, Germany: Hogrefe.

Kendell, R. A. (1975). *The role of diagnosis in psychiatry.* Oxford: Blackwell Scientific.

Korfine, L., & Lenzenweger, M. F. (1995). The taxonicity of schizotypy: A replication. *Journal of Abnormal Psychology, 104,* 26–31.

Lenzenweger, M. F. (1999). Deeper into the schizotypy taxon: On the robust nature of maximum covariance analysis. *Journal of Abnormal Psychology, 108,* 182–187.

Lenzenweger, M. F., & Korfine, L. (1992). Confirming the latent structure and base rate of schizotypy: A taxometric analysis. *Journal of Abnormal Psychology, 101,* 567–571.

Livesley, W. J. (1996). Commentary of "Epistemic value commitments". *Philosophy, Psychiatry, and Psychology, 3,* 223–226.

Livesley, W. J., Schroeder, M. L., Jackson, D. N., & Jang, K. L. (1994). Categorical distinctions in the study of personality disorder: Implications for classification. *Journal of Abnormal Psychology, 103,* 6–17.

Lowrie, G. S., & Raulin, M. L. (1990). *Search for schizotypic and nonschizotypic taxonomies in a college population.* Paper presented at the Sixty-First Annual Convention of the Eastern Psychological Association, Philadelphia, PA.

McCrae, R. R. (1994). A reformulation of axis II: Personality and personality related problems. In P. T. Costa, & T. A. Widiger (Eds.), *Personality disorders and the five-factor model of personality* (pp. 303–310). Washington, DC: American Psychological Association.

Meehl, P. E. (1962). Schizotaxia, schizotypy, schizophrenia. *American Psychologist, 17,* 827–838.

Meehl, P. E. (1990). Toward an integrated theory of schizotaxia, schizotypy, and schizophrenia. *Journal of Personality Disorders, 4,* 1–99.

Meehl, P. E. (1992). Factors and taxa, traits and types, differences of degree and differences in kind. *Journal of Personality, 60,* 117–174.

Meehl, P. E. (1995). Bootstrap taxometrics: Solving the classification problem in psychopathology. *American Psychologist, 50,* 266–275.

Meehl, P. E., & Yonce, L. J. (1994). Taxometric analysis: I. Detecting taxonicity with two quantitative indicators using means above and below a sliding cut (MAMBAC procedure). *Psychological Reports, 74,* 1059–1274.

Meyer, T., & Keller, F. (2001). Exploring the latent structure of the Perceptual Aberration, Magical Ideation and Physical Anhedonia Scales in a German sample—A partial replication. *Journal of Personality Disorders, 15,* 521–535.

Meyer, T., & Keller, F. (2003). Is there evidence for a latent class called "hypomanic temperament"? *Journal of Affective Disorders, 75,* 259–267.

Murphy, E. A. (1964). One cause? Many causes? The argument from the bimodal distribution. *Journal of Chronic Disease, 17,* 301–324.

Nakao, K., Gunderson, J. D., Phillips, K. A., Tanaka, N., Yorifuji, K., Takaishi, J., & Nashimura, N. (1992). Functional impairment in personality disorders. *Journal of Personality Disorders, 6,* 24–33.

Oakman, J. M., & Woody, E. Z. (1996). A taxometric analysis of hypnotic susceptibility. *Journal of Personality and Social Psychology, 71,* 980–991.

Rothschild, L., Cleland, C., Haslam, N., & Zimmerman, M. (2003). Taxometric analysis of borderline personality disorder. *Journal of Abnormal Psychology, 112,* 657–666.

Ruscio, J., Haslam, N., & Ruscio, A. M. (2006). *Introduction to the taxometric method: A practical guide.* Mahwah, NJ: Erlbaum.

Ruscio, J., & Ruscio, A. M. (2002). A structure-based approach to psychological assessment: Matching measurement models to latent structure. *Assessment, 9,* 4–16.

Ruscio, J., & Ruscio, A. M. (2004). A conceptual and methodological checklist for conducting a taxometric investigation. *Behavior Therapy, 35,* 403–447.

Ruscio, J., Ruscio, A. M., Keane, T. M. (2004). Using taxometric analysis to distinguish a small latent taxon from a latent dimension with positively skewed indicators: The case of involuntary defeat syndrome. *Journal of Abnormal Psychology, 113,* 145–154.

Schmidt, N. B., Kotov, R., Lerew, D. R., Joiner, T. E., & Ialongo, N. S. (in press). Evaluating latent discontinuity in cognitive vulnerability to panic: A taxometric investigation. *Cognitive Therapy and Research.*

Simpson, W. B. (1994). *Borderline personality disorder: Dimension or category? A maximum covariance analysis.* Unpublisheddoctoral dissertation, Boston University.

Skilling, T. A., Harris, G. T., Rice, M. T., & Quinsey, V. L. (2001). Identifying persistently antisocial offenders using the Hare Psychopathy Checklist and DSM IV antisocial personality disorder criteria. *Psychological Assessment, 14,* 27–38.

Skilling, T. A., Quinsey, V. L., & Craig, W. M. (2001). Evidence of a taxon underlying serious antisocial behavior in boys. *Criminal Justice and Behavior, 28,* 450–470.

Stern, H. S., Arcus, D., Kagan, J., Rubin, D. B., & Snidman, N. (1995). Using mixture models in temperament research. *International Journal of Behavioral Development, 18,* 407–423.

Strong, D. R., Brown, R. A., Kahler, C. W., Lloyd-Richardson, E. E., & Niaura, R. (2004). Depression proneness in treatment-seeking smokers: A taxometric analysis. *Personality and Individual Differences, 36,* 1155–1170.

Strong, D. R., Greene, R. L., Hoppe, C., Johnston, T., & Olesen, N. (1999). Taxometric analysis of impression management and self-deception on the MMPI-2 in child-custody litigants. *Journal of Personality Assessment, 73,* 1–18.

Strong, D. R., Greene, R. L., & Schinka, J. A. (2000). Taxometric analysis of the MMPI-2 Infrequency scales [F and F(p)] in clinical settings. *Psychological Assessment, 12,* 166–173.

Strube, M. J. (1989). Evidence for the type in type A behavior: A taxometric analysis. *Journal of Personality and Social Psychology, 56,* 972–987.

Taylor, S., Rabian, B., & Fedoroff, I. C. (1999). Anxiety sensitivity: Progress, prospects, and challenges. In S. Taylor (Ed.), *Anxiety sensitivity: Theory, research, and treatment of the fear of anxiety* (pp. 339–353). Mahwah, NJ: Erlbaum.

Trull, T. J., Widiger, T. A., & Guthrie, P. (1990). Categorical versus dimensional status of borderline personality disorder. *Journal of Abnormal Psychology, 99,* 40–48.

Tyrka, A., Cannon, T. D., Haslam, N., Mednick, S. A., Schulsinger, F., Schulsinger, H., & Parnas, J. (1995a). The latent structure of schizotypy: I. Premorbid indicators of a taxon of individuals at risk for schizophrenia-spectrum disorders. *Journal of Abnormal Psychology, 104,* 173–183.

Tyrka, A., Haslam, N., & Cannon, T. D. (1995b). Detection of a longitudinally stable taxon of individuals at risk for schizophrenia spectrum disorders. In A. Raine, T. Lencz, & S. A. Mednick (Eds.), *Schizotypal personality disorder* (pp.168–191). New York: Cambridge University Press.

Waller, N. G., & Meehl, P. E. (1998). *Multivariate taxometric procedures: Distinguishing types from continua.* Thousand Oaks, CA: Sage.

Widiger, T. A., & Clark, L. A. (2000). Toward DSM-V and the classification of psychopathology. *Psychological Bulletin, 126,* 946–963.

Woodward, S. A., Lenzenweger, M. F., Kagan, J., Snidman, N., & Arcus, D. (2000). Taxonic structure of infant reactivity: Evidence from a taxometric perspective. *Psychological Science, 11,* 296–301.

# 3

# Measurement and Assessment

# Assessment of Maladaptive Personality Traits

**13**

Thomas A. Widiger
Paul T. Costa Jr.
Douglas B. Samuel

The purpose of this chapter is to provide recommendations for the assessment of maladaptive personality traits. We consider not only the general method for assessing personality disorders, but also which individual instrument(s) to use. We consider instruments that have been developed to assess general personality structure (as well as instruments to assess personality disorder) because these instruments include maladaptive personality traits. Instruments to assess general personality structure can provide a more comprehensive assessment than instruments confined to the assessment of personality disorders, and the actual boundary between adaptive and maladaptive personality functioning is, at best, unclear.

The primary methods available to clinicians and researchers for the assessment of maladaptive personality traits are unstructured clinical interviews, semistructured clinical interviews, structured interviews, self-report inventories, and projective tests. A structured interview provides a systematic assessment by standardizing the questions used by an interviewer, the sequencing of these questions, and the scoring of the responses (Rogers, 2001). Structured interviews provide little to no allowance for deviation from the specified procedures (e.g., little to no follow-up queries are allowed). Many structured interviews are so straightforward that they can be administered and scored by lay persons.

Large-scale epidemiologic studies generally use structured interviews because of the substantial savings that are provided by the opportunity to employ lay persons to conduct the assessments. The Diagnostic Interview Schedule (DIS; Leaf, Myers, & McEvoy, 1991) is a structured interview that was used by the National Institute of Mental Health (NIMH) for the extensive Epidemiologic Catchment Area study.

The DIS included an assessment of the antisocial personality disorder. No large-scale epidemiologic study has included an assessment of all of the personality disorders in part because of the large number of diagnostic criteria that would need to be assessed and because it has been generally assumed that "for some disorders—particularly the personality disorders, the criteria require much more inference on the part of the observer" (American Psychiatric Association, 1987, p. xxiii). However, the recently completed National Epidemiologic Survey on Alcohol and Related Conditions included a face-to-face structured interview of 43,093 persons to assess the antisocial, avoidant, dependent, obsessive-compulsive, histrionic, and paranoid personality disorders (Grant, Stinson, Dawson, Chou, & Ruan, 2005).

A semistructured interview is a modified version of a structured interview. Semistructured interviews provide a standard set of questions that generally must be administered in a specified sequence, along with explicit rules for scoring responses. However, they also encourage the provision of follow-up queries that can be worded in a manner that is idiosyncratic to the interviewer; they might allow the exclusion of questions when the interviewer judges them to be unnecessary to render a confident assessment; and they often require the scoring of some diagnostic criteria on the basis of the interviewer's visual observation of the respondent. Structured interview questions are generally phrased in a manner that the scoring of the response will be unambiguous (e.g., questions that can be answered by "yes" or "no"). Semistructured interviews, in contrast, will include open-ended questions, the responses to which can be idiosyncratic to the respondent and complex in content.

An unstructured interview consists of a series of questions that were selected by the interviewer. The content, wording, and sequencing of unstructured interview questions will generally be idiosyncratic to the interviewer and will be unspecified prior and subsequent to the interview. Unstructured interviews need not be consistent across respondents even when administered by the same person.

Self-report inventories consist of written statements, adjectives, or questions, to which a person responds in terms of a specified set of options (e.g., true or false, or agree vs. disagree along a 5-point scale). Projective tests consist of relatively ambiguous stimuli or probes, the possible responses to which are largely open-ended. The use of projective tests, such as the Rorschach and the Thematic Apperception Test, will not be considered in this chapter as there is currently no comprehensive or consistently used scoring system of a projective test for the diagnosis of personality disorders, and there is currently only limited research on the use of projective tests for the assessment of most of the *DSM-IV* (*Diagnostic and Statistical Manual of Mental Disorders*, 1994) personality disorders. There is empirical support for the Rorschach oral dependency score (Bornstein, 1999; Wood, Garb, Lilienfeld, & Nezworski, 2002) and effort is being given to the development of a scoring system that would cover all of the personality disorders (Huprich, 2005).

# Assessment Strategy

For the purpose of obtaining an accurate assessment of personality disorder, a general assessment strategy that we recommend in clinical practice is to first administer a self-report inventory to alert oneself to the potential presence of particular maladaptive personality traits, followed by the administration of a semistructured interview to verify and document the presence of these traits (Widiger, 2002; Widiger & Samuel, in press). This integrative strategy is guided by existing evidence suggesting particular strengths of self-report inventories and semistructured interviews, relative to a reliance on unstructured clinical interviews.

## Semistructured Interviews

The predominant method for the assessment of personality disorders in general clinical practice is an unstructured clinical interview (Watkins, Campbell, Nieberding, & Hallmark, 1995; Westen, 1997), whereas the preferred method for research is the semistructured interview (Rogers, 2001; Segal & Coolidge, 2003; Zimmerman, 2003). Semistructured interviews have several advantages over unstructured interviews (Kaye & Shea, 2000; Rogers, 2003). Semistructured interviews ensure and document that a systematic and comprehensive assessment of each personality disorder diagnostic criterion has been made. This documentation can be particularly helpful in situations in which the credibility or validity of the assessment might be questioned, such as forensic or disability evaluations. Semistructured interviews also increase the likelihood of reliable and replicable assessments (Farmer, 2000; Rogers, 2001, 2003; Segal & Coolidge, 2003; Wood et al., 2002). Semistructured interviews provide specific, carefully selected questions for the assessment of each diagnostic criterion, the application of which increases the likelihood that assessments will be consistent across interviewers. In addition, the manuals that often accompany a semistructured interview frequently provide a considerable amount of helpful information for understanding the rationale of each diagnostic criterion, for interpreting vague or inconsistent symptoms, and for resolving diagnostic ambiguities (e.g., Loranger, 1999; Widiger, Mangine, Corbitt, Ellis, & Thomas, 1995).

## Unstructured Interviews

Studies have consistently indicated that assessments based on unstructured clinical interviews do not consider all of the necessary or important diagnostic criteria (Blashfield & Herkov, 1996; Garb, 2005; Zimmerman & Mattia, 1999). Studies have also indicated that personality disorder assessments in the absence of structured clinical interviews are often unreliable (Garb, 2005; Mellsop, Varghese, Joshua, & Hicks, 1982). Clinicians tend to diagnose personality disorders hierarchically, failing to assess additional symptoms, once they reach a conclusion that a particular personality disorder is present (Adler, Drake, & Teague, 1990; Blashfield & Flanagan, 1998; Herkov & Blashfield, 1995). The identified personality disorder may even be based on idiosyncratic interests (Mellsop et al., 1982).

Researchers would be hard pressed to get findings published if they failed to document that their diagnoses were based on a systematic, replicable, and objective method, yet no such requirements are currently provided for clinical diagnoses, with the exception of mental retardation and learning disorders (American Psychiatric Association, 2000). A recommendation of the American Psychiatric Association (APA) and the NIMH *DSM-V* Nomenclature Work Group is to consider incorporating more structured assessments into the *DSM-V* criterion sets to require that they be assessed systematically. "At present, results of psychological testing are not included in *DSM-IV* diagnostic criteria, with the exception of IQ testing and academic skills—[and] this exception points the way for research that could lead to incorporation of psychological test results as diagnostic criteria for other disorders" (Rounsaville et al., 2002, p. 24). Few clinicians would attempt to diagnose mental retardation in the absence of a structured test, yet no structured assessment is required for the diagnosis of most other mental disorders. A proposal for *DSM-V* is to make comparable requirements for the diagnosis of the anxiety, mood, personality, and other mental disorders (Rounsaville et al., 2002; Widiger & Clark, 2000).

Advocates of unstructured clinical interviews raise the compelling criticism that semistructured interviews can degenerate into mindless symptom-counting that does not adequately consider the context of a maladaptive behavior in a broader life history (Westen, 1997). An alternative to the semistructured interview is provided by the Shedler-Westen Assessment Procedure-200 (SWAP-200), which is described as "a method for studying personality and personality pathology that strives to capture the richness and complexity of psychoanalytic constructs and formulations without forsaking the benefits of empirical rigor" (Shedler, 2002, p. 429). The SWAP-200 consists of 200 items (e.g., "tends to be angry or hostile, whether consciously or unconsciously" and "is unable to soothe or comfort self when distressed; requires involvement of another person to help regulate affect;" Westen & Shedler, 2005, pp. 247–248) drawn from the psychoanalytic and personality disorder literature, as well as the *DSM-IV* diagnostic criterion sets (Shedler, 2002; Westen & Shedler, 1999a). SWAP-200 items are rated by a clinician on an 8-point scale in a manner that conforms to a specified distribution. The typical distribution used for the SWAP-200 is to require that half (100) of the items receive a score of 0 (least descriptive), 20 receive a score of 1, 18 receive a score of 2, 16 a score of 3, 14 a score of 4, 12 a score of 5, 10 a score of 6, and only 8 can receive the highest score of 7. SWAP-200 items are not sorted into this specified distribution on the basis of a series of questions administered via a semistructured interview; instead, the SWAP-200 relies on "the empathically attuned and dynamically sophisticated clinician given free rein to practice his or her craft" (Shedler, 2002, p. 433).

Initial research with the SWAP-200 has reported good to excellent convergent and discriminant validity (e.g., Westen & Shedler, 1999b; Westen, Shedler, Durrett, Glass, & Martens, 2003). The positive results obtained with the SWAP-200 are encouraging. However, a consideration of these findings should be tempered by methodological limitations of much of the initial research. For example, clinicians who have provided validity data have generally been the same persons who have provided the SWAP-200 ratings (e.g., Shedler & Westen, 2004; Westen & Shedler, 1999b; Westen et al., 2003). This is comparable to having semistructured interviewers provide the criterion diagnoses in a study addressing the validity of the semistructured interview. It might not be a particularly stringent test of the validity of an interview to determine whether the interviewer's ratings are in agreement with the diagnostic conclusions of the interviewer. An additional methodological concern is the guidelines for the distribution of the ratings. For example, only eight of the 200 SWAP-200 items can be given the highest rankings (e.g., Westen & Shedler, 1999b) no matter the opinions of the raters or the symptoms present. If a clinician has provided a patient with the highest rating of 7 for 12 SWAP-200 items, the clinician is presented with a list of these 12 items and is told to shift four to a lower rating. It is perhaps not surprising that clinicians often shift out of this list those items that are least convergent with the other items. Half of the 200 SWAP-200 items have to be provided the lowest possible score. Convergent and discriminant validity of a semistructured interview would also be improved dramatically if interviewers were instructed to code half of the diagnostic criteria as absent and to identify only a few of the diagnostic criteria as present.

## Self-Report Inventories

The complete administration of a semistructured personality disorder interview generally requires 1–2 hours, with some as long as 4 hours (e.g., IPDE; Loranger, 1999). Hence, it is understandable that clinicians are reluctant to administer an entire semistructured interview. We therefore recommend that one first administers a self-report inventory to identify the principle areas of normal and abnormal personality functioning that warrants additional consideration with a subsequent semistructured interview (Widiger, 2002; Widiger & Samuel, in press). Brief screening questionnaires can also be used, although there is little advantage in using a screening instrument rather than an inventory constructed to provide a comprehensive and valid assessment.

Self-report inventories are also useful in alerting clinicians to maladaptive personality functioning that might otherwise be missed due to false expectations or assumptions, such as failing to notice antisocial personality traits in female patients (Garb, 2005). A further advantage of a well-validated self-report inventory is the presence of normative data to facilitate interpretation. A substantial amount of normative data have been obtained and reported for some of the self-report inventories (e.g., Colligan, Morey, & Offord, 1994; Costa & McCrae, 1992; Millon, Millon, & Davis, 1997).

# Which Instruments to Use?

Quite a few inventories and interviews that would be useful to clinicians for assessing normal and abnormal personality functioning have been developed. A complete summary is beyond the scope of this chapter, but several extensive reviews exist (e.g., Clark & Harrison, 2001; Farmer, 2000; Hilsenroth, Segal, & Hersen, 2004; Kaye & Shea, 2000; McDermut & Zimmerman, 2005; Rogers, 2001; Segal & Coolidge, 2003; Widiger, 2002; Widiger & Coker, 2002).

There are five semistructured interviews for the assessment of the 10 *DSM-IV* (American Psychiatric Association, 2000) personality disorders: (a) Diagnostic Interview for Personality Disorders (DIPD; Zanarini, Frankenburg, Chauncey, & Gunderson, 1987); (b) International Personality Disorder Examination (IPDE; Loranger, 1999); (c) Personality Disorder Interview-IV (PDI-IV; Widiger et.al., 1995); (d) Structured Clinical Interview for *DSM-IV* Axis II Personality Disorders (SCID-II; First & Gibbon, 2004); and (e) Structured Interview for *DSM-IV* Personality Disorders (SIDP-IV; Pfohl, Blum, & Zimmerman, 1997). There are also additional interviews for the assessment of individual personality disorders, such as (but not limited to) the Revised Diagnostic Interview for Borderlines (DIB-R; Zanarini et al., 1989), the Diagnostic Interview for Narcissism (DIN; Gunderson, Ronningstam, & Bodkin, 1990), and the Hare Psychopathy Checklist-Revised (PCL-R; Hare, 2003). There is currently only one semistructured interview for the assessment of general personality functioning, the Structured Interview for the Five-Factor Model (SIFFM; Trull & Widiger, 1997).

There are six commonly used inventories for the assessment of the *DSM-IV* personality disorders: (a) Minnesota Multiphasic Personality Inventory-2 (MMPI-2) personality disorder scales developed originally by Morey, Waugh, and Blashfield (1985) but revised for the MMPI-2 by Colligan et al. (1994); (b) Millon Clinical Multiaxial Inventory-III (Millon et al., 1997); (c) Personality Diagnostic Questionnaire-4 (PDQ-4; Bagby & Farvolden, 2004); (d) Personality Assessment Inventory (PAI; Morey & Boggs, 2004); (e) Wisconsin Personality Disorders Inventory (WISPI; Klein et al., 1993); and (f) Coolidge Axis II Inventory (CATI; Coolidge & Merwin, 1992); as well as questionnaires and rating forms to assess various components of adaptive and maladaptive personality functioning, including the Dimensional Assessment of Personality Disorder Pathology-Basic Questionnaire (DAPP-BQ; Livesley & Jackson, in press), Eysenck Personality Questionnaire-Revised (EPQ-R; Eysenck & Eysenck, 1991), Millon Index of Personality Styles (Millon, 1994; Strack, 2005), Multidimensional Personality Questionnaire (MPQ; Tellegen, in press), OMNI Personality Inventory (OMNI; Loranger, 2001), Personality Assessment Form (PAF; Pilkonis, Heape, Ruddy, & Serrao, 1991), Personality Psychopathology-Five (PSY-5; Harkness, McNulty, & Ben-Porath, 1995), Revised NEO Personality Inventory (NEO PI-R; Costa & McCrae, 1992), Schedule for Nonadaptive and Adaptive Personality Functioning (SNAP; Clark, Simms, Wu, & Casillas, in press), Structural Analysis of Social Behavior (SASB; Benjamin, 1988), Shedler-Westen Assessment Procedure (SWAP-200; Shedler, 2002), and Temperament and Character Inventory (TCI; Cloninger, Przybeck, Svrakic, & Wetzel, 1994).

Table 13.1 provides a comparative listing of most of these instruments, along with a brief indication of their potential advantages and potential disadvantages. Further below, we discuss our characterization of some of the advantages and disadvantages of each instrument with respect to the general issues of (a) personality disorder conceptualization, (b) degree of structure, (c) guidance for interpretation, and (d) diagnosis.

## Personality Disorder Conceptualization

Most of the instruments listed in Table 13.1 are concerned explicitly with the assessment of the *DSM-IV* personality disorder diagnostic criterion sets (American Psychiatric Association, 2000). However, also included within Table 13.1 are instruments developed for the assessment of general personality functioning that can be used to assess maladaptive personality traits. Existing research has indicated that there are maladaptive personality traits of interest to clinicians that are not included within the diagnostic manual (Verheul & Widiger, 2004; Westen & Arkowitz-Westen, 1998). Many (if not all) of these additional traits can perhaps be found within instruments that assess general personality functioning (Widiger & Simonsen, 2005). In addition, clinicians concerned with the boundary between normal and abnormal personality functioning might find it useful to include instruments that assess the primary traits of general personality structure.

The OMNI and the SNAP are unique as they include separate scales for the assessment of normal and abnormal personality functioning. The OMNI includes 25 scales to assess normal personality traits (e.g., aestheticism, dutifulness, and assertiveness), 10 scales to assess the *DSM-IV* personality disorders, and 7 higher order scales derived from joint factor analyses of the normal and abnormal scales. The seven higher order factors are empirically derived higher order constructs (i.e., agreeableness, conscientiousness, extraversion, narcissism, neuroticism, openness, and sensation-seeking) that

Table
13.1

## Instruments for the Assessment of Personality Disorders

| Title and Citation | Acronym | Fmt | Length | Coverage | Advantages | Potential Disadvantages |
|---|---|---|---|---|---|---|
| Coolidge Axis II Inventory; Coolidge & Merwin (1992) | CATI | SRI | 200 | *DSM-III-R* PD diagnostic criteria | Items coordinated with *DSM* criteria; includes validity & a few Axis I scales | Limited empirical support; not revised for *DSM-IV* |
| Diagnostic Interview for Narcissism; Gunderson et al. (1990) | DIN | SSI | 105[a] | Narcissistic PD symptoms | Subscales for components of narcissistic symptomatology; only SSI devoted to narcissism | Substantial amount of time to assess for one PD |
| Diagnostic Interview for Personality Disorders Zanarini et al. (1987) | DIPD | SSI | 398[a] | *DSM-IV* PD diagnostic criteria | Empirical support; less expensive other PD SSIs | Used less frequently than other PD SSIs; manual is limited with respect to scoring guidelines |
| Dimensional Assessment of Personality Disorder Pathology; Livesley & Jackson (in press) | DAPP-BQ | SRI | 290 | PD symptoms | Precise coverage of components of *DSM-IV* PDs | Absence of *DSM-IV* PD scales; absence of validity scales |
| Eysenck Personality Questionnaire–Revised; Eysenck & Eysenck (1991) | EPQ-R | SRI | 100 | Three broad personality dimensions | Heavily researched; rich theoretical model | Ability of -three broad traits to adequately account for personality disorders is unclear |
| Hare Psychopathy Checklist–Revised; Hare (2003) | PCL-R | CRI | Unclear | Psychopathy | Substantial empirical support; covers more aspects of psychopathy than *DSM-IV* | As much a checklist as an interview; relies heavily on legal record |

*(continued)*

317

Table
13.1

**(Continued)**

| Title and Citation | Acronym | Fmt | Length | Coverage | Advantages | Potential Disadvantages |
|---|---|---|---|---|---|---|
| International Personality Disorder Examination Loranger (1999) | IPDE | SSI | 537[a] | *DSM-IV* and ICD-10 criteria | Jointly assesses for ICD-10 PDs; good empirical support | More time-consuming than other PD SSI's; relies on DSM-IV questions to assess for ICD-10 criteria |
| Millon Clinical Multiaxial Inventory–III Millon et al. (1994) | MCMI-III | SRI | 175 | *DSM-IV* PDs | Empirical support; includes validity and Axis I scales | Relatively expensive; hand-scoring impractical; problematic for higher functioning samples; gender bias |
| Millon Index of Personality Styles Millon (1994) | MIPS | SRI | 180 | Normal traits | Rich theoretical model; validity scales | Empirical relationship to personality disorders is unclear |
| Minnesota Multiphasic Personality Inventory–2 Colligan et al. (1994) | MMPI-2 | SRI | 157[b] | *DSM-III* PDs | Embedded within MMPI-2 | May require administration of all 567 MMPI-2 items; unvalidated cut-off points; possible gender bias |
| Multidimensional Personality Questionnaire Tellegen (in press) | MPQ | SRI | 276 | Normal & abnormal traits | Empirical support; includes traits that may facilitate treatment; validity scales | Coverage of *DSM-IV* personality disorder symptoms is unclear |
| NEO Personality Inventory–Revised Costa & McCrae (1992) | NEO PI-R | SRI | 240 | Normal & abnormal traits | Substantial empirical support; includes traits that may facilitate treatment | Emphasis on assessment of normal personality traits; validity scales are experimental |
| Omnibus Personality Inventory; Loranger (2001) | OMNI | SRI | 375 | Normal and abnormal traits | Comprehensive coverage within integrated model | Limited empirical support |

| Instrument | Abbreviation | Type | Items | Assesses | Strengths | Limitations |
|---|---|---|---|---|---|---|
| Personality Assessment Form; Pilkonis et al. (1991) | PAF | CRI | 13[c] | DSM-III-R PDs | Requires no systematic interview | Absence of interview questions to ensure systematic and consistent assessments |
| Personality Assessment Inventory; Morey (1991) | PAI | SRI | 344 | DSM-III-R PDs | Subscales for borderline and antisocial PDs; psychometrically strong; Axis I and validity scales | Absence of scales for eight of the PDs; not revised for DSM-IV |
| Personality Diagnostic Questionnaire—4 Hyler et al. (1988) | PDQ-4 | SRI | 99 | DSM-IV PD diagnostic criteria | Brief and inexpensive; item(s) for each DSM-IV PD criterion; used frequently | Psychometrically weak; inconsistent empirical support |
| Personality Disorders Interview-IV Widiger et al. (1995) | PDI-IV | SSI | 325[a] | DSM-IV PD diagnostic criteria | Empirical support; manual provides detailed rationale and guidelines for each diagnostic criterion | Used less frequently than SIDP-IV, IPDE, or SCID-II |
| Personality Psychopathology–5 Harkness et al. (1995) | PSY-5 | SRI | 139 | Personality disorder symptoms | Embedded within MMPI-2; validity scales | Limited usage; requires administration of complete MMPI-2; only five broad scales |
| Revised Diagnostic Interview for Borderlines Zanarini et al. (1989) | DIB-R | SSI | 106[a] | Borderline PD symptoms | Subscales for components of borderline symptomatology; good empirical support | Original DIB at times preferred over DIB-R; substantial amount of time to assess for one PD |
| Schedule for Nonadaptive and Adaptive Personality Clark (1993) | SNAP | SRI | 375 | PD symptoms and three temperaments | Precise coverage of components of DSM-IV PDs; validity scales | Ability of the three temperament scales to account for personality disorders is unclear |
| Shedler–Westen Assessment Procedure Westen & Shedler (1999a) | SWAP-200 | CRI Qsrt | 200[c] | Abnormal traits symptoms, & defenses | Requires no systematic interview; includes psychodynamic items | Susceptible to halo effects; forced distribution of items; Q-sorting can require substantial time |

*(continued)*

**Table 13.1** (Continued)

| Title and Citation | Acronym | Fmt | Length | Coverage | Advantages | Potential Disadvantages |
|---|---|---|---|---|---|---|
| Structured Clinical Interview for *DSM-IV* Axis II Personality Disorders; First & Gibbon (2004) | SCID-II | SSI | 303[a] | *DSM-IV* PD diagnostic criteria | Screening questionnaire available; empirical support; coordinated with Axis I interview | Perhaps more superficial in questions than most other SSI's; manual limited in its coverage |
| Structured Interview for *DSM-IV* Personality Disorders; Pfohl et al. (1997) | SIDP-IV | SSI | 337[a] | *DSM-IV* and ICD-10 criteria | Good empirical support; support for training | Manual is limited in its instructions for scoring of responses |
| Structured Interview for the Five-Factor Model Trull & Widiger (1997) | SIFFM | SSI | 240[a] | Normal & abnormal traits | Empirical support; includes traits that may facilitate treatment; only SSI for dimensional model | Absence of *DSM-IV* PD scales; limited usage |
| Temperament and Character Inventory Cloninger et al. (1994) | TCI | SRI | 240 | Normal & abnormal traits | Empirical support; assesses temperament and character dimensions; validity scales | Support for theoretical model is unclear |
| Wisconsin Personality Disorders Inventory Klein et al. (1993) | WISPI | SRI | 214 | *DSM-III-R* PD diagnostic criteria | Coordinated with interpersonal, object-relational theory; item(s) for each PD diagnostic criterion | Limited usage; some items involve complex concepts; not revised for *DSM-IV* |

*Note:* FMT = format; Length = relative estimate of length of instrument (for SRIs = number of items; for SSIs = approximate number of questions administered; for CRIs = number of constructs assessed); SRI = self-report inventory; SSI = semistructured interview; CRI = clinician-report inventory; Qsrt = Q-sort; *DSM = Diagnostic and Statistical Manual of Mental Disorder*, either *DSM-III, DSM-III-R,* or *DSM-IV* (American Psychiatric Association, 1980, 1987); ICD-10 = International Classification of Diseases (World Health Organization, 1992).

[a]Number provided for semistructured interviews are only an approximation of number of questions provided in interview form; actual number of questions administered will vary depending upon items or questions skipped during interview and additional, follow-up inquiries that might be administered. Many SSI's also require additional observational ratings (e.g., 32 specified for IPDE, 19 for DIPD-IV, 16 for SIDP-IV, 7 for SCID-II, and 3 for PDI-IV).

[b]MMPI-2 includes 567 items, but Morey et al. (1985) PD scale uses only 157 of them.

[c]Number of constructs assessed by interviewer; actual number of questions provided by an interviewer to assess these constructs will vary substantially.

integrate the normal and abnormal scales within a common hierarchical model. The SNAP, in a similar fashion, also includes 12 scales to assess maladaptive personality traits (e.g., mistrust, detachment, self-harm) and three additional scales that assess three broad personality domains of negative temperament, positive temperament, and disinhibition. However, unlike the OMNI, the three broad personality scales of the SNAP are not higher order factors of the abnormal personality scales. The SNAP normal and abnormal personality scales are independent in their construction and content.

Livesley's (2003) DAPP-BQ was developed in a manner comparable to the development of the 12 SNAP personality disorder symptom scales. Livesley first obtained personality disorder symptoms and features from a thorough content analysis of the literature. An initial list of criteria was then coded by clinicians, with respect to their prototypicality for respective personality disorders. One hundred scales (each with 16 items) were submitted to a series of factor analyses to derive a set of 18 fundamental dimensions of personality disorder that cut across the existing diagnostic categories (e.g., anxiousness, self-harm, intimacy problems, social avoidance, passive opposition, and interpersonal disesteem). Additional analyses indicate that these 18 dimensions can be subsumed within four higher order dimensions: emotional dysregulation, dissocial, inhibitedness, and compulsivity. Joint factor analyses of the DAPP-BQ and the SNAP personality disorder symptom scales typically yield this four-factor solution (Clark & Livesley, 2002; Clark, Livesley, Schroeder, & Irish, 1996).

The TCI, like the OMNI, provides a hierarchical, integrative assessment of both normal and abnormal personality structure. The TCI includes seven higher order factors (e.g., reward dependence, self-transcendence, and cooperativeness) from which the lower order normal (e.g., helpfulness, compassion, and empathy) and abnormal (e.g., disorderliness and dependence) personality scales are derived empirically, as well as conceptually. Cloninger (2000) hypothesizes the existence of four fundamental temperaments (each of which is associated with a particular monoamine neuromodulator) and three additional character dimensions that reflect individual differences that have developed through a nonlinear interaction of temperament, family environment, and life experiences (Svrakic et al., 2002).

The NEO PI-R is the most commonly used measure of the Five-Factor Model (FFM) of general personality structure (Costa & McCrae, 1992). The FFM is the predominant model in general personality research, with extensive applications in the fields of health psychology, aging, developmental psychology, and even animal species comparisons (McCrae & Costa, 1999; Mullins-Sweatt & Widiger, in press). Empirical support for the FFM is extensive, including convergent and discriminant validity at the domain and facet levels across self, peer, and spouse ratings, temporal stability across 7–10 years, cross-cultural generalization, heritability, and molecular genetics, as well as links to a wide variety of important life outcomes, such as mental health, career success, and mortality (Mullins-Sweatt & Widiger, in press). Many of the NEO PI-R scales refer explicitly to maladaptive personality functioning (e.g., vulnerability, anxiousness, and impulsiveness). However, the NEO PI-R might provide somewhat less representation of maladaptive variants of high agreeableness, high conscientiousness, and high openness, relative to its representation of the maladaptive variants of low agreeableness, low conscientiousness, and low openness (Haigler & Widiger, 2001). There is a semistructured interview for the assessment of the FFM that is coordinated explicitly with the NEO PI-R that attempts to provide somewhat more representation of maladaptive variants of high agreeableness, conscientiousness, and openness (i.e., SIFFM; Trull & Widiger, 1997) but it is unclear whether it in fact succeeds in doing so.

All of the semistructured interviews that provide assessments of the *DSM-IV* personality disorders (i.e., DIPD, IPDE, SCID-II, SIDP-IV, and PDI-IV) are coordinated explicitly with the respective *DSM-IV* diagnostic criterion sets. Each of these interviews provides questions to assess each of the *DSM-IV* diagnostic criteria. This is not the case, however, for most of the self-report inventories, as they vary considerably in the extent to which they are coordinated with *DSM-IV*. For example, the CATI (Coolidge & Merwin, 1992), PAI (Morey, 1991), and WISPI (Klein et al., 1993) were constructed in reference to the *DSM-III-R* criterion sets (American Psychiatric Association, 1987) and have not since been revised to be compatible with *DSM-IV*. The Morey et al. (1985) MMPI-2 personality disorder scales were constructed in reference to the *DSM-III* criterion sets (American Psychiatric Association, 1980). MMPI-2 personality disorder scales coordinated with *DSM-IV* have since been developed by Ben-Porath (Hicklin & Widiger, 2000; Jones, 2005), but most researchers and clinicians continue to use the original Morey et al. *DSM-III* scales.

The DIB-R, DIN, and PCL-R are semistructured interviews that are devoted to specific personality disorders. The DIB-R provides an assessment of the borderline personality disorder, the DIN an assessment of the narcissistic, and the PCL-R an assessment of the psychopathic. An advantage of these semistructured interviews is their extensive coverage of the symptoms and features of each of these respective personality disorders. However, with this coverage also comes increased time for administration. The DIB-R and DIN require about as much time to assess the borderline and narcissistic personality disorders as the DIPD and PDI-IV use to assess all of the *DSM-IV* personality disorders. Additionally, their assessments are not necessarily congruent with the *DSM-IV* criterion sets. For instance, the DIB-R places more emphasis on the assessment of cognitive-perceptual aberrations for the assessment of borderline personality disorder than does *DSM-IV*. The PCL-R assessment of psychopathy was constructed explicitly to provide an alternative assessment of antisocial personality disorder; more specifically, an assessment that is more consistent with the construct of psychopathy developed by Cleckley (1941). The primary difference is that the PCL-R includes an assessment of glib charm, arrogance, lack of empathy, and shallow affect that are not included within the *DSM-IV* antisocial criterion set. Missing from both the PCL-R and *DSM-IV*, however, is an assessment of low anxiousness, a feature of psychopathy also emphasized by Cleckley (Widiger & Lynam, 1998).

Even instruments that are coordinated with *DSM-IV* will at times do so from somewhat different theoretical perspectives. WISPI and SWAP-200 items emphasize an object-relational, psychodynamic perspective (Benjamin, 1996; Klein et al., 1993; Shedler, 2002; Westen, 1997). Many of the PAI items emphasize an interpersonal model (Morey, 1991). Some of the MCMI-III personality disorder scales are slanted somewhat toward the theoretical model of Millon et al. (1996). In fact, the MCMI-III obsessive-compulsive personality disorder scale often correlates negatively with the respective scale from other self-report inventories (Widiger & Coker, 2002) due perhaps to its inclusion of adaptive as well as maladaptive components of obsessive-compulsive personality traits (Haigler & Widiger, 2001). This unusual feature of the MCMI-III, however, could be advantageous if one is concerned with the unclear boundary between normal and abnormal personality functioning (Haigler & Widiger, 2001). The PDQ-IV is perhaps the only self-report inventory constructed to assess the *DSM-IV* diagnostic criterion sets as they are de-scribed in the diagnostic manual, although the CATI is reasonably close as its items were written to assess the *DSM-III-R* criterion sets.

## Degree of Structure

Self-report inventories are the most heavily structured assessment instruments. They can in fact be characterized as fully structured interviews that are being self-adminis-tered. None of the personality disorder semistructured interviews are themselves fully structured. Interviewers are encouraged to administer follow-up queries of their own design to provide more thorough assessments, and some of the diagnostic criteria assess-ments are based on the interviewer's observations of the patient's behavior and manner of relating to the interviewer. Semistructured interviewers are not instructed to simply record the patient's responses to each question; they may in fact code diagnostic criteria as being present even if the patient denies that the symptom is present.

All of the semistructured interviews include an explicit set of questions that are to be administered to each patient, contributing to the reliability of their assessments across different interviewers. In contrast, the PAF and SWAP-200 are neither self-report inven-tories nor semistructured interviews. The PAF is essentially a list of the 12 *DSM-III-R* (American Psychiatric Association, 1987) personality disorders, along with a brief narra-tive description of each disorder. The SWAP-200 is a set of 200 items, approximately half of which are the 94 *DSM-IV* personality disorder diagnostic criteria, the other half are additional personality disorder symptoms, defense mechanisms, and adaptive personality traits. Neither the PAF nor the SWAP-200 includes a set of questions to be administered to a patient, nor even a set of guidelines for the assessment of the items.

The PCL-R (Hare, 2003), like the PAF and the SWAP-200, is essentially a set of items that the clinician can use to describe patients. The PCL-R is often described as a semistructured interview but the PCL-R does not in fact include a set of interview questions that are administered consistently across different research sites or clinical set-tings. The manual for the PCL-R (Hare, 2003) offers suggested questions for many of the items and it also provides extensive discussion of how each item could be scored on the basis of biographical data. Nevertheless, many of the PCL-R items are scored primarily on the basis of a person's legal, criminal record rather than on the basis of an interview (e.g., a history of murders or rapes indicates the presence of a lack of empathy; Hare, 2003). PCL-R studies have rarely involved the administration of an explicit set of ques-tions that could be replicated in subsequent studies, and there is often no record of the basis upon which items have been assessed. The availability of a detailed criminal history within prison settings has contributed to the PCL-R's excellent inter-rater reliability and predictive validity, but an application of the PCL-R within most other clinical settings would probably have to rely more heavily on an interview, the administration and scoring of which will be unclear for some PCL-R items (Lilienfeld, 1994; Rogers, 2001).

## Guidelines for Interpretation

Most of the self-report inventories have manuals that provide extensive guidance for the interpretation of test scores, notably the DAPP-BQ (Livesley & Jackson, in press), PAI (Morey, 1991), MCMI-III (Millon et al., 1997), MIPS (Millon, 1994), NEO PI-R

(Costa & McCrae, 1992), SNAP (Clark et al., in press), and TCI (Cloninger et al., 1994). The test manual for the NEO PI-R was not developed primarily for the assessment of maladaptive personality functioning within clinical settings. However, Piedmont (1998) developed a text that can serve well for this purpose.

No published manual has been developed for the PDQ-4, PSY-5, SWAP-200, or the MMPI-2 personality disorder scales. Numerous manuals for the interpretation of the MMPI-2 have been developed, but surprisingly, these manuals often fail to include much information concerning the application of the MMPI-2 for the assessment of the *DSM-IV* personality disorders. A manual for the SWAP-200 (Shedler, 2002) is under construction. In the meantime, readers are encouraged to go to the SWAP-200 website (http://www. psychsystems.net) to obtain information concerning the instrument and to experience how the SWAP-200 is administered. A manual for the MPQ is in press (Tellegen, in press) but perhaps it should be noted that it has been in this state for a number of years.

The absence of a manual for the PDQ-IV could be due in part to the fact that it was constructed to be coordinated explicitly with the *DSM-IV* criterion sets. Individual items of the PDQ-4 can be scored for each of the 94 *DSM-IV* personality disorder diagnostic criteria. Therefore, anything that might be implied by the presence of *DSM-IV* diagnostic criteria (i.e., any chapter or text concerning a *DSM-IV* personality disorder) might presumably be applied to persons who are scored by the PDQ-4 as having the respective criteria. However, clinicians should be quite cautious in providing such straightforward interpretations of PDQ-4 scores, as there are considerable empirical data to indicate that the PDQ-4 provides a substantial number of false-positive diagnoses (Bagby & Farvolden, 2004). The CATI might be somewhat less problematic in this regard as CATI items were also written to represent individual diagnostic criteria and the CATI provides more items for the assessment of each diagnostic criterion.

The manuals for the semistructured interviews vary substantially in the amount of assistance provided for the interpretation of responses. None contain normative data, and all of them are weak in their coverage of basic reliability and validity data (Kaye & Shea, 2000; Rogers, 2001). A clear exception in this regard is the PCL-R (Hare, 2003). The PCL-R manual is itself a small book on the conceptualization, diagnosis, and empirical support for the diagnosis of psychopathy. The PCL-R manual includes a thorough description of the extensive research that has been conducted with this instrument, addresses most (if not all) of the major controversies within the field of psychopathy, and provides extensive guidance as to how individual items could be scored on the basis of biographical and institutional file information. The PDI-IV manual (Widiger et al., 1995) is also a small book, including individual chapters on each personality disorder that provide the history of each diagnostic criterion, the rationale for the precise wording of each diagnostic criterion, and common problems and issues experienced in the assessment of each diagnostic criterion. The PDI-IV manual is an excellent resource for learning the history, rationale, and common issues for the *DSM-IV* criterion sets, but the PDI-IV manual again fails to provide much information concerning the instrument's validity.

## Diagnosis

One particular interpretive decision that is central to this text is the provision of a personality disorder diagnosis. For the instruments coordinated explicitly with *DSM-IV*, this decision can appear to be straightforward. If the person meets the diagnostic criteria for a respective personality disorder, then the clinician would provide that diagnosis. A clear advantage of the *DSM-IV* semistructured interviews (i.e., DIPD, IPDE, PDI-IV, SCID-II, and SIDP-IV) is that the determination of the presence of a personality disorder can be governed by the algorithms provided by the *DSM-IV* (American Psychiatric Association, 2000). The manuals for the semistructured interviews that concern individual personality disorders (e.g., DIB-R, DIN, & PCL-R) also provide explicit rules for the provision of a diagnosis. However, as suggested in the chapter by Samuel and Widiger (this volume, chapter 7), *DSM-IV* diagnoses should perhaps not be so straightforward, given that there is no compelling rationale or empirical support for any of the existing *DSM-IV* personality disorder diagnostic thresholds.

In addition, the semistructured interviews vary substantially in the extent and manner in which they attempt to include cases of personality disorder not otherwise specified (PDNOS). Clinicians provide a diagnosis of PDNOS when they determine that a person has a personality disorder that is not adequately represented by any one of the 10 officially recognized diagnoses (American Psychiatric Association, 2000). PDNOS is perhaps the single most frequently used personality disorder diagnosis in clinical practice (Verheul & Widiger, 2004). *DSM-IV* does provide a general definition of personality (see Samuel & Widiger, this volume, chapter 7) that should be used by clinicians when they provide a PDNOS diagnosis, but the semistructured interviews vary in the extent to which they are explicitly coordinated with this general definition. The manual for the PDI-IV devotes a chapter to the assessment of PDNOS cases, indicates the variety of ways in which a PDNOS diagnosis can be used and requires that PDNOS cases meet the general diagnostic criteria for a personality disorder. However, no questions are provided by the PDI-IV that would encourage or facilitate the assessment of PDNOS. The IPDE and SIDP-IV confine their assessment of PDNOS to instances of "mixed" personality disorders (i.e., "presence of features of more than one specific Personality Disorder that do not meet the full criteria for any one Personality Disorder," American Psychiatric Association, 2000, p. 729) and make no reference to the general diagnostic criteria. The IPDE requires the presence of at least 10 diagnostic criteria of different personality disorders in order for PDNOS to be diagnosed; the SIDP-IV recommends using PDNOS when (and only when) two or more disorders are just one criterion short of diagnostic threshold.

Westen and Shedler (2000) suggest that clinicians simply be provided with a half-page, narrative description of a prototypic case of each personality disorder and then use their professional judgment to decide whether the patient is close enough to the prototype to warrant a diagnosis. No explicit or specific diagnostic criteria would be required or provided, as they suggest that criterion sets are unnecessarily cumbersome and that valid diagnoses are obtained in routine clinical practice in the absence of any use of the *DSM-IV* criterion sets (Shelder & Westen, 2004). The narrative descriptions of each prototype currently proposed by Westen and Shelder (2005) are based largely on SWAP-200 items but the prototype matching procedure would not require a systematic administration of the SWAP-200 items.

The Westen and Shedler (2000) prototype matching procedure would be much easier to use than the existing diagnostic criterion sets but the method is essentially a return to DSM-II (American Psychiatric Association, 1968). It is unlikely that reliable clinical diagnoses will occur in the absence of any explicit diagnostic criteria (Spitzer & Fleiss, 1974), particularly for initial intake assessments that constitute the primary focus of most diagnostic evaluations. Current studies on the prototypal matching procedure have been confined to persons who have been in treatment for many sessions and are well known to the clinician (Westen & Shedler, 2005). The purpose of the diagnostic manual is instead to help clinicians and researchers obtain reliable and valid diagnoses at the initial entry into treatment or the onset of a study; that is, situations in which very little is known about the patient.

Most of the self-report inventories that provide scales for the assessment of the *DSM-IV* personality disorders provide cutoff points for diagnosis, but there are in fact exceptions. For instance, no cutoff points are provided for the MMPI-2 personality disorder scales. Colligan et al. (1994) do relate the Morey et al. (1985) scales to the MMPI-2 normative data collection, but using cutoff points set at 1.5 standard deviations from a population mean for each personality disorder would have little apparent relationship with a *DSM-IV* diagnosis. The cutoff points for the PAI are also based on statistical deviance from a population mean.

A limitation of using normative distributions to set cutoff points is the false assumption that scale interpretation should be governed primarily by statistical deviance (Gorenstein, 1984), let alone the same degree of statistical deviance for each personality disorder. Cutoff scores that are coordinated with the actual base rate of a disorder will provide more accurate diagnoses (Meehl & Rosen, 1955). "An important feature that distinguishes the MCMI from other inventories is its use of actuarial base rate data rather than normalized standard score transformations" (Millon et al., 1997, p. 5). However, the advantages of using base rates to set cutoff points can be undermined if they are not adjusted for changes in the base rates across different settings. The MCMI-III cutoff points are coordinated with the total set of inpatient and outpatient settings that provided the normative clinical pool. Clinicians will find that the MCMI-III cutoff points result in many false-positive assessments when applied to populations that do not include much personality disorder pathology, such as college counseling centers, introductory psychology pools, or child custody and divorce mediation evaluations (King, 1994; Lampel, 1999).

Cloninger (2000) proposes a two-step procedure with the TCI. Cloninger suggests that all personality disorders are characterized by low self-directedness, and most are characterized in addition by low cooperativeness and low self-transcendence. These scales would then be used to determine the presence of a personality disorder, and the temperament scales (e.g., reward dependence and harm avoidance) could be used to determine which personality disorder is present. However, Cloninger does not provide specific cutoff points on the respective scales.

Cutoff points are not provided for SNAP or DAPP-BQ scales. Livesley (2003) does not provide cutoff points on the DAPP-BQ scales as he suggests that the diagnosis of a personality disorder should be based on the presence of a failure to establish and maintain stable representations of self and others, interpersonal dysfunction, and a failure to develop prosocial behavior and cooperative relationships. If these features are present, then a personality disorder diagnosis should be provided and the DAPP-BQ scales could be used to describe the specific nature of the disorder. However, no specific guidelines are provided for the assessment or weighting of the three basic components of a personality disorder. The MPQ and NEO PI-R provide cutoff points (based on statistical deviance) for determining when a meaningful level of a respective personality trait is present, but not for determining the presence of a personality disorder.

Widiger et al. (2002) have proposed a four-step procedure to diagnose the presence of a personality disorder from the perspective of the FFM. The first step is to provide a comprehensive assessment of personality functioning with an existing measure of the FFM (De Raad & Perugini, 2002). Preferably, this step should employ a measure that provides both domain and facet level assessments (e.g., the NEO PI-R). The second step is to identify the problems in living that are typically associated with the individual's characteristic personality traits. For this purpose, Widiger et al. (2002) provided a tentative checklist of problems associated with both poles of all 30 facets of the FFM. McCrae (in press) and McCrae, Lockenhoff, and Costa (in press) have augmented this list with items drawn from existing inventories of clinically relevant problems and symptoms, such as the Personalty Problems Checklist for Adults (PPPC; Schinka, 1985) and the SWAP-200 (Shedler & Westen, 2004). These problems in living can be assessed with the SIFFM (Trull & Widiger, 1997). The third step is to determine whether the dysfunction and distress reach a clinically significant level of impairment. Widiger et al. (2002) provide a quantitative rating scale for this judgment, modeled after Axis V of *DSM-IV* (APA, 2000). The fourth step is a quantitative matching of the individual's personality profile to prototypic profiles of diagnostic constructs. In sum, the four-step procedure provides a straightforward approach but, as yet, there has been no published research to indicate that the four steps can be used effectively in general clinical practice.

# Convergent and Discriminant Validity

The instruments summarized in Table 13.1 should demonstrate substantial convergent validity, as they are attempting to do largely the same thing: identify the fundamental features of personality disorder. Most of the instruments do in fact appear to be readily integrated within a common hierarchical structure (Bouchard & Loehlin, 2001; John & Srivastava, 1999; Krueger & Tackett, 2003; Livesley, 2003; Markon, Krueger, & Watson, 2005; Trull & Durrett, 2005; Widiger & Mullins-Sweatt, in press; Widiger & Simonsen, 2005). Below we review studies on their convergent and discriminant validity.

## Convergent Validity

Only three studies have provided data concerning the convergent validity among the personality disorder semistructured interviews (O'Boyle & Self, 1990; Skodol, Oldham, Rosnick, Kellman, & Hyler, 1991; Pilkonis et al., 1995), only two of these studies administered the interview schedules to the same patients (O'Boyle & Self, 1990; Skodol et al., 1991), and all three were confined to just two of the five semistructured interviews.

The most comprehensive study to date was by Skodol et al. (1991). They administered the IPDE and SCID-II to 100 inpatients of a personality disorders treatment unit. Both interviews were administered blind to one another on the same day (one in the morning, the other in the afternoon). Order of administration was staggered. Kappa for individual diagnoses ranged from 0.14 (schizoid) to 0.66 (dependent), with a median kappa of 0.53 (borderline). The authors considered the agreement for some of the categorical diagnoses to be discouraging. "It is fair to say that, for a number of disorders (i.e., paranoid, schizoid, schizotypal, narcissistic, and passive-aggressive) the two [interviews] studied do not operationalize the diagnoses similarly and thus yield disparate results" (Skodol et al., 1991, p. 22). However, the median agreement does appear to be consistent with rates obtained for many Axis I disorders when their assessments are conducted blind to one another (Loranger, 1992). In addition, agreement with respect to a more quantitative assessment of the extent to which each personality disorder was present was considerably better than the agreement for categorical diagnoses, with correlations ranging from 0.58 (schizoid) to 0.87 (antisocial). Skodol et al. (1991) concluded that "the greater agreement shown by comparing dimensions of disorder than by comparing strict categorical diagnoses suggests that patients are providing interviewers with reliable information about areas of difficulty in personality functioning and interviewers are able to judge when at least some of these reports indicate clinically significant psychopathology" (p. 22).

Several studies have been published on the convergent validity of personality disorder semistructured interviews with self-report inventories, as well as the convergent validity among self-report inventories. Widiger and Coker (2002) tabulated the findings from 41 of these studies. It is apparent from this research that convergent validity increases as the structure of the assessment increases. The weakest convergent validity has been obtained with unstructured clinical interviews; the highest has been obtained with self-report inventories; the convergence of semistructured interviews with self-report inventories falls somewhere in between.

One implication of this convergent validity research is that self-report inventories might provide a more valid assessment of personality disorders than semistructured interviews, yet semistructured interviews are often used as the criterion with which the validity of self-report inventories are tested (Zimmerman, 2003). Rarely are self-report inventories used as criterion measures for the validity of a semistructured interview, although there are exceptions. For example, Trull et al. (1998) used the NEO PI-R, the predominant instrument for the assessment of the FFM, as the criterion with which to evaluate the convergent and discriminant validity of their semistructured interview assessment of the FFM.

Semistructured interviews are generally preferred over self-report inventories in clinical research (Rogers, 2001; Segal & Coolidge, 2003). This preference could be analogous to the preference of clinicians for unstructured interviews. One reason that semistructured interviews are preferred over self-report inventories is that they provide the researcher the opportunity to have a direct, personal impact on the assessment; follow-up queries can be provided and inadequacies in self-insight and awareness can be addressed (Kaye & Shea, 2000; Rogers, 2001; Segal & Coolidge, 2003). However, the opportunity of the interviewer to personally impact the assessment might also contribute to less reliable and ultimately less valid assessments (comparable to the lower reliability obtained with unstructured interviews relative to semistructured interviews). The findings obtained with self-report inventories are more likely to replicate across research sites than findings obtained with semistructured interviews because there is little to no room for inter-rater disagreement in the administration and scoring of a self-report inventory.

There is currently no gold standard for evaluating the validity of a semistructured interview. Perhaps self-report inventories could be used in future studies to at least compare the convergent validity of alternative semistructured interviews. Semistructured interviews are currently evaluated largely on the basis of face validity and frequency of usage (Kaye & Shea, 2000; Rogers, 2001). However, in defense of the validity of semistructured interviews, the most compelling published research concerning etiology, course, pathology, and treatment has been based on assessments provided by semistructured interviews (Rogers, 2001). The results of this extensive research provide support for the construct validity of the semistructured interviews that were administered.

## Discriminant Validity

Only few studies have provided discriminant validity data (Widiger & Coker, 2002). The absence of much attention to discriminant validity reflects in part the recognition that the diagnostic constructs assessed by these measures do not themselves have compelling discriminant validity (Clark & Harrison, 2001; Farmer, 2000). For example, the report by Skodol et al. (1991) was confined to the convergent validity of the IPDE and SCID-II and did not discuss or provide any data on discriminant validity. Instead, Oldham et al. (1992) subsequently used the same data to report an excessive co-occurrence among the personality disorder diagnostic categories and concluded that most of this was due to overlap among the disorders' criterion sets rather than flaws or inadequacies of the IPDE or SCID-II. Because the DSM-IV personality disorders overlap extensively (Bornstein,1998; Farmer, 2000; Lilienfeld, Waldman, & Israel, 1994), a valid assessment of an individual personality disorder should perhaps obtain weak discriminant validity with respect to its near neighbor diagnostic constructs. For example, perhaps a valid assessment of borderline personality disorder should not result in the absence of overlap with the dependent, histrionic, and narcissistic personality disorders. The scales of some personality disorder self-report inventories (e.g., MCMI-III and MMPI-2) overlap substantially in order to compel the obtainment of a particular degree and direction of co-occurrence that would be consistent with theoretical expectations.

Morey et al. (2002) administered the NEO Personality Inventory-Revised (NEO PI-R; Costa & McCrae, 1992), a self-report measure of the Five-Factor Model (FFM) of general personality functioning, to 86 patients diagnosed with schizotypal, 175 with borderline, 157 with avoidant, and 153 with obsessive-compulsive personality disorder in the multi-site Collaborative Longitudinal Personality Disorders Study (CLPS). A discriminant function analysis indicated that the four personality disorders were differentiated significantly in terms of the 30 facets of the FFM, but it was also apparent from a visual inspection of the FFM profiles that "all four of the disorders displayed a similar configuration of FFM traits" (Morey et al., 2002, p. 229). However, there was considerable diagnostic co-occurrence among the personality disorders in their sample. Morey et al. repeated the analyses using a subsample of 24 schizotypals, 72 borderlines, 103 avoidants, and 105 obsessive-compulsives who did not meet criteria for one of the three other respective personality disorders under study. "The elimination of patients with comorbid study diagnoses did appear to sharpen the distinction between the personality disorder groups, whereas only 18 facets revealed substantive differences (i.e., effect sizes larger than .50) among the cell-assigned personality disorder diagnoses, 31 facets achieved this threshold using the non-comorbid groups" (pp. 224–225). Differentiation would probably increase further if the additional diagnostic co-occurrence with the six other personality disorders was also considered. In other words, it is unclear whether the results of Morey et al. indicated weak discriminant validity for the FFM or for the personality disorder constructs.

Lynam and Widiger (2001) explored whether the problematic co-occurrence among the *DSM-IV* personality disorders could itself be explained by the FFM. They had personality disorder researchers describe prototypic cases of each *DSM-IV* personality disorder in terms of the 30 facets of the FFM. They then obtained the correlations among the personality disorders with respect to their FFM descriptions, and found that the personality disorder diagnostic co-occurrence reported in 15 previous studies could be largely accounted for by the covariation among the FFM personality trait profiles. For example, the FFM understanding of the antisocial personality disorder accounted for 85% of its diagnostic co-occurrence reported in nine *DSM-III* (APA, 1980) studies and 76% of its diagnostic co-occurrence reported in the six *DSM-III-R* (American Psychiatric Association, 1987) studies obtained for the authors of the *DSM*-IV criterion sets. "Under the FFM account, disorders appear comorbid to the extent that they are characterized by the same [FFM] facets" (Lynam & Widiger, 2001, p. 409).

## Conclusions

As we indicated at the beginning of this chapter, the general assessment strategy we recommend is to first administer a self-report inventory, followed by a semistructured interview that focuses on the disorders that received elevated scores (Widiger & Samuel, in press). Semistructured interviews substantially facilitate the obtainment of reliable, systematic, comprehensive, and valid assessments, and help avoid the occurrence of the unreliable, idiosyncratic and, at times, biased assessments that can occur with unstructured interviews (Garb, 2005; Wood et al., 2002).

Semistructured interviews, however, can require a considerable amount of time, which is one of the reasons we recommend that they be preceded by the administration of a self-report inventory. The interview can then focus on the particular scale elevations revealed by the self-report inventory. Self-report inventories can also be useful in alerting the clinician to aspects of normal or abnormal personality functioning that might not have been anticipated on the basis of the referral or initial impressions.

We have described several alternative self-report inventories and semistructured interviews that could be used. The choice of which particular instrument(s) to use is hindered by the absence of a gold standard with which to evaluate or compare the alternatives. This is not a problem that is unique to the personality disorders. In response to the fact that large-scale epidemiologic studies have produced inconsistent results, Regier et al. (1998) suggested that researchers agree to confine future studies to just one instrument. However, the inconsistency of findings is itself an argument against relying on just one instrument because it is not yet known which instrument is providing the most valid results or whether a revision to an existing instrument might increase its validity. Our own preference is to first administer the NEO PI-R, followed by the SIFFM (Widiger et al., 2002). The selection for any particular clinician or researcher will of course depend in part on their particular needs and interests. We recommend that clinicians and researchers become familiar with a number of different alternative instruments prior to making their particular selection.

# REFERENCES

Adler, D. A., Drake, R. E., & Teague, G. B. (1990). Clinicians' practices in personality assessment: Does gender influence the use of DSM-III Axis II? *Comprehensive Psychiatry, 31*, 125–133.

American Psychiatric Association. (1968). *Diagnostic and statistical manual of mental disorders* (2nd ed.). Washington, DC: Author.

American Psychiatric Association. (1980). *Diagnostic and statistical manual of mental disorders* (3rd ed.). Washington, DC: Author.

American Psychiatric Association. (1987). *Diagnostic and statistical manual of mental disorders* (3rd ed., rev. ed.). Washington, DC: Author.

American Psychiatric Association. (2000). *Diagnostic and statistical manual of mental disorders* (4th ed., text rev.). Washington, DC: Author.

Bagby, R. M., & Farvolden, P. (2004). The Personality Diagnostic Questionnaire-4 (PDQ-4). In M. J., Hilsenroth, D. L. Segal, & M. Hersen (Eds.), *Comprehensive handbook of psychological assessment. Personality assessment* (Vol. 2, pp. 122–133). New York: Wiley.

Benjamin, L. S. (1988). *Intrex user's manual.* Madison, WI: Intrex Institute.

Benjamin, L. S. (1996). *Interpersonal diagnosis and treatment of personality disorders* (2nd ed.). New York: Guilford Press.

Blashfield, R. K., & Flanagan, E. (1998). A prototypic nonprototype of a personality disorder. *Journal of Nervous and Mental Disease, 186*, 244–246.

Blashfield, R. K., & Herkov, M. J. (1996). Investigating clinician adherence to diagnosis by criteria: A replication of Morey and Ochoa (1989). *Journal of Personality Disorders, 10*, 219–228.

Bornstein, R. F. (1998). Reconceptualizing personality disorder diagnosis in the DSM-V: The discriminant validity challenge. *Clinical Psychology: Science and Practice, 5*, 333–343.

Bornstein, R. F. (1999). Criterion validity of objective and projective dependency tests: A meta-analytic assessment of behavioral prediction. *Psychological Assessment, 11*, 48–57.

Bouchard, T. J., & Loehlin, J. C. (2001). Genes, evolution, and personality. *Behavior Genetics, 31*, 243–273.

Clark, L. A., & Harrison, J. A. (2001). Assessment instruments. In W. J. Livesley (Ed.), *Handbook of personality disorders. Theory, research, and treatment* (pp. 277–306.). New York: Guilford press.

Clark, L. A., & Livesley, W. J. (2002). Two approaches to identifying the dimensions of personality disorder: Convergence on the five-factor model. In P. T. Costa, & T. A. Widiger (Eds.), *Personality disorders and the five-factor model of personality* (2nd ed., pp. 161–176). Washington, DC: American Psychological Association.

Clark, L. A., Livesley, W. J., Schroeder, M. L., & Irish, S. L. (1996). Convergence of two systems for assessing personality disorder. *Psychological Assessment, 8*, 294–303.

Clark, L. A., Simms, L. J., Wu, K. D., & Casillas, A. (in press). *Manual for the schedule for nonadaptive and adaptive personality (SNAP-2).* Minneapolis, MN: University of Minnesota Press.

Cleckley, H. (1941). *The mask of sanity.* St Louis: Mosby.

Cloninger, C. R. (2000). A practical way to diagnosis personality disorders: A proposal. *Journal of Personality Disorders, 14*, 99–108.

Cloninger, C. R., Przybeck, T. R., Svrakic, D. M., & Wetzel, R. D. (1994). *The Temperament and Character Inventory (TCI): A guide to its development and use.* St. Louis, MO: Center for Psychobiology of Personality, Washington University.

Colligan, R. C., Morey, L. C., & Offord, K. P. (1994). MMPI/MMPI-2 personality disorder scales. Contemporary norms for adults and adolescents. *Journal of Clinical Psychology, 50*, 168–200.

Coolidge, F. L., & Merwin, M. M. (1992). Reliability and validity of the Coolidge Axis II Inventory: A new inventory for the assessment of personality disorders. *Journal of Personality Assessment, 59*, 223–238.

Costa, P. T., & McCrae, R. R. (1992). *Revised NEO Personality Inventory (NEO PI-R) and NEO Five-Factor Inventory (NEO-FFI) professional manual.* Odessa, FL: Psychological Assessment Resources.

De Raad, B., Perugini, M. (Eds.). (2002). *Big five assessment.* Bern, Switzerland: Hogrefe & Huber.

Eysenck, H. J., & Eysenck, S. B. G. (1991). *Manual of the eysenck personality questionnaire (EPS Adult).* London: Hodder & Stroughton.

Farmer, R. F. (2000). Issues in the assessment and conceptualization of personality disorders. *Clinical Psychology Review, 20*, 823–851.

First, M. B., & Gibbon, M. (2004). The structured clinical interview for DSM-IV Axis I disorders (SCID-I) and the structured clinical interview for DSM-IV Axis II disorders (SCID-II). In M. J.,

Hilsenroth, D. L. Segal, & M. Hersen (Eds.), *Comprehensive handbook of psychological assessment. Personality assessment* (Vol. 2, pp. 134–143). New York: Wiley.

Garb, H. (2005). Clinical judgment and decision making. *Annual Review of Clinical Psychology, 1*, 67–89.

Gorenstein, E. (1984). Debating mental illness. *American Psychologist, 39*, 50–56.

Grant, B. F., Stinson, F. S., Dawson, D. A., Chou, S. P., & Ruan, W. J. (2005). Co-occurrence of DSM–IV personality disorders in the United States: Results from the National Epidemiologic Survey on Alcohol and Related Conditions. *Comprehensive Psychiatry, 46*, 1–5.

Gunderson, J. G., Ronningstam, E., & Bodkin, A. (1990). The diagnostic interview for narcissistic patients. *American Journal of Psychiatry, 47*, 676–680.

Haigler, E. D., & Widiger, T. A. (2001). Experimental manipulation of NEO PI-R items. *Journal of Personality Assessment, 77*, 339–358.

Hare, R. D. (2003). *Hare Psychopathy Checklist Revised (PCL-R). Technical manual.* North Tonawanda, NY: Multi-Health Systems.

Harkness, A. R., McNulty, J. L., & Ben-Porath, Y. S. (1995). The personality psychopathology five (PSY–5): Constructs and MMPI–2 scales. *Psychological Assessment, 7*, 104–114.

Herkov, M. J., & Blashfield, R. K. (1995). Clinicians diagnoses of personality disorder: Evidence of a hierarchical structure. *Journal of Personality Assessment, 65*, 313–321.

Hicklin, J., & Widiger, T. A. (2000). Convergent validity of alternative MMPI-2 personality disorder measures. *Journal of Personality Assessment, 75*, 502–518.

Hilsenroth, M. J., Segal, D. L., & Hersen, M. (Eds.). (2004). *Comprehensive handbook of psychological assessment. Personality assessment* (Vol. 2). New York: Wiley.

Huprich, J. (Ed.). (2005). *Rorschach assessment of the personality disorders.* Mahwah, NJ: Lawrence Erlbaum.

Hyler, S. E., Rieder, R. O., Williams, J. B. W., Spitzer, R. L., Hendler, J., & Lyons, M. (1988). The Personality Diagnostic Questionnaire: Development and preliminary results. *Journal of Personality Disorders, 2*, 229–237.

John, O. P., & Srivastava, S. (1999). The Big Five trait taxonomy: History, measurement, and theoretical perspectives. In L. A. Pervin, & O. P. John (Eds.), *Handbook of personality: Theory and research* (2nd ed., pp. 102–138). New York: Guilford Press.

Jones, A. (2005). An examination of three sets of MMPI-2 personality disorder scales. *Journal of Personality Disorders, 19*, 370–385.

Kaye, A. L., & Shea, M. T. (2000). Personality disorders, personality traits, and defense mechanisms measures. *Handbook of psychiatric measures* (pp. 713–749). Washington, DC: American Psychiatric Association.

King, R. E. (1994). Assessing aviators for personality pathology with the Millon Clinical Multiaxial Inventory (MCMI). *Aviation, Space, and Environmental Medicine, 65*, 227–231.

Klein, M. H., Benjamin, L. S., Rosenfeld, R., Treece, C., Husted, J., & Greist, J. H. (1993). The Wisconsin Personality Disorders Inventory: I. Development, reliability, and validity. *Journal of Personality Disorders, 7*, 285–303.

Krueger, R. F., & Tackett, J. L. (2003). Personality and psychopathology: Working toward the bigger picture. *Journal of Personality Disorders, 17*, 109–128.

Lampel, A. K. (1999). Use of the Millon Clinical Multiaxial Inventory-III in evaluating child custody litigants. *American Journal of Forensic Psychology, 17*, 19–31.

Leaf, P. J., Myers, J. K., & McEvoy, L. T. (1991). Procedures used in the Epidemiologic Catchment Area study. In L. N. Robins, & D. A. Regier (Eds.), *Psychiatric disorders in America. The Epidemiologic Catchment Area study* (pp. 11–32). New York: Free Press.

Lilienfeld, S. O. (1994). Conceptual problems in the assessment of psychopathy. *Clinical Psychology Review, 14*, 17–38.

Lilienfeld, S. O., Waldman, I. D., & Israel, A. C. (1994). A critical examination of the use of the term "comorbidity" in psychopathology research. *Clinical Psychology: Science and Practice, 1*, 71–83.

Livesley, W. J. (2003). Diagnostic dilemmas in classifying personality disorder. In K. A. Phillips, M. B. First, & H. A. Pincus (Eds.), *Advancing DSM. Dilemmas in psychiatric diagnosis* (pp. 153–190). Washington, DC: American Psychiatric Association.

Livesley W. J., & Jackson, D. (in press). *Manual for the dimensional assessment of personality pathology-basic questionnaire.* Port Huron, MI: Sigma Press.

Loranger, A. W. (1992). Are current self-report and interview methods adequate for epidemiological studies of personality disorders? *Journal of Personality Disorders, 6*, 313–325.

Loranger, A. W. (1999). *International Personality Disorder Examination* (*IPDE*). Odessa, FL: Psychological Assessment Resources.

Loranger, A. W. (2001). *OMNI Personality inventories. Professional manual*. Odessa, FL: Psychological Assessment Resources.

Lynam, D. R., & Widiger, T. A. (2001). Using the five factor model to represent the DSM-IV personality disorders: An expert consensus approach. *Journal of Abnormal Psychology, 110*, 401–412.

Markon, K. E., Krueger, R. F., & Watson, D. (2005). Delineating the structure of normal and abnormal personality: An integrative hierarchical approach. *Journal of Personality and Social Psychology, 88*, 139–157.

McCrae, R. R., & Costa, P. T. (1999). A five-factor theory of personality. In L. A. Pervin, & O. P. John (Eds.), *Handbook of personality: Theory and research* (2nd ed., pp. 139–153). New York: Guilford Press.

McCrae, R. R., Lockenhof, C. E., & Costa, P. T. (in press). A step toward DSM-V: Cataloging personality-related problems in living. *European Journal of Personality, 19,* 269–286.

McDermut, W., & Zimmerman, M. (2005). Assessment instruments and standardized evaluation. In J. Oldham, A. Skodol, & D. Bender (Eds.), *Textbook of personality disorders* (pp. 89–101). Washington, DC: American Psychiatric Press.

Meehl, P. E., & Rosen, A. (1955). Antecedent probability and the efficiency of psychometric signs, patterns, or cutting scores. *Psychological Bulletin, 52*, 194–216.

Mellsop, G., Varghese, F. T. N., Joshua, S., & Hicks, A. (1982). The reliability of Axis II of DSM-III. *American Journal of Psychiatry, 139*, 1360–1361.

Millon, T. (1994). *Millon Index of Personality Styles manual*. San Antonio, TX: Psychological Corporation.

Millon, T., Davis, R. D., Millon, C. M., Wenger, A. W., Van Zuilen, M. H., Fuchs, M., & Millon, R. B. (1996). *Disorders of personality. DSM-IV and beyond*. New York: Wiley.

Millon, T., Millon, C., & Davis, R. (1997). *MCMI-III manual* (2nd ed.). Minneapolis, MN: National Computer Systems.

Morey, L. C. (1991). *The Personality Assessment Inventory professional manual*. Odessa, FL: Psychological Assessment Resources.

Morey, L. C., & Boggs, C. (2004). The Personality Assessment Inventory (PAI). In M. J. Hilsenroth, D. L. Segal, & M. Hersen (Eds.), *Comprehensive handbook of psychological assessment. Personality assessment* (Vol. 2, pp. 15–29). New York: Wiley.

Morey, L. C., Gunderson, J. G., Quigley, B. D., Shea, M. T., Skodol, A. E., McGlashan, T. H., Stout, R. L., & Zanarini, M. C. (2002). The representation of borderline, avoidant, obsessive-compulsive, and schizotypal personality disorders by the five-factor model. *Journal of Personality Disorders, 16*, 215–234.

Morey, L. C., Waugh, M. H., & Blashfield, R. K. (1985). MMPI scales for DSM-III personality disorders: Their derivation and correlates. *Journal of Personality Assessment, 49*, 245–251.

Mullins-Sweatt, S. N., & Widiger, T. A. (in press). The five-factor model of personality disorder: A translation across science and practice. In R. Krueger, & J. Tackett (Eds.), *Personality and psychopathology: Building bridges*. New York: Guilford Press.

O'Boyle, M., & Self, D. (1990). A comparison of two interviews for DSM-III-R personality disorders. *Psychiatry Research, 32*, 85–92.

Oldham, J. M., Skodol, A. E., Kellman, H. D., Hyler, S. E., Rosnick, L., & Davies, M. (1992). Diagnosis of DSM-III-R personality disorders by two semistructured interviews: Patterns of comorbidity. *American Journal of Psychiatry, 149*, 213–220.

Pfohl, B., Blum, N., & Zimmerman, M. (1997). *Structured Interview for DSM-IV Personality*. Washington, DC: American Psychiatric Press.

Piedmont, R. L. (1998). *The Revised NEO Personality Inventory: Clinical and research applications*. New York: Plenum.

Pilkonis, P. A., Heape, C. L., Proietti, J. M., Clark, S. W., McDavid, J. D., & Pitts, T. E. (1995). The reliability and validity of two structured diagnostic interviews for personality disorders. *Archives of General Psychiatry, 52*, 1025–1033.

Pilkonis, P. A., Heape, C. L., Ruddy, J., & Serrao, P. (1991). Validity in the diagnosis of personality disorders: The use of the LEAD standard. *Psychological Assessment, 3*, 46–54.

Regier, D. A., Kaelber, C. T., Rae, D. S., Farmer, M. E., Knauper, B., Kessler, R. C., & Norquist, G. S. (1998). Limitations of diagnostic criteria and assessment instruments for mental disorders. Implications for research and policy. *Archives of General Psychiatry, 55*, 109–115.

Rogers, R. (2001). *Diagnostic and structured interviewing. A handbook for psychologists*. New York: GuilfordPress..

Rogers, R. (2003). Standardizing DSM-IV diagnoses: The clinical applications of structured interviews. *Journal of Personality Assessment, 81*, 220–225.

Rounsaville, B. J., Alarcon, R. D., Andrews, G., Jackson, J. S., Kendell, R. E., & Kendler, K. (2002). Basic nomenclature issues for DSM-V. In D. J. Kupfer, M. B. First, & D. E. Regier (Eds.), *A research agenda for DSM-V* (pp. 1–29). Washington, DC: American Psychiatric Association.

Schinka, J. A. (1985). *Personal problems checklist for adults*. Odessa, FL: Psychological Assessment Resources.

Segal, D. L., & Coolidge, F. L. (2003). Structured interviewing and DSM classification. In M. Hersen, & S. Turner (Eds.), *Adult psychopathology and diagnosis* (4th ed., pp. 72–103, 13–26). New York: Wiley.

Shedler, J. (2002). A new language for psychoanalytic diagnosis. *Journal of the American Psychoanalytic Association, 50*, 429–456.

Shedler, J., & Westen, D. (2004). Refining personality disorder diagnosis: Integrating science and practice. *American Journal of Psychiatry, 161*, 1350–1365.

Skodol, A. E., Oldham, J. M., Rosnick, L., Kellman, H. D., & Hyler, S. E. (1991). Diagnosis of DSM-III-R personality disorders: A comparison of two structured interviews. *International Journal of Methods in Psychiatric Research, 1*, 13–26.

Spitzer, R. L., & Fleiss, J. L. (1974). A re-analysis of the reliability of psychiatric diagnosis. *British Journal of Psychiatry, 125*, 341–347.

Strack, S. (2005). Measuring normal personality the Millon way. In S. Strack (Ed.), *Handbook of personology and psychopathology* (pp. 372–389). Hoboken, NJ: Wiley.

Svrakic, D. M., Draganic, S., Hill, K., Bayon, C., Przybeck, T. R., & Cloninger, C. R. (2002). Temperament, character, and personality disorders: Etiologic, diagnostic, and treatment issues. *Acta Psychiatrica Scandinavica, 106*, 189–195.

Tellegen, A. (in press). *Manual for the Multidimensional Personality Questionnaire*. Minneapolis, MN: University of Minnesota Press.

Trull, T. J., & Durrett, C. A. (2005). Categorical and dimensional models of personality disorder. *Annual Review of Clinical Psychology, 1*, 355–380.

Trull, T. J., & Widiger, T. A. (1997). *Structured Interview for the Five-Factor Model of Personality*. Odessa, FL: Psychological Assessment Resources.

Trull, T. J., Widiger, T. A., Useda, J. D., Holcomb, J., Doan, D.-T., Axelrod, S. R., Stern, B. L., & Gershuny, B. S. (1998). A structured interview for the assessment of the five-factor model of personality. *Psychological Assessment, 10*, 229–240.

Verheul, R., & Widiger, T. A. (2004). A meta-analysis of the prevalence and usage of the personality disorder not otherwise specified (PDNOS) diagnosis. *Journal of Personality Disorders, 18*, 309–319.

Watkins, C. E., Campbell, V. L., Nieberding, R., & Hallmark, R. (1995). Contemporary practice of psychological assessment by clinical psychologists. *Professional Psychology: Research and Practice, 26*, 54–60.

Westen, D. (1997). Divergences between clinical and research methods for assessing personality disorders: Implications for research and the evolution of Axis II. *American Journal of Psychiatry, 154*, 895–903.

Westen, D., & Arkowitz-Westen, L. (1998). Limitations of Axis II in diagnosing personality pathology in clinical practice. *American Journal of Psychiatry, 155*, 1767–1771.

Westen, D., & Shedler, J. (1999a). Revising and assessing Axis II, Part I: Developing a clinically and empirically valid assessment method. *American Journal of Psychiatry, 156*, 258–272.

Westen, D., & Shedler, J. (1999b). Revising and assessing Axis II, Part II: Toward an empirically based and clinically useful classification of personality disorders. *American Journal of Psychiatry, 156*, 273–285.

Westen, D., & Shedler, J. (2000). A prototype matching approach to diagnosing personality disorders: Toward DSM-V. *Journal of Personality Disorders, 14*, 109–126.

Westen, D., & Shedler, J. (2005). Prototype diagnosis of personality. In S. Strack (Ed.), *Handbook of personality and psychopathology* (pp. 238–256). Hoboken, NJ: Wiley.

Westen, D., Shedler, J., Durrett, C., Glass, S., & Martens, A. (2003). Personality diagnoses in adolescence: DSM-IV Axis II diagnoses and an empirically derived alternative. *American Journal of Psychiatry, 160*, 952–966.

Widiger, T. A. (2002). Personality disorders. In M. M. Antony, & D. H. Barlow (Eds.), *Handbook of assessment, treatment planning, and outcome for psychological disorders* (pp. 453–480). NY: Guilford Press.

Widiger, T. A., & Clark, L. A. (2000). Toward DSM-V and the classification of psychopathology. *Psychological Bulletin, 126*, 946–963.

Widiger, T. A., & Coker, L. A. (2002). Assessing personality disorders. In J. N. Butcher (Ed.), *Clinical personality assessment. Practical approaches* (2nd ed., pp. 407–434). New York: Oxford University Press.

Widiger, T. A., Costa, P. T., & McCrae, R. R. (2002). A proposal for Axis II: Diagnosing personality disorders using the five factor model. In P. T. Costa, & T. A. Widiger (Eds.), *Personality disorders and the five factor model of personality* (2nd ed., pp.431–456). Washington, DC: American Psychological Association.

Widiger, T. A., & Lynam, D. R. (1998). Psychopathy from the perspective of the five-factor model of personality. In T. Millon, E. Simonsen, M. Birket-Smith, & R. D. Davis (Eds.), *Psychopathy: Antisocial, criminal, and violent behaviors* (pp. 171–187). New York: Guilford Press.

Widiger, T. A., Mangine, S., Corbitt, E. M., Ellis, C. G., & Thomas, G. V. (1995). *Personality Disorder Interview-IV. A semistructured interview for the assessment of personality disorders. Professional manual.* Odessa, FL: Psychological Assessment Resources.

Widiger, T. A., & Mullins-Sweatt, S. (in press). Categorical and dimensional models of personality disorder. In J. Oldham, A. Skodol, & D. Bender (Eds.), *Textbook of personality disorders*. Washington, DC: American Psychiatric Press.

Widiger, T. A., & Samuel, D. B. (in press). Evidence based assessment of personality disorders. *Psychological Assessment, 17*, 278–287.

Widiger, T. A., & Simonsen, E. (2005). Alternative dimensional models of personality disorder: Finding a common ground. *Journal of Personality Disorders, 19*, 110–130.

Wood, J. M., Garb, H. N., Lilienfeld, S. O., & Nezworski, M. T. (2002). Clinical assessment. *Annual Review of Psychology, 53*, 519–543.

Zanarini, M. C., Frankenburg, F. R., Chauncey, D. L., & Gunderson, J. G. (1987). The Diagnostic Interview for Personality Disorders: Interrater and test–retest reliability. *Comprehensive Psychiatry, 28*, 467–480.

Zanarini, M. C., Gunderson, J. G., Frankenburg, F. R., & Chauncey, D. L. (1989). The Revised Diagnostic Interview for Borderlines: Discriminating BPD from other Axis II disorders. *Journal of Personality Disorders, 3*, 10–18.

Zimmerman, M. (2003). What should the standard of care for psychiatric diagnostic evaluations be? *Journal of Nervous and Mental Disease, 191*, 281–286.

Zimmerman, M., & Mattia, J. I. (1999). Differences between clinical and research practices in diagnosing borderline personality disorder. *American Journal of Psychiatry, 156*, 1570–1574.

## Yossef S. Ben-Porath

The Minnesota Multi-phasic Personality Inventory (MMPI) (Hathaway & McKinley, 1943) has for several decades been the most widely studied and applied instrument in differentiating normal and abnormal personality. There are many reasons why the MMPI, and now its updated version the MMPI-2 (Butcher, Graham, Ben-Porath, Dahlstrom, Tellegen, & Kaemmer, 2001) has maintained this status. The longevity of the test is particularly striking given the skepticism and ambivalence that have characterized its perception among some personality researchers and repeated attempts to introduce psychometrically superior instruments designed to replace the MMPI. This issue is revisited in the Conclusion section.

This chapter will discuss the theoretical background of the MMPI and MMPI-2, review the emergence of this instrument as a leading clinical tool in differentiating normal and abnormal personality, discuss the present status of the MMPI-2, and provide an outlook and recommendations for future directions in MMPI-2 research and application.

## Theoretical Underpinnings and Construction of the MMPI

As chronicled by Dahlstrom (1992a) the MMPI was published during a period of increasing skepticism regarding the utility of self-report personality inventories (e.g., Landis & Katz, 1934; Landis Zubin, & Katz, 1935). The two major inventories of that time, the Bernreuter Psychoneurotic Inventory (Bernreuter, 1933) and the Humm-Wadsworth

Temperament Scales (Humm & Wadsworth, 1935) were viewed as overly transparent, and, as a result, subject to manipulative distortion. They also were considered too narrow in scope to serve as omnibus measures of abnormal personality functioning. Thus, Hathaway and McKinley (1940) sought to "create a large reservoir of items from which various scales might be constructed in the hope of *evolving* a greater variety of valid personality descriptions than are available at the present time" (p. 249; italics added).

It is noteworthy that as early as 1940 Hathaway and McKinley viewed their initial efforts at scale development as only a starting point for what they hoped would be an evolving inventory. In fact, a primary reason for the longevity of the MMPI has been the extensive and continuing research effort that its broad item pool and wide-ranging constructs have engendered. This research tradition has been one of the hallmarks of the MMPI.

## Conceptual Basis

Not with standing Hathaway's well-known skepticism about psychological theories and his heavily empirical approach to scale construction (which appears to have given it the reputation of being the poster child of "blind empiricism") it would be a mistake to view the development of the MMPI as a literally atheoretical enterprise bereft of conceptual guidance. The construction of the MMPI did not take place in a conceptual vacuum and was inevitably and selectively, rather than indiscriminantly, influenced by the nosological, psychological, and measurement concepts available at the time.

The MMPI was constructed in a medical setting, for the express purpose of serving as a screening instrument for the detection of psychopathology. In compiling the test items and constructing the scales targeting certain disorders, Hathaway and McKinley were strongly influenced by the psychiatric thinking and practices of the 1930s. In their words:

> The individual items were formulated partly on the basis of previous clinical experience. Mainly, however, the items were supplied from several psychiatric examination direction forms, from various textbooks of psychiatry, from certain of the directions for case taking in medicine and neurology, and from the earlier published scales of personal and social attitudes. (Hathaway & McKinley, 1940, p. 249)

In selecting items for the MMPI, Hathaway and McKinley followed the diagnostic classification system of the 1930s, which was a derivative of the descriptive nosology developed by Kraepelin. In that respect, the MMPI was conceived originally in a manner that is quite consistent with current diagnostic practices of descriptive categorical classification.

Whereas Kraepelinian nosology supplied the model for the initial compilation of items and designation of scales, an interesting combination of behavioral, psychodynamic, and psychometric thinking can be found in early theoretical writings on the MMPI. All three elements appear in Meehl's (1945) classic article, *The Dynamics of "Structured" Personality Tests*. Meehl (1945) wrote this article in response to a criticism that faulted self-report personality inventories for relying on the assumption that responses to factually accurate test items must always have the same meaning to different individuals.

While agreeing that this assumption is unsupported, Meehl (1945) asserted that its validity was not a requirement for tests such as the MMPI. He stated:

> A "self-rating" constitutes an intrinsically interesting and significant bit of verbal behavior, the non-test correlates of which must be discovered by empirical means. Not only is this approach free from the restriction that the subject must be able to describe his own behavior accurately, but a careful study of structured personality tests built on this basis shows that such a restriction would falsify the actual relationships that hold between what a man says and what he is.(Meehl, 1945, p. 297)

Thus, according to Meehl (1945), the "manifest" content of the stimulus (the item) is entirely unimportant, and even irrelevant and potentially misleading. Sophisticated psychometric use of test items dictates that the test interpreter ignore item content altogether lest he or she be misled. The empirical correlates of scales composed of responses to the item stimuli must be the sole source of test interpretation—they are the empiricists "bottom line". Moreover, Meehl (1945) provided examples of MMPI items that are scored in nonintuitive or counter-intuitive directions, potentially connecting the interpretive approach taken with the MMPI with psychodynamically based assumptions. In Meehl's words:

> The complex defense mechanisms of projection, rationalization, reaction formation, etc., appear dynamically to the interviewer as soon as he begins to take what the client says as itself motivated by other needs than those of giving an accurate verbal report. There is no good apriori reason for denying the possibility of similar processes in the highly structured 'interview', which is the question-answer personality test. (Meehl, 1945, p. 298)

Although he provided a theoretical rationale for not assuming the literal accuracy of item responses, Meehl (1945) was well aware that those who take the MMPI are attuned to the meaning of test items and may, for a variety of motivations, choose to distort their self-presentation through their responses. He recognized that item subtlety could only go so far in preventing such distortions and that other means must also be employed to counter this possibility. The MMPI validity scales L and F and the later addition of K (Meehl & Hathaway, 1946) provided additional psychometric means for detecting and correcting the effects of distortion.

In sum, the theoretical underpinnings of the MMPI included:

1 Initial selection of items and designation of scales based on the then–contemporary Kraepelinian descriptive nosology as a model of psychopathology.
2 Rejection of a naïve belief in the literal veridicality of self–report, and a recognition that it is susceptible to influences of overt (intentional) and covert (unconscious) distortion, but can nonetheless remain informative.
3 Treatment of test items as stimuli for behavioral responses that may have certain empirical correlates including diagnostic group membership.

## Development of the MMPI and Its Initial Use

In keeping with the theoretical outlook just outlined, the MMPI clinical scales were constructed by a method of empirical keying that involved the use of contrasted groups, that is, comparisons of various groups of differentially diagnosed patients called here the "criterion groups", with nonpatients. Hathaway and McKinley described the development of several of the original clinical scales of the MMPI in a series of articles (Hathaway & McKinley, 1940, 1942; McKinley & Hathaway, 1940, 1942, 1944). In essence, statistical analyses were conducted to identify responses to test items that were correlated with criterion group membership. Those items were selected that differentiated both globally between normal and abnormal personality, as well as more narrowly between different criterion groups representing various types of abnormal personality constellations corresponding to the Kraepelinian model of psychopathology.

Actual use of the clinical scales required three important choices: of a psychometric algorithm for obtaining "raw scores" on the scales, of a "normative sample" in which to standardize the scales, and of a psychometric algorithm for standardizing the raw scores in the normative sample.

The normative sample was a subset of the "normals" used in the construction of the scales. It was composed primarily of visitors to the University of Minnesota Hospital who volunteered to answer the test items. This group came to be known as the *Minnesota Normals*, most of whom were rural Minnesotans with an average of 8 years of education and who were employed primarily as skilled and semiskilled laborers and farmers.

To obtain raw scores on the clinical scale, Hathaway and McKinley adopted an additive (cumulative) model: They summed the number of items an individual answered in the direction (True or False) answered more frequently in a given criterion group (e.g., the depressed patients) than in the normative sample. The raw scores were then standardized through a linear transformation to $T$-scores with a mean of 50 and a standard deviation of 10.

The empirical method of scale construction employed by Hathaway and McKinley initially limited the interpretive possibilities of even standardized scale scores. These quasi-continuous scores could only be used to characterize the extent to which an individual responded to the test items in a manner similar to those who served as the criterion group for that scale. Thus, the higher the $T$-score on the Hypochondriasis scale, the more similar were the responses of the individual to those of known hypochondriacs and, by inference, the more likely was that individual to have hypochondriasis.

In spite of the care and ingenuity that characterized the work of Hathaway and McKinley, for various reasons the MMPI never worked as its authors had initially intended. Attempts to replicate the validity of the clinical scales as predictors of diagnostic group membership were only marginally successful for some scales, and mostly unsuccessful for others (Hathaway, 1960). However, rather than fade away as had many of its predecessors, the MMPI underwent a remarkable transformation. As quoted earlier in this chapter, Hathaway and McKinley (1940) viewed the initial development of the MMPI as a starting, not an end point. Led by Paul Meehl, Hathaway's students and followers reinvented the MMPI by directing its use away from the narrow task of differential diagnosis to a considerably broader application. Hathaway (1960) described this process as follows:

> The MMPI began with validity based upon the usefulness of the various diagnostic groups from which its scales were derived. Now the burden of its use rests upon construct validity. Only a small fraction of the published data relating clinical or experimental variables to its scales or profiles can be understood in terms of the original approach.

If the validity views of 1941 were the only support for the inventory, it could not survive. What is happening is that the correlations observed with other variables in normal and abnormal subjects are filling out personality constructs that emerge, to be in turn tested for their ability to survive. It is significant that constructs, in the general sense of construct validity, can be the forerunners of diagnostic classes. (Hathaway, 1960, p. viii)

# Evolution of the Original MMPI

Although no doubt disappointed by the failure of the test to fulfill its original goal, early users of the MMPI observed consistency in the patterns of MMPI scale scores of individuals who shared certain personality characteristics. As a result, researchers began to shift their focus from the validity of individual scales to the identification of replicable empirical correlates of patterns of scale scores. Authors began to use the term *profile* to refer to the complete set of scores on the eight clinical scales and *profile types* to identify certain patterns or combinations of scores. Gough (1946), Meehl (1946), and Schmidt (1945) published a series of articles on the utility of certain profile types in the task of differential diagnosis. Hathaway (1947) and then Welsh (1948) developed coding systems that provided convenient shorthand summaries of the pattern of scores on the profile. This led eventually to adoption of the term *code type* to designate certain classes of profiles. Most early code types were based on the highest one or two scales on the profile.

As investigators were studying the diagnostic accuracy of profile types, they began to expand their studies to identify nondiagnostic correlates as well. Hathaway and Meehl (1951) developed an adjective checklist that was modified by Black (1953) in his study of the empirical correlates of MMPI code types. Examples of adjectives that appeared on Black's (1953) list include honest, orderly, conscientious, worrying, neurotic, cheerful, alert, seclusive, generous, foolish, incoherent, argumentative, peaceable, curious, and versatile.[1]

Within a decade of its initial publication, the nature of the MMPI had changed dramatically. The Kraepelinian nosological model was dropped in favor of a considerably broader and more ambitious goal of describing normal and abnormal personality characteristics, and code types, rather than individual scales, were viewed as the test's primary source of information. Reflecting this change, the original scale names that corresponded to the Kraepelinian nosological system were modified by using either abbreviations (e.g., *Hs* for Hypochondriasis) or digits (e.g., *Scale* 1 for Hypochondriasis).

The empirical literature on the test was expanding at an exponential rate. By the time Welsh and Dahlstrom (1956) published their compendium of basic readings on the MMPI they were able to list 689 references. With such profound changes came a need to rethink the theoretical basis of the MMPI.

---

[1]Examination of these examples should reassure adherents of five- and/or seven-factor models of personality that the MMPI research literature has long incorporated these dimensions of personality into the empirical correlate database.

## Revised Theoretical Foundation of the MMPI

As described earlier, the initial theoretical foundations of the MMPI were spelled out by Meehl (1945) and included elements of Kraepelinian nosology and behavioral, psychodynamic, and psychometric theory. With the move away from the initial narrow diagnostic focus of the MMPI came a more open-ended pursuit of a wider range of empirical correlates.

In 1954, Meehl published his seminal monograph on clinical versus statistical predictions. He presented a series of theoretical and empirical analyses leading to a call for clinical psychologists to use statistical or actuarial methods in predicting behavior. The thrust of his argument was that by using psychological test data and other sources of information to classify individuals into meaningful groups, we may then "enter a statistical or actuarial table which gives the statistical frequencies of behaviors or various sorts of persons belonging to the class" (Meehl, 1954, p. 3).

In effect, Meehl (1954) advocated that psychologists pursue a three-pronged task: first, they must identify meaningful classes within which individuals tend to cluster; second, they must develop reliable and valid ways of identifying to which class a given individual belongs; and finally, researchers were to identify statistical or actuarial correlates of belonging to different classes. This task would entail a fair amount of "bootstrapping": as we would learn to infer more about class membership than what we used initially to allow us to classify individuals into a given class. Eventually, by using actuarial tables clinicians would be able to predict a variety of behaviors and personality characteristics on the basis of knowing the individual's class membership. Moreover, the clinician would be able to attach a probability level to actuarial predictions.

Subsequently, in his presidential address to the Midwestern Psychological Association, Meehl (1956) described how such a method could be developed for the MMPI. In issuing his now famous call for an "MMPI Cookbook", Meehl (1956) described the cookbook method as one in which "any given configuration (holists please note, I said configuration, not sum!) of psychometric data is associated with each facet (or configuration) of personality description, and the closeness of this association is explicitly indicated by a number" (p. 121). Meehl (1956) did not provide a detailed prescription on how to develop a complete set of MMPI types but did note that the number of useful MMPI types is limited by the number of infallible criteria we wish to predict leading to a need to group different profiles into coarser types.

Meehl had now provided MMPI researchers with a theoretical rationale for developing actuarial methods of test interpretation and challenged them to do so. Instead of relying on now-antiquated Kraepelinian nosology, MMPI researchers were to identify a new, clinically useful set of MMPI-based classes. After the development of an actuarial classification system, test interpretation would involve a simple clerical task of using the scores to reveal the individual's class and looking up the empirical correlates of class membership in actuarial tables. Investigators responded with a variety of efforts at developing such systems and demonstrating their validity and clinical utility.

## The Codebook Approach to MMPI Interpretation

As reviewed in the preceding section, precursors to the codebook method of MMPI interpretation can be found in early research efforts, such as those reported by Hathaway and Meehl (1951) Guthrie (1952), and Black (1953). In these early investigations profiles were classified based simply on the highest one or two scales in the Welsh code. Halbower (1955) took this approach a step further by beginning to introduce a more stringent set of criteria for code-type classification. The advantage of using more stringent criteria was the identification of a relatively homogeneous set of individuals who would be classified to each code-type.

Marks and Seeman (1963) followed Halbower's lead in their development of a codebook for MMPI interpretation. They investigated the empirical correlates of 16 code types that occurred frequently enough in their setting to allow for a minimum of 20 subjects in each code type. Rules for code-type classification were quite stringent and detailed. Therapists who were familiar with the subjects in this study but had not been exposed to their MMPI profiles provided Q sorts of 108 descriptive statements that served as the primary source of personality correlate data. Case history and additional psychometric data also were used in the identification of empirical correlates.

The stringency with which Marks and Seeman (1963) defined each of their code types ensured that there would be relatively little overlap in their correlates. However, there was a clear cost associated with this benefit. In contrast to Marks and Seeman's (1963) initial report that nearly 80% of the patients at their facility could be classified into one of the 16 code types, subsequent researchers found that as many as 80% of patients in other facilities *could not* be so classified (Briggs, Taylor, & Tellegen, 1966). Thus, stringent code-type definitions produced discrete, however nonexhaustive profile classes that had empirically replicable correlates.

Subsequent attempts to identify and study stringently defined code types proved equally problematic. In response, researchers began to relax their code-type definitional criteria to allow for broader applicability of their systems. This however reintroduced the problem of less clearly distinctive and more heterogeneous code types with weaker and overlapping correlates. Further discussion on this issue is offered by Tellegen and Ben-Porath (1993).

Another difficulty introduced by loosely defined code types is that they are unstable. For example, the system developed by Gynther, Altman, and Sletten (1973) was intended to be nearly exhaustive. A profile was classified based on the highest two scales on the profile regardless of how distant these two scales were from the remaining scales on the profile. Thus, in a hypothetical case in which an individual scores 70 on scales 1 and 2, and 69 on the remaining scales on the profile, should the MMPI be re-administered a change of one or two $T$-score points would be sufficient to move that individual into an entirely different code-type.

Such instability is in fact found when this less stringent method of classification is employed. Graham, Smith, and Schwartz (1986) reported that only 28% of psychiatric inpatients who were retested with the MMPI within an average of 80 days produced the same two-point code. Ben-Porath and Butcher (1989b) found approximately 40% agreement in the two-point codes of college students who completed the MMPI twice within one week.

A final question regarding the code-type approach to MMPI interpretation is whether configural scale interpretation, implicit in profile coding, actually adds to the validity of MMPI interpretation. The most thoroughly documented answer (albeit limited in scope) to this question was provided by Goldberg (1965), who demonstrated that a linear combination of individual MMPI scale scores was more effective than the configural set of classification rules developed by Meehl and Dahlstrom (1960) to differentiate neurotics from psychotics with the MMPI.

In sum, the codebook method has received considerable research attention. Studies cited in this section have identified a broad range of normal and abnormal personality descriptors that are associated with adequately defined code types. However, recent trends toward the relaxation of classification rules and the absence of empirical evidence that the validity of a code type exceeds the sum (and even optimally weighted sum) of its parts raise questions about the ultimate utility of code-type-based profile interpretation.

## Additional Empirical Scale Developments

The codebook methodology just described represented the primary approach to MMPI interpretation and continues to dominate MMPI-2 interpretation to date. However, soon after the initial publication of the inventory, researchers began harvesting additional scales from the MMPI item pool. These efforts can be viewed as a fulfillment of Hathaway's initial (Hathaway & McKinley, 1940) and continued (e.g., Hathaway, 1960, 1972) calls for improvements and refinements in the MMPI. In their initial collection of basic readings on the MMPI, Welsh and Dahlstrom (1956) reprinted articles describing eight new scales designed to supplement the original clinical scales. These included measures of socioeconomic status (Gough, 1948), anti-Semitism (Gough, 1951), dominance (Gough, McClosky, & Meehl, 1951), caudality (Williams, 1952), ego-strength (Barron, 1953), and control (Cuadra, 1953). An original chapter by Welsh (1956) describing his development of the factor-based scales A and R also was included, as was a reprinted article by Wiener (1948) describing his development of subtle and obvious keys for the MMPI.

These initial efforts at developing supplementary scales for the MMPI represented a variety of approaches to scale construction and conceptualization. Most followed in the footsteps of Hathaway and McKinley by using the contrasted-groups empirical-keying method to select items for their scales (e.g., Cuadra, 1953; Gough, 1948, 1951; Gough et al., 1951; and Williams, 1952). In all these studies, the investigators identified two or more criterion groups and selected items based on their psychometric ability to differentiate between the groups.

This early work was followed by a near-avalanche of similar studies designed to construct empirically keyed scales for the MMPI. By 1975, Volume II of the *MMPI Handbook* (Dahlstrom, Welsh, & Dahlstrom, 1975) listed almost as many supplementary scales (455) as there were test items. With continued efforts, the number of supplementary scales eventually exceeded the number of test items! In contrast to the 10 clinical and three validity scales that were scored from only 383 of the 550 MMPI items, the supplementary scales made full use of the entire item pool. Most, however, remained obscure, and were used rarely in clinical practice.

The new empirically keyed scales, although introducing a near-endless number of personality traits and constructs for measurement with the MMPI, did not necessarily represent psychometric innovation or even advance. They were based on the same premises and theoretical formulations as were described earlier for the original clinical scales. There was, however, innovation to be found in some of the other scales and research efforts compiled by Welsh and Dahlstrom (1956). These were to lay the foundations for a complementary approach to personality assessment with the MMPI—content-based interpretation.

## Content-Based Personality Assessment with the MMPI

The content-based approach to MMPI interpretation has evolved considerably since the initial publication of the test. It began with attempts to control for the obvious nature of some of the MMPI items and continued with the identification of two major content dimensions of the MMPI, the development of content-based subscales to aid in the interpretation of the heterogeneous clinical scales, and the compilation of lists of critical items, and it culminated in a set of content scales developed by Wiggins (1966). Following is a description of the origin of the content-based approach to MMPI interpretation and a discussion of the research foundations of various content-based strategies.

## Origins of the Content-Based Approach

The content-based approach in some respect stands in contradiction to the original designation of the MMPI as a purely empirical instrument. It appears to have evolved more out of necessity than intent. Its origins may be found in early MMPI theoretical writings and scale-development efforts. As reviewed under the heading *Theoretical Underpinnings of the MMPI*, Meehl (1945) argued that the literal content of the item stimulus was irrelevant to test interpretation, which should be based solely on the empirical correlates of the response. However, toward the end of his article Meehl (1945) noted:

> While it is true of many of the MMPI items, for example, that even a psychologist cannot predict on which scale they will appear or in what direction different sorts of abnormals will tend to answer them, still the relative acceptability of defensive answering would seem to be greater than is possible in responding to a set of inkblots. (p. 302)

In a later article Meehl and Hathaway (1946) commented further on this issue:

> One of the important failings of almost all structured personality tests is their susceptibility to "faking" or "lying" in one way or another, as well as their even greater susceptibility to unconscious self-deception and role-playing on the part of individuals who might consciously be quite honest and sincere in their responses. (p. 525)

The issue that was of considerable concern to the developers of the MMPI was that it is possible for an individual completing a highly valid (criterion, construct, and otherwise) measure of personality to produce an absolutely or relatively invalid test protocol. In other words, test validity is necessary, but not sufficient to guarantee the validity of individual test protocols, which may be tainted by any number of distorting strategies employed by the test-taker. Although in their initial empirical construction of the scales Hathaway and McKinley ignored the content of the test items, they could not assume that individuals taking the test would do the same. In fact, they assumed that individual differences in the approach people take to responding to the test items would be a function of both external circumstances (i.e., evaluation for need or eligibility for medical benefits) and internal states (e.g., the operation of unconscious defense mechanisms).

Meehl and Hathaway (1946) described the two initial validity scales L and F as relatively good indicators of conscious distortion. The L scale was made up of 15 items selected rationally (i.e., by examining their content) based on the honesty research of Hartshorne and May. It was keyed so that an elevated score would represent a conscious effort on the part of the individual to present her- or himself in an overly positive manner. It was assumed that people who approach the entire test this way would be detected based on their score on L. Meehl and Hathaway (1946) reported the results of one of the very first simulation studies in which L proved successful at detecting individuals who were instructed to present an overly-favorable picture. The F scale, although not intended initially for this purpose, also proved capable of detecting intentional distortion. Meehl and Hathaway (1946) reported that it was successful at detecting subjects who were instructed to "fake bad."

Meehl and Hathaway (1946) were thus satisfied that scales L and F would be capable of alerting the test-interpreter that conscious distortion has occurred and recommended that profiles with elevated scores on these scales be designated invalid and not interpreted. They remained concerned that these scales would be far less successful at identifying people who were unconscious distorters. Consequently, Meehl set about developing a subtle L scale, one that would identify an unconscious, defensive approach to the MMPI. His work culminated in the K scale. Briefly, the K scale was developed by identifying a sample of 50 patients who had been hospitalized due primarily to behavioral acting out problems (e.g., alcoholism) and who had elevated scores on L and normal range scores on the clinical scales, and contrasting empirically their responses to the MMPI item pool with those of the normative reference group used in other MMPI scale construction efforts. Twenty-two of the K items were identified in this manner and were designated in early writings as scale L6. Meehl was concerned that the L6 scale somewhat underestimated the amount of true psychopathology reported by depressed or schizophrenic patients. To counteract this tendency, he added eight items that did not appear to be sensitive to test-taking attitude but were answered differently (in the keyed direction) by depressed and schizophrenic patients when compared to the Minnesota normals. K is thus made up of the 30 items identified empirically by the two approaches.

Meehl and Hathaway (1946) reported that K was not developed originally to be used as a third validity scale. Rather, it was intended to be used as a correction scale or suppressor variable to correct for the effects of unconscious distortion upon scores on the clinical scales. Through a series of empirical analyses Meehl devised a set of weights to be applied to the raw score on K to correct the raw scores on five of the clinical scales. It is noteworthy and often overlooked that the K-correction works in two ways. Elevated scores on K increase the level of elevation on the K-corrected $T$-score in comparison to the nonK-corrected $T$-score, on the assumption that the individual under-reported their abnormal personality characteristics. Conversely, a lower than average raw score on K leads to a decrease in the K-corrected $T$-score in comparison with the non-K-corrected $T$-score, on the assumption that the individual over-reported pathology.

In sum, it can be seen that awareness of the effect of individual differences in responsiveness to item content led to the development of the MMPI validity scales. These scales have proven to be one of the strongest and most enduring assets of the test. Their present status will be discussed further later in this chapter. These scales also represent the early view that item content was essentially a source of nuisance variance, the effect of which needed to be measured and, to the extent possible, corrected. Subsequent research efforts began gradually to reflect a view of item content as a source of valid variance in its own right.

## Subtle and Obvious MMPI Scales

Concurrent with the development of the K scale, two early MMPI researchers (Wiener & Harmon, 1946) were developing an alternative approach for dealing with the problem of item content. Recognizing that some MMPI items were much more obviously related in content to the scale on which they were scored than were others, Wiener and Harmon (1946) sought to divide the clinical scales into obvious subscales, comprising items whose scoring on a given scale was intuitively clear, and subtle subscales, made up of items whose connection to the scale was either unclear or counter-intuitive based on their scoring direction.

Wiener and Harmon (1946), who worked in a Veterans Administration counseling center, articulated two goals for their efforts: (a) "[To] detect symptoms of emotional disturbance in test-conscious veterans who did not want to indicate them" (p. 7); and (b) "[to distinguish] invalidity on the separate scales of the Multiphasic Inventory" (p. 7). The first goal could be accomplished through the identification of elevated scores on one or more of the subtle subscales in cases where the full scale score was not elevated. The second goal was to be accomplished by contrasting within each scale the individual's score on the subtle and obvious subscales. A considerably higher subtle than obvious subscale score would indicate under-reporting of pathology in the area measured by that scale; an opposite pattern would indicate over-reporting.

Each author examined independently all the items on each of the clinical scales and sorted them into those that were relatively obvious and those that were relatively subtle. Empirical evaluations suggested that useful subtle and obvious keys were developed for five of the clinical scales (Wiener & Harmon, 1946). It is important to note that an implicit and necessary assumption in using these scales for the purposes intended by Wiener and Harmon is that the subtle scales are measures of what the clinical scales assess, but they are not susceptible to faking.

Wiener (1948) conducted one of the first external validation studies of the subtle and obvious subscales. He compared the obvious and subtle $T$-scores of 100 veterans, half of whom had been successful and the other half unsuccessful in school and in on-the-job training. Previous analyses of this data set using the full scales indicated that "the MMPI showed consistent but generally insignificant differences favoring the emotional stability of the successful group" (Wiener, 1948, p. 168). In Wiener's new analyses, all five obvious scales were significantly higher for the unsuccessful group than the successful one, averaging a 6.5 $T$-score point difference. However, none of the subtle scales discriminated significantly between the two groups.

Wiener (1948) interpreted these findings as supporting the distinction between the subtle and obvious scales as the obvious scales were able to discriminate between the two groups much more successfully than the full scales. However, these findings failed to provide any empirical support for the subtle scales and should have raised questions about including the so-called subtle items on the full clinical scales. They did, however, suggest that content-based assessment (as represented by the rationally-derived obvious scales) could yield clinically and statistically significant findings. The history of the subtle and obvious scales of the MMPI is replete with debate and controversy. Wiener's (1948) own findings are representative of much of the subsequent research with these scales. These investigations indicated that whereas the obvious scales can, in fact, be quite useful, there is very limited empirical support for the validity of the subtle scales as measures of psychopathology or as validity indicators. This issue is revisited later in this chapter.

## The Welsh Factor Scales

Although they have never become widely used in clinical applications of the MMPI, the Welsh factor scales, A and R, represented important landmarks in the evolution of content-based MMPI interpretation. Welsh (1956) developed these scales to provide measures of two dimensions that appeared repeatedly in factor analyses of the MMPI scales. The method of construction for these two scales is less important for the present discussion than the manner by which Welsh (1956) went about analyzing them and recommending their use. Prominent among the analyses he reported was a detailed inspection of the content of items that appeared on each scale. His recommendations for their interpretation also were guided, to a significant degree, by their content. This approach, advocated by one of the leading figures in MMPI research, marked a significant departure from the early doctrine of test interpretation, which was based exclusively on the empirical correlates of a response rather than its explicit meaning. Item content was no longer viewed solely as a potential cause of nuisance variance requiring sophisticated methods of correction. Rather, it was considered a potentially valid source of additional information. Although Welsh (1956) did not articulate this view explicitly, it is implied clearly in his methods of analysis.

## The Harris–Lingoes Subscales

One of the most direct attempts to incorporate item content in MMPI interpretation was the development by Harris and Lingoes (1955) of a set of subscales for the clinical scales. These scales were designed to assist in the interpretation of the clinical scales whose item content was very heterogeneous. As noted previously, in assigning items to the clinical scales, Hathaway and McKinley were uninterested in content and unbothered by heterogeneity. However, as users and researchers of the MMPI began to inspect the content of these scales, they discovered that a given clinical scale might comprise a wide range of content areas.

Harris and Lingoes (1955) developed their subscales by examining the content of items on a given clinical scale and assigning them rationally to clusters of item content. The scales were designed to aid the test-interpreter by allowing her or him to determine which of several sources of content may be contributing to an elevated score on the full clinical scale. In contrast to Wiener and Harmon's (1946) subtle and obvious subscales, the assumption underlying and guiding construction of the Harris–Lingoes subscales was that the obvious content of an item carried the brunt of its interpretive meaning. Thus, use of the Harris and Lingoes subscales was based on the assumption that people respond in meaningful ways to the content of MMPI items.

## Critical Items

If the content of items to which an individual is responding is viewed as relevant to assessing their personality, a logical extension of this approach might be the examination of responses to individual items. After all, if one wishes to know what the test-taker said about him- or herself, there is no more direct way to find this out than to read his or her answers to specific test items. Grayson (1951) was the first to propose such an approach. He devised a list of 38 items that he believed to be highly indicative of severe psychopathology and should, if answered in the keyed direction, lead the test-interpreter to pause and take notice. They were designated *critical* or *stop* items. The Grayson list was generated on the basis of a rational inspection of item content and no empirical studies were ever published to support the selection and utility of these items. The same is true of a subsequent list of 68 items proposed by Caldwell (1969).

More recent attempts to develop critical item lists have employed empirical methods of item selection. Koss and Butcher (1973) based their selection of items on the responses of individuals known to be experiencing various types of crisis situations. Lachar and Wrobel (1979) selected their items by contrasting the responses of clinical and nonclinical samples. Both lists have received some additional empirical attention (e.g., Evans, 1984; Koss, Butcher, & Hoffman, 1976).

Critical item lists are, in some respects, the most radical of the content-based approaches to MMPI interpretation. The psychometric limitations of individual items are well known; however, developers of these lists have never proposed that they be used as psychometric indicators. Rather, they are viewed as a useful way for the test-interpreter to get a flavor for some of the specific issues that are of concern to the test-taker and as a means for identifying areas of functioning that might require additional evaluation.

## Content Scales

Content scales are the most direct, reliable means for communication between the test-taker and test-interpreter. In contrast to critical items, when constructed properly, content scales provide psychometrically sound measures for discerning the major content themes of the individual's self-report. Wiggins (1966) set the standard for rigorous construction of content scales for the MMPI.

In providing a rationale for his project, Wiggins (1966) noted the dearth of attempts to develop content-based scales for the MMPI. He attributed this situation to the ambivalence, if not animosity, that existed among the originators of the MMPI toward any deviation from the strict empirical approach to scale construction and interpretation. Wiggins offered cogent arguments in favor of exploring the possibility of constructing content-based scales for the MMPI, citing research that had demonstrated equivalence, if not superiority, of content-based measures over empirically keyed ones, and the desirability of developing psychometrically sound, dimensional means of gauging the communication conveyed by the test-taker to its interpreter.

Wiggins (1966) began his study by examining the internal consistency of the 26 content-based item-groupings described originally (for descriptive, not prescriptive purposes) by Hathaway and McKinley (1940). He found some content areas to be quite promising for further scale-development efforts, whereas others, for a variety of reasons including a dearth of items, clearly were not. He then set about revising the content categories based on a rational-intuitive analysis followed by additional empirical analyses that yielded a set of 15 content dimensions that were promising enough to warrant further analyses. Empirical analyses involving the entire item pool of the MMPI yielded eventually a set of 13 internally consistent and relatively independent content scales.

The significance of Wiggins's (1966) efforts cannot be overstated. His methods served as the prototype for all subsequent efforts to develop content-based scales for the MMPI, and the psychometric success of his endeavor provided much needed empirical support for the still-fledgling content-based approach to MMPI interpretation in particular and personality assessment in general. His method of scale construction was emulated in subsequent efforts to develop content-based measures for the MMPI (e.g., Morey, Waugh, & Blashfield [1985], in their development of *DSM-III*-based personality disorder scales for the MMPI). And, as will be described later, when the revisers of the MMPI sought to expand its item pool, they did so through the development of new content scales, following the tradition and methods originated by Wiggins (1966).

## Evolution of the MMPI: Conclusions

The developments chronicled in this section illustrate that by the 1980s, use of the MMPI followed only nominally the initial intent of its developers. Gone were both the nosological categories into which people were to be classified and the initial goal of developing an instrument to be used primarily for the differential diagnosis of psychopathology. Criticisms of the MMPI that cite its inadequacies in this area (e.g., Helmes and Reddon, 1993) are irrelevant to its present applications.

After recognizing that the MMPI did not serve adequately its initial function, the test's developers and their students established two broad categories or methodologies for its application in clinical assessment and research: the empirical and content-based methods of interpretation. Of the two, the empirical method has dominated both in the extent of its research base and in its actual use in clinical evaluations. Within the empirical framework, the typologically grounded codebook approach continues to prevail; however, it is based on certain assumptions regarding configural scoring that merit further evaluation. A clear trend toward greater acceptance and incorporation of content-based approaches has characterized MMPI interpretation more recently.

The MMPI is without precedent in the amount, extent, and quality of the research efforts that have guided its application in differentiating normal and abnormal personality. Nevertheless, over the years, researchers and users of the MMPI became keenly aware of several shortcomings and deficiencies in the test that might be addressed through its update and revision. These considerations led eventually to the MMPI restandardization project and the publication of the MMPI-2.

## The MMPI-2: 1989

The publication, in 1989, of the revised version of the MMPI represented the culmination of nearly a decade of research. Although not without controversy and debate, 4 years after the MMPI-2's publication the revised version of the inventory had already replaced the original in the vast majority of clinical settings (Webb, Levitt, & Rojdev, 1993). In the next sections, the rationale, goals, methods, and outcome of the revision will be described.

## Rationale for the Revision

A need to update and revise the MMPI had been recognized and expressed for some time prior to the launching of the restandardization project (cf. Butcher, 1972). However, for a variety of reasons, it was not until the early 1980s that the test publisher, the University of Minnesota Press, launched an effort to examine the feasibility, and eventually fund a major revision of what by then had become the most widely used self-report measure of personality (Lubin, Larsen, & Matarazzo, 1984). Following is a discussion of the factors that led eventually to the revision.

Among the various arguments made in favor of revising the MMPI, none was more salient than the need to update the test's norms. As described earlier in this chapter, the MMPI normative sample was collected in the 1930s and consisted almost exclusively of Caucasian working-class rural Minnesotans possessing an average of 8 years of education who happened to be visiting the University Hospital at the time of the project and consented to serve as subjects. This sample, although appropriate for the test's initial application, was no longer adequate as the MMPI became more widely used in a variety of settings throughout the United States and the world over.

A second focus of the revision was MMPI items, which had come under considerable criticism over the years for a number of reasons. Foremost among these was the existence of items whose content was no longer clear, relevant, or appropriate based on modern linguistic patterns, cultural practices (e.g., "drop the handkerchief"), and social norms. One set of MMPI items that had stirred controversy for many years posed questions regarding the test-taker's religious beliefs and practices. Other questions delved into such matters as excretory functions and sexual orientation. Butcher and Tellegen (1966) provided an empirically generated list of objectionable MMPI items. In addition, a relatively large set of MMPI items was not scored on any of the clinical, validity, or widely used supplementary scales. These nonworking items were viewed as an unnecessary burden, and candidates for deletion and replacement. A final item-level issue was the absence of content dealing with issues that are relevant to contemporary clinical personality assessment (e.g., suicidal ideation, type A behavior, use of drugs such as marijuana, work-related difficulties, and treatment readiness). A tradeoff between nonworking and new items was viewed as the appropriate strategy for confronting both problems. The test's revision was an opportunity to eliminate objectionable items, rewrite others that were worded archaically or contained gender-specific references, and to eliminate nonworking items and replace them with the ones addressing contemporary clinical concerns.

## Goals for the Revision

Recognizing the needs and problems just noted, in 1982 the University of Minnesota Press, owner of the MMPI, appointed a committee of MMPI researchers that was charged with the task of carrying out a revision of the MMPI. The committee eventually included James N. Butcher, W. Grant Dahlstrom, John R. Graham, and Auke Tellegen. Beverly Kaemmer, test manager for the University of Minnesota Press, served as the coordinator for the committee that came to be known as the *MMPI Restandardization Committee.*

The restandardization committee was entrusted with two potentially discordant goals: improve the test while maintaining as much continuity as possible with the original

MMPI so as not to lose its vital research base. Improvement was to be attained by updating the normative base (hence the name *restandardization project*) and correcting the item-level deficiencies just noted. Continuity was to be accomplished by minimizing the amount of change to be introduced in the original validity and clinical scales so as to allow test-interpreters to continue to rely on decades of accumulated research and clinical experience with these scales.

Referring to the two main methodologies of MMPI interpretation reviewed earlier in this chapter, the MMPI restandardization committee decided to maintain continuity by retaining the test's ability to rely on the codebook database that had accumulated over the years and which served as the primary source of interpretive information while developing an expanded item pool to be harvested for new content-based scales.

## Methods of the Revision

The first task of the restandardization committee was to develop an experimental MMPI booklet with which the new normative data would be collected and from which new items could be added to the test. The MMPI-AX was developed by retaining all 550 original MMPI items (although 82 were reworded slightly to correct for archaic or otherwise inappropriate language), dropping the 16 repeated items that had been added to the test for ease of scoring, and writing 154 new, experimental items as candidates for replacing nonworking and objectionable items.[2] The new items were to cover content areas identified above as missing from the original MMPI.

Additional instruments developed for the restandardization project included a biographical data form that was used to collect extensive demographic data on normative and other subjects and a life events form designed to identify subjects who had been experiencing extreme stress in 6 months prior to participating in the project. A subset of subjects who participated in the normative data collection along with their spouses or live-in partners also completed a modified version of the Katz and Lyerly (1963) Adjustment Scale and Spanier's (1976) Dyadic Adjustment Scale. These were to be used as sources of validity and correlate data for new scales that might be developed.

The MMPI-2 normative sample was collected throughout the United States, using a variety of procedures designed to produce an adequate sample of the population of individuals with whom the test is used. Over 2,900 individuals completed the test battery, of these 2,600 (1,462 women and 1,138 men) produced valid and complete protocols and were included in the normative sample. Approximately 1,680 members of the normative sample who participated along with their spouses or live-in partners completed the two additional forms. Individual subjects were paid $15 for their participation; couples received $40.

A number of additional clinical and nonclinical data sets were compiled and used in various scale development and validation studies. These included a sample of psychiatric inpatients (Graham & Butcher, 1988), individuals undergoing substance abuse treatment (McKenna & Butcher, 1987), patients at a pain treatment clinic (Keller & Butcher, 1991), college students (Ben-Porath & Butcher, 1989a,b; Butcher, Graham, Dahlstrom,

---

[2]A second booklet, the MMPI-TX, was developed for a separate project designed to explore the feasibility of developing an adolescent version of the MMPI. This project culminated in the publication of the MMPI-A (Butcher, Williams, Graham, Archer, Tellegen, Ben-Porath, & Kaemmer, 1992).

& Bowman, 1990; military personnel (Butcher et al., 1990), mothers at risk for child abuse (Egland, Erickson, Butcher, & Ben-Porath, 1991), and participants in the Boston Normative Aging Study (Butcher et al., [1991]. All told, over 10,000 subjects were tested in conjunction with the restandardization project.

## Outcome of the Revision

The MMPI-2 consists of 567 items. Of the 383 items scored on the basic validity and clinical scales of the MMPI, 372 appear on the MMPI-2. Eleven items were deleted due to objectionable content. No basic scale lost more than four items; most scales did not lose any. A total of 64 MMPI-2 items were revised slightly. Ben-Porath & Butcher (1989b) found these changes to impact negligibly on the psychometric functioning of the scales on which they were scored. Thus, consistent with the goal of maintaining continuity with the original, the basic validity and clinical scales of the MMPI-2 are nearly identical to those of the MMPI. Improvements were made with the introduction of new norms and a new way of calculating MMPI-2 standard scores, new validity scales, and the MMPI-2 content scales (Butcher, Graham, Williams, and Ben-Porath, 1990).

### New Norms

As just described, norms for the MMPI-2 were based on a national sample of 2,600 individuals tested for the restandardization project. For a variety of reasons, members of the MMPI-2 normative sample produced higher raw scores on the test's clinical scales than did their 1930s original MMPI counterparts. A primary factor contributing to this shift was a change in the instructions given to MMPI test takers. At the time it was developed and during the early years of its use, the original MMPI was administered by presenting a test taker with each item on a separate index card and instructing her or him to sort them into three piles of statements that were "true" about them, those that were "false", and those that they could not decide whether they were true or false. The instructions did not discourage the third, so-called "Cannot Say" response option. When MMPI administration shifted from the "Card Form" to booklets, the instructions were changed and item omission was explicitly discouraged. These instructions, which had become the standard for MMPI administration, were used in the normative data collection. As a result, members of the MMPI-2 normative sample responded to more of the test's items than their original counterparts, contributing to the increase in raw scores on the clinical scales.

A second factor leading to the higher clinical scale raw scores in the MMPI-2 restandardization sample involved societal changes over the 40+ years that separated the two normative data collection studies. These include both real changes in how individuals perceive themselves, as well as a greater willingness to admit holding unattractive beliefs and engaging in undesirable behaviors. Regardless of their cause higher raw scores in the new normative sample translated into lower $T$-scores for the same raw score based on the new norms. This led the restandardization committee to lower the cutting point for clinically meaningful elevation on the MMPI-2 from a $T$-score of 70 to 65.

Another potential source of change at the $T$-score level was the development of uniform $T$-scores for the MMPI-2 (Tellegen & Ben-Porath, 1992). Briefly, uniform $T$-scores were developed to correct a long-recognized problem with MMPI $T$-scores. Because the raw score distributions for the clinical scales are differentially skewed when using linear *T*-scores, the same value does not correspond to the same percentile across different scales. The lack of percentile equivalence across scales makes direct comparisons of *T*-scores on different clinical scales potentially misleading. The solution adopted by the restandardization committee was to compute the average distribution of non-K-corrected raw scores for men and women in the normative sample and correct each scale's distribution slightly to correspond to this composite. This is accomplished in the transformation of raw scores to *T*-scores. This approach yields percentile-equivalent *T*-scores while retaining the skewed nature of the distribution of the clinical scales. By comparing profiles based on uniform versus traditional linear *T*-scores (both derived from the new normative sample), Graham, Timbrook, Ben-Porath, and Butcher (1991) demonstrated that the uniform *T*-scores do not alter substantially the nature and characteristics of the MMPI-2 profile.

A final source of potential difficulty in interpreting scores on the clinical scales based on the new norms was the relatively high socio-economic status (SES) of the new normative sample when compared to the 1980 census figures. To address these concerns, Pope, Butcher, & Seelen (1993) produced figures illustrating that the correlation between the MMPI-2 clinical scales and SES indicators, such as education, does not yield clinically meaningful differences between the profiles of various SES groups. Schinka and LaLone (1997) recalculated the MMPI-2 norms based on a reduced sample designed to match national SES distributions and concluded that the resulting norms were not meaningfully different from the MMPI-2 norms. Thus, the relatively high SES standing of the MMPI-2 normative sample does not affect the utility of the revised norms.

In summary, the new MMPI-2 norms more accurately reflected contemporary societal trends without jeopardizing the interpretability of the clinical scales. Nonetheless, shortly after the MMPI-2 was released some authors questioned whether the new norms might impede code-type interpretation, based on observations that when code types were derived, the new norms yielded seemingly discrepant results. Initial data suggesting this possibility were provided in the 1989 MMPI-2 manual, where it was reported that the same 2-point code type is found in only two thirds of cases where the same responses are plotted on MMPI and MMPI-2 norms. Dahlstrom (1992b) reported similar results.

Concerns regarding code-type congruence or comparability across the two sets of norms were not trivial. At issue was the applicability of nearly 50 years of research and clinical experience with the MMPI, to MMPI-2 interpretation, which, as described earlier is heavily influenced by code-type classification. If, in fact, in roughly one-third of the cases the two sets of norms yielded different code types, which set of empirical correlates should be used in interpreting the profile? As it turned out, this concern was based on misleading data analyses including those reported in the 1989 MMPI-2 manual.

As described earlier in this chapter, the codebook approach to MMPI interpretation has undergone tremendous change over the years. The method used to define code types in the analyses reported in the 1989 MMPI-2 manual and by Dahlstrom (1992b) yields highly unstable and thus unreliable code types. A change of one *T*-score point on two scales can lead to an entirely different code-type designation. Because neither MMPI nor MMPI-2 scales are perfectly reliable, meaningful code-type classification schemes cannot be sensitive to such minuscule changes. Rather, a minimal degree of differentiation between the scales in the code type and the remaining scales on the profile must be present for the code type to be stable.

Analyses conducted by Graham et al. (1991) indicated that scales in a code type need to be at least five points higher than the remaining scales in a profile for the code type to be sufficiently stable. Such *well-defined code types* are also quite stable across the MMPI and MMPI-2 norms. Graham et al. (1991) report congruence in 80–95% of clinical and nonclinical profiles when well-defined code types are evaluated. In nearly all of the relatively small proportion of cases where the same code type does not emerge, at least one scale appears in both code types. McNulty, Ben-Porath, and Graham (1998) demonstrated subsequently that as expected, well-defined code types produce more valid empirical correlates than nondefined ones.

## New Scales

As discussed earlier, the MMPI-2 Restandardization Project had two seemingly contradictory goals: to improve the instrument while maintaining continuity with its empirical and experiential database. Continuity was fostered by leaving the 13 basic validity and clinical scales of the MMPI largely intact. Improvement was accomplished primarily through the introduction of 21 new scales in the 1989 manual, including three new validity scales, the MMPI-2 content scales (Butcher et al., 1990), and three supplementary scales, two designed to measure gender roles and a post-traumatic stress disorder (PTSD) indicator.

**New Validity Scales.** Three new validity scales were developed for the MMPI-2. The $F_B$ scale is very similar to the original F scale. It is made up of items that appear in the second half of the booklet that were endorsed infrequently by the MMPI-2 normative sample. The $F_B$ scale allows the interpreter to detect any changes in the test-taker's response pattern that may have occurred after the first part of the booklet where nearly all of the F scale items are located. Studies have shown that the $F_B$ scale contributes successfully to detecting shifting response patterns across the inventory (Berry, Wetter, Baer, & Widiger, 1991; Clark, Gironda, & Young, 2003; Gallen & Berry, 1996, 1997).

Two response consistency scales fashioned after similar scales developed by Tellegen & Waller (in press) for the Multidimensional Personality Questionnaire (MPQ) were added to the MMPI-2. Variable Response Inconsistency (VRIN) measures random responding by considering test-takers' responses to pairs of MMPI-2 items identified through a series of statistical and semantic analyses designed to yield pairs of items that are identical or opposite in meaning. The scale is keyed so that for each item pair that an individual answers inconsistently, she or he will receive a point on VRIN. Raw scores are converted into linear $T$-scores that inform the test-interpreter regarding the extent of random responding in a given protocol. Studies have demonstrated that the VRIN scale is an effective indicator of random responding (e.g., Berry et al., 1991; Paolo & Ryan, 1993; Wetter, Baer, Berry, Smith, & Larsen, 1992).

The second consistency scale introduced with the MMPI-2 is True Response Inconsistency (TRIN). This scale is made up of pairs of items that are opposite in meaning. Item pairs were identified through a series of statistical and semantic analyses. Because each item pair is opposite in meaning, answering both items True or False is inconsistent. Some pairs are inconsistent only when both are answered True, others are inconsistent only when both are answered False, and some are inconsistent with both combinations. The number of inconsistent True and inconsistent False responses is tallied separately, and T-scores were developed so that the test-interpreter can determine the predominant direction of inconsistency ("True" or "False"). TRIN can be used to detect two possible response sets: *yea saying* or *nay saying*. Knowledge of the presence of such response sets is particularly important given the asymmetrical keying that characterizes some of the MMPI-2 scales. For example, all of the items on L and all but one of the items on K are keyed false. Thus, a *nay saying* response set could produce artificially inflated scores on these scales. Examination of TRIN allows the test-interpreter to detect such response sets and consider their effects on the MMPI-2 scales in her or his interpretation. Even for scales with balanced keys, extreme TRIN scores, like high VRIN scores, indicate protocol invalidity.

**The MMPI-2 Content Scales.** As noted earlier, beginning in the 1950s content-based considerations gained increasing acceptance as a supplement to the codebook-based interpretation of scores on the MMPI clinical scales. The Wiggins (1966) content scales represented the most thorough and comprehensive application of this approach to the MMPI. It is, therefore, not surprising that the MMPI restandardization committee opted to introduce interpretive innovation through the adoption of a new set of content scales developed by Butcher et al. (1990).

The MMPI-2 content scales were developed through a series of rational–conceptual and empirical analyses fashioned after the ones used by Wiggins (1966) in developing the original content scales for the MMPI. Items were assigned first to potential scales based on a consensus among judges who conducted a rational examination of their content. Then, a series of statistical analyses was carried out to eliminate items that did not contribute to the internal consistency of a scale and to identify potential items for inclusion that were missed in the first round of rational analyses. The latter were then inspected rationally and added to a scale if they were found by consensus to be related to the domain that it was designed to measure. Final statistical analyses were conducted to eliminate items that created excessive intercorrelation among the content scales.

This process yielded a set of 15 content scales. As might be expected, some of these scales are similar in composition to the ones developed by Wiggins (1966). Nearly all the scales have new items on them; some (e.g., Type A Behaviors and Negative Treatment Indicators) are composed predominantly of new items. As discussed earlier in this chapter, the interpretation of content scales can be based entirely on the actual content of the items endorsed. Empirical identification of correlates can substantiate and enhance content-based interpretation.

Butcher et al. (1990) reported initial empirical correlates for the MMPI-2 content scales. Since their introduction, a substantial body of empirical research has established the validity of these scales, in particular, their incremental validity relative to the clinical scales. For example, Archer, Aiduk, Griffin, and Elkins (1996) examined the incremental validity of the content scales with psychiatric inpatients; Barthlow, Graham, Ben-Porath, and McNulty (1999) demonstrated the incremental validity of the scales with mental health outpatients; Ben-Porath, McCully, and Almagor (1993) explored their incremental validity as predictors of other self-report measures of personality and psychopathology; Ben-Porath, Butcher, and Graham (1991) and Wetzler, Khadivi, and Moser (1998) found that the content scales contribute incrementally to psychodiagnosis; and Palav, Ortega, and McCaffrey (2001) studied the incremental validity of the content scales with neurologically impaired patients.

### Other New Scales

Three additional scales introduced with the 1989 MMPI-2 manual have not fared as well as the new validity and content scales. Two gender role measures, Gender Role–Masculine and Gender Role–Feminine, and a new measure designed to assess symptoms of post traumatic stress disorder (PTSD), the Schlenger PTSD Scale, have received very little attention in the literature and there are no empirical data to support their interpretation.

# The MMPI-2: 2001 Update

During the decade following publication of the MMPI-2, the test was the subject of over 800 journal articles, 70 book chapters, 20 books, and some 360 doctoral dissertations. Some of this research (cited earlier) focused initially on comparing clinical scale scores based on the MMPI versus MMPI-2 norms. Surveys of practitioners (e.g., Webb et al., 1993,) indicated that most were quick to adopt the revised instrument. Consequently, the focus of MMPI-2 research soon shifted to validating the new scales and exploring further scale development based (in part) on the new items added to the inventory. To incorporate the wealth of information just mentioned, in 2001 a revised edition of the MMPI-2 manual was published (Butcher, Graham, Ben-Porath, Tellegen, & Kaemmer, 2001).

## Goals and Content

The 2001 manual was designed to update interpretive guidelines for some scales of the MMPI-2 included in the 1989 manual, formalize the discontinuation of others, and provide guidelines for interpreting several new scales developed during the decade following the revision. The revised manual did not introduce any changes in the norms or item composition of the MMPI-2 scales included in the 1989 manual.

## Discontinued Scales

Several years prior to publication of the 2001 manual, the MMPI-2 publisher, the University of Minnesota Press, decided to discontinue one set of scales that had been included in the 1989 manual, the subtle and obvious subscales. As discussed earlier, empirical support for the validity of the subtle scales was scant from the beginning. Nonetheless, in the interest of continuity, the 1989 MMPI-2 manual authors decided to keep the obvious and subtle subscales in the official scoring materials for the test. This sparked renewed efforts to study these scales (e.g., Timbrook, Graham, Keiller, & Watts, 1993; Weed, Ben-Porath, & Butcher, 1990), which continued to point toward the invalidity of the subtle scales. With the 2001 manual now superseding the 1989 edition, the obvious and subtle scales were no longer included in the official documentation for the test. Another scale omitted from the 2001 manual was the Schlenger PTSD scale (described earlier). During the decade following publication of the MMPI-2 no research had been generated to guide its interpretation and it is largely redundant with the Keane PTSD scale that remains on the list of supplementary scales.

## New Scales and Revised Profile

Many new scales were developed during the decade following publication of the MMPI-2. The authors of the 2001 manual reviewed this research and identified several new scales and sets of scales that had garnered sufficient empirical support to be added to the list of scales incorporated in the manual. These developments led (in some cases) to structural changes in the instrument's profiles.

**Revised Validity Scale Profile.** The 2001 manual introduced a significant structural change in the validity scale profile. The four original validity scales (Cannot Say, L, F, and K) were augmented (as described earlier) by the $F_B$, VRIN, and TRIN scales introduced with the 1989 publication of the MMPI-2. In the following decade, two additional validity scales Infrequency Psychopathology (Fp; Arbisi and Ben-Porath, 1995) and Superlative Self-Presentation (Butcher & Han, 1995) had been introduced and validated sufficiently to warrant their inclusion among the validity indicators. The 2001 revisions to the validity scale profile were designed to place these ten scales within a conceptual framework for assessing test protocol validity and present them in the order in which they should be considered. This framework is guided by the recognition that self-report measures are susceptible to several validity threats inherent to the methodology and there is no way to construct self-report measures that are immune to these challenges. The only way to address these threats, therefore, is to measure them and consider their impact upon scores on the substantive scales of the test. Although these threats are discussed next in the context of the MMPI-2, they are at issue in all self-report-based assessment devices.

The conceptual framework that guided the restructuring of the validity scale profile identifies two classes of threats to the validity of a test protocol. Noncontent-based threats involve any response pattern that is not based on an accurate reading, comprehension, and consideration of the instrument's items. Content-based threats are the product of misleading responses to properly read, comprehend, and consider test items.

The MMPI-2 validity scales target three types of noncontent-based threats. Nonresponding occurs when a test taker fails to answer an item or answers it both true and false. Because of the method used to score the test's scales, a nonresponse introduces bias to these scores. MMPI-2 raw scores are calculated by counting the number of items on a scale that the respondent has answered in the keyed direction (true or false). A nonresponse, therefore, is reflected in a scale's raw score exactly the same as if the test taker had answered the item in the nonkeyed direction. It is implausible to assume that an individual failing to respond to an item would have answered it in the nonkeyed direction had they chosen to respond in the first place. Consequently, a nonresponse artificially deflates MMPI-2 scales' raw scores.

Because this will affect all scales that have nonscorable item responses, considering the extent to which nonresponding has occurred, and if so, which scales (including other validity scales) are affected, is the starting point to any protocol validity analysis. The Cannot Say count (which is not actually a scale, and therefore does not appear on the profile) provides a gross appraisal of the extent of nonresponding. Automated scoring services inform the interpreter of the percentage of items answered on each scale, allowing for a more direct appraisal of the nonresponding threat on a scale-by-scale basis.

The second type of noncontent-based threat is random responding, which occurs when the test taker responds to the items in a nonsystematic manner without accurately considering their content. Random responding may be intentional, as in the case of an individual who marks her or his answers without attempting to read the items. It may also be unintentional, if the individuals lacks the required reading or language comprehension skills to be able to read and comprehend the test items or is confused and disorganized and responds, therefore, based on an inaccurate consideration of their content. The VRIN scale (discussed earlier) assists in identifying random responding, but not in distinguishing between its intentional or unintentional origins. Because random responding affects scores on all other MMPI-2 scales (including those that assess content-based invalid responding), it is the first to appear on the left-hand side of the revised profile.

The third type of noncontent-based responding is fixed responding, which involves a fixed pattern of responding without consideration of an item's content. The MMPI-2 TRIN scale (discussed earlier) provides information on the extent and direction of fixed responding. Unlike random responding, fixed responding, although rare, is almost always volitional. It too threatens the validity of all MMPI-2 scales including measures of content-based invalid responding. Therefore, the TRIN scale appears immediately following VRIN on the revised validity scale profile.

The MMPI-2 validity scales assess for two types of content-based invalid responding. Over-reporting involves any response pattern where the individual describes her- or himself as being worse-off psychologically than an objective assessment would indicate. Three infrequency scales F, $F_B$, and Fp are used to gauge over-reporting. F and $F_B$ have already been discussed. The basic premise underlying the use of infrequency scales to identify over-reporting is that when individuals attempt to overstate their self-reported problems, they will endorse unlikely ones. However, infrequent responding may be the product of four different sources: (a) random responding; (b) fixed responding; (c) severe psychopathology or distress; or (d) intentional over-reporting (also known as faking bad or malingering).

Because VRIN and TRIN should already have been considered, random and fixed responding will have been ruled out before the infrequency scale scores are examined, leaving the interpreter the task of differentiating between severe dysfunction and intentional over-reporting. Arbisi and Ben-Porath (1995) introduced the Fp scale to assist in this task. Fp includes 27 items endorsed infrequently by psychiatric inpatients experiencing severe psychopathology and distress. Individuals who produce an elevated score on this scale present in a manner that is highly unlikely even for individuals experiencing dysfunction. Coupled with an elevation on the other infrequency scales, an elevated score on Fp is a strong indicator of intentional over-reporting. Conversely, a nonelevated score on Fp coupled with elevations on the other infrequency scales indicates that severe psychopathology and distress are more likely present than over-reporting. In a recent meta-analysis, Rogers, Sewell, Martin, and Vitacco (2003) concluded that Fp is the most effective MMPI-2 scale in detecting over-reporting.

The second content-based threat to protocol validity is under-reporting. Here, a comparison between the individual's self-report and an objective assessment would reveal that the test taker has failed to report the nature and/or extent of her/his psychological difficulties. The original MMPI scales L and K are used to detect and quantify the presence, nature, and extent of under-reporting. Butcher and Han (1995) developed the Superlative Self-Presentation (S) scale by contrasting the responses of individuals highly motivated to under-report with those of MMPI-2 normative sample members. Preliminary studies (e.g., Baer & Miller, 2002; Baer, Wetter, Nichols, and Greene, 1995) have indicated that this scale adds to L and K in detecting under-reporting with the MMPI-2. Further research is needed to clarify how it might best be used to augment L and K interpretation in this task.

## The Personality-Psychopathology-Five (PSY-5) Scales

A major MMPI-2 innovation incorporated in the 2001 manual was the addition of the MMPI-2 Personality-Psychopathology-Five (PSY-5) scales to the standard list of measures scales and scoring materials for the test. The scales were introduced first by Harkness, McNulty, and Ben-Porath (1995) as measures of a personality model developed and described in detail in the first edition of this text by Harkness and McNulty (1994). Harkness, McNulty, Ben-Porath, and Graham (2002) provide extensive analyses of the PSY-5 scales' psychometric properties and the most up-to-date definition of the five constructs.

Harkness and McNulty (1994) discussed how the five constructs compare with other Five-Factor models of personality. They reported that the origin for the PSY-5 scales was research done by Harkness (1992) on the *DSM-III-R* criteria for diagnosing personality disorders. Thus, in contrast to other Five-Factor models that have been explored ex-post-facto as dimensional models of personality disorder symptomatology, the PSY-5 constructs originated from the clinical criteria for diagnosing personality disorders. Moreover, the MMPI-2 scales developed by Harkness et al. (1995) to assess the PSY-5 consist of clinically-salient items. Graham, Ben-Porath and McNulty (1999) provided a comprehensive list of empirical correlates for the PSY-5 scales in an outpatient community mental health setting. The following description of the PSY-5 constructs is based on all of the sources just cited.

Aggressiveness (AGGR) is associated with offensive, instrumental aggression designed to achieve a desired goal (as opposed to being reactive). Individuals high on this dimension are more likely to have a history of being physically abusive, and to be viewed by others as aggressive and antisocial. Men high on AGGR are more likely than others to have a history of having committed domestic violence, and women are more likely to have been arrested.

Psychoticism (PSYC), as measured by the PSY-5, assesses a disconnection from reality reflected in unshared beliefs or unusual sensory and perceptual experiences. Alienation and unrealistic expectations of harm are also associated with higher than average standing on this construct. Empirically, individuals who score high on the PSYC scale are more likely to present with disorganized, delusional, bizarre, or circumstantial thought processes as well as hallucinations, loose associations, and flight of ideas.

Disconstraint (DISC) involves risk taking, impulsivity, and the absence of moral restraint. Consistent with this conceptualization, individuals who score high on the DISC scale have been found to be more risk-taking, impulsive, and less traditional. In clinical settings, they are more likely to have a history of substance abuse and be viewed as aggressive and antisocial. Low scores on this scale are associated with greater self-control and boredom tolerance and an increased tendency toward rule-following.

Negative Emotionality Neuroticism (NEGE) involves a disposition to experience negative emotions. Individuals high on this dimension are viewed as worry-prone, overly self-critical, and guilt-prone. Empirically, individuals who produce elevated scores on the NEGE scale are more likely to be diagnosed with depression or dysthymia and described as presenting with anxiety, depression, and a sad mood state.

Introversion/Low Positive Emotions (INTR) scale is related to low hedonic capacity and interpersonal isolation. Empirically, high scorers on the INTR scale have increased rates of depression and dysthymia and are likely to present with sad and depressed mood. Low achievement orientation, anxiety, introversion, pessimism and somatic complaints are also associated with elevated scores on this scale. Since their initial publication, the PSY-5 scales have received considerable attention in the research literature. Bagby, Ryder, Ben-Dat, Bacchiochi, and Parker (2002) replicated the PSY-5 dimensional structure in clinical and nonclinical samples. Rouse, Finger, and Butcher (1999) conducted an Item Response Theory (IRT)-based analysis of the PSY-5 scales and concluded that they assess unidimensional constructs that conform to IRT requirements. Sharpe and Desai (2001) and Trull, Useda, Costa, and McCrae (1995) examined relations between, and the relative predictive abilities of the PSY-5 and NEO-PI-R-based Five-Factor model scales and concluded that although there is substantial overlap between the models, they each provide incrementally valid information in predicting extra-test criteria.

Vendrig, Derksen, and de Mey (2000) examined the ability of the PSY-5 scales to predict treatment outcome for chronic pain patients and reported that the INTR scale had incremental validity in predicting the emotional outcome of treatment.

Petroskey, Ben-Porath, and Stafford (2003) reported empirical correlates for the PSY-5 scales in a pretrial forensic assessment sample and concluded that they were consistent with findings in other settings and provide support for relying on PSY-5 scores in forensic assessments.

They offer a clinical perspective that is advantageous to differentiating normal and abnormal personality. They are particularly helpful as dimensional indicators of possible personality disorder symptomatology. Prior efforts to construct MMPI-2-based personality disorder scales have met with mixed success, in large part because of limitations of the categorical approach to defining and measuring these conditions. However, the advantages of dimensional differentiation between normal and abnormal behaviors are not limited to the Axis II domain. As the field moves more broadly toward a dimensional conceptualization of psychopathology, MMPI-2-based measures of the PSY-5 constructs will likely become even more important in clinical assessment and research. The PSY-5 scales provide MMPI-2 users an important link to a well-studied, influential personality model.

## The MMPI-2 Content Component Scales

Although item analyses designed to maximize their internal consistency ensured that the MMPI-2 content scales would be considerably more homogeneous than the clinical scales, it remains possible to parse some of them even further into relatively independent item clusters. The MMPI-2 content component scales were constructed by Ben-Porath and

Sherwood (1993) to serve as subscales designed to clarify content-scale interpretation much like the Harris Lingoes subscales are used with the clinical scales. The content component scales were derived through a series of principal component and item analyses of each of the content scales separately, resulting in a total of 28 subscales for 12 of the 15 content scales (Anxiety, Obsessiveness, and Work Interference did not produce sufficiently independent subscales). Most content scales yielded only two component subscales.

Initial data reported by Ben-Porath and Sherwood (1993) indicated that the component scales have sufficient within-parent scale discriminant validity to enable the test-interpreter to develop a more refined picture of the test-taker's self-portrayal. Subsequent studies (e.g., Clark, 1996; Englert, Weed, & Watson, 2000) have supported the content component scales' utility in clarifying the interpretation of their parent content scales. The 2001 manual authors recommend that, like the Harris Lingoes subscales, the MMPI-2 content component scales be interpreted only if their parent content scale is elevated.

### New Supplementary Scales

Three new and one old scale were added to the Supplementary Scale Profile in the 2001 manual. The three new scales were developed after the 1989 publication of the MMPI-2, and described in subsequent printings of that document. These are the Marital Distress Scale developed by Hjemboe, Almagor, and Butcher (1992), and two substance abuse measures, the Addiction Potential Scale (APS) and Addiction Admission Scale (AAS) that were developed by Weed, Butcher, McKenna, and Ben-Porath (1992). These authors reported initial data indicating that APS and AAS are incrementally valid with respect to the MAC-R scale. Similar results were reported by Greene, Weed, Butcher, Arrendondo, and Davis (1992). Follow-up studies (e.g., Aaronson, Dent, & Kline, 1996; Rouse, Butcher, & Miller, 1999; Sawrie, Kabat, Dietz, Greene, Arrendondo, & Mann, 1996; Stein, Graham, Ben-Porath, & McNulty, 1999; Svanum, McGrew, & Ehrmann, 1994) have supported the utility of AAS in particular as a predictor of substance abuse. Results for APS are more mixed, and additional research is needed to guide interpretation of this scale. Finally, a slightly revised version of an original MMPI scale that was not included in the 1989 manual, the Cook and Medley (1954) Hostility Scale, was added to the Supplementary Scale Profile following renewed interest in the scale (e.g., Han, Weed, Calhoun, & Butcher, 1995) and the relation between hostility and health (e.g., Smith & Christensen, 1992). The MMPI-2 version of the scale contains 28 of the original 31 items.

# The MMPI-2: Post-2001 Developments

Two major developments have occurred since the 2001 MMPI-2 manual was released: a renewed emphasis on considering non-K-corrected scores when interpreting the clinical scales and publication of the MMPI-2 Restructured Clinical (RC) scales.

### The K Correction

As described earlier, the K correction has been an integral part of scoring and interpreting the MMPI-2 clinical scales for nearly 60 years. However, the K correction poses a challenge to MMPI-2 interpreters who seek to rely on other MMPI-2 sources (e.g., the

Harris–Lingoes subscales, the MMPI-2 content scales, the PSY-5 and other supplementary scales,) none of which are similarly corrected. Non-K-corrected norms were developed for the MMPI-2 clinical scales and included in both the 1989 and 2001 manuals. To address the difficulties in comparing scores on K-corrected scales with the ones on noncorrected scales recommended for use to clarify their interpretation, non-K-corrected clinical scale profiles have recently been made available by the MMPI-2 publisher for both hand scoring and automated services. Differences between corrected and noncorrected scores are of course most likely to occur when the test taker produces a deviant score on K.

The renewed emphasis on non-K-corrected scores has refocused attention on the utility of the correction procedure. Examination of the literature on the correction indicates that questions about its validity have existed since it was first introduced. Initial data analyses, presented by McKinley, Hathaway, and Meehl (1948) to illustrate its effects, showed that in some instances applying the K-correction actually attenuated the validity of the clinical scales. These authors also suggested that alternative correction weights would likely need to be developed for different populations, but this never happened.

Dahlstrom and Welsh (1960, p. 154) observed that "the few studies available that provide cross-validational evidence on the K-corrections have [indicated that] the K scale corrections do not seem to be beneficial, and may actually reduce the effective separations obtained without K-corrections." In updating their review of the literature, Dahlstrom, Welsh, and Dahlstrom (1972) noted that subsequent studies of the K correction continued to fail to support its use. However, they concluded that it is nonetheless necessary to continue to interpret K-corrected scores because most of the empirical correlates of the clinical scales and, in particular, the code types were identified based on K-corrected profiles.

Modern MMPI-2 authors have voiced similar concerns about the K correction. Greene (2000, p. 96) states, "little research justifies the continued widespread use of the Kcorrection of the Clinical Scales. Hopefully, future research will investigate this area more thoroughly … clinicians probably need to avoid using K-corrections in settings in which normal persons are evaluated."

Recent empirical studies have shed additional light on the K-correction. Barthlow, Graham, Ben-Porath, Tellegen, and McNulty (2002) examined the contribution of the correction to the predictive validity of the clinical scales in two outpatient samples, and also explored whether alternative weights could improve upon the ones applied currently to these scales. They concluded that neither the current nor any other correction weights improved the validity of the clinical scales. On the other hand, noncorrected scores were no more valid than corrected ones.

Detrick, Chibnall, and Rosso (2001) explored correlations between scores on the MMPI-2 clinical scales and on the Inwald Personality Inventory (IPI; Inwald, 1992) a measure used commonly in screening candidates for law enforcement positions, in a sample of applicants for such positions. Their results indicated a very substantial attenuation of correlations between MMPI-2 scales and relevant IPI scales as a result of applying the K-correction. This effect was most pronounced (essentially removing all of the scales' predictive validity) for clinical scales 7 and 8, which receive the highest weighted K correction, and least prominent for scale 9, which receives the lowest weighted correction.

Following-up on these findings, Ben-Porath and Forbey (2004) reanalyzed data from six large samples (three clinical and three nonclinical), to examine the effects of the K correction on the corrected clinical scales. They found a consistent pattern where the correction, for the most part, had either no effect or a detrimental effect on the validity of the corrected scales in all three clinical samples (consisting of inpatients, outpatients, and individuals undergoing treatment for substance abuse). Two of the nonclinical samples (a subset of the normative sample of the MMPI-2 and a sample of college students) completed the MMPI-2 anonymously, and therefore had no incentive for defensive responding. The third nonclinical sample was similar to the one studied by Detrick et al. (2001), and its subjects were strongly motivated to appear well adjusted. In the two nonclinical samples where subjects were tested anonymously, adding the K correction substantially attenuated the scales' validity. In the defensively motivated sample, adding the K correction often removed all of the scales' predictive validity and always resulted in a more substantial attenuation of validity than in the other two nonclinical samples.

Ben-Porath and Forbey's (2004) results indicated that there was no advantage to applying the K correction in clinical settings, and in nonclinical settings it was clearly detrimental to the validity of the corrected scales. Correlational patterns for the corrected and noncorrected scores were similar, but the magnitude of the correlations was as great or greater (sometimes substantially) for the latter. As the proportion of the K-corrected score attributable to K increased, the predictive validity of that score diminished. Clearly, at the individual clinical scale level, there is no reason to interpret K-corrected scores and in nonclinical settings in particular, there is good reason not to do so.

As just reviewed, these problems with the K correction are not new or newly discovered. The primary reason why the K correction has not been abandoned is concern over implications for code-type interpretation, which is based mainly on empirical correlates identified in studies of K-corrected profiles. Ben-Porath and Forbey (2004) analyzed data from the three clinical samples to compare the predictive validity of code types when subjects are classified based on non-corrected scores versus K-corrected ones. The two sets of code types yielded very similar correlates (i.e., the same criteria were found to be correlated with membership in a code type); however, almost without exception the magnitude of the correlations for code types classified based on non-K-corrected scales was as high or higher. In some instances correlations for non-K-corrected code types were dramatically higher.

These findings indicate that it is possible to interpret code types generated with non-K-corrected scores based on the existing literature, but with greater confidence. Concerns about whether removing the correction would alter the correlates of MMPI-2 code types, although reasonable, turn out to be unfounded. If these findings are replicated with other samples and criteria, this will constitute compelling evidence that it is time to abandon the K correction. Until then, MMPI-2 users are advised to examine the non-K-corrected profile, which will provide a direct indication of the effect of the correction in a given case as well as a more appropriate reference point for considering scores on all of the other MMPI-2 scales that are not corrected.

After reviewing the literature just described, Graham (2006, p. 224) offers the following recommendation: "In summary, research data do not support the routine use of K-corrected clinical scale scores. Although current practice is to use K-corrected scores routinely, this practice probably needs to be reexamined." Regarding use of the K correction in nonclinical settings Graham (2006, p. 224) notes: "One has to be especially careful in using K-corrected scores in settings where defensiveness is common (e.g., employment screening, child custody evaluations). In these settings, K-corrected scores may over-pathologize test takers.... Fortunately, uncorrected norms are available for the MMPI-2 clinical scales." Graham states further: "it is this author's recommendation that in nonclinical applications of the MMPI-2 both K-corrected and uncorrected scores be generated and that emphasis be placed on the uncorrected scores when K-scale scores are significantly above or below average" (2006, p. 225).

## The MMPI-2 Restructured Clinical Scales

As described earlier, a major emphasis of the MMPI Restandardization Project was to maintain continuity between the original and renormed versions of the test. This was accomplished by leaving the clinical scales essentially intact. This decision made it possible for users to continue to rely on the vast empirical literature and accumulated clinical experience associated with the clinical scales, while accommodating to the revised norms and learning how to incorporate new validity and content scales in MMPI-2 interpretation. Soon after the revision process was completed, one MMPI-2 Restandardization Committee member, Auke Tellegen, began work on a major research project designed to explore the feasibility of improving the clinical scales. A decade later, this work culminated in the publication of the MMPI-2 RC (restructured clinical) scales. Tellegen, Ben-Porath, McNulty, Arbisi, Graham, and Kaemmer (2003) describe in detail the rationale, methods, and results of Tellegen's efforts. Following is a synopsis of this information followed by a summary of research findings subsequent to the Tellegen et al. (2003) publication.

## Why Restructure the Clinical Scales?

In order to succeed, any effort to improve the clinical scales must be informed by an accurate appraisal of their strengths and weaknesses as psychometric devices. The primary strengths of the scales lie in the unusually rich item pool assembled by Hathaway and McKinley for scale development, the unusual care the test's developers exercised in their diagnoses of members of the development samples, and the unparalleled quantity and quality of empirical research available to guide their interpretation and the accumulated experience of applying this literature across a variety of settings, assessment types, and populations. Their weaknesses are a product of limitations faced by Hathaway and McKinley. These included very limited resources to develop and cross-validate the scales, and an effort guided by a then underdeveloped field of applied psychometrics.

The primary limitation of the clinical scales involves their discriminant validity. Because of unexpectedly high correlations between them, amplified by considerable item overlap, the clinical scales individually have limited discriminant abilities. This shortcoming is in part a product of how the empirical keying technique was applied in assigning items to the clinical scales, based primarily on their ability to discriminate between a patient group and a common normal comparison sample. Because (essentially) the same normal reference group was used in constructing them, each of the eight scales includes items that characterize either the patient group or the difference between being a patient and not being one. The latter are essentially reversed adjustment markers (shared to significant but different degrees by all eight scales) that contribute substantially to the unexpectedly high correlations between the clinical scales.

A second significant limitation of the clinical scales concerns their convergent validity. Because Hathaway and McKinley lacked adequate resources to collect large multiple samples, there would be reason to expect that some clinical scale items were selected due to chance findings that would not have held up to adequate cross-validation. As discussed earlier, this is the likely origin of the so-called subtle items that have repeatedly been found to have little or no convergent validity (e.g., Burkhart, Gynther & Fromuth, 1980; Gynther, Burkhart, & Hovanitz, 1979; Snyter & Graham, 1984; Weed, Ben-Porath, & Butcher, 1990). Because these subtle items remain embedded in the clinical scales, they attenuate their convergent validity.

A related limitation of the clinical scales is their heterogeneity, which some, including their developers, viewed as a positive feature of these measures. Because the original target constructs for the clinical scales were complex psychiatric syndromes, Hathaway and McKinley were quite comfortable with their heterogeneous content. For example, McKinley and Hathaway (1944) noted that some of the items on scale 3 were actually negatively correlated with the total scale score, but found their content consistent with the syndrome of hysteria.

McKinley and Hathaway were unable to report in detail how their clinicians had identified the patients for the hysteria criterion group. However, drawing on their own analysis of the content of the Hy scale itself, we assume here for purely illustrative purposes that each patient in the criterion group met the following three diagnostic criteria: (a) "reports certain somatic complaints"; (b) "appears well-socialized"; (c) "avows unhappiness." The heterogeneity of symptoms such as these would not necessarily invalidate the hysteria construct. A group of syndromal indicators might not covary in the general clinical population, but may nonetheless co-occur in a subpopulation of patients suffering from the targeted disorder (which in that case would operate as a moderator variable). However, we need to note an important discrepancy between the algorithmic model embodied by syndromes such as hysteria and the one embodied by the traditional clinical scales.

A syndrome in the strict sense is a conjunction of symptoms; it can be called a "conjunctive" construct. To be diagnosed as having syndrome S, the individual must exhibit each of the $n$ symptoms, s(1), s(2), ... s(n), that identify S. However, in contrast to this conjunctive conception, most multi-item scales, including the MMPI-2 clinical scales, are "additive" measures. For example, in the case of a binary (e.g., True–False) item response format, each item response in the keyed direction would add one point to the total score. The same total score can therefore be achieved by keyed responses to alternative subsets of $n$ items (e.g., to items 1, 2, 3 *or* to items 2, 4, 7, etc.), and in that sense the additive scoring method may therefore also be considered "disjunctive."

Given a disjunctive measure made up of negatively or minimally correlated items, the same total score (unless close enough to the minimum or maximum value) will be the result of often markedly different item response patterns for different respondents. In our example, the same Hy score could reflect primarily somatic complaints, *or* primarily a self-portrayal as well socialized. In other words, even a composite additive measure made up of items deliberately selected to represent the components of a particular syndrome cannot provide an optimal assessment of this syndrome if the measure is heterogeneous, as is true for the Hy scale. In sum, heterogeneous additive (disjunctive) measures do not map well onto syndromal (conjunctive) constructs. To accommodate such constructs, it will often be necessary to develop several measures that are substantively and structurally more homogeneous but that can jointly capture the full syndromal symptom domain. These component measures can then be used in the same way as the syndromal indicators are used to arrive at a diagnosis, namely, conjunctively, as elements of a diagnostically revealing profile.

The psychometric superiority of relatively homogeneous additive measures over markedly heterogeneous ones is of course not limited to diagnostic applications that focus on the domains represented by strict syndromal constructs or, for that matter, on the more fuzzily syndromal "polythetic" construct domains such as those adopted for the *Diagnostic and Statistical Manual of Mental Disorders* (*DSM–IV*; American Psychiatric Association, 1994) disorders, and can also be accepted in other areas. Moreover, since current MMPI-2 interpretive applications encompass a broad array of psychological attributes and extend well beyond the purely diagnostic use originally intended for the original MMPI, even a purely historical rationale for relying primarily on heterogeneous additive measures of syndromal constructs is not sustainable.

In summary, from a psychometric perspective, scoring negatively (or minimally) correlated items on the same scale results in a disjunctive and, therefore, ambiguous total scale score. Developing valid, independent indicators of a syndrome's components, and considering scores on these measures conjunctively, would provide the interpreter a much clearer indication of the presence or absence of various elements of the syndrome. Moreover, as the focus of MMPI interpretation shifted from psychiatric syndromes to empirical correlates, the rationale for relying on disjunctive scales diminished further.

As discussed earlier, Hathaway and McKinley relied on the then state-of-the-art technique of empirical keying to construct eight scales to be used as differential diagnostic indicators. However, soon after their publication, it became evident that the clinical scales did not perform this task adequately. Subsequent research and clinical experience soon pointed to an alternative interpretive approach, based on the empirical correlates of scores (and particularly patterns of scores) on the clinical scales. The shift toward code types in MMPI interpretation drew the test users' attention away from the clinical scales individually. Subsequent introduction of various supplementary and subscales provided additional tools to guide MMPI interpretation. With these aids, MMPI-2 users are able to overcome the limitations of the clinical scales. However, the test's critics (e.g., Helmes and Reddon, 1993) have correctly observed that MMPI-2 interpretation has become a complex process— not necessarily a weakness in itself, unless it can be done more parsimoniously.

A final limitation of the clinical scales is the near-total absence of a theoretical foundation for their interpretation. For the most part, clinical scale interpretation is guided by their empirical correlates. This has been touted as a strength, as the foundation for their interpretation is not based on shifting or unsatisfactory theoretical models and conceptualizations. On the other hand, assessment psychologists have long recognized the importance and advantages of relying on construct validity in test-score interpretation. Indeed several of Cronbach and Meehl's (1955) illustrations of construct validity included MMPI scales as examples. Moreover, considerable progress has occurred over the past several decades in the development and validation of dispositional personality theory and its relation to psychopathology. The ability to interpret MMPI-2 clinical scale scores in part on the basis of their standing within theoretically informed and empirically validated nomological networks may clearly enhance the overall validity of their interpretation. The MMPI-2 PSY-5 scales represent a good example of theoretically informed MMPI-2 scales.

## Goals and Method of Developing the RC Scales

Tellegen's goal in developing the RC scales was to explore the feasibility of restructuring the clinical scales in a manner that would address directly the limitations just reviewed, yielding a parsimonious set of scales with improved discriminant and/or convergent validity that may be linked to contemporary theories and models of personality and psychopathology. Tellegen et al. (2003) describe the methods used in developing the RC scales in detail; they will be summarized briefly here. A critical aspect of the construction effort was reliance on consistent findings in four large samples (composed of male and female psychiatric inpatients and male and female substance abuse treatment patients) in making all empirically based decisions.

Scale development proceeded in four steps. The first, involved devising a measure of the MMPI common factor, which, as discussed previously, is associated differentially with all of the clinical scales. Tellegen labeled this factor *Demoralization*, and described it in the context of Watson and Tellegen's (1985) model of Positive and Negative Affect (PA and NA) as the equivalent of a dimension labeled "Pleasant-Unpleasant" (PU), marked on the unpleasant end by the presence of negative emotions and absence of positive emotional experiences.

Tellegen (1985) conceptualized the dispositional or trait counterpart of high NA (negative emotionality) as a risk factor for difficulties with anxiety, and of low PA (positive emotionality) as increasing vulnerability to depression. These two affect dimensions have recently been renamed more descriptively "Positive Activation" and "Negative Activation", respectively (Watson, Wiese, Vaidya, & Tellegen,1999; Tellegen, Watson, & Clark, 1999a, 1999b), without changing the PA and NA labels. In a subsequent empirical hierarchical elaboration of Watson and Tellegen's model (Tellegen et al., 1999a, 1999b), demonstrated that PU emerges as a broad bipolar dimension, overarching PA and NA, and as such related to but distinctive from these two dimensions, capturing primarily their hedonic (rather than their activational) variance.

Recognizing that demoralization is itself a clinically meaningful construct, but that from a psychometric perspective it is better to measure it only once, rather than repeatedly with each clinical scale and then confounded with other content, Tellegen first constructed a demoralization scale through a series of factor analyses of the combined items of Clinical scales 2 and 7. A set of items correlated with both scales (consistent with the PU dimension), was assigned to a preliminary demoralization scale as the product of Step 1.

Step 2 was designed to identify the distinctive core component of each clinical scale, and it was hypothesized that this would consist of something other than demoralization. Factor analyses were conducted separately with the items of each clinical scale combined with the demoralization markers identified in Step 1. The first factor that emerged in each case included the demoralization markers as well as clinical scale items that are primarily correlated with this construct. The second (and in some cases third) factor included items representing a core component of the clinical scale that was distinct from demoralization, as well as from the core factor of each of the other clinical scales.

In Step 3, these core markers were refined further to yield a maximally distinct set of "Seed" (S) scales. This step included the removal of all item overlap and retention for the S scales of core items that correlated maximally with a given potential S scale and minimally with the remaining candidate S scales. Step 4 involved analyses of the entire MMPI-2 item pool. An item was added to a given S scale and included on the final restructured scale if it correlated more highly with that S scale than with any other; the correlation exceeded a certain specified value and did not correlate beyond a specified level with any other seed scale. The specific criteria varied across scales as detailed by Tellegen et al. (2003).

The result of this four-step process was a set of nine nonoverlapping scales representing Demoralization and the distinct core component of each of the eight original clinical scales. Restructured scales were not developed for clinical scales 5 or 0 because the focus of the RC scales was on measuring psychopathology. Further, ongoing scale development efforts described later include some of the core components of these two scales. The nine RC scales are made up of 192 MMPI-2 items and described briefly in Table 14.1.

| Table 14.1 | Scale Labels and Number of Items of the MMPI-2 Restructured Clinical (RC) Scales and the Clinical Scale Counterparts | | | |
| --- | --- | --- | --- | --- |
| Clinical Scale | # of Items | RC Scale Label | Abbreviated Illustrative Item | Number of Items on RC Scale |
| — | — | Demoralization (RCd) | "Usually happy" (False) | 24 |
| 1 (Hs) | 32 | Somatic Complaints (RC1) | "Much trouble with stomach" (True) | 27 |
| 2 (D) | 57 | Low Positive Emotions (RC2) | "Sometimes full of energy" (False) | 17 |
| 3 (Hy) | 60 | Cynicism (RC3) | "Most people would like to succeed" (True) | 15 |
| 4 (Pd) | 50 | Antisocial Behavior (RC4) | "Stole things when young" (True) | 22 |
| 6 (Pa) | 40 | Ideas of Persecution (RC6) | "Mind is controlled" (True) | 17 |
| 7 (Pt) | 48 | Dysfunctional Negative Emotions (RC7) | "Almost always anxious" (True) | 24 |
| 8 (Sc) | 78 | Aberrant Experiences (RC8) | "Feel things aren't real" (True) | 18 |
| 9 (Ma) | 46 | Hypomanic Activation (RC9) | "Sometimes thoughts race" (True) | 28 |

## Psychometric Findings with the RC Scales

Because they are made up of MMPI-2 items, any data set that includes the MMPI-2 and some extra-test information can be analyzed to explore the psychometric properties of the RC scales. Relying on five large samples of psychiatric inpatients and outpatients other than the ones used in developing the RC scales, Tellegen et al. (2003) presented a series of analyses designed to explore their functioning. These analyses indicated that although they remain substantially correlated with their clinical scale counterparts (with the expected exception of scale 3 as discussed later), the RC scales are considerably less correlated with Demoralization and less correlated with each other. The reliability findings indicated that the much shorter RC scales are at least as reliable as their original counterparts. These "structural" findings have been replicated recently by Wallace and Liljequist (2005).

Tellegen et al. (2003) reported that validity analyses, using external criteria based on therapists' ratings of the outpatients and chart information for the inpatients, indicated considerably improved discriminant validity for most of the RC scales compared with their clinical scale counterparts and in some instances markedly improved convergent validity, as well. Multivariate analyses indicated that, as a set, the RC scales accounted for similar and often considerably greater variance in the criteria compared with the clinical scales. These findings have recently been replicated by Sellbom, Ben-Porath and Graham (in press) with a college counseling clinic sample.

Additional studies completed after the RC scales were published provide further evidence of their promise and utility. Sellbom and Ben-Porath (2005) explored the extent to which the RC scales can be linked to normal personality traits measured by Tellegen's (in press) Multidimensional Personality Questionnaire (MPQ). They found strong convergence between the RC scales and expected MPQ higher order factors and primary scales. These findings indicate that Tellegen's goal of linking measures of the core constructs of the clinical scales with contemporary models and theories of personality and psychopathology has been accomplished, and with additional studies it will be possible to base interpretations of the RC scales in part on their construct validity in addition to empirical correlates. In this context, Abraham (2005) observed that the RC scales' links to contemporary models of personality and psychopathology make the MMPI-2 more accessible to students who are unfamiliar with the dated nomenclature still preserved in the labels of the clinical scales.

Forbey, Ben-Porath and Tellegen (2004) reported findings designed to explore relations between the RC scales and the MMPI-2 content scales. Using the same criteria analyzed by Tellegen et al. (2003) in comparing the RC and clinical scales, Forbey et al. (2004) compared the convergent, discriminant, and incremental validity of the RC and content scales, and concluded that findings point to a distinct advantage for the RC scales over the content scales in most areas covered by the criterion measures. In several instances Forbey et al. (2004) found evidence of substantially better discriminant validity and in others enhanced convergent validity for the RC scales. At the multivariate level, the content scales added very little to the RC scales in predicting the collateral measures, whereas the RC scales showed evidence of modest but significant incremental validity in several domains.

There were three notable exceptions involving some criteria related to anger, family problems, and social introversion. The first two areas represent domains assessed by the content scales that are not targeted by the clinical scales and, therefore, are also not the focus of the RC scales. As discussed earlier, the RC scales also do not cover the area of social introversion. Additional scale development efforts (discussed later) are ongoing to produce restructured MMPI-2 measures of these and other domains not assessed by the RC scales.

McNulty, Ben-Porath, and Arbisi (2004) presented analyses designed to ascertain the extent, origin, and implications of differences in elevation on the clinical and RC scales in a psychiatric inpatient sample. These authors found that in most cases a clinical scale and its RC scale counterpart agreed insofar as elevation versus nonelevation was concerned (although marked differences could nevertheless occur when both scales were elevated). Differential elevation patterns were found in as few as 11.2% of the cases for scale 1 and its restructured counterpart, RC1, and as many as 35.7% of the cases for scale 8 and its counterpart RC8. Consistent with the expected effects of removing demoralization, when differences did occur, the clinical scale was considerably more likely to be elevated than the RC scale.

McNulty et al. (2004) also explored the origin of differential findings when they occurred, and concluded that when the clinical scale was elevated and its RC scale counterpart was not, removal of demoralization variance was the most common source of this difference, followed by the K correction (which is not applied to the RC scales and discussed further later) and the effects of subtle items. When an RC scale was elevated and its clinical scale counterpart was not, the three possible origins just mentioned contributed equally to this outcome.

Finally, McNulty et al. (2004) explored the interpretive implications of differential elevation findings by classifying their subjects into four groups: (a) neither scale elevated; (b) clinical scale elevated and RC scale not elevated; (c) clinical scale not elevated and RC scale elevated; or (d) both scales elevated. Group comparisons showed that individuals classified into groups 3 and 4 were considerably more likely to display symptoms or problems consistent with the scale in question, indicating that when differential elevation patterns occur, more weight should be given to the RC scale result.

Simms, Casillas, Clark, Watson, and Doebbeling (2005) examined the RC scales in samples of college counseling clients and military veterans. They concluded that the RC scales were as internally consistent as the clinical scales and correlated strongly with their original counterparts (except for the expected exception of Hy). The RC scales were less intercorrelated, produced conceptually clearer relations with measures of personality and psychopathology, and yielded somewhat greater incremental utility than the clinical scales. Sellbom, Graham, and Schenk (in press) explored the incremental validity of the RC scales in a private mental health practice, and reported that several RC scales added significantly to the clinical scales in predicting symptoms of psychiatric disorder in this setting. Finally, Sellbom, Ben-Porath, Lilienfeld, Patrick, and Graham (in 2005) demonstrate that the RC scales yield a parsimonious model for predicting psychopathy, an important construct in forensic assessments.

## Current Role and Future Directions for the RC Scales

Tellegen et al. (2003) cautioned that it is not possible to interpret patterns of scores on the RC-scales based on the clinical scale code-type literature because an expected result of the restructuring, is that the two sets of scales do not yield comparable elevation patterns. In light of the central role of code types in MMPI-2 interpretation, a primary challenge for future RC scale research will be to explore whether they can account for criteria predicted by the code types. As discussed earlier, a primary function of the code types is to assist the interpreter in refining clinical scale interpretation. For example, clinical scale 4 is considered traditionally to be a predictor of externalizing acting-out behavior, however scores on this scale are also correlated with emotional dysfunction (i.e., demoralization). Scores on other clinical scales indicate which of these two rather different correlates should be emphasized in the interpretation. If scale 9 is elevated along with scale 4, the externalizing correlates are emphasized. If scale 2 is elevated along with scale 4, the emotional dysfunction correlates will be emphasized. The two types of dysfunction, emotional and externalizing, are assessed by distinct and more discriminantly valid RC scales, considerably reducing the pervasive need to rely on one scale to clarify the interpretation of another.

This is not to suggest that meaningful score patterns cannot also be identified with the RC scales. As mentioned earlier, one of the more challenging of the clinical scales is scale 3 (Hy), which contains several items sets that are negatively correlated with each other. In addition to Demoralization, the scale has three primary components: somatic complaining, naiveté, and extraversion. Because somatic complaints represent the distinctive core component of scale 1 and extraversion is assessed by scale 0 (which, for reasons described earlier, was not included among the RC scales,) naiveté was identified as the distinct core component of scale 3. However, because it is negatively correlated with psychopathology, the scoring key was reversed, with elevations indicating that the test taker professes cynical beliefs about others. Low scores on the restructured version of scale 3 now reflect the naiveté and gullibility sometimes associated with histrionic features. An MMPI-2 protocol marked by elevations on the restructured version of scale 1 (RC1) and a low score on the restructured version of scale 3 (RC3) and clinical scale 0, informs the interpreter that a combination of features associated conjunctively with the syndrome of hysteria is present. In contrast, an elevated score on scale 3 sends a disjunctive, ambiguous signal regarding the individual's standing on the three elements that make up the syndrome. Butcher's (2006, p. 13) concern that "for a patient who has a high Hy score on the Hy scale (or a code type with Hy as a member), the RC3 is not likely to be prominent and is not likely to be a factor in the interpretive process" misses this point when considered in the context of the advantages offered by conjunctive over disjunctive measurement.

With the additional research cited earlier, and users' growing experience with their interpretation, the role of the RC scales can now be broadened beyond clarifying clinical scale scores as Tellegen et al. (2003) first recommended. Sellbom and Ben-Porath (in press, a) provide recommendations for incorporating the RC scales in forensic assessments, and Graham (2006) provides descriptors for RC scale interpretation in his widely used MMPI-2 interpretive text. Some authors have nevertheless expressed concerns about using the RC scales in certain types of assessments. For example, Butcher, Ones, and Cullen (2006, p. 404) state "the RC Scales should not be used in making employment decisions until a substantial number of validity studies are available in personnel settings." This admonition is misplaced on two counts. First, it is rarely necessary to reach any specific MMPI-2-based inference based on the RC scales alone. Rather, the scales, presently, may best be viewed as a roadmap that provides guidance for profile interpretation. Once the user, guided by the RC scales, knows what to look for, it is usually possible to find corroborating information in other standard MMPI-2 sources (e.g., code types, supplementary scales, and subscales). Moreover, studies of the RC scales in personnel screening settings have yielded very positive results. For example, in a sample of individuals undergoing pre-employment assessment for police officer positions, Ben-Porath and Detrick (2004) reported that the RC scales had similar to improved validity when compared with their clinical scale counterparts in predicting scores on the Inwald Personality Inventory (Inwald, 1992), a commonly used measure in law enforcement pre-hire testing. In a longitudinal study of individuals screened for law enforcement positions Fischler (2005) reported that the RC scales had substantially stronger validity as predictors of problematic performance on the job when compared with their clinical scale counterparts. As additional studies establishing further their empirical correlates in various settings are published, it is likely that the RC scales will assume an increasingly major interpretive role.

# Future Directions for the MMPI-2

## Further Restructuring Efforts

As described earlier, when constructing the RC scales Tellegen decided not to include restructured versions of clinical scales 5 and 0 because they are not primary psychopathology indicators. However, several distinct core components were identified for these two scales and are candidates for developing additional restructured scales. Tellegen and Ben-Porath (2005) have developed a set of additional MMPI-2 scales designed to assess areas not targeted specifically by the original clinical scales and, therefore, also not measured directly or specifically by the RC scales. Like the RC scales, these additional scales were developed using methods designed to make them as independent as possible of Demoralization, and maximally distinct from each other. These scales do, however, overlap intentionally with some of the RC scales, and they may, guided by future research, prove helpful in augmenting and complementing RC scale interpretation.

## Computerized Adaptive Testing

Computers are used routinely to administer the MMPI-2 on-line in a variety of settings, most notably the Veterans Administration system. On-line administration is faster and more reliable than booklet-based administration, and research indicates that well-written on-line administration programs produce results that are comparable to those of paper and pencil administration (e.g., Honaker, 1988).

However, current methods of on-line administration of the MMPI-2 do not take advantage of the flexibility offered by the computer. Adaptive testing, in which computer algorithms are developed to administer individually tailored versions of the test, if feasible, could substantially reduce administration time. Item Response Theory (IRT)-based adaptive testing is problematic with the MMPI-2 in light of questions regarding whether its scales represent unidimensional latent constructs analogous to those that are the focus of ability testing. Moreover, the complexities of IRT may inhibit the use of this technology in clinical assessment.

An alternative approach to adaptive testing with the MMPI-2 has shown considerable promise. Butcher, Keller, and Bacon (1985) suggested the *Countdown Strategy*, as an example of a variable termination approach to adaptive testing described by Weiss (1985). The strategy involves terminating item administration on a scale as soon as it is determined whether the score will exceed a designated cutoff. For example, if the cutoff for clinically significant elevation on a 30-item scale is a raw score of 20, item administration is terminated as soon as the individual has answered 11 items in the nonkeyed direction (because clinically significant elevation is no longer possible) or 20 in the keyed direction.

Ben-Porath, Slutske, and Butcher (1989) examined a modified version of this approach termed the *Countdown Method*, where in addition to the *Classification* technique just described, an alternative strategy termed *Full Scores on Elevated Scales* (FSES) was developed. The FSES approach eliminates the rule involving termination when elevation is reached, resulting in full scores (rather than only a designation of elevation) when a scale score exceeds the threshold for clinically significant elevation. Ben-Porath et al. (1989) conducted a *real data simulation*, using existing data from several samples to simulate adaptive administration of the original MMPI based on the Classification and FSES methods. Their findings indicated the potential for substantial reductions in the number of items administered using this technique. Forbey, Handel and Ben-Porath (2000) recently reported similar findings with the adolescent version of the MMPI, the MMPI-A.

Roper, Ben-Porath, and Butcher (1991) conducted the first actual study of an adaptive administration of the MMPI-2 using the Classification and FSES methods with college students. This study also demonstrated considerable reductions in the number of items administered, but left unanswered the all important question of whether altering the order of item administration changes the validity of MMPI-2 scales. Roper, Ben-Porath and Butcher (1995) followed up with a study of college students that included extra-test validity data and found that the adaptive administration produced comparably valid scale scores when contrasted with conventional administration of the MMPI-2. Handel, Ben-Porath, and Watt (1999) conducted the first study of this technology with a clinical sample (of individuals undergoing treatment for substance abuse) and replicated Roper et al.'s (1995) findings that adaptive administration can yield substantial reductions in items administered (and hence administration time) without sacrificing scale validity.

Based on these promising findings, a computerized adaptive version of the MMPI-2 (the MMPI-CA) has been developed and is presently undergoing clinical trials. In addition to choosing a Classification or FSES approach to adaptively administer the test, the MMPI-2-CA allows users to decide which cutoffs to use and which scales to administer, making it possible to tailor the test to more focused assessments or just not administer scales that the user does not plan to interpret. Initial results of these clinical trials are promising, indicating that an MMPI-2-CA-based screening can be accomplished in 20–30 min. Considerable follow-up research will be needed to establish the feasibility and utility of administering the MMPI-2-CA in various settings.

# Conclusions

The MMPI-2 has been a mainstay of psychological assessment for 60 years. During this time period, authors have occasionally predicted the test's impending demise (e.g., Goldberg, 1969), or concluded that it is soon to be replaced by promising alternatives (e.g., Helmes & Reddon, 1993). To the likely wonder of these and similarly minded pundits, the instrument remains the most widely used and studied assessment device. Holden (2000) wondered whether this may be a product of inertia on the part of test users and predicted that more modern psychometric devices will soon replace the MMPI-2. An alternative explanation lies in a crucial point overlooked by Holden. MMPI and MMPI-2 researchers have not been sideline observers of the psychometric advances he mentions. In fact, the instrument has been the focus and conduit of nearly all major controversies and advances in the assessment of personality and psychopathology by self-report. Examples include the merits of clinical versus statistical prediction (Meehl, 1954), linear versus configural scoring and interpretation (Goldberg, 1965, 1969; Meehl, 1950; Meehl and Dahlstrom, 1960), and the influence of response styles on self-report measures of personality (Block, 1965; Jackson & Messick, 1962), to name just a few. Moreover, developments chronicled in this chapter (exemplified by the recent introduction of the RC scales) reflect one of the most enduring features of the MMPI. The test has undergone an unparalleled amount of empirical scrutiny resulting in periodic updates (albeit sometimes belated) that have kept the instrument at the forefront of advances in the science and practice of test construction.

## Acknowledgment

The author thanks Auke Tellegen and Beverly Kaemmer for their helpful feedback on this chapter.

## REFERENCES

American Psychiatric Association. (1994). *Diagnostic and statistical manual of mental disorders* ( 4th ed.). Washington, DC: Author.

Arbisi, P. A., & Ben-Porath, Y. S. (1995). An MMPI-2 infrequent response scale for use with psychopathological populations: The infrequency-psychopathology scale, F(p). *Psychological Assessment, 7*, 424–431.

Archer, R. P., Aiduk, R., Griffin, R., & Elkins, D. E. (1996). Incremental validity of the MMPI-2 content scales in a psychiatric sample. *Assessment, 3*, 79–90.

Baer, R. A., Wetter, M. W., Nichols, D. S., & Greene, R. (1995). Sensitivity of MMPI-2 validity scales to underreporting of symptoms. *Psychological Assessment, 7*, 419–423.

Baer, R. A., & Miller, J. (2002). Underreporting of psychopathology on the MMPI-2: A meta-analytic review. *Psychological Assessment, 14*, 16–26.

Bagby, R. M., Ryder, A. G., Ben-Dat, D., Bacchiochi, J., & Parker, J. D. A. (2002). Validation of the dimensional factor structure of the Personality Psychopathology Five in clinical and nonclinical samples. *Journal of Personality Disorders, 16*, 304–316.

Barron, F. (1953). An ego-strength scale which predicts response to psychotherapy. *Journal of Consulting Psychology, 17*, 327–333.

Barthlow, D. L., Graham, J. R., Ben Porath, Y. S., & McNulty, J. L. (1999). Incremental validity of the MMPI-2 content scales in an outpatient mental health setting. *Psychological Assessment, 11*, 39–47.

Barthlow, D. L., Graham, J. R., Ben-Porath, Y. S., Tellegen, A., & McNulty, J. L. (2002). The appropriateness of the MMPI-2 K correction. *Assessment, 9*, 219–229.

Ben-Porath, Y. S., & Butcher, J. N. (1989a). The psychometric stability of rewritten MMPI items. *Journal of Personality Assessment, 53*, 645–653.

Ben-Porath, Y. S., & Butcher, J. N. (1989b). The comparability of MMPI and MMPI-2 scales and profiles. *Psychological Assessment: A Journal of Consulting and Clinical Psychology, 1*, 345–347.

Ben-Porath, Y. S., Butcher, J. N., & Graham, J. R. (1991). Contribution of the MMPI-2 content scales to the differential diagnosis of psychopathology. *Psychological Assessment: A Journal of Consulting and Clinical Psychology, 3*, 634–640.

Ben-Porath, Y. S., & Detrick P. (2004, May). *MMPI-2 RC Scale correlates in a law enforcement pre-employment screening sample.* Paper presented at the 39th Annual Symposium on Recent Developments in the Use of the MMPI-2 and MMPI-A, Minneapolis, MN.

Ben-Porath, Y. S., & Forbey, J. D., (May, 2004). Detrimental effects of the K correction on Clinical Scale validity. Paper presented at the 39th Annual Symposium on Recent Developments in the Use of the MMPI-2 and MMPI-A. Minneapolis, MN.

Ben-Porath, Y. S., McCully, E., & Almagor, M. (1993). Incremental validity of the MMPI-2 Content Scales in the assessment of personality and psychopathology by self-report. *Journal of Personality Assessment, 61*, 557–575.

Ben-Porath, Y. S., & Sherwood, N. E. (1993). *The MMPI-2 Content Component Scales: Development, psychometric characteristics, and clinical applications.* Minneapolis, MN: University of Minnesota Press.

Ben-Porath, Y. S., Slutske, W. S., & Butcher, J. N. (1989). A real-data stimulation of computerized adaptive administration of the MMPI. *Psychological Assessment, 1*, 18–22.

Bernreuter, R. J. (1933). Theory and construction of the personality inventory. *Journal of Social Psychology, 4*, 387–405.

Berry, D. T., Wetter, M. W., Baer, R. A., & Widiger, T. A. (1991). Detection of random responding on the MMPI-2: Utility of F, back F, and VRIN scales. *Psychological Assessment, 3*, 418–423.

Black, J. D. (1953). The interpretation of MMPI profiles of college women. *Dissertation Abstracts, 13*, 870–871.

Block, J. (1965). *The challenge of response sets: Unconfounding meaning, acquiescence, and social desirability in the MMPI.* Appleton-Century-Crofts, East Norwalk, CT, US.

Briggs, P. F., Taylor, M., & Tellegen, A. (1966). A study of the Marks and Seeman MMPI profile types as applied to a sample of 2,875 psychiatric patients. *Reports from the research laboratories of the Department of Psychiatry, University of Minnesota, Report Number PR-66-5.*

Burkhart, B. R., Gynther, M. D., & Fromuth, M. E. (1980). The relative predictive validity of subtle vs. obvious items on the MMPI Depression scale. *Journal of Clinical Psychology, 36*, 748–751.

Butcher, J. N. (Ed.). (1972). *Objective personality assessment: Changing perspectives.* New York: Academic Press.

Butcher, J. N. (2006). Pathways to MMPI-2 use: A practitioner's guide to test usage in diverse settings. In J. N. Butcher (Ed.), *MMPI-2: A practitioner's guide* (pp. 3–13). Washington, DC: American Psychological Association.

Butcher, J. N., Aldwin, C. L., Levenson, M. R., Ben-Porath, Y. S., Spiro, A, & Bosse, R. (1991). Personality and aging: A study of the MMPI-2 aging elderly men. *Psychology of Aging, 6*, 361–370.

Butcher, J.N., Graham, J.R., Ben-Porath, Y.S., Tellegen, A., & Kaemmer, B. (2001). *Minnesota Multiphasic Personality Inventory: Manual for administration, scoring, and interpretation, revised edition.* Minneapolis, MN: University of Minnesota Press.

Butcher, J. N., Graham, J. R., Dahlstrom, W. G., & Bowman, E. (1990). The MMPI-2 with college students. *Journal of Personality Assessment, 54*, 1–15.

Butcher, J. N., Graham, J. R., Williams, C. L., & Ben-Porath, Y. S. (1990). *Development and use of the MMPI-2 content scales.* Minneapolis, MN: University of Minnesota Press.

Butcher, J. N., & Han, K. (1995). Development of an MMPI-2 scale to assess the presentation of self in a superlative manner: The S Scale. In J. N. Butcher & C. D. Spielberger (Eds.), *Advances in personality assessment* (Vol. 10, pp. 25–50). Hillsdale, NJ: Erlbaum.

Butcher, J. N., Jeffrey, T., Cayton, T. G., Colligan, S., DeVore, J., & Minnegawa, R. (1990). A Study of active duty military personnel with the MMPI-2. *Military Psychology, 2*, 47–61.

Butcher, J. N., Keller, L. S., & Bacon, S. F. (1985). Current developments and future directions in computerized personality assessment. *Journal of Consulting & Clinical Psychology, 53*, 803–815.

Butcher, J. N., Ones, D. S., & Cullen, M. (2006). Personnel screening with the MMPI-2. In J. N. Butcher (Ed.), *MMPI-2: A practitioner's guide* (pp. 381–406). Washington, DC: American Psychological Association.

Butcher, J. N., & Tellegen, A (1966). Objections to MMPI items. *Journal of Consulting Psychology, 46*, 527–534.

Butcher, J. N., Williams, C. L., Graham, J. R., Archer, R. P., Tellegen, A, Ben-Porath, Y. S., & Kaemmer, B. (1992). *Minnesota Multiphasic Personality Inventory (MMPI-A): Manual for administration, scoring and interpretation.* Minneapolis, MN: University of Minnesota Press.

Caldwell, A. B. (1969). *MMPI critical items.* Unpublished manuscript. Available from Alex Caldwell, Ph.D., 1545 Sawtelle Boulevard, Suite 14, Los Angeles, CA 90025–3200.

Clark, M. E. (1996). MMPI-2 Negative Treatment Indicators Content and Content Component Scales: Clinical correlates and outcome prediction for men with chronic pain. *Psychological Assessment, 8*, 32–38.

Clark, M. E., Gironda, R. J., & Young, R. W. (2003). Detection of back random responding: Effectiveness of MMPI-2 and Personality Assessment Inventory validity indices. *Psychological Assessment, 15*, 223–234.

Cook, W. W., & Medley, D. M. (1954). Proposed hostility and Pharisaic-virtue scales for the MMPI. *Journal of Applied Psychology, 38*, 414–418.

Cronbach, L. J., & Meehl, P. E. (1955). Construct validity in psychological tests. *Psychological Bulletin, 52*, 281–302.

Cuadra, C. A. (1953). *A psychometric investigation of control factors in psychological adjustment.* Unpublished doctoral dissertation, University of California.

Dahlstrom, W. G. (1992a). The growth in acceptance of the MMPI. *Professional Psychology: Research and Practice, 23*, 345–348.

Dahlstrom, W. G. (1992b). Comparability of two-point high-point code patterns from the original MMPI norms to MMPI-2 norms for the restandardization sample. *Journal of Personality Assessment, 59*, 153–164.

Dahlstrom, W. G., Welsh, G. S., & Dahlstrom, L. E. (1972). *An MMPI handbook: Clinical Interpretation* (Vol. I). Minneapolis, MN: University of Minnesota Press.

Dahlstrom, W. G., & Welsh, G. S. (1960). *An MMPI Handbook: A guide to use in clinical practice and research.* Minneapolis: University of Minnesota Press, MN.

Dahlstrom, W. G., Welsh, G. S., & Dahlstrom, L. E. (1975). *An MMPI handbook: Research Applications* (Vol. II). Minneapolis, MN: University of Minnesota Press.

Detrick, P., Chibnall, J. T., & Rosso, M. (2001). Minnesota Multiphasic Personality Inventory-2 in police officer selection: Normative data and relation to the Inwald Personality Inventory. *Professional Psychology: Research & Practice, 32*, 484–490.

Egland, B., Erickson, M., Butcher, J. N., & Ben-Porath, Y. S. (1991). MMPI-2 profiles or women at risk for child abuse. *Journal of Personality Assessment, 57*, 254–263.

Englert, D. R., Weed, N. C., & Watson, G. S. (2000). Convergent, discriminant, and internal properties of the Minnesota Multiphasic Personality Inventory (2nd ed.). Low Self-Esteem Content Scale. *Measurement & Evaluation in Counseling & Development, 33*, 42–49.

Evans, R. G. (1984). Normative data for two MMPI critical item sets. *Journal of Clinical Psychology, 40*, 512–515.

Fischler, G. L. (2005, April). MMPI-2 predictors of police officer integrity problems. Paper presented at the 40th Annual Symposium on MMPI-2/MMPI-A Research. Fort Lauderdale, FL.

Forbey, J. D., Ben-Porath, Y. S., & Tellegen, A., (2004). Associations between and relative contributions of the MMPI-2 restructured clinical (RC) and content scales. Paper presented at the Midwinter meeting of the Society for Personality Development. Miami, FL.

Gallen, R. T., & Berry, D. T. R. (1996). Detection of random responding in MMPI-2 protocols. *Assessment, 3*, 171–178.

Gallen, R. T., & Berry, D. T. R. (1997). Partially random MMPI-2 protocols: When are they interpretable? *Assessment, 4*, 61–68.

Goldberg, L. R., (1965). Diagnosticians vs. diagnostic signs: The diagnosis of psychosis versus neurosis for the MMPI. *Psychological Monographs, 79*, (9, whole no. 602).

Goldberg, L. R. (1969). The search for configural relationships in personality assessment: The diagnosis of psychosis vs. neurosis from the MMPI. *Multivariate Behavioral Research, 4*, 523–536.

Gough, H. G. (1946). Diagnostic patterns on the MMPI. *Journal of Clinical Psychology, 2*, 23–37.

Gough, H. G. (1948). A new dimension of status: I. Development of a personality scale. *American Sociology Review, 13*, 401–409.

Gough, H. G. (1951). Studies of social intolerance: I. Psychological and sociological correlates of anti-semitism. *Journal of Social Psychology, 33*, 237–246.

Gough, H. G., McClosky, H., & Meehl, P. E. (1951). A personality scale for dominance. *Journal of Abnormal and Social Psychology, 46*, 360–366.

Graham, J. R. (2006). *MMPI-2: Assessing personality and psychopathology* (4th ed.). New York: Oxford University Press.

Graham, J. R., Ben-Porath, Y. S., & McNulty, J. L. (1999). *MMPI-2 correlates for outpatient community mental health settings.* Minneapolis, MN: University of Minnesota Press.

Graham, J. R., & Butcher, J. N. (1988, March). Differentiating schizophrenia and major affective disorders with the revised form of the MMPI. Paper presented at the *23rd Annual Symposium on Recent Developments in the Use of the MMPI*, SI. Petersburg Beach, FL.

Graham, J. R., Smith, R. L., & Schwartz, G. F. (1986). Stability of MMPI configurations for psychiatric inpatients. *Journal of Consulting and Clinical Psychology, 54*, 375–380.

Graham, J. R., Timbrook, R. E., Ben-Porath, Y. S., & Butcher, J. N. (1991). Congruence between MMPI and MMPI-2: Separating fact from artifact. *Journal of Personality Assessment, 57*, 205–215.

Grayson, H. M. (1951). *A psychological admissions testing program and manual*. Los Angeles: Veterans Administration Center, Neuropsychiatric Hospital.

Greene, R. L. (2000). *The MMPI-2: An interpretive manual* (2nd ed.). Needham Heights, MA: Allyn & Bacon.

Greene, R. L., Weed, N. C., Butcher, J. N., Arrendono, R., & Davis, H. G. (1992). A cross validation of the MMPI-2 substance abuse scales. *Journal of Personality Assessment, 58*, 405–410.

Guthrie, G. M. (1952). Common characteristics associated with frequent MMPI profile types. *Journal of Clinical Psychology, 8*, 141–145.

Gynther, M. D., Altman, H., & Sletten, I. W. (1973). Replicated correlates of MMPI two-point code types: The Missouri actuarial system. *Journal of Clinical Psychology, 29*, 263–289.

Gynther, M. D., Burkhart, B. R., & Hovanitz, C. (1979). Do face-valid items have more predictive validity than subtle items? The case of the MMPI Pd scale. *Journal of Consulting & Clinical Psychology, 47*, 295–300.

Halbower, C. C. (1955). *A comparison of actuarial versus clinical prediction to classes discriminated by the MMPI*. Minneapolis, MN: Unpublished doctoral dissertation.

Han, K., Weed, N. C., Calhoun, R. F., & Butcher, J. N. (1995). Psychometric characteristics of the MMPI-2 Cook-Medley Hostility Scale. *Journal of Personality Assessment, 65*, 567–585.

Handel, R. W., Ben-Porath, Y. S., & Watt, M. (1999). Computerized adaptive assessment with the MMPI-2 in a clinical setting. *Psychological Assessment, 11*, 369–380.

Harkness, A. R. (1992). Fundamental topics in the personality disorders: Candidate trait dimensions from lower regions of the hierarchy. *Psychological Assessment, 4*, 251–259.

Harkness, A. R., & McNulty, J. L. (1994). The Personality Psychopathology Five (PSY-5): Issues from the pages of a diagnostic manual instead of a dictionary. In S. Strack & M. Lorr (Eds.), *Differentiating normal and abnormal personality* (pp. 291–315). New York: Springer.

Harkness, A. R., McNulty, J. L., & Ben-Porath, Y. S. (1995). The Personality Psychopathology Five (PSY-5): Constructs and MMPI-2 scales. *Psychological Assessment, 7*, 104–114.

Harkness, A. R., McNulty, J. L., Ben-Porath, Y. S., & Graham, J. R. (2002). *MMPI-2 Personality-Psychopathology Five (PSY-5) Scales: Gaining an overview for case conceptualization and treatment planning*. Minneapolis, MN: University of Minnesota Press.

Harris, R., & Lingoes, J. (1955). *Subscales for the Minnesota Multiphasic Personality Inventory*. Mimeographed materials, The Langley Porter Clinic.

Hathaway, S. R. (1947). A coding system for MMPI profiles. *Journal of Consulting Psychology, 11*, 334–337.

Hathaway, S. R. (1960). Foreword. In W. G. Dahlstrom & G. S. Welsh (Eds.), *An MMPI handbook: A guide to use in clinical practice and research*. Minneapolis, MN: University of Minnesota Press.

Hathaway, S. R. (1972). Forward. In W. G. Dahlstrom, G. S. Welsh, & L. E. Dahlstrom (Eds.). *An MMPI handbook: Clinical Interpretation* (Vol. 1). Minneapolis, MN: University of Minnesota Press.

Hathaway, S. R., & McKinley, J. C. (1940). A multiphasic personality schedule (Minnesota): I. Construction of the schedule. *Journal of Psychology, 10*, 249–254.

Hathaway, S. R., & McKinley, J. C. (1942). A multiphasic personality schedule (Minnesota): III. The measurement of symptomatic depression. *Journal of Psychology, 14*, 73–84.

Hathaway, S. R., & McKinley, J. C. (1943). *The Minnesota Multiphasic Personality Inventory*. Minneapolis, MN: University of Minnesota Press.

Hathaway, S. R., & Meehl, P. E. (1951). The Minnesota Multiphasic Personality Inventory. In *Military clinical psychology*. Department of the Army technical manual TM 8:242; Department of the Air Force Manual AFM, 160–145. Washington, DC: U.S. Government Printing Office.

Helmes, E., & Reddon, J. R. (1993). A perspective on developments in assessing psychopathology: A critical review of the MMPI and MMPI-2. *Psychological Bulletin, 113*, 453–471.

Hjemboe, S., Almagor, M., & Butcher, J. N. (1992). Empirical assessment of marital distress: The Marital Distress Scale (MDS) for the MMPI-2. In J. N. Butcher, & C. D. Spielberger (Eds.), *Advances in personality assessment* (Vol. 9). Hillsdale, NJ: Erlbaum.

Holden, R. R. (2000). Are there promising MMPI substitutes for assessing psychopathology and personality? Review and prospect. In R.H. Dana (Ed.), *Handbook of cross-cultural and multicultural personality assessment* (pp. 267–302). Mahwah, NJ: Erlbaum.

Honaker, L. M. (1988). The equivalency of computerized and conventional MMPI administration: A critical review. *Clinical Psychology Review, 8*, 561–577.

Humm, D. G., & Wadsworth, G. W. (1935). The Humm-Wadsworth temperament scale. *American Journal of Psychiatry, 92*, 163–200.

Inwald, R. (1992). *Inwald Personality Inventory technical manual (revised)*. New York: Hilson Research.

Jackson, D. N., & Messick, S. (1962). Response styles on the MMPI: Comparison of clinical and normal samples. *Journal of Abnormal & Social Psychology, 65*, 285–299.

Katz, M. M., & Lyerly, S. B. (1963). Methods for measuring adjustment and social behavior in the community. *Psychological Reports, 13*, 503–535.

Keller, L. S., & Butcher, J. N. (1991). *Use of the MMPI-2 with chronic pain patients*. Minneapolis, MN: University of Minnesota Press.

Koss, M. P., & Butcher, J. N. (1973). A comparison of psychiatric patients' self-report with other sources of clinical information. *Journal of Research in Personality, 7*, 225–236.

Koss, M. P., Butcher, J. N., & Hoffman, N. G. (1976). The MMPI critical items: How well do they work? *Journal of Consulting and Clinical Psychology, 44*, 921–928.

Lachar, D., & Wrobel, T. A (1979). Validating clinicians' hunches: Construction of a new MMPI critical item set. *Journal of Consulting and Clinical Psychology, 47*, 277–284.

Landis, C., & Katz, S. E. (1934). The validity of certain questions which purport to measure neurotic tendencies. *Journal of Applied Psychology, 18*, 343–356.

Landis, C., Zubin, J., & Katz, S. E. (1935). Empirical validation of three personality adjustment inventories. *Journal of Educational Psychology, 26*, 321–330.

Lubin, B., Larsen, R. M., & Matarazzo, J. (1984). Patterns of psychological test usage in the United States 1935–1982. *American Psychologist, 39*, 451–454.

Marks, P. A., & Seeman, W. (1963). *The actuarial description of abnormal personality: An atlas for use with the MMPI*. Baltimore, MD: The Williams & Wilkins Company.

McKenna, T., & Butcher, J. N. (1987, March). Continuity of the MMPI with alcoholics. Paper presented at the *22nd Annual Symposium on Recent Developments in the use of the MMPI*, Seattle, WA.

McKinley, J. C., & Hathaway, S. R. (1940). A multiphasic personality schedule (Minnesota): II. A differential study of hypochondriasis. *Journal of Psychology, 10*, 255–268.

McKinley, J. C., & Hathaway, S. R. (1942). A multiphasic personality schedule (Minnesota): IV. Psychasthenia. *Journal of Applied Psychology, 26*, 614–624.

McKinley, J. C., & Hathaway, S. R. (1944). A multiphasic personality schedule (Minnesota): V. Hysteria, Hypomania, and Psychopathic Deviate. *Journal of Applied Psychology, 28*, 153–174.

McKinley, J. C., Hathaway, S. R., & Meehl, P. E. (1948). The Minnesota Multiphasic Personality Inventory: VI. The K Scale. *Journal of Consulting Psychology, 12*, 20–31.

McNulty, J. L., Ben-Porath, Y. S., & Arbisi, P. A. (March, 2004). Accounting for Elevation Differences between Individual Clinical and RC Scales. Paper presented at the Midwinter meeting of the Society for Personality Assessment. Miami, FL.

McNulty, J. L., Ben-Porath, Y. S., & Graham, J. R. (1998). An empirical examination of the correlates of well-defined and not defined MMPI-2 code types. *Journal of Personality Assessment, 71*, 393–410.

Meehl, P. E. (1945). The dynamics of "structured" personality tests. *Journal of Clinical Psychology, 1*, 296–303.

Meehl, P. E. (1946). Profile analysis of the MMPI in differential diagnosis. *Journal of Applied Psychology, 30*, 517–524.

Meehl, P. E. (1950). Configural scoring. *Journal of Consulting Psychology, 14*, 165–171.

Meehl, P. E. (1954). *Clinical versus statistical prediction: A theoretical analysis and a review of the evidence.* Minneapolis, MN: University of Minnesota Press.

Meehl, P. E. (1956). Wanted—A good cookbook. *American Psychologist, 11*, 263–272.

Meehl, P. E., & Dahlstrom, W. G. (1960). Objective configural rules for discriminating psychotic from neurotic MMPI profiles. *Journal of Consulting Psychology, 24*, 375–387.

Meehl, P. E., & Hathaway, S. R. (1946). The K factor as a suppressor variable in the MPI. *Journal of Applied Psychology, 30*, 525–564.

Morey, L. C., Waugh, M. H., & Blashfield, R. K. (1985). MMPI scales for DSM-III personality disorders: Their derivation and correlates. *Journal of Personality Assessment, 49*, 245–251.

Palav, A., Ortega, A., & McCaffrey, R. J. (2001). Incremental validity of the MMPI-2 content scales: A preliminary study with brain-injured patients. *Journal of Head Trauma Rehabilitation, 16*, 275-283.

Paolo, A. M., & Ryan, J. J. (1992). Detection of random response sets on the MMPI-2. *Psychotherapy in Private Practice, 11*, 1-8.

Petroskey, L. J., Ben-Porath, Y. S., & Stafford, K. P. (2003). Correlates of the Minnesota Multiphasic Personality Inventory-2 (MMPI-2) Personality Psychopathology Five (PSY-5) scales in a forensic assessment setting. *Assessment, 10*, 393-399.

Pope, K. S., Butcher, J. N., & Seelen, J. (1993). *MMPI, MMPI-2, & MMPI-A in court: A practical guide for expert witnesses and attorneys.* Washington, DC: American Psychological Association.

Rogers, R., Sewell, K. W., Martin, M. A., & Vitacco, M. J. (2003). Detection of feigned mental disorders: A meta-analysis of the MMPI-2 and malingering. *Assessment, 10*, 160-177.

Roper, B. L., Ben-Porath, Y. S., & Butcher, J. N. (1991). Comparability of computerized adaptive and conventional testing with the MMPI-2. *Journal of Personality Assessment, 57*, 278-290.

Roper, B. L., Ben Porath, Y. S., & Butcher, J. N. (1995). Comparability and validity of computerized adaptive testing with the MMPI-2. *Journal of Personality Assessment, 65*, 358-371.

Rouse, S. V., Butcher, J. N., & Miller, K. B. (1999). Assessment of substance abuse in psychotherapy clients: The effectiveness of the MMPI-2 substance abuse scales. *Psychological Assessment, 11*, 101-107.

Rouse, S. V., Finger, M. S., & Butcher, J. N. (1999). Advances in clinical personality measurement: An item response theory analysis of the MMPI-2 PSY-5 scales. *Journal of Personality Assessment, 72*, 282-307.

Sawrie, S. V., Kabat, M. H., Dietz, C. B., Greene, R. L., Arrendondo, R., & Mann, A. W. (1996). Internal structure of the MMPI-2 Addiction Potential Scale in alcoholic and psychiatric inpatients. *Journal of Personality Assessment, 66*, 177-193.

Schinka, J. A., & LaLone, L. (1997). MMPI-2 norms: Comparisons with a census-matched subsample. *Psychological Assessment, 9*, 307-311.

Schmidt, H. O. (1945). Test profiles as a diagnostic aid: The Minnesota Multiphasic Inventory. *Journal of Applied Psychology, 29*, 115-131.

Sellbom, M., & Ben-Porath, Y. S. (2005). Mapping the MMPI-2 Restructured Clinical (RC) Scales onto normal personality traits: Evidence of construct validity. *Journal of Personality Assessment, 85*, 179-187.

Sellbom, M., & Ben-Porath, Y. S. (in press). Forensic applications of the MMPI-2. In R. P. Arhcer (Ed.), *Forensic uses of clinical assessment instruments.* Hillsdale, NJ: Erlbaum.

Sellbom, M., Ben-Porath, Y. S., & Graham J. R. (in press). Correlates of the MMPI-2 Restructured Clinical (RC) Scales in a college counseling setting. *Journal of Personality Assessment.*

Sellbom, M., Ben-Porath, Y. S., Lillienfeld, S. O., Patrick, C. J., & Graham, J. R. (2005). Assessing psychopathic traits with the MMPI-2. *Journal of Personality Assessment, 85*, 334-343.

Sellbom, M., Graham, J. R., & Schenk, P. W. (in press). Incremental validity of the MMPI-2 Restructured Clinical (RC) Scales in a Private Practice Sample. *Journal of Personality Assessment.*

Sharpe, J. P., & Desai, S. (2001). The revised Neo Personality Inventory and the MMPI-2 Psychopathology Five in the prediction of aggression. *Personality & Individual Differences, 31*, 505-518.

Simms, L. J., Casillias, A., Clark, L. A., Watson, D., & Doebbeling, B. I. (2005). Psychometric evaluation of the Restructured Clinical Scales of the MMPI-2. *Psychological Assessment, 17*, 345-358.

Smith, T. W., & Christensen, A. J. (1992). Hostility, health, and social contexts. In H.S. Friedman (Ed.), *Hostility, coping, & health* (pp. 33-48). Washington, DC: American Psychological Association.

Spanier, G. B. (1976). Measuring dyadic adjustment: New scales for assessing the quality of marriage and similar dyads. *Journal of Marriage and the Family, 38*, 15-28.

Stein, L. A. R., Graham, J. R., Ben-Porath, Y. S., & McNulty, J. L. (1999). Using the MMPI-2 to detect substance abuse in an outpatient mental health setting. *Psychological Assessment, 11*, 94-100.

Svanum, S., McGrew, J., & Ehrmann, L. (1994). Validity of the substance abuse scales of the MMPI-2 in a college student sample. *Journal of Personality Assessment, 62*, 427-439.

Synter, C. M., & Graham, J. R. (1984). The utility of subtle and obvious MMPI subscales based on scale-specific ratings. *Journal of Clinical Psychology, 40*, 981-985.

Tellegen, A. (1985). Structures of mood and personality and their relevance to assessing anxiety, with an emphasis on self-report. In A.H. Tuma & J.D. Maseer (Eds.), *Anxiety and the anxiety disorders* (pp. 681-706). Hillsdale, NJ: Erlbaum.

Tellegen, A., & Ben-Porath, Y. S. (1992). The new uniform T-scores for the MMPI-2: Rationale, derivation, and appraisal. *Psychological Assessment, 4*, 145-155.

Tellegen, A., & Ben-Porath, Y. S. (1993). Code-type comparability of the MMPI and MMPI-2: Analysis of recent findings and criticisms. *Journal of Personality Assessment, 61*, 489-500.

Tellegen, A., & Ben-Porath, Y. S. (April, 2005). Restructured MMPI-2 Scales: A Progress Report on Further Developments. Paper presented at the 40th Annual Symposium on Recent Research with the MMPI-2/MMPI-A. Fort Lauderdale, FL.

Tellegen, A., Ben-Porath, Y. S., McNulty, J. L., Arbisi, P. A., Graham, J. R., & Kaemmer, B. (2003). *The MMPI-2 Restructured Clinical Scales: Development, validation, and interpretation.* Minneapolis, MN: University of Minnesota Press.

Tellegen, A., & Waller, N. G. (in press). Exploring personality through test construction: Development of the Multidimensional personality questionnaire. In S. R. Briggs, & J. M. Cheek (Eds.), *Personality measures: Development and evaluation.* Greenwich, CN: JAI Press.

Tellegen, A., Watson, D., & Clark, L. A. (1999a). Further support for a hierarchical model of affect: Reply to Green and Salovey. *Psychological Science, 10,* 307–309.

Tellegen, A., Watson, D., & Clark, L. A. (1999b). On the dimensional and hierarchical structure of affect. *Psychological Science, 10,* 297–303.

Timbrook, R. E., Graham, J. R., Keiller, S. W., & Watts, D. (1993). Comparison of the Wiener-Harmon Subtle-Obvious scales and the standard validity scales in detecting valid and invalid MMPI-2 profiles. *Psychological Assessment, 5,* 53–61.

Trull, T. J., Useda, J. D., Costa, P. T., & McCrae, R. R. (1995). Comparison of the MMPI-2 Personality Psychopathology Five (PSY-5), the NEO-PI, and NEO-PI–R. *Psychological Assessment, 7,* 508–516.

Vendrig, A. A., Derksen, J. J. L., & de Mey, H. R. (2000). MMPI-2 Personality Psychopathology Five (PSY-5) and prediction of treatment outcome for patients with chronic back pain. *Journal of Personality Assessment, 74,* 423–438.

Wallace, A., & Liliequist, L. (2005). A comparison of the correlational structures and elevation patterns of the MMPI-2 Restructured Clinical (RC) and Clinical Scales. *Assessment, 12,* 290–294.

Watson, D., & Tellegen, A. (1985). Toward a consensual structure of mood. *Psychological Bulletin, 98,* 219–235.

Watson, D., Wiese, D., Vaidya, J., & Tellegen, A. (1999). The two general activation systems of affect: Structural findings, evolutionary considerations, and psychobiological evidence. *Journal of Personality & Social Psychology, 76,* 820–838.

Webb, J. T., Levitt, E. E., & Rojdev, R. (1993, March). After three years: A comparison of the clinical use of the MMPI and MMPI-2. Paper presented at the *53rd Annual Meeting of the Society for Personality Assessment,* San Francisco, CA.

Weed, N. C., Ben-Porath, Y. S., & Butcher, J. N. (1990). Failure of the MMPI Weiner and Harmon subtle scales as measures of personality and as validity indicators. *Psychological Assessment: A Journal of Consulting and Clinical Psychology, 2,* 281–285.

Weed, N. C., Butcher, J. N., McKenna, T., & Ben-Porath, Y. S. (1992). New measures for assessing alcohol and drug abuse with the MMPI-2: The APS and AAS. *Journal of Personality Assessment, 58,* 389–404.

Weiss, D. J. (1985). Adaptive testing by computer. *Journal of Consulting & Clinical Psychology, 53,* 774–789.

Welsh, G. S. (1948). An extension of Hathaway's MMPI profile coding system. *Journal of Consulting Psychology, 12,* 343–344.

Welsh, G. S. (1956). Factor dimensions A and R. In G. S. Welsh, & W. G. Dahlstrom (Eds), *Basic readings on the MMPI in psychology and medicine* (pp. 264–281). Minneapolis, MN: University of Minnesota Press.

Welsh, G. S., & Dahlstrom, W. G. (Eds.). (1956). *Basic readings on the MMPI in psychology and medicine.* Minneapolis, MN: University of Minnesota Press.

Wetter, M. W., Baer, R. A., Berry, D. T. R., Smith, G. T., & Larsen, L. H. (1992). Sensitivity of MMPI-2 validity scales to random responding and malingering. *Psychological Assessment, 4,* 369–374.

Wetzler, S., Khadivi, A., & Moser, R. K. (1998). The use of the MMPI-2 for the assessment of depressive and psychotic disorders. *Assessment, 5,* 249–261.

Wiener, D. N. (1948). Subtle and obvious keys for the MMPI. *Journal of Consulting Psychology, 12,* 164–170.

Wiener, D. N., & Harmon, L. R. (1946). *Subtle and obvious keys for the MMPI: Their development.* Minneapolis, VA, Advisement Bulletin, no. 16.

Wiggins, J. S. (1966). Substantive dimensions of self-report in the MMPI item pool. *Psychological Monographs, 80,* (22, whole no. 630).

Williams, H. L. (1952). The development of a caudality scale for the MMPI. *Journal of Clinical Psychology, 8,* 293–297.

# Interpersonal Circumplex Measures

## 15

### Kenneth D. Locke

nspired by Sullivan's theoretical framework (Sullivan, 1953), the interpersonal model conceptualizes interpersonal processes as the vital foundations of both normal and abnormal personality. Indeed, an examination of normal personality terms across many languages reveals that more traits refer to aspects of interpersonal functioning than to any other domain of functioning ( John, 1990). Likewise in the domain of abnormal functioning, the majority of the criteria for diagnosing personality disorders in the current Diagnostic and Statistical Manual of Mental Disorders (American Psychiatric Association, 2000) refer to interpersonal acts or reactions to actual, imagined, desired, or feared interpersonal situations. The topic of several recent books has been the centrality and utility of interpersonal models for understanding, diagnosing, and treating various forms of psychopathology (Horowitz, 2004; Kiesler, 1996), with a particular focus on personality disorders (Benjamin, 1996a). But the seminal book on applying interpersonal models to psychopathology was Leary (1957), which elaborated and popularized the interpersonal circle model developed by Freedman, Leary, Ossorio, and Coffey (1951).

The interpersonal circle or interpersonal circumplex (IPC) has in recent decades become the most popular model for conceptualizing, organizing, and assessing interpersonal dispositions (Kiesler, 1983; Wiggins, 2003). The IPC is defined by two orthogonal axes: a vertical axis (of status, dominance, power, or control) and a horizontal axis (of solidarity, friendliness, warmth, or love). In recent years, it has become conventional to identify the vertical and horizontal axes with the broad metaconcepts of *agency* and *communion* (Horowitz, 2004; Wiggins, 2003). Thus, each point in the IPC space can be specified as a weighted combination of agency and communion; or, in other words, the IPC offers a place for interpersonal dispositions reflecting all combinations of agency and communion.

Placing a person near one of the poles of the axes implies that the person tends to convey clear or strong messages (of warmth, hostility, dominance or submissiveness). Conversely, placing a person at the midpoint of the agentic dimension implies the person conveys neither dominance nor submissiveness (and pulls neither dominance nor submissiveness from others). Likewise, placing a person at the midpoint of the communal dimension implies the person conveys neither warmth nor hostility (and pulls neither warmth nor hostility from others).

The IPC can be divided into broad segments (such as fourths) or narrow segments (such as sixteenths), but currently most IPC inventories partition the circle into eight octants, as shown in Figure 15.1. As one moves around the circle, each octant reflects a progressive blend of the two axial dimensions. Also note that, by convention, each octant has a generic two-letter code (shown in parentheses). In this chapter I will review a variety of inventories designed to measure these eight IPC octants. I will focus on measures of interpersonal traits, interpersonal problems, interpersonal values, and interpersonal impacts. However, I will also briefly mention several more specialized IPC measures, as well as the SASB/INTREX questionnaires, which measure an alternative model of the interpersonal space. After introducing these measures, I will describe how they can help differentiate normal and abnormal interpersonal dispositions.

For an inventory to be considered an IPC measure, its octant scales should have the following properties: (a) scales that are closer to one another on the circle should have higher correlations than scales that are farther apart; (b) the scales' communalities on

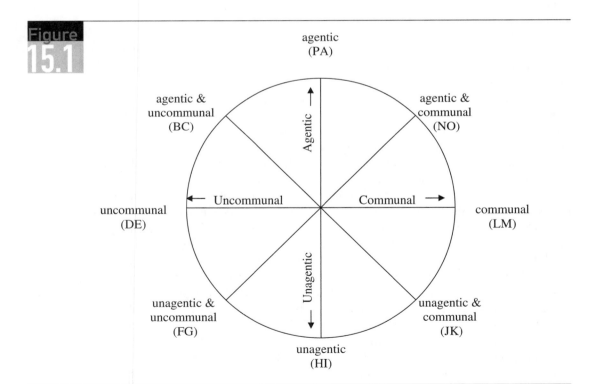

**Figure 15.1**

The interpersonal circumplex.

the two underlying dimensions of agency and communion should all be high and approximately equal; and (c) plotting the octant scales on the two underlying axes should show them to be distributed at approximately equal 45-degree intervals. Measures whose scales meet these criteria have the advantage of being amenable to the types of geometric analyses described in Pincus and Gurtman (this volume, chapter 4). The IPC measures reviewed below generally meet these criteria, albeit some better than others.

Although the IPC inventories described below typically are used as self-report measures of global dispositions, almost all of the measures can be and have been used in other ways. For example, most of the self-report measures (with perhaps a slight change in the wording of the instructions or the items) also have been used to obtain ratings by peer or observers. Likewise, IPC measures have been used to ask not only about a target's general dispositions, but also about the target's dispositions in specific situations (e.g., at work or at home), in specific relationships (e.g., with your spouse or with your therapist), or under specific conditions (e.g., when under stress or when relaxed). The benefit of greater specification is that it may yield greater understanding and predictive power; the cost is that the respondent is faced with more complex instructions to read and more items to answer, and the clinician or researcher is faced with more scales to interpret. Typically, the cost is greater than the benefit unless the clinician or researcher has an *a priori* reason for inquiring about those specific situations, relationships, or conditions.

# Measures

## Assessing Interpersonal Traits

The Interpersonal Check List (ICL; LaForge & Suczek, 1955) was the first IPC inventory. The ICL was designed to assess 16 segments of the interpersonal circle. Each segment was assessed by eight adjectives or verb-phrases (yielding a total of 128 items), each of which was weighted according to one of four levels of extremity. The ICL has been used in numerous studies (for a bibliography, see Clark & Taulbee, 1981). However, it has psychometric inadequacies. Specifically, the ICL has noteworthy measurement gaps in the top-right and bottom-left quadrants, and scales opposite each other on the circle are not actually polar opposites (Kiesler, 1983; Lorr & McNair, 1965; Paddock & Nowicki, 1986a,b; Wiggins, 1979, 1982). Wiggins (1979) and Wiggins, Trapnell, and Phillips (1988) developed the Interpersonal Adjective Scales (IAS) to address these inadequacies. Since the IAS has proven to have more desirable psychometric and circumplex properties than the ICL, IAS is now the preferred measure of interpersonal traits. Moreover, the basic methods used to develop the IAS have served as the model for developing all subsequent IPC measures.

The most recent version of the IAS (Wiggins, 1995) consists of 64 interpersonal adjectives. Example items are shown in Table 15.1. Respondents rate each adjective with respect to how accurately it describes a target (typically the self) on a scale ranging from 1 (Very Inaccurate) to 8 (Very Accurate) scale. The adjectives are combined into eight scales that assess each octant of the IPC. The IAS has acceptable internal consistency and a clear circumplex structure (Gurtman & Pincus, 2000; Wiggins et al., 1988), and its scales show a sensible sinusoidal pattern of correlations with numerous other

**Table 15.1** Examples of Items from Each Octant of the IAS, IIP, CSIV, and IMI

| Octant Scale | Sample IAS Items (Rate how accurately each describes you) | Sample IIP Items (Rate how distressing each problem has been) | Sample CSIV Items "When I am with him/her/them, it is important that..." | Sample IMI Items "When I am with this person, he/she makes me feel..." |
|---|---|---|---|---|
| LM (Communal) | Sympathetic | I try to please other people too much | they show concern for how I am feeling | appreciated by him/her |
| NO (Agentic and communal) | Perky | I tell personal things to other people too much | they respect what I have to say | that I could relax and he/she'd take charge |
| PA (Agentic) | Forceful | I try to control other people too much | they acknowledge when I am right | bossed around |
| BC (Agentic and uncommunal) | Boastful | I fight with other people too much | I keep the upper hand | that I want to stay away from him/her |
| DE (Uncommunal) | Ruthless | It is hard for me to show affection to people | they not know what I am thinking or feeling | distant from him/her |
| FG (Unagentic and uncommunal) | Unsociable | I am too afraid of other people | I not say something stupid | that I should tell him/her not to be so nervous around me |
| HI (Unagentic) | Timid | It is hard for me to be assertive with another person | I not make them angry | in charge |
| JK (Unagentic and communal) | Unargumentative | I am too gullible | they like me | that I could tell him/her anything and he/she would agree |

self-report personality measures (Wiggins & Broughton, 1985, 1991) as well as ratings of nonverbal interpersonal behavior (Gifford, 1991; Gifford & O'Connor, 1987). One problem with the IAS is that respondents may find some of the adjectives (such as "uncrafty" and "uncunning") odd and unfamiliar.

## Assessing Interpersonal Problems

The most common self-report measure of problems associated with each octant of the interpersonal circle is the Inventory of Interpersonal Problems (IIP; Horowitz, Alden, & Pincus, 2000). The IIP consists of eight 8-item***(CH REP) scales that assess problematic dispositions associated with each octant of the interpersonal circumplex. Example items are shown in Table 15.1. Respondents indicate how distressed they have been by each problem on a 0 (not at all) to 4 (extremely) scale. The items are divided into two sections, namely, "things you find hard to do with other people" and "things that you do too much". The octant scores show adequate internal and 1-week test–retest reliability (Horowitz et al., 2000), and meet the criteria for circumplex structure (Alden, Wiggins, & Pincus, 1990; Pincus, Gurtman, & Ruiz, 1998; Vittengl, Clark, & Jarrett, 2003). The scales also show convergent validity with circumplex measures of interpersonal traits (Alden et al., 1990) and interpersonal motives (Locke, 2000).

The IIP has been successfully applied to a variety of research questions. For example, Locke (2005) studied if there were connections between how people expected others to treat them in their everyday lives and the interpersonal problems assessed by the IIP. Some of the findings were that anticipating others being critical or dismissive predicted problems with being too agentic, whereas anticipating others being uninviting or unsupportive predicted problems with being too uncommunal. As another example, numerous studies of psychotherapy process and outcome have used the IIP (e.g., Alden & Capreol, 1993; Borkovec, Newman, Pincus, & Lytle, 2002; Gurtman, 1996; Horowitz, Rosenberg, & Bartholomew, 1993; Maling, Gurtman, & Howard, 1995; Muran, Segal, Samstag, & Crawford, 1994). While the findings have not been completely consistent, they generally suggest that problems in the "agentic and uncommunal" region predict poorer progress, at least in psychodynamic treatment.

## Assessing Interpersonal Values and Motives

Individuals' feelings and behaviors in interpersonal situations depend in part on their interpersonal values. For example, being told what to do may be a relief to someone who values submission, but a humiliation to someone who values dominance. Consequently, many psychotherapies seek to change feelings and behavior by changing values; for example, cognitive and rational–emotive therapies often have clients question the extreme value they place on certain interpersonal experiences, such as *needing* others to show respect. The Circumplex Scales of Interpersonal Values (CSIV; Locke, 2000) is a 64-item measure of the value individuals place on interpersonal experiences associated with each octant of the IPC. The values the CSIV measures are akin to the "subjective values" of cognitive social learning theory (Mischel, 1973) and "incentive values" of expectancy-value theory (Atkinson, 1964; Eccles & Wigfield, 2002). While these are sometimes referred to as "motives" (Horowitz, 2004), the term "values" follows McClelland's (1980, 1985) distinction between implicit "motives" that are measured by the Thematic Apperception Test and "values" that are measured by self-report inventories such as the CSIV.

The CSIV asks respondents to rate the importance of 64 interpersonal experiences, with eight items associated with each octant of the IPC. For each item, respondents indicate, on a scale from 0 (not important) to 4 (extremely important) how important it is that they act or appear or are treated that way in interpersonal situations. Sample items are shown in Table 15.1. The CSIV form, scoring program, and norms are available at www.class.uidaho.edu/klocke/csiv.htm. The scales have adequate internal consistency and test–retest reliability, a circumplex structure, and convergent and discriminant validity in relation to measures of interpersonal traits, interpersonal goals, interpersonal problems, personality disorders, and implicit power and intimacy motives assessed by the Thematic Apperception Test (Locke, 2000).

## Assessing Interpersonal Impacts

The Impact Message Inventory-Circumplex (IMI; Kiesler & Schmidt, 1993; Kiesler, Schmidt, & Wagner, 1997) assesses the interpersonal dispositions of a target person, not by asking the target person directly, but by assessing the covert responses or "impact messages" (i.e., feelings, thoughts, and behavioral tendencies) that the target evokes in another person. The IMI asks the respondent to describe the covert reactions he or she typically experiences in the presence of the target. The IMI consists of 56 items grouped into eight 7-item octant scales. The items are designed to assess the types of reactions evoked by interpersonal behaviors from all regions of the interpersonal circle. Thus, items on the dominant scale are reactions likely to be evoked by a dominant target, whereas the items on the friendly scale are reactions likely to be evoked by a friendly target. Respondents indicate how accurately each item describes their reaction to the target using a 4-point scale ranging from *not at all* (1) to *very much so* (4). Example items are shown in Table 15.1.

The IMI scales show convergent validity with measures of interpersonal behavior; for example, the types of problems a target reports on the IIP predict the types of impacts they have on the IMI (Wagner, Kiesler, & Schmidt, 1995). The IMI octant scales have acceptable internal consistencies and also approximate a circumplex structure (Schmidt, Wagner, & Kiesler, 1999b). However, the IMI does not meet circumplex criteria as well as the other IPC measures reviewed above. Although the octant scales show a circular ordering around the interpersonal axes, they also show unequal spacing around the circumference and inconsistent vector lengths (Schmidt et al., 1999b). The IMI has been used successfully in numerous studies, but when conducting research using the IMI it would be prudent to verify that the IMI scales in your data set meet the criteria for a circumplex prior to combining them using trigonometric formulas of the sort described below.

## Specialized IPC Measures

Various other IPC measures exist that may be useful within particular contexts. I will briefly mention three of these.

### The Support Actions Scale-Circumplex

The Support Actions Scale-Circumplex (SAS-C; Trobst, 2000) is a 64-item measure of dispositions to provide agentic and communal support to those in need of assistance. Example of items are "give advice" (PA), "remind them whining doesn"t help" (DE), and "give them a hug" (LM). The SAS-C might be particularly useful for identifying the difficulties or conflicts experienced by people who are members of support groups or people who are giving support to physically or mentally challenged individuals.

### The Check List of Interpersonal Transactions

The Check List of Interpersonal Transactions (CLOIT; Kiesler, Goldston, & Schmidt, 1991) is a 96-item measure of the degree to which a person has enacted interpersonal behaviors in each of 16 segments of the IPC. There is a version specifically for ratings of clients or counselors called the Check List of Psychotherapy Transactions (CLOPT). Examples of items are "act in a relaxed, informal, warm, or nonjudgmental manner" (LM) and "act in a stiff, formal, unfeeling, or evaluative manner" (DE). For each item the respondent simply indicates whether or not the target enacted that behavior; thus, the CLOIT and CLOPT are behavioral checklists, rather than measures of enduring dispositions. The CLOIT and CLOPT may be particularly useful for identifying patterns of behavior within particular situations or interactions, such as within a therapy session.

### The Chart of Interpersonal Reactions in Closed Living Environments

The Chart of Interpersonal Reactions in Closed Living Environments (CIRCLE; Blackburn & Renwick, 1996) is a 49-item set of observer ratings that were designed to sample the interpersonal behavior of psychiatric inpatients. Examples of items are "dominates conversations" (PA), "sits alone or keeps to himself" (FG), and "helpful to other patients" (LM). The frequency of each behavior is rated on a 4-point scale. The eight octant scales demonstrate acceptable psychometric and circumplex properties. Being based on observer ratings, the CIRCLE may be particularly useful for assessment in inpatient populations or when self-reports are likely to be invalid (e.g., Blackburn, 1998).

## SASB/INTREX Questionnaires

Whereas the preceding interpersonal inventories were based on the IPC model, the INTREX questionnaires are based on an alternative structural model of interpersonal space—the Structural Analysis of Social Behavior (SASB; Benjamin, 1974, 1996b). SASB codes interpersonal stances on two circles rather than just one. When the "focus" is on the other person, the interpersonal stance is coded on the transitive behavior circle. When the "focus" is on the self (reacting to the other person), the interpersonal stance is coded on the intransitive behavior circle. Both circles are defined by a horizontal dimension of affiliation (like that of the IPC) and a vertical dimension of independence–enmeshment (ranging from *give-autonomy* to *dominate* on the transitive circle and from *take-autonomy* to *submit* on the intransitive circle). Thus, theoretically, whatever reaction a particular transitive action pulls for is coded at the corresponding point on the intransitive circle; for example, dominance and submission are coded at the same points on the transitive and intransitive circles, respectively. The full INTREX questionnaire contains 36 items for each circle (i.e., 4 or 5 items per octant).

While some find SASB/INTREX an appealing system for describing dyadic transactions, it has serious theoretical and psychometric problems. For example, the research does not support the existence of distinct transitive and intransitive dimensions of affiliation (Pincus et al., 1998). The most serious problems concern the independence dimension. In the IPC model, independence is maximized at the IPC origin (where stances do not exert interpersonal pulls in any direction), and interpersonal enmeshment increases as a person's stances deviate from the center (in any one direction or in multiple directions). In the SASB model, independence increases as one moves from the bottom to the top of the circle. Consequently, the IPC model puts the extremes of affiliation (e.g., *love* and *attack*) among the least independent stances, whereas the SASB model puts them at the midpoint of the independence dimension—a position that I find counterintuitive. Moreover, analyses of trait terms across numerous language groups reliably reveal the IPC dimensions, but not an independence dimension (Rolland, 2002). Even on the INTREX, friendly acts tend to co-occur and unfriendly acts tend to co-occur regardless of the autonomy those acts grant or deny, suggesting that independence is a less salient dimension. Because the affiliation dimension differentiates items better than does the independence dimension, the INTREX scales produce unequally spaced ellipses that fail to meet the "constant radius" and "equal spacing" criteria for circumplex measures (Pincus et al., 1998); consequently, the type of geometric formulas that can be applied to the IPC scales cannot be applied to the INTREX scales.

## Other Noncircular Interpersonal Measures

There are many other instruments that measure aspects of interpersonal behavior, but whose scales conform to neither the IPC nor SASB circles for one of two reasons. First, some tests measure only subsets of the interpersonal space. For example, tests of the extroversion factor of the Five-Factor model (FFM) typically measure the FG-NO axis of the IPC, whereas tests of the agreeableness factor of the FFM typically measure the BC-JK axis (McCrae & Costa, 1989; Trapnell & Wiggins, 1990). Other examples would be a Machiavellianism scale or an interpersonal dependency scale (Gurtman, 1992; Pincus & Gurtman, 1995). Second, some instruments measure both interpersonal and non-interpersonal dispositions. An example is the Interpersonal Style Inventory (ISI; Lorr & Youniss, 1986). The ISI is a well-constructed 300-item self-report inventory consisting of fifteen bipolar scales that show good internal and temporal reliability. However, while some of the scales are specifically interpersonal (e.g., *Directive–Nondirective, Nurturant–Help Withholding*), other are not (e.g., *Conscientious–Expedient, Deliberate–Impulsive*). Consequently, factor analyses of the ISI scales (Lorr & DeLong, 1984) yield, not the two IPC factors, but instead five factors that are similar to the FFM factors. While any personality trait—including the "noninterpersonal" traits of the FFM (conscientiousness, emotionality, and culture)—*can* be expressed in and have effects on interpersonal situations, the IPC dimensions define the specifically interpersonal aspects of a relationship or interaction. That is why this chapter focuses on IPC inventories.

# Scoring and Interpreting IPC Inventories

Typically, the initial scoring of an IPC inventory yields eight raw octant scores. You can plot and compare the raw scores, but since people generally tend to report more agentic and communal dispositions than unagentic and uncommunal dispositions, it may be more informative to standardize the raw scores as follows: standardized score = (raw score − $M$)/$SD$, where $M$ and $SD$ are the mean and standard deviation from a relevant standardization sample. Of course, only examining the octant scores one at a time fails to take advantage of the remarkable capacity of IPC measures to systematically fuse together scales using trigonometric formulas. Different approaches to fusing or summarizing the scales exist, and the most useful approach for you will depend on how you will use the scores—for example, whether will you use the scores in research or will give feedback to individual patients or health care providers in a clinical context. The following approach is one way to quickly (and by hand) compute an individual's overall interpersonal trends; Gurtman (1994) offers a more sophisticated approach.

The first step is to compute the individual's overall dispositions to approach agency, avoid agency, approach communion, or avoid communion as follows:

$$\text{Agentic Vector} = (0.414)(\text{PA} + (0.707)(\text{BC} + \text{NO})$$
$$\text{Unagentic Vector} = (0.414)(\text{HI} + (0.707)(\text{FG} + \text{JK})$$
$$\text{Communal Vector} = (0.414)(\text{LM} + (0.707)(\text{JK} + \text{NO})$$
$$\text{Uncommunal Vector} = (0.414)(\text{DE} + (0.707)(\text{BC} + \text{FG})$$

To the extent that an individual is above average in both communal and uncommunal tendencies, or above average in both agentic and unagentic tendencies, that individual may be prone to problematic conflicts such as simultaneously wanting and fearing power, or alternately seeking and avoiding closeness. Moreover, dispositions to approach versus avoid may be associated with distinct neurophysiological, affective, cognitive, and behavioral patterns (Amodio, Shah, Sigelman, Brazy, & Harmon-Jones, 2004). For example, Locke (2005) found that more of any type of interpersonal problem measured by the IIP predicted more distress, but whereas agentic and communal dispositions predicted *too much* negative feeling (of anger or shame), unagentic and uncommunal dispositions predicted *too little* positive feeling (of confidence or connection). Thus, dispositions to approach versus avoid agency and communion may be related to the individual's broader pattern of affect (e.g., too much anger versus too little confidence), cognition (e.g., focus on rewards versus costs), and behavior (e.g., using approach versus avoidance to solve problems).

The second step is to compute the overall X and Y vectors. The agentic vector score minus the unagentic vector score yields the individual's overall tendency to be agentic versus unagentic (or Y coordinate). The communal vector score minus the uncommunal vector score yields the individual's overall tendency to be communal versus uncommunal (or X coordinate). The point in the IPC space defined by these X and Y coordinates shows the individual's overall interpersonal tendencies. The angle of this vector shows where the individual's pattern of octant scores has its predicted peak, and should reveal the individual's predominant interpersonal disposition. The length of this vector shows how intensely and consistently the target manifests this interpersonal disposition; the longer the vector, the more the pattern of scores reflects a well-defined interpersonal pattern with a clear peak in one region, a clear trough in the opposite region, and moderate scores in between.

# Using IPC Measures to Assess Abnormality

## General Indicators

A maladaptive interpersonal disposition is one that contributes to *unnecessary* distress in the self or others *across relationships*. Note that to be maladaptive, the distress must be unnecessary. For example, sometimes arguing with your boss can be distressing yet necessary to protect the safety of your co-workers; at other times, not arguing with your boss can be distressing yet necessary to protect your job. Your behavior in these instances may be uncomfortable to you or your boss, but nonetheless be adaptive. Note also that to be a disposition, the distress must not be limited to just one relationship or situation; for example, if you get into arguments with your boss and nobody else, then blaming the arguments on your having a maladaptive interpersonal disposition would be an oversimplification.

The IPC model maps normal and abnormal dispositions onto the same interpersonal space, and does not define any particular segment of the interpersonal space as necessarily adaptive or maladaptive (Leary, 1957; Kiesler, 1996). In support of this view, analyses of clinical intake interviews shows that people complain of interpersonal problems associated with all segments of the IPC (Alden et al., 1990). Approaching agency and communion can be adaptive, and avoiding status or solidarity can be adaptive (Wiggins, 2003). Indeed, evolutionary psychology suggests that it is exactly because there are both costs and benefits of agency and communion that there exists variance in agentic and communal behaviors across persons and across situations. For example, communing with others creates opportunities not only for resource exchange and social support (that can have physiological, psychological, and material benefits), but also for contracting diseases or social responsibilities (that can have physiological, psychological, and material costs). Likewise, agency can increase not only access to valued resources, but also the likelihood of costly interpersonal competition.

The IPC model predicts that abnormal profiles generally will be either more rigid and extreme or more conflicted and chaotic (Kiesler, 1996). With respect to rigidity, being close or distant or controlling or yielding can be adaptive when done judiciously, but being *indiscriminately* or *excessively* close or distant or controlling or yielding tends to be maladaptive. Consequently, normal (moderate and flexible) dispositions tend to be located near the center of the IPC, whereas abnormal (extreme and rigid) dispositions tend to be located near the periphery of the IPC (Sim & Romney, 1990). Because rigid and extreme behaviors, values, and impacts can all contribute to interpersonal distress, any of the measures reviewed above can be used to identify potentially maladaptive dispositions.

Conflicted interpersonal profiles (higher than average scores on opposing vectors) may also be problematic because they suggest internal conflicts and the likelihood of sending messages that are confusing and ambiguous or that are inconsistent either across time or across different channels (Kiesler, 1996). For example, with respect to motives, a person who strongly values both closeness and distance (i.e., who wishes to be loved and embraced but fears being exploited or suffocated) is likely to experience distressing conflicts. The person who then actually does both—pulling another person close, and then pushing them away—is likely to cause unnecessary distress in themselves and others. The person who communicates "mixed messages" across verbal and nonverbal channels also tends to create confusion and distress.

## Specific Disorders

While there are some inconsistent findings, overall the research shows that people who score high on measures of negative affectivity (such as depression, anxiety, low self-esteem, or the emotionality or neuroticism dimension of the Five-Factor model) tend to describe themselves and to be described by others as having less $+$ A $+$ C dispositions or more $-$ A $-$ C dispositions on interpersonal circle measures (e.g., Alden & Phillips, 1990; McCullough et al., 1994; Schmidt, Wagner, & Kiesler, 1999a; Trapnell & Wiggins, 1990).

Since interpersonal dispositions are key features of most personality disorders, IPC measures are particularly useful for identifying or differentiating personality disorders (Kiesler, 1996; Leary, 1957). A number of studies have examined correlations between personality disorder measures and IPC measures (e.g., Blackburn, 1998; Locke, 2000; Matano & Locke, 1995; Pincus & Wiggins, 1990; Soldz, Budman, Demby, & Merry, 1993; Sim & Romney, 1990; Wiggins & Pincus, 1989). Across a variety of measures and samples, personality disorders and IPC dispositions tend to be related as follows.

Interpersonal dispositions (e.g., values, behaviors, problems) in the "low agency and low communion" region are associated with avoidant, schizoid, and (to a lesser extent) schizotypal personality styles. Individuals with these personality disorders tend to avoid connections with and attention from others, presumably as a means of self-protection (Horowitz, 2004). Whereas schizoid and schizotypal individuals tend to show non-specific interpersonal discomfort and withdrawal, avoidant persons tend to be especially sensitive to and avoidant of social situations and interactions in which they might experience rejection, criticism, and humiliation.

Interpersonal dispositions in the "low agency and high communion" region are associated with the dependent personality style. Dependent individuals perceive others as having more status and competence than themselves. Thus, they seek from others not only solidarity but also protection and guidance, and they offer up trust and submission to others in return. Interpersonal dispositions at the opposite end of the IPC—in the "high agency and low communion" region—are associated with antisocial or paranoid personality styles. Individuals with these personality disorders tend to view interpersonal interactions in cynical or hostile terms, and are prone to insensitive or aggressive interpersonal behaviors. However, whereas the "controlling and unfriendly" actions of antisocial persons tend to be pre-emptive or instrumental, the actions of paranoid persons tend to be reactive or self-protective (in response to perceived abuse or malice).

Interpersonal dispositions in the "high agency and high communion" region are associated with the histrionic personality style, and dispositions in the "high agency" (but neither high nor low in communion) region are associated with a narcissistic personality style. The positive feelings and self-worth of histrionic individuals appear highly dependent on the status and solidarity they are currently experiencing in their interpersonal relationships, and therefore they tend to display inviting yet controlling interpersonal behaviors that demand attention and engagement. While narcissistic persons are also sensitive to how they believe others perceive them, they are more concerned with status (respect, admiration) and less concerned with solidarity (support, love) than are histrionic persons, and are correspondingly less likely to use warm, inviting behaviors as a means to gain status.

Finally, the borderline and obsessive–compulsive personality disorders do not appear to be associated with any one segment of the IPC. One reason may be that the core problems in these disorders are not interpersonal, but instead reflect extreme levels of noninterpersonal traits, such as neuroticism in the case of borderline personality disorder and conscientiousness in the case of obsessive–compulsive personality disorder (Widiger & Hagemoser, 1997). Another reason may be that the interpersonal dispositions associated with these disorders are complicated, and thus not limited to one IPC region. Obsessive–compulsive persons who want to avoid mistakes and blame may act remarkably dutiful and compliant (in the lower right of the IPC) when accepting another's authority, but act critical and controlling (in the upper left of the IPC) when in authority themselves. Likewise, borderline persons who crave being nurtured and fear being abandoned may be trusting and deferent (in the lower right) when they perceive the other person to be nurturing, but quickly become demanding and vindictive (in the upper left of the IPC) when they perceive the other person to be withdrawing.

## Examples of IPC Profiles

In order to illustrate some of the points the preceding sections made concerning interpreting and using IPC measures, let us consider three examples. The examples will be the CSIV scores of the three individuals from the sample of participants in Locke (2000, Study 3) whose MCMI-III (Millon, 1994) profiles most clearly suggested an antisocial, a dependent, or a borderline personality disorder. Specifically, these three individuals were the ones whose BR score on the antisocial, dependent, or borderline scale was (a) greater than 85; (b) at least 10 units higher than their scores on any other personality disorder scale; (c) and higher than the scores of anyone else who met the first two criteria.

The CSIV octant means for these individuals are shown in Figures 15.2–15.4, and are consistent with the predictions made in the previous section. (Recall that CSIV scores can range from 0, "not at all important", to 4, "extremely important"). Experiencing agency without communion was very important to the antisocial person but not the dependent person, whereas experiencing communion without agency was very important to the dependent person but not the antisocial person. The wishes and fears of the borderline person were not limited to particular regions. The arrows on Figures 15.2 to 15.4 point to the mean (X,Y) coordinate or vector, and are consistent with the preceding observations. The overall interpersonal tendencies of the antisocial and dependent persons were in the "uncommunal and agentic" and "communal and unagentic" regions, respectively. The borderline person's overall tendencies were in the agentic region, but because her interpersonal tendencies were less consistent, her vector was shorter than that of the antisocial or dependent person.

Table 15.2 shows the four "cardinal" vectors (agentic, unagentic, communal, and uncommunal) for each individual. The scores have been standardized to show how many

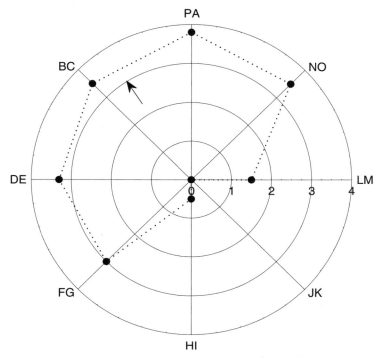

CSIV octant scores of a person with antisocial personality disorder symptoms.

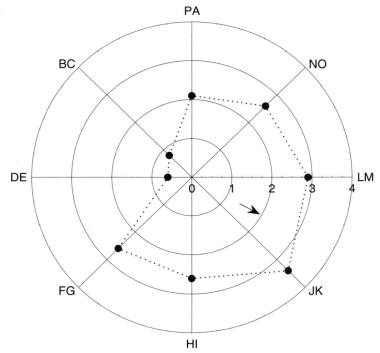

CSIV octant scores of a person with dependent personality disorder symptoms.

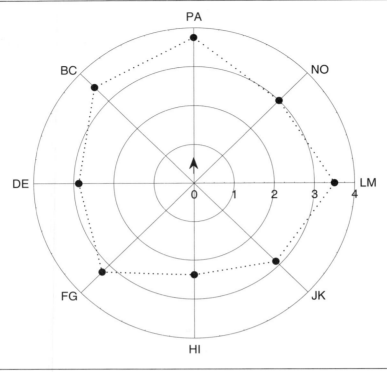

CSIV Octant scores of a person with borderline personality disorder symptoms.

### Table 15.2 — Standardized CSIV Vector Scores of Persons with an Elevation on the MCMI-III Antisocial Scale, Dependent Scale, or Borderline Scale

| CSIV Vector | Antisocial | Dependent | Borderline |
|---|---|---|---|
| Communal | −2.01 | 0.25 | 0.63 |
| Uncommunal | 3.05 | −0.17 | 2.92 |
| Agentic | 2.43 | −0.82 | 2.16 |
| Unagentic | −1.43 | 1.30 | 1.26 |

*Note:* The values shown represent the number of standard deviations above or below the vector means of the standardization sample ($n = 1,200$).

standard deviations each score is above or below the mean of the CSIV standardization sample. Note that since most people value getting along with others, the tendencies of the dependent person—when viewed as standardized scores—do not appear too extreme. Conversely, the tendencies of the antisocial person—when viewed as standardized scores—appear very extreme. Note also the borderline person scored above average on all of the scales. Consequently, the borderline person may be prone to distressing conflicts, especially between wanting control (since her "agentic" vector was over two standard deviations above average) and wanting to give in to avoid friction (since her "unagentic" vector, while smaller, is still over one standard deviation above average).

# Caveats and Conclusions

The IPC measures reviewed above were designed to differentiate interpersonal dispositions with respect to levels of agency and communion, not with respect to levels of normality and abnormality. While unusually extreme or conflicting interpersonal tendencies tend to be maladaptive, IPC measures by themselves cannot determine whether or not a disposition is adaptive. Indeed, the scales and norms for most IPC measures were derived using normal samples. More research is needed on the efficacy and incremental validity of IPC instruments in clinical populations, and may show the need to revise existing instruments (or develop new instruments) in order to enhance their utility in clinical settings. Furthermore, there are many other personality dimensions, in addition to those assessed by IPC inventories, that contribute to adaptive versus maladaptive functioning. Therefore, when used for diagnostic purposes, IPC measures are used in conjunction with other measures of functioning.

On the other hand, problematic interpersonal dispositions are a major impetus for seeking psychotherapy, and play an important role in a wide variety of disorders and in the process and outcome of psychotherapy (Horowitz, 2004). Therefore, it is important to include measures of interpersonal dispositions when conducting assessments that inform judgments concerning the causes, nature, and treatment of abnormality. The IPC measures reviewed in this chapter give researchers and clinicians a variety of ways to efficiently assess and summarize the domain of interpersonal dispositions described by the IPC, which remains the most geometrically elegant and empirically robust model of the cardinal vectors on which people chart the course of their interpersonal lives.

## REFERENCES

Alden, L. E., & Capreol, M. J. (1993). Avoidant personality disorder: Interpersonal problems as predictors of treatment response. *Behavior Therapy, 24*, 357–376.

Alden, L. E., & Phillips, N. (1990). An interpersonal analysis of social anxiety and depression. *Cognitive Therapy & Research, 14*, 499–512.

Alden, L. E., Wiggins, J. S., & Pincus, A. L. (1990). Construction of circumplex scales for the Inventory of Interpersonal Problems. *Journal of Personality Assessment, 55*, 521–536.

American Psychiatric Association. (2000). *Diagnostic and statistical manual of mental disorders* (4th ed., text revision). Washington, DC: Author.

Amodio, D. M., Shah, J. Y., Sigelman, J., Brazy, P. C., Harmon-Jones, E. (2004). Implicit regulatory focus associated with asymmetrical frontal cortical activity. *Journal of Experimental Social Psychology, 40*, 225–232.

Atkison, J. W. (1964). *An introduction to motivation*. Oxford, England: Van Nostrand.

Benjamin, L. S. (1974). Structural analysis of social behavior. *Psychological Review, 81*, 392–425.

Benjamin, L. S. (1996a). Interpersonal diagnosis and treatment of personality disorders. New York, NY: Guilford Press.

Benjamin, L. S. (1996b). A clinician-friendly version of the Interpersonal Circumplex: Structural Analysis of Social Behavior (SASB). *Journal of Personality Assessment, 66*, 248–266.

Blackburn, R. (1998). Criminality and the interpersonal circle in mentally disordered offenders. *Criminal Justice & Behavior, 25*, 155–176.

Blackburn, R., & Renwick, S. J. (1996). Rating scales for measuring the interpersonal circle in forensic psychiatric patients. *Psychological Assessment, 8*, 76–84.

Borkovec, T. D., Newman, M. G., Pincus, A. L., & Lytle, R. (2002). Component analysis of cognitive-behavioral therapy for generalized anxiety disorder and the role of interpersonal problems. *Journal of Consulting and Clinical Psychology, 70*, 288–298.

Clark, T. L., & Taulbee, E. S. (1981). A comprehensive and indexed bibliography of the Interpersonal Check List. *Journal of Personality Assessment, 45*, 505–525.

Eccles, J. S., & Wigfield, A. (2002). Motivational beliefs, values, and goals. *Annual Review of Psychology, 53*, 109–132.

Freedman, M. B., Leary, T., Ossorio, A. G., & Coffey, H. S. (1951). The interpersonal dimension of personality. *Journal of Personality, 20*, 143–161.

Gifford, R. (1991). Mapping nonverbal behavior on the interpersonal circle. *Journal of Personality and Social Psychology, 61*, 279–288.

Gifford, R., & O'Connor, B. (1987). The interpersonal circumplex as a behavior map. *Journal of Personality and Social Psychology, 52*, 1019–1026.

Gurtman, M. B. (1992). Trust, distrust, and interpersonal problems: A circumplex analysis. *Journal of Personality & Social Psychology, 62*, 989–1002.

Gurtman, M. B. (1994). The circumplex as a tool for studying normal and abnormal personality: A methodological primer. In S. Strack & M. Lorr (Eds.), *Differentiating normal and abnormal personality* (pp. 243–263). New York: Springer.

Gurtman, M. B. (1996). Interpersonal problems and the psychotherapy context: The construct validity of the Inventory of Interpersonal Problems. *Psychological Assessment, 8*, 241–255.

Gurtman, M. B., & Pincus, A. L. (2000). Interpersonal adjective scales: Confirmation of circumplex structure from multiple perspectives. *Personality & Social Psychology Bulletin, 26*, 374–384.

Horowitz, L. M. (2004). *Interpersonal foundations of psychopathology*. Washington, DC: American Psychological Association.

Horowitz, L. M., Alden, L. E., Wiggins, J. S., & Pincus, A. L. (2000). *Inventory of Interpersonal Problems manual*. Odessa, FL: The Psychological Corporation.

Horowitz, L. M., Rosenberg, S. E., & Bartholomew, K. (1993). Interpersonal problems, attachment styles, and outcome in brief dynamic psychotherapy. *Journal of Consulting and Clinical Psychology, 61*, 549–560.

John, O. P. (1990). The "Big Five" Factor Taxonomy: Dimensions of Personality in the Natural Language and in Questionnaires. In L. Pervin (Ed.), *Handbook of personality: Theory and research* (pp. 66–100). New York: Guilford Press.

Kiesler, D. J. (1983). The 1982 interpersonal circle: A taxonomy for complementarity in human transactions. *Psychological Review, 90*, 185–214.

Kiesler, D. J. (1996). *Contemporary interpersonal theory and research: Personality, psychopathology and psychotherapy*. New York: Wiley.

Kiesler, D. J., Goldston, C. S., & Schmidt, J. A. (1991). *Manual for the Check List of Interpersonal Transactions–Revised (CLOIT-R) and the Check List of Psychotherapy Transactions–Revised (CLOPT-R)*. Richmond: Virginia Commonwealth University.

Kiesler, D. J., & Schmidt, J. A. (1993). *The Impact Message Inventory: Form IIA octant scoring version*. Redwood City, CA: Consulting Psychologists Press.

Kiesler, D. J., Schmidt, J. A. & Wagner, C. C. (1997). A circumplex inventory of impact messages: An operational bridge between emotional and interpersonal behavior. In R. Plutchik, & H. R. Conte (Eds.), *Circumplex models of personality and emotions* (pp. 221–244). Washington, DC: American Psychological Association.

LaForge, R., & Suczek, R. F. (1955). The interpersonal dimension of personality: An interpersonal check list. *Journal of Personality, 24*, 94–112.

Leary, T. (1957). *Interpersonal diagnosis of personality*. New York: Ronald Press.

Locke, K. D. (2000). Circumplex Scales of Interpersonal Values: Reliability, validity, and applicability to interpersonal problems and personality disorders. *Journal of Personality Assessment, 75*, 249–267.

Locke, K. D. (2005). Interpersonal problems and interpersonal expectations in everyday life. *Journal of Social and Clinical Psychology, 24*, 915–931.

Lorr, M., & DeLong, J. (1984). Second-order factors defined by the ISI. *Journal of Clinical Psychology, 40*, 1378–1382.

Lorr, M., & McNair, D. M. (1965). Expansion of the interpersonal behavior circle. *Journal of Personality and Social Psychology, 2*, 823–830.

Lorr, M., & Youniss, R. P. (1986). *The Interpersonal Style Inventory*. Los Angeles: Western Psychological Services.

Maling, M. S., Gurtman, M. B., & Howard, K. I. (1995). The response of interpersonal problems to varying doses of psychotherapy. *Psychotherapy Research, 5*, 63–75.

Matano, R., & Locke, K. D. (1995). Personality disorder scales as predictors of interpersonal problems of alcoholics. *Journal of Personality Disorders, 9*, 62–67.

McClelland, D. C. (1980). Motive dispositions: The merits of operant and respondent measures. In L. Wheeler (Ed.), *Review of personality and social psychology* (Vol.1, pp. 10–41). Beverly Hills, CA: Sage.

McClelland, D. C. (1985). How motives, skills and values determine what people do. *American Psychologist, 40*, 812–825.

McCrae, R. R., & Costa, P. T., Jr. (1989). The structure of interpersonal traits: Wiggins' circumplex and the five-factor model. *Journal of Personality and Social Psychology, 56*, 586–595.

McCullough, J. P., McCune, K. J., Kaye, A. L., Braith, J. A., Friend, R., Roberts, W. C., Belyea-Caldwell, S., Norris, S. C. W., & Hampton, C. (1994). Comparison of a community dysthymia sample at screening with a matched group of nondepressed community controls. *Journal of Nervous and Mental Disease, 182*, 402–407.

Millon, T. (1994). *Manual for the Millon Clinical Multiaxial Inventory-III*. Minneapolis: National Computer Systems.

Mischel, W. (1973). Toward a cognitive social learning reconceptualization of personality. *Psychological Review, 80*, 252–283.

Muran, J. C., Segal, Z. V., Samstag, L. W., & Crawford, C. E. (1994). Patient pretreatment interpersonal problems and therapeutic alliance in short-term cognitive therapy. *Journal of Consulting and Clinical Psychology, 62*, 185–190.

Paddock, J. R., & Nowicki, S. (1986a). An examination of the Leary circumplex through the Interpersonal Check List. *Journal of Research in Personality, 20*, 107–144.

Paddock, J. R., & Nowicki, S. (1986b). The circumplexity of Leary's Interpersonal Circle: A multidimensional scaling perspective. *Journal of Personality Assessment, 50*, 279–289.

Pincus, A. L., & Gurtman, M. B. (1995). The three faces of interpersonal dependency: Structural analyses of self-report dependency measures. *Journal of Personality & Social Psychology, 69*, 744–758.

Pincus, A. L., Gurtman, M. B., & Ruiz, M. A. (1998). Structural analysis of social behavior (SASB): Circumplex analyses and structural relations with the interpersonal circle and the five-factor model of personality. *Journal of Personality & Social Psychology, 74*, 1629–1645.

Pincus, A. L., & Wiggins, J. S. (1990). Interpersonal problems and conceptions of personality disorders. *Journal of Personality Disorders, 4*, 342–352.

Rolland, J. (2002). The cross-cultural generalizability of the Five-Factor model of personality. In R. R. McCrae & J. Allik (Eds.), *The Five-Factor model of personality across cultures* (pp. 7–28). New York: Kluwer Academic Publishers.

Schmidt, J. A., Wagner, C. C., & Kiesler, D. J. (1999a). Covert reactions to big five personality traits: The Impact Message Inventory and the NEO-PI-R. *European Journal of Psychological Assessment, 15*, 221–232.

Schmidt, J. A., Wagner, C. C., & Kiesler, D. J. (1999b). Psychometric and Circumplex Properties of the Octant Scale Impact Message Inventory (IMI-C): A structural evaluation. *Journal of Counseling Psychology, 46*, 325–334.

Sim, J. P., & Romney, D. M. (1990). The relationship between a circumplex model of interpersonal behaviors and personality disorders. *Journal of Personality Disorders, 4*, 329–341.

Soldz, S., Budman, S., Demby, A., & Merry, J. (1993). Representation of personality disorders in a circumplex and five-factor space: Explorations with a clinical sample. *Psychological Assessment, 5*, 41–52.

Sullivan, H. S. (1953). *The interpersonal theory of psychiatry.* New York: Norton.

Trapnell, P. D., & Wiggins, J. S. (1990). Extension of the Interpersonal Adjective Scales to include the Big Five dimensions of personality. *Journal of Personality & Social Psychology, 59,* 781–790.

Trobst, K. K. (2000). An interpersonal conceptualization and quantification of social support transactions. *Personality & Social Psychology Bulletin, 26,* 971–986.

Vittengl, J. R., Clark, L. A., & Jarrett, R. B. (2003). Interpersonal problems, personality pathology, and social adjustment after cognitive therapy for depression. *Psychological Assessment, 15,* 29–40.

Wagner, C. C., Kiesler, D. J., & Schmidt, J. A. (1995). Assessing the interpersonal transaction cycle: Convergence of action and reaction interpersonal circumplex measures. *Journal of Personality and Social Psychology, 69,* 938–949.

Widiger, T. A., & Hagemoser, S. (1997). Personality disorders and the interpersonal circumplex. In R. Plutchik, & H. R. Conte (Eds.), *Circumplex models of personality and emotions* (pp. 299–325). Washington, DC: American Psychological Association.

Wiggins, J. S. (1979). A psychological taxonomy of trait-descriptive terms: The interpersonal domain. *Journal of Personality and Social Psychology, 33,* 409–420.

Wiggins, J. S. (1982). Circumplex models of interpersonal behavior in clinical psychology. In P. S. Kendall, & J. N. Butcher (Eds.), *Handbook of research methods in clinical psychology* (pp. 183–221). New York: Wiley.

Wiggins, J. S. (1995). *Interpersonal Adjective Scales: Professional manual.* Odessa, FL: Psychological Assessment Resources.

Wiggins, J. S. (2003). *Paradigms of personality assessment.* New York, NY: Guilford Press.

Wiggins, J. S., & Broughton, R. (1985). The interpersonal circle: A structural model for the integration of personality research. In R. Hogan, & W. H. Jones (Eds.), *Perspectives in personality* (Vol. 1, pp. 1–47). Greenwich, CT: JAI Press.

Wiggins, J. S., & Broughton, R. (1991). A geometric taxonomy of personality scales. *European Journal of Personality, 5,* 343–365.

Wiggins, J. S., & Pincus, A. L. (1989). Conceptions of personality disorders and dimensions of personality. *Psychological Assessment, 1,* 305–316.

Wiggins, J. S., Trapnell, P., & Phillips, N. (1988). Psychometric and geometric characteristics of the Revised Interpersonal Adjective Scales (IAS-R). *Multivariate Behavioral Research, 23,* 517–530.

# The Dimensional Assessment of Personality Pathology (DAPP) Approach to Personality Disorder

16

W. John Livesley

The overall objective of the program of research on the classification of personality disorder that led to the construction of the Dimensional Assessment of Personality Pathology (DAPP) measures is to explicate and validate the basic components of personality disorder. The research program, initiated in the early 1980s, was originally designed to validate *DSM-III* (*Diagnostic and Statistical Manual of Mental Disorders*; American Psychiatric Association, 1980) personality disorders. Each disorder was systematically defined by a cluster of traits identified from a review of the clinical literature. Self-report scales were developed to assess the 100 traits used to define the 11 *DSM-III* personality disorders. Because scales were developed to assess clinical concepts, the DAPP incorporates the features of personality disorder that clinicians have traditionally considered important. The program was initiated with the expectation that multivariate studies would reveal factors that resembled DSM diagnostic constructs. When this proved not to be the case, attention focused on explicating the dimensional structure of personality disorder. These studies provided multiple opportunities to evaluate categorical versus dimensional models of personality disorder and test assumptions of the categorical model that a boundary or discontinuity occurs between normal and disordered personality and that the structure or organization of traits of disordered personality differs from that of normal personality.

# Overview of the DAPP Constructs and Measures

Results of multivariate analyses were used to define 18 basic or primary traits underlying clinical concepts of personality disorder. These traits formed the basis of a self-report inventory, the DAPP-Basic Questionnaire (DAPP-BQ). The 18 scales of the DAPP-BQ are: Affective Lability, Anxiousness, Callousness, Cognitive Dysregulation, Compulsivity, Conduct Problems, Identity Problems, Insecure Attachment, Intimacy Problems, Narcissism, Oppositionality, Rejection, Restricted Expression, Self Harm, Social Avoidance, Stimulus Seeking, Submissiveness, and Suspiciousness. A social desirability scale is included.

Subsequent studies showed that these traits are organized into four higher-order factors labeled Emotional Dysregulation, Inhibitedness, Dissocial Behavior, and Compulsivity. Because the 18 scales were derived from an initial set of 100 traits, each basic trait is divided into from two to seven subtraits so that a total of 69 subtraits define the 18 basic dimensions. These are assessed by a second self-report measure: the DAPP-Differential Questionnaire (DAPP-DQ). The items forming the DAPP-BQ are a subset of the DAPP-DQ items. Thus the DAPP system has three levels of construct—higher-order factors, basic traits, and subtraits—whereas most personality measures typically incorporate two levels, higher-order domains and their facets. This permits a detailed analysis of trait structure that has been particularly useful in exploring the genetic architecture of personality disorder.

# Conceptual Foundations

The conceptual foundations for research leading to the DAPP were provided by: (a) the metaphor that a classification of mental disorders may be viewed as a psychological test (Blashfield & Livesley, 1991) with disorders being considered equivalent to scales and diagnostic criteria analogous to items; (b) the construct validation approach to test construction as expounded by Loevinger (1957) and applied to psychiatric classification by Skinner (1981, 1986) and Livesley and Jackson (1992); and (c) a modification of the lexical hypothesis which assumed that traditional clinical constructs provide the best starting point for nosological research. With this approach, the development of a classification of personality disorder involves defining disorders (scales) and compiling criteria sets (items) that are distinct and meet the usual psychometric criteria for a sound test. Conceptualizing a classification of mental disorders in this way emphasizes that the system should be constructed using explicit assumptions and that the requirements for validity should be built into the system from the beginning (Livesley & Jackson, 1992).

As conceptualized by Loevinger, construct validity has three components (Livesley & Schroeder, 1990). First, a theoretical taxonomy needs to be constructed that defines diagnostic constructs and items. This forms the substantive component of construct validity. Second, it needs to be demonstrated that diagnostic items combine empirically to form the diagnostic entities proposed by the theoretical taxonomy. This is the structural component of construct validity which describes the extent to which relationships among constructs and items are congruent with the postulated structure. Third, it needs to be demonstrated that the diagnostic constructs are systematically related to external criteria such as other measures, outcome, and etiology. This is the external component of construct validity. These components form an iterative process in which the postulated theoretical structure is tested and modified on the basis of empirical findings leading to incremental increases in validity.

# Constructing a Theoretical Taxonomy: A Lexical Approach

Since research began shortly after the publication of *DSM-III* in 1980, it could be argued that this system provided a satisfactory theoretical taxonomy. There were, however, several problems with the *DSM-III* that have remained unresolved in subsequent editions. First, the classification was arbitrary in terms of diagnoses included and the diagnostic criteria proposed for each disorder. Criteria were developed on the basis of informal and unsystematic samplings of clinical opinion rather than systematic definitions of diagnoses. Second, many criteria were too poorly specified for measurement purposes. This created problems developing items to assess them and in differentiating among different criteria. For example, it was not clear how "incessant drawing attention to oneself " (*DSM-III* histrionic personality disorder) differed from "exhibitionism" (*DSM-III* narcissistic personality disorder). Third, most criteria sets contained only a few of the terms used to describe a given disorder, and there was no reason to believe that the items selected were representative of all features of the disorder. For these reasons, the 11 personality disorders proposed by *DSM-III* were only used to provide the initial structure to the theoretical taxonomy, and more systematic definitions of each disorder were developed using a modification of the lexical hypothesis used to explicate the structure of normal personality (Saucier & Goldberg, 1996).

The lexical hypothesis assumes that the natural language of personality is a repository of wisdom about personality that embodies distinctions having important implications for adaptation. Similarly, it was assumed that there is accumulated clinical wisdom about personality disorder consisting of ideas or concepts that clinicians have traditionally used to describe and explain personality problems, and that this knowledge forms the most appropriate starting point for a theoretical taxonomy. Although this knowledge is largely informally organized, more explicit accounts are found in the general clinical literature. Hence the clinical literature was content-analyzed to identify the terms and phrases used to describe each disorder. This began by examining texts by Millon (1981) and Lion (1981), Vaillant and Perry's chapter in the *Comprehensive Textbook of Psychiatry* (1980), and the *DSM-III*. References cited in these sources were examined and additional references identified through computerized literature searches. Items were edited by combining synonyms and deleting non-personality features. This eventuated in lists of between 57 and 83 items for each disorder.

The next step was to organize these lists of items by identifying the most important features of each disorder. This was achieved using the concept of prototypical categorization (Rosch, 1978). Prototypical categories are organized around prototypical examples, the best examples of the concept, with less prototypical examples forming a continuum away from these central cases. With personality disorder, both cases and descriptive items may be considered to fall along a gradient of prototypicality (Livesley,

| | |
|---|---|
| **Table 16.1** | **Dimensions Used to Classify Highly Prototypical Traits for Paranoid Personality Disorder** |

| | |
|---|---|
| Vindictiveness: | seeks revenge for any perceived harm |
| *Traits:* | carries grudges; tries to "get back" at people |
| Suspiciousness: | mistrustful of the intent of others |
| *Traits:* | questions the loyalty of others; searches for special meanings; readily perceives hidden motives; sees the world as hostile and opposed to him/her; expects trickery or harm; unwarranted suspiciousness and mistrust of people; feels persecuted and oppressed; misinterprets the intentions and actions of others |
| Hypervigilance: | overalert, ready to respond to any sign of threat |
| *Traits:* | hypervigilant; continually scans the environment for signs of threat; easily slighted; quick to take offense |
| Hypersensitivity to Negative Evaluation: | reacts adversely to any negative input, low threshold for perceiving criticism |
| *Traits:* | interprets minor slights as major insults; difficulty in accepting criticism; hypersensitive to real or imagined criticism; easily slighted; quick to take offense |
| Reluctance to Self-Disclose: | reluctant to disclose personal information |
| *Traits:* | guarded, defensive |
| Blame Avoidance: | avoids accepting blame or responsibility even when justified |
| *Traits:* | blames others for difficulties and problems |
| Externalization: | attributes problems to external world |
| *Traits:* | blames others for difficulties and problems |
| Rigid Cognitive Style: | processes information on the basis of fixed ideas |
| *Traits:* | rigid personality; rigid view of things; unable to compromise |
| Anger at Conditional Positive Regard: | reacts angrily when positive regard is not forthcoming |
| *Traits:* | angry when judgment questioned |
| Resents Authority Figures: | dislike, resentment, and jealousy toward authority figures |
| *Traits:* | jealous and resentful of those in power |
| Fearful of Interpersonal Hurt: | fearful of being hurt, embarrassed or humiliated in any type of relationship |
| *Traits:* | fearful of personal attachments; fears intimacy |

1985a,b). For example, the term "socially withdrawn" is more typical of schizoid personality disorder than the term "eccentric." The idea was used to organize descriptions of each *DSM-III* disorder by asking samples of psychiatrists to rate the prototypicality of items for each diagnosis. The results indicated substantial agreement on the most prototypical feature of each disorder (Livesley, 1986). These ratings were then used to rank items according to their prototypicality.

Examination of the highly prototypical items for each disorder revealed that many referred to the same characteristic. For example, items highly prototypical of paranoid personality disorder included "mistrustful," "searches for hidden meanings," and "sees the world as hostile and opposed to him/her." All are aspects of "suspiciousness." Consequently, the prototype of each disorder was reduced to fewer items by grouping together items referring to the same trait. Traits were then defined based on these items with the greatest weight given to items with the highest prototypicality ratings. This procedure was followed for all 11 *DSM-III* personality disorders. Definitions of each trait were then scrutinized across all disorders to ensure that definitions were distinctive. This procedure as applied to paranoid personality disorder is illustrated in Table 16.1.

This process resulted in a theoretical taxonomy in which 79 dimensions were used to define the 11 disorders of *DSM-III*. This number subsequently increased to 100 as a result of psychometric studies. These dimensions could be considered to constitute a lexicon of personality pathology derived from clinical concepts.

The important question was whether the *DSM-III* assumption that the features of personality disorder are organized into 11 diagnoses was supported empirically. It was assumed that preliminary support for the taxonomy would be provided by evidence that internally consistent and distinct scales can be constructed to assess each dimension and that dimensions cluster into the 11 diagnoses proposed by DSM-III.

## Scale Construction

Scales were constructed using the structured approach developed by Jackson (1971) which emphasizes the selection of items for conformity to theoretical definitions and suppression of response biases. Items were selected to assess all facets or subtraits of each dimension and a rigorous process of item development was used to foster convergent and discriminant validity. Approximately 50 items were compiled for each dimension from multiple sources including literature review, expert judgment, and interviews with personality-disordered patients. Preliminary item sets were reduced to 30 items by eliminating items that did not conform to the definition of the dimension, referred to several behaviors, or were judged to be at the extremes of social desirability. Ratings rather than a true/false format were used because they tend to yield higher item variance and greater scale reliability. Subjects were required to rate how characteristic each item was of them on a 5-point scale ranging from "very unlike me" to "very like me." The following are typical items: Social Apprehensiveness: "I do not feel very sure of myself when I am with other people." Grandiosity: "I am exceptionally good at daydreaming about being powerful and successful". Attention seeking: "I feel happiest when all eyes are on me." Conscientiousness: "I do everything thoroughly."

## Preliminary Psychometric Analyses

The internal consistency of scales was established using responses obtained by mailing questionnaires to a general population sample selected randomly from a street directory. The study was designed to provide approximately 100 responses per scale, which was considered adequate for psychometric purposes. Responses were received from 3,256 subjects. Each subject received items for only three personality scales, two measures of social desirability—the Marlowe-Crowne Scale (Crowne & Marlowe, 1960) and a scale used to develop the Personality Research Form and the Differential Personality Inventory (Jackson, 1984)—and a short version of the General Health Questionnaire (Goldberg, 1972), which was used to identify items that are strongly related to general psychiatric symptomatology. Coefficient alpha ranged from 0.98 (Secure Base) to 0.64 (Need for Adulation). Each item was correlated with its own scale score (minus that item), each social desirability scale, and the symptom measure. Items were eliminated if they: (a) correlated less than 0.3 with their own scale; (b) had a highly skewed pattern of endorsement; that is, if less than 5% of the endorsements were located on two adjacent rating points on the 5-point scale (such items provide little information); (c) correlated higher with a desirability scale than with their own scale, or greater than 0.5; (d) correlated higher with the symptom measure than with their own scale, or greater than 0.5. Scales were reduced to the best 18 to 20 items using these criteria.

During the course of establishing internally consistent scales it was necessary to revise the theoretical taxonomy by adding scales to accommodate changes introduced by the *DSM-III-R* (APA, 1987). Also some dimensions had to be combined and others redefined because it was not possible to identify behaviors that discriminated between them. The internal consistency analyses also led to the revision of some dimensions. Scales with an alpha coefficient less than 0.80 were examined with principal components analysis. These analyses sometimes indicated that scales contained several sets of items. Such scales were divided and new items were developed. For example, a scale labeled Control, originally proposed to describe the need to control situations and feelings, was found to comprise two sets of items: need to exercise control over interpersonal situations and fear of losing emotional control. The dimensions were redefined to accommodate these observations. The changes led to the increase in number of dimensions from 79 to 100.

The next step was to cross-validate the internal consistency of the revised scales and construct distinctive scales by eliminating items that correlated higher with irrelevant scales than the scale for which they were developed. This required subjects to endorse items for all scales (1,943 items). A second, heterogeneous general population sample (N=110; 62 women) was obtained. Scales were found to cross-validate satisfactorily; coefficient alpha was above 0.90 for 22 scales, 0.80 to 0.89 for 67 scales, 0.70 to 0.79 for 6 scales, and 0.68 for 1 scale. Using these data, scales were reduced to 16 items.

# Structure of Personality Disorder

The development of psychometrically satisfactory scales made it possible to test the hypothesis that dimensions are organized into the 11 categories described in *DSM-III*. Evaluation of this hypothesis in general population and clinical samples provided an opportunity to test the assumption implicit in the *DSM* that there is a clear distinction between normal personality and personality disorder. If this is the case, the distributions of scores should show discontinuities across samples that differ in the presence of personality disorder, and there should be important differences in the structure of their principal component loadings in the two samples (Eysenck, 1987).

# Primary Structure

To investigate these questions, the 16-item per scale questionnaire was first administered to a heterogeneous sample of 274 subjects (125 men, 149 women: mean age 29.7 years, range 17–70 years; Livesley, Jackson & Schroeder, 1989). Internal consistency of the final scales was satisfactory: coefficient alpha was above 0.90 for 31 scales, between 0.80 and 0.89 for 64 scales, and between 0.72 and 0.79 for 5 scales. The structure underlying the 100 scales was examined using principal component analysis. Decomposition of the correlation matrix yielded 15 eigenvalues greater than unity. Because a scree plot of eigenvalues did not reveal the number of components to retain, several solutions were evaluated for simple structure and theoretical meaningfulness. An oblique rotation was used because it would predictably be more interpretable than an orthogonal solution and other studies demonstrated high correlations between personality diagnoses (Kass, Skodol, Charles, Spitzer, & Williams, 1985; Livesley & Jackson, 1986).

A 15-component, obliquely rotated solution accounting for 75.1% of the total variance appeared to have the greatest theoretical meaning. Solutions with fewer than 15 components contained a greater degree of factorial complexity and solutions with more yielded components with only one salient loading. The 15 components were labeled: affective reactivity, rejection, social apprehensiveness, compulsive behaviors, stimulus seeking, insecure attachment, diffidence (later relabeled submissiveness), intimacy problems, interpersonal disesteem (later relabeled callousness), narcissism, conduct problems, restricted expression, cognitive distortion, identity disturbance, and obsessionality.

A similar study was subsequently conducted on a clinical sample of 158 patients with a primary diagnosis of personality disorder (Livesley, Jackson, & Schroeder, 1992). Although decomposition of the correlation matrix yielded 19 eigenvalues greater than unity, a 15-component solution accounting for 74.4% of the variance was adopted after examining different solutions. This solution was preferred because solutions with more components were less readily interpretable and yielded components with a single salient loading.

Examination of the distribution of scores on all scales for the two samples yielded no evidence of discontinuity (Livesley et al., 1992). Congruence coefficients computed between the two solutions indicated considerable similarity (see Table 16.2).

These studies offered little support for the diagnostic constructs included in *DSM-III* and *DSM-III-R* and hence indicated the need for considerable revision of the theoretical taxonomy. They also provided strong evidence that personality disorder is best represented by a dimensional framework, and individual differences in personality disorder represent the extremes of behavioral tendencies that are present to a lesser extent in the general population.

| Table 16.2 | Congruence Coefficients for the 15-Component Solution of Principal Components Analysis for Clinical and General Population Samples | | |
|---|---|---|---|
| | | Off-diagonal Element | |
| Factor | Congruence Coefficients | Highest | Mean |
| 1 | 0.98 | −0.57 | 0.24 |
| 2 | 0.97 | 0.61 | 0.24 |
| 3 | 0.93 | −0.54 | 0.17 |
| 4 | 0.88 | −0.31 | 0.09 |
| 5 | 0.93 | 0.61 | 0.22 |
| 6 | 0.68 | 0.26 | 0.12 |
| 7 | 0.94 | −0.57 | 0.20 |
| 8 | 0.77 | 0.25 | 0.09 |
| 9 | 0.62 | 0.20 | 0.09 |
| 10 | 0.80 | −0.31 | 0.14 |
| 11 | 0.83 | −0.22 | 0.14 |
| 12 | 0.65 | −0.16 | 0.07 |
| 13 | 0.82 | −0.44 | 0.15 |
| 14 | 0.86 | 0.39 | 0.12 |
| 15 | 0.67 | 0.20 | 0.01 |

*From:* Livesley, W. J., Jackson, D.N., & Schroeder, M.L. (1992). Factorial structure of traits delineating personality disorders in clinical and general population samples. *Journal of Abnormal Psychology, 101(3)*; 432–440.

# Primary Traits

The results of the principal components analyses were used to define the basic or primary dimensions of personality disorder and construct a self-report measure—the DAPP-BQ—to assess them. Although 15 components were extracted from the correlational matrices for the general population, clinical, and combined samples, 18 scales were developed for several reasons. First, many scales were salient on the first component which appeared to represent general distress and resemble neuroticism (Eysenck & Eysenck, 1975) or negative affectivity (Watson & Clark, 1984). In particular, it combined traits resembling affective traits and problems with self or identity. Because these features have different clinical and theoretical implications, the factor was divided into two separate scales, labeled anxiousness and identity problems. Second, although suspiciousness was not salient on any component, it was retained as a separate scale because of its clinical significance. Finally, a scale of self-harm was developed that included chronic suicidal ideation and self-harming acts for use in clinical assessment although the scale does not actually represent a personality trait. This resulted in a new theoretical structure of 18 basic or primary

## Table 16.3 — DAPP Primary and Specific Traits

| | |
|---|---|
| **Affective Instability:** | Labile Anger, Affective Over-Reactivity, Affective Lability, Irritability, Generalized Hypersensitivity |
| **Anxiety:** | Indecisiveness, Trait Anxiety, Rumination, Guilt Proneness |
| **Callousness:** | Lack of Empathy, Exploitation, Egocentrism, Sadism, Contemptuousness, Interpersonal Irresponsibility, Remorselessness |
| **Cognitive Dysregulation:** | Depersonalization or Derealization, Schizotypal Cognition, Brief Stress Psychosis |
| **Compulsivity:** | Orderliness, Conscientiousness, Precision |
| **Conduct Problems:** | Interpersonal Violence, Addictive Behaviors, Juvenile Antisocial Behavior, Failure to Adopt Social Norms |
| **Identity Problems:** | Chronic Feelings of Emptiness and Boredom, Labile Self-Concept, Pessimism, Anhedonia |
| **Insecure Attachment:** | Feared Loss, Secure Base, Proximity Seeking, Separation Protest, Intolerance of Aloneness |
| **Intimacy Problems:** | Avoidant Attachment, Desire for Improved Attachment Relationships, Inhibited Sexuality |
| **Narcissism:** | Need for Approval, Attention-Seeking, Need for Adulation, Grandiosity |
| **Oppositionality:** | Passivity, Oppositional, Lack of Organization |
| **Rejection:** | Dominance, Rigid Cognitive Style, Interpersonal Hostility, Judgmental |
| **Restricted Expression:** | Restricted Affective Expression, Restricted Expression of Angry Affects, Restricted Expression of Positive Affects, Reluctant Self-Disclosure, Self-Reliance |
| **Self Harm:** | Ideas of Self-Harm, Self-Damaging Acts |
| **Social Avoidance:** | Low Affiliation, Fearful of Interpersonal Hurt, Defective Social Skills, Desire for Improved Affiliative Relationships, Social Apprehensiveness |
| **Stimulus Seeking:** | Recklessness, Impulsivity, Sensation Seeking |
| **Submissiveness:** | Need for Advice and Reassurance, Suggestibility, Submissiveness |
| **Suspiciousness:** | Suspiciousness, Hypervigilance |

traits and the 69 specific traits that define them (see Table 16.3). The extent to which this structure could be confirmed empirically in the two samples was evaluated using a procrustes rotation (Helmes & Jackson, 1994). Only two dimensions, suspiciousness and intimacy problems, failed to show strong convergence across samples (see Table 16.4). This confirmed the hypothesis that the basic scales are defined and organized the same way in samples of patients with personality disorder and the general population.

| Table 16.4 | Factor Congruence in General Population and Clinical Samples | |
|---|---|---|
| Factor | DAPP Scale | Congruence Coefficient |
| I | Affective Lability | 0.971 |
| II | Anxiousness | 0.923 |
| III | Cognitive Distortion | 0.963 |
| IV | Compulsivity | 0.979 |
| V | Conduct Problems | 0.954 |
| VI | Diffidence | 0.905 |
| VII | Identity Problems | 0.963 |
| VIII | Insecure Attachment | 0.901 |
| IX | Callousness | 0.986 |
| X | Intimacy Problems | 0.747 |
| XI | Narcissism | 0.970 |
| XII | Passive Opposition | 0.966 |
| XIII | Rejection | 0.956 |
| XIV | Restricted Expression | 0.980 |
| XV | Self Harm | 0.911 |
| XVI | Social Avoidance | 0.979 |
| XVII | Stimulus Seeking | 0.972 |
| XVIII | Suspiciousness | 0.832 |

Based on Helmes, G., & Jackson, D.N. (1994). Evaluating normal and abnormal personality using the same set of constructs. In: S. Strack and M. Lorr, (Eds.), *Differentiating normal and abnormal personality*. Springer Publishing.

## Secondary Structure

The next step in explicating the structure of personality disorder traits was to investigate the higher-order structure underlying the 18 basic traits. The DAPP-BQ was administered to 939 general population subjects, 656 patients with a primary diagnosis of personality disorder, and 686 twin pairs (Livesley, Jang, & Vernon, 1998). Principal components analysis yielded four components labeled emotional dysregulation, dissocial behavior, inhibitedness, and compulsivity that were remarkably similar across the three samples: congruence coefficients ranged from 0.94 to 0.99. The four-component structure has cross-cultural stability being reported in studies from North America (Livesley et al., 1998), Germany (Pukrop, Gentil, Steinbring, & Steinmeyer, 2001), Holland (van Kampen, 2002), and China (Zheng et al., 2002) (see Table 16.5). The robustness of the four-factor structure across cultures suggests a universal structure to personality disorder traits and raises the possibility that this structure reflects the way personality is organized at a biological level.

## Table 16.5 — Higher-Order Structure of the DAPP-BQ in Different Cultures

| DAPP-BQ Scales | Livesley et al. 1998 Factors | | | | Pukrop et al. 2001 Factors | | | | van Kampen 2002 Factors | | | | Zheng et al. 2002 Factors | | | |
|---|---|---|---|---|---|---|---|---|---|---|---|---|---|---|---|---|
| | I | II | III | IV | I | II | III | IV | I | II | III | IV | I | II | III | IV |
| Submissiveness | 0.84 | | | | 0.83 | | | | 0.80 | | | | 0.86 | | | |
| Cognitive distortion | 0.75 | | | | 0.66 | | | | 0.83 | | | | 0.71 | | | |
| Identity Problems | 0.74 | | | | 0.75 | | 0.48 | | | 0.84 | | | | 0.67 | | |
| Affective lability | 0.78 | | | | 0.53 | 0.62 | | | 0.82 | | | | 0.52 | | | |
| Stimulus seeking | 0.67 | | | | 0.71 | | | 0.49 | 0.57 | | −0.43 | | | 0.52 | −0.40 | |
| Compulsivity | 0.88 | | | | 0.88 | | | | 0.78 | | | | 0.91 | | | |
| Restricted expression | 0.74 | | | 0.52 | | 0.53 | | 0.67 | | | | | | | 0.70 | |
| Callousness | 0.74 | | | | 0.72 | | | | 0.83 | | | | 0.87 | | | |
| Oppositionality | 0.69 | | | −0.40 | 0.73 | | | 0.78 | 0.45 | | | | 0.79 | | | |
| Intimacy Problems | | | 0.86 | | | 0.84 | | | | 0.86 | | | | | | |
| Rejection | 0.82 | | | | 0.71 | | | 0.80 | | | | 0.53 | 0.44 | | | |
| Anxiousness | 0.89 | | | | 0.86 | | | | 0.90 | | | 0.83 | | | | |
| Conduct problems | 0.76 | | | | | 0.76 | | | 0.75 | | | | 0.80 | | | |
| Suspiciousness | 0.41 | 0.46 | | | 0.62 | | | | 0.72 | 0.57 | | | | 0.58 | | |
| Social avoidance | 0.69 | | | | 0.82 | | | | 0.82 | | | | 0.75 | | | |
| Narcissism | 0.60 | | | | 0.43 | 0.55 | | | 0.62 | 0.57 | | | | −0.43 | | |
| Insecure Attachment | 0.81 | | | | 0.53 | | −0.46 | 0.69 | | | | 0.65 | | | −0.44 | |
| Self Harm | | | | | | | 0.51 | | | | | | | | | |

411

# Genetic Architecture of the DAPP

The identification of a robust structure to personality disorder traits led to investigations of the genetic and environmental etiology of these traits and the relationships among them using behavioral genetic methods. These studies are also relevant to the distinction between normal and disordered personality because they suggest that observed continuity between normality and disorder reflects genetic continuity between measures of normal and disordered personality.

Behavioral genetic studies of the DAPP began with simple heritability studies that revealed a substantial heritable component to all three levels of trait structure (Jang, Livesley, Vernon, & Jackson, 1996; Livesley, Jang, Jackson, & Vernon, 1993) with heritability in the 40–60% range typically reported for normal personality traits (Plomin, Chipeur, & Loehlin, 1990). Estimates of the heritability of the secondary patterns of emotional dysregulation, dissocial behavior, inhibitedness and compulsivity were 53, 50, 51, and 38%, respectively. The heritability of the 18 basic or primary traits ranged from 56% for callousness and conduct problems to 35% for rejection and all of the 69 subtraits that define the 18 basic DAPP-BQ dimensions were heritable, except judgmental (a component of rejection), self-harming acts, and depersonalization (a component of cognitive dysregulation; Jang et al., 1996; Livesley et al., 1993).

Subsequent studies suggested that the four-factor secondary structure of the DAPP reflects the structure of genetic predispositions. These studies used multivariate genetic analyses to explicate genetic contributions to the covariance structure underlying the 18 traits (Carey & DiLalla, 1994). The degree to which genetic and environmental effects on two variables are correlated is indexed by genetic and environmental correlation coefficients. Genetic and environmental correlation or covariance matrices may then be factored to provide information about the structures underlying these influences (Crawford & DeFries, 1978). These analyses extend univariate analysis of etiological influences on a single trait to estimate genetic and environmental contributions of the covariation between two or more traits (DeFries & Fulker, 1985).

Comparisons of the factors extracted from matrixes of phenotypic, genetic, and environmental correlations computed among the 18 traits indicated that the four-factor phenotypic structure closely corresponds to genetic structure, as does the structure of non-shared environmental effects (Livesley et al., 1998). Congruence coefficients computed between genetic and phenotypic factors derived from data from a sample of twin pairs yielded values of 0.97, 0.97, 0.98, and 0.95 for emotional dysregulation, dissocial, inhibition, and compulsivity, respectively. Those between phenotypic and non-shared environmental factors were 0.99, 0.96, 0.99 and 0.96, respectively. These observations are consistent with other studies showing that the structure of genetic and environmental influences corresponds to phenotypic structure (Loehlin, 1987; Plomin, DeFries, & McClearn, 1990). For example, the phenotypic and genetic structures of the NEO-PI-R are highly congruent (Jang, Livesley, Angleitner, Riemann, & Vernon, 2002).

The similarity between phenotypic and genetic structures suggests that environmental influences do not change patterns of trait covariation. This was a somewhat surprising finding. This raises the question of how the environment influences personality. Twin studies clearly show that environmental effects are pervasive; they contribute to more than 50% of the variance. In the case of trait covariation, it seems likely that the environment acts to consolidate genetic influences. This is probably achieved through the mechanisms of gene–environment correlation and situational coactivation of traits. Many environmental events are likely to activate several traits simultaneously, especially traits in the same cluster. For example, events that evoke submissive behavior are also likely to evoke anxiousness and perhaps social apprehensiveness. All three traits are part of the emotional dysregulation pattern. Over time, these patterns of trait coactivation are likely to consolidate genetic influences. This suggests that trait structure is a self-organizing structure that emerges under the influence of genetic predispositions.

# Genetic Influences on Basic Traits

Decomposition of the matrix of genetic correlations into four genetic factors suggests the occurrence of common genetic dimensions that affect all basic traits in a given domain. This raises questions about the nature and genetic etiology of basic or primary traits. Trait theory has largely neglected primary traits in the search for a universal higher-order structure and has tended to imply that primary traits are merely facets of secondary constructs rather than distinct entities. Consequently, it was assumed that primary traits were heritable because they are components of broader heritable entities (Loehlin, 1982). This does not appear to be the case, however, because primary traits have a specific heritable component when the heritable component of secondary traits is partialled out (Jang, McCrae, Angleitner, Riemann, & Livesley, 1998; Livesley et al., 1998). For example, 11 of 18 traits assessed by the DAPP-BQ had substantial residual heritabilities ranging from 0.48 for Conduct Problems to 0.26 for Intimacy Problems (Livesley et al., 1998). The 30 NEO–PI–R facet scales showed even greater evidence of the specificity of genetic influences with 26 scales showing residual heritabilities ranging from 0.21 to 0.37 ( Jang et al., 1998).

These analyses used regression to partial out the effects of secondary traits from primary traits and applied standard heritability analyses to the residuals. Similar results are obtained when genetic effects are modeled directly. Multivariate analysis of the genetic correlations among the subtraits for each primary trait showed that from one to three specific genetic dimensions contribute to each primary trait (Livesley, Jang, & Vernon, 2003). For example, two genetic dimensions contributed to the primary trait of affective lability that appear to the reactive and irritable and intensity of arousal components of this trait (see Table 16.6). It appears from these analyses that each primary trait is influenced by a common genetic factor and one or more specific factors, and that personality is inherited as a large number of genetic dimensions or modules each consisting of multiple genes with each gene probably making a modest contribution to phenotypic variance (Jang et al., 2002). A few genetic modules appear to influence the expression of other modules giving rise to trait covariation. The implication is that primary traits are not simply components of secondary traits but rather the fundamental building blocks of personality that are probably as important, or even more important, for understanding personality than the secondary traits that have traditionally been the focus of research and explanation.

| Table 16.6 | Multivariate Genetic Analysis of the Sub-traits of Affective Lability | | | | | | |
|---|---|---|---|---|---|---|---|
| | Common Factors | | | | | | |
| | Genetic | | Environmental | | Specific Trait | | |
| Unique Factors | A1 | A2 | E1 | E2 | A | C | E |
| Lability | 0.53 | 0.42 | 0.39 | 0.36 | – | – | 0.51 |
| Over-reactivity | 0.34 | 0.50 | 0.35 | 0.36 | 0.24 | – | 0.58 |
| Hypersensitivity | 0.41 | 0.38 | 0.58 | 0.33 | 0.36 | – | 0.34 |
| Labile anger | 0.53 | 0.32 | – | 0.73 | 0.31 | – | – |
| Irritability | 0.68 | – | 0.16 | 0.40 | – | – | 0.60 |

# Relationship with Other Models of Normal and Disordered Personality

Studies of the DAPP discussed thus far offer little support for the *DSM-IV* model of personality disorder. Confidence in the alternative dimensional model emerging from this work would be strengthened by evidence of convergence between the DAPP and other measures of personality disorder traits. Similarly, the conclusion that individual differences in personality disorder are continuous with normal personality variation and that the same constructs may be used to represent normal and disordered personality would be supported by evidence of convergence with commonly used measures of normal personality.

# Personality Disorder

There is remarkable agreement across studies that four broad factors underlie the domain of personality disorder (Mulder & Joyce, 1997). Mulder and Joyce (1997) labeled these dimensions: asthenic, asocial, antisocial, and anankastic. They resemble the DAPP secondary dimensions of emotional dysregulation, inhibitedness, dissocial, and compulsivity, respectively. This structure first emerged in clinical studies in the 1970s (Presly & Walton, 1973; Tyrer & Alexander, 1979) that examined the factor structure underlying traits selected to represent personality disorder. Since then the structure has been confirmed by studies based on *DSM* personality disorder criteria (Austin & Deary, 2000; Kass et al., 1985; Mulder & Joyce, 1997) and shown to be robust across different methods of measurement including structured interviews (Austin & Deary, 2000; Tyrer & Alexander, 1979) and self-report (Livesley et al., 1998).

There is also a good agreement across studies using different starting points and methods on the primary traits of personality disorder (Harkness, 1992). Clark (1990) used cluster analysis of clinicians' ratings to identify 22 traits. A self-report measure—the

Schedule for Nonadaptive and Adaptive Personality (SNAP)—was developed to assess these clusters (Clark, 1993a). An iterative series of analyses resulted in 15 scales. Conceptual comparison of the SNAP and DAPP showed high convergence (Clark & Livesley, 1994, 2002; Clark, Livesley, Schroeder, & Irish, 1996). Neither measure incorporated content which was not included in the other. Differences in number of scales were due to some traits being divided into several scales by the other approach. For example, the SNAP dependency scale is represented in the DAPP by two scales, submissiveness and insecure attachment. Empirical comparison of the two measures substantiated these conclusions. Twenty-two of the 24 predicted convergent correlations were above 0.40, and the average correlation was 0.53. The average discriminant correlation was 0.22. This degree of convergence is encouraging given the different origins of these measures.

# Normal Personality

The DAPP also shows meaningful relationships with normal personality scales. This suggests that DAPP dimensions are clinical variants of normal personality traits and that individual differences in personality disorder may be represented by the same constructs used to describe normal personality. Examination of the four secondary dimensions suggests similarity with four of the Big Five factors of normal personality: neuroticism, introversion, (dis)agreeableness, and conscientiousness (Widiger, 1998). This convergence was explored by administering the DAPP-BQ and NEO-PI to a sample of 300 subjects (Schroeder, Wormsworth, & Livesley, 1992). Principal components analysis of the 18 scales and five NEO-PI domains yielded five factors (see Table 16.7).

Neuroticism and eight DAPP scales defined the first factor. The second factor consisted of extraversion and DAPP stimulus seeking. NEO-PI-R extraversion and agreeableness and DAPP restricted expression of affects (negative loading) defined the third factor. The fourth factor consisted of agreeableness and negative loadings of DAPP scales related to psychopathic or antisocial features along with suspiciousness. The final factor was defined by conscientiousness and compulsivity. These results suggest that the domain of personality disorder can be explained reasonably well with the Five-Factor Model of personality. Consistent with other studies, a factor of openness was not obtained (Clark, 1993b).

Despite the convergence between the NEO-PI-R and the DAPP, the two measures are not equivalent. The DAPP has specific content that is not captured by the NEO-PI-R (Schroeder et al., 1992). Clinically important traits such as insecure attachment and cognitive dysregulation are poorly represented by the NEO-PI-R. The SNAP also seems to capture clinically relevant behaviors not included in the NEO-PI-R (Reynolds & Clark, 2001). This suggests caution in accepting the suggestion that the Five-Factor Model might provide an integrating framework for personality disorder. There is only partial overlap between the domains of normal and disordered personality (Davis & Millon, 1995), important components of personality pathology are missing in the Five-Factor Model, and the primary or facet structure in particular needs further development before it captures clinical concepts (Livesley,

Table
16.7
## A Combined Analysis of the NEO-PI Five Factor Model of Normal Personality Traits and the DAPP-BQ 16 Factor Model of Personality Disorders

| Factor | 1 | 2 | 3 | 4 | 5 |
|---|---|---|---|---|---|
| *NEO-PI Scales* | | | | | |
| Neuroticism | **0.84** | −0.21 | 0.02 | −0.16 | −0.13 |
| Extraversion | −0.18 | **0.72** | −0.42 | −0.05 | 0.08 |
| Openness | −0.05 | 0.06 | −0.41 | 0.09 | −0.16 |
| Agreeableness | −0.06 | 0.11 | −0.09 | **0.86** | 0.01 |
| Conscientiousness | 0.04 | −0.05 | 0.08 | **0.94** | −0.14 |
| *DAPP-BQ Scales* | | | | | |
| Anxiousness | **0.83** | −0.19 | 0.09 | −0.11 | 0.06 |
| Affective Lability | **0.68** | −0.01 | −0.17 | −0.35 | 0.00 |
| Diffidence | **0.64** | 0.08 | 0.32 | 0.25 | −0.07 |
| Insecure Attachment | **0.61** | 0.22 | −0.02 | −0.10 | 0.04 |
| Social Avoidance | **0.59** | −0.15 | **0.42** | −0.07 | −0.09 |
| Identity Problems | **0.58** | −0.04 | **0.53** | −0.14 | −0.11 |
| Narcissism | **0.58** | 0.32 | 0.00 | −0.29 | −0.06 |
| Stimulus Seeking | −0.01 | **0.64** | −0.03 | 0.27 | 0.00 |
| Restricted Expression | 0.15 | 0.01 | **0.81** | 0.03 | −0.03 |
| Intimacy Problems | −0.16 | **0.58** | −0.12 | −0.08 | −0.11 |
| Callousness | 0.11 | 0.09 | 0.19 | −0.76 | 0.01 |
| Rejection | 0.11 | 0.32 | −0.03 | −0.62 | 0.05 |
| Suspiciousness | 0.30 | 0.10 | 0.32 | −0.58 | 0.13 |
| Conduct Problems | 0.12 | 0.16 | −0.08 | −0.48 | −0.18 |
| Compulsivity | 0.12 | 0.06 | 0.13 | −0.05 | **0.72** |
| Oppositionality | **0.51** | 0.09 | 0.22 | −0.06 | −0.55 |

*From:* Schroeder, M. L., Wormsworth, J. A., & Livesley, W. J. (1992). Dimensions of personality disorder and their relationships to the big five dimensions of personality. *Psychological Assessment, 4;* 47–53

2001). The latter point is especially important given behavioral genetic evidence of the importance of the primary traits.

Although the secondary structure of personality disorder is consistent with the Five-Factor Model, it is equally consistent with other models, especially the three-factor structure proposed by Eysenck (1987). This was demonstrated in a principal components analysis of the EPQ-R, NEO-PI-R, and DAPP-BQ higher-order factors which found four factors related to neuroticism, psychopathic traits, introversion, and compulsivity (Larstone, Jang, Livesley, Vernon, & Wolf, 2002; see Table 16.8). A similar analysis

| Table 16.8 | Varimax Rotated Principal Components Analysis of the EPQ-R Scales, NEO-PI-R Domain Scales, and the DAPP-BQ Higher-Order Dimensions |

| | Factors | | | |
| --- | --- | --- | --- | --- |
| Measures & Scales | 1 | 2 | 3 | 4 |
| **EPQ-R** | | | | |
| Psychoticism | −0.06 | −0.04 | **0.70** | −0.24 |
| Extraversion | −0.15 | **0.86** | 0.07 | 0.05 |
| Neuroticism | **0.71** | −0.17 | 0.23 | 0.07 |
| Lie | −0.21 | −0.07 | **−0.56** | 0.14 |
| **NEO-PI-R** | | | | |
| Neuroticism | **0.81** | −0.30 | 0.12 | −0.17 |
| Extraversion | −0.35 | **0.82** | 0.09 | −0.05 |
| Openness | **−0.50** | −0.22 | 0.37 | −0.20 |
| Agreeableness | **−0.65** | 0.20 | **−0.49** | −0.19 |
| Conscientiousness | −0.32 | 0.11 | 0.24 | **0.82** |
| **DAPP-BQ** | | | | |
| Emotional Dysregulation | **0.84** | −0.19 | 0.04 | −0.28 |
| Dissocial Behavior | 0.22 | 0.37 | **0.72** | 0.14 |
| Inhibition | 0.07 | **−0.78** | −0.01 | −0.07 |
| Compulsivity | 0.12 | −0.01 | −0.01 | **0.93** |

*From:* Larstone, R. M., Jang, K. L., Livesley, W. J., Vernon, P. A., & Wolf, H. (2002). The Relationship Between Eysenck's P-E-N Model of Personality, the Five-Factor Model of Personality, and Traits Delineating Personality Disorder. *Personality and Individual Differences, 33(1):* 25–37.

of the DAPP-BQ and the Zuckerman-Kuhlman Personality Questionnaire yielded a five factor structure in which four factors resembled the four secondary components of the DAPP with the fifth factor being defined by ZKPQ impulsive sensation seeking and DAPP conduct problems, self-harm, and compulsivity (negatively) (Wang, Du, Wang, Livesley, & Jang, 2004; see Table 16.9).

Although there is substantial evidence that personality disorders can be accommodated by models of normal personality, it is possible that distinct genetic factors contribute to extreme variation. The limited evidence available, however, suggests genetic continuity between normal and disordered personality, a finding that lends further support for a dimensional taxonomy. Jang and Livesley (1999), for example, showed that the genetic and nonshared environmental factors shared by the DAPP-BQ and NEO–FFI accounted for the significant phenotypic correlations between them. In most cases, the magnitude of the genetic correlations was higher than the environmental or phenotypic correlations.

| Table 16.9 | Principal Components Analysis of the DAPP-BQ and ZKPQ Scales | | | | |
|---|---|---|---|---|---|

| | Factors | | | | |
| Trait Scale | I | II | III | IV | V |
|---|---|---|---|---|---|
| **ZKPQ** | | | | | |
| Impulsive Sensation–Seeking | 0.07 | 0.29 | 0.46 | 0.33 | 0.13 |
| Neuroticism–anxiety | **0.77** | −0.07 | −0.02 | 0.02 | −0.11 |
| Aggression–hostility | 0.11 | **0.46** | 0.05 | **0.47** | −0.38 |
| Activity | −0.12 | 0.01 | 0.08 | 0.08 | **0.83** |
| Sociability | 0.01 | 0.12 | −0.02 | **0.66** | 0.16 |
| **DAPP-BQ** | | | | | |
| Affective Lability | **0.74** | 0.38 | 0.15 | 0.23 | 0.06 |
| Anxiousness | **0.79** | 0.28 | 0.04 | −0.26 | 0.00 |
| Callousness | 0.16 | **0.67** | 0.40 | −0.07 | −0.08 |
| Cognitive Distortion | **0.77** | 0.21 | 0.28 | −0.04 | 0.01 |
| Compulsivity | 0.19 | 0.23 | −0.61 | −0.17 | **0.54** |
| Conduct Problems | 0.07 | **0.42** | **0.68** | 0.15 | −0.14 |
| Identity Problems | **0.60** | 0.22 | 0.30 | −0.22 | −0.26 |
| Insecure Attachment | **0.73** | 0.15 | −0.04 | 0.26 | 0.10 |
| Narcissism | 0.22 | **0.83** | −0.02 | −0.07 | 0.17 |
| Oppositionality | **0.56** | **0.46** | 0.09 | 0.02 | −0.26 |
| Rejection | 0.14 | **0.81** | 0.06 | 0.18 | −0.02 |
| Restricted Expression | 0.30 | 0.04 | −0.20 | **−0.73** | 0.20 |
| Self Harm | 0.35 | 0.09 | **0.71** | −0.10 | 0.17 |
| Social Avoidance | **0.65** | 0.31 | 0.02 | **−0.47** | −0.06 |
| Stimulus Seeking | 0.30 | **0.57** | 0.25 | 0.29 | 0.00 |
| Submissiveness | **0.74** | 0.12 | 0.10 | −0.28 | 0.03 |
| Suspiciousness | 0.38 | **0.48** | 0.33 | −0.21 | 0.14 |
| Eigenvalue | 7.33 | 2.93 | 1.69 | 1.34 | 1.16 |
| % Total variance | 33.31 | 13.31 | 7.62 | 6.07 | 5.26 |

*From:* Wang, W., Du, W., Wang, Y., Livesley, W. J., & Jang K. L. (2004). The relationship between the Zuckerman Kuhlman Personality Questionnaire and traits delineating personality pathology. *Personality and Individual Differences, 36*; 155–162.

# The Distinction Between Normal and Disordered Personality

Empirical research on the DAPP has yielded several findings that are directly relevant to the distinction between normal and disordered personality: (a) the structure of primary and secondary personality traits is similar in clinical samples of patients with personality disorder and general population samples; (b) the distribution of scores in general population and clinical samples overlap substantially with no evidence of discontinuity; (c) the secondary structure of personality disorder identified using the DAPP-BQ is remarkably similar to models of normal personality traits; and (d) there appears to be genetic continuity between traits representing normal and disordered personality. From a trait perspective, the distinction between normal and disordered personality appears to be quantitative rather than qualitative. These findings are consistent with the substantial literature indicating that personality disorder traits represent the extremes of normal variation and with a dimensional rather than a categorical representation of individual differences in personality disorder (Livesley, 2003; Livesley, Schroeder, Jackson, & Jang, 1994; Widiger, 1993).

Although a dimensional representation of personality disorder is consistent with empirical findings, adoption of a dimensional classification would create the conceptual and practical problem of how to determine when an extreme position on a trait dimension is indicative of personality disorder. There are four possibilities. Personality disorder could be viewed as: (a) extreme personality variation; (b) maladaptive expressions of extreme personality variation; (c) specific constellations of extreme traits; or (d) personality dysfunction defined independently of trait extremity. The first three approaches conceptualize personality disorder largely in terms of extreme variation. In contrast, the latter approach seeks to define disorder using criteria that are independent of trait function.

# Extreme Variation

The problem of having to specify when extreme variation constitutes personality disorder could be circumvented by assuming that personality disorder simply represents an extreme position on a trait dimension; that is, it involves either too much or too little of a given characteristic (Eysenck, 1987; Kiesler, 1986; Leary, 1957, Wiggins & Pincus, 1989). Unfortunately, the idea confuses extremity with disordered functioning (Clark, 2002; Parker & Barrett, 2000). As Wakefield (1992) pointed out, statistical deviance alone is neither a necessary nor sufficient criterion for disorder. Moreover, it is difficult to see how an extreme score on dimensions such as conscientiousness, extraversion, or agreeableness is necessarily pathological.

To distinguish between normal and disordered personality, we need additional criteria besides trait extremity. Schneider (1923/1950) made this point several generations ago when he distinguished between abnormal personality and psychopathic personality (personality disorder). The term "abnormal personality" was used in the statistical sense to refer to extremes of normal variation. Personality disorders were considered forms of abnormal personality that cause either personal suffering or society to suffer. Although this distinction continues to be useful, the criteria that Schneider proposed to distinguish them are less helpful. The problem is that it is not clear how much suffering is needed to warrant a diagnosis. Traits such as shyness may cause discomfort but not all shy individuals have personality disorder. There is also the problem that suffering is dependent on social context so that some traits may be problematic in some contexts and not in others.

# Maladaptive Trait Expression

An extension of the extreme trait definition of personality disorder that avoids problems created by equating extremity with disorder is Widiger's (1994) proposal that personality disorders be diagnosed at that point along the continuum of personality functioning that is associated with clinically significant impairment. This is considered to involve "dyscontrolled impairment" or "maladaptivity" in psychological functioning (Widiger & Trull, 1991; Widiger & Sankis, 2000). The attractive feature of this proposal is that it places the definition of personality disorder within the general framework of a definition of mental disorders. Widiger and Sankis (2000) consider mental disorders to be "dyscontrolled organismic impairments in psychological functioning" (p. 383) and suggest that "fundamental to a judgment of mental disorder is perhaps the ability to control one's thoughts, behaviors, or feelings adequately" (p. 383). By extension, personality disorder would involve "dyscontrolled maladapativity" in the various expressions of traits central to a given disorder. The idea has merits but it raises the question of how to define "dyscontrolled maladapativity" in trait expression in a way that leads to reliable assessment. Without a general definition, one would have to catalog the various maladaptive manifestations of each trait.

This approach was followed by McCrae (1994) who listed the problems, difficulties, and impairments associated considered to be secondary to the traits incorporated in the Five-Factor Model. This list was subsequently expanded by Trull and Widiger (1997) and Widiger, Costa, & McCrea (2002). For example, potential problems with anxiousness, a facet of neuroticism, are listed as "extremely nervous, anxious, tense, or jittery; is excessively apprehensive, prone to worry, inhibited, and uncertain" (p. 438). Anyone with these problems would no doubt experience difficulties and probably adjustment problems but would they necessarily have personality disorder? Similarly, problematic expressions of assertiveness, a facet of extraversion in the Five-Factor Model, said to involve being "domineering, pushy, bossy, dictatorial, or authoritarian" (Widiger et al., 2000, p. 439). But are all domineering, pushy, and dictatorial individuals personality disordered? The diagnosis of personality disorder as traditionally used by clinicians implies something more pervasive than dysfunctional traits. As Rutter (1987) noted, it usually refers to chronic and pervasive impairment in interpersonal functioning. We are also left with troublesome point that the criteria used to identify problems and difficulties associated with each trait are not specified. That is, maladaptive expressions or dyscontrolled maladaptivity is not explicitly defined. This is a problem because implicit definitions lead to unreliable assessment; different observers are likely to hold idiosyncratic notions about what constitutes a maladaptive expression of a trait and hence make different determinations.

Because of these difficulties, Widiger and colleagues (2002) suggest that diagnosis of personality disorder using the Five-Factor Model includes four cumulative steps: (a) describe personality using the five domains and 30 facets of the model; (b) identify problems, difficulties, and impairments secondary to each trait; (c) determine whether these impairments are clinically significant; and (d) determine whether the constellation of traits matches the profile for a given *DSM-IV* personality disorder. The fourth step is puzzling. If one accepts the extensive evidence on the limitations of *DSM-IV*, it is not clear why it is necessary to link dimensional assessment to a set of categories with dubious reliability and validity. If, however, one holds the opinion that *DSM-IV* diagnoses are valid clinical concepts then it is not clear why a dimensional evaluation is also needed. However, the first three steps are of interest. Widiger and colleagues also recognize that the second step is insufficient to diagnose personality disorder. They discuss the value of simply using the first two steps and focusing only on maladaptive expressions of traits because this avoids forcing the clinician to make arbitrary decisions as to whether an individual has clinically significant maladaptive traits. They note, however, that clinicians often need to make a distinction between the presence and absence of personality disorder. This requires a cut-off that "indicates a clinically significant level of impairment" (Widiger et al., 2002; p. 444). They suggest that this be based on a score on the *DSM-IV-TR* Global Assessment of Functioning Scale (GAF; APA, 1994). With this proposal, they have largely adopted a variant of Schneider's original proposal. In which case, it is not clear why the second step—that of determining maladaptive expression of each trait—is needed. Essentially, the diagnosis of personality disorder is based on extreme trait variation that is associated with a GAF score that is below a cut-off.

# Specific Trait Constellations

An alternative approach to defining personality disorder is Cloninger's (2000) proposal that personality disorder involves a specific constellation of extreme traits. He suggested that individuals with personality disorder show low levels of specific traits as measured with the Temperament and Character Inventory (TCI; Cloninger, Przybeck, Svrakic, & Wetzel, 1994). Four characteristics are described: self-directedness, cooperativeness, affective stability, and self-transcendence. Two of these characteristics are required to diagnose disorder. The order in which the four traits are listed has some significance. Self-directedness appears first because empirical studies suggest it is the most consistent feature of personality disorder. Self-transcendence is listed last because it is only associated with severe personality disorder.

The strength of this proposal is its foundation in a theoretical model of personality disorder and a measure of empirical support. The list also includes features that clinicians traditionally consider defining features of personality disorder, namely chronic interpersonal problems and self-pathology. Nevertheless, the rationale for selecting these particular traits is a little unclear. Within the Cloninger model, the rationale for using these traits to define personality disorder is that they are character dimensions as opposed to temperament dimensions. The latter are used to describe individual differences in personality disorder. The implication is that because the model postulates that character traits are largely environmental in origin, personality disorder is assumed to arise from adverse experiences. However, low affective stability does not feature in the original models. Cloninger (2000) suggested that this trait is associated with low self-directedness. However, empirical studies suggest that low affective stability is a feature of neuroticism. Although the character/temperament distinction is interesting and could introduce a measure of clarity into ideas about the nature of origins of personality disorder, it is not supported by the evidence. Twin studies indicate that character traits are as heritable as temperament traits (Ando et al., 2002, 2004) and much of the variance in some character traits is shared with temperament dimensions (Gillespie, Cloninger, Heath, & Martin, 2003). Once the distinction between character and temperament becomes unclear, the rationale for basing the definition of personality disorder in these qualities is unspecified.

# Personality Failure

Many of the difficulties created by using extreme trait levels to define disorder occur because trait constructs represent proclivities—tendencies to exhibit a given class of behaviors—whereas the concept of disorder refers more to competencies and disturbances of function. This suggests the need to define disorder independently of trait extremity. There is also the problem that the concept of personality is not confined to individual differences in personality traits and the clinical concept of personality disorder refers to more maladaptive traits (Livesley & Jang, 2000). For these reasons, the DAPP system makes a clear distinction between the assessment of personality and the diagnosis of personality disorder. DAPP questionnaires are considered measures of personality disorder traits—ways to describe individual differences in personality— not measures of personality disorder. Personality disorder is conceptualized separately as a disturbance in personality structure and functioning. Trait extremity is not a sufficient condition to determine the diagnosis although it increases the risk of disorder. It remains an unanswered empirical question of whether trait extremity is a necessary condition for diagnosis.

When considering the nature of the dysfunction associated with personality disorder, it is useful to think of personality as a system of interrelated structures and processes (Costa & McCrae, 1995; Livesley, 2003: Mischel, 1999; Vernon, 1964) that includes: traits, personal concerns and motives, and coping strategies. It also includes the self-system and autobiographical sense of self that integrates past, present, and future experiences and events (McAdams, 1994). The psychopathology of personality disorder extends to all aspects of this system: it includes symptoms, situational problems, dysregulation of affects and impulses, maladaptive expressions of traits, interpersonal problems, and self-pathology (Livesley, 2003). Pathology also extends beyond the contents of the personality system to include its structure and functioning. For example, personality disorder invariably includes disturbances of self and identity that extends beyond maladaptive beliefs about the self and problems of self-esteem to more fundamental problems with the structure of self-experience as shown in a fragmented and unstable experience of the self or an impoverished self-concept. The idea implies that personality disorder arises from extreme variation leading to disturbances in the normal functions of personality (Livesley & Jang, 2005). This proposal is consistent with Wakefield's (1992) definition of the mental disorders as "harmful dysfunctions" that prevent internal mental mechanisms from performing their naturally selected functions.

To complete this definition, we need to explicate the normal functions of personality and specify the way these functions are disturbed in personality disorder. Allport originally noted that "personality is something and personality does something." Trait theory is largely concerned with individual differences in what personality is. In contrast, social cognitive approaches are more concerned with what personality does. Some years ago, Cantor (1990) drew attention to Allport's comment and in the process described the functions of personality in terms of the personal tasks that individuals face and set for themselves; the schemata used to construe these tasks, the self and life situations; and the strategies used to achieve personal tasks. This analysis provides a conceptualization of personality functions that forms the foundation for a definition of personality disorder. The functions that Cantor described include specific dysfunctions such as problems with construal mechanisms and life tasks that are more pervasive in their effects. Although many of the specific dysfunctions have important implications for understanding and treating personality disorder, the concept of personality disorder implies something more pervasive. This suggests that personality disorder should be defined at the more abstract level of life tasks.

Life tasks are the problems individuals face as a consequence of cultural expectations and underlying biology. The solution of these tasks is essential for satisfactory adjustment. Many life tasks vary with culture and stage of life such as the tasks faced by adolescents as compared to those of their middle-aged parents. However, some life tasks are shared by everyone because they are part of a common human nature. These life tasks have evolutionary significance. They probably emerged from universal challenges that faced our remote ancestors in their struggle to survive and reproduce in the ancestral environment on the African savanna. This idea suggests that personality disorder occurs when "the structure of personality prevents the person from achieving adaptive solutions to universal life tasks" (Livesley, 1998, p. 141). This is a deficit definition which considers personality disorder to be a "harmful dysfunction" in the sense that it involves the failure to acquire the personality structures and functions required for successful adaptation. We now need to specify universal life tasks.

Plutchik (1980) described four universal challenges: The development of identity; the solution to the problems of dominance and submissiveness created by the hierarchy that is characteristic of primate social hierarchies; development of a sense of territoriality or belongingness; and solution to the problems of temporality, that is, problems of loss and separation. The life tasks posed by these universal challenges are remarkably similar to definitions of personality disorder from the clinical literature. Clinical psychiatry has traditionally considered personality disorder to involve either chronic interpersonal dysfunction or problems with self or identity, or both.

Chronic interpersonal dysfunction is emphasized by Rutter (1987) who suggested that personality disorder is "characterized by a persistent, pervasive abnormality in social relationships and social functioning generally" (p. 454). Similarly, Vaillant and Perry (1980) noted that personality disorder "almost always occurs in an interpersonal context" (p. 1562). Self-pathology tends to be emphasized by psychoanalytic thinkers. This is illustrated by the importance of identity diffusion in

Kernberg's (1984) construct of borderline personality organization. Identify diffusion involves

> ... a poorly integrated concept of the self and of significant others ... reflected in the subjective experience of chronic emptiness, contradictory self-perceptions, contradictory behavior that cannot be integrated in an emotionally meaningful way, and shallow, flat, impoverished perceptions of others. (1984, p. 12)

In the same way, failure to develop a cohesive sense of self is central to Kohut's (1971) account of narcissism. Cloninger's (2000) suggestion that personality disorder involves low self-directedness and low cooperativeness combines both components. The apparent similarity of clinical concepts and ideas of universal personality functions makes it possible to express the failure to attain universal life tasks in traditional clinical language, while retaining an evolutionary perspective. With this approach, personality disorder could be said to involve the failure to achieve one or more of the following: (a) stable and integrated representations of self and others; (b) the capacity for intimacy, to function adaptively as an attachment figure, and/or to establish affiliative relationships; and (c) adaptive functioning in the social group as indicated by the failure to develop the capacity for prosocial behavior and/or cooperative relationships. This definition is probably not specific to personality disorder. Most severe mental disorders are probably associated with these problems. To differentiate personality disorder from other mental disorders, we need to introduce the caveat that one or more of these failures should be enduring and traceable to adolescence or at least early adulthood and due to extreme personality variation rather than another pervasive mental disorder, such as a cognitive or schizophrenic disorder. Several advantages accrue from defining personality as the failure to achieve adaptive solutions to universal life tasks. First, it separates the diagnosis of personality disorder from the assessment of individual differences in personality dimensions such as traits, thereby avoiding the problems created by defining disorder only in terms of extreme levels of a given characteristic. Second, it emphasizes the severity of personality disorder and clarifies the distinction between disordered personality and dysfunctions in relatively discrete aspects of personality such as an isolated trait. Such dysfunctions may cause distress but they do not always lead to the extensive difficulties seen in patients considered to have personality disorder. Finally, the definition of disorder is based on an understanding of the functions of normal personality rather than on an arbitrary set of characteristics.

# Classification and Diagnosis

Application of the ideas discussed in the previous section would separate the diagnosis of personality disorder from the assessment of individual differences in personality. A classification of personality disorder structured in this way would have two components: (a) a systematic definition of personality disorder and associated diagnostic items; and (b) a system for describing clinically important differences in personality (Livesley, 2003). With this arrangement, personality disorder could be classified on Axis I with all other mental disorders, thereby avoiding the taxonomic and practical problems created by spreading mental disorders across two axes. Clinically important individual differences in personality would be represented on a separate axis.

Diagnosis would involve first determining the presence of personality disorder and then assessing personality using a representative set of dimensions if this was considered warranted either because the individual was deemed to have personality disorder or personality was considered relevant to the evaluation and treatment of another mental disorder. The proposal incorporates categorical and dimensional models. The diagnosis of personality disorder would be recorded as a categorical diagnosis because the decision to treat is binary. However, the characteristics used to make the diagnosis are continuously distributed so that empirically-derived cutting scores would need to be developed. Individual differences would be recorded as a profile of scores or ratings on a set of dimensions.

A two-step diagnosis has also been suggested by Cloninger (2000) and is consistent with the structure of *DSM-IV* (APA, 1994) and ICD-10, which both incorporate criteria for general personality disorder along with specific categories describing individual variation. The emphasis on personality disorder as a single entity that is the first step in the diagnostic process is also consistent with evidence that the global diagnosis of personality disorder has greater temporal stability than diagnoses of specific categories of disorder (David & Pilkonis, 1996).

Clinically significant individual differences would be described using a comprehensive set of primary traits, such as those evaluated by the DAPP-BQ. For convenience these traits could be hierarchically organized using the four-factor secondary structure. This would create a classification that reflects the etiological structure of personality disorder (Livesley, 2005). These secondary patterns introduce structure to the description of personality disorder. Clinical evidence also suggests that this structure is useful for the boarder aspects of treatment planning because the four patterns require somewhat different management strategies. For many clinical and research purposes, description at this level will be sufficient. Nevertheless, detailed treatment planning and research into the etiology and biological correlates of personality disorder requires an evaluation of the primary traits because most clinical interventions are directed toward the specific components of personality disorder rather than global diagnoses or secondary patterns and the etiology of personality disorder demonstrates considerable specificity.

# Concluding Comments

The overall picture emerging from research leading the DAPP is one of continuity between the trait structure of normal and disordered personality. Personality disorder traits seem to be phenotypically and genetically continuous with those of normal personality and traits specific to personality disorder have not been identified. Although in retrospect this finding seems mundane and even inevitable, it was not anticipated when these studies were initiated. It is somewhat remarkable that the structure of personality that emerges from analyses of clinical observations is almost identical to that underling everyday language of personality description. The significance of this finding is that a common structure and language is available to describe normal and disordered personality. The study of personality disorder can only be enriched as a result. Currently there is considerable opportunity to integrate models of normal and disordered personality at the secondary trait level. Less agreement occurs at the primary trait level so that an important area of research is to explicate the primary trait structure of personality and develop a set of primary traits that are both pertinent to the study of normal personality and relevant to clinical practice. Despite the progress being made in understanding individual differences, it seems important to remind ourselves that personality is not simply the study of traits, and that the defining features of personality disorder are likely to be found in the integrative and regulatory mechanisms and structures that are responsible for the organization and coherence of personality.

## REFERENCES

American Psychiatric Association. (1980). *The diagnostic and statistical manual of mental disorders* (3rd ed.). Washington, DC: Author.

American Psychiatric Association. (1987). *Diagnostic and statistical manual of mental disorders* (3rd ed., rev.). Washington, DC: Author.

American Psychiatric Association. (1994). *Diagnostic and statistical manual of mental disorders* (4th ed.). Washington, DC: Author.

American Psychiatric Association. (2000). *Diagnostic and statistical manual of mental disorders* (4th ed., text revision). Washington, DC: Author.

Ando, J., Ono, Y., Yoshimura, K., Onoda, N., Shinohara, S., Kanba, S., Asai, M. (2002). The genetic structure of Cloninger's seven-factor model of temperament and character in a Japanese sample. *Journal of Personality, 70*, 583–609.

Ando, J., Suzuki, A., Yamagata, S., Kijima, N., Maekawa, H., Ono, Y., & Jang, K. L. (2004). Genetic and environmental structure of Cloninger's temperament and character dimensions. *Journal of Personality Disorders, 18*, 379–393.

Austin, E. J., & Deary, I. J. (2000). The "four As": A common framework for normal and abnormal personality? *Personality and Individual Differences, 28*, 977–995.

Blashfield, R. K., & Livesley, W. J. (1991). A metaphorical analysis of psychiatric classification as a psychological test. *Journal of Abnormal Psychology, 100*, 262–270.

Cantor, N. (1990). From thought to behavior: "Having" and "doing" in the study of personality and cognition. *American Psychologist, 45*, 735–750.

Carey, G., & DiLalla, D. L. (1994). Personality and psychopathology: Genetic perspectives. *Journal of Abnormal Psychology, 103*, 32–43.

Clark, L. A. (1990). Toward a consensual set of symptom clusters for assessment of personality disorder. In J. Butcher, & C. Spielberger (Eds.), *Advances in Personality Assessment* (Vol. 8, pp. 243–266). Hillsdale, NJ: Erlbaum.

Clark, L. A. (1993a). *Manual for the Schedule for Non-adaptive and Adaptive Personality* (*SNAP*). Minneapolis, MN: University of Minnesota Press.

Clark, L. A. (1993b). Personality disorder diagnosis: Limitations of the five factor model. *Psychological Inquiry, 4*, 100–104.

Clark, L. A. (2002). Evaluation and devaluation in personality assessment. In J. Z. Sadler (Ed.), *Descriptions and prescriptions: Values, mental disorders, and the DSMs* (pp. 131–147). Baltimore, MD: Johns Hopkins University Press.

Clark, L. A., & Livesley, W. J. (1994). Two approaches to identifying the dimensions of personality disorder. In P. T. Costa & T. A. Widiger (Eds.), *Personality disorders and the five factor model of personality* (pp. 261–277). Washington DC: American Psychological Association.

Clark, L. A., & Livesley, W. J. (2002). Two approaches to identifying the dimensions of personality disorder: Convergence on the five-factor model. In P. T. Costa, Jr., & T. A. Widiger (Eds), *Personality disorders and the five-factor model of personality* (2nd ed., pp. 161–176). Washington, DC: American Psychological Association.

Clark, L. A., Livesley, W. J., Schroeder, M. L., Irish, S. L. (1996). Convergence of two systems for assessing specific traits of personality disorder. *Psychological Assessment, 8*(3), 294–303.

Cloninger, C. R. (2000). A practical way to diagnose personality disorder: A proposal. *Journal of Personality Disorders, 14*, 99–108.

Cloninger, C. R., Przybeck, T. R., Svrakic, D., & Wetzel, R. D. (1994). *The Temperament and Character Inventory (TCI): A guide to its development and use.* St. Louis, MO: Washington University, Center for Psychobiology of Personality.

Costa, P. T., & McCrae, R. R. (1995). Domains and facets: Hierarchical personality assessment using the Revised NEO Personality Inventory. *Journal of Personality Assessment, 64,* 21–50.

Crawford, C. B., & Defries, J. C. (1978). Factor analysis of genetic and environmental correlation matrices. *Multivariate Behavioral Research, 13,* 297–318.

Crowne, D. P., & Marlowe, D. (1960). A new scale of social desirability independent of psychopathology. *Journal of Consulting Psychology, 24,* 349–354.

David, J. D., & Pilkonis, P. A. (1996). The stability of personality disorder diagnoses. *Journal of Personality Disorders, 10,* 1–15.

Davis, R., & Millon, T. (1995). On the importance of theory to a taxonomy of personality disorders. In W. J. Livesley (Ed.), *The DSM-IV personality disorders,* (pp. 377–396). New York: Guilford Press.

DeFries, J. C., & Fulker, D. W. (1985). Multiple regression analysis of twin data. *Behavior Genetics, 15,* 467–473.

Eysenck, H. J. (1987). The definition of personality disorders and the criteria appropriate for their description. *Journal of Personality Disorders, 1,* 211–219.

Eysenck, H. J., & Eysenck, S. B. G. (1975). *Manual of the Eysenck Personality Inventory.* San Diego, CA: Educational and Industrial Testing Service.

Gillespie, N. A., Cloninger, C. R., Heath, A. C., & Martin, N. G. (2003). The genetic and environmental relationship beween Cloninger's dimensions of temperament and character. *Personality and Individual Differences, 35,* 1931–1946.

Goldberg, L. R. (1972). Some recent trends in personality assessment. *Journal of Personality Assessment, 36,* 547–560.

Harkness, A. R. (1992). Fundamental topics in the personality disorders: Candidate trait dimensions from the lower regions of the hierarchy. *Psychological Assessment, 4,* 251–259.

Helmes, E., & Jackson, D. N. (1994). Evaluating normal and abnormal personality using the same set of constructs. In S. Strack, & M. Lorr (Eds), *Differentiating normal and abnormal personality* (pp. 341–360). New York: Springer.

Jackson, D. N. (1971). The dynamics of structured personality tests. *Psychological Review, 78,* 229–248.

Jackson, D. N. (1984). *The Personality Research Form.* Sigma Assessment Systems, ON.

Jang, K. L., & Livesley, W. J. (1999). Why do measures of normal and disordered personality correlate? A study of genetic comorbidity. *Journal of Personality Disorders, 13,* 10–17.

Jang, K. L., Livesley, W. J., Vernon, P. A., & Jackson, D. N. (1996). Heritability of personality disorder traits: A twin study. *Acta Psychiatrica Scandinavica, 94,* 438–444.

Jang, K. L., Livesley, W. J., Angleitner, A., Riemann, R., & Vernon, P. A. (2002). Genetic and environmental influences on the covariance of facets defining the domains of the five-factor model of personality. *Personality and Individual Differences, 3,* 83–101.

Jang, K. L., McCrae, R. R., Angleitner, A., Riemann, R., & Livesley, W. J. (1998). Heritability of facet-level traits in a cross-cultural twin sample: Support for a hierarchical model of personality. *Journal of Personality and Social Psychology, 74,* 1556–1565.

Kass, F., Skodol, A. E., Charles, E., Spitzer, R. L., & Williams, J. B. (1985). Scaled ratings of *DSM-III* personality disorders. *American Journal of Psychiatry, 142*(5), 627–630.

Kernberg, O. F. (1984). *Severe personality disorders.* New Haven, CT: Yale University Press.

Kiesler, D. J. (1986). The 1982 interpersonal circle: An analysis of *DSM-III* personality disorders. In T. Millon, & G. L. Klerman (Eds.), *Contemporary directions in psychopathology: Toward the DSM-IV* (pp. 571–597). New York: Guilford Press.

Kohut, H. (1971). *The analysis of the self.* New York: International Universities Press.

Larstone, R. M., Jang, K. L., Livesley, W. J., Vernon, P. A., & Wolf, H. (2002). The relationship between Eysenck's P-E-N model of personality, the five-factor model of personality, and traits delineating personality disorder. *Personality and Individual Differences, 33*(1), 25–37.

Leary, T. (1957). *Interpersonal diagnosis of personality: A functional theory and methodology for personality evaluation.* New York: Ronald Press.

Lion, J. R. (Ed). (1981). *Personality disorders: Diagnosis and management.* Baltimore: Williams & Wilkins.

Livesley, W. J. (1985a). The classification of personality disorder: I. The choice of category concept. *Canadian Journal of Psychiatry, 30,* 353–358.

Livesley, W. J. (1985b). The classification of personality disorder: II. The problem of criteria. *Canadian Journal of Psychiatry, 30*, 359–362.

Livesley, W. J. (1986). Trait and behavioral prototypes of personality disorder. *American Journal of Psychiatry, 143*, 728–732.

Livesley, W. J. (1998). Suggestions for a framework for an empirically based classification of personality disorder. *Canadian Journal of Psychiatry, 43*, 137–147.

Livesley, W. J. (2001). Conceptual and taxonomic issues. In W. J. Livesley (Ed.), *Handbook of personality disorders: Theory, research, and treatment* (pp. 3–38). New York: Guilford Press.

Livesley, W. J. (2003). *Practical management of personality disorder.* New York: Guilford Press.

Livesley, W. J. (2005). Behavioral and molecular genetic contributions to a dimensional classification of personality disorder. *Journal of Personality Disorders, 19*, 131–155.

Livesley, W. J., & Jackson, D. N. (1986). The internal consistency and factorial structure of behaviors judged to be associated with DSM-III categories of personality disorders. *American Journal of Psychiatry, 143*, 1473–1474.

Livesley, W. J., & Jackson, D. N. (1992). Guidelines for developing, evaluating, and revising the classification of personality disorders. *Journal of Nervous and Mental Disease, 180*, 609–618.

Livesley, W. J., Jackson, D. N., & Schroeder, M. L. (1989). A study of the factorial structure of personality pathology. *Journal of Personality Disorders, 3*, 292–306.

Livesley, W. J., Jackson, D. N., & Schroeder, M. I. (1992). Factorial structure of traits delineating personality disorders in clinical and general population samples. *Journal of Abnormal Psychology, 101*, 432–440.

Livesley, W. J., & Jang, K. L. (2000). Toward an empirically based classification of personality disorder. *Journal of Personality Disorders, 14*, 137–151.

Livesley, W. J., & Jang, K. L. (2005). Genetic contributions to personality structure. In S. Strack (Ed.), *Handbook of personology and psychopathology* (pp. 103–119). Hoboken, NJ: Wiley.

Livesley, W. J., Jang, K. L., Jackson, D. N., & Vernon, P. A. (1993). Genetic and environmental contributions to dimensions of personality disorder. *American Journal of Psychiatry, 150*, 1826–1831.

Livesley, W. J., Jang, K. L., & Vernon, P. A. (1998). Phenotypic and genetic structure of traits delineating personality disorder. *Archives of General Psychiatry, 55*, 941–948.

Livesley, W. J., Jang, K. L., & Vernon, P. A. (2003). Genetic basis of personality structure. In T. Millon, & M. J. Lerner (Eds.), *Handbook of psychology: Personality and social psychology* (Vol. 5, pp. 59–83). New York: Wiley.

Livesley, W. J., & Schroeder, M. L. (1990). Dimensions of personality disorder: The *DSM-III-R* Cluster A diagnoses. *Journal of Nervous and Mental Disease, 178*, 627–635.

Livesley, W. J., Schroeder, M. L., Jackson, D. N., & Jang, K. L. (1994). Categorical distinctions in the study of personality disorder: Implications for classification. *Journal of Abnormal Psychology, 103*, 6–17.

Loehlin, J. C. (1982). Are personality traits differentially heritable? *Behavior Genetics, 12*, 417–428.

Loehlin, J. C. (1987). Heredity, environment, and the structure of the California Psychological Inventory. *Multivariate Behavioral Research, 22*, 137–148.

Loevinger, J. (1957). Objective tests as instruments of psychological theory. *Psychological Reports, 3*, 635–694.

McAdams, D. P. (1994). Personality, modernity, and the storied self: A contemporary framework for studying persons. *Psychological Inquiry, 7*, 295–321.

McCrae, R. R. (1994). A reformulation of Axis II: Personality and personality-related problems. In P. T. Costa, & T. A. Widiger (Eds.), *Personality disorders and the Five-Factor model of personality* (pp. 303–310). Washington, DC: American Psychological Association.

Millon, T. (1981). *Disorders of personality: DSM-III, Axis II.* New York: Wiley.

Mischel, W. (1999). Personality coherence and dispositions in a Cognitive-Affective Personality System (CAPS) approach. In D. Cervone, & Y. Shoda (Eds.), *The coherence of personality* (pp. 37–60). New York: GuilfordPress.

Mulder, R. T., & Joyce, P. R. (1997). Temperament and the structure of personality disorder symptoms. *Psychological Medicine, 27*, 99–106.

Parker, G., & Barrett, E. (2000). Personality and personality disorder: Current issues and directions. *Psychological Medicine, 30*, 1–9.

Plomin, R., Chipeur, H. M., & Loehlin, J. C. (1990). Behavior genetics and personality. In L. A. Pervin (Ed.), *Handbook of personality: Theory and research* (pp. 225–243). New York: Guilford Press.

Plomin, R., DeFries, J. C., & McClearn, G. E. (1990). *Behavioral genetics: A primer* (2nd ed.). New York: W. H. Freeman.

Plutchik, R. (1980). A general psychoevolutionary theory of emotion. In R. Plutchik, & H. Kellerman (Eds.), *Emotion, theory, research, and experience* (pp. 3–33). San Diego, CA: Academic Press.

Presly, A. J., & Walton, H. J. (1973). Dimensions of abnormal personality. *British Journal of Psychiatry, 122,* 269–276.

Pukrop, R., Gentil, I., Steinbring, I., & Steinmeyer, E. (2001). Factorial structure of the German version of the Dimensional Assessment of Personality Pathology-Basic Questionnaire in clinical and nonclinical samples. *Journal of Personality Disorders, 15,* 450–456.

Reynolds, S. K., & Clark, L. A. (2001). Predicting dimensions of personality disorder from domains and facets of the five-factor model. *Journal of Personality, 69,* 199–222.

Rosch, E. (1978). Principles of categorization. In E. Rosch, & B. B. Lloyd (Eds), *Cognition and categorization.* Hillsdale, NJ: Lawrence Erlbaum Associates.

Rutter, M. (1987). Temperament, personality, and personality disorder. *British Journal of Psychiatry, 150,* 443–458.

Saucier, G., & Goldberg, L. R. (1996). The language of personality: Lexical perspectives on the five-factor model. In J. S.Wiggins (Ed.), *The five factor model of personality* (pp. 21–50). New York: The Guilford Press.

Schneider, K. (1950). *Psychopathic personalities* (9th ed.). London: Cassell. (Original work published 1923)

Schroeder, M. L., Wormsworth, J. A., & Livesley, W. J. (1992). Dimensions of personality disorder and their relationship to the big five dimensions of personality. *Psychological Assessment, 4,* 47–53.

Skinner, H. A. (1981). Toward the integration of classification theory and methods. *Journal of Abnormal Psychology, 90,* 68–87.

Skinner, H. A. (1986). Construct validity approach to psychiatric classification. In T. Millon, & G. L. Klerman (Eds.), *Contemporary directions in psychopathology: Towards DSM-IV* (pp. 307–330). New York: Guilford Press.

Trull, T. J., & Widiger, T. A. (1997). *Structured interview for the five-factor model of personality.* Odessa, FL: Psychological Assessment Resources.

Tyrer, P., & Alexander, J. (1979). Classification of personality disorder. *British Journal of Psychiatry, 135,* 163–167.

Vaillant, G. E., & Perry, J. C. (1980). Personality disorders. In H. Kaplan, A. M. Freedman, & B. Sadock (Eds.), *Comprehensive textbook of psychiatry/III* (pp. 1562–1590). Baltimore: Williams & Wilkins.

van Kampen, D. (2002). The DAPP-BQ in the Netherlands: Factor structure and relationship with basic personality dimensions. *Journal of Personality Disorders, 16,* 235–254.

Vernon, P. E. (1964). *Personality assessment: A critical survey.* London: Methuen.

Wakefield, J. C. (1992). The concept of mental disorder: On the boundary between biological facts and social values. *American Psychologist, 47,* 373–388.

Wang, W., Du, W., Wang, Y., Livesley, W. J., & Jang K. L. (2004). The relationship between the Zuckerman-Kuhlman Personality Questionnaire and traits delineating personality pathology. *Personality and Individual Differences, 36,* 155–162.

Watson, D., & Clark, L. A. (1984). Negative affectivity: The disposition to experience aversive emotional states. *Psychological Bulletin, 96,* 465–490.

Widiger, T. A. (1993). The DSM-III-R categorical personality disorder diagnoses: A critique and an alternative. *Psychological Inquiry, 4,* 75–90.

Widiger, T. A. (1994). Conceptualizing a disorder of personality from the five-factor model. In P. T. Costa, Jr. & T. A. Widiger (Eds.), *Personality disorders and the five-factor model of personality* (pp. 311–317). Washington, DC: American Psychological Association.

Widiger, T. A. (1998). Four out of five ain't bad. *Archives of General Psychiatry, 55,* 865–866.

Widiger, T. A., Costa, P. T., Jr., & McCrae, R. R. (2002). A proposal for Axis II: Diagnosing personality disorders using the five-factor model. In P. T. Costa, Jr., & T. A. Widiger (Eds.), *Personality disorders and the five-factor model of personality* (2nd ed., pp. 431–456). Washington, DC: American Psychological Association.

Widiger, T. A., & Sankis, L. M. (2000). Adult psychopathology: Issues and controversies. *Annual Review of Psychology, 51,* 377–404.

Widiger, T. A., & Trull, T. J. (1991). Diagnosis and clinical assessment. *Annual Review of Psychology, 42,* 109–133.

Wiggins, J. S., & Pincus, A. L. (1989). Conceptions of personality disorders and dimensions of personality. *Psychological Assessment, 1,* 305–316.

Zheng, W., Wang, W., Huang, Z., Sun, C., Zhu, S., & Livesley, W. J. (2002). The structure of traits delineating personality disorder in China. *Journal of Personality Disorders, 16,* 477–486.

# The Schedule for Nonadaptive and Adaptive Personality (SNAP)

## A Dimensional Measure of Traits Relevant to Personality and Personality Pathology

**Leonard J. Simms**
**Lee Anna Clark**

The Schedule for Nonadaptive and Adaptive Personality (SNAP; Clark, 1993) and its second edition (SNAP-2; Clark, Simms, Wu, & Casillas, in press) were developed to provide a means for assessing trait dimensions relevant to the diagnosis of personality pathology. Traditional nosological systems of personality pathology, such as those provided by the fourth edition of the *Diagnostic and Statistical Manual of Mental Disorders* (*DSM-IV*; American Psychiatric Association [APA], 1994/2000), have postulated that disordered personality can be described reliably and validly using a categorical system within which a particular pathological syndrome is viewed as being either present or absent. However, research has identified a number of problems with this conceptualization and has led many to call for a dimensional approach to personality pathology (e.g., Ball, 2001; Clark, Livesley, & Morey, 1997; Tyrer, 2000; Widiger, 1993; Widiger & Clark, 2000; Widiger & Frances, 1994). Clark (1990) anticipated this movement, and the SNAP is an early example of a dimensional approach to personality disorder assessment. In this chapter, we review problems associated with categorical models, describe the development and primary features of the SNAP, suggest directions for future research, and discuss the practical application of the SNAP using a clinical case example.

Although the inclusion of personality disorders (PDs) on Axis II as an independent domain in *DSM-III* (APA, 1980) was an important advance, the categorical model used by that and all subsequent editions of the *DSM*—in which PDs are described as distinct clinical entities—suffers from a number of significant problems that limit its usefulness in research and clinical practice. Perhaps the most concerning problem is the high rate of diagnostic comorbidity observed among personality disorders. Numerous studies have revealed that it is more common for patients to receive multiple PD diagnoses than a single diagnosis (e.g., Clark, Watson, & Reynolds, 1995; Dolan, Evans, & Norton, 1995; Fossati et al., 2000; Oldham et al., 1995; Stuart et al., 1998; Watson & Sinha, 1998). The robustness of this finding suggests that the present system is not effectively "carving nature at its joints" with respect to personality pathology. Moreover, the presence of more than one PD leads to an important question: What exactly does it mean to have more than one personality disorder? For example, if a patient satisfies the criteria for borderline, histrionic, and avoidant PDs, is it the case that he or she has three distinct disease processes operating simultaneously? (In the extreme case, one might even ask if having multiple personality disorders means having multiple personalities as well.) Or, rather, might he or she simply be exhibiting certain traits (e.g., interpersonal problems, affective dysregulation, and unstable self-concept) that are consistent to varying degrees with the defining criteria of all three PDs? If the latter is correct, then dimensional models can be helpful in identifying those traits that robustly describe individual differences relevant to normal- and abnormal-range personality.

Another important problem with the current categorical system is within-class heterogeneity (e.g., Clark et al., 1995; Widiger, 1993). Axis II is a polythetic classification system, which means that individuals are diagnosed with a given disorder on the basis of meeting a subset of criteria from a larger pool. For example, *DSM-IV* specifies that borderline PD be diagnosed when at least any five of nine criteria are satisfied. Thus, there are 256 distinct combinations of criteria that satisfy this diagnostic threshold, and it is possible for two individuals with the same borderline PD diagnosis to share only one criterion. Such heterogeneity is problematic for a number of reasons. At a minimum, within-class heterogeneity limits the clarity of the diagnostic picture and, at the extreme, can lead to prejudicial attitudes among clinicians or other professionals who mistakenly believe that all members of a particular diagnostic class share all core features of that class. Two important functions of any diagnostic system are to foster effective communication among professionals and to aid in treatment planning; heterogeneity clearly interferes with both of these functions. Dimensional models, when implemented rigorously, yield relatively distinct dimensions that are internally consistent. Thus, instead of heterogeneous criteria sets that do not cohere well, internally consistent trait scales yield estimates of the degree to which a given patient exhibits the corresponding traits.

A final major point of contention with categorical classification systems is the arbitrary boundary between normal and abnormal personality (e.g., Clark et al., 1995; Livesley, 2001; Trull & Durrett, in press; Widiger & Clark, 2000). As described above, *DSM-IV* requires only a subset of criteria to be satisfied for each PD, but empirical support is limited for the particular cut points it has imposed. Practically speaking, it is difficult to argue, for example, that a person meeting only four schizotypal PD criteria is significantly different from one who meets five criteria. In fact, dichotomizing the distributions underlying PD criteria is associated with decreased reliability (Dreessen & Arntz, 1998; Pilkonis et al., 1995; Zanarini et al., 2000) and lower convergent validity across categorical measures of personality pathology (see Clark et al., 1997, for a review), as compared to dimensional classification systems in which no arbitrary cut point is used. Moreover, categorical systems result in significant information loss, especially for individuals who manifest clinically significant signs and symptoms that do not reach the arbitrary thresholds specified by the *DSM*.

Of course, these points assume that personality pathology can be described validly along dimensional lines. Correlational techniques, such as factor analysis, are ideal for revealing dimensionality, for example of personality pathology, but are not well suited for revealing categories, if they exist. However, a group of statistical techniques, collectively labeled *taxometrics* (Gangestad & Snyder, 1985; Meehl, 1992; Waller & Meehl, 1998), have been applied with increasing frequency to PDs (see Haslam, 2002, for a review). The basic premise of taxometric analyses is that members of a particular class (or taxon) will covary significantly less strongly on variables that reflect taxon membership than will nonmembers of the class because of restriction of range within the taxon. Thus, by looking for significant changes in covariation along multiple dimensions relevant to a particular disorder, the techniques seek to assess the dimensionality or taxonicity of that disorder.

A number of taxometric studies have provided initial support for taxa underlying several PDs, in particular those using traits theoretically related to antisocial (e.g., Harris, Rice, & Quinsey, 1994; Kotov, Aumer-Ryan, & Clark, 2003) and schizotypal (e.g., Blanchard, Gangestad, Brown, & Horan, 2000; Lenzenweger & Korfine, 1992) PDs. However, the most that these techniques can do is provide results that *are consistent with* taxonicity, and such results can be obtained for a number of reasons—some interesting and relevant to the question of taxonicity and some not—so additional research is needed to determine the meaning and practical significance of the potential taxa that have emerged from these studies (Lenzenweger, 2003; Schmidt, Kotov, & Joiner, 2004; Widiger, 2001). Also, interestingly, taxometric analyses have relied to a large extent on questionnaires developed under the assumption that the constructs assessed are dimensional in nature. Thus, another advantage of dimensional measurement of personality pathology is that it provides a strong foundation upon which to study important questions of continuity versus discontinuity among the personality disorders (Clark, 1993; Clark et al., in press; Krueger & Tackett, 2003; Trull & Durrett, 2005).

# Dimensional Assessment

Two basic methods have been proposed and used to dimensionalize Axis II. The first method is to maintain the current PD category labels and simply measure them along continua, either by summing the *DSM* criteria or by creating measures to tap the relevant aspects of each PD construct. Such methods generally lead to increased stability of measurement (e.g., Zanarini et al., 2000); however, diagnostic overlap and within-class heterogeneity still are problems (Clark, 1999) because the PDs share various traits or behaviors, and the PD diagnostic criteria were not selected to be internally consistent.

The second method involves (a) discarding the *a priori* assumption that personality pathology is categorical (and, consequently, discarding the *DSM* PD labels) and (b) identifying and measuring the trait dimensions that underlie phenotypic manifestations of personality pathology. The SNAP and SNAP-2 reflect this method, but other examples also exist. Most notably, the Five-Factor Model (FFM)—which historically has been focused on normal-range personality—has gathered support in recent years as a potential model for personality pathology in general (e.g., McCrae, this volume, chapter 2) and perhaps for Axis II in *DSM-V* (e.g., Widiger, Costa, & McCrae, 2002). The interpersonal circumplex also has been proposed as an alternative dimensional framework for understanding personality pathology (e.g., Pincus & Gurtman, this volume, chapter 4). These latter models represent *"top-down"* models that attempt to explain personality pathology in terms of existing structural models of personality. In contrast, *"bottom-up"* models—such as the SNAP—first identify lower order trait dimensions relevant to personality disorder and then let the empirical relations among those dimensions determine the ultimate structure of the domain.

In either case, the primary descriptive units in dimensional models of this second broad type are the basic traits that characterize the domain of personality pathology. Patients are rated on a number of distinct traits or potential problem areas that are relevant to personality dysfunction, rather than being placed in one or more diagnostic categories. The distinction between normal and abnormal functioning then can be determined on the basis of empirical criteria. Statistical infrequency is a common criterion of abnormality in dimensional models, with individuals scoring one-and-a-half or two standard deviations above or below the norm considered to be in the "abnormal" or "pathological" range. These choices of cut points along dimensions are no less arbitrary than the choice of criteria thresholds in the *DSM*, so many eschew the use of cutoffs and only interpret dimensional scores quantitatively both relative to norms and to other dimensions in the same clinical profile. Moreover, statistical extremity per se is insufficient to diagnose pathology, which also requires independent evidence of subjective distress and/or interpersonal dysfunction (Livesley, 2001; Trull & Durrett, 2005).

# The SNAP

The SNAP was published originally in 1993 following a series of content- and factor-analytic studies designed to identify traits underlying personality pathology (Clark, 1990, 1993; Clark, McEwen, Collard, & Hickok, 1993). The original instrument included 375 true–false items measuring 12 relatively distinct trait dimensions relevant to personality pathology, three broad temperament dimensions, six profile validity indicators, and diagnostic scales tapping each PD described in *DSM-III-R* (American Psychiatric Association, 1987). Clark selected the primary trait dimensions following several studies in which she (a) over inclusively identified PD descriptors from Axis II of *DSM-III* and *-III-R* as well as other possible manifestations of personality pathology, such as those on Axis I (e.g., dysthymia) or Cleckley's (1964) psychopathy criteria, and (b) had psychologists and psychology graduate students sort these descriptors into conceptually related groups, which resulted in 22 consensual symptom clusters that provided the basis for trait scale development (see Clark, 1990, for a detailed description of this process).

Scale construction then proceeded through an iterative process of item writing, scale administration, and construct and scale refinement. Several rounds of data collection, including participants from a variety of psychiatric and undergraduate settings, resulted in 12 primary trait scales: Mistrust, Manipulativeness, Aggression, Self-Harm, Eccentric Perceptions, Dependency, Exhibitionism, Entitlement, Detachment, Impulsivity, Propriety, and Workaholism. In addition, scales measuring three broad temperament dimensions—Negative Temperament, Positive Temperament, and Disinhibition (Clark & Watson, 1990)—were added to tap additional variance relevant to normal- and abnormal-range personality (see Clark, 1993, or Clark et al., in press, for a thorough discussion of the scale construction process). These 15 scales are known collectively as the *trait and temperament scales*. Brief descriptions of these scales are presented in Table 17.1.

| Table **17.1** | Listing and Brief Descriptions of SNAP-2 Scales | |
|---|---|
| **Scale (Abbreviation)** | **Brief Description** |
| **Trait and temperament scales:** | |
| **Negative Temperament (NT)** | Taps the tendency to experience a wide range of negative emotions and to overreact to the minor stresses of daily life |
| Mistrust (MST) | Measures a pervasive suspicious and cynical attitude toward other people |
| Manipulativeness (MAN) | Reflects an egocentric willingness to use people and to manipulate systems for personal gain without regard for the rights or feelings of others |
| Aggression (AGG) | Measures the frequency and intensity of the experience of anger and its behavioral expression in aggression |
| Self-Harm (SFH) | Includes two highly related components: low self-esteem and suicide proneness |
| Eccentric Perceptions (EP) | Measures unusualness in somatosensory perceptions, cognitions, and beliefs |
| Dependency (DEP) | Reflects individual differences in self-reliance, locus of control, and self-confidence in decision-making |
| **Positive Temperament (PT)** | Reflects the tendency to experience a wide variety of positive emotions and to be pleasurably, actively, and effectively involved in one's life |
| Exhibitionism (EXH) | Measures overt attention-seeking versus withdrawal from the attention of others |
| Entitlement (ENT) | Measures unrealistically positive self-regard and the feeling that one should be treated as a special person |
| Detachment (DET) | Taps emotional and interpersonal distance |
| **Disinhibition (DIS)** | Reflects broad differences in the tendency to behave in an under- versus over-controlled manner |
| Impulsivity (IMP) | Measures the specific tendency to act on a momentary basis without an overall plan |
| Propriety (PRO) | Taps the preference for traditional, conservative morality versus rejection of social rules and convention |
| Workaholism (WRK) | Reflects preferences for work versus leisure time, a tendency to perfectionism, and self-imposed demands for excellence |

*(continued)*

| Table 17.1 | (Continued) | |
|---|---|---|
| **Scale (Abbreviation)** | **Brief Description** | |
| **Validity Indices:** | | |
| Variable Response Inconsistency (VRIN) | Measures inconsistency related to random responding, carelessness, poor reading ability, etc. | |
| True Response Inconsistency (TRIN) | Assesses the tendency to admit to items (i.e., respond "True") or deny items (i.e., respond "False"), regardless of the content | |
| Desirable Response Inconsistency (DRIN) | Measures the tendency to respond to items on the basis of their social desirability features rather than on the basis of their content | |
| Rare Virtues (RV) | Identifies subjects who are presenting themselves in a very favorable light | |
| Deviance (DEV) | Identifies test-takers who are presenting themselves as broadly deviant | |
| Invalidity Index (II) | Provides an overall index of the degree of invalidity in the profile | |
| Back Deviance (BDEV)[a] | Detects careless, inconsistent, or deviant responding on the second half of the instrument | |

*Note:* Temperament scales are shown in boldface.
[a] Back Deviance can be scored using the SNAP-2 only.

Recently, the SNAP underwent a series of studies to improve its normative base (the original norms were based on a relatively homogenous group of undergraduates), update the diagnostic scales to reflect *DSM-IV*, and add a new validity scale. The resulting revision—the 390-item SNAP-2 (Clark et al., in press)—left the item content of the trait and temperament scales unchanged, ensuring continuity with the original instrument. However, the norms were updated to reflect a broader, more representative sampling of the United States population. The updated norms are based on responses provided by community-based adults from three sites, Iowa City, Minneapolis, and Dallas, who were recruited using lists of randomly generated phone numbers. For simplicity's sake, the abbreviation "SNAP" will be used throughout the remainder of the chapter except when discussing features relevant only to the SNAP-2.

As described above, the SNAP trait scales were selected and constructed in a bottom-up fashion with no assumptions made as to their structural relations. However, factor analytic studies have indicated that when factored on their own, the trait and temperament scales usually group into three higher order factors—*Negative Affectivity* (NA), *Positive Affectivity* (PA), and *Disinhibition vs. Constraint* (DvC)—that have been identified consistently in the normal-range personality literature (e.g., Eysenck & Eysenck, 1975; Gough, 1987; Tellegen & Waller, in press). Exemplifying this pattern, Table 17.2 includes varimax-rotated loadings of the trait and temperament scales on three principal factors. These data, which were collected in the community-based SNAP normative sample ($N = 561$) and a mixed psychiatric patient sample ($N = 611$), confirmed that three higher order factors largely account for relations underlying these scales. However, the factor-loading pattern differs somewhat between the two types of samples.

**Table 17.2** Varimax Factor Loadings of the Trait and Temperament Scales on Three Principal Factors in the SNAP-2 Normative Sample and a Mixed Psychiatric Patient Sample

| Scale | Negative Affectivity | | Positive Affectivity | | Disinhibition vs. Constraint | |
|---|---|---|---|---|---|---|
| | Norms | Patients | Norms | Patients | Norms | Patients |
| **Negative Temperament** | .72 | .57 | −.03 | −.35 | −.03 | .43 |
| Mistrust | .74 | .51 | .08 | −.23 | −.05 | .55 |
| Manipulativeness | .53 | .74 | .14 | .11 | .51 | −.02 |
| Aggression | .56 | .59 | .05 | −.05 | .16 | .24 |
| Self-Harm | .66 | .55 | −.27 | −.50 | .21 | .34 |
| Eccentric Perceptions | .63 | .52 | .25 | −.01 | .06 | .38 |
| Dependency | .31 | .40 | −.12 | −.32 | .07 | .15 |
| **Positive Temperament** | −.21 | −.10 | .76 | .76 | −.13 | .14 |
| Exhibitionism | −.01 | .32 | .58 | .63 | .40 | −.14 |
| Entitlement | .14 | .08 | .59 | .64 | −.05 | .09 |
| Detachment | .46 | .18 | −.42 | −.59 | −.19 | .30 |
| **Disinhibition** | .38 | .80 | .14 | .12 | .72 | −.21 |
| Impulsivity | .22 | .72 | .10 | .02 | .71 | −.19 |
| Propriety | .10 | −.11 | .14 | −.04 | −.58 | .53 |
| Workaholism | .30 | .04 | .34 | .06 | −.42 | .69 |
| **Percent of common variance** | 46% | 54% | 26% | 29% | 31% | 17% |

*Note:* Norms = community-based normative sample (*N* = 561); Patients = mixed psychiatric patient sample (*N* = 611) Loadings ≥ |.35| are shown in boldface. The non-overlapping version of Disinhibition was used in these analyses.

In the community sample, the core Negative Temperament scale as well as Mistrust, Manipulativeness, Aggression, Self-Harm, and Eccentric Perceptions loaded primarily on the NA factor, and Manipulativeness split evenly with the DvC factor. The PA factor was marked most strongly by the core Positive Temperament scale as well as Exhibitionism, Entitlement, and low Detachment (which split with the NA factor). Finally, the DvC factor consisted primarily of the broader Disinhibition scale as well as Impulsivity, low Propriety, low Workaholism, and Manipulativeness (which, as noted, split with the NA factor). As has been typical in most samples, Dependency did not load strongly on any factor, but had a modest loading on NA.

This structure has been identified robustly across a number of community and undergraduate samples (see Clark et al., in press). In psychiatric patient samples, however, aspects of the structure often appear to be somewhat less differentiated. For instance, the mixed patient sample data presented in Table 17.2 yielded a larger first factor than the community participants that included all of the expected NA factor markers with, in addition, very strong loadings by Disinhibition and Impulsivity, which separated from Workaholism and Propriety as markers of the third factor. Thus, these psychiatric patients showed an interrelated presentation of negative emotions and disinhibitory processes. Interestingly, this factor can be identified as Digman's (1997) "alpha" factor—the first of two very broad factors at the very top of the personality structural hierarchy (see Markon, Krueger, & Watson, 2005).[1]

These data suggest that emotional distress and behavioral undercontrol may be more tightly entwined in some psychiatric patient samples, whereas these processes remain relatively independent in nonpatients and perhaps also in patient samples rigorously screened for research purposes in which behavioral undercontrol may be less strongly represented (see Clark et al., in press, for an example). Moreover, behavioral overcontrol (represented by Propriety and Workaholism) form an independent factor in this patient sample, along with Mistrust and a secondary loading by Negative Temperament. Conversely, behavioral over- and undercontrol appear more clearly as opposites in non-patients (i.e., Disinhibition-Impulsivity vs. Propriety-Workaholism is a single bipolar factor in the community sample). Investigating these structural differences may be important in understanding the nature of personality pathology in relation to normal-range personality.

As discussed briefly in the preceding text, the Five-Factor model (FFM) of personality—which includes traits typically labeled *neuroticism* (vs. *emotional stability*), *extraversion* (or *surgency*), *conscientiousness*, *agreeableness* (vs. *antagonism*), and *openness to experience* (or *intellectance* or *culture*)—has developed a strong base in the normal-range personality literature and has been offered as an alternative for dimensional assessment of personality pathology (e.g., Costa & Widiger, 2002). Thus, it is interesting that the SNAP has meaningful relations with the FFM. In Table 17.3, we present correlations between the SNAP and FFM factor scores based on two common measures of the FFM—the NEO Five-Factor Inventory (NEO-FFI; Costa & McCrae, 1992) and the Big Five Inventory (BFI; John & Srivastava, 1999)—in a subset of the community-based normative sample. The relevance of the FFM to the maladaptive traits of personality pathology is apparent from these data. Three SNAP scales—Negative Temperament, Self-Harm, and Dependency—were moderately to strongly related to neuroticism, whereas three other NA scales—Mistrust, Manipulativeness, and Aggression—were most strongly related to the agreeableness (low) dimension of the FFM. SNAP Positive Temperament, Exhibitionism, and Detachment (low) were strongly related to extraversion, and Entitlement correlated moderately with this dimension. The conscientiousness dimension of the FFM related most strongly to three scales—Disinhibition (low), Impulsivity (low), and Workaholism—all from the DvC factor, with a secondary loading by Manipulativeness (low), whereas the fourth DvC-factor scale, Propriety, correlated moderately with both FFM conscientiousness and openness. However, as with most measures of personality pathology, the openness dimension is not otherwise well represented in the SNAP, although the modest

---

[1]Indeed, when only two factors are extracted in the patient data, the resemblance to "alpha" is unmistakable; Extraversion and Openness (discussed below), represented primarily by (low) SNAP Detachment, form the second, "beta" factor.

| Table 17.3 | Correlations Between the SNAP Trait and Temperament Scales and Five-Factor Model Factor Scores in the Normative Sample | | | | |
|---|---|---|---|---|---|
| | **Five-Factor Model Factor Scores** | | | | |
| **SNAP Scale** | **N** | **E** | **C** | **A** | **O** |
| **Negative Temperament** | .79 | −.02 | −.16 | −.17 | .02 |
| Mistrust | .26 | .01 | −.01 | **−.39** | −.06 |
| Manipulativeness | .13 | .10 | **−.31** | **−.35** | .18 |
| Aggression | .24 | .00 | −.06 | **−.40** | −.02 |
| Self-harm | **.48** | −.22 | −.10 | −.13 | .09 |
| Eccentric Perceptions | .24 | .09 | −.04 | −.24 | .24 |
| Dependency | **.40** | .10 | −.24 | .11 | −.09 |
| **Positive Temperament** | −.23 | **.58** | .21 | −.08 | .15 |
| Exhibitionism | −.13 | **.59** | −.07 | −.18 | .26 |
| Entitlement | −.19 | **.33** | .18 | −.25 | .15 |
| Detachment | .17 | **−.61** | .10 | −.27 | .02 |
| **Disinhibition** | .07 | .24 | **−.50** | −.25 | .19 |
| Impulsivity | .03 | .24 | **−.47** | −.13 | .11 |
| Propriety | .03 | .00 | **.30** | .09 | **−.37** |
| Workaholism | .11 | −.01 | **.38** | −.19 | .00 |

*Note:* $N = 245$. rs $\geq$ |.30| are shown in boldface. All rs $\geq$ |.16| are significant, $p < .01$.

correlation also with Eccentric Perceptions suggests that these two SNAP scales might be used to assess extreme- and low-openness, respectively. Taken together, these data suggest considerable overlap among the SNAP and the higher order dimensions of the FFM, although the magnitude of the correlations indicates that the two instruments do not provide simply redundant sets of information.

The SNAP also yields predictable relations with structured interview ratings of *DSM-IV* personality disorder. In Table 17.4, we present correlations between the SNAP trait and temperament scales and dimensional PD ratings from the Structured Interview for *DSM-IV* Personality (*SIDP-IV*; Pfohl, Blum, & Zimmerman, 1997) in a sample of 94 mixed psychiatric patients. The correlational pattern illustrates the *DSM* conceptualization of PDs as *sets of traits*, as the average PD correlated moderately to strongly (i.e., $r \geq .35$) with three SNAP traits (range $= 1 – 6$). Conversely, on average, each SNAP scale correlated with two *DSM* PDs (range $= 0$ [Eccentric Perceptions and Propriety] to 4 [Mistrust, Self-harm, Exhibitionism]). Importantly, the SNAP scales were related in meaningful and predictable ways with PD ratings (see Clark, 1993; Clark et al., in press, for hypothesized relations between the SNAP and PD ratings). In eight cases (80% of the PDs and over 50% of the SNAP scales), a one-to-one relation was found; that is, a particular SNAP-PD correlation was the highest for both the scale and the disorder: These seven pairs are Mistrust–Paranoid PD,

**Table 17.4** Correlations Between the SNAP Scales and Interview-Based Ratings of Personality Disorder in a Mixed-Patient Sample

| SNAP Scale | Interview-Based Ratings of Personality Disorder[a] | | | | | | | | | |
|---|---|---|---|---|---|---|---|---|---|---|
| | PAR | SZD | STP | ANT | BDL | HIS | NAR | AVD | DPN | OC |
| Negative Temperament | .41 | .13 | .21 | .11 | **.59**<u>*</u> | .31 | .13 | .23 | <u>.33</u> | <u>.23</u> |
| Mistrust | <u>**.52**</u>*† | <u>.17</u> | **.36**† | .23 | **.52*** | .34 | .15 | <u>.31</u> | .39 | .12 |
| Manipulativeness | .12 | −.32 | .03 | <u>.43</u>* | .18 | .17 | <u>.34</u> | −.12 | .23 | .16 |
| Aggression | **.43*** | .10 | .15 | .30 | <u>.37</u> | .21 | .25 | −.06 | .12 | .15 |
| Self-Harm | .38 | .17 | .31 | .18 | <u>**.65**</u>*† | .25 | .05 | .41 | .48 | .22 |
| Eccentric Perceptions | .04 | .12 | <u>.32</u>* | .03 | .20 | .24 | .19 | −.02 | .10 | .07 |
| Dependency | .24 | .01 | .18 | .09 | .50 | .22 | −.08 | .43 | <u>.59</u>*† | .00 |
| Positive Temperament | −.23 | −.35 | −.09 | .04 | −.21 | .26 | .24 | **−.52*** | −.27 | .11 |
| Exhibitionism | .06 | **−.42** | −.13 | .33 | −.03 | <u>**.42**</u>† | <u>**.50**</u>*† | **−.45** | −.12 | −.04 |
| Entitlement | −.12 | −.26 | −.15 | .08 | −.23 | .14 | **.40*** | **−.40*** | **−.35** | .06 |
| Detachment | <u>.34</u> | <u>**.56**</u>*† | <u>.32</u> | −.06 | .23 | −.21 | −.18 | **.56***† | .24 | .18 |
| Disinhibition | .07 | −.26 | −.05 | <u>**.56**</u>*† | .23 | .23 | .26 | −.14 | .18 | −.07 |
| Impulsivity | .07 | −.10 | .01 | <u>.39</u>* | <u>.30</u> | <u>.20</u> | .09 | −.03 | .18 | −.09 |
| Propriety | <u>.20</u>* | .13 | .14 | −.04 | .20 | .10 | .17 | .10 | .09 | <u>.19</u> |
| Workaholism | .11 | .22 | .19 | −.07 | .16 | .13 | .14 | .05 | .07 | <u>**.45**</u>*† |

*Note:* $N = 94$. $rs \geq |.26|$ are significant, $p < .01$. All $rs \geq |.35|$ are shown in **boldface**. PAR, paranoid; SZD, schizoid; STP, schizotypal; ANT, antisocial; BDL, borderline; HIS, histrionic; NAR, narcissistic; AVD, avoidant; DPN, dependent; OC, obsessive-compulsive. Hypothesized relations are <u>underlined</u>.

[a] Dimensional ratings from the Structured Interview for *DSM-IV* Personality (SIDP-IV; Pfohl, Blum, & Zimmerman, 1997).

* Highest correlation of a SNAP scale.

† Highest correlation of a SIDP-IV PD dimension.

Self-Harm–Borderline PD, Dependency–Dependent PD, Exhibitionism–Narcissistic PD, Detachment–Schizoid and Avoidant PDs, Disinhibition–Antisocial PD, and Workaholism–Obsessive–Compulsive PD. In addition to these one-to-one relations, the "supporting scale" relations also were quite systematic. For example, antisocial PD related not only to Disinhibition, but also to Manipulativeness and Impulsivity and, to a lesser extent, Exhibitionism and Aggression.

Similar SNAP-PD relations were found in a large recent study of personality pathology—the Collaborative Longitudinal Personality Disorders Study (Morey et al., 2003)—in which the authors presented correlations between the SNAP trait and temperament scales and another well-known interview measure of personality pathology, the Diagnostic Interview for Personality Disorders-IV (*DIPD-IV*; Zanarini, Frankenburg, Sickel, & Yong, 1996). Morey et al. (2003) presented a table of correlations similar to those in Table 17.4, finding a largely comparable pattern. They also commented that the SNAP "appeared to successfully distinguish specific PDs, a property that represents a particular challenge for dimensional models of personality" (p. 326).

To assess the similarity of the two correlation matrices (i.e., those presented here and by Morey et al., 2003), we correlated the corresponding coefficients, which yielded an overall correlation of .79 (95% confidence interval = .72 to .84), indicating moderately strong consistency in the correlational relations between the SNAP trait and temperament scales and interview ratings of PD. This consistency is particularly notable given that two different interview measures of personality pathology were used in these studies. Taken together, these data demonstrate that SNAP scales provide meaningful information regarding personality pathology as traditionally assessed.

Thus, the SNAP yields meaningful relations with the FFM as well as traditional PD conceptualizations. One might then ask, how do the SNAP and FFM compare in their ability to predict traditional PD diagnoses? Several investigations have addressed this question (Morey et al., 2002, 2003; Reynolds & Clark, 2001), finding that the SNAP trait and temperament scales generally predict PD diagnoses better than the five higher order factors of the FFM and at least as well as the 30 lower-order facet scales of the FFM assessed by the NEO Personality Inventory-Revised (NEO PI-R; Costa & McCrae, 1992). In fact, studies by Morey and colleagues (2002, 2003) revealed that the SNAP trait and temperament scales classified PDs more accurately than the 30 facet scales of the NEO PI-R. At minimum, the studies reported to date indicate that the dimensional model of personality pathology represented by the SNAP is as viable as the FFM. Additional comparative studies are needed to compare the SNAP to other competing models of personality pathology (e.g., interpersonal models).

# Other SNAP Scales

To provide maximum utility, especially in applied settings, the SNAP also contains validity scales to aid in the detection of biased or inconsistent responding. Identification of individuals who respond inconsistently or less than forthrightly is an important assessment consideration, and failure to take profile validity into account both affects the quality of clinical interpretations and increases error variance in research investigations. Thus, most omnibus personality tests used in clinical practice include some attempt to detect such forms of responding. The SNAP's seven validity indices were designed to detect a wide range of invalid approaches to the test. Three of the validity scales—Variable Response Inconsistency (VRIN), True Response Inconsistency (TRIN), and Desirable Response Inconsistency (DRIN)—include matched pairs of items that, when endorsed inconsistently, suggest a range of interpretations, including random responding, carelessness, poor reading ability, yea-saying, nay-saying, or endorsing items simply based on their social desirability characteristics.

The fourth validity scale—Rare Virtues—is a rationally derived scale consisting of 12 highly socially desirable behaviors that are rarely seen (e.g., *I have never made a promise that I didn't keep*). It is similar to the "Lie" scales of other instruments, such as the L scale of the MMPI-2. On the other end of the spectrum, Deviance and Back Deviance are scales that include a broad range of infrequently endorsed items on the first and second halves of the SNAP-2, respectively. High scorers on these scales may, in fact, exhibit socially deviant thoughts, feelings, and behaviors, or they simply may be trying to portray themselves in this way. However, high scores also may result from carelessness, poor reading skills, or other random responding. Finally, the Invalidity Index is a linear combination of the original validity scales (i.e., all but Back Deviance) designed to provide an overall measure of profile invalidity. Studies of the validity scales have indicated that Rare Virtues and Deviance detect simulated impression management and malingering, respectively, as well as other established validity scales do (Simms & Clark, 2001). Moreover, Monte Carlo analyses have indicated that: (a) VRIN, Deviance, Back Deviance, and the Invalidity Index effectively detect general random responding; (b) only Back Deviance successfully identifies profiles in which random responding begins after item 200; and (c) both TRIN and the Invalidity Index effectively detect all-true or all-false response patterns (Clark, 1993; Clark et al., in press).

Finally, although the SNAP was designed primarily as an alternative to traditional PD assessment, the SNAP-2 includes an updated set of diagnostic scales that provide indices of personality pathology linked to *DSM-IV*. For each PD, one or more items measure each criterion, and scores can be computed categorically (i.e., present vs. absent) or dimensionally (by summing all criteria or all items within each PD scale).

# Potential Research Applications

The SNAP is a useful tool for studies of normal- and abnormal-range personality. Among the wide range of potential research applications for the SNAP, there are several topics that the SNAP is particularly well suited to investigate. For example, given its dimensional nature, the SNAP would be quite useful in studies aiming to understand the personality and temperament dimensions underlying personality disorders as currently described in *DSM-IV*. Indeed, it was for this reason that the SNAP was developed in the first place (Clark, 1993; Clark et al., in press). Data such as those presented in Table 17.4 highlight the points of overlap and distinctiveness in our current Axis II nosology, but additional studies are needed using other measures and with participants selected primarily for personality disorder. With an eye toward building a better system for describing personality pathology in *DSM-V*, studies of this variety could be expanded, for example, to identify clusters of SNAP traits that cohere to form empirically derived personality disorders. Forming new personality disorder categories in such a bottom-up manner still might result in diagnostic overlap among PDs, but the overlap would be intentional (or at least not unexpected, if disorders had one or more traits in common) and, importantly, based on empirical findings, neither of which is true in the current system.

Alternatively, traits from the SNAP, or similar dimensional measures of personality pathology, could be investigated as potential building blocks for a purely dimensional system of personality disorder description in *DSM-V* (e.g., Widiger et al., 2002; Widiger & Clark, 2000). The strong movement in this direction is attested to by the December, 2004, *DSM-V* Research Agenda Personality Disorders Workgroup Conference jointly sponsored by the American Psychiatric Association and the National Institutes of Health, specifically entitled "Dimensional Models of Personality Disorder: Etiology, Pathology, Phenomenology, and Treatment."

The SNAP also is well suited to study the basic structure of personality pathology and whether this basic structure varies systematically as a function of sample type. For example, in this chapter we present exploratory factor analytic data showing that SNAP scales generally give rise to a three-factor structure that has been identified in many studies of normal-range personality. However, the data also suggest that the emotional distress and behavioral undercontrol represented by the higher order factors of NA and DvC, respectively, may be more closely related in psychiatric patients than in non-patients. Multi-sample confirmatory factor analytic (CFA) studies across patient and nonpatient samples would be useful for better understanding the similarities and differences in the organization of these traits as a function of sample type. In such analyses, competing structural models can be specified *a priori*, and their relative fits to the observed data can be assessed systematically by constraining certain parameters (e.g., factor intercorrelations, loading patterns, etc.) to be the same across samples. The results of such studies could highlight points of similarity and difference across models of normal- and abnormal-range personality structure.

Another structural question that the SNAP is well suited to study is whether personality pathology is better understood as a categorical or dimensional construct. Said differently, do persons who score high on measures of personality pathology represent a distinct class of individuals (i.e., a difference in kind) or simply the high end of continuous underlying traits or dimensions (i.e., a difference in degree)? As described briefly earlier, taxometric analyses[2] of the SNAP trait and temperament scales may be useful in trying to understand this question in at least two distinct ways. First, one common approach would be to examine the dimensional or categorical nature of the standard *DSM-IV* personality disorders (e.g., Haslam, 2002). To do this with the SNAP, trait and temperament scales that are strongly related to a given personality disorder could be used as indicators in a standard taxometric analysis. In one such analysis, for example, Kotov et al., (2003) used the Disinhibition, Manipulativeness, Aggression, and Impulsivity scales of the SNAP as indicators to examine the taxonicity of antisocial PD in a large combined sample of psychiatric patients, community-based

---

[2]A complete description of taxometrics is far beyond the scope of this chapter; see books by Waller and Meehl (1998) or Schmidt, Kotov, and Joiner (2004) for comprehensive coverage of taxometric methods.

adults, and undergraduates. Their results replicated previous findings suggesting that antisocial PD may be best understood as a category rather than a dimension of psychopathology. They conducted similar analyses for each of the remaining nine PDs, finding equivocal evidence of taxonicity for borderline and avoidant PDs, and clear evidence of dimensionality for all other PDs.

Alternatively, one might be interested in understanding whether the three higher-order factors that emerge in most factor analyses of the SNAP—NA, PA, and DvC—are better understood as categories or continua. As described above, factor analytic studies are well suited for identifying apparent dimensions but are incapable of testing the relative merits of a categorical or dimensional structure underling these constructs. Thus, in this type of analysis, for example, one might use the Positive Temperament, Exhibitionism, Entitlement, and Detachment scales of the SNAP (i.e., the four markers of the PA factor) as indicators in a taxometric analysis of the higher order positive affectivity temperament construct.

A final research opportunity for the SNAP relevant to the topic of this book would be to use it in comparative predictive validity studies along with measures of normal-range personality, such as those tapping the three- or five-factor models of personality or those modeling the interpersonal components of personality. A number of interesting outcome domains—such as psychotherapy process and outcome, life satisfaction, physical health, interpersonal relationship functioning, educational and occupational achievement, and legal problems—might show interesting correlates with measures of personality and related pathology. In particular, it would be especially interesting to see "head-to-head" studies using the SNAP and normal-range personality measures to examine how normal-range and pathological personality features contribute similarly or uniquely to the prediction of such variables. For example, studies might reveal that SNAP scales provide better information for predicting clinically relevant outcomes (e.g., therapy compliance and outcome), whereas normal-range measures might do a better job in predicting nonclinical outcomes (e.g., educational achievement). Alternatively, the data could show great similarity across measures with regard to all outcome domains. Thus, such studies would help us better understand the nature of the territory between normal and abnormal personality functioning and whether or not a discrete boundary exists.

# Clinical Case Example

In addition to helping researchers better understand the nature of personality pathology, the dimensional structure of the SNAP can be useful in clinical practice as well. We present the following case example as a demonstration of SNAP integration into clinical practice. "Margaret" was a therapy client of the first author and initially presented for therapy following a self-described "nervous breakdown" during the Christmas holiday season. She was 64 years of age, Caucasian, and a devoutly Christian woman who had been married to her husband, "Harold," for 49 years. They lived in a small rural town where she worked primarily as a homemaker, raising six children who now were grown and living out of the house, and he as a farmer, until a recent series of mini-strokes forced him to retire. In brief, they reported living a conventional rural and religious existence within which Margaret valued traditional rules of behavior, morality, and, above all else, family. Harold's illness and decision to retire from farming meant that they soon would need to sell the farm and move out of the home that they had occupied for the duration of their marriage. Margaret's "stress" level increased precipitously in the months following this decision as she began preparing for the transition, culminating in the following events that led her to seek psychotherapy for the first time in her life.

Margaret first presented to a local emergency room several days prior to Christmas following an emotionally charged evening during which she was preparing for a large Christmas dinner with her family. Margaret wanted the evening to go well since she believed that this very likely would be the last time that she would be able to accommodate all of her children and grandchildren during the holidays. To make matters more stressful, Margaret, a self-described perfectionist, refused to allow any of her grown children to help her prepare the meal. When two of them noticed that Margaret was overwhelmed with all that was left to do, they asked if they could help, but she told them that she "had it all under control" and did not need any help. Irritated by their mother's stubbornness and refusal to allow them to help, they abruptly told her that they were leaving with their respective families. As the family began to leave, Margaret reportedly began to "lose it," sensing that the dinner to which she had so looked forward was not turning out as she had hoped and planned. She became quite emotional, yelling and screaming at those who were leaving and threatening to hurt herself and others; thus, she subsequently was taken to the emergency room, where she was involuntarily committed for several days until she could be stabilized on medication.

Upon her release, Margaret was compelled to seek outpatient psychotherapy as a condition of her outpatient commitment. At her first session, she reported significant sadness, anger, and anxiety related to the events that led to her hospitalization. In particular, she was highly mistrustful of her children, because she believed that they thought she was "crazy" and wanted her to be permanently "locked up." She had not spoken with her children since the incident. In addition, she refused to shop in her small town, because she was afraid that her neighbors all knew about the incident and also would think that she was crazy. Margaret denied any history of psychopathology or contact with mental health counselors of any kind. However, Harold indicated that he had long noticed similar symptoms—as well as a rigid, perfectionistic, self-sufficient interpersonal style—but never to the extent that he had seen in recent months.

Margaret completed a number of measures during the assessment phase of the treatment, but we limit our discussion to her SNAP profile, shown in Figure 17.1, in which SNAP scale scores are plotted as $T$ scores (i.e., scaled to $M = 50$, $SD = 10$, using community-based norms). Validity scales are presented first, followed by the 15 trait and temperament scales, grouped by factor. The dotted lines marked at $T$s $= 65$ and 35 represent scores that are one-and-a-half standard deviations above and below the normative mean, respectively. Assuming a normal distribution underlies the SNAP scales (which is accurate for most scales), individuals scoring above the upper clinical threshold are scoring higher than 93% of individuals randomly selected from the community. Clearly, as discussed earlier, strict interpretation of the clinical thresholds as cutoffs distinguishing normality from psychopathology runs counter to the dimensional conceptualization and construction of the measure. Thus, the upper and lower thresholds are provided merely as a guide to the relative significance of scale elevations and are not interpreted rigidly.

Figure
17.1

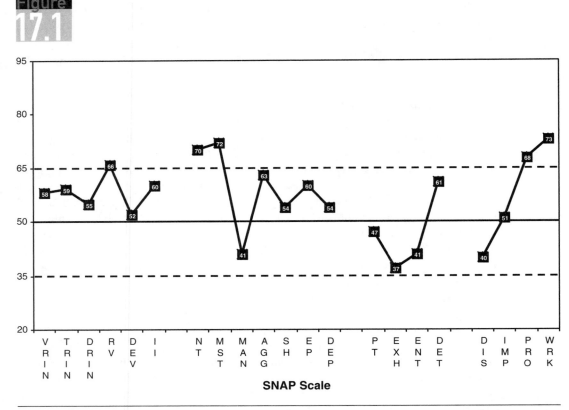

SNAP Profile for "Margaret." SNAP, Schedule for Nonadaptive and Adaptive Personality; VRIN, Variable Response Inconsistency; TRIN, True Response Inconsistency; DRIN, Desirable Response Inconsistency; RV, Rare Virtues; DEV, Deviance; II, Invalidity Index; NT, Negative Temperament; MST, Mistrust; MAN, Manipulativeness; AGG, Aggression; SH, Self-harm; EP, Eccentric Perceptions; DEP, Dependency; PT, Positive Temperament; EXH, Exhibitionism; ENT, Entitlement; DET, Detachment; DIS, Disinhibition; IMP, Impulsivity; PRO, Propriety; WRK, Workaholism.

Margaret's SNAP profile included significant and meaningful elevations on the following trait and temperament scales (in descending order of $T$ scores)— Workaholism, Mistrust, Negative Temperament, and Propriety—as well as moderate elevations on Aggression and Detachment. Her Workaholism elevation was consistent with her self-described perfectionism and suggested that she enjoys work more than play and drives herself extremely hard to complete projects even when exhausted. Margaret's Mistrust score highlighted the suspiciousness that she reported, but more generally suggested that she is cynical about interpersonal relationships and believes that it is best to keep others from knowing her too well. Her Propriety score suggested that she is greatly concerned about proper standards of conduct, values her reputation, and places good appearances over personal comfort or convenience. Further, her Negative Temperament elevation revealed that she is moody, chronically nervous or stressed, and easily irritated and angered. Finally, her Aggression and Detachment scores hinted that she may be somewhat prone to anger and aggression, and tends to prefer emotional and interpersonal distance, respectively.

Taken together, the SNAP portrayed Margaret as a self-sufficient, self-righteous, and perfectionistic woman who had developed significant cynicism and suspiciousness regarding others' motives. Although these features were highlighted during her Christmas dinner breakdown, it was clear from the interviews with her and other family members that she had embodied these traits, albeit at a more moderate and less dysfunctional level, for much of her lifetime. Coupled with her tendency to experience negative emotions such as anxiety, sadness, and explosive anger, these personality characteristics were particularly problematic for Margaret during times of stress. When the time came to consider diagnoses, it was clear that she met the primary *DSM* threshold for personality pathology; however, no single PD accurately and fully captured the unique constellation of traits that characterized her dysfunctional orientation to her world, thus yielding the relatively uninformative PD-NOS (not otherwise specified) diagnosis. By contrast, the traits measured by the SNAP conveyed a much richer and more accurate picture.

In the spirit of therapeutic assessment (e.g., Finn & Tonsager, 1997), the results of the assessment were shared with Margaret and were helpful in setting treatment goals and informing the therapy process. Given the interpersonal nature of her presenting complaint, therapy focused on her familial relationships and her role in instigating and maintaining conflict in those relationships. During twelve sessions of psychotherapy, we considered the themes suggested by the SNAP, arriving at the following dysfunctional pattern that we worked to change: (a) her high self-standards and preference for doing things alone creates distance between herself and others, particularly her family members; (b) distance with family runs counter to the high value she places on having a close-knit family and ultimately makes her feel rejected and unloved; and (c) in this context, she acts impulsively and aggressively toward those who she believes are rejecting her, particularly during times of stress, further creating distance. Therapy helped Margaret identify and accept this pattern, and she learned various tools to help manage its various elements. By the time of therapy termination, Margaret had reconciled with her family and had begun trusting them again. In addition, she had learned to exercise self-control when feeling strong emotions such as anger, to make use of the social support systems that were available to her (e.g., family and church), and to ask for help when she needed it. Given the time-limited nature of the therapy, personality change was not the goal; rather, therapy focused on providing Margaret with insight into her personality dynamics, as well as concrete tools that she could use in the future to cope with her interpersonal tendencies, especially during times of stress.

## Summary and Conclusions

The purposes of this chapter were to discuss the rationale for dimensional models of personality pathology, to introduce the SNAP as one such dimensional model and measure, to discuss possible research applications, and to provide a clinical example describing the use of the SNAP in applied psychotherapy settings. The SNAP and the revised SNAP-2 provide an alternative conceptualization of personality pathology that has shown promise in studies comparing it to the FFM of personality, as well as traditional interview ratings of personality pathology. In contrast to top-down models, such as the FFM, in which the personality structure defined in the normal personality literature is assumed to apply equally well to abnormal-range personality, the SNAP was designed in a bottom-up fashion primarily to assess traits specifically relevant to personality pathology. Interestingly, although in normal-range and some psychiatric samples the trait and temperament scales typically form the three higher order dimensions of the Big Three model, this structure appears to be modified somewhat in other psychiatric samples. Specifically, the first dimension appears to represent the first factor of Digman's Big Two model, combining the NA (emotional distress) and DvC (behavioral undercontrol) dimensions, leaving smaller second (PA/Extraversion) and third (behavioral overcontrol) factors. Thus, further work is needed to study SNAP structural differences across varied psychiatric and nonpatient samples. Such studies not only will clarify the structural nature of personality as assessed by the SNAP in different populations, but also may provide insight into the important question of continuity versus discontinuity across the range from normal- to abnormal-range personality.

## Acknowledgments

This work was supported by grants from the University of Minnesota Press. We thank Alex Casillas, Kevin Wu, and Sarah Reynolds for their help in collecting portions of the data presented herein.

## REFERENCES

American Psychiatric Association. (1980). *Diagnostic and statistical manual of mental disorders* (3rd ed.). Washington, DC: Author.

American Psychiatric Association. (1987). *Diagnostic and statistical manual of mental disorders* (3rd ed., rev.). Washington, DC: Author.

American Psychiatric Association. (1994/2000). *Diagnostic and statistical manual of mental disorders* (4th ed., text revision). Washington, DC: Author.

Ball, S. (2001). Reconceptualizing personality disorder categories using personality trait dimensions: Introduction to Special Section. *Journal of Personality, 69*, 147–153.

Blanchard, J. J., Gangestad, S. W., Brown, S. A., & Horan, W. P. (2000). Hedonic capacity and schizotypy revisited: A taxometric analysis of social anhedonia. *Journal of Abnormal Psychology, 109*, 87–95.

Clark, L. A. (1990). Toward a consensual set of symptom clusters for assessment of personality disorder. In J. N. Butcher & C. D. Spielberger (Eds.), *Advances in personality assessment* (Vol. 8, pp. 243–266). Hillsdale, NJ: L. Erlbaum.

Clark, L. A. (1993). *Schedule for nonadaptive and adaptive personality (SNAP)*. Minneapolis, MN: University of Minnesota Press.

Clark, L. A. (1999). Dimensional approaches to personality disorder assessment and diagnosis. In C. R. Cloninger (Ed.), *Personality and psychopathology* (pp. 219–244). Washington, DC: American Psychiatric Press.

Clark, L. A., Livesley, W. J., & Morey, L. (1997). Personality disorder assessment: The challenge of construct validity. *Journal of Personality Disorders, 11*, 205–231.

Clark, L. A., McEwen, J. L., Collard, L. M., & Hickok, G. (1993). Symptoms and traits of personality disorder: Two new methods for their assessment. *Psychological Assessment, 5*, 81–91.

Clark, L. A., Simms, L. J., Wu, K. D., & Casillas, A. (in press). *Schedule for nonadaptive and adaptive personality (SNAP-2)* (2nd ed.). Minneapolis, MN: University of Minnesota Press.

Clark, L. A., & Watson, D. (1990). *General temperament survey.* Unpublished manuscript, Southern Methodist University.

Clark, L. A., Watson, D., & Reynolds, S. (1995). Diagnosis and classification of psychopathology: Challenges to the current system and future directions. *Annual Review of Psychology, 46,* 121–153.

Cleckley, H. (1964). *The mask of sanity* (4th ed.). St. Louis, MO: Mosby.

Costa, P. T., Jr., & McCrae, R. R. (1992). *Revised NEO Personality Inventory (NEO-PI-R) and NEO Five Factor Inventory (NEO-FFI) professional manual.* Odessa, FL: Psychological Assessment Resources.

Costa, P. T., Jr., & Widiger, T. A. (2002). *Personality disorders and the five-factor model of personality* (2nd ed.). Washington, DC: American Psychological Association.

Digman, J. M. (1997). Higher-order factors of the Big Five. *Journal of Personality and Social Psychology, 73,* 1246–1256.

Dolan, B., Evans, C., & Norton, K. (1995). Multiple axis-II diagnoses of personality disorder. *British Journal of Psychiatry, 166,* 107–112.

Dreessen, L., & Arntz, A. (1998). Short-interval test-retest interrater reliability of the Structured Clinical Interview for *DSM-III-R* Personality Disorders (SCID-II) in outpatients. *Journal of Personality Disorders, 12,* 138–148.

Eysenck, H. J., & Eysenck, S. B. G. (1975). *Eysenck Personality Questionnaire manual.* San Diego, CA: Educational and Industrial Testing Service.

Finn, S. E., & Tonsager, M. E. (1997). Information-gathering and therapeutic models of assessment: Complementary paradigms. *Psychological Assessment, 9,* 374–385.

Fossati, A., Maffei, C., Bagnato, M., Battaglia, M., Donati, D., Donini, M., Fiorilli, M., Novella, L., & Prolo, F. (2000). Patterns of covariation of *DSM-IV* personality disorders in a mixed psychiatric sample. *Comprehensive Psychiatry, 41,* 206–215.

Gangestad, S. W., & Snyder, M. (1985). "To carve nature at its joints": On the existence of discrete classes in personality. *Psychological Review, 92,* 317–349.

Gough, H. G. (1987). *California Psychological Inventory administrator's guide.* Palo Alto, CA: Consulting Psychologists Press.

Harris, G. T., Rice, M. E., & Quinsey, V. L. (1994). Psychopathy as a taxon: Evidence that psychopaths are a discrete class. *Journal of Consulting and Clinical Psychology, 62,* 387–397.

Haslam, N. (2002). The dimensional view of personality disorders: A review of the taxometric evidence. *Clinical Psychology Review, 23,* 75–93.

John, O. P., & Srivastava, S. (1999). The Big Five Trait taxonomy: History, measurement, and theoretical perspectives. In L. A. Pervin & O. P. John (Eds.), *Handbook of personality: Theory and research* (2nd ed., pp. 102–138). New York: Guilford Press.

Kotov, R., Aumer-Ryan, K., & Clark, L. A. (2003). *Categories or continua: Taxometric analysis of personality disorders.* Poster presented at 37th Annual Conference of the Association for Advancement of Behavior Therapy, Boston, MA.

Krueger, R. F., & Tackett, J. L. (2003). Personality and psychopathology: Working toward the bigger picture. *Journal of Personality Disorders, 17,* 109–128.

Lenzenweger, M. F. (2003). On thinking clearly about taxometrics, schizotypy, and genetic influences: Correction to Widiger (2001). *Clinical Psychology: Science & Practice, 10,* 367–369.

Lenzenweger, M. F., & Korfine, L. (1992). Confirming the latent structure and base rate of schizotypy: A taxometric analysis. *Journal of Abnormal Psychology, 101,* 567–571.

Livesley, W. J. (2001). Conceptual and taxonomic issues. In W. J. Livesley (Ed.), *Handbook of personality disorders: Theory, research, and treatment* (pp. 3–38). NY: Guilford Press.

Markon, K. E., Krueger, R. F., & Watson, D. (2005). Delineating the structure of normal and abnormal personality: An integrative hierarchical approach. *Journal of Personality and Social Psychology, 88,* 139–157.

Meehl, P. E. (1992). Factors and taxa, traits and types, differences in degree and differences in kind. *Journal of Personality, 60,* 117–174.

Morey, L. C., Gunderson, J. G., Quigley, B. D., Shea, M. T., Skodol, A. E., McGlashan, T. H., Stout, R. L., & Zanarini, M. C. (2002). The representation of borderline, avoidant, obsessive-compulsive, and schizotypal personality disorders by the five-factor model. *Journal of Personality Disorders, 16,* 215–234.

Morey, L. C., Warner, M. B., Shea, M. T., Gunderson, J. G., Sanislow, C. A., Grilo, C., Skodol, A. E., & McGlashan, T. H. (2003). The representation of four personality disorders by the Schedule for

Nonadaptive and Adaptive Personality dimensional model of personality. *Psychological Assessment, 15*, 326–332.

Oldham, J. M., Skodol, A. E., Kellman, H. D., Hyler, S. E., Doidge, N., Rosnick, L., & Gallaher, P. E. (1995). Comorbidity of axis I and axis II disorders. *American Journal of Psychiatry, 152*, 571–578.

Pfohl, B., Blum, N., & Zimmerman, M. (1997). *Structured Interview for DSM-IV Personality (SIDP-IV)*. Washington, DC: American Psychiatric Press.

Pilkonis, P. A., Heape, C. L., Proietti, J. M., Clark, S. W., McDavid, J. D., & Pitts, T. E. (1995). The reliability and validity of two structured diagnostic interviews for personality disorders. *Archives of General Psychiatry, 52*, 1025–1033.

Reynolds, S. K., & Clark, L. A. (2001). Predicting dimensions of personality disorder from domains and facets of the five-factor model. *Journal of Personality, 69*, 199–222.

Schmidt, N. B., Kotov, R., & Joiner, T. E., Jr. (2004). *Taxometrics: Toward a new diagnostic scheme for psychopathology*. Washington, DC: American Psychological Association.

Simms, L. J., & Clark, L. A. (2001). Detection of deception on the schedule for nonadaptive and adaptive personality: Validation of the validity scales. *Assessment, 8*, 251–266.

Stuart, S., Pfohl, B., Battaglia, M., Bellodi, L., Grove, W., & Cadoret, R. (1998). The cooccurrence of *DSM-III-R* personality disorders. *Journal of Personality Disorders, 12*, 302–315.

Tellegen, A., & Waller, N. (in press). Exploring personality through test construction: Development of the Multidimensional Personality Questionnaire. In S. R. Briggs, & J. M. Cheek (Eds.), *Personality measures: Development and evaluation* (Vol. 1). Greenwich, CN: JAI Press.

Trull, T. J., & Durrett, C. A. (2005). Categorical and dimensional models of personality disorder. *Annual Review of Clinical Psychology, 1*, 355–380.

Tyrer, P. (2000). Improving the assessment of personality disorders. *Criminal Behaviour & Mental Health*, 10, S51–S65.

Waller, N. G., & Meehl, P. E. (1998). *Multivariate taxometric procedures: Distinguishing types from continua*. Thousand Oaks, CA: Sage.

Watson, D. C., & Sinha, B. K. (1998). Comorbidity of *DSM-IV* personality disorders in a nonclinical sample. *Journal of Clinical Psychology, 54*, 773–780.

Widiger, T. A. (1993). The *DSM-III-R* categorical personality disorder diagnoses: A critique and an alternative. *Psychological Inquiry, 4*, 75–90.

Widiger, T. A. (2001). What can be learned from taxometric analyses? *Clinical Psychology: Science & Practice, 8*, 528–533.

Widiger, T. A., & Clark, L. A. (2000). Toward *DSM-V* and the classification of psychopathology. *Psychological Bulletin, 126*, 946–963.

Widiger, T. A., & Frances, A. J. (1994). Toward a dimensional model for the personality disorders. In P. T. Costa & T. A. Widiger (Eds.), *Personality disorders and the five-factor model of personality* (pp. 19–39). Washington, DC: American Psychological Association.

Widiger, T. A., Costa, P. T., Jr., McCrae, R. R. (2002). A proposal for Axis II: Diagnosing personality disorders using the five-factor model. In P. T. Costa, & T. A. Widiger (Eds.), *Personality disorders and the five-factor model of personality* (2nd ed., pp. 431–456). Washington, DC: American Psychological Association.

Zanarini, M. C., Frankenburg, F. R., Sickel, A. E., & Yong, L. (1996). *The Diagnostic Interview for DSM-IV Personality Disorders (DIPD-IV)*. Belmont, MA: McLean Hospital.

Zanarini, M. C., Skodol, A. E., Bender, D., Dolan, R., Sanislow, C., Schaefer, E., et al. (2000). The Collaborative Longitudinal Personality Disorders Study: Reliability of Axis I and II diagnoses. *Journal of Personality Disorders, 14*, 291–299.

# The Personality Assessment Inventory and the Measurement of Normal and Abnormal Personality Constructs

Leslie C. Morey
Christopher J. Hopwood

An array of instruments resulting from a variety of approaches to test construction are available to the investigator attempting to measure important constructs related to normal and abnormal personality. This chapter provides a brief overview of the theory and procedures employed in developing one of these instruments, the *Personality Assessment Inventory* (PAI; Morey, 1991), reports evidence of validity in a variety of clinical endeavors, discusses the empirical differences between normal and abnormal personality, and examines the PAI in the context of these differences. Since its introduction, the PAI has become widely taught in graduate and internship training settings (Belter & Piotrowski, 2001; Piotrowski, 2000; Piotrowski & Belter, 1999) and has received widespread acceptance in settings such as correctional (e.g., Edens, Cruise, & Buffington-Vollum, 2001; Duellman & Bower, 2004) and legal (Boccaccini & Brodsky, 1999; Lally, 2003) applications. More detailed coverage than is possible in this chapter can be found in several primary sources (Morey, 1991, 1996, 2003), as well as various review articles regarding the use of the instrument for specific purposes (e.g., Edens et al., 2001).

## An Overview of the PAI

The PAI is a self-administered, multi-scale inventory intended to provide clinically useful information about client variables in professional and research settings. It contains

344 items that are answered on a four-point Likert-type scale, with the options of *Totally False, Slightly True, Mainly True,* and *Very True.* The 344 items encompass 22 nonoverlapping full scales: 4 validity, 11 clinical, 5 treatment consideration, and 2 interpersonal. The clinical syndromes assessed by the PAI were selected on the basis of the stability of their importance within the nosology of psychopathology and their significance in contemporary diagnostic practice. Ten of the full scales contain conceptually derived subscales that were designed to facilitate interpretation and coverage of the full breadth of clinical constructs. The literature on each clinical syndrome was examined to identify those components most central to the definition of the disorder, and items were written to provide an assessment of each component of the syndrome in question.

# Theoretical Basis and Test Development

The development of the PAI was based on a construct validation framework that emphasized a theoretical/rational as well as a quantitative method of scale development. This framework places a strong emphasis on a theoretically informed approach to the development and selection of items, as well as on the assessment of their stability and correlates. As a first step, the theoretical and empirical literature for each of the constructs to be measured was closely examined because this articulation had to serve as a guide to the content of information sampled and to the subsequent assessment of content validity. The development of the test then went through four iterations in a sequential construct validation strategy similar to that described by Loevinger (1957) and Jackson (1970), although item selection involved the consideration of a number of item parameters that were not described by those authors. Of paramount importance at each point of the development process was the assumption that no single quantitative item parameter should be used as the sole criterion for item selection. An over-reliance on a single parameter in item selection typically leads to a scale with one desirable psychometric property and numerous undesirable ones. Both the conceptual nature and empirical adequacy of the items played an important role in their inclusion in the final version of the PAI.

The construction of the PAI sought to develop scales that provided a balanced sampling of the most important elements of the constructs being measured. This content coverage was designed to include both a consideration of *breadth* as well as *depth* of the construct. The *breadth* of content coverage refers to the diversity of elements subsumed within a construct. For example, in measuring depression it is important to inquire about physiological and cognitive symptoms as well as features of affect. Depression scales that focus exclusively on one of these elements have limited breadth of coverage and compromised content validity. The PAI sought to insure breadth of content coverage through the use of subscales representing the major elements of the measured constructs, as indicated by the theoretical and empirical literature.

The *depth* of content coverage refers to the need to sample across the full range of construct severity. To assure adequate depth of coverage, the scales were designed to include items reflecting both its milder and most severe forms. The use of four-alternative scaling provides each item with the capacity to capture differences in the severity of the manifestation of a feature of a particular disorder, and is further justified psychometrically in that it allows a scale to capture more true variance per item, meaning that even scales of modest length can achieve satisfactory reliability. This item type may also be preferred by clinicians considering particular items (e.g., risk indicators) or by clients themselves, who often express dissatisfaction with forced choice alternatives because they feel that the truth is between the two extremes presented.

In addition to differences in depth of severity reflected in response options, the items themselves were constructed to tap different levels of severity. For example, cognitive elements of depression can vary from mild pessimism to severe feelings of hopelessness, helplessness, and despair. Item characteristic curves were used to select items that provide information across the full range of construct severity. The nature of the severity continuum varies across the constructs. As an example, severity on the Suicidal Ideation (SUI) scale involves the imminence of the suicidal threat. Thus, items on this scale vary from vague and ill-articulated thoughts about suicide to immediate plans for self-harm.

One implication of a careful consideration of content validity in the construction of a test is that it is assumed that item content is critical in determining an item's ability to capture the phenomenology of various disorders and traits, and hence its relevance for the assessment of the construct. Empirically derived tests may include items on a construct scale that have no apparent relation to the construct in question. However, research (e.g., Holden, 1989; Holden & Fekken, 1990; Peterson, Clark, & Bennett, 1989) has consistently indicated that such items add little or no validity to self-report tests. The available empirical evidence is entirely consistent with the assumption that the content of a self-report item is critical in determining its utility in measurement. This assumption does not preclude the potential utility of items that are truly "subtle" in the sense that a lay audience cannot readily identify the relationship of the item to mental health status. However, the assumption does suggest that the implications of such items for mental health status should be apparent to the expert diagnosticians for the item to be useful.

Although discriminant validity has been long recognized as an important facet of construct validity, it traditionally has not played a major role in the construction of psychological tests, and it continues to represents one of the largest challenges in the assessment of psychological constructs. There are a variety of threats to validity where discriminability plays a vital role. One such area of involves *test bias*. A test that is intended to measure a psychological construct should not be measuring a demographic variable, such as gender, age, or sex. This does not mean that psychological tests should never be correlated with demographic variables, but that the magnitude of any such correlations should not exceed the theoretical overlap of the demographic feature with the construct. For example, nearly every indicator of antisocial behavior suggests that it is more common in men than in women; thus, it would be expected that an assessment of antisocial behavior would yield average scores for men that are higher than that for women. However, the instrument should demonstrate a considerably greater correlation with other indicators of antisocial behavior than it does with gender; otherwise it may be measuring gender rather than measuring the construct it was designed to assess.

The issue of test bias is one that is particularly salient in light of past abuses of testing and current legislation designed to prevent such abuses. However, such bias is just one form of potential problems with discriminant validity. It is particularly common in the field of clinical assessment to find that a measure that supposedly measures one construct (such as anxiety or schizophrenia) is in fact highly related to many constructs. It is this tendency that makes many instruments quite difficult to interpret. How does the clinician evaluate an elevated score on a scale measuring "schizophrenia" if that scale is also a measure of alienation, indecisiveness, family problems, and depression? At each stage of the development of the PAI, items were selected that had maximal associations with indicators of the pertinent construct and minimal associations with the other constructs measured by the test.

# Normative Data

The PAI was developed and standardized for use in the clinical assessment of individuals in the age range of 18 through adulthood. Items were written to be easily understood and applicable across cultures; the initial reading level analyses of the PAI test items indicated that reading ability at the fourth-grade level was necessary to complete the inventory. A comparative study of similar instruments by Schinka and Borum (1993) supported the conclusion that the PAI items are written at a grade equivalent lower than estimates for comparable instruments.

PAI scale and subscale raw scores are transformed to $T$-scores (mean of 50, standard deviation of 10) in order to provide interpretation relative to a standardization sample of 1,000 community-dwelling adults. This sample was selected to match 1995 U.S. census projections on the basis of gender, race and age; the educational level of the standardization sample (mean of 13.3 years) was representative of a community group with the required fourth-grade reading level. For each scale and subscale, the $T$-scores were linearly transformed from the means and standard deviations derived from the census-matched standardization sample. Unlike many other similar instruments, the PAI does not calculate $T$-scores differently for men and women; instead, combined norms are used for both genders. Separate norms are only necessary when the scale contains some bias that alters the interpretation of a score based on the respondent's gender. To use separate norms in the absence of such bias would only distort the natural epidemiological differences between genders. In the example discussed above, women are less likely than men to receive the diagnosis of antisocial personality disorder, and this is reflected in the lower mean scores for women on the Antisocial Features (ANT) scale. A separate normative procedure for men and women would result in similar numbers of each gender scoring in the clinically significant range, a result that does not reflect the established gender ratio for this disorder. The PAI included several procedures to eliminate items that might be biased due to demographic features, and items that displayed any signs of being interpreted differently as a function of these features were eliminated in the course of selecting final items for the test. As it turns out, with relatively few exceptions, differences as a function of demography were negligible in the community sample. The most noteworthy effects involve the tendency for younger adults to score higher on the Borderline Features (BOR) and ANT scales, and the tendency for men to score higher on the ANT and Alcohol Problems (ALC) relative to women.

Because $T$-scores are derived from a community sample, they provide a useful means for determining if certain problems are clinically significant, as relatively few normal adults will obtain markedly elevated scores. As described later in this chapter, for measures of abnormal constructs, mean differences between community and clinical samples are expected and serve as a foundation for making determinations of the normality or abnormality of a particular person's presentation. However, other normative comparisons are often of equal importance in clinical decision making. For example, nearly all patients report depression at their initial evaluation; the question confronting the clinician considering a diagnosis of Major Depressive Disorder is one of relative severity of symptomatology. Knowing that an individual's score on the PAI Depression scale is elevated in comparison to the standardization sample is of value, but a comparison of the elevation relative to a clinical sample may be more critical in forming diagnostic hypotheses.

To facilitate these comparisons, the PAI profile form also indicates the *T*-scores that correspond to marked elevations when referenced against a representative clinical sample. This profile "skyline" indicates the score for each scale and subscale that represents the raw score that is two standard deviations above the mean for a clinical sample of 1,246 patients selected from a wide variety of different professional settings. Scores above this skyline represent a marked elevation of scores relative to those of patients in clinical settings. When contrasted with the comparable line for a community sample (i.e., 70t), the differences in configurations of these lines alerts the interpreter about base rate differences for scale elevations in the two settings. Thus, interpretation of the PAI profiles can be accomplished in comparison to both normal and clinical samples.

The PAI manual provides normative transformations for a number of different comparisons. Various appendices provide *T*-score transformations referenced against the clinical sample and a large sample of college students, as well as for various demographic subgroups of the community standardization sample. Although the differences between demographic groups were generally quite small, there are occasions where it may be useful to make comparisons with reference to particular groups. Thus, the raw score means and standard deviations needed to convert raw scores to *T*-scores with reference to normative data provided by particular groups are provided in the manual for this purpose. However, for most clinical and research applications, the use of *T*-scores derived from the full normative data is strongly recommended because of its representativeness and larger sample size.

# Reliability

The reliability of the PAI scales and subscales has been examined in a number of different studies that have evaluated the internal consistency (Alterman et al., 1995; Boyle & Lennon, 1994; Morey, 1991; Rogers, Flores, Ustad & Sewell, 1995; Schinka, 1995), test–retest reliability (Boyle & Lennon, 1994; Morey, 1991; Rogers et al., 1995) and configural stability (Morey, 1991) of the instrument. Internal consistency alphas for the full scales are generally found to be in the 0.80s, whereas the subscales yield alphas in the 0.70s. Although these numbers are acceptable, internal consistency estimates are generally not the ideal basis for deriving the standard error of measurement (SEM) in clinical measures because temporal instability is often of greater concern than inter-item correlations.

For the standardization studies, median test-retest reliability values, over a 4-week interval, for the 11 full clinical scales was 0.86 (Morey, 1991), leading to SEM for these scales on the order of three to four *T*-score points, with 95% confidence intervals of ± six to eight *T*-score points. Absolute *T*-score change values over time were quite small across scales, on the order of two to three *T*-score points for most of the full scales (Morey, 1991). Boyle and Lennon (1994) reported a median test–retest reliability of 0.73 in their normal sample over 28 days. Rogers et al. (1995) found an average stability of 0.71 for the Spanish version of the PAI, administered over a 2-week interval.

Because multi-scale inventories are often interpreted configurally, additional questions should be asked concerning the stability of configurations on the 11 PAI clinical scales. One such analysis involved determining the inverse (or Q-type) correlation between each subject's profile at Time 1 and the profile at Time 2. Correlations were obtained for each of the 155 subjects in the full retest sample, and a distribution of the within-subject profile correlations was obtained. Conducted in this manner, the median correlation of the clinical scale configuration was 0.83, indicating a substantial degree of stability in profile configurations over time (Morey, 1991).

# Validity

In the examination of test validity presented in the manual (Morey, 1991), a number of the best available clinical indicators were administered concurrently to various samples to determine their convergence with corresponding PAI scales. Diagnostic and other clinical judgments concerning clinical behaviors (as rated by the treating clinician) have also been examined to determine if their PAI correlates were consistent with hypothesized relations. Finally, a number of simulation studies have been performed to determine the efficacy of the PAI validity scales in identifying response sets. A comprehensive presentation of available validity evidence for the various scales is beyond the scope of this chapter; the PAI manual alone contains information about correlations of individual scales with over 50 concurrent indices of psychopathology (Morey, 1991). The following paragraphs provide some of the more noteworthy findings from such studies, divided into the four broad classes of PAI scales: validity scales, clinical scales, treatment consideration scales, and interpersonal scales.

## Validity Scales

The assessment of profile validity is vital in any measure intended for use in an evaluative context. The PAI validity scales were developed to provide an assessment of the potential influence of certain response tendencies on PAI test performance, including both random and systematic influences upon test responding. To model the performance of subjects completing the PAI in a random fashion, computer-generated profiles were created by generating random responses to individual PAI items and then scoring all scales according to their normal scoring algorithms. A total of 1,000 simulated protocols were generated for this analysis. Comparison of profiles derived from normal subjects, clinical subjects, and the random response simulations demonstrated a clear separation of scores of actual respondents from the random simulations, and 99.4% of these random profiles were identified as such by either Inconsistency (ICN) or Infrequency (INF) scales (Morey, 1991).

Numerous studies have been performed in which subjects were instructed to simulate positive or negative response styles. Comparison of profiles for normal subjects, clinical subjects, and the corresponding response style simulation group demonstrated a clear separation between Negative Impression Management (NIM) and Positive Impression Management (PIM) scores of actual respondents and those of simulators. In the initial validation studies described in the test manual, individuals scoring above the critical level of NIM were 14.7 times more likely to be a member of the malingering group than of the clinical sample, while those scoring above threshold on PIM were 13.9 times more likely to be in the positive dissimulation sample than a community sample (Morey, 1991). Subsequent studies have generally supported the ability of these scales to distinguish simulators from actual protocols under a variety of response set conditions. For example, the studies described in the test manual found that the point of rarity on PIM between the distributions of the impression management sample (i.e., "fake good") and the community normative sample was at a raw score of 57t; application of this cut score resulted in a sensitivity in the identification of defensiveness of 82%, and a specificity with respect to normal individuals of 70%. These findings have been well replicated (Morey & Lanier, 1998); for example, a study by Cashel, Rogers, Sewell, and Martin-Cannici (1995) also identified 57t as their optimal cutting score. Their study, in which respondents were coached regarding believability of results, yielded sensitivity and specificity rates of 48% and 81%, respectively. Peebles and Moore (1998) also found a cutting score of 57t to be optimal for their sample, resulting in a hit rate of 85.1% in distinguishing forthright from fake-good responders. Finally, a study by Fals-Stewart (1996) found that the 57t cut-score on PIM had a sensitivity of 88% in identifying "questionable responding" in substance abusers (e.g., forensic patients who denied substance use but had positive urine screens), with a specificity of 80% in honest responding groups.

A number of examinations of the utility of the NIM scale in the evaluation of malingering have also been reported in the literature. Rogers, Ornduff, and Sewell (1993) examined the effectiveness of the NIM scale in identifying both naive and sophisticated simulators (advanced graduate students in clinical and counseling psychology) who were given a financial incentive to avoid detection as malingerers while attempting to feign specific disorders. Rogers et al. found that the recommended NIM scale cutoff successfully identified 90.9% of participants attempting to feign schizophrenia, 55.9% of participants simulating depression, and 38.7% of participants simulating an anxiety disorder. In contrast, only 2.5% of control participants were identified as simulators. Rogers et al. concluded that the NIM scale is most effective in identifying the malingering of more severe mental disorders. Interestingly, there was no effect of subject sophistication; the scale was equally effective in identifying naive and sophisticated malingerers. Gaies (1993) conducted a similar study of malingering, focusing upon the feigning of clinical depression, and reported average scores on NIM of 92t for sophisticated malingerers and 81t for naive malingerers. Although both simulation groups were elevated relative to honest responding groups, the results are similar to those of Rogers et al. (1993), suggesting that individuals attempting to simulate milder forms of mental disorder (in this case, depression) will obtain more "moderate" elevations on NIM. Finally, Scragg, Bor and Mendham (2000) reported a sensitivity of 54% and a specificity of 100% for distinguishing malingered from true post-traumatic stress disorder for the NIM scale.

Several validity indices have been developed in addition to PAI profile scales. For example, the Malingering Index (Morey, 1996), a composite of several configural indicators, was introduced to measure malingering more directly than NIM, which is often affected by response styles consequent to psychopathology in addition to overt attempts at negative dissimulation. Rogers and colleagues (1996) have developed the Rogers Discriminant Function, an index that appears able to indicate malingering nearly totally unassociated with psychopathology (Morey & Lanier, 1998). The Defensiveness Index (Morey, 1996) is a composite of configural indices of positive impression management. This index can be supplemented by the Cashel Discriminant Function (Cashel et al., 1995), which appears to measure positive dissimulation unassociated with psychopathology (e.g., naiveté). The combination of three scales provides representative of positive and negative distortion provides the evaluator with the ability to tease out the relative influences of psychopathology and intentional distortion in making decisions about invalidity (Morey, 2003). In addition to indicators of invalid response sets, Morey and Hopwood (2004) developed an indicator of back random responding involving short-form/full-form scaled score discrepancies on ALC and SUI, with satisfactory positive and negative predictive power across levels and base rates of back random responding.

## Clinical Scales

The clinical scales of the PAI were assembled to provide information about 11 important clinical constructs. A number of instruments have been used to provide information on the convergent and discriminant validity of the PAI clinical scales. Correlations tend to follow hypothesized patterns; for example, strong associations are found between neurotic spectrum scales such as Anxiety (ANX), Anxiety Related Disorder (ARD), and Depression (DEP) and other psychometric measures of neuroticism (Costa & McCrae, 1992; Montag & Levin, 1994; Morey, 1991). The ARD scale has also been found to correlate with the probability of experiencing nightmares, with ARD-T in particular being associated with night terrors (Greenstein, 1993). The ARD scale (particularly ARD-T) has also been found to differentiate women psychiatric patients who were victims of childhood abuse from other women patients who did not experience such abuse (Cherepon & Prinzhorn, 1994). Similarly, the DEP scale demonstrates its largest correlations with various widely used indicators of depression, such as the Beck Depression Inventory (BDI; Beck & Steer, 1987), the Hamilton Rating Scale for Depression (Hamilton, 1960), and the Wiggins (1966) Minnesota Multiphasic Personality Inventory (MMPI; Hathaway & McKinley, 1967) Depression content scale (Ban, Fjetland, Kutcher, & Morey, 1993; Morey, 1991). Several indicators have been found useful in discriminating PTSD from ASD among individuals traumatized in motor-vehicle accidents (Holmes, Williams, & Haines, 2001), and the PAI has demonstrated effectiveness in distinguishing true from malingered PTSD in psychiatric (Liljequist, Kinder, & Schinka, 1998) and VA (Calhoun, Earnst, Tucker, Kirby, & Beckham 2000) samples. It has also been suggested that the PAI provides important diagnostic information about individuals with pain (George & Wagner, 1995) and eating disorder (Tasca, Wood, Demidenko, & Bissada, 2002) problems.

Within the psychotic spectrum, PAI scales such as Paranoia (PAR), Mania (MAN), and Schizophrenia (SCZ) have been correlated with a variety of other indicators of severe psychopathology (Morey, 1991). Of these scales, the PAR scale has been found to correlate particularly well with diagnostic assessments of paranoia made via structured clinical interview (Rogers, Ustad, & Salekin, 1998). Also, the SCZ scale has been found to distinguish schizophrenic patients from controls (Boyle & Lennon, 1994). In that study the schizophrenic sample did not differ significantly from a sample of alcoholics on SCZ scores, although certain characteristics of their criterion group (patients on medication maintenance) and their alcoholic group (alcoholics undergoing detoxification) might have in part accounted for their findings (Morey, 1996). Nonetheless, further research along these lines is needed; at this point, the SCZ scale in particular might more safely be interpreted as a measure of general impairment, rather than as a specific marker of schizophrenia (Rogers et al., 1998). Combining the PAI profile with information from other assessment sources may be particularly important for differential diagnosis of psychotic disorders.

Two scales on the PAI directly target character pathology, the Borderline Features (BOR) scale and the Antisocial Features (ANT) scale. The choice to include these two constructs on the PAI was based on the fact that the majority of the literature on personality disorders centers around these two constructs. Both the BOR and ANT scales have been found to relate to other measures of these constructs as well as to predict relevant behavioral outcomes (e.g., Trull, Useda, Conforti, & Doan, 1997; Salekin, Rogers, Ustad, & Sewell, 1998). The BOR scale has been found to correlate with the MMPI Borderline scale (Morey, 1991), the Bell Object Relations Inventory (Bell Inventory; Bell, Billington, & Becker, 1985; Kurtz, Morey, & Tomarken, 1993), and the NEO-PI Neuroticism scale (Costa & McCrae, 1992). Other studies have supported the validity and utility of this scale in borderline treatment samples (e.g., Evershed et al., 2003; Yeomans, Hull, & Clarkin, 1994). In addition, it has been demonstrated that an assessment of BOR increments the information provided by a diagnosis of MDD (Kurtz & Morey, 2001). The BOR scale in isolation has been found to distinguish borderline patients from unscreened controls with an 80% hit rate, and successfully identified 91% of these subjects as part of a discriminant function (Bell-Pringle, Pate, & Brown, 1997). Classifications based upon the BOR scale have been validated in a variety of domains related to borderline functioning, including depression, personality traits, coping, Axis I disorders, and interpersonal problems (Trull, 1995). These BOR scale classifications were also found to be predictive of two-year outcome on academic indices in college students, even after controlling for academic potential and diagnoses of substance abuse (Trull et al., 1997).

The ANT scale demonstrated its largest correlations in initial validation studies (Morey, 1991) with the MMPI Antisocial personality disorder scale (Morey, Waugh, & Blashfield, 1985) and the Self-Report Psychopathy test designed by Hare (Hare, 1985) to assess his model of psychopathy. Subsequent studies have also been supportive of the validity of ANT. Salekin, Rogers, and Sewell (1997) examined the relationship between ANT and psychopathic traits in a sample of female offenders and found that elevations on ANT in this population were primarily the result of endorsements on Antisocial Behaviors (ANT-A). Also, support was found for the convergent validity of ANT with other measures including the Psychopathy Checklist-Revised (PCL-R; Hare, 1985) Total score and the Personality Disorder Examination (Loranger, 1988)

Antisocial scale. In a similar study, Edens, Hart, Johnson, Johnson, and Olver (2000) examined the relationship of the ANT scale to the screening version of the Psychopathy Checklist (PCL:SV; Hart, Cox, & Hare, 1995) and the PCL-R. Moderately strong correlations were found between ANT and the PCL:SV and the PCL-R total score, with the highest correlations with these measures being found ANT-A. Salekin, Rogers, Ustad, and Sewell (1998) investigated the ability of the ANT and the Aggression (AGG) scales of the PAI to predict recidivism among female inmates over a 14-month follow-up interval. Findings indicated that the ANT scale was significantly related to recidivism, as was the Aggression (AGG) scale. ANT has also demonstrated validity in predicting violence in a sample of incarcerated mentally ill individuals (Wang & Diamond, 1999), and in predicting treatment course for a sample of borderline females (Clarkin et al., 1994).

The PAI contains two scales, Alcohol Problems (ALC) and Drug Problems (DRG), that inquire directly about behaviors and consequences related to alcohol and drug use, abuse, and dependence. These scales demonstrate a similar pattern of correlates: strong correlations with corresponding measures of substance abuse, such as the interview-based Addiction Severity Index (Parker, Daleiden, & Simpson, 1999) and moderate associations with indicators of behavior problems and antisocial personality (Alterman, et al., 1995). The ALC scale has been found to differentiate patients in an alcohol rehabilitation clinic from patients with schizophrenia (Boyle & Lennon, 1994) as well as normal controls (Ruiz, Dickinson, & Pincus, 2002). The DRG scale has also been found to successfully discriminate drug abusers and methadone maintenance patients from general clinical and community samples (Alterman et al., 1995; Kellogg et al., 2002). Because the items for ALC and DRG inquire directly about substance use, the scales are susceptible to denial. Thus, there are empirically derived procedures to assess the likelihood that a profile under-represents the extent of alcohol or drug problems (Fals-Stewart, 1996; Morey, 1996). Overall, the PAI appears to be especially useful in a forensic context, because of its ability to measure constructs related to that population (e.g., BOR, ANT, DRG, ALC) as well as its ability to detect invalid profiles (e.g., Douglas, Hart, & Kropp, 2001, Edens et al., 2001, Wang et al., 1997).

## Treatment Consideration Scales

The treatment consideration scales of the PAI were assembled to provide indicators of potential complications in treatment that would not necessarily be apparent from diagnostic information. There are five of these scales: two indicators of potential for harm to self or others, two measures of environmental circumstances, and one indicator of motivation for treatment. These scales have been compared to a number of measures of related constructs. In addition to the NEO-PI, IAS-R, and the MMPI, the scales have been correlated with numerous specialized assessment instruments. The BDI and BHS (Beck & Steer, 1988) provide convergent correlates for suicidal ideation. Also, the Suicide Probability Scale (SPS; Cull & Gill, 1982) serves as a concurrent indicator of suicide potential. The SPS has four subscales, which assess hopelessness, suicidal ideation, negative self-evaluation, and hostility, in addition to yielding a total score for suicide probability. The State-Trait Anger Expression Inventory (STAXI; Spielberger, 1988) provides a marker for aggression, which is broken down into six scales and two subscales. The Perceived Social Support scales (Procidano & Heller, 1983) provide an assessment of the subjective impact of supportive transactions between the subject and the subject's social system; two separate scales assess support provided by the subject's family and by the subject's friends. Finally, the Schedule of Recent Events (SRE) is a unit-scoring adaptation of the widely used Holmes and Rahe (1967) checklist of recent stressors, where subjects are asked to indicate major life changes that have taken place in the 12 months prior to evaluation.

Correlations between the PAI treatment consideration scales and such validation measures provide support for the construct validity of these scales (Costa & McCrae, 1992; Morey, 1991). Substantial correlations have been identified between the Aggression (AGG) scale and NEO-PI Hostility (.83) and STAXI Trait Anger (.75) scales. AGG was also negatively correlated with the STAXI Anger Control scale (−.57). The Suicidal Ideation (SUI) scale was most positively correlated with the BHS (.64), the BDI (.61), the Suicidal Ideation (.56) and Total Score (.40) of the SPS, and also found to be negatively correlated with perceived social support measures. As expected, the Nonsupport (NON) scale was found to be highly (and inversely) correlated with the social support measures; −.67 with PSS-Family, −.63 with PSS-Friends. It was also moderately associated with numerous measures of distress and tension. The Stress (STR) scale displayed its largest correlations with the SRE (.50) and was also associated with various indices of depression and poor morale. Finally, the Treatment Rejection (RXR) scale is found to be negatively associated with Wiggins Poor Morale (−.78) and the NEO-PI Vulnerability (−.54) scales, consistent with the idea that distress can serve as a motivator for treatment. RXR has been shown to be positively associated with indices of social support, implying that people are less likely to be motivated for treatment if they have an intact and available support system as an alternative, and has predicted treatment noncompliance in a sample of sex-offending inmates (Caperton, Edens, & Johnson, 2004).

## Interpersonal Scales

The interpersonal scales of the PAI were designed to provide an assessment of the interpersonal style of subjects along two dimensions: (a) a warmly affiliative versus a cold rejecting axis, and (b) a dominating, controlling versus a meekly submissive style. These axes provide a useful way of conceptualizing variation in normal personality as well as many different mental disorders, and persons at the extremes of these dimensions may present with a variety of disorders. The PAI manual describes a number of studies indicating that diagnostic groups differ on these dimensions; for example, spouse-abusers are relatively high on the Dominance (DOM) scale, while schizophrenics are low on the Warmth (WRM) scale (Morey, 1991). Correlations with related measures also provide support for the construct validity of these scales. For example, the correlations with the IAS-R vector scores are consistent with expectations, with PAI DOM associated with the IAS-R dominance vector (.61) and PAI WRM associated with the IAS-R love vector (0.65). The NEO-PI Extraversion scale roughly bisects the high DOM/high WRM quadrant, as it is moderately positively correlated with both scales; this finding is consistent with previous research (Trapnell & Wiggins, 1990). The WRM scale was also correlated with the NEO-PI Gregariousness scale, while DOM was associated with the NEO Assertiveness facet (Costa & McCrae, 1992).

## The PAI and the Differentiation of Normal and Abnormal Personality

The differentiation of normal and abnormal personality has been a particular challenge to the psychopathology researcher as well as to the mental health professional. In part, this difficulty not only stems from the heterogenous behaviors of individuals bearing diagnoses such as "personality disorder," but also reflects the vague and ill-defined nature of the boundaries between normal and abnormal personality, whether these boundaries are considered natural or artificial. As a further complication, the definition of "abnormal personality" (e.g., personality disorder) has undergone substantial changes in recent years, and despite admirable attempts to objectify many critical distinctions, the American Psychiatric Association's *Diagnostic and Statistical Manual* (most recent edition *DSM-IV-TR*; APA, 2000), is still unclear on distinctions between normal personality, abnormal personality, and clinical syndromes. However, it is clear that there are differences between instruments as to whether they are designed to measure "normal" or "abnormal" constructs. For example, catalogs from test publishers often present such tests in separate sections, suggesting that the differences between them are implicit.

The remainder of this chapter proposes certain empirical criteria that we believe may help to identify whether a construct captures an element of "normal personality" or whether it represents something abnormal. Each of these criteria will be discussed with respect to the PAI, and the general conclusion will be drawn that the PAI measures elements of both normal and abnormal personality, although measurements of the latter type of constructs predominate. Furthermore, these criteria are easily applied to other instruments, and their application may help to clarify some of the differences between psychopathology, abnormality personality, and normative personality traits.

*Criterion 1. Normal and abnormal personality constructs differ in the distribution of their related features in the general population.*

Differentiating normal and abnormal personality in this manner is similar to the approach taken by Foulds (1971). Foulds separated what he called personality deviance from personal illness (i.e., psychopathology), and he proposed a model of the overlapping but conceptually independent domains. In making this distinction, he focused upon quantitative aspects of these conditions, namely the distributions of symptoms (features of personal illness) and traits (features of personality deviance) in various populations.

In distinguishing between features associated with these conditions, Foulds hypothesized that abnormal symptoms should have distributions which have a marked positive skew (i.e. occur infrequently) in normal samples, while roughly normally distributed in clinical samples. In contrast, normative personality traits should be distributed in a roughly Gaussian (i.e, bell-shaped) manner in the general population; a sample of individuals with "deviant" personalities are distinguished by the personality trait being manifest to a degree rarely encountered in the general population. It should be noted that both types of constructs may be of clinical interest. Various regions of each type of construct may represent an area of concern; a person can have difficulties because he or she manifests a particular normative trait to an extreme degree (e.g., introversion), or because he or she manifests an abnormal construct to even a slight degree (e.g., social anxiety). The primary difference is in the nature of the construct; the individual with

**Table 18.1**

## Distributional Differences Between Clinical and Community Samples on the PAI Full Scales

| PAI Scale | Skewness | | Mean Score | |
|---|---|---|---|---|
| | Community | Clinical | Community | Clinical |
| ICN | 0.98 | 0.51 | 5.39 | 6.57 |
| INF | 1.59 | 1.03 | 2.66 | 3.18 |
| NIM | 2.88 | 1.41 | 1.69 | 4.38 |
| PIM | −0.32 | −0.01 | 15.07 | 12.24 |
| SOM | 1.70 | 0.80 | 11.09 | 19.34 |
| ANX | 1.18 | 0.43 | 16.47 | 28.50 |
| ARD | 0.86 | 0.40 | 19.91 | 28.27 |
| DEP | 1.24 | 0.42 | 14.28 | 27.38 |
| MAN | 0.52 | 0.43 | 23.01 | 25.34 |
| PAR | 0.64 | 0.54 | 18.45 | 24.86 |
| SCZ | 0.96 | 0.71 | 13.99 | 21.03 |
| BOR | 0.79 | 0.21 | 18.03 | 31.39 |
| ANT | 1.18 | 0.72 | 13.16 | 18.88 |
| ALC | 1.83 | 0.87 | 4.83 | 10.44 |
| DRG | 1.95 | 1.01 | 4.09 | 8.62 |
| AGG | 0.86 | 0.60 | 8.42 | 19.69 |
| SUI | 2.52 | 1.13 | 4.86 | 9.09 |
| STR | 1.18 | 0.12 | 5.80 | 11.91 |
| NON | 1.09 | 0.48 | 4.90 | 8.44 |
| RXR | −0.41 | 0.41 | 13.76 | 9.10 |
| DOM | −0.01 | −0.27 | 20.60 | 19.41 |
| WRM | −0.21 | −0.29 | 23.48 | 21.16 |

a clinical trait (i.e., psychopathology) may be somehow qualitatively different from normals, whereas individuals with an "abnormal amount" of a normative personality trait are quantitatively distinct; there is a difference of degree rather than kind.

The PAI was designed to be used with clinical populations, and as such many of the scales it includes would be considered to provide an assessment of psychopathological rather than normative personality constructs under this criterion. Support for this conclusion may be found in comparison the distributions of the PAI scales in community and clinical populations, as shown in Table 18.1. Most of the PAI scales and subscales demonstrate a pronounced positive skew in a community sample, with some (e.g., SUI, DRG) being quite skewed and as such meet this criterion as abnormal or pathological personality characteristics. Furthermore, for most of the PAI scales, the distributions in clinical samples are more nearly Gaussian, as would be expected of a measure of a construct representing abnormality. For example, the distribution of the DEP scale is far more skewed in the community sample than in the clinical sample, suggesting that according to this criterion, depression qualifies as an abnormal facet of an individual's functioning.

However, some scales, in particular the interpersonal scales, demonstrate distributions that are quite similar in both community and clinical samples and are nearly normal. Furthermore, some of the clinical scales demonstrate rather small distributional differences across populations; for example, MAN and PAR have fairly similar skewness values in the two populations. These results suggest that there are important elements of normal personality measured by these two constructs, perhaps self-esteem and interpersonal wariness, respectively.

The PAI includes scales designed to provide an assessment of "personality disorder" concepts, conceptually represented in the *DSM* manual as being extreme manifestations of normal personality traits. The PAI scales for BOR and ANT are direct measures for antisocial personality disorder and borderline personality disorder. However, it is interesting to note that there are substantial skewness differences between populations for the BOR and ANT scales, suggesting that by this definition these are measures of abnormal aspects of functioning rather than of normative personality traits. This implies that the instantiation of these constructs on the PAI more resembles a psychopathological construct than an extreme manifestation of normal personality traits.

However, there are indications suggesting that other *DSM* personality disorder constructs may indeed reflect extremes of normal variation, if this criterion is applied to PAI data. For example, relationships between DOM and WRM dimensions of personality and personality disorders have been frequently identified (DeJong, van den Brink, Jansen, & Schippers, 1989; Morey, 1985; Wiggins, 1987), with the results obtained using the two PAI scales being quite similar to those found in previous research (Morey, 1991). Dependent and avoidant personality disorders were found to be negatively related to DOM and narcissistic personality disorder was positively related to DOM. Avoidant, schizotypal, and schizoid personalities are negatively associated with WRM. Histrionic personality is positively associated with both the WRM and DOM scales, with stronger associations with WRM. These consistent patterns of associations do support the conclusion that some of the personality disorder diagnoses included in the DSM may indeed be manifestations of extreme degrees of normative personality traits.

Morey, Warner, and Boggs (2002) have applied this criterion to the issue of gender bias in personality disorder diagnoses. If, by the logic of criterion 1, the distribution of personality disorder criteria approached normality in a distribution of nonclinical males or females, that criterion may be pathologizing normative, gender-specific behavior. This study indicated that this was not the case, and that personality disorder indicators are, on the whole, largely indicators of abnormal personality functioning rather than more normal, gender-linked behaviors.

In summary, the criterion of distributional differences suggests that the preponderance of PAI scales would be considered to measure abnormal or psychopathological personality traits. However, this criterion also indicates that various aspects of personality constructs that are more normative in nature are assessed by certain PAI scales, particularly by the interpersonal scales.

*Criterion 2. Normal and abnormal personality constructs differ dramatically in their social desirability.*

Assessment investigators have long recognized that self-report personality tests can be vulnerable to efforts at impression management. In particular, much concern has been expressed about the influence of efforts to respond in a socially desirable fashion on such tests. Various diverse and creative efforts have been directed at resolving this dilemma, including the empirical keying strategy behind the development of the original MMPI, the subsequent use of the "k-correction", and the forced choice matched item alternatives employed in the Edwards Personal Preference Schedule (Edwards, 1959). However, for self-report tests that focus on abnormal constructs, these strategies tend not to work very well. It is suggested that the reason for these problems is that abnormal constructs are inherently socially undesirable. As such, most measures of social desirability responding will correlate quite highly with measures of abnormal constructs. In contrast, the social desirability of normative personality features is more ambiguous, less evaluative, and more likely to be tied to a specific context. For example, the trait adjective "talkative" might be a socially desirable characteristic in a salesperson but not in a librarian. There is likely to be little consensus among people as to whether being talkative is a desirable or undesirable characteristic, whereas characteristics, such as "depressed" or "delusional" will invariably be viewed consensually as undesirable.

This implies that the social desirability of a construct may be useful as an indicator of its status in capturing normal or abnormal variation between people. The desirability of the construct may be measured in many ways; for example, correlations with social desirability scales can yield an estimate of the desirability loading of a measure of some construct. Another means to assess the desirability of a construct measured by a particular scale is to gauge the impact that efforts at impression management have upon scale scores. Each of these techniques was used in the development of the PAI, and the results of those studies suggested that these two desirability metrics are related although not identical. In these studies, two desirability metrics were examined: (a) intercorrelation with a short form of the Marlowe-Crowne Social Desirability Scale (Reynolds, 1982); and (b) the F value from a one way analysis of variance comparing mean scales scores under positive impression, negative impression, and standard instructional sets (Morey, 1991). Some scales (such as DOM, and MAN-G) demonstrated little correlation with the Marlowe-Crowne and also little effect of impression management, while others (such as PAR-P and SCZ-T) showed the opposite pattern, suggesting that features of persecutory beliefs and thought disorder have strong desirability connotations.

As was the case with the criterion of distributional differences, the use of social desirability to distinguish normal from abnormal constructs suggests that the preponderance of PAI scales appear to measure the latter. The majority of PAI scales demonstrate significant negative associations with social desirability measures and substantial effects of impression management instructional sets. Once again, however, this criterion also indicates that more normative aspects of personality are assessed as well, and again the interpersonal scales (particularly the DOM scale) appear as the strongest candidates as measures of normal personality traits by this criterion.

*Criterion 3. Scores on measures of abnormal personality constructs differ dramatically between clinical and community samples, whereas scores of normal constructs do not.*

This criterion is based on the assumption that, in dealing with an abnormal personality construct, "more" is worse; that is, the more of the construct a person has, the greater the impairment the person manifests and the more likely the person is to come to the attention of mental health professionals. For example, when considering disordered thinking as a personal characteristic, greater amounts of thought disorder will be associated with greater impairment and need for intervention. Thus, a clinical population should invariably obtain higher scores on measures of such constructs than a community sample. In contrast, for a normative personality trait, the adaptive direction of scores is less clear-cut. Given the assumption that such traits are normally distributed, then the traits are inherently bipolar, and extreme scores at either end of the trait may be maladaptive. Thus, even if clinical samples were restricted to persons with problems on a particular normative trait (e.g., extreme scores on Introversion–Extraversion), there would still be no reason to suspect mean differences between clinical and community subjects as the extreme scores of the clinical subjects at either end of the continuum would be expected to balance out.

Most of the PAI scales demonstrate much higher mean scores in a clinical sample, with the difference generally on the order of a standard deviation on many scales (means listed in Table 18.1; standard deviations are presented in Morey, 1991). Particularly large differences are noted on the DEP and BOR scales, which have emerged on other criteria as noteworthy candidates for "abnormal" personality constructs. Once again, however, there are certain scales that demonstrate negligible mean differences between populations. For example, both of the interpersonal scales, as well as the MAN scale, again seem to show little overall difference between community and clinical samples. These results point to the likelihood that these measures most heavily tap what may be considered to be normative personality traits.

*Criterion 4. Measures of normative personality traits should demonstrate factorial/ correlational invariance across clinical and community samples, while measures of abnormal traits may not.*

The basic assumption behind this criterion is that the correlation pattern that gives abnormal constructs their syndromal coherence should only emerge in samples where there is adequate representation of individuals manifesting the syndrome (i.e., clinical samples). In community samples, which may include relatively few individuals who have a clinical syndrome, the association between features of the same syndrome may be no greater than that between any two features selected randomly. As an example, if depression were defined by five necessary and sufficient criteria, and these five criteria were intercorrelated in a community sample that contained no depressed subjects, the average correlation between these features might well be zero. In a sample of nonde-pressed individuals, sleep problems and low self-esteem may only be associated at chance levels since individuals who share the putative causal process that underlies the clinical association of these features have been removed from the sample. It is the covariation of these features in individuals considered to be depressed that lends a correlation pattern to these features. Thus, highly intercorrelated sets of features (i.e., syndromes) might emerge from a factor analysis of clinical subjects that would not be identified in a sample of subjects selected from the community.

In contrast, those traits that describe normal variation in personality would be expected to capture this variability among clinical as well as normal subjects. Even though the clinical subjects may be, as a group, more extreme on normal personality traits, similar correlational patterns among elements of the trait should be obtained. For example, the construct of extraversion/introversion should identify meaningful differences among clinical subjects as well as normal subjects, and the intercorrelation of the behaviors that make up this construct should be similar in the two populations. This should yield predictable empirical results with respect to the factor structure (for multifaceted scales/constructs) and the average item intercorrelation (i.e., coefficient alpha, for unidimensional constructs); for a normative trait, these results should be similar in clinical and nonclinical samples. In contrast, these values may well differ if an abnormal construct is being examined.

The most ambitious examination of this assumption to date was conducted by O'Connor (2002), who conducted a statistical review of data from 37 personality and psychopathology inventories to determine whether there were dimensional structure differences between clinical and nonclinical respondents. O'Conner tested correlation and factor-loading matrices from a variety of multiscale inventories and from specialized measures (both clinical and nonclinical in nature) for structural invariance across the two populations. There was considerable evidence for similarity between normal and abnormal populations both in the number of factors that exist in the data matrices and in the factor patterns. Consistent with this conclusion, factor analyses of the PAI in clinical and community samples yield factor structures that are quite similar (Morey, 1991). In both samples, the first factor appears to involve negative affect, and the second factor impulsivity and poor judgment. The third factor, which emerges primarily in clinical samples rather than community samples, appears to involve egocentricity, callousness, and exploitativeness, once again suggesting that the construct of antisocial personality is better described as an abnormal construct rather than as an extreme of normal variation. The fourth and final factor was quite different in the two samples; in the clinical sample, it appeared related to profile validity, while in the community sample it involved interpersonal sensitivity and detachment. This latter factor may again reflect a normal personality trait which, when extreme, may be maladaptive in either high (undue caution, paranoia) or low (dependency, gullibility) degree.

# Summary

This chapter has presented four criteria for distinguishing between normal and pathological aspects of personality, and has demonstrated how the PAI illustrates empirical differences between the two types of constructs. The PAI was developed to provide assessments of constructs that for the most part would be considered in the abnormal spectrum. However, according to the criteria described above, the test includes many scales that are related to constructs which show considerable variation even within the general population. In part, this may be due to the assumption of inherent dimensionality of all clinical constructs that was the foundation of the development of the instrument; despite the positive skew of most scales, the scales were constructed to have a relatively "soft floor" so that meaningful variation could be captured, even within the normal range. Nonetheless, with the exception of the interpersonal scales, the PAI was designed to ascertain abnormality, not to capture the possible variants of normality. As noted, the four criteria discussed above suggest strongly that the PAI is heavily slanted in that direction. To provide a thorough evaluation of both domains of interest, the PAI is probably best used in conjunction with an instrument designed specifically for the assessment of normative personality traits.

## REFERENCES

Alterman, A. I., Zaballero, A. R., Lin, M. M., Siddiqui, N., Brown, L.S., Rutherford, M.J., & McDermott, P.A.l. (1995). Personality Assessment Inventory (PAI) scores of lower-socioeconomic African American and Latino methadone maintenance patients. *Assessment, 2*, 91–100.

American Psychiatric Association. (2000). *Diagnostic and statistical manual of mental disorders* (4th ed., text-revised). Washington, DC: Author.

Ban, T. A., Fjetland, O. K., Kutcher, M., & Morey, L. C. (1993). CODE-DD: Development of a diagnostic scale for depressive disorders. In I. Hindmarch, & P. Stonier (Eds.), *Human psychopharmacology: Measures and methods*. Chichester, UK: Wiley. (Vol. 4, pp. 73–85).

Beck, A. T., & Steer, R. A. (1987). *Beck Depression Inventory manual*. San Antonio, TX: The Psychological Corporation.

Beck, A. T., & Steer, R. A. (1988). *Beck Hopelessness Scale manual*. San Antonio: The Psychological Corporation.

Bell, M. J., Billington, R., & Becker, B. (1985). A scale for the assessment of object relations: Reliability, validity, and factorial invariance. *Journal of Clinical Psychology, 42*, 733–741.

Bell-Pringle, V. J., Pate, J. L., & Brown, R. C. (1997). Assessment of borderline personality disorder using the MMPI-2 and the Personality Assessment Inventory. *Assessment, 4*, 131–139.

Belter, R. W., & Piotrowski, C. (2001). Current status of doctoral-level training in psychological testing. *Journal of Clinical Psychology, 57*, 717–726.

Boccaccini, M.T. & Brodsky, S.L. (1999). Diagnostic test usage by forensic psychologists in emotional injury cases. *Professional Psychology: Research and Practice, 30*, 253–259.

Boyle, G. J., & Lennon, T. (1994). Examination of the reliability and validity of the Personality Assessment Inventory. *Journal of Psychopathology & Behavioral Assessment, 16*(3), 173–187.

Calhoun, P. S., Earnst, K. S., Tucker, D. D., Kirby, A. C., & Beckham, J. C. (2000). Feigning combat-related posttraumatic stress disorder on the Personality Assessment Inventory. *Journal of Personality Assessment, 75*(2), 338–350.

Caperton, J. D., Edens, J. F., & Johnson, J. K. (2004). Predicting Sex Offender Institutional Adjustment and Treatment Compliance Using the Personality Assessment Inventory. *Psychological Assessment, 16*, 187–191.

Cashel, M. L., Rogers, R., Sewell, K., & Martin-Cannici, C. (1995). The Personality Assessment Inventory (PAI) and the detection of defensiveness. *Assessment, 2*(4), 333–342.

Cherepon, J. A., & Prinzhorn, B. (1994). Personality Assessment Inventory (PAI) profiles of adult female abuse survivors. *Assessment, 1*(4), 393–399.

Clarkin, J. F., Hull, J. W., Yeomans, F., Kakuma, T. & Cantor, J. (1994). Antisocial traits as modifiers of treatment response in borderline inpatients. *Journal of Psychotherapy Practice & Research, 3*(4), 307–312.

Costa, P. T., & McCrae, R. R. (1992). Normal personality in clinical practice: The NEO Personality Inventory. *Psychological Assessment, 4*, 5–13.

Cull, J. G., & Gill, W. S. (1982). *Suicide Probability Scale manual*. Los Angeles, CA: Western Psychological Services.

DeJong, C. A., Van den Brink, W., Jansen, J. A., & Schippers, G. M. (1989). Interpersonal aspects of DSM-III Axis II: Theoretical hypotheses and empirical findings. *Journal of Personality Disorders, 3*, 135–146.

Douglas, K. S., Hart, S. D., & Kropp, P. R. (2001). Validity of the Personality Assessment Inventory for forensic assessments. *International Journal of Offender Therapy & Comparative Criminology, l, (45)*, 183–197.

Duellman, R. M., & Bower, T. G. (2004). Use of the Personality Assessment Inventory in forensic and correctional settings: Evidence for concurrent validity. *International Journal of Forensic Psychology, 1*, 42–57.

Edens, J. F., Cruise, K. R., & Buffington-Vollum, J. K. (2001). Forensic and correctional applications of the Personality Assessment Inventory. *Behavioral Sciences & the Law, 19 *, 519–543.

Edens, J. F., Hart, S. D., Johnson, D. W., Johnson, J. K., & Olver, M. E. (2000). Use of the Personality Assessment Inventory to assess psychopathy in offender populations. *Psychological Assessment, 12*, 132–139.

Edwards, A. L. (1959). *Edwards personal preference schedule*. New York: Psychological Corporation.

Evershed, S., Tennant, A., Boomer, D., Rees, A., Barkham, M., & Watson, A. (2003). Practice-based outcomes of dialectical behaviour therapy (DBT) targeting anger and violence, with male forensic patients: A pragmatic and non-contemporaneous comparison. *Criminal Behaviour & Mental Health, 13*, 198–213.

Fals-Stewart, W. (1996). The ability of individuals with psychoactive substance use disorders to escape detection by the Personality Assessment Inventory. *Psychological Assessment, 8*(1), 60–68.

Foulds, G. A. (1971). Personality deviance and personal symptomatology. *Psychological Medicine, 1*, 222–233.

Gaies, L. A. (1993). Malingering of depression on the Personality Assessment Inventory. (Doctoral dissertation, University of South Florida, 1993). *Dissertation Abstracts International, 55*, 6711.

George, J. M., & Wagner, E. (1995). Correlations between the Hand Test Pathology score and Personality Assessment Inventory scales for pain clinic patients. *Perceptual & Motor Skills, 80*(3, Pt 2), 1377–1378.

Greenstein, D. S. (1993). Relationship between frequent nightmares, psychopathology, and boundaries among incarcerated male inmates. Unpublished doctoral dissertation, Adler School of Professional Psychology, Chicago IL.

Hamilton, M. (1960). A rating scale for depression. *Journal of Neurology, Neurosurgery, and Psychiatry, 23*, 56–62.

Hare, R. D. (1985). Comparison of procedures for the assessment of psychopathy. *Journal of Consulting and Clinical Psychology, 53*, 7–16.

Hart, S. D., Cox, D. N., & Hare, R. D. (1995). *Psychopathy checklist: Screening version*. Toronto, Ontario, Canada: Multi-Health Systems.

Hathaway, S. R., & McKinley, J. C. (1967). *MMPI manual* (revised edition). New York: Psychological Corporation.

Holden, R. R. (1989). Disguise and the structured self-report assessment of psychopathology: II. A clinical replication. *Journal of Clinical Psychology, 45*(4), 583–586.

Holden, R. R., & Fekken, G. C. (1990). Structured psychopathological test item characteristics and validity. *Psychological Assessment, 2*(1), 35–40.

Holmes, T. H., & Rahe, R. H. (1967). The social readjustment rating scale. *Journal of Psychosomatic Research, 11*, 213–218.

Holmes, G. E., Williams, C. L., & Haines, J. (2001). Motor vehicle accident trauma exposure: Personality profiles associated with posttraumatic diagnoses. *Anxiety, Stress & Coping: An International Journal, 14*(3), 301–313.

Jackson, D. N. (1970). A sequential system for personality scale development. In C. D. Spielberger (Ed.), *Current topics in clinical and community psychology* (Vol. 2, pp. 62–97). New York: Academic Press.

Kellogg, S. H., Ho, A., Bell, K., Schluger, R. P., McHugh, P. F., McClary, K. A., & Kreek, M. J. (2002). The Personality Assessment Inventory Drug Problems Scale: A validity analysis. *Journal of Personality Assessment, 79*(1), 73–84.

Kurtz, J. E., & Morey, L. C. (2001). Use of structured self-report assessment to diagnose borderline personality disorder during major depressive episodes. *Assessment, 8*(3), 291–300.

Kurtz, J. E., Morey, L. C., & Tomarken, A. J. (1993). The concurrent validity of three self-report measures of borderline personality. *Journal of Psychopathology and Behavioral Assessment, 15*, 255–266.

Lally, S. J. (2003). What tests are acceptable for use in forensic evaluations? A survey of experts. *Professional Psychology Research and Practice, 34*, 491–498.

Liljequist, L., Kinder, B. N., & Schinka, J. A. An investigation of malingering posttraumatic stress disorder on the Personality Assessment Inventory. *Journal of Personality Assessment, 71*, 322–336.

Loevinger, J. (1957). Objective tests as instruments of psychological theory. *Psychological Reports, 3*, 635–694.

Loranger, A. W. (1988). Personality Disorders Examination Manual. Yonkers, NY: DV Communications.

Montag, I., & Levin, J. (1994). The Five Factor Model and psychopathology in nonclinical samples. *Personality & Individual Differences, 17*, 1–7.

Morey, L. C. (1985). An empirical comparison of interpersonal and DSM-III approaches to classification of personality disorders. *Psychiatry, 48*, 358–364.

Morey, L. C. (1991). *The Personality Assessment Inventory Professional manual.* Odessa, FL: Psychological Assessment Resources.

Morey, L. C. (1995). Critical issues in construct validation: Comment on Boyle and Lennon (1994). *Journal of Psychopathology & Behavioral Assessment, 17*, 393–401.

Morey, L. C. (1996). *An Interpretive Guide to the Personality Assessment Inventory.* Odessa, FL: Psychological Assessment Resources, Inc.

Morey, L. C. (2003). *Essentials of PAI assessment.* Hoboken, NJ: Wiley.

Morey, L. C., & Hopwood, C. J. (2004). Efficiency of a Strategy for Detecting Back Random Responding on the Personality Assessment Inventory. *Psychological Assessment, 16*, 197–200.

Morey, L. C., & Lanier, V. W. (1998). Operating characteristics of six response distortion indicators for the Personality Assessment Inventory. *Assessment, 5*, 203–214.

Morey, L. C., Warner, M. G., & Boggs, C. D. (2002). Gender bias in the personality disorders criteria: An investigation of five bias indicators. *Journal of Psychopathology and Behavioral Assessment, 24*, 55–65.

Morey, L. C., Waugh, M. H., & Blashfield, R. K. (1985). MMPI scales for DSM-III personality disorders: Their derivation and correlates. *Journal of Personality Assessment, 49*, 245–251.

O'Connor, B. P. (2002). The search for dimensional structure differences between normality and abnormality: A statistical review of published data on personality and psychopathology. *Journal of Personality & Social Psychology, 83*, 962–982.

Parker, J. D., Daleiden, E. L., & Simpson, C. A. (1999). Personality assessment inventory substance-use scales: Convergent and discriminant relations with the Addiction Severity Index in a residential chemical dependence treatment setting. *Psychological Assessment, 11*, 507–513.

Peebles, J., & Moore, R. J. (1998). Detecting socially desirable responding with the Personality Assessment Inventory: The Positive Impression Management Scale and the Defensiveness Index. *Journal of Clinical Psychology, 54*, 621–628.

Peterson, G. W., Clark, D. A., & Bennett, B. (1989). The utility of MMPI subtle, obvious scales for detecting fake good and fake bad response sets. *Journal of Clinical Psychology, 45*, 575–583.

Piotrowski, C. (2000). How popular is the Personality Assessment Inventory in practice and training? *Psychological Reports, 86*, 65–66.

Piotrowski, C., & Belter, R. W. (1999). Internship training in psychological assessment: Has managed care had an impact? *Assessment, 6*, 381–385.

Procidano, M. E., & Heller, K. (1983). Measures of perceived social support from friends and from family: Three validation studies. *American Journal of Community Psychology, 11*, 1–24.

Reynolds, W. M. (1982). Development of reliable and valid short forms of the Marlowe-Crowne Social Desirability Scale. *Journal of Clinical Psychology, 38*, 119–125.

Rogers, R., Flores, J., Ustad, K., & Sewell, K. W. (1995). Initial validation of the Personality Assessment Inventory—Spanish version with clients from Mexican American communities. *Journal of Personality Assessment, 64*, 340–348.

Rogers, R., Ornduff, S. R., & Sewell, K. (1993). Feigning specific disorders: A study of the Personality Assessment Inventory (PAI). *Journal of Personality Disorders, 60*, 554–561.

Rogers, R., Sewell, K. W., Morey, L. C., & Ustad, K. L. (1996). Detection of feigned mental disorders on the Personality Assessment Inventory: A discriminant analysis. *Journal of Personality Assessment, 67*, 629–640.

Rogers, R., Sewell, K. W., Ustad, K., Reinhardt, V. & Edwards, W. (1995). The Referral Decision Scale with mentally disorder inmates: A preliminary study of convergent and discriminant validity. *Law & Human Behavior, 19*, 481–492.

Rogers, R., Ustad, K. L., & Salekin, R. T. (1998). Convergent validity of the Personality Assessment Inventory: A study of emergency referrals in a correctional setting. *Assessment, 5*, 3–12.

Ruiz, M. A., Dickinson, K. A., & Pincus, A. L. (2002). Concurrent validity of the Personality Assessment Inventory Alcohol Problems (ALC) Scale in a college student sample. *Assessment, 9*, 261–270.

Salekin, R. T., Rogers, R., & Sewell, K. W. (1997). Construct validity of psychopathy in a female offender sample: A multitrait-multimethod evaluation. *Journal of Abnormal Psychology, 106*, 576–585.

Salekin, R. T., Rogers, R., Ustad, K. L., & Sewell, K. W. (1998). Psychopathy and recidivism among female inmates. *Law and Human Behavior, 22*, 109–128.

Schinka, J. A. (1995). PAI profiles in alcohol-dependent patients. *Journal of Personality Assessment, 65,* 35–51.

Schinka, J. A., & Borum, R. (1993). Readability of adult psychopathology inventories. *Psychological Assessment, 5,* 384–386.

Scragg, P., Bor, R, & Mendham, M. C. (2000). Feigning post-traumatic stress disorder on the PAI. *Clinical Psychology and Psychotherapy, 7,* 155–160.

Selzer, M. L. (1971). The Michigan Alcoholism Screening Test: The quest for a new diagnostic instrument. *American Journal of Psychiatry, 127,* 1653–1658.

Spielberger, C. D. (1983). *Manual for the State-Trait Anxiety Inventory.* Palo Alto, CA: Consulting Psychologists Press.

Spielberger, C. D. (1988). *State-Trait Anger Expression Inventory.* Odessa, FL: Psychological Assessment Resources.

Tasca, G. A., Wood, J., Demidenko, N., & Bissada, H. (2002). Using the PAI with an eating disordered population: Scale characteristics, factor structure and differences among diagnostic groups. *Journal of Personality Assessment, 79,* 337–356.

Trapnell, P. D., & Wiggins, J. S. (1990). Extension of the Interpersonal Adjective Scale to include the big five dimensions of personality. *Journal of Personality and Social Psychology, 59,* 781–790.

Trull, T. J. (1995). Borderline personality disorder features in nonclinical young adults: I. Identification and validation. *Psychological Assessment, 7,* 33–41.

Trull, T. J., Useda, J. D., Conforti, K., & Doan, B. T. (1997). Borderline personality features in nonclinical young adults: Two year outcome. *Journal of Abnormal Psychology, 106,* 307–314.

Wang, E. W., & Diamond, P. M. (1999). Empirically identifying factors related to violence risk in corrections. *Behavioral Sciences & the Law, 17,* 377–389.

Wang, E. W., Rogers, R., Giles, C. L., Diamond, P. M., Herrington-Wang, L. E., & Taylor, E. R. (1997). A pilot study of the Personality Assessment Inventory (PAI) in corrections: Assessment of malingering, suicide risk, and aggression in male inmates. *Behavioral Sciences & the Law, 15,* 469–482.

Wiggins, J. S. (1966). Substantive dimensions of self-report in the MMPI item pool. *Psychological Monographs, 80,* 22 (whole no. 630).

Wiggins, J. S. (1987, August). *How interpersonal are the MMPI personality disorder scales?* Paper presented at the meeting of the American Psychological Association, New York.

Yeomans, F. E., Hull, J. W., & Clarkin, J. C. (1994). Risk factors for self-damaging acts in a borderline population. *Journal of Personality Disorders, 8,* 10–16.

# Rorschach Assessment of Normal and Abnormal Personality

Ronald J. Ganellen

The Rorschach Ink-blot Test is one of the most widely used and researched measures of personality and psychological functioning. Surveys of the frequency with which specific tests are used in applied clinical settings have consistently shown that the MMPI-2 (Butcher, Dahlstrom, Graham, Tellegen, & Kaemmer, 1989) and Rorschach (Exner, 2003) are the two most commonly used measures of personality and emotional functioning (Archer, Maruish, Imhof, & Piotrowski, 1991; Archer & Newsom, 2000; Groth-Marnat, 1997; Lubin, Larsen, Matarazzo, & Seever, 1985; Piotrowski & Zalewski, 1993; Watkins, 1991; Watkins, Campbell, Nieberding, & Hallmark, 1995). Vigorous interest in studying these tests' conceptual underpinnings, psychometric properties, and clinical utility is reflected in the large and still growing theoretical and empirical literature concerning these tests. For instance, Butcher and Rouse (1996) found that the most frequently researched psychological assessment measures in adults were the MMPI and Rorschach; between 1974 and 1994, 4,452 articles were published investigating the MMPI, whereas 1,969 articles were published investigating the Rorschach.

The Rorschach provides a method of assessing the psychological characteristics, traits, and processes underlying enduring patterns of thinking, behavior, emotional responses, self-responses, and interpersonal functioning in clinical and nonclinical groups that differs from the methods used by self-report personality measures, such as the MMPI-2. Unlike self-report measures, which assess personality by asking an individual to describe himself or herself, the Rorschach assesses personality characteristics based on their responses to a standard series of images. This approach to personality assessment, which has been labeled a performance-based method by some authors, provides a sample of how the individual organizes, perceives, and interprets stimuli. Responses to the Rorschach are the end product of a complex, cognitive–perceptual problem–solving process. Whereas self-report methods provide information based on how an individual *describes* himself or herself, Rorschach findings are based on the individual's *behavior* in the testing situation. In other words, self-report methods provide information based on what a person *says*, while performance methods provide information based on what a person *does*.

Current procedures for administering, coding, and interpreting responses to the Rorschach have evolved considerably since Hermann Rorschach first introduced this method for use in studying psychopathology and personality in 1921. Rorschach, a psychiatrist, was not the first to use inkblots as stimulus figure. In fact, other early pioneers in the field of psychological assessment, such as Binet and Henri (1895, 1896), considered using inkblots to assess an ability they conceptualized as "visual imagination" as part of a test of intelligence, but abandoned this approach as it was not practical for group administration.

Rorschach (1921) developed a set of inkblots which he administered to 188 schizophrenic patients being treated at a psychiatric institution and to 117 nonpatients. Initially, he was interested in using the inkblots as a means of identifying schizophrenics. While he found the inkblot method was useful for diagnostic purposes, he also observed that certain kinds of responses were related to distinctive psychological and behavioral characteristics. Rorschach recognized there was a potential to use the inkblot method to classify individuals in terms of the nature of psychopathology, on the one hand, and to identify certain psychological features, personality traits, or behaviors, on the other.

Since Rorschach's untimely death in 1922 at the age of 37, a number of approaches to administering, scoring, and interpreting the inkblots were developed (Exner, 1969). These systems differed in a number of important respects. Variations in use of the inkblot method included different scores and different emphases on the extent to which the content of responses were interpreted for their symbolic or dynamic meanings as opposed to which specific features of the inkblots were articulated, such as referring to colors or movement. The Rorschach method most widely used in contemporary practice was developed and refined by Exner (2003) who attempted to integrate the systems developed by his predecessors to establish a standardized set of administration procedures, a standardized set of rules for coding responses, and objective, empirically based guidelines for interpretation of scores. One goal of Exner's work has been to develop standardized, objective procedures that would meet accepted standards for inter-rater reliability and criterion-related validity.

The history of the development of the inkblot test and the method it employs to assess psychological functioning have several implications. First, it should be noted that the Rorschach test was not developed in accordance with a specific theory of personality or psychopathology. Historically, in the USA the Rorschach was initially embraced and championed by psychologists with a psychoanalytic orientation. While psychoanalytically oriented psychologists may view Rorschach data as providing rich material about an individual's dynamics, the method is not inherently wedded to a psychodynamic conceptualization of psychological functioning or, for that matter, to any one theoretical model. The clinician using Rorschach data may opt to formulate findings within the framework of any theory of personality and psychopathology. Exner has attempted to ground Rorschach theory, interpretation, and application on a bedrock of empirical research, rather than any particular theory of personality and psychopathology.

As Rorschach coding and interpretation methods were not developed to operationalize specific dimensions of psychological functioning central to any theoretical model, Rorschach findings may not fully capture certain dimensions relevant to some theories. For instance, while the psychological constructs assessed by the Rorschach may overlap with constructs identified in particular theories, such as the Five-Factor Model (Costa & Widiger, 2002), one would not expect Rorschach data to adequately measure all of these constructs. Conversely, one might expect the Rorschach to provide meaningful information about other dimensions of psychological functioning not contained in a specific theory.

# Symptoms, Diagnoses, and the Rorschach

It is important for clinicians using the Rorschach to recognize which psychological constructs the Rorschach measures in a valid, reliable manner (discussed in more detail later in this chapter in the section titled "Dimensions of Personality Functioning Assessed by the Rorschach") and which it does not. Given how data is collected using the Rorschach inkblot method, the Rorschach may yield information about some personality characteristics, behaviors, or symptoms reported by an individual, but not others. As a performance-based measure which assesses how an individual responds to and perceives standard test stimuli, the Rorschach does not directly inquire about particular problems, specific thoughts, or emotions an individual currently experiences nor does it provide detailed data about an individual's history. For example, the Rorschach does not directly ask about a history of alcohol abuse; the amount typically consumed when drinking; the period of time over which an individual has abused alcohol; or whether the individual has ever had a blackout, DUI, or lost a job because of drinking. In contrast, assessment using a self-report inventory or diagnostic interview can address these specific areas. Similarly, the Rorschach does not directly ask whether a person has been the victim of sexual abuse at any time in his or her life. As a general principle, therefore, one should not expect the Rorschach to provide information about particular behaviors, thoughts, emotions, or historical experiences unless they are related to specific Rorschach variables.

This point is relevant when considering the position taken by some commentators who criticized the Rorschach on the grounds that it does not identify a past history of child sexual abuse (Lohr, Fowler, & Lilienfeld, 2002). As discussed above, Rorschach variables are not linked to specific historical experiences, such as a history of sexual abuse. Since sexual abuse is not a construct directly measured by the Rorschach, there is no reason to expect the Rorschach to flag victims of sexual abuse. Thus, the fact that the Rorschach does not identify a past history of sexual abuse has no bearing on the Rorschach's criterion-related validity. As will be discussed below, substantial evidence exists demonstrating that the Rorschach's construct validity is quite respectable for a number of dimensions of personality functioning.

Recognizing how the Rorschach inkblot method obtains information about personality characteristics and psychological functioning is also important in conceptualizing the relationship between criteria used to make *Diagnostic and Statistical Manual of Mental Disorders* (*DSM-IV-TR*; American Psychiatric Association, 2000) diagnoses and Rorschach findings. Since the Rorschach does not directly inquire about specific symptoms, behaviors, thoughts, patterns of interpersonal functioning, or historical data, Rorschach data do not map neatly onto many *DSM-IV-TR* diagnostic criteria. For instance, Rorschach data do not bear directly on a history of recurrent episodes of binge eating followed by self-induced vomiting, a pattern seen in bulimia; a pervasive pattern of unlawful behavior and disregard for the rights of others, a history consistent with an antisocial personality disorder; or periods of time involving a decreased need for sleep, excessive energy, spending sprees, and sexual indiscretions, common manifestations of a bipolar disorder.

Although Rorschach variables may not provide information about specific symptoms, behaviors, or emotions, this does not mean that Rorschach findings are irrelevant when one goal of a psychological evaluation is to formulate a *DSM-IV-TR* diagnosis. There are Rorschach variables that are strongly associated with particular disorders, such as psychotic disorders. For example, evidence of illogical, disorganized thinking, and inaccurate perceptions of events on the Rorschach can provide important evidence of a psychotic disorder (Exner, 2003; Ganellen, 1996). Rorschach findings can also highlight important features of various other psychological disorders, such as patterns in an individual's thinking, feeling, and interacting with others characteristic of personality disorders (Huprich & Ganellen, 2005). The excessive emotionality associated with an histrionic personality disorder (Blais & Baity, 2005), the passivity and submissive orientation associated with a dependent personality disorder (Bornstein, 2005), and the self-doubt, fear of humiliation, and sense of isolation associated with an avoidant personality disorder (Ganellen, 2005) are all associated with specific Rorschach variables.

Even though there may not be a one-to-one correspondence between all *DSM-IV* criteria and Rorschach variables, Rorschach findings complement the information a clinician can obtain from a diagnostic interview or self-report inventory by identifying or highlighting certain difficulties as well as areas of competence. Perhaps more importantly, Rorschach data can help describe the unique features of an individual. Exner (2003), for instance, commented that "the greatest utility of the Rorschach is when an understanding of a person, *as an individual*, becomes important" (p. 4). This information may be particularly relevant for treatment planning when an understanding of an individual's strengths and weaknesses may be just as important as their *DSM-IV-TR* diagnosis. For example, the treatment needs of a patient with an Axis I diagnosis of major depression whose Rorschach reveals signs of narcissistic vulnerabilities may differ greatly from another depressed patient whose Rorschach shows they feel lonely and isolated from others and have trouble establishing and maintaining satisfying interpersonal relationships.

# Implicit and Explicit Measures of Personality

McClelland et al. (1989) distinguished between implicit and explicit methods of personality assessment. *Explicit* measures, such as self-report instruments, assess psychological characteristics and needs individuals recognize about themselves and which they can articulate. In contrast, by analyzing a representative sample of an individual's behavior during the assessment process, *implicit* or performance-based measures, such as the

Rorschach or Thematic Apperception Test (Morray, 1943), tap into automatic patterns of behavior and motivations individuals may not be aware of or may not be willing or able to verbalize. Although implicit or performance-based measures of personality may provide relatively limited information about the content of people's thoughts or the specific symptoms they experience, performance-based measures, such as the Rorschach, may be particularly revealing of an individual's underlying attitudes, coping styles, behavioral dispositions, and implicit motivations, even those about which they have little awareness.

McClelland, Koestner, and Weinberger (1989) suggested that because implicit measures assess underlying patterns of thinking, reacting, and behaving that individuals may not recognize in themselves or which may not be consciously represented and articulated, implicit measures may be less susceptible to conscious control or filtering than explicit measures. In other words, implicit measures are less likely to be skewed by self-presentational concerns than explicit measures. For this reason, implicit measures may provide meaningful information about important psychological functioning that may not otherwise be acknowledged because an individual is not aware of certain aspects of their psychological operations, has not consciously formulated or labeled certain aspects of their functioning, or is not willing to acknowledge what they do know (cf., Shedler, Mayman, & Manis, 1993).

One implicit Rorschach measure of dependency needs is the number of responses coded for Texture. The link between Texture responses and a sense of basic security and trust in others that affects one's comfort and willingness to become attached to others is not explicit. In nonclinical populations, women who are coping with the effects of marital separation or divorce produced an elevated number of Texture responses, suggesting that their reaction to the loss of a marital relationship contributed to a sense of emotional deprivation and increased needs for closeness (Exner, 1993). Similarly, children placed in foster care for the first time also produced an elevated number of Texture responses compared to their peers. This reflects their reaction to separation from or loss of one or both parents. Other studies found that children in foster care who had frequent moves from one placement to another produced significantly fewer Texture responses than their same-age peers who had lived with their parents since birth (Exner, 1993). These findings suggested the children in foster care did not have secure attachments and tended to back away from emotional involvement with others, most likely because they did not have consistent experiences of caretakers responding to their feelings and needs.

Another example of an implicit measure related to social functioning is the number of cooperative movement responses (COP) produced on the Rorschach. COP signals an interest in being involved with others and an expectation that interactions have the potential to be friendly, harmonious, and mutually satisfying. Note that even though the Rorschach does not directly inquire about social expectations or attitudes, the number of responses involving COP are related to social functioning. For example, Exner (1993) described a study of college freshman living in the same dormitory who rated one another on a number of dimensions. The college students who gave more than an average number of COP responses were five times more likely than others to be rated as being "the most fun to be with" or "the easiest to be around." As individuals who produce COP responses tend to have positive expectations concerning social interactions, their behavior is likely to be characterized as friendly, agreeable, and open to others and they are likely to be regarded positively by the people with whom they are involved.

Other studies investigating interpersonal dependency needs have found that scores obtained on explicit and implicit measures of dependency diverge in ways that are theoretically meaningful. Bornstein et al. (1993), for instance, compared male and female college students on a self-report measure of dependency and the Rorschach Oral Dependency Scale (ROD; Masling, Rabie, & Blondheim, 1967), an implicit measure of dependency based on responses to the Rorschach. Bornstein et al. (1993) hypothesized that since males are socialized to be strong, assertive, and independent, they are less likely to acknowledge dependent feelings and behaviors than women on objective, face valid measures. Consistent with this hypothesis, they found that although female college students consistently obtained higher scores than male college students when compared on self-report questionnaires assessing dependent traits, attitudes, and behaviors, male and female participants produced comparable scores on the ROD, an implicit measure of interpersonal dependency. They concluded that men and women have comparable underlying dependency needs, but that women are more willing than men to openly acknowledge these needs when asked directly about them using explicit measures of this construct.

As discussed previously, McClelland et al. (1989) suggested that individuals can more easily control the impression they create on explicit than implicit psychological measures. Bornstein, Rossner, Hill, and Stepanian (1994) investigated this proposition in a series of studies examining whether individuals could consciously skew results on the ROD and a self-report measure, the Interpersonal Dependency Inventory (IDI; Blatt, D'Afflitti, & Quinlan, 1976). They found that scores on the IDI but not the ROD changed in response to experimental manipulations, such as instructions to respond to the measures as a dependent person would or when told that dependent characteristics were negative or positive. For instance, some participants were told that dependent characteristics interfered with interpersonal relationships and one's ability to express emotions, while other participants were told that people who had more dependent characteristics had better relationships and were particularly good at reading other people. Consistent with predictions, scores on the IDI shifted in response to experimental manipulations, while scores on the ROD did not.

Bornstein et al. (1996) concluded that objective, explicit self-report measures of dependency are more susceptible to conscious manipulation than implicit dependency measures. This has the following implication: self-report measures can be quite effective when assessing psychological characteristics an individual recognizes and is willing to acknowledge. However, in other situations, such as when assessing traits or behaviors that are socially undesirable or which clash with an individual's self-image, an implicit test which has low face validity may be preferable to a test with high face validity. In the latter situation, implicit measures, such as the Rorschach, may be preferred as they are less likely to be consciously biased or distorted by self-presentational concerns or deliberate efforts to create a desired impression than self-report methods. The Rorschach should be viewed as a valuable assessment tool because the empirically derived information it provides complements material obtained through self-report measures or clinical interview or provides a means to access data that otherwise may not be readily available (Ganellen, 1996).

A study by Blais, Hilsenroth, Castelbury, Fowler, and Baity (2001) provides another example of how the Rorschach functions as an implicit measure of psychological characteristics related to specific personality disorders. Blais et al. (2001) examined relationships among select Rorschach and MMPI-2 variables and *DSM-IV-TR* Cluster B personality disorder criteria. They entered theoretically relevant MMPI-2 and Rorschach variables into hierarchical regression analyses predicting *DSM-IV-TR* criteria for anti-social, borderline, histrionic, and narcissistic personality disorders. They found that both MMPI-2 and Rorschach variables added incrementally to the prediction of borderline and narcissistic personality disorder criteria scores while Rorschach variables independently predicted diagnostic criteria for histrionic personality disorder. For instance, the Rorschach variable that predicted histrionic personality disorder (FC+CF+C) relates to emotional reactivity and expressiveness, a key component of this disorder, whereas the Rorschach variable that predicted narcissistic personality disorder, the number of Reflection responses, relates to an inflated sense of self-worth, need for affirmation from others, and a tendency to be more focused on oneself than others.

Consistent with the distinction drawn by McClelland et al. (1989), Blais et al. (2001) suggested that MMPI-2 scores tap material an individual is aware of and able to acknowledge, whereas Rorschach variables tap material that may be outside of his or her or awareness. It is interesting to note that Rorschach variables, such as the number of Reflection responses and the number of responses involving color, were related to narcissistic and histrionic personality disorder criteria, respectively. As discussed previously, these Rorschach variables do not directly assess specific behaviors, mood states, or symptoms, such as narcissistic self-absorption, inflated self-image, or emotional reactivity. Thus, the significant relationship between these Rorschach variables and diagnostic criteria was not found because these Rorschach variables are face valid, explicit measures of specific characteristics, experiences, or patterns of thinking and reacting an individual recognizes as being true for them. Instead, Rorschach variables presumably captured a dimension of personality functioning which the individual may not be aware applies to himself or herself or may not be able to articulate. These findings suggest that implicit measures can be used in a powerful manner to assess certain meaningful dimensions of psychological functioning.

Meyer and Archer (2001) have raised some intriguing issues concerning the relationship between Rorschach variables, overt behavior and internal experiences, which may refine the distinction between explicit and implicit personality measures. They observed that no Rorschach variables are direct measures of specific psychological constructs or personality dimensions. For example, although some Rorschach variables are related to self-esteem issues and others are related to mood disorders, the Rorschach does not assess these constructs explicitly by asking directly how a person perceives himself or herself, as a self-report self-esteem questionnaire might, or whether they feel sad, have decreased levels of energy, and have trouble concentrating, as a self-report depression inventory might. In other words, the Rorschach "gets at" these constructs implicitly by relying on variables which are not face valid or obvious, but which have been shown empirically to be related to specific criterion variables, such as negative self-perceptions or aspects of a mood disorder or personality disorder.

Meyer and Archer (2001) noted that while Rorschach variables in general can be considered implicit measures of criterion variables, certain Rorschach variables may be more closely related to observable behavior than others. For instance, Meyer and Archer (2001) observed that Rorschach signs of disorganized thought processes, illogical thinking, and distorted, unrealistic perceptions are likely to be manifested in psychotic symptoms. In contrast, the link between other Rorschach variables, such as Reflection responses, and overt behavior, such as a need to elicit affirmation of self-worth from others, may be less direct and obvious. Meyer and Archer suggest that although both sets of variables (e.g., thought processes and perception, on the one hand, and Reflection responses on the other) are implicit measures of psychological constructs, the strength of relationship between a Rorschach variable and an external criterion variable is likely to be stronger for those variables which are more directly linked to an external criterion variable than for those which are less clearly related to a criterion variable.

# Dimensions of Personality Functioning Assessed by the Rorschach

As described previously, based on investigations of both clinical and nonclinical groups, Rorschach variables have been related to different aspects of psychological functioning, including thought processes, emotions, self-perception, and the quality of interpersonal relationships. In clinical samples, investigators recognized that schizophrenic patients deviated markedly from nonclinical individuals on a number of Rorschach variables, while in nonpatient samples investigators have found Rorschach variables to be related to personality traits and characteristic patterns of behavior. For instance, Rorschach observed that individuals who produced a preponderance of responses coded for human movement have a strong tendency to turn to his or her inner life as a primary source of gratification rather than looking outward to external experiences.

Exner (1993) summarized findings from research, which examined relationships between Rorschach variables and extra–test criterion variables. A number of these studies involved nonclinical samples. This research provides evidence that the Rorschach can be used effectively to assess a range of personality characteristics for individuals with and without a history of psychological difficulties.

Based on the results of empirical findings and logical analyses, Exner (1993) grouped the Rorschach variables on the Structural Summary into seven major domains. These groupings are the product of a series of cluster analyses Exner conducted studying interrelationships among Rorschach variables. He identified seven clusters of intercorrelated, conceptually related variables that are linked with distinct aspects of psychological functioning. As noted above, these dimensions of psychological functioning are relevant for both clinical and nonclinical evaluations. As described by Exner (1993) and Weiner (2003), the seven clusters identified by this logical, empirical approach are related to the following dimensions of psychological functioning:

1 *Control and Stress Tolerance*: Variables in this cluster provide information about an individual's adaptive resources; that is, their capacity to respond to challenges and problems in his or her life. Individuals with adequate personal resources are able to initiate action to handle the demands of their current situation and maintain their psychological equilibrium when dealing with problems. In contrast, individuals with inadequate internal strength are likely to have difficulty figuring out how to respond when difficulties occur and tend to become disorganized and feel overwhelmed.

Variables in the Control and Stress Tolerance cluster also distinguish between two types of individuals identified as experiencing considerable distress at the time the Rorschach was administered. Some individuals have solid ego strength, but become overwhelmed when faced with a situation that involves unusually intense or uncommonly high levels of stress. Other individuals are chronically vulnerable to becoming disorganized and feeling upset when things do not go smoothly in their lives because they have not developed adequate personal resources to draw on to deal with problems.

One should not assume that inadequate resources or poor capacity to maintain one's emotional equilibrium occur only for patients with a psychiatric disorder. There is considerable variability in the capacity for control and stress tolerance in both clinical and nonclinical samples. Variables loading on this dimension provide information about specific aspects of coping style and an individual's potential to respond constructively to stressful situations.

2 *Affect*: These cluster variables provide information about an individual's emotional state, characteristic style of expressing emotions, and capacity to manage feelings effectively. Information from this cluster also shows whether people are able to modulate and control feelings, how they usually respond to the feelings of others, and how they handle emotionally charged situations. For instance, variables in the Affect cluster show whether an individual's reactions tend to be based on intuition and guided by emotions as opposed to being shaped by logical analysis. Other variables show whether an individual characteristically is comfortable with affect and expresses feelings naturally and spontaneously or tends to be constricted and prefers to withdraw from and avoid situations which are emotionally charged.

Differences in emotional responsivity, self-control, and style of expressing feelings are found among individuals with and without psychological difficulties. For instance, some individuals by nature are warm, expressive, and emotionally demonstrative, while others are calm and even-tempered. Rorschach data describe individual differences in emotional style and the capacity to modulate expressions of feelings, as well as the implications these findings have for interpersonal functioning and psychological adjustment.

3 *Information Processing*: This group of measures describes the approach people used as they responded to the set of standard inkblots. This manner of responding is presumed to describe not only how an individual approached the Rorschach, but also to show the processes people use more generally to learn about and make sense of their world. This includes the perceptual operations they typically use to focus on, take in, and organize available information. Some individuals, for instance, put so much effort into taking stock of all the data available to them and making sure they do not overlook any details that "they may not see the forest for the trees." Individuals whose style is overly cautious, meticulous, and perfectionistic may function well in situations that reward attention to detail, but may be less effective in situations that require rapid completion of tasks and the ability to make decisions quickly. In contrast, others are open to available information. They notice and take into account the most central pieces of information while also integrating small details. Still others tend to jump to conclusions and respond to events in a hasty, careless, if not reckless manner because they put little effort into collecting and taking stock of relevant information. Considerable variability exists in information processing styles in clinical and nonclinical populations.

4 *Cognitive Mediation*: Variables in the Cognitive Mediation cluster show how accurately an individual perceives events. Stated differently, this group of measures addresses the extent to which people see themselves, others, and situations in their lives in a reasonable, realistic manner that others can understand. The likelihood that an individual will have problems dealing with situations increases if their impressions of other people's actions are inaccurate or if their view of events are distorted and unrealistic.

Although serious distortions in perceptual accuracy occur frequently among patients with a psychotic disorder, problems in adjustment, poor judgment, or a tendency to act inappropriately are also likely to characterize the history of individuals without a psychological disorder if the way they gauge events and read other people's words, actions, and intentions are unrealistic and unreasonable. The implications of the variables in the Cognitive Medication cluster for positive adjustment in a nonclinical population was suggested by findings from a study which will be described in more detail below which found that higher levels of perceptual accuracy predicted success in military training among candidates for the Norwegian Navy's Special Forces (Hartman, Sunde, Kristensen, & Martinussen, 2003).

5 *Ideation*: The Rorschach yields information about an individual's characteristic patterns of thinking about their experiences, the information they are continuously acquiring about themselves, other people, and the world. The variables in the Ideation cluster have a bearing on the extent to which perceptions of events are organized and interpreted in a logical, coherent manner that others can readily understand. Whereas some people form reasonable, rational conclusions about what events mean, others arrive at conclusions in an arbitrary manner, force the facts to fit their preconceived notions in a rigid, inflexible fashion, or exhibit rambling, fragmented, irrational patterns of thinking.

As might be expected, more severe psychopathology is typically associated with Rorschach signs of bizarre, distorted, disjointed, unrealistic thinking. There is considerable variability in the aspects of thinking assessed by the Rorschach even in nonclinical populations. In some instances, variables in the Ideation cluster may show that an individual who generally functions effectively can think clearly and logically, but tends to become stubborn, inflexible, and argumentative when others offer a competing point of view. Findings on this cluster might suggest other well-functioning people's "take" on events tend to be colored by an apprehensive sense of mistrust. This may lead these individuals to emphasize the significance of information that confirms their anticipation they will be hurt or blindsided by others or to constantly scrutinize, appraise, and question others' motivations and intentions.

6 *Self-Perception*: Data in the Self-Perception cluster provides information about an individual's self-regard as well as their tendency to be focused on themselves. In terms of self-regard, these variables show whether a person's self-image tends to be realistically positive and whether he or she usually feels self-confident. Variables in this cluster can also highlight whether an individual tends to act as though they are the center around whom everything else revolves and to be preoccupied with themselves to such an extent they appear disinterested in or insensitive to the needs and feelings of others. Other variables in this cluster provide a gauge of an individual's capacity for introspection and self-awareness.

Available data indicates there is considerable variability in scores on Rorschach variables related to self-perception in both clinical and nonclinical populations. It may be reasonable to assume that many depressed patients, for instance, are bothered by self-critical thoughts, a sense of guilt, and feelings of inadequacy. However, this is not true of all depressed patients. Rorschach findings may identify individuals who become depressed because they feel others have insulted them and have not shown the appreciation admiration, and respect they believe they deserve. Among nonclinical subjects, Rorschach variables may similarly identify individuals whose self-perception and responses to others are influenced by narcissistic dynamics as opposed to individuals who are prone to depreciate themselves, who are chronically bothered by a sense of inferiority, and whose willingness to take on new challenges and risks is affected by a fear of failure and humiliation.

7  *Interpersonal Perception*: Although no Rorschach variable is a direct measure of general social adjustment or of specific behaviors in social interactions, variables contained in the Interpersonal Perception cluster address some of the needs, attitudes toward others, expectations, and styles of coping that can contribute to positive interpersonal relationships or that can lead to problems in social interactions and feelings of loneliness and alienation. These variables show, for instance, whether an individual anticipates relationships will provide a sense of security and foster development of intimacy or whether they take a stance of constant vigilance and are prepared to protect their personal space. In general, variables in this cluster provide information as to whether people are usually comfortable interacting with others; view interpersonal closeness as rewarding or threatening; tend to assume a submissive, subservient role when they become involved with other people; and are able to see others and interpret their actions in a realistic manner or are prone to misread and misinterpret their behavior and intentions.

## Factor-Analytic Studies

A different approach to identifying the dimensions of psychological functioning measured by Rorschach was taken by Meyer (1996). In collaboration with several colleagues, Meyer developed the Rorschach Rating Scale (RRS) to operationalize constructs measured by Rorschach variables. The goal of this project was to generate items that clearly and accurately describe each construct the Rorschach is believed to measure. For instance, because scores on specific Rorschach variables identify an individual who has self-critical, denigrating thoughts, an item was developed linked to this variable. Similarly, items describing an individual who is passive, dependent, and submissive were written to be linked to other Rorschach variables. Items were developed to measure both constructs addressed by Comprehensive System (CS) variables and constructs derived from other approaches to the Rorschach, such as the Mutuality of Autonomy Scale (Urist, 1977, Urist & Shill, 1982). Two different forms of the RRS were developed, one a self-report to be completed by an individual to describe themselves, and the other a form to be completed by an observer familiar with a target person.

Meyer, Bates, and Gacono (1999) factor analyzed the RRS using observer ratings of target participants with psychological difficulties. Items clustered in six factors, which the authors labeled (a) Narcissism, Aggression, and Dominance; (b) Perceptual Distortions and

Thought Disorder; (c) Passive Dependence, Vulnerability, and Inferiority; (d) Emotional Health and Coping Effectiveness versus Emotional Control Problems; (e) Social and Emotional Engagement versus Constriction; and (f) Intellectual Defenses and Obsessive Character. Although these factors are related to the clusters described above, there are several reasons why they do not correspond entirely with the clusters identified by Exner (1993). First, the RRS included variables that were not contained in the CS. Second, the clusters were derived from analysis of data derived from Rorschach protocols administered and coded using standard procedures whereas RRS data were collected using observer ratings of another person.

Meyer et al. (1999) also conducted a factor analysis involving both the observer form of the RRS and a 50-item observer rating form that measured the Five-Factor Model (FFM) personality dimensions of neuroticism, extraversion, agreeableness, conscientiousness, and intellect/openness to experience (Goldberg, 1992). Although considerable overlap between the two measures was found, the RRS and FFM did not overlap completely. For instance, the RRS did not adequately define two dimensions contained in the FFM, Extraversion and Openness. At the same time, the FFM did not adequately define the following three RRS factors: Perceptual Distortions and Thought Disorder; Passive Dependence, Vulnerability, and Inferiority; and Intellectual Defenses and Obsessive Character. This suggests overlap between the RRS and FFM for some constructs measured by each while also showing that each independently measures certain dimensions of personality functioning.

Mihura, Meyer, Bel-Bahar, and Gunderson (2003) conducted a follow-up to the Meyer et al. (1999) study. Mihura et al. first revised the RRS to lower its level of reading difficulty and added items to assess constructs not adequately addressed in the RRS. Although items on the RRS on average were written at the 12th-grade level, items on the revised scale, called the Rorschach Construct Scale (RCS), were written at the 7th-grade level. This indicates that they succeeded in making RCS items easier to read and understand. A factor analysis of the RCS yielded six factors, five of which closely paralleled the factors found for the RRS. No factor corresponding to the RRS Intellectual Defenses and Obsessive Character factor was found.

Mihura et al., (2003) recruited college students to use the observer form of the RCS to rate someone they knew well, such as a friend, relative, or partner, who had psychological difficulties. Participants also rated the target individual on a FFM measure, Goldberg's (1999) International Personality Item Pool (IPIP), and on a measure designed to assess criteria for *DSM-IV* (American Psychiatric Association, 1994) personality disorders (the Personality Questionnaire-4).

Mihura et al. (2003) conducted factor analyses in which variables from the IPIP, PDQ-4 and RCS were entered. As might be expected given differences in how these three scales were developed, their theoretical underpinnings, and item pool, the scales were found to have significant overlap as well as to measure independent dimensions of psychological functioning. A high degree of overlap was found for the three measures on two factors, the first labeled Self-Centeredly Exploitive and the second Poor Ego Resiliency. A factor labeled Extraversion was most strongly associated with the IPIP and then with the PDQ-4 and RCS. The IPIP had the strongest association with a factor labeled Conscientiousness and Openness to Ideas. Finally the RCS defined a factor titled Emotional and Expressive Constriction that was independent of the IPIP and PDQ-4. Although no factor of psychotic processes was found, Mihura et al. noted that the distorted thinking and perception measured by the RCS was independent of the IPIP.

The ratings scales used by Meyer et al. (1999) and Mihura et al. (2003) allowed observers to rate target individuals on dimensions of personality functioning assessed by the Rorschach, FFM, and *DSM-IV* personality disorders criteria. Interrelationships among the scales were then examined. As scores from each perspective were based on observer-ratings, the impact of method-specific variance (Meyer, 1997c; Meyer et al., 2001), which could obscure associations among these measures, was reduced. As described previously, meaningful relationships were found.

The studies by Meyer et al. (1999) and Mihura et al. (2003) suggest, first, that Rorschach variables can be reliably clustered to define specific, important aspects of psychological functioning. Second, these findings also show substantial overlap between the constructs tapped by the Rorschach and other assessment methods including the FFM and descriptions of personality disorders defined by the *DSM-IV*. These dimensions are relevant for both clinical and nonclinical populations. Third, their studies indicate each method, including the Rorschach, independently measures dimensions of psychological functioning not captured by the other methods. With regard to the Rorschach, the dimensions uniquely associated with the RRS and RCS involved distorted thinking and perceptions, on the one hand, and a dimension of emotional expressiveness as opposed to self-control, on the other.

It should be noted that Meyer et al.'s (1999) and Mihura et al.'s (2003) findings are based on ratings using the RRS and RCS, rather than responses to the Rorschach itself. Mihura et al. (2003) suggested that because the RRS and RCS operationalized constructs measured by the Rorschach it would be reasonable to assume that similar relationships would be found if associations among these measures were examined using Rorschach variables obtained from standard Rorschach administration. They acknowledged, however, it is possible a different pattern of results would be found if associations among the same measures were investigated using data from actual Rorschach protocols.

# Reliability

Research has examined two aspects of the Rorschach's reliability, inter-coder agreement of variables comprising the test and test-retest or temporal stability.

## Inter-rater Reliability

As described previously, a number of early Rorschach systems developed which varied in the methods used to administer the test, focused on different variables for interpretation, and in some instances differed in how they defined common variables. Given the unsystematic nature of early approaches to the Rorschach, as well as differences during an accepted standard for psychological assessment in an earlier era in psychological science evaluation, it is not surprising that basic psychometric properties of the method were not adequately investigated or established.

Contemporary use of the Rorschach has evolved considerably since the CS (Exner, 2003) was introduced in the early 1970's. Exner established a standardized set of administration procedures, detailed guidelines for scoring or coding individual Rorschach responses, and methods for tabulating and combining these scores to be interpreted. When considering which variables to incorporate from earlier Rorschach systems into the CS, for instance, Exner (2003) only included variables for which a minimum level of inter-rater reliability could be established: "no coding category was included in the 'new' system unless a minimum .85 level could be achieved easily for groups of 10 to 15 scorers across at least 10 to 20 protocols (p. 25).

Adherence to the procedures of the CS ensures that Rorschach data can be collected and scored in a reliable manner. A number of research articles have investigated the inter-rater reliability of Comprehensive System variables. These studies provide solid empirical evidence that well-trained raters can reliably score the Rorschach (Acklin, McDowell, & Verschell, 2000; McDowell & Acklin, 1996; Meyer, 1997a, 1997b). Meyer (1997a), for instance, reported a meta-analytic study of inter-rater reliability data in published Rorschach research studies. Using Kappa to assess these data for chance-corrected inter-rater reliability, Meyer obtained a mean coefficient of 0.88. He noted that Kappa values greater than 0.75 are generally considered to demonstrate excellent agreement.

There has been concern expressed by some observers that psychologists in clinical settings may not adhere to the standardized administration and scoring procedures of the Comprehensive System (CS). Hunsley and Bailey (1999) for instance, stated that "the significant question of how reliably the Rorschach is scored in clinical practice" (p. 268) has not been established. Their reservation is based on doubts that psychologists can learn and then maintain proficiency with the standard procedures required by the CS to administer and code responses; a concern that over the years many psychologists have scored and interpreted Rorschach protocols in an idiosyncratic manner; and the refusal of some practitioners to adopt the CS. As the previous discussion shows, however, well-trained examiners who adhere to the detailed procedures of the CS can achieve acceptable levels of inter-rater agreement.

## Test–Retest Reliability

Exner (1993) reported several studies examining the temporal consistency of Rorschach scores over relatively brief (e.g., 7 days), moderate (e.g., 1 year), and lengthy (e.g., 3 years) periods of time in clinical and nonclinical samples. These findings show high levels of test–retest reliability for variables relating to trait characteristics. Substantial (e.g., greater than 0.75) short- and long-term reliability correlations were found for most variables. The exception occurred for Rorschach variables, which are conceptualized as measuring current emotional distress.

Given these and similar findings, even critics of the CS acknowledge that "Exner and his colleagues have reported test-retest reliability coefficients that are generally quite good." However, Garb, Wood, Nezworski, Grove, and Stejskal (2001) objected that test–retest reliability data have not been reported for a number of CS variables. A number of the variables to which Garb et al. called attention are formed by combining two or more Rorschach scores. For instance, the Isolation Index is a composite variable created by adding together the number of responses containing specific content features.

Viglione and Hilsenroth (2001) questioned whether Garb et al.'s (2001) objection is well-founded. For instance, Viglione and Hilsenroth acknowledged that while test–retest stability may not have been examined for several composite variables, adequate test-retest reliability has been established for the individual variables which contribute to those composite variables. Viglione and Hilsenroth (2001) asserted that if the individual components of composite Rorschach variables have established temporal stability, it is reasonable to assume that the composite variables incorporating those variables will similarly be stable over time. They also pointed out that several of the variables Garb et al. (2001) identified as lacking adequate evidence of test–retest reliability do not exist. Meyer and Archer (2001) commented that while test–retest data exist for most CS variables, some, particularly newer, variables have not been adequately studied and called for additional research to address the "evidentiary holes (that) exist in the literature" (p. 496).

Viglione and Hilsenroth (2001) compared the test-retest reliability of the Rorschach against the test–retest reliability of the WAIS (e.g., Weschler, 1981) and MMPI-2. The values for temporal consistency were culled from published meta-analyses investigating various assessment measures. This comparison showed that test–retest coefficients for CS Rorschach variables compare quite favorably with those for other tests" (p. 453). These findings replicate those reported in a previous meta-analysis, which investigated the test–retest reliability of the Rorschach, MMPI, and WAIS (Parker, Hanson, & Hunsley, 1992). Overall, these studies show, first, high levels of temporal consistency exist for most CS variables and, second, that reliability for Rorschach data is comparable to that for other assessment measures.

# Validity

## Global Construct Validity

A number of meta-analyses have examined the construct validity of the Rorschach (Atkinson, Quarrington, Alp, & Cyr, 1986; Garb, Florio, & Grove, 1998; Hiller, Rosenthal, Bornstein, Berry, & Brunell-Neuleib, 1999; Meyer & Archer, 2001; Parker, Hanson, & Hunsley 1992). These meta-analyses aggregated findings from studies which examined the association between a Rorschach variable and an external criterion variable, such as diagnosis, response to treatment, or manifestation of psychotic symptoms. In addition to examining the Rorschach's construct validity, several of the meta-analyses also examined the construct validity of the MMPI and WAIS.

Results from Hiller et al.'s (1999) meta-analysis were based on 2,276 Rorschach protocols and 5,007 MMPI protocols. They reported an unweighted mean validity coefficient of 0.29 for the Rorschach and 0.30 for the MMPI. Hiller et al. concluded not only that the validity coefficients for the Rorschach and MMPI were comparable, but also that the "validity for these instruments is about as good as can be expected for personality tests" (p. 291). Given the magnitude of the obtained effect sizes, they endorsed the use of both the Rorschach and MMPI in clinical practice and commented that consumers and users of both tests should have confidence that they are effective when used for their intended purposes. Their findings also suggested that the Rorschach variables may be superior to MMPI variables in some areas, such as predicting objective criterion variables, while MMPI variables may be superior to Rorschach variables in other areas, such as when psychiatric diagnosis or self-report variables were the criterion variables. These conclusions are in accordance with those reached by Parker et al. (1992) as they stated that the Rorschach is a valid measure which may have greater utility than the MMPI in certain domains.

To address concerns raised by Garb et al. (1998) about the adequacy of Parker et al.'s (1992) meta-analysis examining the construct validity of the Rorschach, MMPI, and WAIS, Meyer and Archer (2001) re-analyzed Parker et al.'s (1992) findings. They attempted to correct potential confounds in Parker et al.'s data by expanding the number of scales included, computing focused effect sizes to avoid overestimates or underestimates of effect sizes, limiting analyses to those studies which had *a priori*, theoretically sound hypotheses, and examining the impact of method variance on results. Meyer and Archer pointed out that effect sizes could be inflated because of shared method variance if results for studies which examined associations between one method (e.g., two self-report tests) were combined with studies that examined different assessment methods (e.g., self-report and observer ratings). In other words, they cautioned that when predictor and criterion variable used the same assessment method, findings could be stronger because of shared method variance than when predictor and criterion variables used different assessment methods.

As predicted, Meyer and Archer (2001) found higher effect sizes in analyses which did not control for method variance than when method variance was controlled by excluding studies in which the predictor and criterion variables had the same method. This was true not only for studies concerning the Rorschach, but also for studies involving the MMPI and WAIS. Meyer and Archer concluded that "when all three tests are placed on a comparable methodological footing that excludes concurrent validity yielded by an alternative test of the same type, the Rorschach, MMPI, and WAIS obtain generally similar estimates of global validity" (p. 490). They also stated that their meta-analyses showed that "the Rorschach, MMPI, and WAIS all have positive and meaningful evidence of construct validity" (p. 491).

## Alternative Approaches to Investigating Construct Validity

Several other approaches that have investigated the construct validity of specific Rorschach variables will be described in the following section. Bornstein (1996) reviewed published studies examining the construct validity of the Rorschach Oral Dependency Scale (ROD; Masling et al., 1967), a measure of interpersonal dependency described previously. He concluded that laboratory, clinical, and field studies show the ROD is a significant predictor of dependency-related behavior in clinical and nonclinical samples. For instance, studies have shown that ROD scores predict help-seeking behavior, cooperativeness, and compliance with authority figures in college samples.

Furthermore, Bornstein (1996) cited studies which showed that high ROD scores are associated with an increased risk for several forms of psychopathology that are theoretically related to interpersonal dependency, including depression, alcoholism, and eating disorders. Individuals who obtain high scores on the ROD scale were also found to be more sensitive to interpersonal cues than individuals who scored low on the ROD scale and were also more upset by interpersonal conflict and rejection. Bornstein concluded that the ROD scale is a valid measure of interpersonal dependency in both clinical and nonclinical populations. Scores on the ROD have implications for interpersonal functioning, are associated with vulnerability to psychological difficulties, and predict health-related behaviors, such as a tendency to seek and accept support and compliance with treatment recommendations.

A second approach to examining the Rorschach's validity was taken by Meyer et al. (2001). Meyer et al. presented a review of studies examining the efficacy of assessment procedures used by a number of disciplines. Their review included measures of personality functioning, including the Rorschach and MMPI, measures of intellectual functioning, including the WAIS, and diagnostic procedures used in medicine and dentistry. They concluded, first, that the validity of psychological diagnostic procedures in general are comparable to the validity of diagnostic procedures used in medicine and dentistry. Second, they noted that findings supporting the construct validity of the Rorschach were comparable to those supporting the construct validity of other psychological measures, such as the MMPI and WAIS.

Weiner (2002) presents a third approach to considering the Rorschach's construct validity based on a conceptual understanding of various psychological phenomena. For instance, the developmental psychology literature recognizes that level of egocentricity decreases with age as part of normal development. Weiner examined age-related changes of a Rorschach measure of self-centeredness, the Egocentricity Index, in a sample of 1,390 5 to 16 year-old nonpatient children and adolescents. Consistent with the developmental psychology literature, the Egocentricity Index is highest in young children and decreases in a linear fashion until the age of 16.

Weiner (2003) observed similar developmental trends in Rorschach variables which address control over expression of emotions (e.g., FC: CF+C). It is widely accepted that young children are less able to modulate affective expression than older children and adolescents. With age, we expect children to gradually become less reactive, develop more stable emotional states, and establish more mature ways of expressing themselves. Consistent with these developmental trends, in the sample of nonpatient children and adolescents described above, Rorschach variables related to the capacity for self-control change in a predictable manner from childhood through adolescence; relevant Rorschach variables show that a) young children tend to be much more spontaneous, uninhibited, labile, and emotionally intense than adolescents and (b) the capacity for restraint increases gradually with age.

Another example supporting the Rorschach's construct validity comes when nonpatient adults are compared to psychiatric inpatients on relevant variables. For instance, Exner (1993) presented Rorschach data for a sample of 600 nonpatient adults, 279 psychiatric inpatients with a diagnosis of an episode of Major Depression, and 328 psychiatric inpatients admitted for a first episode of schizophrenia. These groups may be thought of as falling at different points on a continuum of psychological functioning, with the nonpatient sample exhibiting little or no disturbance in thinking or perception, psychotic patients exhibiting substantial impairment in thinking and perception, and depressed patients in between. Consistent with this, the mean value for a measure of impaired reality testing, the X-%, increases from 0.07 in the nonpatient sample to 0.20 in the depressed sample and 0.37 in the schizophrenic sample. Similarly, the mean value for a measure of disorganized, illogical thinking, WSum6, is low and nonsignificant for nonpatients (4.48), is moderately elevated among depressed inpatients (18.36), and is extremely high for schizophrenics (42.17).

## Incremental Validity

A number of studies have examined the incremental validity of the Rorschach, the extent to which findings from the Rorschach increase the accuracy of information derived from other sources, such as other psychological tests or diagnostic interviews. This is an important issue to consider as administration, coding, and interpretation of the Rorschach is more time-intensive than for some other measures of personality functioning.

Some authors have asserted that the Rorschach adds little to what can be learned from other clinical data. For instance, Garb (1984) summarized literature showing that the accuracy of clinical judgment based on demographic information, a clinical interview, and self-report inventory did not improve when findings from the Rorschach were added. Garb (1998) recently restated this position using the same body of literature. It should be noted, however, that Garb's conclusions are based on a very restricted set of literature published between 1954 and 1982 and does not include *any* studies using the CS, the Rorschach system accepted as the standard of contemporary clinical practice.

In contrast to the Garb's (1984, 1998) position, other authors provide evidence supporting the incremental validity of the Rorschach. Meyer (2000), for instance, reported the results of two meta-analyses which compared the incremental validity of the Rorschach Prognostic Rating Scale (PRS) to the MMPI Ego Strength scale (Es) in predicting treatment outcome. The results of six studies in which both the PRS and Es were used found a nonsignificant relationship between treatment outcome and the Es with effect sizes ranging from $-0.03$ to $0.03$. In contrast, the Rorschach PRS was significantly related to treatment outcome with a corrected effect size of $0.48$.

In a subsequent meta-analysis, Meyer included both the PRS and intelligence test findings in prediction of treatment outcome. The Rorschach PRS accounted for a significant amount of variance above and beyond that explained by intelligence. These findings provide clear evidence that the Rorschach PRS demonstrated incremental validity over the MMPI Es Scale and intelligence.

Viglione (1999) summarized a number of studies which supported the Rorschach's incremental validity. For instance, Archer and Gordon (1988) compared how accurately MMPI Scale 8 and the Rorschach Schizophrenia Index (SCZI) classified psychiatric inpatients as being schizophrenic or nonschizophrenic. Using traditional cutoff scores (e.g., T score $> 69$ for Scale 8 and a score $> 3$ for the SCZI), they reported that the hit rate for Scale 8 was 60% while the hit rate for the SCZI was 69%. Their findings suggested the accuracy of the MMPI and Rorschach for identifying schizophrenia were comparable.

Several studies, described in the following section, have examined the incremental validity of the Ego Impairment Index (EII; Perry & Viglione, 1991), a Rorschach measure of pathological thinking. For instance, Perry and Braff (1994) found that the EII was more strongly related to neuropsychological markers of schizophrenia than scores on thought disorder scales rated using a structured clinical interview, the Schedule for Positive Symptoms and Schedule for Negative Symptoms. Similar findings were reported by Perry (2001) who found that the EII predicted positive symptoms of schizophrenia after other variables, including a measure of social competence, were entered into a regression analysis.

Dawes (1999) questioned predictive power of the Rorschach, in general, and the EII, in particular. Dawes re-analyzed data sets provided by other investigators with an intent of demonstrating how the Rorschach's incremental validity should be examined. In a series of correlational analyses Dawes found that the EII correlated significantly with two ratings of severity of psychopathology ($rs = 0.35$ and $0.20$, respectively). Furthermore, similar correlations were found between these ratings and average scale elevations on the MMPI ($rs = 0.31$ and $0.27$, respectively). The correlational analyses also showed that the MMPI Goldberg Index, a weighted combination of MMPI clinical scales developed to differentiate between psychotic and nonpsychotic psychiatric disorders, was not as strongly related to ratings of severity of psychopathology as the EII ($rs = 0.17$ and $-0.03$, respectively).

Dawes (1999) investigated the EII's incremental validity by including the EII in hierarchical regression analyses predicting severity of impairment and a second predicting social competence after MMPI scores (the average clinical scale elevations and Goldberg Index) were included. He also entered the EII score in these analyses after two other Rorschach variables, the number of Rorschach responses (R), and a variable Dawes created to assess form quality (XQUAL). Dawes claimed that the EII had little predictive power above and beyond the MMPI and Rorschach variables. This conclusion was challenged by Weiner (2001), however, who noted that Dawes' analyses provided strong evidence for the Rorschach's incremental validity. Weiner (2001) pointed out that the multiple R was 0.37 when both the average MMPI clinical scale elevations and Goldberg Index were included in the regression analysis and increased to 0.49 when Rorschach variables were added.

Viglione and Hilsenroth (2001) raised methodological questions about the approach Dawes (1999) used, concerns also voiced by Perry (2001). Both Viglione and Hilsenroth (2001) and Perry (2001) agreed that the approach advocated by Dawes biased the analyses by reducing the chances positive findings for Rorschach variables would be obtained. Viglione and Hilsenroth re-analyzed one of the data sets Dawes (1999) had used and concluded that their findings provided "clear empirical support for criterion validity and incremental validity of the EII and Rorschach" (p. 460). Dawes subsequently acknowledged that the EII can account for a statistically significant amount of the variance of a criterion variable after other predictor variables were entered in a regression equation.

Stokes et al., (2003) used a revised version of the EII to investigate its treatment utility in a sample of child psychiatric inpatients. Ratings of symptom severity were made by the patient's parents at admission, 30 days after discharge, and 120 days after discharge. Stokes et al. found that the revised EII was significantly related to initial levels of symptom severity. Although the revised EII did not predict short-term response to the intensive, inpatient treatment program, it was strongly related to long-term outcome and long-term negative symptoms, including disruptive behaviors, affective symptoms and symptoms associated with psychotic disorders. Furthermore, the results of hierarchical regression analyses predicting relapse for the ratings made for 30 and 120 days after discharge showed the revised EII predicted long-term outcome even after initial symptom severity was entered into the equation. These findings provide evidence of the incremental validity of the revised EII for predicting long-term vulnerability to psychological and behavioral problems. Overall, these findings show that incremental validity can be achieved for the Rorschach EII.

The incremental validity of Rorschach variables was examined in a nonclinical population in a study conducted by Hartman et al. (2003) discussed briefly above. Hartman et al. examined the extent to which psychological measures predicted success or failure of applicants entering training for the Naval Special Forces of Norway. The predictor variables included measures of cognitive ability (e.g., subtests of the WAIS and the Ravens Advanced Progressive Matrices test) and personality measures. Personality measures included a Norwegian version of the FFM of personality and The Rorschach. Although measures of cognitive ability and the FFM showed little relation to success in military training,

5 of 7 Rorschach variables were significantly correlated with the outcome. Completion of training was associated with low vulnerability to stress (low scores on m + Y), accurate perceptions of self and others (high scores on X + % and low scores on X − %), and the ability to think clearly and logically (low scores on WSum6). Hartman et al. (2003) commented that the Rorschach captured personality characteristics critical to success in military training that were not identified by an interview or scores on ability tests or the FFM.

In addition, Hartman et al. (2003) conducted regression analyses predicting success or failure of the military trainees in which scores on ability tests were entered on the first step, scores from the Norwegian measure of the FFM were entered on the second step, and Rorschach variables entered on the third step. It should be noted that this approach provides a conservative estimate of the contribution made by Rorschach variables as these variables were deliberately entered into the analysis after other relevant predictor variables were entered. They found that success in military training was predicted by two dimensions of the FFM (Extraversion and Emotional Stability) and Rorschach variables. The largest amount of variance was accounted for by Rorschach variables reflecting stress tolerance, reality testing, and clear, logical patterns of thinking.

The incremental validity of the Rorschach was also investigated in a study conducted by Blais et al. (2001) described previously. They examined the relationships among select Rorschach and MMPI-2 variables and *DSM-IV* Cluster B personality disorder criteria. Consistent with findings from other research, modest correlations were found between Rorschach and MMPI-2 variables.

Blais et al. (2001) entered selected, theoretically relevant MMPI-2 and Rorschach variables into hierarchical regression analyses predicting *DSM-IV* criteria for antisocial, borderline, histrionic, and narcissistic personality disorders. They found that both MMPI-2 and Rorschach variables added incrementally to the prediction of borderline and narcissistic personality disorder criteria scores. For instance, as predicted, the combination of Rorschach Reflection responses and MMPI-2 NPD scale score were the best predictor variables in regression analyses involving narcissistic personality disorder. Although criteria for antisocial personality disorder was best predicted by MMPI-2 variables alone, Rorschach variables independently were associated with diagnostic criteria for histrionic personality disorder.

Blais et al. (2001) concluded, first, that both Rorschach and MMPI-2 variables are meaningfully related to personality disorder criteria. Second, they found a differential pattern of inter-relationships among these variables and criteria for specific personality disorder: Some disorders were best predicted by a combination of MMPI-2 and Rorschach variables while others were best predicted by Rorschach variables independent of MMPI-2 variables or by MMPI-2 variables independent of Rorschach variables.

In summary, the studies described above provide compelling evidence for both the construct validity of Rorschach variables and the incremental validity of Rorschach variables in clinical and nonclinical populations.

# Racial and Ethnic Differences

One important issue to consider when using any psychological measure is whether differences will be found if the measure is used with different ethnic or racial groups. For instance, concerns that the MMPI-2 (Butcher et al., 1989) is biased has been debated in the literature for many years. This debate was sparked by suggestions that Caucasians and African-Americans scored differently on the MMPI (Greene, 1987; Graham, 2000) and led to concerns that MMPI scores might overpathologize African American psychiatric patients.

The evolution of the controversy concerning racial and ethnic differences on the MMPI-2 is informative in identifying relevant issues to consider when examining whether any psychological test, including the Rorschach, is biased. For instance, Greene (1987) pointed out that differences between ethnic groups could be explained by differences in socio-economic status, level of education, or acculturation. Other studies have suggested that observed differences between African American and Caucasian psychiatric inpatients reflected different symptom patterns and types of psychopathology (Butcher, Braswell, & Raney, 1983; Dahlstrom, Lachar, & Dahlstrom, 1986).

Other authors have pointed out that significant differences between ethnic groups on MMPI-2 scales do not necessarily indicate bias. According to these writers, bias would be indicated if a differential pattern of validity was found for MMPI-2 scales across ethnic groups (Greene, 1987, Timbrook & Graham, 1994). From their perspective, bias would be demonstrated if particular MMPI-2 scales were differentially related to conceptually related extra-test criterion variables in different ethnic or racial groups.

This possibility was examined in a study by Arbisi, Ben-Porath, & McNulty (2002). They examined not only whether African American and Caucasian psychiatric inpatients produced differentially elevated profiles, but also whether MMPI-2 scores produced by the two groups were comparable in their relationship to external criteria. Arbisi et al. (2001) used the Record Review Form, which extracted clinical data from hospital records, to assess the external criteria. The results of multiple regression analyses produced some evidence of prediction bias. Unexpectedly, however, rather than providing evidence that the MMPI-2 overpathologizes minority group members, Arbisi et al. found evidence that "when bias was present, it was overwhelmingly in the direction of *underprediction* of psychopathology in African Americans" (p. 10, italics added). Their results conflict with claims that MMPI-2 findings yield inaccurate and overly negative conclusions about the presence and severity of psychopathology for minorities.

The MMPI-2 literature provides a backdrop against which concerns about ethnic and racial bias of the Rorschach can be viewed. For instance, some writers (e.g., Wood & Lilienfeld, 1999) have cited a study by Krall, Sachs, Lazar, et al. (1983) as evidence that different scores are obtained by African-Americans and Caucasians. Wood and Lilienfeld viewed these findings as evidence of racial bias. In a similar vein, Frank (1992, 1993) conducted a review of potential bias on the Rorschach with African-Americans and Hispanics. No evidence for bias among Hispanic Americans was found. Based on seven studies published between 1930 and 1990, Frank (1992) found one consistent finding when Rorschachs produced by African-Americans and Caucasians were compared: African-Americans tended to give fewer responses than Caucasians. No other meaningful ethnic differences were found.

As noted, before concluding that differences in scores between ethnic or racial groups are signs of bias, one first must consider whether demographic factors, such as level of education or socioeconomic status, might account for these differences. This is an important consideration as the sample described by Krall et al. (1983) was comprised of inner city African-American youngsters most of whom came from impoverished, disadvantaged backgrounds. It is not surprising that this group scored differently on the Rorschach than the sample of middle class children that comprised Exner's normative sample given differences in demographic characteristics that may affect scores obtained by these groups.

Support for this perspective is provided by a study which compared Rorschach data produced by 44 Black and 44 White nonpatient adults matched on sociodemographic variables including age, gender, education, marital status, and socioeconomic status (Presley, Smith, Hilsenroth, & Exner, 2001). Both groups were drawn from the CS normative sample (Exner, 1993). The two groups were compared on 23 Rorschach variables prior research had identified as potentially being biased by race. No significant differences between Black and White groups were found for twenty of the twenty-three Rorschach variables. Contrary to Frank's (1992) conclusions, the two groups produced comparable number of responses.

Presley et al. (2001) noted that while there were statistically significant differences for three variables, the differences were not clinically meaningful for two of these variables. For instance, although Blacks obtained significantly higher scores than Whites on the Schizophrenia Index (0.48 vs. 0.16, respectively), these differences were not clinically meaningful as the scores were well below the established cutoff points used in clinical practice to identify psychotic disorders. That is, the higher mean score obtained by Blacks on the SCZI did not result in an elevated rate of false positive identification of black participants as having a psychotic disorder.

Presley et al. (2001) found Blacks produced significantly fewer cooperative movement responses than Whites. They concluded this finding was interpretively meaningful as 23% of Whites but 43% of Blacks had no cooperative movement responses. They speculated this finding indicated Black Americans may be less likely than Whites to anticipate positive interactions with others given differences in the groups' life experiences. Overall, however, Presley et al. noted that their findings showed Blacks and Whites matched on key demographic variables earned similar scores on the Rorschach. They commented that these findings supported the view that results from earlier studies investigating racial differences on the Rorschach may have been confounded by the effects of demographic variables that were not controlled.

Meyer (2002) conducted a study that (a) controlled for demographic variables and that (b) conceptually parallels the Arbisi et al. (2002) study described previously. When 120 African-American and 147 Caucasian psychiatric inpatients were matched in terms of age, education, gender, and martial status, "ethnicity was not associated with 188 Comprehensive System scores at a level beyond chance" (p. 125). Meyer then examined whether a differential pattern of associations were found for minority and majority group members when Rorschach scores predicted external criteria. In this study, associations between Rorschach and conceptually relevant MMPI variables were examined. He found that, "across 17 predictor-criterion pairs, there was no evidence to indicate the Rorschach was more valid for one group than the other" (p. 125). Meyer did find some evidence of bias. Similar to Arbisi et al.'s (2002) findings, Meyer reported that Rorschach scores tended to underestimate psychotic disorders for minority group members:

> [T]he intercept differences observed in this study created a form of bias that *favored* minorities and worked against the European Americans. Specifically, if the majority regression equations were used to predict psychotic disorders for minority patients, they would consistently underestimate this type of problem. As such, the findings were

directly opposite the pattern that should be seen if the Rorschach was biased against minorities. (p. 125)

The findings from the Presley et al. (2001) and Meyer (2002) studies conflict with the concerns expressed by some writers (Frank, 1992, 1993; Wood & Lilienfeld, 1999) that the Rorschach may be racially biased. These contemporary studies provide evidence that earlier findings of racial differences on the Rorschach likely reflected the effects of demographic variables which were not adequately considered or controlled. Overall, research using appropriate methods to control for the effects of variables which may confound test performance, such as level of education and socioeconomic status, indicates that the Rorschach is as valid a measure of personality functioning for Blacks as for Whites.

# Directions for Future Research

Since it was developed, the Rorschach method has been used to describe individual differences in personality characteristics and psychological functioning in normal and clinical populations. Although some writers refer to the Rorschach as a measure of psychopathology primarily useful for diagnostic evaluations, the range of variability on many Rorschach variables in both clinical and nonclinical populations demonstrates that it provides meaningful information relevant to understanding individual's strengths and weaknesses in a number of domains of psychological functioning. These include individuals' capacity to manage stress; their self-concept; capacity to form and maintain satisfying interpersonal relationships; comfortably and effectively manage emotions; and to perceive, analyze, and understand situations in an accurate, realistic, and logical manner. Although information culled from the Rorschach overlaps with information provided by other assessment sources, given the nature of its procedures the constructs addressed by the Rorschach do not and should not be expected to overlap entirely with the constructs that typical self-report measures address. Furthermore, investigations of possible racial bias show the Rorschach provides valid information about the personality characteristics of Blacks and Whites without bias.

A number of potential avenues for research incorporating the Rorschach in nonclinical populations is suggested by the preceding text. For example, the Rorschach is recognized as being a robust measure of perceptual distortions and may be more sensitive to illogical thinking and cognitive slippage than some self-report measures (Mihura et al., 2003). This suggests that researchers studying the psychological functioning of biological relatives of schizophrenics might profitably include the Rorschach if they are investigating this population's coping resources, perceptual accuracy, thought processes, and indications of cognitive disorganization.

It may also be fruitful to include the Rorschach in studies investigating schizotypy, a personality dimension characterized by magical thinking, unusual perceptual experiences, anhedonia, and impaired social functioning (Meehl, 1962). Accurate assessment of thought processes and content is contingent on whether the participant is willing to openly and candidly discuss his or her thoughts. For reasons discussed earlier in this chapter, the use of a performance-based measure of these constructs may be particularly useful for this purpose as both self-report and interview-based ratings of these constructs may be subject to confounding variables, such as reluctance to acknowledge information that may not be flattering. Furthermore, some researchers have suggested that certain groups, such as biological relatives of schizophrenic patients, are defensive when completing paper-and-pencil measures of characteristics associated with schizotypy.

Some writers have suggested that although self-report, implicit measures may identify the presence or absence of disturbances in thinking, performance-based methods can "reach beyond symptom description and into the processes of disorganization" (Hurt, Holzman, & Davis, 1983, p. 1281). One might predict that scores on Rorschach variables, such as the Ego Impairment Index (EII; Perry & Viglione, 1991), indices of disorganized thinking, or distorted, inaccurate perceptions of events, may discriminate between nonclinical individuals with high and low scores on measures of schizotypy and complement findings obtained from commonly used paper-and-pencil measures, such as the Magical Ideation Scale or Perceptual Aberration Scale. This possibility is supported by previous research showing that the EII is positively correlated with the Magical Ideation Scale, as well as clinical ratings of psychotic symptoms and thought disorder in psychiatric patients (Perry & Braff, 1996).

The work of Bornstein (1996) summarized previously has shown a dissociation between explicit, self-report measures of dependency and implicit, performance-based measures of dependency, such as the Rorschach Oral Dependency scale. These studies have shown that dependency needs in both clinical and nonclinical populations are related to aspects of psychopathology, such as vulnerability to depression, as well as to aspects of health psychology, including compliance with medical care, help-seeking behavior, and use of medications. These findings should be pursued to investigate the implications different levels of dependency assessed using both self-report and performance-based measures have for health-related behaviors, the risk for developing psychopathology, treatment effectiveness, and compliance with care.

Another intriguing avenue of research is suggested by the work of Shedler et al. (1993) who found the risks of both physical and psychological problems differed for nonclinical individuals classified as having *genuine* as opposed to *illusory* positive psychological adjustment. Shedler et al. (1993) distinguished between individuals presenting with genuine or illusory mental health by comparing their responses to explicit, self-report and implicit, performance-based measures of emotional distress. They found that scores indicating positive psychological adjustment were congruent on both self-report and performance-based measures for some individuals; these individuals were identified as reporting being psychologically healthy in a genuine manner.

In contrast, other individuals appeared well-adjusted when their responses to self-report measures were reviewed, but expressed significant distress on an implicit, performance-based measure. Shedler et al. (1993) described these individuals as creating an illusion of effective coping by defensively denying emotional distress and personal difficulties. Compared to individuals whose psychological adjustment is genuine, individuals who project a facade of positive psychological adjustment were found to have an elevated risk for developing medical and emotional problems. Their findings present compelling reasons why researchers (a) should not assume that individuals identified as having a particular psychological characteristic based on their score on a self-report measure (e.g., positive psychological health), form a homogenous group and; (b) should investigate the intriguing possibility that important differences in behavior, coping strategies, and risk of developing physical and psychological problems may be found between individuals who obtain concordant and those who obtain discordant scores on explicit, self-report and implicit, performance-based measures of personality functioning, such as the Rorschach.

In summary, substantial empirical evidence shows that when used according to the guidelines for administration, coding, and interpretation of the CS, the Rorschach is a valid, reliable, *implicit* or performance-based measure of personality functioning that can complement and enhance the understanding of an individual based on findings from *explicit* assessment methods. Although the information from explicit assessment methods, such as self-report measures and clinical interviews, may be sufficient for some evaluation purposes, the information from implicit measures, such as the Rorschach, can provide meaningful data that in some instances could not be accessed either because an individual lacked self-awareness or was reluctant to disclose certain information Overall, when used to assess the dimensions of personality functioning for which it is designed, the Rorschach is a sound, robust method of assessing individual differences in clinical and nonclinical settings.

# REFERENCES

Acklin, M. W., McDowell, C. J., & Verschell, M. S. (2000). Interobserver agreement, intraobserver reliability, and the Rorschach Comprehensive System. *Journal of Personality Assessment, 74,* 15–47.

American Psychiatric Association (1994). *Diagnostic and statistical manual of mental disorders* (4th ed.). Washington, DC: Author.

American Psychiatric Association (2000). *Diagnostic and statistical manual of mental disorders* (4th ed., text revision). Washington, DC: Author.

Arbisi, P. A., Ben-Porath, Y. S., & McNulty, J. (2002). A comparison of MMPI-2 validity in African American and Caucasion psychiatric inpatients. *Psychological Assessment, 14,* 3–15.

Archer, R. P., & Gordon, R. A. (1988). MMPI and Rorschach indices of schizophrenic and depressive diagnoses among adolescent inpatients. *Journal of Personality Assessment, 52,* 276–287.

Archer, R. P., Maruish, M., Imhof, E. A., & Piotrowski, C. (1991). Psychological test usage with adolescent clients: 1990 survey findings. *Professional Psychology: Research and Practice, 22,* 247–252.

Archer, R. P., & Newsom, C. R. (2000). Psychological test usage with adolescent clients: Survey update. *Assessment, 7,* 227–235.

Atkinson, L., Quarrington, B., Alp, I. E., & Cyr, J. J. (1986). Rorschach validity: An empirical approach to the literature. *Journal of Clinical Psychology, 42,* 360–362.

Binet, A., & Henri, V. (1895–1896). La psychologie individuelle. *Annee Psychologiquem 2,* 411–465.

Blais, M. A., & Baity, M. R. (2005). Rorschach assessment of histrionic personality disorder (pp. ). In S. K. Huprich (Ed.), *Rorschach assessment of the personality disorders.* Mahwah, NJ: Erlbaum.

Blais, M. A., Hilsenroth, M. J., Castlebury, F., Fowler, J. C., & Baity, M. R. (2001). Predicting DSM-IV Cluster B Personality Disorder criteria from MMPI-2 and Rorschach data: A test on incremental validity. *Journal of Personality Assessment, 76,* 150–168.

Blatt, S. J., D'Afflitti, J. P., & Quinlan, D. M. (1976). Experiences of depression in normal young adults. *Journal of Abnormal Psychology, 85,* 383–389.

Bornstein, R. F. (1996). Construct validity of the Rorschach Oral Dependency Scale: 1967–1995. *Psychological Assessment, 8,* 200–205.

Bornstein, R. F. (2005). Rorschach assessment of dependent personality disorder (pp. ). In S. K. Huprich (Ed.), *Rorschach assessment of the personality disorders.* Mahwah, NJ: Erlbaum.

Bornstein, R. F., Krukonis, A. B., Manning, K. A., Mastrosimone, C. C., et al. (1993). Interpersonal dependency and health service utilization in a college student sample. *Journal of Social & Clinical Psychology, 12,* 262–279.

Bornstein, R. F., Rossner, S. C., Hill, E. L., & Stepanian, M. L. (1994). Face validity and fakability of objective and projective measures of dependency. *Journal of Personality Assessment, 63,* 363–386.

Butcher, J. N., Braswell, L., & Raney, D. (1983). A cross-cultural comparison of Amerian Indian, Black, and White inpatients on the MMPI and presenting symptoms. *Journal of Consulting and Clinical Psychology, 51,* 587–594.

Butcher, J. N., Dahlstrom, W. G., Graham, J. R., Tellegen, A., & Kaemmer, B. (1989). *Minnesota Multiphasic Personality Inventory-2 (MMPI-2): Manual for administration and scoring.* Minneapolis: University of Minnesota.

Butcher, J. N., & Rouse, S. (1996). Personality: Individual differences and clinical assessment. *Annual Review of Psychology, 47,* 87–111.

Costa, P. T., Jr., & Widiger, T. A. (2002). *Personality disorders and the five-factor model of personality* (2nd ed.). Washington, DC: American Psychological Association.

Dahlstrom, W. G., Lachar, D., & Dahlstrom, L. E. (1986). *MMPI patterns of American minorities.* Minneapolis: University of Minnesota Press.

Dawes, R. N. (1999). Two methods for studying the incremental validity of a Rorschach variable. *Psychological Assessment, 131,* 297–302.

Exner, J. E. (1969). *The Rorschach systems.* New York: Grune & Stratton.

Exner, J. E. (1993). *The Rorschach: A comprehensive system, Vol. 1: Basic foundations* (3rd ed.). New York: Wiley.

Exner, J. E. (2003). *The Rorschach: A comprehensive system* (4th ed.). New York: Wiley.

Frank, G. (1992). The response of African Americans to the Rorschach: A review of the research. *Journal of Personality Assessment, 59,* 317–325.

Frank, G. (1993). The use of the Rorschach with Hispanic Americans. *Psychological Reports, 72,* 276–278.

Ganellen, R. (1996). Integrating the Rorschach with the MMPI. Hillsdale, NJ: Erlbaum.

Ganellen, R. J. (2005). Rorschach assessment of avoidant personality disorder (pp. ). In S. K. Huprich (Ed.), *Rorschach assessment of the personality disorders.* Mahwah, NJ: Erlbaum.

Garb, H. N. (1984). The incremental validity of information used in personality assessment. *Clinical Psychology Review, 4,* 641–655.

Garb, H. N. (1998). *Studying the clinician: Judgment research and psychological assessment.* Washington, DC: American Psychological Association.

Garb, H. N., Florio, C. M., & Grove, W. M. (1998). The validity of the Rorschach and the Minnesota Multiphasic Personality Inventory: Results from meta-analyses. *Psychological Science, 9,* 402–404.

Garb, H. N., Wood, J. M., Nezworski, M. T., Grove, W. M., & Stejskal, W. J. (2001). Toward a resolution of the Rorschach controversy. *Psychological Assessment, 13,* 433–448.

Goldberg, L. R. (1999). A broad-bandwidth, public domain, personality inventory measuring the lower-level facets of several five-factor models. In I. Mervielde, I. Deary, F. De Fruyt, & F. Ostendorf (Eds), *Personality psychology in Europe* (Vol. 7, pp. 7–28). Tilburg, The Netherlands: Tilburg University Press.

Graham, J. R. (2000). *MMPI-2: Assessing personality and psychopathology* (3rd ed.). New York: Oxford University Press.

Greene, R. L. (1987). Ethnicity and MMPI performance: A review. *Journal of Consulting and Clinical Psychology, 55,* 497–512.

Groth-Marnat, G. (1997). *Handbook of psychological assessment* (3rd ed.). New York: Wiley.

Hartman, E., Sunde, T., Kristensen, W., & Martinussen, M. (2003). Psychological measures as predictors of military training performance. *Journal of Personality Assessment, 80,* 87–98.

Hiller, J. B., Rosenthal, R., Bornstein, R. F., Berry, D. T. R., & Brunell–Neuleib, S. (1999). A comparative meta-analysis of Rorschach and MMPI validity. *Psychological Assessment, 11,* 278–296.

Hunsley, J., & Bailey, J. M. (1999). The clinical utility of the Rorschach: Unfulfilled promises and an uncertain future. *Psychological Assessment, 11,* 266–277.

Huprich, S. K., & Ganellen, R. J. (2005). The advantages of assessing personality disorders with the Rorschach (pp. ). In S. K. Huprich (Ed.), *Rorschach assessment of the personality disorders.* Mahwah, NJ: Erlbaum.

Hurt, S. W., Holzman, P., & Davis, J. M. (1983). Thought disorder. *Archives of General Psychiatry, 40,* 1281–1285.

Hyler, S. E. (1994). Personality Diagnostic Questionnaire-4+ (PDQ-4+). Unpublished manuscript, New York State Psychiatric Institute, New York.

Krall, V., Sachs, H., Lazar, B., Rayson, B., & Growe, G. (1983). Rorschach norms for inner city children. *Journal of Personality Assessment, 47,* 155–157.

Lohr, J. M., Fowler, K. A., & Lilienfeld, S. O. (2002). The dissemination and promotion of pseudoscience in clinical psychology: The challenge to legitimate clinical science. *The Clinical Psychologist, 55,* 4–10.

Lubin, B., Larsen, R. M., Matarazzo, J. D., & Seever, M. (1985). Psychological test usage patterns in five professional settings. *American Psychologist, 40,* 857–861.

Masling, J. M., Rabie, L., & Blondheim, S. H. (1967). Obseity, level of aspiration, and Rorschach and TAT measures of oral dependence. *Journal of Consulting Psychology, 31*, 233–239.

McClelland, D. C., Koestner, R., & Weinberger, J. (1989). How do self-attributed and explicit motives differ? *Psychological Review, 96*, 690–702.

McDowell, C. J., & Acklin, M. W. (1996). Standardizing procedures for calculating Rorschach interrater reliability: Conceptual and empirical foundations. *Journal of Personality Assessment, 66*, 308–320.

Meehl, P. E. (1962). Schizotaxia, schizotypy, schizophrenia. *American Psychologist, 17*, 827–838.

Meyer, G. J. (1996). Construct validation of scales derived from the Rorschach method: A review of issues and introduction to the Rorschach Rating Scale. *Journal of Personality Assessment, 67*, 598–628.

Meyer, G. J. (1997a). Assessing reliability: Critical corrections for a critical examination of the Rorschach Comprehensive System. *Psychological Assessment, 9*, 480–498.

Meyer, G. J. (1997b). Thinking clearly about reliability: More critical correlations regarding the Rorschach Comprehensive System. *Psychological Assessment, 9*, 495–498.

Meyer, G. J. (1997c). On the integration of personality assessment methods: The Rorschach and MMPI-2. *Journal of Personality Assessment, 68*, 297–330.

Meyer, G. J. (2000). The incremental validity of the Rorschach Prognostic Rating Scale over the MMPI Ego Strength Scale and IQ. *Journal of Personality Assessment, 74*, 356–370.

Meyer, G. J. (2002). Exploring possible ethnic differences and bias in the Rorschach Comprehensive System. *Journal of Personality Assessment, 78*, 104–129.

Meyer, G. H., & Archer, R. P., (2001). The hard science of Rorschach research: What do we know and where do we go? *Psychological Assessment, 13*, 486–502.

Meyer, G. J., Bates, M., & Gacono, C. (1999). The Rorschach Rating Scale: Item adequacy, scale development, and relations with the Big Five model of personality. *Journal of Personality Assessment, 73*, 199–244.

Meyer, G. J., Finn, S. E., Eyde, L., Kay, G. G., Moreland, K. L., Dies, R. R., Eisman, E. J., Kubiszyn, T. W., & Reed, G. M. (2001). Psychological testing and psychological assessment: A review of evidence and issues. *American Psychologist, 56*, 128–165.

Mihura, J. L., Meyer, G. J., Bel-Behar, T., & Gunderson, J. (2003). Correspondence among observer ratings of Rorschach, Big Five Model, and DSM-IV personality disorder constructs. *Journal of Personality Assessment, 81*, 20–39.

Murray, H. A. (1943). *Thematic Apperception Test manual.* Cambridge, MA: Harvard University Press.

Parker, K. C., Hanson, R. K., & Hunsley, J. (1992). MMPI, Rorschach, and WAIS: A meta-analytic comparison of reliability, stability, and validity. In A. E. Kazdin (Ed), *Methodological issues and strategies in clinical research* (pp. 217–232). Washington, DC: American Psychological Association.

Perry, W. (2001). Incremental validity of the Ego Impairment Index: A reexamination of Dawes (1999). *Psychological Assessment, 13*, 403–407.

Perry, W., & Braff, D. L. (1994). Information-processing deficits and thought disorder in schizophrenia. *American Journal of Psychiatry, 151*, 363–367.

Perry, W., & Braff, D. L. (1996). Disturbed thought and information processing deficits in schizophrenia. *Biological Psychiatry, 39*, 549.

Perry, W., & Viglione, D. J. (1991). The Ego Impairment Index as a predictor of outcome in melancholic depressed patients treated with tricyclic antidepressants. *Journal of Personality Assessment, 56*, 487–501.

Piotrowski, C., & Zalewski, C. (1993). Training in psychodiagnostic testing in APA-approved PsyD and PhD clinical psychology programs. *Journal of Personality Assessment, 61*, 394–405.

Presley, G., Smith, C., Hilsenroth, M., & Exner, J. (2001). Clinical utility of the Rorschach with African Americans. *Journal of Personality Assessment, 77*, 491–507.

Rorschach, H. (1921). *Psychodiagnostik* (Transl. Hans Huber Verlag, 1942).

Bern: Bircher. Saucier, G. (1994). Mini-markers: A brief version of Goldberg's unipolar Big-Five markers. *Journal of Personality Assessment, 63*, 506–516.

Shedler, J., Mayman, M., & Manis, M. (1993). The *illusion* of mental health. *American Psychologist, 48*, 1117–1131.

Stokes, J. M., Pogge, D. L., Powell-Lunden, J., Ward, A. W., Bilginer, L., & DeLuca, V. A. (2003). The Rorschach Impairment Index: Prediction of treatment outcome in a child psychiatric population. *Journal of Personality Assessment, 81*, 11–19.

Timbrook, R. E., & Graham, J. R. (1994). Ethnic differences on the MMPI-2? *Psychological Assessment, 6*, 212–217.

Urist, J. (1977). The Rorschach test and the assessment of object relations. *Journal of Personality Assessment, 41*, 3–9.

Urist, J., & Shill, M. (1982). Validity of the Rorschach mutuality of autonomy scale: A replication using excerpted responses. *Journal of Personality Assessment, 46,* 450–454.

Viglione, D. H. (1999). A review of recent research addressing the utility of the Rorschach. *Psychological Assessment, 11,* 251–265.

Viglione, D. H., & Hilsenroth, M. J. (2001). The Rorschach: Facts, fictions, and future. *Psychological Assessment, 13,* 452–471.

Watkins, C. E. (1991). What have surveys taught us about the teaching and practice of psychological assessment? *Journal of Personality Assessment, 56,* 426–437.

Watkins, C., Campbell, V., Nieberding, R., & Hallmark, R. (1995). Contemporary practice of Psychological assessment by clinical psychologists. *Professional Psychology: Research and Practice, 26,* 45–60.

Weiner, I. B. (2001). Advancing the science of psychological assessment: The Rorschach Inkblot Method as examplar. *Psychological Assessment, 13,* 423–432.

Weiner, I. B. (2002). Scientific psychology and the Rorschach Inkblot Method. *The Clinical Psychologist, 55,* 7–12.

Weiner, I. B. (2003). *Principles of Rorschach interpretation* (2nd ed.). Mahwah, NJ: Erlbaum.

Weiner, I. B. (2005). Integrative personality assessment with self-report and performance-based measures (pp. 317–331). In S. Strack (Ed.), *Handbook of personology and psychopathology.* Hoboken, NJ: Wiley.

Weschler, D. (1981). *Manual for the Weschler Adult Intelligence Scale-Revised.* New York: Psychological Corporation.

Wood, J. M., & Lilienfeld, S. O. (1999). The Rorschach Inkblot Test: A case of overstatement? *Assessment, 6,* 341–349.

# Name Index

Aalto, S., 73
Aaronson, A. L., 362
Abraham, P. P., 370
Abrahamson, A. C., 266–267
Abramson, L. Y., 292
Acklin, M. W., 486
Adams, R. S., 94
Adler, D. A., 313
Aiduk, R., 356
Akbudak, E., 73
Akiskal, H. S., 157
Alarcon, R. D., 170, 180, 314
Albrecht, B., 51
Alden, L. E., 89, 97–98, 387, 392, 393
Aldwin, C. L., 353
Alexander, J., 414
Alexopoulos, G. S., 173
Alford, B. A., 124
Allmon, D., 129
Alloy, L. B., 292
Allport, G. W., xvii, 34, 53, 66, 68
Almagor, M., 357, 362
Almasy, L., 275
Alp, I. E., 487
Alper, J. S., 176
Alterman, A. I., 455, 460
Altman, H., 343
Altom, M. W., 17
Amell, J. W., 149
Amodio, D. M., 391
Amos, C. I., 275
Anchin, J. C., 84
Anderson, T. W., 229
Ando, J., 422
Andreasen, N., 142
Andree, B., 73
Andrews, G., 180, 314
Angleitner, A., 412, 413
Annable, L., 84
Ansell, E. B., 83, 84–86, 92, 103, 105, 107

Anthony, E. J., 159
Antoni, M., 40
Arbisi, P. A., 358, 359, 365, 367–368, 370–372, 493–494
Archer, R. P., 352, 356, 473, 479–480, 487–489, 490
Arcus, D., 290–291
Arieti, S., 123
Arkowitz-Westen, L., 167, 316
Armstrong, H. E., 129
Arnau, R. C., 289
Arntz, A., 127, 128, 432
Aron, A., 159
Arrendondo, R., 362
Asai, M., 422
Asendorpf, J., 305
Atkinson, J. W., 387
Atkinson, L., 487
Aubé, J., 99
Auerbach, J. S., 86
Aumer-Ryan, K., 433, 443
Austin, E. J., 414
Axelrod, S. R., 328
Ayers, W., 296

Bacchiochi, J., 361
Bacon, S. F., 374
Baer, B. A., 97
Baer, R. A., 355, 360
Bagby, R. M., 51, 316, 324, 361
Bagnato, M., 432
Bailer, U. F., 73
Bailey, J. M., 290, 486
Baity, M. R., 476, 478–479, 492
Bakan, D., 90, 98–99
Baker, L. A., 263–264, 265, 266–267, 271
Balakrishnan, J. D., 84, 89, 93, 95, 97, 98
Ball, S., 431
Ball, S. A., 52, 128
Balla, J. R., 233
Ban, T. A., 458
Bandura, A., 12

Barash, D. P., 23–24
Bargh, J. A., 175
Barkham, M., 130, 459
Barrantes, N., 157
Barrett, E., 419
Barrett, P., 15, 255
Barriga, A. Q., 60
Barron, F., 344
Barthlow, D. L., 356–357, 363
Bartholomew, D. J., 240, 242
Bartholomew, K., 387
Bartlett, F. C., 115
Bartlett, M. S., 229
Barton, M., 271
Bates, M., 483–485
Battaglia, M., 432
Bauer, D. J., 242
Baumeister, R. F., 53
Baumgardner, M. H., 233
Baxter, L. R., 140
Bayer, R., 178
Baylis, N., 65
Bayon, C., 74–75, 78, 321
Beauchaine, T. P., 297, 302–303
Beck, A. T., 114–115, 116, 118–120, 122–131, 173, 458
Beck, J. S., 125, 127–128
Becker, B., 459, 460
Beckham, J. C., 458
Beevers, C. G., 292
Bel-Behar, T., 484–485, 495
Bell, K., 460
Bell, M. J., 459
Bellodi, L., 127, 432
Bell-Pringle, V. J., 459
Belmaker, R. H., 270, 277, 278
Belter, R. W., 451
Belyea-Caldwell, S., 393
Bemporad, J., 123
Ben-Dat, D., 361
Bender, D., 433
Bengel, D., 277
Benjamin, J., 270, 277, 278
Benjamin, L., 125, 128
Benjamin, L. S., 19, 84, 86, 89, 100, 105–106, 107, 173, 316, 322, 383, 389
Bennett, B., 453
Ben-Porath, Y. S., xx, 19, 201, 316, 319, 337, 343, 352–354, 356–368, 370–373, 493–494
Bentall, R. P., 140, 155, 156
Bergner, R. M., 174
Berman, S., 138
Bernreuter, R. J., 337–338
Bernstein, D., 296
Berrettini, W. H., 156
Berrios, G. E., 141, 156
Berry, D. T. R., 355, 487

Bieling, P. J., 123, 124
Bigelow, G. E., 57
Bilginer, L., 491
Billington, R., 459
Bindseil, K., 51
Binet, A., 474
Bishop, T., 275
Bissada, H., 458
Black, D. W., 130
Black, J. D., 341, 343
Blackburn, I.- M., 124
Blackburn, R., 389, 393
Blaine, D., 277
Blair, R. J. R., 150
Blais, M. A., 476, 478–479, 492
Blanchard, J. J., 293, 433
Bland, R. C., 263–264
Blaney, P. H., 123
Blangero, J., 275
Blashfield, R. K., 19, 125–126, 168–169, 199, 313, 316, 322, 350, 402, 459
Blatt, S. J., 86, 118, 123, 478
Bleske, A., 263–264
Bleuler, E., xviii
Block, J., 19, 191, 375
Block, P., 124
Blondheim, S. H., 478, 488
Blum, K., 277
Blum, N., 167, 168–169, 199, 315, 439
Boccaccini, M. T., 451
Bodkin, A., 315
Boggs, C., 316
Boggs, C. D., 464
Bolton, L. S., xxvi
Boomer, D., 459
Boothroyd, L. J., 263–264
Bor, R., 457–458
Borg, J., 73
Borkovec, T. D., 95, 387
Bornstein, R. F., 166, 312, 329, 478, 487, 488
Borum, R., 454
Bosse, R., 353
Bouchard, T. J., Jr., 270, 273, 327
Boudewyns, P., 51
Bower, T. G., 451
Bowers, K. S., 4, 23
Bowers, W., 130
Bowlby, J., 120, 123
Bowman, E., 355, 356
Boyd, S., 51
Boyle, G., 156
Boyle, G. J., 455–456, 459, 460
Bradley, R., 195
Braff, D. L., 157, 490
Braith, J. A., 393
Braithwaite, A., 139, 149

Brandenberg, N., 210
Braswell, L., 51, 493
Braverman, E., 277
Brazy, P. C., 391
Breakefield, X. O., 265
Breuer, J., 55
Briggs, P. F., 343
Brink, J., 150
Brockington, J. F., 156
Brod, J. H., 154–155
Brodsky, S. L., 451
Brody, A. L., 140
Brokaw, D. W., 83
Broome, M., 140
Brooner, R. K., 57
Broughton, R., 387
Brown, G. K., 123–129
Brown, L. L., 159
Brown, L. S., 171, 455, 460
Brown, R. A., 292
Brown, R. C., 459
Brown, S. A., 293, 433
Brunell-Neuleib, S., 487
Brunner, H. G., 265
Budman, S., 393
Buffington-Vollum, J. K., 451, 460
Burk, C., 278
Burkhart, B. R., 366
Burnham, B. L., 125
Burns, D. D., 124
Burr, E. J., 228–229
Buss, A. H., 148, 149
Buss, K. A., 271
Butcher, J. N., xx, 39, 201, 337, 343, 349, 351–358, 360–362, 366, 372, 374, 473, 492–493
Butler, A. C., 127–128
Butti, G., 144

Cadoret, R., 432
Cai, T., 52, 61
Caldwell, A. B., 349
Calhoun, P. S., 458
Calhoun, R. F., 362
Campbell, D. T., 189, 191
Campbell, V., 313, 473
Cannon, T. D., 152–154, 293, 295
Cantor, J., 460
Cantor, N., 423
Caperton, J. D., 461
Cappeliez, P., 124–125
Capreol, M. J., 398
Cardno, A. G., 155, 156, 258
Carey, G., 274, 412
Carmichael, L., 53
Carson, R. C., 19, 84, 89, 90, 92, 94, 101
Cashel, M. L., 457–458

Casillas, A., 316, 323–324, 371, 431, 434–439, 442
Caspi, A., xxi, 139, 149, 263–264, 265, 266–267, 277
Castlebury, F., 478–479, 492
Castonguay, L. G., 95
Cattell, R. B., xxvi, xxviii, 15, 209, 221, 225, 230
Cayton, T. G., 353
Cecero, J. J., 128
Chambless, D. L., 129
Chan, T., 178–179
Chapman, A. L., 129
Chapman, J. P., 152, 157
Chapman, L. J., 152, 157
Charles, E., 166–168, 407, 414
Charlesworth, S. E., 129
Chartrand, T. L., 175
Chauncey, D. L., 315
Chen, E. C., 106
Cherepon, J. A., 458
Cherny, S. S., 275
Chess, S., 148
Chibnall, J. T., 363
Chipeur, H. M., 412
Chou, S. P., 312
Christal, R. E., 51
Christensen, A. J., 362
Claridge, G., 138, 142–144, 146, 151, 152, 154–156, 196
Clark, C. M., 54
Clark, D. A., 123, 124, 453
Clark, F., 150
Clark, L. A., xx, 52, 55, 57, 98, 168, 188, 199, 203, 255, 294, 315, 316, 321, 323–324, 329, 368, 371, 385, 408, 414–415, 431–439, 441–443
Clark, M. E., 355, 362
Clark, S. W., 327, 432
Clark, T. L., 387
Clarkin, J. F., 52, 61, 459, 460
Cleckley, H., 149, 322, 434
Cleland, C., 296, 303
Cloninger, C. R., xx, 65–79, 138–139, 146, 147, 257, 272, 316, 321, 326, 421–423, 425
Coffey, H. S., 86–88, 94–95
Cohen, J., 193, 200
Cohler, B. J., 159
Coker, L. A., xx, 166, 188, 315, 322, 328, 329
Cole, L. C., 33
Cole, S. W., 178–179
Collard, L. M., 434
Colledge, E., 150
Colligan, R. C., 315–316, 326
Colligan, S., 353
Collins, P. F., 146
Colon, F., 157
Comings, D., 277
Conforti, K., 459
Conklin, H. M., 139
Conway, C. G., 175

Cook, W. W., 362
Cooke, R. G., 51
Coolidge, F. L., 313, 315, 316, 322, 328
Cooper, A. M., 166
Corbitt, E. M., 167–168, 199, 313, 315, 324
Corley, R. P., 259
Cornblatt, B. A., 152–154, 293
Coryell, W., 54, 166–167
Costa, P. T., Jr., 15, 19, 51–53, 55, 57–61, 68, 94, 124–125,
    128, 143, 146, 176, 191, 199, 202, 225, 230, 231, 294,
    315, 316, 321, 323–324, 327, 361, 390, 420–422, 433,
    438, 441, 443, 458–459, 461, 475
Cowdry, R. W., 127
Cox, D. N., 460
Craddock, N., 157
Craig, I. W., 139, 265, 274
Craig, W. M., 296
Craighead, L. W., 124–125
Crawford, C. B., 412
Crawford, C. E., 387
Crits-Christoph, P., 129
Cronbach, L. J., 367
Crow, T. J., 156
Crowne, D. P., 406
Cruise, K. R., 451, 460
Cuadra, C. A., 344
Cull, J., 277, 460
Cullen, M., 372
Cumsille, P. E., 216
Curran, P. J., 243
Cyr, J. J., 487

D'Afflitti, J. P., 123, 478
Dahlsgaard, K. K., 127–128
Dahlstrom, L. E., 344, 363, 493
Dahlstrom, W. G., xx, 39, 201, 337, 341, 344, 352–354,
    356, 363, 375, 473, 492–493
Dai, X., 52, 61
Daleiden, E. L., 460
Daneluzzo, E., 144
Darwin, C. R., xvii
David, J. D., 425
Davies, M., 329
Davis, C., 142–143, 144
Davis, D. D., 114–117, 119–120, 125–126, 128–131
Davis, H. G., 362
Davis, J. M., 496
Davis, R. D., 10, 16, 19, 38, 42, 43, 315–316, 322–324,
    326, 415
Dawes, R. M., 229
Dawes, R. N., 490–491
Dawson, D. A., 312
Dawson, D. V., 54
Day, D., 154
de Charms, R., 32
De Clercq, B., 148

De Fruit, F., 148
de Mey, H. R., 52, 361
De Raad, B., 230, 327
Deary, I. J., 414
DeFries, J. C., 258, 259, 261, 265, 269, 271–274, 412
DeJong, C. A., 464
deJong-Meyer, R., 127
del Rio, C., 38
DeLong, J., 390
DeLuca, V. A., 491
DelVecchio, W. F., 149
Demby, A., 393
Demidenko, N., 458
Dent, O. B., 362
Depue, R. A., 146, 173
Derksen, J. J. L., 361
Desai, S., 361
Detrick, P., 363, 373
DeVore, J., 353
Di Dio, L., 99
Diamond, P. M., 460
DiCicco, L., 144
Dickinson, K. A., 460
DiClemente, C. C., 210, 224
Dies, R. R., 489
Dietz, C. B., 362
Dietzel, R., 127
Digman, J. M., 19, 51, 225, 234, 438
DiLalla, D. L., 412
Doan, B. T., 459
Doan, D.- T., 328
Doebbeling, B. I., 371
Doidge, N., 432
Dolan, B., 432
Dolan, R., 433
Dolan-Sewall, R. T., 202
Donati, D., 432
Donini, M., 432
Doren, R., 97
Douglas, K. S., 460
Draganic, S., 321
Drake, R. E., 313
Dreessen, L., 127, 128, 432
Du, W., 417–418
Duellman, R. M., 451
Dunn, J., 126–127
Durant, W., xvii
Durrett, C. A., 314, 327, 432–433, 434
Dyce, J. A., xx, 94–95
Dye, D. A., 230

Earl, N. L., 54
Earnst, K. S., 458
Eaton, C. A., 222–224
Eaves, L. J., 271, 272, 275
Ebstein, R. P., xxi, 270, 277, 278

Eccles, J. S., 387
Echemendia, R. J., 95
Edelson, S. M., 17
Edens, J. F., 451, 460, 461
Edwards, A. L., 465
Edwards, W., 465
Egger, J. I. M., 52
Egland, B., 353
Ehrmann, L., 362
Eisman, E. J., 489
Elek-Fisk, E., 216
Elkins, D. E., 356
Ellicott, A., 124
Ellis, C. G., 167–168, 199, 313, 315, 324
Emery, G., 115, 119, 123
Endicott, J., 144
Endler, N. S., 187
Englert, D. R., 362
Epstein, N., 123
Epstein, S., 58
Erickson, M., 353
Erickson, M. T., 271
Erlenmeyer-Kimling, L., 152–154, 293
Evans, C., 432
Evans, D. M., 258, 265
Evans, R. G., 349
Everett, J. E., 225
Evershed, S., 459
Exner, J. E., 473–474, 476, 477, 480, 484–486, 489, 494–495
Eyde, L., 489
Eysenck, H. J., xxvi, xxviii, 15, 124, 146, 147, 151, 195, 199, 230, 255, 272, 316, 406–408, 416, 419, 436
Eysenck, S. B. G., 124, 151, 255, 316, 408, 436

Fabrega, H., 166
Fagan, P. J., 56
Falkei, P., 143–144
Fals-Stewart, W., 457, 460
Farias, M., 154
Farmer, A. E., 156
Farmer, M. E., 179, 330
Farmer, R. E., 148
Farmer, R. F., 313, 315, 329
Farvolden, P., 316, 324
Fava, J. L., 210, 211, 214, 217, 219, 222–223, 229
Federoff, I. C., 292
Feifel, D., 157
Feinstein, A. R., 17–18, 201–202
Fekken, G. C., 453
Felske, U., 129
Fenichel, O., xviii
Ferrando, P. J., 254
Fetch, L. J., 57
Fidell, L. S., 188, 200
Fillenbaum, G. G., 54

Finch, J. F., xx
Fine, J. A., 124
Finger, M. S., 361
Finn, S. E., 447, 489
Fiore, C., 210
Fiorilli, M., 432
First, M. B., xvi, 125, 128, 169, 172, 180, 187, 320
Fischler, G. L., 373
Fisher, H. E., 159
Fisher, R. A., 275
Fjetland, O. K., 458
Flanagan, E., 313
Fleiss, J. L., 325–326
Flores, J., 455–456
Florio, C. M., 487–488
Foley, D., 156
Follette, W. C., 179
Forbey, J. D., 363–364, 371, 374
Forman, J. B. W., 168
Forster, B. B., 150
Forth, A. E., 144
Fossati, A., 432
Foulds, G. A., 144, 462
Fournier, M. A., 99
Fowler, J. C., 478–479, 492
Fowler, K. A., 475
Fowles, D. C., 147
Fraley, R. C., 290
Frances, A. J., 169, 172, 179, 180, 431
Frank, G. K., 73, 494–495
Frankenburg, F. R., xx, 315, 441
Fredrickson, B. L., 67, 68, 73
Freedman, M. B., 86–88, 94–95, 383, 387
Freeman, A., 58–59, 114–117, 119–120, 125–131, 173
Freko, D., 17
Fresco, D. M., 124–125
Freud, S., xvii, xxii, 3, 23, 25–26, 46, 55, 177
Friend, R., 393
Fritz, H. L., 98, 99–100
Fromm, E., 32, 34
Fromuth, M. E., 366
Fuchs, M., 322
Fulford, K. W. M., 140
Fulker, D. W., 267, 268, 272, 275, 412
Funder, D. C., 89, 91, 101–102

Gabel, J., 130
Gacono, C., 483–485
Gaies, L. A., 457
Galbaud du Fort, G., 263–264
Gallaher, P. E., 432
Gallen, R. T., 355
Gandhi, M. K., 73
Ganellen, R. J., 476, 478
Gangestad, S. W., 284, 288, 289, 290, 291, 293, 433

Gao, B., 52, 61
Garamoni, G. L., 171
Garb, H. N., 312, 315, 330, 486–488, 490
Gardner, D. L., 127
Gasperini, M., 127
Gentil, I., 410
George, A., 144
George, J. M., 458
Gerrity, D. M., 124
Gershuny, B. S., 328
Gibb, B. E., 292
Gibbon, M., 125, 128, 144, 315
Gibbs, J. C., 60
Gifford, R., 387
Gilbert, P., 124–125
Giles, C. L., 460
Gill, W. S., 460
Gillespie, N. A., 65–66, 258, 265, 422
Gilligan, C., 33
Gilmore, M. M., 166
Gironda, R. J., 355
Gitlin, M., 124
Glass, S., 314
Gleaves, D. H., 289
Glicksohn, J., 264
Golan, H., 264
Goldberg, L. R., 15, 19, 199, 211, 218, 225, 230–233, 255,
    343, 374, 403, 406, 484
Golden, R. R., 152–154, 293, 295
Golding, S. L., 176
Goldman, H., 173
Goldsmith, H. H., 271
Goldstein, A. J., 129
Goldstein, K., 35
Goldstein, M. G., 210
Goldston, C. S., 389
Gollwitzer, P. M., 86
Goodstein, L. D., xviii, 188, 194
Goodwin, C. J., xvii
Gordon, R. A., 490
Gorenstein, E., 171, 326
Gorsuch, R. L., 210, 233
Gosling, S. D., 148
Gottesman, I. I., 155, 270, 273
Gough, H. G., 341, 344, 436
Goulding, A., 154
Graham, J. R., xx, 201, 337, 343, 352–358, 360, 362–368,
    370–372, 473, 492–493
Graham, J. W., 216
Grant, B. F., 312
Gray, J. A., 147
Grayson, D., 233
Grayson, H. M., 349
Green, B. A., 289
Green, C. J., 41
Greenberg, B. D., 277

Greenberg, D., 129
Greenberg, R. L., 115, 119
Greene, R. L., 291, 360, 362, 363, 493
Greenstein, D. S., 458
Greenwald, A. G., 233
Greist, J. H., 316, 322
Griffin, R., 356
Griffith, P., 54
Grilo, C. M., 433, 441
Grossman, S. D., xx, 38, 40, 41, 195
Groth-Marnat, G., 473
Grove, W. M., 15, 19, 76, 300, 432, 486–488
Growe, G., 493
Guadagnoli, E., 213–214
Gunderson, J. D., 294
Gunderson, J. G., xx, 166, 315, 329, 441, 485–486, 495
Gurtman, M. B., xx, 84, 89, 93, 94–95, 97, 98, 101–102,
    107, 125, 197, 385, 387, 390, 391, 433
Gusnard, D. A., 73
Guthrie, G. M., 343
Guthrie, P., 296
Gynther, M. D., 343, 366

Haaga, D. F., 124
Hagemoser, S., 394
Haigler, E. D., 321, 322
Haines, J., 458
Hakstian, A. R., 144
Halbower, C. C., 343
Hall, C. S., xviii
Hallikainen, T., 278
Hallmark, R., 313, 473
Hamer, D. H., 75, 277
Hamilton, M., 458
Hammen, C., 124
Hampton, C., 393
Han, K., 358, 360, 362
Handel, R. W., 374
Handlesman, L., 296
Hanson, R. K., 487–488
Hardy, G., 130
Hare, R. D., 144, 150, 315, 323, 324, 459–460
Harkness, A. R., xx, 54, 316, 319, 360, 414–415
Harlow, L. L., 210
Harman, H. H., 210
Harmon, L. R., 347–348
Harmon-Jones, E., 391
Harpur, T. J., 144
Harrington, D. M., 189
Harrington, H., 139, 149
Harris, G. T., 295–296, 433
Harris, R., 348
Harrison, J. A., xx, 199, 315, 329
Harrison, R. P., 123
Hart, S. D., 144, 460
Hartman, E., 482, 491–492

Haslam, N., 152–154, 196, 242, 247, 288, 290, 293–298, 303, 433, 443
Hathaway, S. R., 51, 337–341, 344–346, 349, 363, 366, 458
Hau, K.- T., 233
Hay, D. A., 156
Hayes, A. M., 124
Heape, C. L., 316, 327, 432
Heard, H. L., 129
Heath, A. C., 65–66, 156, 257, 271, 272
Heck, S. A., 86, 91
Heils, A., 277
Heinen, T., 242–243
Helgeson, V. S., 92, 98, 99–100
Heller, K., 461
Helmes, E., 350, 375, 409–410
Helmreich, R. L., 99
Hempel, C. G., 12–14, 21–22
Hendler, J., 319
Hendrickson, A. E., 227
Hennen, J., xx
Hennig, J., 278
Henri, V., 474
Herbst, J. H., 54
Hergenhahn, B. R., xvii
Herkov, M. J., 313
Heron, J., 157
Herrington-Wang, L. E., 460
Hersen, M., 315
Hewitt, J. K., 259, 271, 272
Hicklin, J., 322
Hickok, G., 434
Hicks, A., 168, 313
Hill, E. L., 478
Hill, K., 321
Hiller, J. B., 487
Hilsenroth, M. J., 315, 478–479, 486–487, 491, 492, 494–495
Hirschfeld, R. M. A., 54
Hjemboe, S., 362
Hmel, B. A., 100
Ho, A., 460
Hoffman, N. G., 349
Hofstee, W. K. B., 230
Hoijtink, H., 155
Holahan, C. K., 99
Holcomb, J., 328
Holden, R. R., 453
Hollon, S., 127
Holmes, G. E., 458
Holmes, J. G., 97
Holmes, T. H., 461
Holzman, P., 496
Honaker, L. M., 373
Hong, S., 214
Hoppe, C., 291

Hopwood, C. J., 458
Horan, W. P., 293, 433
Horn, J. L., 222
Horney, K., 117
Horowitz, L. M., 92, 94, 97, 98, 105, 383, 387, 393, 397
Hotelling, H., 209
Hough, L. M., 19
Houts, A. C., 179
Hovantiz, C., 366
Howard, G. S., 175
Howard, K. I., 387
Huang, Z., 410
Hull, J. W., 459, 460
Humm, D. G., 337–338
Hunsley, J., 486, 487–488
Huppert, F. A., 65
Huprich, J., 312
Huprich, S. K., 476
Hurt, S. W., 496
Husted, J., 316, 322
Hyer, L., 51
Hyler, S. E., 57, 125, 327–328, 329, 432, 484

Iacono, W. G., 139, 254
Ialongo, N. S., 292
Imhof, E. A., 473
Inwald, R., 363, 373
Irish, S. L., 321, 415
Israel, A. C., 166, 329

Jackson, D., 316
Jackson, D. N., 19, 20, 52, 55, 58, 60, 217, 294, 375, 402, 405–410, 412, 419, 424, 452
Jackson, J. S., 180, 314
Jackson, M. A., 176
Jackson, M. C., 140, 152, 154
Jahn, T., 293
Jahoda, M., 29
Jang, K. L., 54, 272–273, 294, 410, 412–414, 416–419, 422, 424
Jansen, J. A., 464
Jarrett, R. B., 98, 203, 387
Jaschik-Herman, B., 101–102
Jaspers, K., xviii
Jeffrey, T., 353
Jeste, D., 173
Joffe, R. T., 51
John, O. P., 225, 327, 383, 438
Johnson, D. W., 460
Johnson, J. K., 460, 461
Johnson, R. C., 178–179
Johnson, T., 168
Johnston, T., 291
Joiner, T. E., 126, 292, 433, 443
Jones, A., 322
Jones, I., 157

Jones, L., 150
Jones, L. A., 157
Joreskog, K. G., 219
Joshua, S., 168, 313
Joyce, P. R., xx, 414
Judd, C. M., 188–189
Jung, C. G., 35, 44, 57

Kaasinen, V., 73
Kabat, M. H., 362
Kaelber, C. T., 179, 330
Kaemmer, B., xx, 201, 337, 352, 353, 365, 367–368, 370–372, 473, 492–493
Kagan, J., 116, 290–291
Kahler, C. W., 292
Kaiser, H. F., 222, 226, 227
Kakuma, R., 263
Kakuma, T., 460
Kalehzan, B. M., 97–98
Kanba, S., 422
Kaplan, E. B., 54
Kaplan, M., 171
Kaplan, R. D., 166
Kass, F., 166–167, 168, 407, 414
Katz, M. M., 352
Katz, S. E., 337–338
Kay, G. G., 489
Kaye, A. L., 313, 315, 324, 328–329, 393
Kaye, W., 73
Kazdin, A. E., 188–192, 194, 205
Keane, T. M., 303
Keiller, S. W., 357–358
Keller, F., 292, 293
Keller, L. S., 374
Keller, M. B., 54
Kelley, H. H., 97
Kellman, H. D., 327–329, 432
Kellogg, S. H., 460
Kelly, G., 115
Keltikangas-Jaervinen, L., 73
Kendall, P., 127
Kendall, R. E., 19, 20–21
Kendell, R. A., 286
Kendell, R. E., 156, 180, 314
Kendler, K. S., 180, 271, 314
Kennedy, S. H., 51
Kenny, D. A., 106
Kerksen, J. J. L., 52
Kernberg, O. F., 55, 173, 423–424
Kerr, N. L., 97
Kessler, R. C., 179, 330
Khadivi, A., 357
Kiehl, K. A., 150
Kiesler, D. J., 56, 83, 84, 89, 92–94, 100–106, 231, 383, 385, 388, 389, 392–393, 419
Kijima, N., 422

Kim, H., 288, 298
Kinder, B. N., 458
King, R. E., 326
Kirby, A. C., 458
Kirk, K .M., 156
Kirk, R. E., 191
Kirk, S. A., 179
Kirmayer, L. J., 174
Klein, C., 293
Klein, D. N., 174
Klein, M. H., 316, 322
Klerman, G. L., 54
Kline, C. D., 362
Kline, P., 15
Klosko, J. S., 118–119, 126, 130
Kluger, A. N., xxi
Knauper, B., 179, 330
Knott, M., 240, 242
Knutson, B., 178–179
Koch, S., xvii
Kocovski, N. L., 187
Koenig, H. G., 75
Koenigsberg, H. W., 166
Koestner, R., 99, 476–479
Kohut, H., 423
Koob, G. F., 73
Koons, A. N., 124–125
Korfine, L., xix, xxiii, 196, 291, 293, 296, 433
Koss, M. P., 349
Kotov, R., 292, 433, 443
Kraepelin, E., xviii
Kraft, D., 203
Krall, V., 493
Kramer, R. J., 124
Kreek, M. J., 460
Kretschmer, E., xviii, 151
Kristensen, W., 482
Kropp, P. R., 460
Krueger, R. F., xx, 196, 199, 201, 254, 255, 263–264, 270, 273, 327, 433, 438
Krug, S. E., xxvi
Krukonis, A. B., 478
Kubiszyn, T. W., 489
Kuhn, T. S., xxiii
Kupfer, D. J., xvi, 180, 187
Kurtz, J. E., 459
Kutcher, M., 458
Kutchins, H., 179
Kvale, J. N., 75
Kwapil, T. R., 155, 157

Lachar, D., 349, 493
Lachman, H. M., 278
Ladd, J., 123
LaForge, R., 86–88, 94–95, 385
Laing, R. D., 142

Lalljee, M., 154
Lally, S. J., 451
Lalone, L., 354
Lampel, A. K., 326
Landis, C., 337–338
Landt, O., 278
Lanier, V. W., 457, 458
Lanyon, R. I., xviii, 188, 194
Larsen, L. H., 355
Larsen, R. M., 351, 473
Larstone, R. M., 416–417
Lavori, P., 54
Lazar, B., 493
Leaf, P. J., 311
Leary, D. E., xvii
Leary, T. F., 84, 86–89, 93–95, 100, 102, 383, 392, 419
Lee, C. W., 126–127
Lehman, A. F., 173
Leibenluft, E., 127
Leibing, E., 130
Leichsenring, F., 130
Leippe, M. R., 233
Lemery, K. S., 271
LeMoal, M., 73
Lencz, T., 152
Lennon, T., 455–456, 460
Lenzenweger, M. F., xix, xxiii, 146, 196, 290, 291, 293, 296, 433
Leonard, A., 150
Lerew, D. R., 292
Lerner, M., 25
Lesch, K. P., 277
Levenson, M. R., 353
Levesque, M. J., 106
Levin, J., 458
Levitan, R. D., 51
Levitt, A. J., 51
Levitt, E. E., 350
Levy, K. N., 86
Lewin, K., 86
Li, H., 159
Li, L., 277
Lichtermann, D., 156
Licinio, J., 277
Liddle, P. F., 150
Lilienfeld, S. O., 166, 174, 312, 313, 323, 329, 330, 371, 475, 493, 495
Liljequist, L., 370, 458
Lin, M. M., 455, 460
Lindzey, G., xviii
Linehan, M. M., 129
Lingoes, J., 348
Linney, Y., 155
Lion, J. R., 403
Liotti, G., 117
Little, R. J. A., 216

Livesley, W. J., xv–xvii, xx, xxi, xxiii, 19, 20, 51–55, 60, 166, 187, 196, 198, 199, 202, 272–273, 294, 297, 316, 321, 323–324, 326, 327, 402, 403–405, 407–408, 410, 412, 413, 415–419, 422–425, 431–432, 434
Lloyd-Richardson, E. E., 292
Locke, K. D., 84, 387, 388, 390, 393
Lockenhoff, C. E., 327
Loeber, R., 271
Loehlin, J. C., xxi, 241, 259, 261, 265, 273, 327, 412, 413
Loevinger, J., 19, 40, 402, 452
Lohr, J. M., 475
Loper, A. B., 128
Loranger, A. W., xviii, 166, 167, 203–204, 313, 315, 316, 328, 459–460
Lorr, M., xviii, xix, xxi, 84, 187, 195, 385, 390
Lowrie, G. S., 293
Lubin, B., 128, 351, 473
Luborsky, L., 129–130
Lucas, P. B., 127
Lyerly, S. B., 352
Lykken, T. D., 68, 263–264
Lynam, D. R., 322, 330
Lyons, M., 319
Lytle, R., 387

MacCallum, R. C., 214
MacDonald, A., 155
Madden, P. A., 257, 272
Maekawa, H., 422
Maes, H., 271, 275
Maffei, C., 432
Maier, W., 143–144, 156
Maling, M. S., 387
Mallinckrodt, B., 106
Mangine, S., 167–168, 199, 313, 315, 324
Manis, M., 477, 496
Mann, A. W., 362
Manning, K. A., 478
Marcus, B. H., 210
Mardia, K. V., 93
Marinangeli, M. G., 144
Marino, L., 174
Markey, P. M., 91, 101–102
Markon, K. E., xx, 196, 199, 254, 255, 270, 273, 327, 438
Marková, I. S., 142
Marks, I., 129
Marks, P. A., 343
Marlowe. D., 406
Marsh, H. W., 233
Marshall, R. D., 57
Martens, A., 314
Martin, C. L., 94–95, 97
Martin, J., 139, 149, 265
Martin, M. A., 359
Martin, N. G., 156, 257, 258, 265, 272, 273, 290, 422
Martin-Cannici, C., 457–458

Martinussen, M., 482
Maruish, M., 473
Mashek, D., 159
Masling, J. M., 478, 488
Maslow, A. H., 27, 29, 31, 34, 35
Mason, O., 152, 156
Mastrosimone, C. C., 478
Matano, R., 393
Matarazzo, J. D., 351, 473
Mattia, J. I., 166, 313
Mayman, M., 477, 496
McAdams, D. P., 92, 422
McCaffrey, R. J., 357
McCartney, K., 265
McCay, E. A., 51
McClary, K. A., 460
McClay, J., 139, 149, 265
McClearn, G. E., 258, 259, 261, 265, 269, 272–273, 412
McClelland, D. C., 387, 476–479
McClosky, H., 344
McCrae, R. R., xx, 15, 19, 51–53, 55, 58–61, 68, 124–125, 128, 146, 176, 191, 199, 202, 225, 230, 231, 294, 315, 316, 321, 323–324, 327, 361, 390, 413, 420–422, 433, 438, 441, 443, 458–459, 461
McCreery, C., 154–156
McCullough, J. P., 393
McCully, E., 357
McCune, K. J., 393
McDavid, J. D., 327, 432
McDermott, P. A., 455, 460
McDermut, W., 315
McDonald, R. P., 210, 228–229
McDowell, C. J., 486
McEvoy, L. T., 311
McEwan, J. L., 434
McGlashan, T. H., xx, 329, 432, 433, 441
McGrew, J., 362
McGuffin, P., 155, 156, 257–259, 261, 265, 269, 272–274
McHugh, P. F., 460
McKenna, T., 352, 362
McKinley, J. C., 51, 337–338, 340, 344, 345, 349, 363, 366, 458
McLellan, T., 129–130
McLemore, C. W., 83, 84
McMain, S., 116–117
McNair, D. M., 84, 385
McNulty, J. L., xx, 54, 316, 319, 356–357, 360, 362, 363, 365, 367–368, 370–372, 493–494
Meagher, R. B., Jr., 41
Meagher, S., 40
Medin, D. L., 13, 17, 21
Medley, D. M., 362
Mednick, S. A., 152, 294, 295
Meehl, P. E., 12, 152, 284, 288, 291, 293, 297–301, 303, 326, 338–346, 363, 367, 375, 433, 443, 495
Meier, P., 58

Melancon, J. G., 289
Mellsop, G., 168, 313
Mendham, M. C., 457–458
Mendrek, A., 150
Menninger, K., 15
Merikangas, K. R., 277
Merry, J., 393
Mervielde, I., 148
Merwin, M. M., 316, 322
Messick, S., 375
Meyer, G. J., 474, 479–480, 483–485, 487–489, 490, 494–495
Meyer, J. M., 271
Meyer, T., 292, 293
Mezzich, J. E., 166
Mihura, J. L., 484–485, 495
Mill, J., 139, 149, 265
Miller, I. W., 292
Miller, J., 360
Miller, J. D., 61
Miller, K. B., 362
Miller, M. B., 157
Miller, M. J., 60
Miller, T., 54
Millon, C. M., 38, 40–43, 315–316, 322–324, 326
Millon, R. B., 322
Millon, T., xv, xx, xxiii, 10, 13, 15, 16, 18–20, 22, 25–27, 29, 38, 39, 41–44, 55, 196, 199–204, 315–316, 322–324, 326, 394, 403, 415
Milne, B., 149
Milofsky, E., 66, 68, 73
Minassian, A., 157
Minnegawa, R., 353
Miranda, J., 124
Mischel, W., 387, 422
Mitchell, D. G. V., 150
Mitchell, S. A., 85, 100
Moffitt, T. E., 139, 149, 257, 263–265, 273
Mohr, C. D., 106
Moldin, S. O., 258
Monahan, P., 130
Montag, I., 458
Moore, E. A., 178–179
Moore, R. G., 124
Moore, R. J., 457
Moreland, K. L., 489
Morey, L. C., xx, 51, 125–126, 166–169, 188, 315, 316, 322–324, 326, 329, 350, 431, 433, 441, 451, 455–461, 464, 466–467
Morse, J. Q., 61
Moser, R. K., 357
Moskowitz, D. S., 84, 95–97, 99, 107, 197
Mulaik, S. A., 210
Mulder, R. T., xx, 414
Mullins-Sweatt, S. N., 321, 327
Muran, J., 387

Murphy, D. L., 277
Murphy, E. A., 286
Murphy, G. L., 14
Murray, H. A., xvii, 8
Murray, L., 150
Murray, R. A., 155
Murray, R. M., 156
Mutén, E., 57
Myers, J. K., 311

Naboisek, H., 86, 94–95
Nakao, K., 294
Narrow, W. E., 176
Nashimura, N., 294
Neale, M. C., 271, 272, 275
Nee, J., 168
Nelen, M., 265
Nelson-Gray, R. O., 148
Netter, P., 278
Nettle, D., 154
Newman, C. F., 127–128, 129
Newman, J. P., 144
Newman, M. G., 387
Newman, S. C., 263
Newsom, C. R., 473
Nezworski, M. T., 312, 313, 330, 486–487
Niaura, R., 292
Nichols, D. S., 360
Nieberding, R., 313, 473
Noble, E. P., 138
Norman, W., 15, 19
Norquist, G. S., 179, 330
Norris, S. C. W., 393
Norton, K., 432
Novella, L., 432
Novick, O., 277
Nowicki, S., 385
Nunnally, J., 225

Oakman, J. M., 292
O'Boyle, M., 327
O'Brien, C. P., 129–130
O'Connor, B. P., xx, 94–95, 211, 255, 387, 467
Offer, D., xxi, 8
Offord, K. P., 315–316, 326
Oldham, J. M., 327–329, 432
O'Leary, K. M., 127
Olesen, N., 291
Ollinger, J. M., 73
Olshan, S., 123, 124
Oltmanns, T. F., 213
Ones, D. S., 372
Ono, Y., 422
Onoda, N., 422
Orford, J., 101
Ornduff, S. R., 457

Ortega, A., 357
Osher, Y., 277
Ossorio, A. G., 86–88, 383
Owen, M. J., 157
Ozer, D. J., 91, 101–102
Ozkaragoz, Y., 138

Paddock, J. R., 385
Padesky, C. A., 131
Palav, A., 357
Paolo, A. M., 355
Pap, A., 12
Paris, J., 196
Parker, G., 419
Parker, J. D., 361, 460
Parker, K. C., 487–488
Parks, A. C., 67, 68
Parnas, J., 140, 144, 293, 295
Pate, J. L., 459
Patrick, C. J., 254, 371
Patterson, C., 277
Paulhus, D. L., 94–95, 97
Paunonen, S. V., xx, 19
Peabody, D., 230, 231
Pearson, K., 209
Pedersen, N. L., 263–264
Peebles, J., 457
Perloff, J. M., 124
Perry, J. C., 403, 423
Perry, K. J., 129
Perry, W., 157, 490–491, 496
Persons, J. B., 124
Perugi, G., 157
Perugini, M., 327
Peselow, E. D., 124
Peters, E., 154, 155
Peterson, C., 67
Peterson, G. W., 453
Petri, S., 277
Petrill, S., 271
Petroskey, L. J., 361
Petruzzi, C., 144
Pfohl, B., 167, 168–169, 199, 315, 432, 439
Phillips, K. A., 294
Phillips, N., 92, 93–95, 176, 385, 392, 393
Piaget, J., 115
Pickering, A. D., 147, 156
Pickles, A., 255, 271
Piedmont, R. L., 51, 324
Pilkonis, P. A., 61, 166, 316, 327, 425, 432
Pinard, G., 84
Pincus, A. L., xx, 52, 83–86, 89, 91, 94, 95, 97–98, 100, 103–105, 107, 125, 197, 225, 385, 387, 390, 393, 419, 433, 460
Pincus, H. A., 169, 171, 180
Piotrowski, C., 451, 473

Pitts, T. E., 327, 432
Plomin, R., xxi, 148, 149, 258, 259, 261, 265, 269, 271–274, 277, 412
Plutchik, R., 423
Pogge, D. L., 491
Pohjalainen, T., 278
Ponticas, Y., 57
Pope, K. S., 354
Popplewell, D., 156
Poulton, R., 139, 149, 265
Powell-Lunden, J., 499
Pratkanis, A. R., 233
Presley, G., 494–495
Presly, A. J., 414
Preston, J., 126
Pretzer, J. L., 120, 127
Priel, B., 277
Prinzhorn, B., 458
Prochaska, J. O., 210, 224
Procidano, M. E., 461
Proietti, J. M., 327, 432
Prolo, F., 432
Prolo, P., 277
Provenza, M., 127
Przybeck, T. R., 65, 66, 68, 77, 138–139, 147, 316, 321, 421
Pukrop, R., 410

Quarrington, B., 487
Quigley, B. D., 329, 441
Quine, W. V. O., 13–14, 21
Quinlan, D. M., 123, 478
Quinsey, V. L., 295–296, 433

Rabe-Hesketh, S., 240
Rabian, B., 292
Rabie, L., 478, 488
Radloff, L. S., 76
Rado, S., 152
Rae, D. S., 179, 330
Raeikkoenen, K., 73
Ragusea, S. A., 95
Rahe, R. H., 461
Raine, A., 152, 271
Rakowski, W., 210
Raney, D., 493
Rasmussen, P. R., 138
Raulin, M. L., 152, 293
Rawlings, D., 152
Rayson, B., 493
Rector, N. A., 51
Redding, C. A., 210
Reddon, J. R., 350, 375
Reed, G. M., 489
Rees, A., 130, 459
Regier, D. A., xvi, 176, 179, 180, 187, 330

Reich, B., xx
Reich, J., 128
Reich, W., xviii
Reinhardt, V., 455
Reis, H. T., 97, 188–189
Reise, S. P., 255
Renneberg, B., 129
Renwick, S. J., 389
Reus, V. I., 178–179
Reuter, M., 278
Revelle, W., 146
Reynolds, C. A., 263–264, 271
Reynolds, S. K., 124–125, 130, 415, 432, 441
Reynolds, W. M., 465
Rhee, S. H., 259
Rice, M. E., 295–296, 433
Rice, M. T., 296
Rieder, R. O., 57, 125, 319
Riemann, R., 412, 413
Rietschel, M., 156
Rijsdijk, S. A., 155
Risch, N. J., 277
Riskind, J. H., 115–116
Roberts, B. W., 149
Roberts, W. C., 393
Robins, C. J., 123, 124, 129
Roesch, R., 176
Rogers, C. R., 29, 35
Rogers, R., 166, 311, 313, 315, 323, 328–329, 359, 455–460
Rogler, L. H., 179
Rojdev, R., 350
Rolf, J. E., 159
Rolland, J., 390
Romney, D. M., 392, 393
Ronchi, P., 127
Ronningstam, E., 315
Roper, B. L., 374
Ropers, H. H., 265
Rorschach, H., 474
Rosch, E., 403
Rosen, A., 326
Rosen, D. H., 289
Rosenbaum, M., 127
Rosenberg, S. E., 97–98, 387
Rosenbloom, D., 210
Rosenfeld, R., 316, 322
Rosenthal, R., 487
Rosnick, L., 327–329, 432
Rossi, A., 144
Rossi, J. S., 210, 224
Rossi, S. R., 210
Rossner, S. C., 478
Rosso, M., 363
Rothschild, L., 296
Rounds, J., 98

Rounsaville, B. J., 180, 314
Rousar, E. E., 57
Rouse, S. V., 361, 362, 473
Ruan, W. J., 312
Rubin, D. B., 216, 290–291
Rubin, H., 229
Ruddy, J., 316
Rude, S. S., 125
Ruiz, M. A., 95, 98, 387, 390, 460
Rusbult, C. E., 97
Ruscio, A. M., 285, 297, 303
Ruscio, J., 285, 297, 303
Rushton, J. P., 33
Russell, B., xvii
Russell, J. A., 83
Rutherford, M. J., 455, 460
Rutter, M., 271, 423
Ryan, J. J., 355
Ryan, J. M., 101–102
Ryder, A. G., 361
Ryynanen, O. P., 278

Sabol, S., 277
Sabshin, M., xxi, 8, 179, 195
Sachs, H., 493
Sadler, P., 84, 101–102
Safran, J. D., 103, 116–117
Saito, T., 278
Salekin, R. T., 459, 460
Salkovskis, P. M., 139–140
Sampson, W. S., 124–125
Samstag, L. W., 387
Samuel, D. B., 166, 195, 200, 313, 314, 315, 325, 330
Sanderson, C., 52, 61
Sanislow, C. A., xx, 433, 441
Sankis, L. M., 174, 420
Saragovi, C., 99
Sass, L. A., 140, 141–142
Saucier, G., 19, 211, 230, 231, 403, 484
Sawrie, S. M., 362
Saxena, S., 140
Scarr, S., 265
Schaefer, E. S., 84, 433
Schafer, J. L., 216
Schenk, P. W., 371
Scherillo, P., 127
Schinka, J. A., 291, 327, 354, 454, 455, 458
Schippers, G. M., 464
Schluger, R. P., 460
Schmidt, C., Jr., 54
Schmidt, C. W., 57
Schmidt, H. O., 341
Schmidt, J. A., 89, 103, 106, 388, 393
Schmidt, N. B., 126, 292, 433, 443
Schneider, K., 419

Schneider, P. L., 89
Schroeder, M. L., 20, 52, 55, 60, 294, 321, 402, 407–408, 415–416, 419, 424
Schuller, D. R., 51
Schulsinger, F., 293, 295
Schulsinger, H., 293, 295
Schwartz, G. F., 343
Schwartz, J. M., 140
Schwartz, R. M., 171
Scinto, A., 144
Scragg, P., 457–458
Seelen, J., 354
Seeman, M. V., 51
Seeman, W., 343
Seever, M., 473
Segal, D. L., 313, 315, 328
Segal, Z. V., 116–117, 387
Self, D., 327
Seligman, M. E. P., 67, 68
Sellars, C., 150
Sellbom, M., 370, 371
Serlin, R. C., 226
Serrao, P., 316
Sewell, K. W., 359, 455–456, 457–458, 459, 460
Shafer, A. B., 148
Shah, J. Y., 391
Sham, P. C., 156, 258, 261, 275
Shapiro, D., 55, 59–60
Shapiro, D. A., 130
Sharpe, J. P., 361
Shea, M. T., xx, 54, 198, 202, 203, 313, 315, 324, 328–329, 441
Shedler, J., 314, 322, 324, 325–326, 327, 477, 496
Sherwood, N. E., 361–362
Shields, J., 155
Shiner, R. L., 148, 149
Shinohara, S., 422
Sickel, A. E., 441
Siddiqui, N., 455, 460
Siegfried, Z., xxi
Siegler, I. C., 54
Sigelman, J., 391
Silberg, J. L., 271
Silk, K. R., xx
Silva, P. A., 149, 263–264
Sim, J. P., 392, 393
Simms, L. J., 316, 323–324, 371, 431, 434–439, 442
Simola, S. K., 177
Simonoff, E., 271
Simonsen, E., xvi, xviii, xx, xxi, 143, 144, 316, 327
Simpson, C. A., 460
Simpson, W. B., 296
Sinha, B. K., 432
Skeem, J. L., 176
Skilling, T. A., 296
Skinner, H. A., 402

Skodol, A. E., xx, 166–168, 173, 327–329, 407, 414, 432, 433, 441
Skrondal, A., 240
Slade, P., 156
Sletten, I. W., 343
Slutske, W. S., 374
Smeraldi, E., 127
Smith, A. M., 150
Smith, C., 494–495
Smith, E. E., 13, 21
Smith, G. T., 355
Smith, L. L., 255
Smith, M., 150
Smith, R. L., 343
Smith, T. W., 362
Snidman, N., 290–291
Snyder, M., 284, 288, 289, 291, 433
Snyter, C. M., 366
Soldz, S., 393
Soloff, P. H., 144
Somer, O., 232
Spanier, G. B., 352
Spearman, C., 209
Spence, J. T., 99
Spencer, H., 29
Spieker, S. J., 290
Spielberger, C. D., 460–461
Spiro, A., 353
Spitzer, R. L., 125, 128, 144, 166–169, 172–173, 176, 178, 179, 319, 325–326, 407, 414
Springen, K., 75
Sprock, J., 19
Srivastava, S., 327, 438
Stafford, K. P., 361
Stallings, M. C., 259
Stanghellini, G., 140
Stanley, J. C., 189, 191
Steer, R. A., 458, 460
Stein, L. A. R., 362
Steinberg, L., 244
Steinbring, I., 410
Steinmeyer, E., 410
Stejskal, W. J., 486–487
Stepanian, M. L., 478
Stern, B. L., 328
Stern, D. N., 85
Stern, G. G., 231
Stern, H. S., 290–291
Stewart, B. L., 124
Stiles, W. B., 130
Stinson, F. S., 312
Stokes, J. M., 491
Stopa, L., 126
Stout, R. L., xx, 329, 441
Strack, S., xix, xx, xxi, 38, 42, 187, 195, 316
Stravynski, A., 129

Strickland, I., 150
Strong, D. R., 291, 292
Strube, M. J., 289
Strycker, L. A., 232
Stuart, S., 432
Suarez, A., 129
Suczek, R. F., 86, 385
Sudgen, K., 139
Sullivan, H. S., 84–86, 100, 102, 104, 383
Sun, C., 410
Sunde, T., 482
Suzuki, A., 422
Svanum, S., 362
Svrakic, D. M., 68, 70–75, 77, 79, 138–139, 147, 316, 321, 421

Tabachnick, B. G., 188, 200
Tackett, J. L., 327, 433
Takaishi, J., 294
Talbert, S., 51
Tanaka, N., 294
Tasca, G. A., 458
Taulbee, E. S., 385
Taylor, A., 139, 265
Taylor, E. R., 460
Taylor, G., 126–127
Taylor, M., 343
Taylor, S., 292
Teague, G. B., 313
Telch, M. J., 126
Tellegen, A., xx, 15, 19, 68, 76, 89, 147, 201, 263–264, 316, 337, 343, 351–353, 355, 363, 365, 367–368, 370–372, 373, 436, 473, 492–493
ten Berge, J. M. F., 215, 216
Tennant, A., 459
Terpstra, J., 178–179
Terril, D. R., 124
Thapar, A., 257, 273
Theodore, R. F., 139, 149
Thissen, D., 244
Thomas, A., 148
Thomas, C., 213
Thomas, G. V., 167–168, 199, 313, 315, 324
Thomas, K., 155
Thompson, J. S., 255
Thorne, P., 126
Thornton, T., 140
Thurstone, L. L., 209, 219, 229
Tice, D. M., 53
Timbrook, R. E., 354, 357–358, 493
Tomarken, A. J., 459
Tonsager, M. E., 447
Tracey, T. J. G., 89, 94, 98, 101–102
Trapnell, P. D., 84, 92, 93–05, 176, 385, 390, 393, 461
Treece, C., 316, 322
Treloar, S. A., 156

Tringone, R., 41
Trivers, R. L., 33
Trobst, K. K., 84, 89, 100, 389
Truett, K. R., 271
Trull, T. J., 52, 54, 57, 61, 166, 177, 296, 315–316, 321, 327, 328, 361, 420, 432–434, 459
Tryon, W. T., 296
Tubre, T., 289
Tucker, D. D., 458
Tupes, E. C., 51
Turkheimer, E., 213
Turner, R. A., 178–179
Tutek, D. A., 129
Tversky, A., 13, 17
Tyrer, P., 168, 414, 431
Tyrka, A., 152–154, 293, 295

Ulrich, R., 166
Umansky, R., 277
Ureño, G., 97
Useda, J. D., 328, 361, 459
Ustad, K. L., 455–456, 458–460
Ustun, B., 173

Vaidya, J., 147, 368
Vaillant, G. E., 66, 68, 73, 403, 423
van den Bosch, R. J., 155
Van den Brink, W., 464
van den Oord, E. J. C. G., 255
van der Staak, C. P. F., 52
Van Driel, O. P., 219
van Kampen, D., 410
Van Lange, P. A. M., 97
Van Leeuwen, K., 148
van Oost, B. A., 265
Van Zuilen, M. H., 322
Varghese, F. T. N., 168, 313
Velicer, W. F., 15, 210, 211, 213–214, 217, 219, 220, 222–224, 229
Vendrig, A. A., 361
Verheul, R., 166–167, 316, 325
Vermunt, J. K., 242–243
Vernon, P. A., 272, 410, 412–414, 416–417
Vernon, P. E., 230, 422
Verschell, M. S., 486
Viding, E., 150
Viglione, D. J., 486–487, 490, 491, 496
Villaseñor, V. S., 97
Vitacco, M. J., 359
Vitkus, J., 97
Vittengl, J. R., 98, 203, 387
Volavka, J., 278
Vollema, M. G., 155

Wadsworth, G. W., 337–338
Wagner, C. C., 89, 103, 106, 388, 393

Wagner, E., 458
Wagner, M., 143–144
Wakefield, J. C., 56, 172–174, 179, 419, 423
Waldman, I. D., 166, 255, 329
Walker, L. E. A., 177
Wallace, A., 370
Waller, N. G., 19, 68, 255, 290, 297, 298, 301, 303, 370, 433, 436
Walton, H. J., 414
Wang, E. W., 460
Wang, W., 410, 417–418
Wang, Y., 417–418
Ward, A. W., 491
Ward, R. M., 210
Warner, M. B., xx, 441
Warner, M. G., 464
Warren, H. D., 53
Waters, A., 126
Waters, E., 302–303
Watkins, C. E., 313, 473
Watson, A., 459
Watson, D., xx, 57, 147, 188, 199, 255, 327, 368, 371, 408, 432, 434, 438, 459
Watson, G. S., 362
Watt, M., 374
Watt, N. F., 159
Wattenmaker, D., 131
Wattenmaker, R., 131
Watts, D., 357–358
Waugh, M. H., 125–126, 316, 322, 350, 459
Webb, J. T., 350
Webster, C., 176
Weckler, D. A., 97
Weed, N. C., 357–358, 362, 366
Wegner, D. M., 175
Weinberger, D. R., 154–155
Weinberger, J., 476–479
Weiner, I. B., 480, 489, 491
Weishaar, M. E., 118–119, 126, 130
Weiss, D. J., 374
Weiss, L., 38, 43
Weissman, A. N., 127
Welkowitz, J., 123
Welsh, G. S., 341, 344, 348, 363
Welsh, K. A., 54
Wenger, A. W., 322
Wenk, E., 255
Wesner, R., 130
Westen, D., 167, 195, 313, 314, 316, 322, 325–326, 327
Wetter, M. W., 355, 360
Wetzel, R. D., 147, 316, 421
Wetzler, S., 357
Wheatley, T., 175
White, P. O., 227
White, R. W., 32

Whitehead, C., 74
Wicklund, R. A., 86
Widaman, K. F., 214
Widiger, T. A., xvi, xviii, xx, xxi, 51–54, 60–61, 94, 116, 119, 143, 144, 166–169, 174, 177, 179, 188, 199, 200, 294, 296, 313–316, 321, 322, 324, 325, 327–330, 355, 394, 415, 419–421, 431–433, 438, 443, 475
Wiener, D. N., 344, 347–348
Wiese, D., 147, 368
Wigfield, A., 387
Wiggins, J. S., 86–90, 92–95, 97–98, 100, 106–107, 176, 225, 231, 345, 349–350, 356, 375, 383, 385, 387, 390, 392, 393, 419, 458, 461, 464
Wildenauer, D. B., 156
Williams, A. O., 150
Williams, B., 152, 196, 242
Williams, C. L., 353, 458
Williams, H. L., 344
Williams, J. B., 157, 166–167, 169, 173, 176, 407, 414
Williams, J. B. W., 125, 128, 319
Willner, P., 141
Wilson, E. O., 3, 23, 33, 46
Wise, T. N., 57
Wolf, H., 416–417
Wolkowitz, O. M., 178–179
Wood, J., 458
Wood, J. M., 312, 313, 486–487, 493, 495
Woodward, K. L., 75
Woodward, S. A., 290
Woody, E., 84, 101–102
Woody, E. Z., 292
Woody, G. E., 129–130
Wormsworth, J. A., 415–416
Wright, J. C., 14
Wrobel, T. A., 349

Wu, K. D., 316, 323–324, 431, 434–439, 442
Wynne, L. C., 159

Yamagata, S., 422
Yang, J., 52, 61
Yao, S., 52, 61
Yen, S., xx, 203
Yeomans, F. E., 459, 460
Yonce, L. J., 299
Yong, L., 441
Yorifuji, K., 294
Yoshimura, K., 422
Young, A., 174
Young, J. E., 118–119, 125–126, 128, 130–131
Young, L. T., 51
Young, R. McD., 138
Young, R. W., 355
Young, S. N., 84
Youniss, R. P., 390
Yule, W., 129

Zaballero, A. R., 455, 460
Zalewski, C., 473
Zanarini, M. C., xx, 315, 329, 432, 433, 441
Zapf, P. A., 176
Zegers, F. E., 216
Zhang, S., 214
Zheng, W., 410
Zhu, S., 410
Zimmerman, M., 166–167, 296, 313, 315, 328, 439
Zinser, M. C., 157
Zonderman, A. B., 54
Zubin, S., 337–338
Zuckerman, M., 128, 146, 151
Zuroff, D. C., 84, 89, 95–97, 107, 118, 123, 197
Zwick, W. R., 220, 222–224

# Subject Index

Page numbers followed by f or t indicate figures and tables, respectively.

Abnormal personality
  biology and, xxii
  causes of, 10
  classification of, 12
  defining, xxi
  as disease, 15
  genetics and, xxii–xxiii
  historical context of, xvii–xxi
  IPC and, 392–397
  normal v., 8–11, 169–170, 283–286, 462–467
  trait differences in, 92–100
  trait structure of, 255
Abridged Big Five-dimensional Circumplex
    (AB5C), 231
Abstraction, 25
Acceptance, 31
Accommodation, 33
Acomplementary patterns, 102
Adaptation, 6, 24
  modes of, 29–32
  passive v. active, 30
Adaptive testing, 373–374
Adaptivity, 24–25
Addiction Admission Scale (AAS), 362
Addiction Potential Scale (APS), 362
Addiction Severity Index, 460
ADHD, 141
  association studies of, 276
  DRD4 and, 277
Adjustive personality, 93–94
Adjustment Scale, 352
Adolescent personality inventories, 41–42
Adoption studies, 267–269
Affect cluster, 481
Affective system, 114
Agency, 90–91, 91f, 383. *See also* Unmitigated agency
AGGR, 360

Aggression (AGG) scale, 460
Aggressiveness, in PSY-5, 360
Aggrieved-masochistic (AM) spectrum, 31
Agreeableness (A), 51
  nontaxonic models of, 289
Alcohol Problems (ALC) scale, 460
Alcoholism, molecular genetic studies of, 277–278
AM. *See* Aggrieved-masochistic spectrum
American Psychiatric Association (APA), xv, 165
Animal temperament, 148
Anticomplementary patterns, 102
Antisocial Features (ANT) scale, 454, 459
Antisocial personality disorder (APD), 144
  DIS and, 312
  IPC of, 395f
  nonrandom mating for, 263
  taxometric studies of, 295–296
Anxiety
  gradient, 85
  mode, 114–115
  sensitivity, 292
  sociotropy and, 124
Anxiety Related Disorder (ARD) scale, 458
Anxiety (ANX) scale, 458
Aristotle, 17
Assessment instruments, 317–320t
  diagnoses, 324–327
  interpretation guidelines, 323–324
  structure of, 323
  validity of, 327–330
Association designs, 276–277
Asymmetry, 141–145
Attachment, 120
Automatic Thoughts Questionnaire (ATQ), 127
Autonomy, 120–125
Avoidance, in TCI, 67
Axiomatics, formalized, 22

Axis I
    FFM and, 54
    genetic influences on, 257
    personality and, 201
    personality disorders and, 119
Axis II, xv, xxi
    cognitive behavior therapy and, 128–130
    criticisms of, 431–432
    dimensionality in, 143–144
    dimensionalizing, 433–434
    disorders, 125
    FFM and, 54–56
    taxometric studies of, 296–297

Basic gene-environment model, 260–263
Basic Personality Inventory (BPI), 51
Behaving styles, 45–46
    MIPS-R and, 43–44
Behavior, expressive, 289
Behavioral genetics, 258
    research design, 258–273
Behavioral intensity, 89
Behavioral rigidity, 89
Behaviorism, extreme, 138
Behaviors
    maladaptive, 171
    medicalization of, 141
    motivations for, 209
    QTLs and, 277
Belonging, 34
Bernreuter Psychoneurotic Inventory, 337
Bimodality, 286–287
Biology, abnormal personality and, xxii
Biophysical dispositions, 13
Bipolar disorder
    schizotypy and, 156–167
    temperament and, 157
    vulnerability to, 292
Borderline Features (BOR) scale, 454, 459
Borderline personality disorder (BPD)
    DBT and, 129
    diagnosing, 168–169
    IPC and, 394, 396f
    neuroticism and, 57
    taxometric studies of, 296
Brain regions, 73

Cashel Discriminant Function, 458
Categorical classification systems, 431–433
Categorical models, 196
Categorical types, 15–16
CC. See Conscientious-compulsive spectrum
CD. See Cooperative-dependent spectrum
Center for Epidemiological Studies, 76
Center for Well-being, 78
CFA. See Confirmatory factor analysis

Character
    TCI and, 67
    temperament and, 72–73, 421–422
Chart of Interpersonal Reactions in Closed Living
        Environments (CIRCLE), 389
Check List of Interpersonal Transactions
        (CLOIT), 389
Checklist response format, 215n2
Children, behaviorally inhibited, 290–291
Chi-square test, 223
Circular profile, 93f
Circumplex. See also Interpersonal circumplex
    interpersonal tendencies in, 93
    interpersonal theory v., 73
    of interpersonal traits, 88f
Circumplex Scales of Interpersonal Values (CSIV),
        387–388
    scores, 394–397
    vector scores, 396f
Classification, 14
    concepts, 14
    taxonomy v., 21
Clinical data collection, self-reporting v., 40
Clinical scales. See Scales
Clinical syndromes, personality traits v., 54
Cluster B, 130
Code types, in MMPI-2, 354–355
Cognition, 43
Cognitive behavior therapy
    Axis II and, 128–130
    tests of, 128–130
Cognitive distortions, 58–59
    schemas and, 115
Cognitive dysregulation, 415
Cognitive Mediation cluster, 482
Cognitive shifts, 119
Cognitive systems, 114
Cognitive theory, of personality disorders, 127–128
Cognitive therapy, 113
    principles of, 130–131
    sociotropy and, 124
Coherence, 66–67
Collaboration, 130
Collaborative Longitudinal Personality Disorders Study
        (CLPS), 329–330, 441
Common origins, 13
Communalities, 220, 221f
Communion, 90–91, 91f, 383. See also Unmitigated
        communion
Comorbidity, 201–202
Complementarity, 101
    interpersonal, 103
Component analysis, 209–210
    congruence coefficients and, 408t
    factor v., 217–218
    loading, 218

minimum average partial-correlation and, 223–224
    model, 218–219
Comprehensive Systems, 486
*Comprehensive Textbook of Psychiatry*, 403
Computerized adaptive testing, 373–374
Conceptual categories, 13–14
Concordance rates, 259
Confidence, 34
Confident-narcissistic (CN) spectrum, 31
    others and, 34
Confirmatory analysis, 233–234
Confirmatory factor analysis (CFA), 443
Conflicts
    in human thought, 71t
    unconscious, 173
Congruence coefficients, 408t, 410t
Conscientious-compulsive (CC) spectrum, 31
Conscientiousness (C), 51
Conscious distortion, 345–346
Consciousness, spiral path of, 69f
Consistency, 194
    checking, 301
    taxometrics and, 288
Content scales
    in MCMI-III-E, 39
    MMPI and, 349–350
    in MMPI-2, 356–357, 361–362
Continuity, 141–145
Control
    behavioral, 174–175
    Rorschach Inkblot Test and, 480–481
Convergence
    evidence of, 301
    of FFM, 20
Co-occurrence, 202
Coolidge Axis II Inventory (CATI), 316
Cooperative movement responses (COP), 477
Cooperative-dependent (CD) spectrum, 31
    self-actualization and, 35
Cooperativeness
    human thought and, 72
    PD and, 424
    in TCI, 67
Core beliefs, 115
    dysfunctional, 116
Correlation
    coefficients, 216
    gene-environment, 265
    genetic, 262–263
Countdown Strategy, 374
Covariance structure models, 242
Creativity, schizotypy and, 154–155
Critical item lists, 348–349
CSIV. *See* Circumplex Scales of Interpersonal
    Values
Cultural expectation, 170–171

D2 dopamine receptor gene, 138–139
Danger avoidance, 26–27
DAPP. *See* Dimensional Assessment of Personality
    Pathology
DAPP-BQ. *See* Dimensional Assessment of Personality
    Disorder Pathology-Basic Questionnaire
Darwin, Charles, xvii
DAS. *See* Dysfunctional Attitude Scale
Data
    cleaning, 215–216
    hypotheses and, 189
    likelihoods, 247–248
    management, 215–217
    matrices, 217
    missing, 216
DBT. *See* Dialectical Behavior Therapy
Decisional Balance Inventory (DBI), 210
Defensiveness Index, 458
Dementia praecox, 17
Demoralization, 368
Dependent personality disorder, 395f
Depression
    attachment and loss and, 120
    distinguishing, 123
    SAS and, 123–124
    TCI and, 76
    theories, 123
    treatment comparisons, 129–130
    vulnerability to, 292
Depression (DEP) scale, 458
Depressive Experiences Questionnaire (DEQ), 123
Desirable Response Inconsistency (DRIN), 442
Deviance
    normality and, xxii
    psychobiology and, 145–151
DF extremes analysis, 271–272
Diagnoses
    of PDs, 200, 324–327
    Rorschach Inkblot Test and, 475–476
    thresholds for, 168–169
    tools, 199–200
*Diagnostic and Statistical Manual of Mental Disorders.*
    *See* DSM
Diagnostic criteria, 166–168
    flexibility of, 175
Diagnostic Interview for Borderlines-Revised (DIB-R),
    315, 322
Diagnostic Interview for Narcissism (DIN), 315, 322
Diagnostic Interview for Personality Disorders
    (DIPD), 315
Diagnostic Interview for Personality Disorders-IV
    (DIPD-IV), 441
Diagnostic Interview Schedule (DIS), 311–312
Dialectical Behavior Therapy (DBT), 129
Differential Personality Questionnaire, 406
Dimensional assessment, 433–434

Dimensional Assessment of Personality Disorder
　　Pathology-Basic Questionnaire (DAPP-BQ),
　　316, 321, 402
　component analysis of, 417t, 418t
　diagnoses with, 425–426
　in different cultures, 411t
　NEO-PI-R and, 415–417
Dimensional Assessment of Personality Pathology
　　(DAPP), 401
　architecture, 412–413
　conceptual foundation of, 402–403
　congruence coefficients of, 410t
　constructs, 402
　*DSM-IV* and, 414
　psychometric analyses of, 405–406
　scales in, 405
　secondary structure, 410
　traits, 409t
Dimensional models, 195–196
Dimensional traits, 14–16
　character v. temperament, 421–422
　in *DSM-V*, xix
　personality types and, xxii
Dimensionality, 143–144
　in *DSM-V*, 158
　primary psychopathy and, 150–151
　of psychosis, 151–157
DISC, 360–361
Disconstraint, 360–361
Disease, 15
　PDs v., 140
Disinhibition *vs.* Constraint (DvC), 436
Disordered cognition, 58–59
Distress, 177–178
　psychotherapy and, 57
Distribution
　bimodal, 286–287
　continuous normal, 255
　discrete, 246f
　latent, 245–257
　non-normal, 246f
　normal, 245f
　of traits, 255–256
Distributional differences, 462–464
DNA markers, 274
Dominance (DOM) scale, 461
Dominance-submission polarity, 45
Dopamine
　novelty seeking and, xxi
　research, 138–139
Dopamine D4 receptor (DRD4), 277
DRD4. *See* Dopamine D4 receptor
DRIN. *See* Desirable Response Inconsistency
Drug Problems (DRG) scale, 460
*DSM (Diagnostic and Statistical Manual of Mental Disorders)*
　disorders in, 9

　normality and, 195
　pedophilia and, 172
　personality-related disorders and, 60–61
　psychobiology in, 141
　Task Force, 17
*DSM-III*
　influence of, xviii
　PDs in, 431–432
　personality in, xv
　prototypes in, 403–405
*DSM-IV*
　assessment instruments, 322–323
　criticisms of, 51–52
　DAPP and, 414
　EMS and, 118
　FFM and, 51
　on impairment, 176
　mental disorders in, 54
　nosology and, 143
　PD diagnoses via, 165–168
　personality disorders in, 54–55
　personality functioning and, 180
　Rorschach Inkblot test and, 476
　SNAP and, 431
*DSM-IV-TR*, 168. *See also* Axis II
　eating disorders in, 203–205
　PD in, 170
*DSM-V*
　dimensional traits in, xix
　dimensionality in, 158
　mental disorder in, 180
　normality in, xxi
　personality taxonomy in, xvi
　SNAP and, 442–443
DSM-V Research Planning Nomenclature Work Group,
　　180, 313
Dyadic Adjustment Scale, 352
Dynamisms, 84–85
Dyscontrol, 174–176
Dyscontrolled maladaptivity, 420
Dysfunction pathology, 171–174
Dysfunctional Attitude Scale (DAS), 127

Early Maladaptive Schemas (EMS), 118
　PDs and, 128
　YSQ and, 126–127
EAS. *See* Emotionality-Activity-Sociability triad
Eating disorders, 203–205
Ecology, 24, 30–31
Edwards Personal Preference Schedule, 465
Effectance, 32
Ego Impairment Index (EII), 490
Ego Strength scale (Es), 490
Eigenvalues, 220–223, 221f
　plotting, 222f
Einheitpsychose theory, 156–157

EM. *See* Exuberant–manic spectrum
Emotionality-Activity-Sociability (EAS) triad, 149
Emotions
    reciprocal, 100–101
    TCI and, 76
EMS. *See* Early Maladaptive Schemas
Environment, 114
    genetics v., 257
Environmental influences, 260–261
    on genetic influences, 279
EPAQ. *See* Extended Version of the Personal Attributes
        Questionnaire
Epidemiologic studies, 311–312
Epistasis, 261*n*1
EPQ. *See* Eysenck Personality Questionnaire
Esoteric Thinking scale, 58
Ethnic differences, 492–495
Evolution, xvii, 23–24
    PDs and, 173–174
    personology and, 4
Evolutionary biology, 33
Existence, 25–29
Experiential technique, 131
Experiments, 188
    types of, 189–191
Extended Version of the Personal Attributes
        Questionnaire (EPAQ), 99
Extremeness, 56
Extremity, 93–97
Extroversion, 29, 51, 147
    nontaxonic models of, 289
    RC scales and, 372
    structure of, 230
Exuberant–manic (EM) spectrum, 29
    SH spectrum and, 31
Eysenck, Hans, 146
Eysenck Personality Questionnaire (EPQ)
    latent variable models and, 254–255
    maladaptive personality traits and, 316
    in quantitative genetic studies, 272
    revised, 417t
    SAS and, 124–125

Factor analysis, 18–19
    component v., 217–218
    decisions regarding, 217–230
    design, 212–215
    exploratory, 209–212
    Eysenck and, 146
    maximum-likelihood, 223
    optimal structure for, 225
    psychobiological processes and, 67
    of Rorschach Inkblot Test, 483–485
    schematic flow diagram, 218f
    of SNAP, 444
    taxometrics and, 287

Factor loading, 213, 214t
    of SNAP-2 scales, 437t
Factor patterns, 226f
    simple, 227
    varimax, 228f
Factors
    to extract, 232
    optimal number of, 219–225
    orthogonal, 227
    rotating, 225–228
    scales, 229–230
    scores, 228–230
    structures, 230–232
Faith, 66
Family studies, 266
*Feeling Good: The Science of Well-Being* (Cloninger), 69f
FFM. *See* Five-Factor Model
Fitness, 24
Five-Factor Model (FFM), xx
    Axis I and, 54
    Axis II and, 54–56, 433
    diagnoses with, 60, 421
    discriminant validity and, 330
    Eysenck and, 146
    history of, 51
    NEO PI-R and, 321–322
    nontaxonic models and, 289
    personality disorder and, 416
    Rorschach Inkblot Test and, 475
    RRS and, 484
    SA spectrum and, 27–29
    SNAP and, 438–439
    support of, 19–20
    taxometrics and, 287
Fluvoxamine, 130
Flux, 95–97, 197
Formes furstes, 151
Free will, 174
Freud, Sigmund, xvii
F-scale, 345–346
Full Scores on Elevated Scales, 374
Functional genomics, 279

GAF. *See* General Assessment of Functioning Scale
Gender
    in evolutionary biology, 33
    limitation, 265–266
    roles, 355
    scales, 357
Gene-behavior associations, 279
Gene-environment model, 271f
General Assessment of Functioning Scale (GAF), 421
Generalized linear latent variable model (GLLVM),
        239–243
    deriving models from, 241
Generalized linear model (GLM), 240

Generalized mixture covariance theorem, 298
Genes, 276
Genetic influence, on harm avoidance, 138–139
Genetic influences
    on basic traits, 413
    effects of, 261
    environmental influences on, 279
    nonadditive, 269
    twin studies and, 269
Genetic studies
    of DAPP, 412
    of lability, 414t
    longitudinal, 270–271
    multivariate, 270
    quantitative, 258–273
Genetics, 65–66, 138–139
    abnormal personality and, xxii–xxiii
    environment v., 257
    of psychopathology, 257
    schizophrenia and, 155
    trait variance and, 257
GLLVM. *See* Generalized linear latent variable model
GLM. *See* Generalized linear model
Global Assessment of Functioning, 61
Goldstein, Kurt, 35

*Handbook of Personality* (Millon & Lerner), 25
Harm avoidance
    genetic influence on, 138–139
    serotonin receptors and, 73
    in TCI, 67
Hereditarianism, 138
Heritability, 260
    DAPP and, 412
    types of, 261
Heterogeneity, within class, 432
Hierarchical structures, 231–232
Hippocrates, 67
Histograms, 247
Histrionic personality disorder, 55
HIV/AIDS, 5
Homosexuality, 178
    taxometric studies of, 289–290
Hope, 66
5-HTTLPR. *See* Serotonin transporter gene
Human relations, 90–91
Humm-Wadsworth Temperament Scales, 337–338
Hypomania-Impulsive Nonconformity, 156n6
Hypotheses, 189
    lexical, 212, 403–405
Hysteria criterion group, 366

IAS. *See* Interpersonal Adjectives Scale
ICD-10 (International Classification of Diseases), 171
ICL. *See* Interpersonal Check List
Ideation cluster, 482

Identity development, 423
IDI. *See* Interpersonal Dependency Inventory
Impact Message Inventory (IMI), 106
    Circumplex, 388–390
Impact messages, 105–106
Impairment, 172–173
    clinically significant, 176–179
Impulsive Nonconformity, 156
Impulsivity, 291
Index of association, 216–217
Indicators, 297
    minimum number of, 302
Individuation, 35–37
Inference, 18
Inflexibility, 56, 174–176
Information Processing cluster, 481
Information sources, 44
Information-theoretic criteria, 248–249
Insecure attachment, 415
Interbehavioral contingency, 104–106
Internal processes, covert, 104–106
*International Classification of Diseases* (WHO), 143
International Personality Disorder Examination (IPDE),
    167, 199
    eating disorders and, 204–205
International Personality Item Pool (IPIP), 484
Interpersonal acts, 383
Interpersonal Adjectives Scale (IAS), 94, 385–387, 386t
Interpersonal Check List (ICL), 385
Interpersonal circumplex (IPC), xvi, 56, 83–84, 92t,
    383–385, 384f
    abnormal personality and, 392–397
    Axis II and, 433
    evolution of, 86–90
    interpreting, 391–392
    mechanisms, 87f
    origins of, 86–90
    profiles, 394–397
    specialized measures, 388–389
Interpersonal Dependency Inventory (IDI), 478
Interpersonal impacts, 388–390
Interpersonal mechanisms, 86–87
Interpersonal Perception cluster, 482–483
Interpersonal problems, 97–100, 387
Interpersonal relations, disturbed, 86, 104–106
Interpersonal situation, 84–86
    impact messages, 106
Interpersonal theory, xx
    circumplex v., 73
Interpersonal tradition, 83
    in personality, 84–91
Interpersonal traits, 89
    circumplex of, 88f
Interpersonal transaction, 100–104
Interviews, 323
    convergent validity of, 328

diagnoses via, 166
epidemiologic studies and, 311–312
maladaptive personality traits and, 311
manuals, 324
semistructured, 313, 330
SNAP v., 439, 440t
structured, 200
unstructured, 313
INTR, 361
INTREX, 384
    questionnaires, 389–390
Introversion, 361
Inventory of Interpersonal Problems (IIP), 97, 386t, 387
Inwald Personality Inventory, 363, 373
IPC. *See* Interpersonal circumplex
IPDE. *See* International Personality Disorder Examination
IQ, 177
Items
    characteristics, 253
    critical, 349
    RC scale, 369t
    response theory, 242

Jung, Carl
    on individuation, 35
    on neuroticism, 57

K correction, 362–365
K-scale, 346
Kaiser Foundation Health Plan, 86
K-strategy, 33

L-scale, 345–346
Lability, 414t
Language, clinical, 20
Latent distribution models, 245–247
    distinguishing, 254
    in practice, 249–253
Latent variable models
    comparing, 247–253
    complexity of, 248–249
    estimating, 243–244
    generalized linear, 239–243
    logistic, 242
    representing traits in, 253
    of traits, 244–247
Leary, Timothy, 86–90
    on adjustive personality, 93–94
Lewin, Kurt, 86
Liability threshold model, 259f
Life enhancement, 25–29
Life preservation, 25–29
Linkage designs, 274–276
Linnaeus, 4
L-Mode, 301
    indicators for, 302

Log-likelihoods, 244
Loss, 34, 120
Love, 34, 66

MACI (Millon Adolescent Clinical Inventory), 38, 40–41, 41–42
*Madness Explained* (Bentall), 140
Magical Ideation Scale, 496
Magnetic resonance imaging (fMRI), 73
Maladaptive personality traits, 168
    assessment of, 311–312
    assessment strategy, 312–315
    expression, 420–421
    instruments, 315–327
    PDs and, 127
    personality failure and, 422–424
MAMBAC, 299
    indicators for, 302
    plot, 300f
Manic-depressive disease, 17
MAP. *See* Minimum average partial-correlation
MAPI (Millon Adolescent Personality Inventory), 38, 41–42
Marital Distress Scale, 362
Marlow-Crowne Scale, 406
Maslow, Abraham
    on acceptance, 31
    self-actualization and, 35
Mating
    assortative, 266
    nonrandom, 263–265
    phenotypic assortative, 263–264
Matrices
    correlational, 211, 217
    factor, 218–219
    reproduced, 219
    residual, 220f
    rotating factor, 225–228
Matrix algebra, 241
Mature personality, 34
Maturity
    cognitive, 85
    levels of, 73–76
MAXCOV, 298–299
    indicators for, 302
MAXEIG, 298–299
    indicators for, 302
Maximum likelihood estimation, 243
    principle of, 247–248
MAXSLOPE, 300
    indicators for, 302
MBHI (Millon Behavioral Health Inventory), 38, 40–41
MBMD (Millon Behavioral Medicine Diagnostic), 38, 40–41
MCMI. *See* Millon Clinical Multiaxiom Inventory

Measurements, 190–191
    format, 215
    reliability of, 193–194
Measures, explicit v. implicit, 476–477
Medicine, 4–5
    psychology v., 14
Meehl, Paul, 283
Mental disorders
    definition of, 170
    in *DSM-IV*, 54
    in *DSM-V*, 180
    homosexuality and, 178
    personalities v., xv
    statistical deviance view of, 56
Mental illness, 145
    theories, 142
Mental retardation, 176–177
Methodology, 188–189
Midwestern Psychological Association, 342
Millon Clinical Multiaxial Inventory-III (MCMI-III),
    38, 39, 199–200, 316
Millon Clinical Multiaxial Inventory (MCMI), 38–40
    Compulsive scale of, 59
    eating disorders and, 204–205
    FFM and, 51
    MIPS-R v., 43
Millon Index of Personality Styles (MIPS-R), 38, 42–46
Minimum average partial-correlation (MAP),
    223–224, 224f
    computing, 224$n$4
    function, 210
Minnesota Multiphasic Personality Inventory (MMPI)
    codebook approach to, 342–344
    conceptual basis of, 338–339
    construction of, 337–341
    contemporizing, 351
    content-based approach to, 345–347
    criticisms of, 350
    development of, 339–341
    empirical scale developments, 344
    evolution of, 341–357
    FFM and, 51
    personality assessment with, 345
    Personality Disorder, 125–126
    quantitative genetic studies and, 273
    Rorschach Inkblot Test and, 473
    Rorschach Inkblot Test validity and, 487–488
    scales, 347–348
    theoretical foundation of, 342
    validity scales, 339
Minnesota Multiphasic Personality Inventory-2
    (MMPI-2), 200, 315, 322, 350
    2001 update, 357–362
    content scales, 356–357
    future of, 373–374
    goals of, 351–352

methods of revision, 352–353
*Mf*, 290
new scales in, 358–360
norms of, 353–354
post-2001 developments, 362–365
PSY-5 and, xx
rationale for, 351
restructured clinical scales, 365
restructuring, 373
revised validity scales, 358–360
revision outcome, 353–357
Rorschach v., 478–479
scales in, 355
validity scales in, 355–356
Minnesota Normals, 340
MIPS. *See* Millon Index of Personality Styles
Mitigation, 99
MMPI Restandardization Committee, 351–352
MMPI. *See* Minnesota Multiphasic Personality Inventory
MMPI-2. *See* Minnesota Multiphasic Personality Inventory-2
Model-fitting procedures, 259
Modes, 114
    latent, 301
    schema, 118–119
Molecular genetic studies, 273–278
Monoamine oxidase (MAO) deficiency, 265
Mood disorders, 292
Morgan, Thomas Hunt, 274
Motivating styles, 44
    MIPS-R and, 43
Motives, 387–388
M-PACI (Millon PreAdolescent Clinical Inventory), 41–42
MPQ. *See* Multidimensional Personality Questionnaire
Multidimensional Personality Questionnaire (MPQ), 68
    maladaptive personality traits and, 316
Multiple Affect Adjective Checklist-Revised
    (MAACL-R), 128

NA. *See* Nonconforming-antisocial personality spectrum
Naiveté, 372
Narcissistic Personality Disorder, 143–144
National Epidemiologic Survey on Alcohol and Related
    Conditions, 312
National Law Center for Children and Families, 172
Needs, 27
Negative Affectivity (NA), 436
Negative Impression Management (NIM), 457
NEGE, 361
NEO Personality Inventory (NEO-PI), 20
    FFM and, 51–52
    hierarchical structures and, 231
    Openness in, 68
    SAS and, 124–125
NEO-Five Factor Inventory (NEO-FFI), 128
NEO-PI-R, 199
    component analysis of, 417t

DAPP-BQ and, 415–417
discriminant validity and, 329–330
FFM and, 321–322
maladaptive personality traits and, 316
Nervous typological theory, 146
Neurochemical dysregulation, 173
Neurology, psychiatry and, 142
*Neurotic Styles* (Shapiro), 59
Neuroticism, 51, 147
  borderline personality disorder and, 57–58
  distribution, 245, 249–250
  negative emotionality, 361
  nontaxonic models of, 289
  personality-related disorders and, 57–58
  SSRIs and, 178–179
NIM. Negative Impression Management
Nonconforming-antisocial (NA) personality spectrum, 27
  others and, 34
Normal behavior, xx
Normal personality, 93–97
  abnormal v., 8–11, 169–170, 283–286, 462–467
  classification of, 12
  criteria, 462–467
  DAPP and, 415–418
  disordered v., 419–420
  historical context of, xvii–xxi
  PDs v., 143
  stability of, xix
  taxometric studies, 288–291
  trait differences in, 92–100
  trait structure of, 255
Normal-abnormal personality science
  developments in, xix–xxi
  dimensional models of, 195–196
  research, 187–188
Normality, xxi–xiii
  criteria for, 25
  defining, xxi, xxii, 195
  *DSM* and, 195
Normality-oriented personality instruments, 42–46
Normative data, 454–456
Nosology, 17–18
  *DSM-IV* and, 143
  Kraepelinian, 338
Novelty seeking, xxi
  genetic influence on, 138–139
  in TCI, 67
Nuclear families, 267f
  in adoption studies, 267–268

Observations, 17–18
  generating, 22
Obsessive-compulsive personality disorder, 59–60
  IPC and, 394
  psychobiology and, 139–140

O-LIFE. *See* Oxford-Liverpool Inventory of Feelings and Experiences
OMNI Personality Inventory, 316
Ontogenic development, 24
Openness, 51, 68
Order, 33
Others, 34
Overcontrollers, 305
Oxford-Liverpool Inventory of Feelings and Experiences (O-LIFE), 152
  schizotypy and, 156

PACL. *See* Personality Adjective Check List
PAI. *See* Personality Assessment Inventory
Pain avoidance, 26–27
Paralimbic hypothesis, 150
Parallel analysis, 222–223
  computing, 224n4
  procedure, 223f
Parameter estimates, 251t
Paranoid personality disorder, 404f
Parataxic distortions, 104–106
Parkinson's disease, 139
Paroxetine, 178–179
Parsimony, 248
Passive-active polarity, 29–32
Path models
  in adoption studies, 268f
  for nuclear families, 267f
  for twin studies, 269
Pathological interpersonal introject, 173
Pathology, xxi–xiii
Pavlovian theory, 138
PDNOS. *See* Personality disorder not otherwise specified
PDs. *See* Personality disorders
Pedophilia, diagnosing, 172
Peer samples, 213
Perceived Social Support scale, 461
Perception cluster, 482–483
Perceptual Aberration scale, 152, 496
Persistence, 67
Personal Styles Inventory (PSI), 123
Personality. *See also* Abnormal personality; Normal personality
  adjustive, 93–94
  Axis I and, 201
  characteristics, 11
  cognitive theory of, 113–119
  conceptualizing, 11–16
  definition of, 53–54
  diagnosing, 199–200
  diagnostic criteria for, 169–170
  differentiation, 462–467
  dimensional conceptualizations of, xix
  dimensional models of, 443
  dimensional traits and, xxii

Personality (*Continued*)
 dimensions, 143–145
 disordered, 419–420
 effect of, 202–203
 etymology of, 8
 factor structures in, 230–232
 failure, 422–424
 genetic effects on, 278
 history of, xvii
 interpersonal tradition in, 84–91
 inventories, 38–46
 measures of, 476–480
 mental disorders v., xv
 modeling, xviii, 67
 models, 68–69
 molecular genetic studies of, 277–278
 pattern, 10
 prototypes, 6
 psychobiology and, 145–151
 psychopathology and, 3, 119–125
 range of, 68–70
 spectra, 10–11, 36f, 37f
 syndromes, 12–13
 taxonomy of, xvi
 temperament v., 147
 variables, 202–203
 variations, 137
Personality Adjective Check List (PACL), 38, 42
 MIPS-R v., 43
Personality assessment, 188
 content-based, 345–347
Personality Assessment Form (PAF), 316
Personality Assessment Inventory (PAI), 322, 451–452
 clinical scales, 458–460
 clinical v. community scales, 463t
 development, 452–454
 FFM and, 51
 interpersonal scales, 461
 maladaptive personality traits and, 316
 psychopathology and, 459
 reliability of, 455–456
 theoretical basis, 452–454
 treatment consideration scales, 460–461
 validity, 456–467
 validity indices, 458
Personality Belief Questionnaire (PBQ), 125–126
Personality Circulargram I, 28f
Personality Circulargram IIA, 36f
Personality Circulargram IIB, 37f
Personality Diagnostic Questionnaire-4 (PDQ-4),
 316, 484
Personality diatheses, 291–294
Personality Disorder Interview-IV (PDI-IV), 199, 315, 322
Personality disorder not otherwise specified (PDNOS),
 166–167
 diagnosing, 325

Personality Disorder Questionnaire-Revised (PDQ-R),
 125–126
Personality Disorder Questionnaire-4 (PDQ-4), 316,
 322–323
 neuroticism and, 57
Personality disorders (PDs), xv, 9
 assessment instruments, 125–127, 317–320t
 Axis I and, 119
 classification, 424–425
 clinical diagnosis of, 200
 Cluster B, 130
 cognitive profiles of, 120, 121–122t
 cognitive theory of, 127–128
 cognitive therapy for, 130–131
 conceptualization, 316–323
 control and, 174–175
 cultural expectation of, 170–171
 cultural influences on, 197
 DAPP and, 414–415
 definition of, 54–55
 diagnoses, 117, 324–327, 424–425
 diagnoses via *DSM-IV*, 165–168
 diagnostic thresholds, 168–169
 discontinuity in, xix
 disease v., 140
 in *DSM-III*, 431–432
 EMS and, 128
 FFM and, 52, 416
 future taxometric studies of, 304–305
 impairment and, 176–177
 inheritability of, 258
 longitudinal studies of, xix
 maladaptive beliefs and, 127
 maturity and, 74
 molecular genetic studies of, 278–279
 normal personality v., 143
 PAI scales and, 464
 per *DSM-IV-TR*, 170
 predisposition for, 159
 primary structure, 407
 recognized, 167
 research, 94
 self-directedness and, 75t
 SNAP correlations, 441
 SSRIs and, 178–179
 structure of, 406–407
 taxometric studies of, 294–297
 taxonomy of, xix
 TCI and, 67, 74
 trait dimension and, 419
 trait stability, xx
 traits v., 143–144
 treatment comparisons, 129–130
 treatment of, xviii
 vulnerability to, 5
 WHO on, 171

Personality functioning, 180
    Rorschach Inkblot Test and, 480–485
Personality pathology, xx
    SNAP and, 444–447
Personality profiles
    schemas and, 116
    syndromes and, 61
Personality Psychopathology-Five (PSY-5), 316,
        360–361
Personality Research Form, 406
Personality subtypes, 6
Personality theories
    competing, xix
    evolutionary scaffold for, 23–37
Personality traits. *See also* Maladaptive personality traits;
        Trait(s)
    clinical syndromes v., 54
    factor structure of, 272
    factors in, 225
    hierarchical models of, 230
    horizontal model of, 231
    interpreting, 53
    PACL and, 42
    PDs v., 143–144
    taxonic, 285
Personality-related disorders, 56–59
    curability of, 59
    *DSM* and, 60–61
Personological assessment, 38–46
Personology, xvii–xviii
    basis for, 5
    evolutionary model of, 4
    history of, 8–9
    physical sciences v., 23
    state of, 4
    subject domains of, 7t
    systemizing, 6
Phenomena, 13–14
Phenotypic assortment, 263–264
Philosophy, xvii
Phylogenesis, 24
Physical analysis, 12
Physics, 11–12
Physiological system, 114
PIM. *See* Positive Impression Management
P-Impulsive Unsocialized Sensation Seeking
        (P-ImpUSS), 151
Pleasure-pain polarity, 25–29
    MIPS-R and, 44
Pleasures, 29
Polymorphism, 274
    in 5-HTTLPR, 277–278
    in DRD4, 277
Positive Affectivity (PA), 436
Positive Impression Management (PIM), 457
Positron emission tomography, 73

Post-traumatic stress disorder (PTSD)
    indicators, 355
    scales, 357
Pragmatism, xxii
Preadolescents, personality inventory for, 41–42
Primary psychopathy, 149–151
Profiles, 341
    codebook approach to, 342–344
    cognitive, 120, 121–122t
Prognostic Rating Scale (PRS), 490
*Project for a Scientific Psychology* (Freud), 3, 23
Projective tests, 312
Proportionality coefficients, 216–217
Prototypal trait domains, 16
Prototypes, 403–405
PSY-5. *See* Personality Psychopathology-Five
PSYC, 360
Psyche, 65–66
Psychiatric disorders, 201–202
Psychiatric patients, as subjects, 205
Psychiatry
    neurology and, 142
    Sullivan on, 85
Psychoanalytic theory, 55
Psychobiological processes, 66–67
Psychobiology, 65, 137–140
Psychologists, clinical, xviii
Psychology
    medicine v., 14
    philosophy and, xvii
Psychometric analyses, 370–371
    of DAPP, 405–406
Psychopathology, 3
    defining, 195
    FFM and, 51–52
    genetics of, 257
    nonrandom mating for, 263
    PAI and, 459
    personality and, 119–125
    prevalence of, 179
    psychopathy and, 150
    schizotypy and, 154–155
    subject domains of, 7t
    temperament and, 148–149
Psychopathology-5 (PSY-5), xxiv, 316, 360–361
Psychopathy, 150
Psychopathy Checklist-Revised (PCL-R), 315
    structure of, 323
Psychoses
    cause of, 151
    dimensionality of, 151–157
Psychotherapy
    distress and, 57
    transaction cycles and, 103–104
Psychoticism
    definition of, 151

Psychoticism (*Continued*)
  in PSY-5, 360
  schizotypy v., 157
Pulse, 95–97, 197
Pythagoras, 67

Quantitative discriminations, 16
Quantitative trait loci (QTLs), 273
  associations, 279
  behavior and, 277
Questionnaires, self-report, 201

R language, 303
Racial differences, 492–495
Randomization, 198–199
Rare Virtues scale, 442
Raw cross products, 216
RCS. *See* Rorschach Construct Scale
Reciprocity, 100–104
Record Review Form, 493
Reductionism, 141–145
Reference vectors, 228
Relatedness coefficients, 263t
Relatives, correlations between, 264t
Reliability
  inter-rater, 485–486
  of measurements, 193–194
  PAI, 455–456
  Rorschach Inkblot Test, 485–487
  test-retest, 486–487
Replication strategies, 32–37
Reproductive nurturance, 33–35
Reproductive propagation, 35–37
Research
  common pitfalls in, xvi
  past, 212
  Rorschach Inkblot Test, 495–497
  SNAP and, 442–444
Research design, 188–189
  behavioral genetic, 258–273
  case-control, 189–190
  correlational, 189–190
  criteria for, 196–197
  experimental, 189–190
  gene-environment, 260–263
  issues, 188–194
  in practice, 203–205
  quasiexperimental, 189–190
  specific issues, 194
  subjects and, 197–199
  types of, 189–191
  validity of, 191–193
Resilients, 305
Restructured clinical (RC) scales, 365–367
  developing, 367–368
  items, 369t

psychometric findings with, 370–371
  role of, 371–373
Retiring-schizoid (RS) spectrum, 29
Reward Dependence, 67
Rewards, 27–29
Rigidity, 93–97
Rogers Discriminant Function, 458
Rorschach Construct Scale (RCS), 484–485
Rorschach, Hermann, 474
Rorschach Inkblot Test, 473–475
  construct validity of, 488–489
  diagnoses and, 475–476
  ethnic differences, 492–495
  factor analysis of, 483–485
  future research in, 495–497
  global construct validity, 487–488
  incremental validity of, 489–492
  inter-rater reliability, 485–486
  limitations of, 475
  MMPI-2, 478–479
  personality functioning and, 480–485
  racial differences, 492–495
  reliability, 485–487
  symptoms and, 475–476
  test-retest reliability, 486–487
Rorschach Oral Dependency Scale (ROD), 478
  construct validity and, 488
Rorschach Rating Scale (RRS), 483–485
RRS. *See* Rorschach Rating Scale
*r*-strategy, 33

SA. *See* Shy-avoidance (SA) spectrum
Salience, 24
Sample(s)
  clinical v. community, 463t, 465–466
  size, 213–214
  taxometrics and, 302
SAS. *See* Sociotropy-Autonomy Scale
SAS software, 210
SASB. *See* Structural Analysis of Social Behavior
Scales. *See also* Content scales; Restructured clinical scales
  clinical, 458–460
  content component, 361–362
  in DAPP, 405
  discontinued, 357–358
  empirical, 344
  Harris-Lingoes subscales, 348
  interpersonal, 461
  MMPI, 347–348
  MMPI-2, 355
  PAI and, 452–453
  revised validity, 358–360
  SNAP, 434, 446t
  SNAP-2, 435–436t
  treatment consideration, 460–461
  Welsh factor, 348

Schedule for Nonadaptive and Adaptive Personality
        (SNAP), 316, 414–415, 431–433
    development of, 434–441
    factor analyses of, 444
    FFM and, 438–439
    interview-based ratings v., 440t
    PD correlations, 441
    profile, 445
    research applications, 442–444
    scales, 441–442, 446t
    scoring, 445–446
    therapy and, 447
Schedule for Nonadaptive and Adaptive Personality-2
        (SNAP-2)
    development, 436–437
    scales, 435–436t
    scales in, 437t
Schedule of Recent Events (SRE) scale, 461
Schema(s), 115–119. *See also* Self-schemas
    confronting, 130–131
    Diary, 131
    domains, 118
    Flashcard, 131
    interpersonal, 117–119
    irrational cognitive, 173
    modes, 118–119
    orienting, 114
    therapy, 118
Schematic modification, 131
Schematic reinterpretation, 131
Schematic restructuring, 131
Schizoid personality disorder, diagnosing, 166, 168–169
Schizophrenia
    genetics and, 155
    psychobiology and, 139
    schizotypy and, 152
    vulnerability to, 293
Schizophrenia Index (SCZI), 490
Schizophrenia Personality Disorder, 143–144
Schizotypal personality disorder (SPD), 58
    taxometric studies of, 295
Schizotypy, 151–157
    diagnosing, 168–169
    features of, 154t
    IPC and, 393
    latent structure of, 293
    model of, 153f
    Rorschach Inkblot Test and, 495–496
    taxometric studies of, 293–294
Schlenger PSTD Scale, 357
Security, 90
Selective placement, 269
Selective serotonin reuptake inhibitors (SSRIs)
    abuse of, 141
    PDs and, 178–179
Self-actualization, 35–37

Self-awareness, 66–67
Self-control, 175–176
Self-Control Schedule (SCS), 127
Self-Directedness, 66
    in TCI, 67
Self-directedness
    human thought and, 72
    PDs and, 75t, 424
Self-dynamism, 102
Self-esteem, 90
Self-evaluations, 117
Self-instructions, 117
Self-reporting, 323
    clinical data collection v., 40
    inventories, 315, 330
    IPC and, 385
    maladaptive personality traits and, 312
    PAI and, 451–452
    v. peer samples, 213
    questionnaires, xvi, 201
    scales, 326
    taxometric studies of, 289
Self-schemas, 117–119
Self-transcendence, 66
    human thought and, 72
    in TCI, 67
Serotonin receptors, 73
Serotonin transporter gene (5-HTTLPR), 139, 277–278
Sexual orientation, 178
    MMPI and, 351
    taxometric studies of, 289–290
Shedler-Westen Assessment Procedure-200 (SWAP-200),
        314, 316, 322
    structure of, 323
Shy-avoidance (SA) spectrum, 27
SIDP-IV, 167–168
SIFFM. *See* Structured Interview for the Five-Factor
        Model
Simulation studies, 212–213
Sixteen Personality Factors Questionnaire, 225
SNAP. *See* Schedule for Nonadaptive and Adaptive
        Personality
SNAP-2. *See* Schedule for Nonadaptive and Adaptive
        Personality-2
Sociability
    measuring, 193
    MIPS-R and, 45
Sociable-histrionic (SH) spectrum, 31
Social adhedonia, 293
Social affiliation, 178–179
Social desirability, 464–465
Social hierarchies, 423
Social tolerance, 70–72
*Sociobiology* (Wilson), 3, 23
Sociotropy, 120–125
Sociotropy-Autonomy Scale (SAS), 123–125

Soma, 65–66
SPD. *See* Schizotypal personality disorder
Spin, 95–97, 197
Spirituality, 66
   schizotypy and, 154–155
   value of, 79
Spitzer, Robert, 17
S-Plus, 303–304
SPSS, 210
SSRIs. *See* Selective serotonin reuptake inhibitors
Stability, 194
Standardization studies, 456
State-Trait Anger Expression Inventory (STAXI),
     460–461
Statistics
   factor analysis and, 210
   information-theoretic, 248
   methods, 20–21
   parsimony and, 248
Stress Tolerance cluster, Rorschach Inkblot Test and,
     480–481
Structural Analysis of Social Behavior (SASB), 100, 316
   INTREX questionnaires and, 389–390
   IPC and, 384
Structural equation models, 242
Structured Clinical Interview for DSM-IV Axis II
     Personality Disorders (SCID-II), 315
Structured Interview for the Five-Factor Model
     (SIFFM), 315–316, 330
Subjects, 197–199
   abnormal v. normal, 213
   in factor analysis, 213–214
   psychiatric patients, 205
   sample size and, 213–214
Suicide Probability Scale (SPS), 460
Sullivan, Harry S., 84–86
Supplementary Scale Profile, 362
Support Actions Scale-Circumplex (SAS-C), 389
Supportive expressive therapy, 129–130
Survival, 6
SWAP-200. *See* Shedler-Westen Assessment
     Procedure-200
Symptomatology, 4
Symptoms
   disorders, 119
   Rorschach Inkblot Test and, 475–476
   syndromes and, 366
   traits v., 143–145
Syndromes, 12–13
   personality profiles and, 61
   symptoms and, 366
SYSTAT, 210

Talmud, 29
Taxa, 16–17
   definition of, 283–284

latent, 16–23
   manifest, 16–23
Taxometrics, 283–285, 433
   considerations for, 301–303
   consistency and, 288
   developments in, 303
   factor analysis and, 287
   Five-Factor Model and, 287
   future of, 304–305
   methodologies, 297–304
   methods, 286–288
   personality studies, 288–297
   procedures, 287
   software, 303–304
Taxonomy
   classification v., 21
   of personalities, xvi
   theoretical, 403
TCI. *See* Temperament and Character Inventory
Temperament, 13
   in animals, 148
   bipolar disorder and, 157
   brain regions and, 73
   character and, 72–73, 421–422
   DBT and, 129
   nongenetic factors of, 158
   personality v., 147
   psychobiology and, 145–151
   psychopathology and, 148–149
   theories, 147–148
Temperament and Character Inventory (TCI),
     65, 321
   character dimensions, 70
   emotional aspects of, 70
   forms of, 77–78
   junior version, 77–78
   maladaptive personality traits and, 316
   PDs and, 74
   in practice, 77
   purpose of, 67
   revised, 77
   validity of, 78
Temporality, 423
Territoriality, 423
Test bias, 453–454
Thematic Apperception Test, 477
Theoretical models, 21
*Theoretical Underpinnings of the MMPI* (Meehl), 345
Theory, formal, 22
Therapy
   interpersonal, 130
   psychodynamic, 130
   SNAP and, 447
Thinking Disorder scale, 58
Thinking styles, 44–45
   MIPS-R and, 43

Thought
    conflicts in, 71t
    content of, 70–73
    movement of, 70–73
    scope of, 69
    stages of, 72t
Threat avoidance, 26–27
TPQ. *See* Tridimensional Personality Questionnaire
Trait(s), 408–409. *See also* Personality traits
    continuous distribution of, 255–256
    continuous v. categorical, 258–260
    covariance of, 13
    DAPP, 409t
    deviant, 145
    differences in, 92–100
    dimensions, 419
    domains, 6
    extremity of, 419–420
    genetic determination of, 257
    genetic influences on, 413
    interpersonal, 385–387
    latent variable models of, 244–247
    models, 242–243
    molecular genetic studies of, 273–274
    normative v. abnormal, 466–467
    for paranoid personality disorder, 404f
    stability, xx
    structures, 230–232
    symptoms v., 143–145
    variance, 257
    vertical v. horizontal, 232–233
Transaction cycles, 102–104
Transactional systems, xxii
Transformation, 44–45
Transmission disequilibrium tests (TDT), 276–277
Treatment
    consideration scales, 460–461
    lopsided, xix
Tridimensional Personality Questionnaire (TPQ), 77
    in quantitative genetic studies, 272
True Response Inconsistency (TRIN), 355–356
    in SNAP, 442
*T*-scores, 353–354
    PAI and, 454
Twin studies, 269–270
    DF extremes analysis and, 271–272

Undercontrollers, 305
University of California, 86

Unmitigated agency (UA), 98–100
Unmitigated communion (UC), 98–100

Valence, 116
Validity, 191–193, 327–330
    construct, 193, 488–489
    convergent, 327–329
    discriminant, 329–330, 453
    global construct, 487–488
    incremental, 489–492
    internal v. external, 192t
    PAI, 456–467
    of Rorschach Inkblot Test, 487–492
    statistical conclusion, 193
Values, 387–388
Variable Response Inconsistency (VRIN), 355
    in SNAP, 442
Variables
    categorical v. continuous, 258–260
    monotonic, 216
    Rorschach Inkblot Test, 489
    sampling, 212–213
    selecting, 212–213, 232
Variance components linkage analysis, 275
Varimax algorithm, 227
    plotted, 228f
Vector length (VL), 93
    rigidity and, 94–95
Vision, 70
VRIN. *See* Variable Response Inconsistency
Vulnerability hypothesis, 123

WAIS, 487
Warmth (WRM) scale, 461
Well-being
    levels of, 73–76
    TCI and, 78
Wisconsin Personality Disorders Inventory (WISPI),
        316, 322
World Health Organization (WHO), 171
World War II, xviii

XQUAL, 491

Young Schema Questionnaire (YSQ), 125–127

Zuckerman-Kuhlman Personality Questionnaire, 417
    component analysis, 418t

# Pioneers of Personality Science
## *Autobiographical Perspectives*

**Stephen Strack,** PhD
**Bill N. Kinder,** PhD, Editors

The field of personology, or personality, is enjoying great growth, spurred by findings coming from behavior genetics, evolutionary psychology, rethinking of the *Diagnostic and Statistical Manual of Mental Disorders* definition of personality disorders, and advances in test construction and psychometrics.

Sixteen biographical chapters written by those who were the pioneers of personality assessment trace the development of the field. With accompanying photos and a concise bibliography from each contributor, this one-of-a-kind compilation of the history, present, and future of personology chronicles the following leaders:

Jack Block • Arnold H. Buss • James N. Butcher • Richard Dana • Leonard Handler • Robert R. Holt • Wayne Holtzman • Samuel Karson • Paul M. Lerner • Jane Loevinger • Joseph Masling • Theodore Millon • Edwin S. Shneidman • Norman Sundberg • Irving B. Weiner • Marvin Zuckerman

**Partial Contents:**
• My Unexpected Life
• A Report on Myself: The Science and/or Art of Assessment
• A Psychologist Grows in Brooklyn: Reflections From the Past
• A Life-Long Attempt to Understand and Assess Personality
• Have PhD, Will Travel
• From Freud to Gehrig to Rapaport to DiMaggio
• Confessions of an Iconoclast: At Home on the Fringe
• A Blessed and Charmed Personal Odyssey
• The Shaping of Personality: Genes, Environments, and Chance Encounters

2006 • 448pp • 0-8261-3205-7 • hardcover

**11 West 42nd Street, New York, NY 10036-8002 • Fax: 212-941-7842**
**Order Toll-Free: 877-687-7476 • Order On-line: www.springerpub.com**